German Military Collectibles Price Guide

Collector items of historical interest from Imperial Germany and the Third Reich

Ron Manion

Edited by Eric J. Johansson

Antique Trader Books
P. O. Box 1050
Dubuque, IA 52004

ISBN: 0-930625-44-7
Library of Congress Catalog Card No. 94-73111

**Other books and magazines published by
Antique Trader Publications:**

American Military Collectibles Price Guide
Japanese & Other Foreign Military Collectibles Price Guide
Antiques & Collectibles Annual Price Guide
American Pressed Glass & Bottles Price Guide
American & European Decorative & Art Glass Price Guide
Ceramics Price Guide
American & European Furniture Price Guide
American & European Art Pottery Price Guide
Maloney's Antiques & Collectibles Resource Directory
Comics Values Annual
Rockin' Records Buyers-Sellers Reference Book & Price Guide
The Antique Trader Weekly
Collector Magazine & Price Guide
Toy Trader Magazine
Postcard Collector Magazine
Discoveries Magazine
Big Reel Magazine
Military Trader Magazine
Baby Boomer Collectibles Magazine

To order additional copies of this book
or other publications listed above, contact:
**Antique Trader Publications
P. O. Box 1050
Dubuque, IA 52004
Phone: 1-800-334-7165**

TABLE OF CONTENTS

FOREWORD

It gives me great pleasure to offer a new *Price Guide* for German Militaria to both the collector and the dealer. This guide is unique in may ways.

The price posted in this Guide reflect 'real time' values, that is to say, they are indicative of the prices realized for merchandise sold within the past two years. All of the data has been carefully culled from previous auctions handled by Manion's International Auction House, Inc., of Kansas City, Kansas.

Being the largest military auction house in the world, Manion's handles literally thousands and thousands of items from the mundane to the rare. With a customer base of over 12,000 and an international operation, the company has data showing the prices realized of merchandise sold on a world-wide basis.

Another unique feature of this Price Guide is that it is flexible and can be used in conjunction with the other two Guides in this series—*American Militaria* and *Other Countries' Militaria*—all have the same category structures that allow cross indexing and speedy recovery of data.

The field of Militaria Collectibles is one of the fastest growing areas of investment and collector activity today and it is vitally important to have a reliable, clearly understandable and comprehensive guide that will allow for quick access to vital data without undue delay.

Extensive and long descriptions of material have been kept to a minimum in order to facilitate the maxim input of data on individual lots and prices.

It is hoped that this guide and continuing editions, updated to future sales, will offer collectors and dealers a solid, in-depth work that will assist them in both collecting and marketing decisions.

Ron Manion
Kansas City, Kansas

HOW TO UTILIZE THE GUIDE

Militaria of Germany has been divided into sections—helmets, visor caps, badges, medals, insignia, etc. Each section has a description of a specific item most often encountered by collectors and dealers. Following the description there appears a price. This is the actual price the item sold for within the past 12 months. It reflects a competitive bidding environment and is a 'real' price, not a hypothetical one.

Price is determined by rarity and condition. The prices shown in this guide reflect items in very fine condition. Militaria in damaged array or missing parts will subsequently sell for lesser amounts, the loss in value being determined by the extent of damage suffered by the material.

We have attempted in all cases to offer a broad spectrum of items with equivalent prices ranging from the exotic to the common.

In an effort to satisfy the needs of collectors and dealers who will handle most items found in this guide, we have not covered esoteric areas that are virtually impossible to find—Napoleonic period headgear, 18th century badges, etc.

All items in this guide are currently on the market and can often be encountered.

The guide has been divided into two major section—Imperial Germany and the Third Reich with the Weimar period of 1921–33 being represented by transitional militaria.

Current West and East German militaria is not covered because it is in a state of flux with the unification of Germany the insignia of the DDR or East Germany is flooding the market and at the moment does not command enough value to warrant its addition to this guide. West German militaria has never achieved any significant value and is thus not covered.

Photographs appearing in the price sections show items in very fine condition and they have simple captions for quick identification. Space does not allow for photographs of all items listed. Those photographs appearing in the guide are representative of a wide range of collectible militaria found on the market.

INTRODUCTION

A collector may generally be defined as one who accumulates articles, data, relics and information for scientific, cultural, historical or educational purposes. For those collectors interested in the physical memorabilia of the past as evidenced by documents, material and historical items of military oriented nature, the field is relatively new.

The collecting of Militaria is a relatively recent phenomena that has manifested itself as a strong hobby and investment area only within the last forty to fifty years.

Prior to the end of the Second World War (1945), there was scant evidence of any large collecting community. Previous wars had of course generated tremendous amounts of material—booty, relics, uniforms, badges, etc., but it was not exploited for its collector value as it is today.

Companies such as Francis Bannermann offered a wide assortment of muskets, cannons, uniforms, swords, armor and related equipment at what would today be considered bargain prices but which, in the time of offering, were somewhat high.

During the American Civil War there were some exhibitions of captured Confederate flags, muskets and swords but the items were not considered collectible in the modern sense of the word. Indeed, with the advent of cartridge weapons, all of the nuzzle loaders were relegated to the category of outdated weaponry and were only used by those who could not afford the newest improvement in firearms.

The Spanish American War of 1898 brought home few souvenirs and there was again no collectible market for relics of the conflict.

During the First World War (1914–1919), the American government sponsored Victory Loan drives and utilized captured German spiked helmets as an attraction to gather curious crowds for the purpose of soliciting donations to the war. After the conflict, scores of these helmets languished in civic centers, schools, libraries and VFW and American Legion halls to gather dust.

It would not be until the end of the Second World War (1939–1945) that the beginnings of collector hobby community could develop. American soldiers returned from this conflict laden with war souvenirs—colorful German flags, daggers, pistols, swords, uniforms, belts, buckles, etc. American veterans who fought in the Pacific brought back samurai and Japanese military swords along with flags and uniforms.

In the mid-1950s the first stirrings of a collector movement began. At first it consisted of younger people buying war souvenirs from the veterans; it progressed into the appearance of early books on German and Japanese badges, insignia, daggers and swords.

The centennial celebration of the American Civil War in 1961 through 1965 brought attention to the old uniforms and equipment of the conflict and this in turn agitated the collector market. Suddenly muskets that previously sold for $40 now commanded $150 and up. Investment became a strong probability and collectors began amassing material with an eye both to its historical value and its future potential in terms of money.

Within the space of ten years a marked change occurred in the military collectible sphere. From 1965 until the mid-70s it was still possible to obtain fine material from local military and gun shows. There was a wide exchange of trade and swapping. Then, with the realization of cash value opportunity in amassing material, the items began to disappear into private collections.

By the 1990s, almost all the material that had been so plentiful disappeared and could only be purchased through dealers who well understood the value of the merchandise they possessed.

This of course must not be construed to say that ALL collectibles of a military nature are in the hands of dealers. However, it would be safe to assume that a large percentage of the material that once flooded the 1970s gun shows is no longer available on an open market.

The same law applies to other countries that govern the market in the United States. Rarely does one encounter militaria in the open market overseas unless it is in such distressed condition that no dealer wants it. The Germans, who once had little interest in the spiked helmets of the Second Reich or the memorabilia of the Third Reich, are not avid collectors of the artifacts. British buyers scour their Arms Fairs for bargains in Victorian and Edwardian headgear only to find most of it in the hands of dealers.

The great flea markets of Paris rarely yield bargains—dealers have picked up whatever will command future potential profit.

The same applied to Western and Eastern Europe—the myth of the country with untold treasures of militaria for sale at cheap prices is, in the end, only a myth. The former states of the Warsaw Pact are as aware of value and price as their Western European and American cousins.

When collectible militaria was relatively cheap, there was little need for price guides. What then was important were books on identification and history if the material.

Today, when there are more than enough books on identification, the price guide has become valuable, if for no other purpose than to identify material of high value as opposed to low end items.

It is important to target collectibles that have a high yield value both for purchase, sale, appraisal and insurance purposes. Material purchased in the past has continued to climb in price and what one paid for a sword in 1980 is not currently indicative of the true value of the item in 1995.

Current evaluations have absolutely nothing to do with the actual price of the material at the time of it creation. Today's collector seeks a 'historical' price as opposed to a 'production' price. Today's collectibles have no commercial value per se as their worth is not tied to the economic production value at the time of production. Value accrues from the item's worth as an educational, historical or collectible relic.

The vast impedimenta of militaria has little real value even in collector terms—mess tins, ponchos, worn canteens, and the like do not possess a strong collector value. They are too common and are not highly sought after. However a chained SS officer dagger, the presentation Civil War sword, a spiked helmet or a historical banner have great value. It is important to know the difference between what is worthy of acquisition and what should be avoided.

In an extreme case, beginning collectors might visit the equivalent of an Army & Navy Store selling used military uniforms, jackets, field gear, etc. Very rarely do such stores have anything that might rightfully be called 'collectible.' Their offerings are the low end of what most collectors want.

On the other hand, antique stores will often have an occasional cuirass, sword or article of great value. Sometimes, because the dealer is unaware of the significance of the item he owns, this can be cheaply purchased.

In an attempt to address the relative values of the common and the rare for both collectors, dealers and handlers of merchandise of a military nature, this Guide will reflect a broad spectrum of material that will be encountered on the market place.

It is hoped that effort will introduce the reader to the nature of what is of value and what is of little worth. The prices reflect 'real time' transactions that took place in the past two years.

CONDITION, RATING AND EVALUATION OF COLLECTIBLE MILITARIA

All militaria collectibles, whether common or rare, are profoundly affected by their condition at time of sale or trade. Damage, repairs, alterations and lack of parts adversely reflect on sale value.

An item with a legitimate field repair done by a soldier at the time of its use is not as badly affected as one which has a repair made long after the conflict in which it was employed.

For all practical purposes, highest values are obtained from, material that is, as closely as possible, reflective of the nature of the item when it was issued.

Replaced insignia, pins, badges and parts can reduce the insignia nature of a collectible by almost 50–60%.

All items listed in this price guide will reflect the OPTIMUM VALUE (i.e. the highest current value without alternation). For any item with alterations, the price will be effected and descend toward a lower end. Consultation with this Guide will establish 'best' price.

Another factor that often determines value is rank. Officer equipment, being of high quality and quite often privately purchased, commands high value than the equipment utilized by Non-Commissioned Officer and enlisted ranks.

For example, an officer Grade du Corps eagle top helmet will reach a value of around $10,000 while the same helmet, in enlisted issue pattern sells for approximately $4500. There is almost a $6000 price differential.

Speaking of Reproduction . . .

A reproduction is any item that attempts to copy or approximate a real counterpart. The Military Collectibles field is filled with a vast amount of reproductions that cover the entire spectrum of collecting from paper documents to swords, daggers, badges, insignia, uniforms, headgear, etc. By and large a reproduction has NO value as it is not original nor was it used in the time period it purports to represent.

Some items are reproduced because originals are almost non-existent or are in such current condition that they could not be used for their original purpose. War games and re-enactors often utilize reproduction uniforms and insignia to recreate battle situations. Other reproductions are spawned to take advantage of collectors who cannot tell the real from the false. The latter category is the most injurious to the collecting field. A reproduction has neither an intrinsic nor a collector/historical value as it currently made.

Reproductions, even if very well crafted, will never achieve the value of the true thing and should be avoided both for investment and collector potential.

IMPERIAL GERMAN CLOTH JACKETS, UNIFORMS, BREECHES

22ND INF. EM OVERCOAT: Dark blue wool with double row of flat-brass buttons. Red shd. bds. with yellow #22. Red stand-up collar. Also has red lapels, red piping, & closure. Below avg. cond. $76.00

ARMY EM FATIGUE PANTS: 1915. White. 4 metal gray button fly. Patch style watch pocket. Unit marked BAX 1915.73. Avg. cond. $145.00

ARMY EM FATIGUE PANTS: White body with 4 gray metal button fly. Patch watch pocket & rear. High tapered back. Faint inked *Arbeits Zentrale Darmstadt*. Type worn with stable, drill & parade tunics. Avg. cond. $65.00

ARTILLERY OFFICER STABLE DRESS TUNIC, PANTS & BELT: Tunic is of white khaki cloth with stand-up mouse-gray collar & subdued crown buttons, sew-in style shoulder straps with red backing, silver tops, black flecking, gilt brass flaming bomb & #80. Two lower slash pockets. Corduroy stable dress pants with matching brown leather belt having roller style buckle with single claw. Avg. cond. $950.00

AUSTRIAN GENERAL
STAFF PIPED TUNIC

AUSTRIAN GENERAL STAFF PIPED TUNIC: Dark blue wool body, red wool piping, blue velvet cuffs & collar with dark silver embr. litzen. 12 frosted silver eagle buttons show darkening. 3 sewn grommet holes for screwback badges. Loops for boards. Full lining with pocket. Avg. cond. $750.00

AUSTRIAN HUSSAR NCO TAILORED
ATTILA WITH FLEECE COLLAR

AUSTRIAN HUSSAR NCO TAILORED ATTILA WITH FLEECE COLLAR: Blue twill wool body, white piping, 16 gold buttons, white cuffs with dark brocade tape, gold front cord & dark gold shouldercord. Black fleece collar & full black satin lining with pocket & bevo marked *Alexander Sohr Wien etc*. Exc. cond. $282.00

AUSTRIAN NCO TUNIC & MATCHING PANTS: WWI. Blue-gray wool body with two upper scalloped pockets. Stand-up collar. Concealed button closure. Collar tabs are dark green with 3 gold wire rank stars. Straight-leg wool pants with 3 green rows of piping. Two orders loops on right pocket. Above avg. cond. $192.00

AUSTRIAN OFFICER DOUBLE BREASTED TUNIC: Light blue doeskin body, red piping, red cuffs & standing collar with gold brocade tape. 16 gold buttons with design. Full lining with bevo label *Kriegsministerium Wien etc*. Above avg. cond. $370.00

BAVARIAN 12TH INF REGT ONE YEAR VOLUNTEER TUNIC: Double dated 1903, 1905 inside with 12th Inf. regt. stamps & contract issue marks. Full liner. Faint owner name below collar. Dark blue wool body with red piping & stand-up collar. Brandenburg style cuffs. Brass buttons. Blue/white piping on red shoulder boards with yellow embr. #12, company buttons numbered 5. Avg. cond. $225.00

UNIFORMS

BAVARIAN 1ST INF. REGT. EM TUNIC: M1910/15. Gray wool body with turn down collar, red piping & tails. Belt ramp buttons present. Brandenburg cuffs with subdued lion style buttons; same on front & rear. Partial style lining for summer issue. Named to owner inside with hand embroidered name. Red embr. #1 on shoulder straps with 8th company buttons. Tunic has two lower slash style pockets. Near mint cond. $480.00

BAVARIAN 2ND LT LITEWKA: Polished copper double row of buttons. Slate-gray body with red piping & light green wool turn down collar. Red tabs with matching buttons. Silver wire shd. bds. with red piping & Bavarian-blue flecking. Two lower slash style pockets. Exc. cond. $276.00

BAVARIAN ARTY LT SERVICE TUNIC: Gray body has repaired red cord/wool piping to front opening. 8 brass lion buttons. Black piped cuffs & red to back. Loops for ribbon bar. Narrow slip-on boards. Lining inked with size *B.A.?1910, 6.fd.A.R.etc..1913* & etc. Avg. cond. $912.00

BAVARIAN CHEVAULEGER REGT IV PLASTRON: Dark red with blue wool backing. Owner name tag intact- *Trumpeter Sergeant Goschl, IV. Chev.-Regt. 4 Esk.* Above avg. cond. .. $76.00

BAVARIAN GENERAL FIELD GRAY TUNIC: 1915. Feldgrau wool with stand-up gray collar having subdued gold wire general collar tabs. Red piped to include collar, closure, cuffs. Two lower slash pockets. Subdued bronze colored Bavarian lion buttons. Red wool slip-on general shoulder boards in subdued gold & silver with blue-white flecking. Large deluxe parade furled ribbon bar with 6 ribbons: Bav. Military Service Cross, 1st, 2nd class + EK 1914 + 1916 Ludwig Cross + Hungarian + Austrian Campaign medals. Group also includes a *ko* hmkd flat-style wartime EK 1914 1st class + black wound badge. Tunic is fully lined. Near mint cond. $2,565.00

BAVARIAN MEDICAL OBERLT PIPED WOOL SERVICE TUNIC: Gray body has red piped front opening & back. 8 brass lion buttons, blue piped cuffs & collar. Blue twill collar tabs with red piping. Darkening to slip-on boards that have been sewn in, pip & snake/staff to each. Full lining with couple patches & slash pocket. Loops for 1 badge. Above avg. cond. $1,250.00

BAVARIAN MEDICAL OFFICER BRO-CADE BELT WITH GILT BUCKLE:

Round buckle with wreath, Bavarian crown. Belt is of silver brocade with 2 wide blue stripes & blue cloth backed. Very interesting buckle adjustment. Above avg. cond. $155.00

BLACK WOOL PANTS WITH YELLOW PIPING: 14th Inf Regt unit marked. Front slash pockets. Yellow piping. Avg. cond. $116.00

CAVALRY EM BELT WITH SWORD HANGER & BUCKLE: Open face brass buckle, blue felt lined white leather dress belt. Avg. cond. $101.00

COLLAR LINER: 3" wide brown satin body tapers down to 1.5" at slot adjustment. White satin inner lining with inked *7 1/2 otm*. Near mint cond. $22.00

COLONIAL ASKARIS/BLACK-TROOPER TAN TUNIC

COLONIAL ASKARIS/BLACK-TROOPER TAN TUNIC: Tan/brown twill cotton body, 4 patch pockets & red wool piped cuffs. Green wool sew-in shoulder straps. Partial tan lining with faint ink stamps & padded shoulders. Above avg. cond. $222.00

COLONIAL SOUTH-WEST AFRICA LT SERVICE TUNIC & BREECHES: Blue piped for SW Africa. Tan corduroy cloth with 2 upper scalloped pockets, two lower pockets. Frosted silver crown colonial buttons with nice hallmarks. Red-white-black cord shoulder straps of Lt. aide-de-camp fouraguerre in white cord with red-black flecking. Full liner. Loops onboth breasts for medals & badges. Matching breeches (straight-leg) with proper blue cord piping. Right sleeve has cloth colonial shield in white with black bars,

red canton, & white stars.
Above avg. cond. $700.00

COLONIAL SOUTHWEST AFRICA
SCHUTZTRUPPE NCO TUNIC

COLONIAL SOUTHWEST AFRICA
SCHUTZTRUPPE NCO TUNIC: The
Schutztruppe was a very small elite unit.
Less than 100 NCO were ever in this unit.
Tan corduroy with blue piping on fold
down collar, cuffs & front. Silver NCO
braid. Polished brass buttons. Four
pleated patch pockets. NCO rank buttons
on the collar. Shoulder strap buttons are
also present. Above avg.
cond. $375.00
DICKEY FOR TUNIC: Gray cloth, wrap
around. Avg. cond. $29.00
EISENBANN 2ND REGT OFFICER FIELD
GRAY LITEWKA: The Eisenbann was a
technical branch of the military &
responsible for rail movement of troops &
supplies. Wartime 2nd lt. dbl. breasted
tunic Standard litewka with dbl. row of
silvered domed buttons. EK2 rb. in 2nd
button hole. Black tech svc. collar tabs
with red piping & silver buttons. 2nd lt.
shoulder straps with gilt E2 device for an
Eisenbahn unit. Full lining. Lower slash
pockets. Has original Hamburg maker's
label. Above avg. cond. $428.00
FATIGUE TROUSERS: White cotton with
BA marks inside. Cord lace up waist.
Avg. cond. $65.00
FATIGUE TROUSERS: White. Still has
paper maker/size label sewn to front. 4
gray metal buttons to fly & for suspenders. Inked size, *191?* & *5.G.B.*
Near mint cond. $48.00

GARDE NCO BANDSMAN TUNIC
WITH SWALLOWS' NESTS

GARDE NCO BANDSMAN TUNIC WITH
SWALLOWS' NESTS: Dark Prussian-
blue body. Red piping. NCO lace on
sleeves & collar. Yellow shd. bds. with
matching yellow, blue swallows' nests
having cord hangers. Yellow Garde
matching litzen on each sleeve. Domed
copper style buttons on front & sleeves.
Exc. cond. $325.00

GENERAL STAFF OFFICER TUNIC

GENERAL STAFF OFFICER TUNIC: Pre-
WWI. Dark Prussian-blue wool tunic with

red piping on closures & collar. Large Garde style gold braid on collar with matching cuff litzen. Copper domed buttons. Full silken black liner. Loops present for slip-on shoulder straps. Near mint cond. $400.00

HUSSAR 1 YEAR VOLUNTEER TAILORED LANCE-CORPORAL ATTILA: Cornflower-blue wool body with gold ornamentation & buttons. Lining has nice bevo maker label at neck *Budapesten etc.* Avg. cond. $195.00

HUSSAR ATTILA (SERVICE TUNIC): This looks like an enlisted uniform with lt. shoulder straps. Dark orange-red body with gilt barrel roundels & buttons. Golden-yellow cord froging. Lt. shoulder straps. Name marked on inside. Avg. cond. $370.00

HUSSAR MUSICIAN ATTILA (DRESS TUNIC): Light blue with dark yellow cording & brass buttons. Complete with yellow-blue matching swallows' nests. NCO style braid piping. Avg. cond. $219.00

NAVAL EM DRESS 'MONKEY' JACKET: Dark blue wool, gilt crown, & anchor buttons. *BAK 18.5.06* issue date inside body. Above avg. cond. $158.00

NAVAL EM DRESS JACKET: 1915. Blue wool body with 18 nickel button front & 6 on each cuff. Black lining, slash pocket & faint inked *BAW 6.3.15 3.* Above avg. cond. $145.00

NAVAL EM FATIGUE SHIRT: Heavy white cotton body, slash pocket, slash cuffs & flap to collar. Pullover with slash having tie string. Flap underside inked *BAW 4.11.03 3* & owner tag *Posse.* Avg. cond. $45.00

NAVAL EM JACKET: Blue wool body with hallmarked naval buttons. Tunic has all buttons & also white wool chevron on left arm. Inside dated Sept. 4, 1895 with Wilhelmshaven quartermaster issue marks. Owner name tag (*Sexter*) sewn inside with unit marks below. Two small eyelet hooks for bib retention on back. Avg. cond. $180.00

NAVAL EM SHIRT FOR TROPICAL CLIMATES, DRESS, ETC.: 1906. White pullover style with blue cuffs & attached dickey. Issue marked *BAK 30.11.06.3.* Tie string front. Avg. cond. $75.00

NAVAL EM UNIFORM LOT: Pre-WWI. Each article of clothing has cloth tag with *Paul Muller* name. Dark blue cap has Kiel issue stamp with Nov. 5, 1914 date & silver bevo tally, *SMS Bremen.* Tunic has

silver buttons, yellow rank chevron & date May 10, 1907 with Kiel issue marks. Wool pants named to sailor with June 1, 1910 date & Wilhelmshafen issue marks. The chain closure is still present & intact. Near mint cond. $555.00

NAVAL PO DRESS JACKET: With petty officer's engineer silver crowned anchor sleeve rating. Deluxe blue wool body with high relief crown buttons. Silver chain & buttons on front. Has silver PO tressing to each cuff. Near mint cond. $300.00

NAVAL TORPEDO BOAT SEAMAN
DRESS BLUE WOOL JACKET

NAVAL TORPEDO BOAT SEAMAN DRESS BLUE WOOL JACKET: High quality with silver crown & anchor buttons (dbl. breasted) to include cuffs. Yellow embroidered Mine Specialist patch on left sleeve with red-white-black inverted chevron above. Jacket marked *II.T.1. 42/ 11 WILHELMSHAVEN 1910.* Near mint cond. $265.00

NAVAL WERFT-DIVISION PO BLUE WOOL JUMPER: Custom purchase. Black silken liner. Silver buttons on front (hallmarked). Silver tressing on sleeves. Avg. cond. $175.00

OFFICER DICKEY FOR INSIDE OF STANDING COLLAR: Blue-gray cloth with full tabs. Tie cords present. Two green litzen sewn on front for a jaeger unit. Nicely stamped with eagle mark on back. Near mint cond. $45.00

PRUSSIAN 23RD FIELD ARTILLERY NCO TUNIC: Dark blue wool with black stand-up collar & cuffs. NCO gold braid trim. Tombak domed buttons. Fine quality blue wool shoulder straps with red embroidered flaming bomb & #23. Has black silk lining. Red piped. Loops on breast are for decorations. Avg. cond. $275.00

PRUSSIAN CHILD TUNIC: Pre-WWI. Dark blue wool body with red piping & stand-up collar. Brandenburg cuffs. Brass domed buttons. Full tails, piping & buttons on rear. Red shoulder boards with white #20 embr. 8th company buttons. Partial liner. Above avg. cond. $85.00

body with red piping to cuffs, collar, closure & tails. Deluxe copper style domed buttons. Slip-on, 4th Artillery major shd. bds. with gilt cipher of unit. Black velour stand-up collar. Has full & lining. Matching velour cuffs. Avg. cond. $350.00

PRUSSIAN GARDE OFFICER BLUE DRESS TUNIC: Has fancy Erfurt maker label inside. Dark blue wool with stand-up collar having heavy silver bullion Garde litzen. Matching litzen on cuff. Red piped. Copper buttons. Large silver & black loops for the shoulder epaulettes. Shoulder buttons also present. Size looks to be about a 40. Above avg. cond. $350.00

PRUSSIAN EM GREATCOAT

PRUSSIAN GARDE OFFICER
DRESS TUNIC

PRUSSIAN EM GREATCOAT: M1910. Stone-gray doeskin body, 6 nickel buttons, 2 slash pockets, French cuffs, white wool collar tabs & shoulder boards with red cord WR II & red wool crown. Full lining with pocket. Avg. cond. $275.00

PRUSSIAN FIELD ARTILLERY OFFICER DRESS TUNIC: Dark Prussian-blue wool

PRUSSIAN GARDE OFFICER DRESS TUNIC: Dark Prussian-blue wool body with domed silver buttons. Silver Garde litzen on full stand-up collar. Matching litzen to sleeves. Service shd. bds. of a captain with rank insignia, silver field, & black flecking. Black velour collar & cuffs with matching litzen & buttons. Full liner. About 1912 period. Near mint cond. $375.00

PRUSSIAN HUSSAR NCO ATTILA FOR HUSSAR: Blue wool with white cloth frogging. Silvered metal buttons. White cord shoulder straps, no ciphers. Avg. cond. $250.00

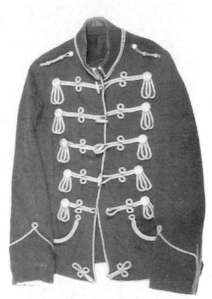

PRUSSIAN HUSSAR OFFICER
ATTILA (TUNIC)

PRUSSIAN HUSSAR OFFICER ATTILA (TUNIC): Sherwood-green with silver frogging & frosted silver round buttons. Stand-up collar with matching piping. Black flecking in cording. Lt. shd. bds. Full liner. Near mint cond. $300.00

PRUSSIAN HUSSAR OFFICER TUNIC: Black wool with silver frogging & buttons. Black flecking. Quatrefoil style shoulder bds. in silver wire. Full liner & inner belt. Loops for medals present. Stand-up collar. Special sewn hole for a breast order of some princely house. Above avg. cond. $340.00

PRUSSIAN HUSSAR ONE YEAR VOLUNTEER TUNIC: Dark Prussian-blue. White/black cording on loops, collar & frogging. Silvered buttons. Full liner. Stand-up collar. Silver shd. bd. buttons. Above avg. cond. $325.00

PRUSSIAN HUSSAR TUNIC: Attila style. Powder-blue. Silver frogging with black flecking. Army style shd. bds. with black flecking. Stand-up collar. Full silken liner with collar liner present. Avg. cond. $325.00

PRUSSIAN KURASSIER OFFICER BREAST FRONTPLATE: 18th century. Black Japanned tin style frontplate with original liner remaining in light rust-red color. Remains of flared padding. Brass scalloped side & neck trim with iron rivets. Brass FR device on chest. Brass

studs remain for shoulder straps. Raised shoulder guides for straps remain. Type worn & associated with 1, 2, 6 & 8th kurassier regts. Officer pieces were always light. EM & NCOs wore heavier steel bodies. Avg. cond. $2,100.00

PRUSSIAN RESERVIST LT. GREATCOAT: M1910. Stone-gray body with 12 crown buttons, 2 slash pockets, fake French cuffs & blue wool collar. Slip-on gray boards with green piping & white bases. 7 crown button back with strap. Full gray satin lining inside. Above avg. cond. $232.00

SAXON JAGER #12 EM GREATCOAT

SAXON JAGER #12 EM GREATCOAT: Light gray almost lilac wool body, black wool collar tabs & sewn in large black shoulder straps with red wool piping, horn/12 & nickel #3 button to each. Full satin lining with slash pocket. Exc. cond. $200.00

STRAIGHT LEG TROUSERS: White twill body. White cloth covered buttons around waist. 2 slash pockets. Avg. cond. $50.00

TROPICAL SHORTS: 1915 unit marked. Gray canvas. Patch style small front & 2 slash side pockets. 5 gray metal button fly & suspender buttons. Adjustment belt across back. Inked *1915 F.A.14.* Summer & tropical use. Above avg. cond. $95.00

UHLAN 2ND REGT OFFICER TUNIC: Wartime corduroy configuration. Plain style red piped shoulder boards with subdued wire finish. Black flecked with subdued metallic #2. Red piped closure with stand-up collar. Gray subdued buttons. Very unusual with rough corduroy layering. Full tails & two lower slash style pockets. Above avg. cond. $1,350.00

UHLAN 3RD GARDE NCO DRESS ULANKA (TUNIC): Dark blue wool with dark yellow piping, stand-up collar & lapels. Silver domed button. NCO litzen & silver rank pip of a feldwebel. Double lance chevrons on right sleeve. Avg. cond. $475.00

UHLAN EM PLASTRON: Lemon-yellow. Owner name handwritten on cloth backing. Above avg. cond. $69.00

UHLAN EM ULANKA

UHLAN EM ULANKA: Dark blue wool body, pink piping, black velvet cuffs & collar. Darkening to silver tape sleeve rank, 12 nickel buttons & blue wool shoulder straps. Full black lining. Above avg. cond. $265.00

UHLAN OFFICER RABATTE: With many loops for decorations. Lemon-yellow. Light yellow silk lining. Above avg. cond. $81.00

UHLAN OFFICER ULANKA: Dark blue wool body, yellow wool piping overall, yellow cuffs, standing collar & sew-on plastron front. 14 nickel buttons. Full lining with

pocket & inked out area to back. Exc. cond. $271.00

IMPERIAL GERMAN BELT BUCKLES

AUSTRIAN EM BELT BUCKLE: 50mm. Stamped brass. Stamped crowned shield proof to top corner. Above avg. cond. $45.00

AUSTRIAN EM BELT BUCKLE: Stamped steel body with gray painted finish. Avg. cond. $58.00

BAVARIAN EM BELT BUCKLE WITH BELT

BAVARIAN EM BELT BUCKLE WITH BELT: Stamped steel with gray paint. Black leather belt with steel hook, leather tongue, stamped *5 Fd.A.R.1916* & size 95. Avg. cond. $118.00

BRUNSWICK OFFICER BUCKLE: Stamped buckle has frosted silver finish to laurel leaf wreath. 92nd tradition skull with crossbones below is nickel cap style with 2 prongs through buckle holes. Belt loop to back-side. Above avg. cond. $164.00

BUTCHER BELT BUCKLE

BUTCHER BELT BUCKLE: 45mm. Dark brass body with 2 rivets to nickel. Silver cow head & cleavers at center. Cast brass prong bar & soldered hook. Styled after M1850. Avg. cond. $95.00

DUCAL BELT BUCKLE: Brass plate with attached decor including initials G & C bracketing a royal crest. Topped by a crown, shows 4 fields meeting at a center of 3 fleur-de-lis in oval. Fields contain two castles & two lions each positioned at opposing corners. Barcelona hallmark. Avg. cond. $65.00

FRENCH INFANTRY EM BELT BUCKLE: 1870. 2.5x2.25" plain rectangular brass plate with loop & retainer on reverse. Above avg. cond. $67.00

GARDE DU CORPS GALA CROSS-STRAP WITH POUCH: Red & white cotton cross-strap has silver strips & pouch to end. Painted details to affixed silver garde star. Roller buckles to bottom. Avg. cond. $460.00

HANNOVER EM BELT BUCKLE: 65mm. Brass body with brass roundel. Above avg. cond. $68.00

HATE BELT WITH 10 DEVICES & PRUSSIAN EM BELT BUCKLE: Brass with nickel roundel & unmarked leather tab. Maker to brown belt with brass hook & tongue. 9 different buttons & silver badge with profiles of Wilhelm II/Franz Josef etc. Pb. Avg. cond. $40.00

HATE BELT WITH 18 DEVICES: Brown body with steel hook & leather tongue. Was size 100. Most buttons & devices are affixed with catches or loops & are intact. Unique silver disc with early race car, enamel 1914 EK with oak leaves on arty. ring, etc.. Above avg. cond. $95.00

HATE BELT WITH 24 DEVICES & PRUSSIAN EM BELT BUCKLE: Brass with nickel roundel. Brown belt with various buttons, pips, cockades, 2 patriotic EK finger rings & silver wound badge. Avg. cond. $26.00

NAVAL OFFICER BELT BUCKLE WITH BELT: 1.5" wide. Dark brown russet leather with circular gilt buckle having wreath, W & anchor. Complete with two lion head slides having hook for dagger hanger. Brass keepers present. Above avg. cond. $85.00

NAVAL OFFICER BELT BUCKLE WITH BROCADE BELT: Gold crowned anchor buckle. Silver brocade facing with 2 black stripes & center red strip. Blue wool backing & grommet size adjustment for about 90. One hidden hinged brass hanger loop. 2 brocade loops. Above avg. cond. $139.00

NAVAL OFFICER BELT BUCKLE WITH BROCADE BELT: Large circular gilt

buckle with anchor, W & crown. Silver brocade belt with backing. Black/gold stripes. Above avg. cond. $177.00

NAVAL OFFICER BELT BUCKLE: Large brass round body with oak leaf trim. Fouled anchor with crown & W cipher. Above avg. cond. $54.00

NAVAL OFFICER DAGGER BELT BUCKLE: 40mm brass disc with gold finish to laurel leaf wreath with crowned W anchor center. Loop to back side. Exc. cond. $80.00

PRUSSIAN CAVALRY BELT BUCKLE WITH BELT: Gray buckle with bronks. Brown leather belt stamped 116. Back inked *J.R.49.* Avg. cond. $35.00

PRUSSIAN CAVALRY BRASS BELT BUCKLE: M1857. Size 2x2.5". Rectangular style with raised edges. Two piece keeper construction. Above avg. cond. $40.00

PRUSSIAN EM BELT BUCKLE WITH BELT

PRUSSIAN EM BELT BUCKLE WITH BELT: 45mm. Brass body with nickel roundel. Brown leather belt, brass hook & leather tongue. Avg. cond. $71.00

PRUSSIAN EM BELT BUCKLE WITH BELT: Brass body with nickel crown. Black leather belt with leather tongue & brass hook. Approx. 90cm long. Avg. cond. $45.00

PRUSSIAN EM BELT BUCKLE WITH BELT: Brass body, 2 solder holes & nickel roundel with dented crown. Prong bar is stamped *DRGM.* Black leather belt with leather tongue & steel hook intact. Avg. cond. $30.00

PRUSSIAN EM BELT BUCKLE WITH BELT: Stamped steel with gray paint. Black belt, tongue, steel hook & size 105. Avg. cond. $28.00

PRUSSIAN EM BELT BUCKLE WITH BELT: Stamped steel with gray paint. Black leather belt with steel hook, leather tongue & size 108. Leipzig maker, 1916 & Army issue *BAXIX 16.* Above avg. cond. $50.00

PRUSSIAN EM BELT BUCKLE WITH BELT:
Stamped steel with gray paint. Brown
leather tab by *Lieferungs-Gen. Itzehoe
1918*. Black leather belt with leather tongue,
steel hook, faint 1916/maker & size 105.
Above avg. cond. $82.00

PRUSSIAN EM BELT BUCKLE WITH
WHITE PARADE DRESS BELT: 40mm.
This is a smaller size than the standard.
Brass body with nickel roundel. White
patent leather belt with leather tongue,
gray hook & white felt backing. Size 104.
Avg. cond. $49.00

PRUSSIAN EM BELT BUCKLE WITH
WHITE PARADE DRESS BELT: 45mm.
Brass body with silver roundel. White
patent leather belt with red felt backing,
leather tongue & brass hook stamped
DRGM 75604. Size 88.
Above avg. cond. $55.00

PRUSSIAN EM BELT BUCKLE
WITH WHITE WOVEN BELT

PRUSSIAN EM BELT BUCKLE WITH
WHITE WOVEN BELT: 45mm. Brass body
with nickel roundel. Brass hook to variation
white string woven belt body & tongue.
Above avg. cond. $169.00

PRUSSIAN EM BELT BUCKLE: 45mm. The
difference on this piece is the oak leaf 1/2
wreath. On the standard pattern the half
wreath is laurel leaves! Brass body with
nickel roundel.
Near mint cond. $72.00

PRUSSIAN EM BELT BUCKLE: Stamped
steel with gray finish. Brown leather tab with
stamped *Carl Remers & Co. Altona 1917*.
Exc. cond. $79.00

PRUSSIAN EM BELT BUCKLE: 50mm.
Brass body with nickel roundel. *DRGM*
stamped prong bar.
Avg. cond. $36.00

PRUSSIAN EM BELT BUCKLE: 50mm.
Polished brass body, nickel roundel & 3
solder holes. Early style.
Above avg. cond. $66.00

PRUSSIAN EM BELT BUCKLE

PRUSSIAN EM BELT BUCKLE: Stamped
steel body with gray paint is still
wrapped in the original paper.
Mint cond. $20.00

PRUSSIAN EM BELT BUCKLE: Stamped
steel with gray finish. Brown leather tab is
dated 1915 & marked with maker.
Avg. cond. $32.00

PRUSSIAN EM BELT BUCKLE: Stamped
steel with gray paint. Brown leather
stamped *Werkgen.Sattler
Innung.Hamburg 1916* & *BAG*.
Exc. cond. $25.00

PRUSSIAN EM BELT BUCKLE: Stamped
steel with gray paint. Brown tab by
L.Regensburgers Nachf. Mannheim 1915.
Avg. cond. $28.00

PRUSSIAN OFFICER BELT BUCKLE
WITH BROCADE BELT

PRUSSIAN OFFICER BELT BUCKLE WITH
BROCADE BELT: Brocade facing with 2
gray stripes. Two brocade loops with green
twill wool backing. Leather tongue with
pronged loop. Gold finish to brass buckle
with affixed *WII* center by 3 prongs.
Exc. cond. $111.00

PRUSSIAN OFFICER BELT BUCKLE:
Matte silver finish with keeper. Circular
oak leaf pattern with W & crown device in
center. Near mint cond. $85.00

PRUSSIAN OFFICER BELT BUCKLE:
Wartime variation. Construction with

UNIFORMS

stamped steel laurel leaf wreath body having affixed crowned *W II* center & back fitting with loop & prong loop. Gold paint. Above avg. cond. $75.00

PRUSSIAN OFFICER SASH BELT: Pre-1896. Darkening to brocade with white cloth backing, large tassels & large loop with grommets to adjust size. Avg. cond. $33.00

PRUSSIAN OFFICER SASH BELT: Scharpe. Large 17x3x3" stiff cardboard case in dark green with original tissue paper inside. Inside printed litho label from firm of Franz Klein, Breslau, Konigssplatz. Many printed medallions of quality. Belt has silvered buckle (hook style) with white silk backing. Silver wire field with dbl. black stripes. Full tassels. Mint cond. $168.00

PRUSSIAN OFFICER SASH BELT

PRUSSIAN OFFICER SASH BELT: Silver body with 2 gray stripes, large tassels, white cloth backing & only has metal loop fitting with no hook device. Above avg. cond. $41.00

PRUSSIAN OFFICERS BELT BUCKLE: 48mm dia. Gilt buckle with crowned *W II* cipher, has hinged left rectangular anchor for belt & broad hook on reverse. Above avg. cond. $55.00

PRUSSIAN TELEGRAPHER BELT BUCKLE WITH BELT: Brass buckle. Belt marked *IR118* with brass keeper. Extended leather tab. Avg. cond. $250.00

PRUSSIAN TELEGRAPHER BELT BUCKLE: Stamped steel. Avg. cond. $225.00

SAXON EM BELT BUCKLE WITH BELT: Friction latch is experimental pattern. Tomback buckle with nickel roundel. Stamped *DRGM 171230*. 45mm black leather belt. Above avg. cond. $95.00

SAXON EM BELT BUCKLE: 45mm. Stamped steel. Avg. cond. $48.00

WURTTEMBERG EM BELT BUCKLE: Brass body, nickel roundel & 2 solder holes. Above avg. cond. $51.00

WURTTEMBURG EM BELT BUCKLE: 50mm. Nickel body & nickel roundel. Avg. cond. $60.00

THIRD REICH UNIFORMS

BELL BOTTOM PANTS NAVAL EM: White. Flap front, stamped metal buttons & tie string back. Owner name *Fimmat*. Above avg. cond. $66.00

BROWN SHIRT NSDAP ORTSGRUPPE BLOCK LEADER: Tan twill cotton body, blue cord piping to collar showing tan wool tabs with swastika tape stripes & blue cord piping. 2 pleated patch pockets, 6 pebbled brass belt ramps with RZM, 3 gold eagle buttons & oilcloth tag *RZM PO Diensthemd etc*. Avg. cond. $239.00

BROWN SHIRT NSDAP ORTSGRUPPE MITARBEITER: Tan twill cotton body with 3 removable nickel/eagle button front. 2 pleated patch pockets. 4 gold pebbled belt ramps. Bevo size tag *52*. Blue cord piping to collar. Tan wool tabs with blue cord piping & dark silver/gold tape stripe. Machine sewn on tabs. Above avg. cond. $225.00

BROWN SHIRT NSDAP WITH BREECHES

BROWN SHIRT NSDAP WITH BREECHES: Light brown gabardine body, 3 gold eagle buttons & 2 eagle button lower closure. Partial satin lining with oilcloth RZM tag. Brown cotton collar liner. Inked inside *48 38 62* & maker/party marks to material. Twill wool

breeches with oil cloth RZM tag marked *Stiefelhose W etc.* & inked *48*.
Near mint cond. $795.00
BROWN SHIRT SA: 2 pleated patch pockets, 3 pebbled nickel button front & 6 gray pebbled belt ramps with RZM M5/276. Composite cotton armband. Pink wool tabs have white cord piping & machine sewn on. Inked neck *50 40*.
Above avg. cond. $405.00
CAMO CHEMICAL PROTECTIVE TROUSERS ARMY: Water pattern camo. Step in short leg, bib front camo suit that matches the army camo parka. Was used at the same time as the winter camo parka.
Mint cond. $200.00
CAMO JACKET ARMY WITH TROUSERS: Water pattern camo. Matched set with camo print on tan & purple satin lining. Thin camo hood with string. All buttons & fittings are intact except for suspenders. Inked RB# & size *III* to coat & RB# *II* to trousers. Mint cond $1,313.00

CAMO JACKET SS-WAFFEN

CAMO JACKET SS-WAFFEN: Field made. Reversible. Green oakleaf side has 4 pleated patch pockets & 5 black resin button front. Large hood lacks drawstring. Slash cuffs with resin button to each. Drawstring at waist. Period made from shelter quarter.
Exc. cond. $495.00
CAMO SMOCK ARMY SNIPER: Reversible, water pattern camo to winter white. Hood still has camo gauze for face cover with hole near seam. Tie string to slash neck, drawstring waist, 2 slash openings for tunic pocket use with inked with RB# & size *II*.
Above avg. cond. $1,000.00
CAMO SMOCK LUFTWAFFE PARATROOPER: Printed water pattern camo on heavy twill cotton body, 4 white plastic *RiRi* zippers on pockets & 4 glass buttons remain to front. Variation gray embr. eagle is on gray cloth & zigzag-sewn. Tan/brown flight suit material is used for rank backing with 4 white felt gulls sewn to each. Inked RB#, *IIa* size & 45 date to inside.
Above avg. cond. $1,785.00
CAMO TROUSERS SS-WAFFEN *PEAS-44* HBT: Reinforced seat, 3 slash pockets, watch patch pocket, 6 button fly & side adjustment belts. Tan pocket lining & style of HBT with camo design to off-white side.
Avg. cond. $840.00
COVERALLS ARMY: Gray cloth body. 1940 date. Near mint cond. $235.00

CAMO JACKET ARMY

CAMO JACKET ARMY: Reversible water pattern camo to winter white. Camo print on light brown, white side, hood, 2 pockets, waist-belt & etc. Near mint cond. $706.00
CAMO JACKET ARMY: Splinter pattern camo reversible to winter white. Hood has drawstring, waist-belt, 2 slash pockets & all buttons to front. Inked with RB# & marked size *III*. Above avg. cond. $685.00

DRESS CAPE ARMY OFFICER: Gray doeskin wool body with green collar. 5 button front & button strap at collar with hook. Mint cond. $328.00

DRESS CAPE LUFTWAFFE OFFICER: Blue-gray wool body & collar. 5 button front. Dark alum. eagle head clasp with chain. Bevo maker tag at neck marked *W.Bentrup & Sohn Panderborn etc.* Above avg. cond. $350.00

DRESS JACKET NAVAL PETTY OFFICER: Dark blue wool. Gilt brass KM buttons. Gilt braid on cuffs. Named inside. Embr. breast eagle. PO rate in gilt metal with anchor over chevron. Red flaming bomb, chevron below. With breast chain. Near mint cond. $315.00

DRILL SHIRT NAVAL EM WHITE HBT: Slash pocket front & tie string. Issue stamp to flap. Avg. cond. $55.00

DRILL SHIRT NAVAL REED-GREEN HBT: Pullover with patch pocket front. Short collar. Slash cuffs. Lacks tie strings at front slash. Avg. cond. $120.00

DRILL TROUSERS ARMY REED-GREEN HBT: Straight-leg style, 3 slash pockets & watch slash with paper button. 6 button fly, suspender buttons & side adjustment belts. Avg. cond. $355.00

DRILL TROUSERS NAVAL EM WHITE HBT: Flap front, gray buttons & tie-string back. Avg. cond. $80.00

DRILL TUNIC ARMY ARTY EM REED-GREEN HBT: Dark green body, 4 patch pockets, 6 removable button front, machine sewn on gray bevo eagle & collar tape tabs. Slip-on arty. straps. Partial gray satin lining. Inked size & 1942 date. 2 alum. belt ramps. Above avg. cond. $425.00

DRILL TUNIC ARMY INF EM REED-GREEN HBT: 4 patch pockets, 6 button front, machine sewn on gray bevo eagle & collar tape tabs. Slip-on wool straps with white cord piping. Partial satin lining. Avg. cond. $285.00

DRILL TUNIC ARMY INF NCO REED-GREEN HBT: Green body with 4 patch pockets & removable 6 button front. Gray embr. eagle on green felt, hand sewn. Dark green wool collar with alum. NCO edge & gray/green tape tabs machine sewn to green wool backings. Slip-on straps in dark green with white piping & worn alum. NCO. Inked size inside. Avg. cond. $370.00

DRILL TUNIC ARMY JAGER EM REED-GREEN: Body & bevo sleeve Jager oval intact. Loops & buttons for strap use. Loops for 2 badges. Avg. cond. $217.00

DRILL TUNIC ARMY NCO
REED-GREEN DENIM

DRILL TUNIC ARMY NCO REED-GREEN DENIM: Not the HBT style body. 4 patch pockets & removable buttons. Zigzag sewn bevo eagle, machine sewn on bevo tabs on green bases & hand sewn gray tape stripe to collar. Loops & buttons for strap use. Partial satin lining. Above avg. cond. $265.00

DRILL TUNIC ARMY UNBLEACHED HBT: 5 removable button front with 2 patch pockets & tie string at back. Above avg. cond. $50.00

DRILL TUNIC LUFTWAFFE EM REED-GREEN HBT: 2 pleated patch upper pockets & appears lower pockets have been removed. Slash cuffs, 6 removable blue-gray pebbled button front & loops with buttons for slip-on strap use. Stitches from removed eagle. Partial purple satin lining with bandage pouch & inked RB#, size, & M43. Above avg. cond. $215.00

DRILL TUNIC NSKK WITH BREECHES: Brown HBT. Both are with black inked *NSKK T.F.Mu* & oilcloth tags marked *Drell-Jacke RZM etc.* & *Drell-Hose etc.* Mint cond. $700.00

FLIGHT JACKET LUFTWAFFE CUSTOM MADE WITH FLIGHT TROUSERS: Brown leather. Commercial style waist length with loops for badge. *Elless* metal zipper front. 2 slash lower pockets with flaps. Down tail alum. hand embr. tunic eagle on wool. Cloth lined matching straight-leg trousers with leather suspenders, 3 slash pockets, 4 button fly with hook & cloth lining inked *1944 etc.* Avg. cond. $2,785.00

FLIGHT JACKET LUFTWAFFE WINTER PATTERN: Dark blue-gray body with dark brown fleece lining & collar. Plastic *Ri-Ri* white front zipper & metal *Zipp* cuff zippers. Three slash pockets & hidden waist belt with snap closure. Avg. cond. $556.00

FLIGHT JACKET LUFTWAFFE
WINTER PATTERN

FLIGHT JACKET LUFTWAFFE WINTER PATTERN: Dark gray suede body with large brown fleece collar. *Ries* metal zipper front, waist-belts & 2 snap closure lacks 1 stud. 2 slash pockets with snap/ strap closures. Full white fleece inside. *Zipp* metal zipper at each cuff with snap closures. Above avg. cond. $430.00

FLIGHTSUIT LUFTWAFFE
SUMMER PATTERN

FLIGHTSUIT LUFTWAFFE SUMMER PATTERN: Tan cotton. Emergency escape to left side. Bevo maker tag marked *Bekleidungsfabrik Habelt Crailsheim Wrttbg. 1940 Grosse I.* Avg. cond. $375.00

FLIGHTSUIT LUFTWAFFE
WINTER PATTERN

FLIGHTSUIT LUFTWAFFE WINTER PATTERN: Brown body has dark brown fleece collar & full lining. Button closure front with various metal zippers to pockets. Oilcloth maker tag intact. Avg. cond. $325.00

FLIGHTSUIT LUFTWAFFE WINTER PATTERN: Gray/brown body with thick brown fleece lining & collar. 8 gray resin button front. Metal zippers by *Zipp* & various pockets. Avg. cond. $276.00

FLIGHTSUIT LUFTWAFFE WINTER PATTERN: Heavy gray cloth body with thick brown fleece collar & white fleece lining. Metal zippers & buttons appear intact. Above avg. cond. $384.00

FLIGHT TROUSERS LUFTWAFFE SUMMER PATTERN: Made from same tan/brown material as flightsuit. Rein- forced seat, metal zippers by *Zipp*, equipment pockets with snaps to flaps & built-in waist belt with suspender fittings. Inked RB# & *Ia*. Exc. cond. $538.00

FLIGHT TROUSERS LUFTWAFFE WINTER PATTERN: Natural suede body with fleece lined inside. 5 metal zippers are intact & hidden waist belt with button closure. Above avg. cond. $292.00

UNIFORMS

FLIGHT TUNIC LUFTWAFFE ADMIN OFFICIAL: Blue-gray wool body, 4 hidden buttons & 2 slash pockets. Bullion eagle, twisted alum. collar piping, 2 green tabs with alum. fittings, sew-in boards, green base, red cord, & alum. body gray pip to each. Full satin lining wlth 2 pockets & dagger D-ring. Exc. cond. $559.00

FLIGHT TUNIC LUFTWAFFE ENGINEER GENERAL WITH TROUSERS & VISOR CAP: Smooth blue-gray wool body, 4 hidden buttons, 2 slash pockets, loops for 3 badges & long ribbon bar. Excellent gold celleon hand embr. eagle, twisted celleon collar piping, pink wool tabs with celleon wreath & 2 blade prop. Sew-in boards of plaited gold celleon & alum. on pink wool. Full gray lining with pocket. Matching wool straight-leg trousers with pink wool side stripes. Blue-gray twill wool body visor cap with saddle shape, gold celleon piping, hand embr. eagle, wreath/cockade & chincord. Black band & visor with trim. Leather sweatband. Blue satin lining with diamond having bevo tag *marked L.V.A. etc..Berlin.*
Near mint cond. $4,320.00

FLIGHT TUNIC LUFTWAFFE FLIGHT EM: Blue-gray wool body with insignia. Purple satin partial lining with 2 pockets & inked RB#, size & *LBA(S)43.*
Near mint cond. $744.00

FLIGHT TUNIC LUFTWAFFE FLIGHT EM: Blue-gray wool body. Embr. gray eagle, embr. 2 tone radio/gunner badge, yellow collar tabs with single gull & slip-on shoulder straps. Partial gray lining with 2 pockets. Avg. cond. $385.00

FLIGHT TUNIC LUFTWAFFE
FLIGHT EM

FLIGHT TUNIC LUFTWAFFE FLIGHT NCO: Blue-gray wool body, 2 slash pockets & 4 hidden wood buttons. No partial lining, just pocket linings. Printed white eagle on gray felt is zigzag-sewn. 3 gulls to yellow tabs, alum. tape stripe to collar & slip-on straps with 2 mismatched pips each. Exc. cond. $550.00

FLIGHT TUNIC LUFTWAFFE
FLIGHT NCO

FLIGHT TUNIC LUFTWAFFE FLIGHT NCO: Blue-gray wool body. Embr. gray eagle, yellow tabs with 4 gulls & slip-on shoulder straps. Many loops for badges, 4 to left side, 1 to right side & 1 clasp. 1939 EK ribbon & Afrika ribbon at button hole. *Kreta, Afrika* embr. cufftitles. Partial gray lining with pockets & inked maker, size *LBA40.*
Above avg. cond. $1,437.00

FLIGHT TUNIC LUFTWAFFE SIGNAL EM: Blue-gray wool body with 4 hidden brown plastic button front. Gray embr. eagle is zigzag-sewn. Brown tabs with single gray gull. Slip-on straps. Partial gray lining with inked date, size & Paris/maker. Avg. cond. $244.00

FLIGHT TUNIC LUFTWAFFE SIGNAL NCO: Blue-gray wool body, 4 hidden blue glass buttons & 2 slash pockets. Gray embr. eagle, alum. tape to collar, brown tabs with 4 gray gulls each & slip-on straps with 2 gray pips each. Partial satin lining with inked maker, size & *BAS42.*
Avg. cond. $301.00

FOUL WEATHER JACKET NAVAL WITH TROUSERS: Black leather. Below waist style with 5 gold fouled anchor button front. 3 slash pockets with flaps. Short stand-up collar. Button strap to cuffs. Black wool lined. Gray leather pants. 5 button front. Gray cloth lined with bevo maker *Hela Kleiderjabrik Kiel 46*. Avg. cond. $300.00

FOUL WEATHER JACKET NAVAL: Below waist length, 3 slash pockets, 10 buttons. Fully lined with wool. Avg. cond. $133.00

FOUL WEATHER JACKET NAVAL: Black leather. Above knee length body. 4 black plastic button front 2 slash chest pockets & 2 lower slash/flap pockets. Stamped Eagle-M to front between buttons. Full black wool lining with pocket & bevo neck label *Hilbert Chemnitz etc..1941* & size 52. Type associated the submarine service as opposed to gray leather worn by surface ship personnel. Avg. cond. $196.00

FOUL WEATHER JACKET NAVAL WITH TROUSERS: Black leather. Black wool lining to 5 anchor button body with stand-up collar & 3 slash pockets. Inked maker/date to straight-leg trousers. Avg. cond. $298.00

FOUL WEATHER TROUSERS NAVAL: Black leather. Cloth lining. 3 metal button fly with hook. Suspender buttons marked *Solide Neuheit*. Tall back with leather adjustment straps intact. Exc. cond. $203.00

FOUL WEATHER TROUSERS NAVAL: Black leather. Straight-leg pattern with gray cloth lining. 3 button fly & hook. Large stamped Eagle-M to left front. 2 slash pockets & watch pocket. Adjustment belt at back & suspender buttons. Inked maker tag with date. Avg. cond. $170.00

FROCK COAT NAVAL RESERVE OFFICER KORVETTENKAPITAN: Blue wool body with 10 button front. Celleon hand embr. eagle, dark bullion winged arty. shell sleeve ovals with oak leaves & 3 gold cuff tape-stripes. Loops for 1 badge & 7 place ribbon bar. Wingtips to silver plaited boards & silver tape loop to each side. Full black satin lining with bevo tag *Harnasch Hofschneider Magdeburg* & inked *1937*. Name. Pre-war quality. Exc. cond. $290.00

GREATCOAT ARMY EM: Gray wool body & collar. Partial satin lining with inked size & *M42/II*. Avg. cond. $153.00

GREATCOAT ARMY EM: Gray wool body & large collar. Partial lining with pocket, inked size & RB#. Avg. cond. ... $126.00

GREATCOAT ARMY EM: Gray wool body & collar. Partial gray lining with inked size & date. Exc. cond. $184.00

GREATCOAT ARMY GRAY RUBBERIZED

GREATCOAT ARMY GRAY RUBBERIZED: Pliable body is cut just like greatcoat. Bevo tag size *48*. Exc. cond. $145.00

GREATCOAT ARMY INF NCO: Gray wool body, green collar & slip-on straps with pip to each. Inked maker, size & *M39*. Avg. cond. .... $185.

GREATCOAT ARMY INF OFFICER OBERSTLT: Gray doeskin body. Buttons

FOUL WEATHER JACKET NAVAL

& fittings intact. Full gray satin lining with bevo maker label at neck & oil cloth label to pocket with owner name. Sew-in boards. Avg. cond. $200.00

GREATCOAT LUFTWAFFE EM: Variation. Looks to be for female use with short/small blue-gray wool body, pleated patch upper pockets, 2 slash lower & 6 button front. French cuffs, loops & buttons for strap use. Partial gray lining with slash pocket, inked size, maker & *LBA(S)40*. Avg. cond. $161.00

GREATCOAT LUFTWAFFE OFFICER

GREATCOAT LUFTWAFFE OFFICER: Dark blue-gray wool body, full satin lining with pocket & bevo neck label is marked *Minovsky Stuttgart*. Above avg. cond. $200.00

GREATCOAT NAVAL ADMIRAL: Smooth black wool body instead of dark-blue. Cornflower-blue wool lapels, 12 button front, 2 slash pockets & fake French cuffs. Full black satin lining with 2 slash pockets. Above avg. cond. $850.00

GREATCOAT NAVAL OFFICER GRAY LEATHER: Pliable body. Anchor buttons for removable boards. Anchor buttons on front. Plaid wool lining, 2 slash pockets. Avg. cond. $387.00

GREATCOAT VOLKSSTURM: Green wool body & green collar. Sew-in gray pleated boards on green & no traces of collar

tabs. Embr. Tirol eagle over title on green sleeve diamond, hand sewn. Full satin lining with pocket & dagger clip. Near mint cond. $225.00

MESS DRESS JACKET LUFTWAFFE FLIGHT OFFICER OBERLT: Short blue-gray wool body with 8 pebbled button front, flat-silver bevo eagle is zigzag sewn to wool backing & hand sewn. Twisted alum. piping to collar & sewn in boards with 1 gold pip each. Gray satin lining with 2 slash pockets. Loops for 1 badge. Above avg. cond. $280.00

MESS DRESS JACKET NAVAL OFFICER KORVETTENCAPTAIN ING. WITH WHITE VEST

MESS DRESS JACKET NAVAL OFFICER KORVETTENCAPTAIN ING. WITH WHITE VEST: Blue wool body, 10 button front, closure chain button, dark bullion eagle, three gold sleeve stripes & dark bullion cogwheel. Full black satin lining with 1 pocket. White linen vest, 4 gold buttons & 2 pockets. Near mint cond. $800.00

MESS DRESS JACKET NAVAL OFFICER LT WITH VEST: Blue doeskin jacket & vest. Bullion hand embr. eagle. Gold tape stripe to each cuff with bullion stars. Oilcloth maker label *Frdr. ???? Kiel* with inked name & 37 date. Pre-war quality outfit. Exc. cond. $468.00

PARADE DRESS TUNIC ARMY ADMIN OFFICIAL: Gray twill wool body, dark green collar & cuffs. Green piped overall. Alum. bullion eagle, thick collar & cuff tabs with orange piping. Loops for 2 badges & ribbon bar. Sew-in boards with gold pip & silver *HV* to each. Satin lining with pocket having oilcloth tag *Lothar Heinze Dresden* & typed *Herr Inspektor*

Helmholdt Juli 1939. Same maker to bevo neck label. Mint cond. $800.00

PARADE DRESS TUNIC ARMY ARTY NCO WITH TROUSERS: Gray twill wool body, green collar, red wool piped collar, front, cuffs & back. 8 button front. Alum. tape tabs to red wool cuff & collar tabs. Alum. NCO tape to cuffs & collar. Officer bullion eagle. Sewn in straps with gray *XVII* & pip to each. Full lining with slash pocket & removed labels. Different shade gray twill wool straight-leg trousers with red wool piping. Early marksmanship lanyard with alum. eagle shield. Avg. cond. $440.00

PARADE DRESS TUNIC ARMY CAV EM: Tailor made with golden-yellow piping, standard pattern, with flat-silver bevo breast Eagle. Gray green wool body. Shoulder strap have #13 devices & #3 pebbled alum. buttons. Full gray lining, Single slash inside pocket with 2 bevo labels *Aug.Koster Luneburg* & *Guezeichen etc.* 2 hidden tail pockets. Near mint cond. $433.00

stripes. Loops for long ribbon bar. Red wool to backside of front opening. Avg. cond. $300.00

PARADE DRESS TUNIC ARMY PIONEER EM: Smooth gray wool body, green collar, cuffs & black piping. flat-silver bevo insignia & sew-in green straps with chain stitched B&W #19. Tag inked with maker, size & *H38.* Above avg. cond. ... $324.00

PARADE DRESS TUNIC ARMY SMOKE TROOP OFFICER LT: Gray twill wool body with green cuffs & collar. Bordeaux piped front, cuffs, collar & back. Alum. cuff & collar tabs. Alum. sew-in boards on bordeaux. Full satin lining with slash pocket & inked *Gepruft 14./J.R.67.* 1939 EK 1st & black 1939 wound badge. Alum. aiguillette with silver metal tips. Avg. cond. $660.00

PARADE DRESS TUNIC ARMY SUPPLY OFFICER OBERLT: Tailored gray twill wool body with green cuffs & collar. Light blue wool piping overall & 8 button front. Alum. bullion eagle, sew-in boards, thick collar & cuff tabs. Full satin lining with pocket & neck bevo maker label *Wilhelm Welhausen Hannover Kassel.* Avg. cond. $385.00

PARADE DRESS TUNIC ARMY
JAGER OFFICER-HAUPTMANN

PARADE DRESS TUNIC ARMY JAGER OFFICER-HAUPTMANN: Smooth gray wool body, green piping overall, green collar & cuffs. Thick alum. tabs to cuffs & collar. Bullion eagle & embr. Jager oak leaf oval to sleeve. Loops for 2 badges & ribbon bar. Bright alum. boards with painted gold pips & mismatched gold #38. Full lining with pocket, inked size & *M35.* Above avg. cond. $319.00

PARADE DRESS TUNIC ARMY NCO: Gray twill wool body & green piping. Flat-silver bevo insignia & darkening to silver tape

PARADE DRESS TUNIC ARMY
SMOKE TROOP OFFICER LT

PEA JACKET NAVAL SIGNAL EM WITH TROUSERS: Both dark blue wool const. 12 anchor buttons, 2 slash pockets with flaps, yellow embr. eagle, 1 blue wool collar tab & yellow embr. lightning bolt to sleeve disc. Wool lined with 2 slash pockets & owner name to neck. Straight-leg trousers with flap. Above avg. cond. $200.00

PEA JACKET NAVAL: Thick navy blue wool heavy wool jacket. 2 slash pockets. Wool lined with 2 pockets. Above avg. cond. $145.00

PIPED SERVICE TUNIC ARMY ADMIN HIGH RANKING OFFICIAL: Early gray doeskin body, green collar & red wool piped front edges. Loops for 1 badge, bullion eagle, gold celleon sawtooth litzen to green tabs with red cord piping & sew-in alum. plaited boards on red/green wlth HV device to each. Full lining with padded chest & shoulders. Pre-war quality. Near mint cond. $851.00

PIPED SERVICE TUNIC CUSTOM OFFICIAL WITH BREECHES: Green-gray wool body, green collar with twisted piping, flat-silver bevo collar tabs with alum pip each, slip-on boards with gold *RFV* & pip to each. Flat-silver bevo eagle cufftitle. Full satin lining with 2 pockets. Includes twill wool breeches. Above avg. cond. $300.00

PIPED SERVICE TUNIC FIRE POLICE OFFICER WITH BREECHES

PIPED SERVICE TUNIC FIRE POLICE OFFICER WITH BREECHES: Blue wool tunic with carmine piping. 2 alum. pips to sew-in boards of black with carmine *V's* to alum cord & carmine bases. Bevo alum litzen on carmine tabs. Carmine sleeve eagle. Luftschutz medal ribbon bar. Full black satin lining. Black wool straight-leg trousers with carmine piping. Exc. cond. $276.00

PIPED SERVICE TUNIC FORESTRY OFFICIAL WITH PANTS: Green twill wool body with green velvet collar & green piped front, pockets, French cuffs & back. 4 alum. button front & smaller button for alum. aiguillette. 2 pleated patch upper pockets & 2 slash lower. Super bullion hand embr. eagle on wool. Twisted alum. piping to collar with gray velvet tabs with alum. piping & hand embr. 2 oak leaves with half-wreath. Sewn in boards of green plaited bodies on gray wool with silver acorn to each. Green lining with 1 pocket. Matching piped straight-leg trousers. Near mint cond. $480.00

PIPED SERVICE TUNIC LUFTWAFFE FLAK EM: Blue-gray wool body, twisted red cord piping to collar with red wool tabs having single gray gull each. Sew-in wool straps with red wool piping. Full gray lining with pocket & inked size & *LBA35 Flak Wei.* Crimea 1941/42 bronze sleeve shield on wool. Avg. cond. $400.00

PIPED SERVICE TUNIC LUFTWAFFE FLAK OFFICER OBERST: Blue-gray twill wool body with padded shoulders, 4 button front, 4 pleated patch pockets & French cuffs. Loops for 7 badges & long ribbon bar. Bullion hand embr. eagle, oberst tabs & sewn in boards. Twisted alum. piping to collar. Full gray satin lining with pocket, dagger D-ring, bevo maker neck label & bevo pocket label *Hermann Frank Berlin* with hand inked *Fiohler 6429 30.12.42.* Avg. cond. $765.00

PIPED SERVICE TUNIC LUFTWAFFE FLIGHT NCO WITH SHIRT: Blue-gray wool body, 4 pleated patch pockets, 4 button front & French cuffs. 3 place ribbon bar is sewn on. Officer alum. hand embr. eagle, twisted yellow piping, alum. tape stripe & yellow tabs with 3 gulls to collar. Sew on straps. Gray lining with pocket & inked maker, size, date. Light gray cotton shirt with 7 white button front. Avg. cond. $653.00

PIPED SERVICE TUNIC LUFTWAFFE FLIGHT OFFICER-HAUPTMANN: Blue-gray twill wool tailored body with padded shoulders. 4 button front, 4 pleated patch pockets, French cuffs & loops for 4 badges. Alum. hand embr. eagle, twisted alum. piping to collar, machine sewn on tabs & sew-in boards with 2 pips each. Dark green satin lining with pocket. Above avg. cond. $779.00

PIPED SERVICE TUNIC
LUFTWAFFE MEDICAL OFFICER
HAUPTMANN WITH BREECHES

PIPED SERVICE TUNIC LUFTWAFFE MEDICAL OFFICER HAUPTMANN WITH BREECHES: Blue-gray twill wool body, bullion eagle, twisted alum. piping to collar with machine-sewn blue tabs with alum. details. Sew-in boards with gold snake/staff & 2 pips. Full satin lining, bevo necklabel *Roger Kauert Berlin etc.* & slash pocket with oilcloth tag having inked script owner. Matching straight-leg trousers with fittings intact. Avg. cond. $400.00

PIPED SERVICE TUNIC NSDAP KREISLEITUNG: Tan twill wool body with silver eagle buttons, black piping to collar & to hand-sewn collar tabs. Wool composite armband. Full gold satin lining with oilcloth maker tag to pocket. RZM ink stamp *August Senger Munchen etc.* Avg. cond. $471.00

PIPED SERVICE TUNIC NSDAP ORTSGRUPPE WITH BREECHES: Matching tan twill wool to each. Blue cord collar piping, brown velvet tabs with gold eagle & 4 faded gray pips. Wool armband, blue cord piping, gold oakleave tape with gold borders & composite swastika center with gold piping. Full gold lining with inked *50* & faded oil cloth RZM tag to pocket. Trousers with oil cloth *PL. Stiefelhose W etc.* RZM tag. Exc. cond. $664.00

PIPED SERVICE TUNIC POLICE WITH RIDING BREECHES: Gray twill wool body, brown collar & cuffs. Red wool piped collar, front, cuffs & back. 8 button front, 2 pleated patch upper pockets with loops for badge & 2 patch lower. 2 place ribbon bar. Red machine embr. sleeve eagle on wool oval with hand embr. sewn in boards with brown centers having 2 alum. pips. Bevo tape tabs on wool with twisted alum. piping. Full satin lining with slash pocket. Exact matching breeches with reinforced seat. Near mint cond. $505.00

PIPED SERVICE TUNIC POLICE: Green wool body, green piping, brown cuffs & collar. Green embr. sleeve eagle, bevo alum. litzen on green tabs with alum. piping, slip-on boards. Hand embr. bullion SS runes. Full green lining with pocket & inked *PO 1943 etc.* Avg. cond. $450.00

PIPED STRAIGHT LEG TROUSERS ARMY GENERAL STAFF: Gray twill wool straight-leg bodies. Carmine wool piped seam & 1 5/8" wide stripes to either side. 3 slash pockets with button-flap back. Adjustment side belts, 4 button fly with hook & gray satin waist-trim. Watch slash pocket. Unmarked. Exc. cond. .. $563.00

PIPED STRAIGHT LEG TROUSERS ARMY GENERAL: Gray twill wool straight-leg bodies with red doeskin sides. 3 slash pockets & watch pocket. 6 button fly, side adjustment belts & suspender fittings. Above avg. cond. $650.00

PIPED STRAIGHT LEG TROUSERS ARMY: Straight legged twill wool bodies, dark green cord piping, 4 slash pockets & watch slash. Back adjustment belt & suspender buttons. Avg. cond. , $135.00

REEFER JACKET NAVAL CHAPLAIN: Dark blue twill wool body, 8 button front, 3 slash pockets & right side pocket has small patch pocket inside. Dark gold bullion & celleon hand embr. eagle, M1942 purple velvet tabs, gold twisted piping, gold bullion wreath with cross center & both hand-sewn to collar. Full black satin lining with pocket. Exc. cond. $695.00

REEFER JACKET NAVAL OFFICER-KAPITANLT WITH TROUSERS: Dark blue twill wool body, 2 slash pockets, 10 anchor buttons, gold bullion eagle, bullion sleeve stars & 3 gold tape stripes to cuffs. Black satin lining with 2 slash pockets & bevo neck label *Steinmetz & Hehl Hamburg.* Comes with black twill wool straight-leg trousers with metal *Talon* zipper. Above avg. cond. $538.00

REEFER JACKET NAVAL TECH OFFICIAL-KAPITANLT

REEFER JACKET NAVAL TECH OFFICIAL-KAPITANLT: Dark blue doeskin body, 3 alum. brocade sleeve stripes, alum. bullion eagle & sleeve oval eagles with 2 triangles. Black satin lining with 2 pockets. Loops for one badge. Avg. cond. $250.00

RIDING BREECHES ARMY: Gray salt & pepper twill cotton body with reinforced seat. 3 slash pockets, 3 button fly with hook, belt loops, suspender buttons & back adjustment belts. Metal zipper to each tapered leg. Inked *Rudolf Wentz Nurnberg 1942*. Mint cond. $162.00

RIDING BREECHES ARMY: Gray wool body with gray leather covered seat & inner legs. Standard fittings intact. Avg. cond. $118.00

RIDING BREECHES LUFTWAFFE: Blue-gray body, 3 pockets with button flaps, watch slash, belt loops, side adjustment belts & etc. Avg. cond. $225.00

SERVICE JUMPER NAVAL EM: White cotton body. Blue dickey with white stripes. No breast eagle, has blue embr. engine room sleeve anchor on white. Anchor buttons at cuffs. Red numbers N1934T/35. Above avg. cond. $75.00

SERVICE TUNIC ARMY ARTY NCO: Gray wool body & green collar with tape stripe. Bevo eagle, tabs & slip-on straps with 2 pips each. Loops for 3 badges & 1 badge to right pocket. Partial gray

lining with inked size tag. Above avg. cond. $850.00

SERVICE TUNIC ARMY ARTY OFFICER-HAUPTMANN: Gray twill wool body, green collar, 6 button front, 4 pleated patch pockets & French cuffs. Bullion eagle, thick tabs & sewn in boards. Full gray satin lining with pocket & dagger clip. Above avg. cond. $450.00

SERVICE TUNIC ARMY CAV OFFICER-MAJOR: Gray twill wool body & green collar. Thick gray tabs & removable boards. Bullion eagle & 1939 EK ribbon at button hole. Loops for 1 badge. Above avg. cond. $616.00

SERVICE TUNIC ARMY CAV OFFICER-OBERST: Gray twill wool body, green collar & thick insignia. Loops for ribbon bar & 1 badge. Avg. cond. $1,000.00

SERVICE TUNIC ARMY EM M43

SERVICE TUNIC ARMY EM M43: Rough texture gray wool body, collar & 4 patch pockets. Bevo eagle is zigzag stitched & bevo tabs are machine sewn on. Loops & buttons for shoulder straps. Partial gray satin lining with inked size, RB# & *E44*. Near mint cond. $710.00

SERVICE TUNIC ARMY INF EM: Gray wool body, green collar with bevo tabs & embr. eagle. 1939 EK ribbon to button hole. Partial gray lining with inked maker & size. Exc. cond. $650.00

SERVICE TUNIC ARMY INF OFFICER-LT: Late-war light gray wool body & green collar. Insignia & 3 loops for ribbon bar. Full brown satin lining, 2 slash pockets, dagger clip & bevo neck label *L.Kielleuthner etc..Munchen*. Named maker envelope & dated bill, paid 135 marks for tunic & 165 marks for greatcoat. Mint cond. $903.00

SERVICE TUNIC ARMY INF OFFICER-LT

SERVICE TUNIC ARMY INF OFFICER-OBERLT M44: Custom made. Short-cut styled after M44 in tan cotton. 6 large stamped metal buttons to front, 2 pleated patch pockets & slash cuffs. Loops for 3 badges, 1939 EK ribbon to button hole, machine sewn on triangle gray bevo eagle & slip-on boards with pipe. Above avg. cond. $345.00

SERVICE TUNIC ARMY MEDICAL OFFICER-MAJOR: Gray twill wool body. Green collar, 5 button front, French cuffs & 4 pleated patch pockets. Loops for 3 badges & ribbon bar, hand embr. eagle. Silver bullion collar tabs with twisted blue cords. sewn in silver plaited boards on blue wool with gold Aesculapius to each. Full green satin lining. Above avg. cond. $365.00

SERVICE TUNIC ARMY MT TROOP OFFICER-MAJOR: Field made from gray doeskin greatcoat, waist length with 2 pleated patch pockets & 7 alum. button front. Hidden waist buckle/hook. Thick bullion insignia, hand embr. bullion sleeve edelweiss & slip-on boards. Russian front ribbon at button hole, 6 loops for ribbon or medal bars, 3 badge loops & German cross loops to right pocket. Full satin lining with slash pocket. Near mint cond. $595.00

SERVICE TUNIC ARMY NCO

SERVICE TUNIC ARMY NCO: Austrian gray twill wool body, 4 slash pockets with scallops to flaps, 5 button front & green collar. Loops for 3 badges & ribbon bar. 1939 EK ribbon to button hole, flat-silver bevo eagle & red signal blitz. Alum. tape to collar with gray bevo tabs on green wool bases & green centers. Sew-in green wool straps, alum. tape, 2 alum. tape loops, 3 pips & faded green/white piping. Partial padded gray lining. Above avg. cond. $300.00

SERVICE TUNIC ARMY NCO: Gray wool body & collar. Machine-sewn gray tape & bevo gray tabs to collar. Slip-on straps. Hand sewn white bevo eagle. 1939 black/brass Wound Badge is affixed through pocket. Partial gray lining with inked *Steinmeyer*, size, *F40* & inked tag *Lenk 1./Beob.=Abt.22.* Near mint cond. $1,369.00

SERVICE TUNIC ARMY OKW OFFICER-HAUPTMANN WITH BREECHES(DETAIL)

SERVICE TUNIC ARMY OKW OFFICER-HAUPTMANN WITH BREECHES: Gray twill body, 2 pleated patch upper pockets, 2 slash lower, 8 button front & green collar. *Krim 1941/1942* sleeve shield, alum. eagle, gold celleon sawtooth litzen to green collar tabs & sew-in bright alum. boards on crimson bases with 2 pips. Full satin lining with bevo maker label at neck & oilcloth *Wilh.Hoffmann, Glogau etc.* tag to pocket with inked *Herrn Seidel 16.12.36.* Different shade gray twill wool breeches with crimson piping & fittings intact. Avg. cond. $1,450.00

SERVICE TUNIC ARMY PIONEER
OFFICER-OBERST

SERVICE TUNIC ARMY PIONEER OFFICER-OBERST: Gray twill wool body with green collar. Thick alum. tabs are machine sewn on. Sew-in boards with gold *4* & 2 gray pips each. Bullion eagle. Full gray lining, 2 slash pockets & dagger clip. 8 place WWI service ribbon bar. Alum./bullion plaited aiguillete. Above avg. cond. $525.00

SERVICE TUNIC ARMY RECRUITING OFFICER-OBERLT WITH BREECHES: Thick gray wool body with matching breeches. Green collar, 6 button front & 4 pleated patch pockets. bullion eagle, sew-in bright alum. boards on orange with pip & missing removable button to each. Poorly hand sewn orange tabs with alum. litzen. 1939 EK ribbon at button hole. Full satin lining with pocket & dagger clip. Avg. cond. $428.00

SERVICE TUNIC ARMY SMOKE TROOP OFFICER-HAUPTMANN: Gray twill wool body, 4 pleated patch pockets, 6 button front & green collar. Bullion eagle, sew-in boards with 2 pips & thick collar tabs. Full satin lining with pocket & dagger clip. Avg. cond. $750.00

SERVICE TUNIC ARMY SMOKE TROOP OFFICER-LT: Gray wool body, green collar & rest of fittings intact. Loops for 2 badges, 1939 EK & Russian Front ribbons. embr. eagle, thick collar tabs with bordeaux centers & sew-in boards. Full satin lining with slash pockets. Rare *Cholm 1942* campaign shield on wool oval. Above avg. cond. $857.00

SERVICE TUNIC BAHNSCHUTZ POLIZEI EM: Light blue wool body & blue collar. No traces of sleeve eagle. Loops & buttons for strap use. Partial cloth lining with inked maker name & size. Avg. cond. $198.00

SERVICE TUNIC BDM *WEST SAARPFALZ*: Brown suede like body, 5 imitation leather button front & 4 patch pockets. White bevo title sleeve triangle, bevo HJ diamond, bevo HJ armband & enamel HJ diamond badge. Avg. cond. $325.00

SERVICE TUNIC BDM *WEST WESTMARK*: Brown suede-like body with 5 plastic BDM/JM button front. 2 pockets, bevo HJ diamond, bevo white title sleeve triangle & green plaited lanyard. Full satin lining with oilcloth RZM *BDM-Weste etc.* Bevo size 40 necktag. Avg. cond. $195.00

SERVICE TUNIC COASTAL ARTY EM: Gray wool body with 5 gray anchor buttons. 2 pleated patch upper pockets with 2 slash style lower pockets & matching slash pattern cuffs. Yellow bevo breast eagle. Single rank chevron. Loops & buttons for shoulder straps. No collar tabs. Full gray lining with ink size marks. Avg. cond. $252.00

SERVICE TUNIC FORESTRY OFFICIAL

SERVICE TUNIC FORESTRY OFFICIAL:
Green twill wool body, green collar has
direct hand embr. alum. oakleave wreath
to each side & sew-in boards, green
wool bases, plaited alum. & green body.
8 place WWI ribbon bar lacks backing &
is sewn in place. Full gray lining has 2
pockets & metal ID tag *Heinr.Timm
Berlin etc.* 1939 EK 1st, 1939 Silver
Wound badge, Silver Inf. badge faded
gray & bronze SA sports badge.
Avg. cond. $370.00

SERVICE TUNIC HITLER YOUTH
LEADER WITH BREECHES

SERVICE TUNIC HITLER YOUTH
LEADER WITH BREECHES: 3rd type.
Light brown twill wool body, 2 pleated
patch upper pockets & 2 slash lower
pockets. 4 silver button front, 2 alum.
RZM belt ramps, bevo HJ armband,
bevo *Nord Nordsee* sleeve triangle,
painted NSDAP member badge, enamel
HJ diamond & sew-in black straps with
twisted alum. piping, 4 silver pips, *20*
devices each. Full gold satin lining, one
slash pocket & oilcloth RZM *HJ-
Dienstrock etc.* tag. Black corduroy
riding breeches with all of the fittings
complete. Near mint cond. $1,795.00
SERVICE TUNIC LUFTWAFFE CIVILIAN
OFFICIAL: Blue-gray twill wool body with
insignia having dark green backing. 1939
EK ribbon at button hole, loops for ribbon
bar & 2 badges. Full satin lining with
pocket, dagger D-ring & closure belt.
Avg. cond. $355.00
SERVICE TUNIC LUFTWAFFE FLAK EM:
Blue-gray wool. 4 alum. button front, 4
pleated patch pockets & French cuffs.
Loops for 1 badge. Embr. eagle,
machine-sewn red wool tabs with single

gull. Slip-on wool straps with red cord
piping. Gray cloth lining with pocket bevo
tag *Materla*, unit *I./E/R.7 11.Batt.II.*
Above avg. cond. $397.00
SERVICE TUNIC LUFTWAFFE FLAK NCO:
Blue-gray wool body, 4 button front & 4
pleated patch pockets. Loops for 1
badge, *F* specialist patch. Eagle on wool
is machine zigzag-sewn. 1939 EK ribbon
at button hole. Alum. NCO tape to collar
with red wool tabs having 3 gray gulls
each. Sewn in straps of wool with alum.
tape, red wool piping & 1 pip each. Full
black lining with 1 slash pocket.
Near mint cond. $381.00
SERVICE TUNIC NSDAP ORTSGRUPPE
BLOCKLEITER *ORDENSBURGEN*:
Short dark blue wool body, 3 silver eagle
button front, 2 pleated patch pockets, 6
belt ramps & slash cuffs with 2 eagle
buttons. Flat-silver bevo title cuffband,
wool armband with blue piping & gold
details. Sew-in blue wool straps with blue
cord piping & brown velvet tabs, blue
cord piping, gold tape, 4 gray pips & gold
eagle to each. Full black lining with slash
pocket. 1939 EK ribbon to button hole &
painted NSDAP member badge.
Near mint cond. $381.00
SERVICE TUNIC NSKK: Olive brown wool
body, brown collar, black collar tabs, flat-
silver bevo sleeve eagle & black sleeve
diamond with silver eagle on 6 spoke
wheel. Partial brown lining, inked *52* &
large RZM mark to wool material. Oilcloth
RZM *Feldbluse NSKK etc.* tag to
beltramp strap. Large size. Near mint
cond. $230.00
SERVICE TUNIC RAD OFFICER: Brown
twill wool body, darker brown collar.
Loops for 1 badge, bevo party armband,
bevo flat-silver spade with nos. alum.
collar tabs on black velvet & sew-in
boards. Full satin lining with bevo neck
label *Hugo Grenwelge etc.* & oil cloth
label to pocket. Avg. cond. $300.00
SERVICE TUNIC REICHSWEHR ARTY
EM: Field-gray wool body, 8 pebbled
button front, 2 pleated patch style upper
pockets & 2 hidden lower. Bronze DRA
sports badge. Sleeve chevron with 2
alum. stripes & pip on green wool with
cuff having bevo alum./green tape stripe,
& V-chevron below. Sewn in green wool
straps with red wool piping & chain-
stitched #22. Gray collar has machine
sewn red wool tabs with dark patina silver
bars. Full gray lining with 2 pockets,
bandage pocket & stamped *1926 J.R. 12
9.K. 1925 II.B.A.B.* Avg. cond. .. $334.00

SERVICE TUNIC SS-WAFFEN INF
OBERSTURMFUHRER (DETAIL)

SHIRT NAVAL EM

SERVICE TUNIC SS-WAFFEN INF
OBERSTURMFUHRER: Gray wool body
& green collar. 4 pleated patch pockets,
6 button front & French cuffs. 1939 EK
ribbon at button hole. Loops for 2
badges & clasp. Gray embr. sleeve
eagle on black is machine zigzag-sewn.
Hand sewn Old Fighter chevron & SS
embr. runes collar tab with twisted alum.
piping. Rank tab is machine sewn-on.
Sewn in boards with worn silver finished
pip & #5 to each. Full satin lining with
pocket & dagger clip.
Above avg. cond. $2,100.00
SERVICE TUNIC VOLKSTRUM WITH
RIDING BREECHES: This is a 1920
early 1930 tunic reworked to closely
resemble the war time pattern uniform,
in fact the pants were even let out to fit
an older & fatter patriot. Gray wool body
with slightly different gray collar. 4 slash
pockets & 7 button front. Gray bevo
eagle hand sewn. 1939 EK ribbon at
button hole. Machine sewn on bevo
gray collar tabs. Gray wool slip-on straps
with white cord piping. Gray padded
upper body lining with pocket & ink
stamps. Loops for 1 badge. Matching
gray wool riding breeches with size
increase added to each side. 2 slash
pockets & watch pocket. 4 button fly with
hook. Adjustment belt back & suspender
buttons. Avg. cond. $801.00
SHIRT HITLER YOUTH: Tan cotton twill,
pullover body with 3 button front slash,
slash cuffs have imitation leather button.
Bevo size label at neck *100*. Above avg.
cond. $85.00
SHIRT NAVAL EM: White HBT. Body with
slash pocket, tie string & inked *BAW
1.1.43 etc*. Near mint cond. $55.00
SHIRT NAVAL EM: White pullover body with
blue cuffs & collar. Bevo blue eagle is
zigzag sew on. Inked maker *Schaffer &
Vogel etc*. Exc. cond. $250.00

SKI TROUSERS HITLER YOUTH: Dark
blue twill body, 3 slash pockets with
button flaps, 5 button fly, belt loops, side
adjustment belts & suspender buttons. All
buttons marked *HJ/DJ* with oakleaves.
Avg. cond. $126.00
SMOCK ARMY DOCTOR: Below knee
length, lightweight, tan cotton body. 5
wood button front. 3 patch pockets. Cuffs
with wood buttons. Half belt at back with
wood buttons. Slashes at sides for
reaching pants. Inked RZM#.
Near mint cond. $82.00
SPORT SHIRT ARMY WITH SHORTS:
White tank top with black stripe around
neck. Black bevo eagle to front & inked
lower edge *E./I.R.83 15.(E)Kp*. Black
cotton shorts with drawstring waist &
slash back pocket. Avg. cond. $34.00
SPORT SHIRT LUFTWAFFE: White cotton
tank top with small bevo eagle. Inked
maker & size. Above avg. cond. . $75.00

SPORT SHIRT SS

SPORT SHIRT SS: White tank-top body with 4" diam. B & W runes disc to front. Inked maker to lower edge. Near mint cond. $244.00

STRAIGHT-LEG DRILL TROUSERS ARMY REED-GREEN HBT: Straight-leg style, 3 slash pockets & watch slash with paper buttons. 6 stamped steel buttons to fly, suspender buttons & side adjustment belts. Avg. cond. $285.00

STRAIGHT-LEG TROUSERS ARMY EM: Gray wool straight-leg body. 3 slash pockets with black resin buttons, watch slash, back adjustment belt, 5 button fly & stamped metal suspender buttons. Inked *Hannover H41 76 86 109 100*. Near mint cond. $643.00

STRAIGHT-LEG TROUSERS ARMY PANZER STYLE: Black wool. 3 slash pockets & watch slash. 5 button fly , suspender buttons, back adjustment belt, & straight legs style. Inked 1942 maker inside. Near mint cond. $276.00

STRAIGHT-LEG TROUSERS ARMY: Tunic shade to thick wool construction. Stamped gray metal buttons overall, 5 button fly, 3 slash pockets, watch slash, back adjustment belt & suspender buttons. Inked size to white inside *80 88 109 106*. Mint cond. $685.00

STRAIGHT-LEG TROUSERS BAHNSCHUTZ POLIZEI: Light blue wool straight-leg bodies with gray wool piping. 3 slash pockets & watch slash. 5 button fly, suspender buttons & back adjustment belt. Inked maker & size inside. Above avg. cond. $156.00

STRAIGHT-LEG TROUSERS LUFTWAFFE: Blue-gray twill straight-leg style. Avg. cond. $205.00

STRAIGHT-LEG TROUSERS NAVAL EM: White body with flap front, gray metal buttons & adjustment side belts. Near mint cond. $65.00

STRAIGHT-LEG TROUSERS SA: Color is a greenish-brown wool. Taper to legs with slash cuff & black stirrup loops. 3 slash pockets with back having button/flap. Adjustment belt in the back, & suspender buttons. 3 button fly with hook. Mint cond. $250.00

SUMMER TUNIC ARMY OFFICER: White linen body, 8 pebbled buttons sewn to front & has fold down collar instead of stand-up. 4 pleated patch pockets, French cuffs, loops/buttons for boards & loops for eagle, ribbon bar, 1 badge, & grommet holes for badge. Above avg. cond. $276.00

TROPICAL BREECHES ARMY M43: Cotton twill body with slash to tapered cuffs & tie strings. 3 slash pockets & watch pocket. 6 metal button fly, built-in web belt with 3 prong buckle & suspender buttons. Inked maker, size & *M43/N*. Near mint cond. $591.00

TROPICAL MOTORCYCLE JACKET ARMY: Olive twill cotton body, belt & buttons. Inked *Lago-Mu M43/N* & size. Cloth loops for shoulder straps. Near mint cond. $285.00

TROPICAL RIDING BREECHES ARMY DAK: Olive corduroy-style body with built-in waist belt, 6 metal button fly, 3 slash pockets & watch slash. Slash cuffs with tie strings. Inked RB#, size & *F42*. Near mint cond. $141.00

TROPICAL SERVICE TUNIC
ARMY PIONEER NCO

TROPICAL SERVICE TUNIC ARMY DAK ARTY NCO: Olive body with 4 patch pockets & late war gray pebbled removable buttons. Tan tape & bevo tabs machine sewn on to collar, blue bevo eagle & slip-on olive shoulder straps with tan tape & red cord piping. Loops for 2 badges. Inked RB#, size & *M43*. Near mint cond. $750.00

TROPICAL SERVICE TUNIC ARMY PIONEER NCO: Field made. Tan canvas body, 4 pleated patch pockets, 5 removable buttons & green collar. Loops for 1 badge, KVK ribbon at button hole, flat-silver bevo eagle, bevo collar tabs,

alum. tape border & slip-on straps.
Above avg. cond. $402.00

TROPICAL SERVICE TUNIC
LUFTWAFFE FLIGHT EM

TROPICAL SERVICE TUNIC LUFTWAFFE
FLIGHT EM: Tan twill cotton body, 6
removable brown button front, 2 pleated
patch upper pockets & 2 patch lower.
Gray embr. eagle on tan & slip-on tan
straps with yellow cord piping. Inked
inside with maker, size & *UB41*.
Above avg. cond. $652.00
TROPICAL SERVICE TUNIC NAVAL
OFFICER-OBERLT: Corduroy style body
with 6 removable button front, pin on gold
alum. eagle & wing-tip shoulder boards.
Exc. cond. $381.00
TROPICAL SHIRT LUFTWAFFE: Pullover
tan cotton body, 4 button slash & 2
pleated patch pockets. Gray embr. eagle
on tan triangle. Loops & buttons for
shoulder straps. Avg. cond. $386.00
TROPICAL STRAIGHT LEG TROUSERS
ARMY DAK: Corduroy style olive body
has slash to tapered cuffs & 6 bakelite
button fly. 3 slash pockets & watch pocket
with ring. No belt fittings. Suspender
loops & buttons. Inked size.
Near mint cond. $250.00
TROPICAL STRAIGHT LEG TROUSERS
LUFTWAFFE: Tan twill body with built-in
waist belt, cuff belts, 6 button fly, patch
left leg pocket & 4 pockets. Inked size.
Above avg. cond. $299.00
UNIFORM GROUP ARMY GENERAL-
FELDMARSCHALL VON KUCHLER:
Tailor made gray twill wool body, green
collar, 4 pleated patch pockets, 5 gold
button front with 3 snaps, red wool
piped collar, front & French cuffs.
Loops for long ribbon bar & 5 badges.

gold hand embr. eagle, collar tabs on
red wool & sewn in boards with affixed
dark silver batons device to each. Full
satin lining with pocket having oilcloth
Alfred Rietz, Berlin etc. & typed title
name with date *3.11.42*. Different
shade gray twill wool straight-leg
trousers with red wool side stripes. No
name tag. Kuchler earned Oakleaves to
his KC, survived war & lived to age 87.
Near mint cond. $5,850.00
UNIFORM GROUP ARMY GRENADIER
NCO: Parade Dress Tunic - gray twill
wool body, green collar & cuffs. 8 button
front, light green wool piping, alum.
tape stripes & tape tabs on green wool.
alum. bullion eagle. 2nd shooting
lanyard with 3 acorns & 1939 black
wound badge of stamped brass. Sew-in
straps with 2 pips each & EK & KVK
ribbons at button hole. Wool straight-leg
trousers with piping. Brocade belt with
alum. buckle having prongs to loop.
Avg. cond. $1,755.00
UNIFORM GROUP BDM: Brown suede-like
jacket, 5 brown plastic *BDM/JM* button
front & 4 patch pockets. Full lining &
oilcloth RZM tag *BDM-West etc.* Hand
sewn scarce gray bevo cuff title on brown
for duty on Eastern Front. Bevo HJ
diamond & bevo white triangle *Nord
Niedersachsen* are both hand sewn.
Extra matching triangle in pocket. Bevo
size *38* at neck & nickel swastika brooch-
pin to collar. Black neckerchief with tan
leather slide. Female black wool trousers
with bloused slash cuffs & metal side
zipper opening. 2 slash pockets.
Exc. cond. $1,200.00
UNIFORM GROUP SA SUDWEST: This is
a very colorful outfit & comes with wool
pants with cotton shirt & brown leather
cross strap. Brown twill tunic with 2
pleated patch upper pockets, 2 patch
lower, French cuffs & 4 pebbled alum.
button front. Wool composite armband.
Loops for 1 badge. Machine sewn on
orange wool tabs with black chain
stitched *I/122* & other with silver pip with
black/orange tape stripe. Black &
Orange twisted piping. Orange wool
base to sewn in strap with black &
orange cord body. Gold satin lining with
pocket. Pullover brown cotton shirt with
cufflinks & button on collar. Inked *SA 50/
2 37*. Matching wool breeches. Dark
brown leather cross-strap nickel RZM
clips. Near mint cond. $1,063.00
UNIFORM GROUP SS-WAFFEN INF REGT
DEUTSCHLAND OFFICER-LT: Service
tunic with gray wool body, green collar, 4

pleated patch pockets & 6 button front. Loops for 3 badges, ribbon bar & 1939 EK/Russian Front ribbons at button hole. Machine embr. alum. *Deutschland* cuff-title, hand embr. bullion eagle, sew-in boards & machine sewn on SS runes & rank tabs. Full green satin lining, dagger clip, white collar liner *Uniform 4 39* & early alum. plaited adjutant aiguillette with tips. Matching wool breeches with slash cuffs having 4 buttons. 19" tall black leather boots with wood forms inside. Exc. cond. $2,855.00

WINTER COVERALLS LUFTWAFFE: Black leather. Pliable body with bevo maker tag *Leder-Kuhne Dresden etc.* & bevo owner *Rindleder*. Inked 43-date & size 3. *Zipp* alum. zipper front.
Avg. cond. $300.00

WINTER GREATCOAT ARMY

WINTER GREATCOAT ARMY: Paris made. Long suede body with 3 wood toggle front closure & 2 slash pockets. Fleece lining. Inked *A.Pilain etc, Paris* & size. Above avg. cond. $350.00

WINTER GREATCOAT LUFTWAFFE EM: Blue-gray body with black wool inside. 4 pockets, button & loops for straps. Inked *Bulag 43 54 102 129 66* & 40 dated. Near mint cond. $126.00

WINTER TROUSERS ARMY: Gray reversible to white. Heavy cotton quilted body. 2 slash pockets, 4 button fly,

suspender straps & inked RB #.
Avg. cond. $180.00

WORK JACKET LUFTWAFFE RUSSIAN FRONT DRIVERS: Reed-green HBT body. Silver-gray machine embr breast eagle on blue-gray wool. Blue-gray wool sleeve chevron with single silver braid 'V'. Motor Vehicle Driver Spec Patch. 2 lower patch style pockets. Pebble finish buttons. The work jacket was worn with shoulder boards or collar tabs.
Avg. cond. $250.00

WRAP-AROUND TUNIC
ARMY RECON NCO

WRAP-AROUND TUNIC ARMY RECON NCO: Black wool, army cut body with partial gray satin lining having 2 patch pockets & inked size. Drawstring adjustments at each side. 7 black resin buttons. White bevo eagle is machine sewn on, black wool collar tabs with yellow cord piping & alum. skulls. Yellow cord piping to collar & 2 slip-on wool straps with alum. tape border & 2 loops.
Above avg. cond. $2,445.00

WRAP-AROUND TUNIC LUFTWAFFE PANZER DIV GORING NCO: Wool body with 4 large & 3 smaller black resin buttons. Gray embr. eagle on dark blue wool, black wool tabs with white cord piping & affixed gray skulls with two rim prongs. Slip-on black wool straps, white wool piping, alum. tape stripe, alum. pip & blue-gray felt backsides. Exc. cond. $3,500.00

WRAP-AROUND TUNIC NAVAL WITH TROUSERS: Black leather. Short waist length jacket with large stamped Eagle-M between 10 black plastic button front. Tan canvas pocket inside with inked maker *C.Steuernagel Worms 4 44 4 179 188 94*. Trousers with 2 slash pockets with button flaps, leather suspenders & inked on tan canvas pocket *Fritz Habell 1944 etc.* Near mint cond. $1,424.00

THIRD REICH FOOTWEAR

CAVALRY BOOTS: Black leather. 18.5" tall, scalloped tops, 2 broken cloth loops, leather soles & heels with heavy duty horseshoes. Spur tabs above heels. Avg. cond. $66.00

DRESS SHOES: Hmkd *RZM 1/35 1938*. Brown leather. 6" tall bodies with 14 brass grommets & original laces. Leather soles, leather heels with steel plates & toe plates. Mint cond. $265.00

FLIGHT BOOTS LUFTWAFFE: Black leather. 16.5" tall bodies with 3 suede upper panels. Adjustment belts to top & at ankles. Black plastic *Ri-Ri* zippers. Fleece lined. Black rubber soles & heels show use & nail repairs. Larger size for mannequin display. Avg. cond. $177.00

JACK BOOTS

JACK BOOTS: Black leather. 16" tall bodies. Leather soles & heels. Has hobnails, toe plates, & horseshoes. Avg. cond. $126.00

JACK BOOTS: Black leather. 16" tall. Side stamped *31.5.39*. About size 11 with leather soles showing remains of

hobnails. Leather heels with horseshoes & rubber centers. Avg. cond. $205.00

LACE-UP BOOTS SA: Brown leather. 16" tall bodies with 18-grommets & 22-hooks. Brown cloth laces. Leather soles & heels & removed/missing toe plates/horse-shoes. Avg. cond. $244.00

LEGGINGS: Black leather. 12" tall formed bodies with brass hook fitting & buckle strap closure. Inked *3A etc.* Above avg. cond. $20.00

LEGGINGS: Black leather. 12.5" tall formed bodies with hook & buckle strap closure. Issue stamped *B.A.Fu.737* & inked *H33 W43 rechts 1937 etc.* Exc. cond. $133.00

LOW-CUT SHOES HITLER YOUTH: Black leather. Size 37 all leather soles with wood peg construction. Mint rubber heels marked continental 164 which is sometimes seen on military shoes & boots. Has 5 sets of steel eyelets & black laces. Near mint cond. $160.00

LOW-QUARTER COMBAT BOOTS

LOW-QUARTER COMBAT BOOTS: 6" tall black leather bodies, 8 grommets & 6 hook fronts. Leather soles & heels with hobnails, large toe plates, horseshoes & stamped with *1010 40*. Near mint cond. $447.00

LOW-QUARTER COMBAT BOOTS: 6" tall brown leather bodies, 8 grommets & 6 hook fronts. Leather soles & heels with hobnails, large toe plates, horseshoes & stamped *1032 40*. Marked cloth lining *Wasser Abstossend Impragniert*. Near mint cond. $368.00

MOUNTAIN BOOTS

MOUNTAIN BOOTS: 5.5" tall dark brown leather bodies with gray wool trim to openings. 12 grommets. Leather soles & heels with hobnails & border cleats. Avg. cond. $115.00

MOUNTAIN BOOTS: Black leather. 6" tall with gray wool trim to opening, 14 grommets & cloth laces. Leather soles & heels filled with steel cleats. Stamped *28 5*. Avg. cond. $229.00

OFFICER BOOTS: Black leather. 15" tall, leather lined upper & buckle strap sides. Luftwaffe style sewn leather soles & heels with horseshoes. Above avg. cond. $114.00

FFICER BOOTS: Black leather. 15.5" tall, leather lined uppers with cloth/leather loops, leather soles, heels & horseshoes. Avg. cond. $65.00

OFFICER BOOTS: Black leather. 16" tall with leather lined uppers, cloth loops & looks to be 41 dated. Polished bodies. Leather soles & heels with toe plates & horseshoes. Avg. cond. $110.00

OFFICER BOOTS: Black leather. 16" tall, leather lined upper with cloth loops. Leather soles & heels with toe plates & horseshoes. Avg. cond. $60.00

OFFICER BOOTS: Black leather. 16.5" tall with leather lining & cloth loops. Leather soles with metal toe plates & black rubber heels by *Berson*. Above avg. cond. $82.00

OFFICER BOOTS: Black leather. 17" tall with leather lined uppers & cloth loops. Leather soles lack toe plate. Black rubber/leather heels. Avg. cond. $95.00

OFFICER BOOTS: Black leather. 17" tall, leather lined uppers inked *Harb W. etc 1940* & cloth loops. Leather soles & heels. Avg. cond. $55.00

OFFICER BOOTS: Black leather. 17.5" tall, leather lined uppers & cloth loops. Leather soles & heels show use. Avg. cond. $67.00

OFFICER BOOTS: Black leather. 17.5" tall, leather lined uppers, cloth loops & lace work at ankle. Leather soles & heels. Avg. cond. $50.00

OFFICER BOOTS: Black leather. 20" tall with partial leather lined uppers, cloth loops & soft bodies. Leather soles with toe plates & rubber to leather heels. Avg. cond. $122.00

OFFICER BOOTS: Black leather. About 17.5" tall with leather lined uppers by *Baren-Shefel K.G.*. Replacement leather loops. Leather soles & heels with toe plates & black rubber *Continental 169* heel covers. Avg. cond. $71.00

OFFICER BOOTS: Black leather. In original factory box. 17.5" tall, leather lined uppers, cloth & leather loops. Light use to leather soles & heels stamped *8 1/2 F* size. Tan cardboard box embossed *Josef Witt Weiden-Oberpfalz etc.* Above avg. cond. $175.00

OFFICER COMBAT BOOTS

OFFICER COMBAT BOOTS: 16.5" tall black leather bodies, leather lined uppers & cloth loops. Leather soles & heels with hobnails & 4 toe plates to each. Avg. cond. $135.00

OFFICER COMBAT BOOTS: Black leather. 16.5" tall leather lined uppers with loops. Leather soles & heels with added hobnails to edge, toe plates & horse-shoes. Avg. cond. $135.00

OFFICER WINTER BOOT LUFTWAFFE: Style favored by officers & generals on Eastern front. 17" tall smooth black leather & suede bodies. Adjustment strap

OFFICER BOOTS

around top & across ankle. Metal zipper to side. White felt lined. Unused double stitched leather soles & heels. Mint cond. $350.00

PARATROOPER BOOTS

PARATROOPER BOOTS: Black leather. Side lace. 10" tall, 6 grommet & 12 hooks to sides with laces. Luftwaffe style sewn leather soles & heels with toe/heel plates. Avg. cond. $801.00

SENTRY BOOTS: 11" tall gray wool bodies with black leather lowers, fittings & soles. Soles & heels. 2 roller buckle closure front & inside leather tab dated 1939. Above avg. cond. $90.00

SENTRY BOOTS: 12" tall gray felt bodies with black leather fittings & wood soles. 2 roller buckle closure straps. Inked cloth maker tags with date. Soles inked *32*. Exc. cond. $82.00

SENTRY BOOTS: 12" tall gray wool bodies, black leather lowers & solid wood soles/ heels. 2 roller buckle closure straps & inked maker tags. Size 32. Above avg. cond. $50.00

SENTRY BOOTS

SENTRY BOOTS: Brown leather & felt. 11.5" tall bodies with 2 roller buckle closure straps to front openings. Printed cloth tag to each *Herm.Muller Hartha*

I.Sa.1943 31. Wood soles/heels inked *31*. Near mint cond. $110.00

SKI BOOTS: 10" tall with green canvas uppers, brown leather lowers & wood soles. 4 leather roller-buckle closure straps. Steel horseshoe & toe fitting to each. Wood stamped *28 Rata 42 623*. French fleece/leather liners with zipper sides. Above avg. cond. $135.00

TROPICAL BOOTS

TROPICAL BOOTS: 17" tall, rust brown canvas uppers, brown leather lowers with ankle leather guards to each side, 18 grommets & 14 hooks with brown laces. Leather soles & heels appear unused & are stamped *27 1/2 6 Lingel*. Mint cond. $1,651.00

TROPICAL LOW-QUARTER BOOTS: 6.5" tall, off-white canvas uppers, 2 roller buckle closure straps, black leather lowers, wood soles/heels stamped *28/44 RB Nr. etc.* 9 hobnails, toe plates & horseshoes. Near mint cond. $125.00

WINTER BOOTS

WINTER BOOTS: 14.5" tall with gray felt uppers, cloth loops, 2 closure straps to front slash & black lowers. Leather soles & heels with horseshoes. Above avg. cond. $129.00

THIRD REICH BELTS & BUCKLES

BELT ARMY DAK: Olive-green web body with leather tongue, green steel hook, inked 88 size & maker/1941 Near mint cond. $72.00

BELT BUCKLE ARMY EM TROPICAL: Stamped steel by *CTD 1941* with olive paint. Above avg. cond. $42.00

BELT BUCKLE ARMY EM WITH BELT: Pebbled alum. body & 4 tab roundel. Black leather belt. Avg. cond. $40.00

BELT BUCKLE ARMY EM WITH BELT: Pebbled gray body with 4 tab roundel having silver painted finish. Black patent leather belt, gray felt backing, riveted hooks, leather tongue, about size 85. Avg. cond. $50.00

BELT BUCKLE ARMY EM WITH BELT: Stamped pebbled alum. body with gray paint. Brown leather tab with 1938/maker. Black leather belt with tongue, alum. hook, 1936/maker & unit stamp. SIze 92. Avg. cond. $61.00

BELT BUCKLE ARMY EM WITH BELT

BELT BUCKLE ARMY EM WITH BELT: Stamped pebbled alum. body. By *F.K.O.* & same maker to black leather tab. Black leather combat belt, leather tongue, steel hook, 1940/maker, size 115 & inked *R.L.M.* Avg. cond. $72.00

BELT BUCKLE ARMY EM WITH BELT: Stamped steel buckle with gray paint. Black leather belt, tongue, alum. hook & size 100. Avg. cond. $72.00

BELT BUCKLE ARMY EM WITH BELT: Stamped steel with gray paint. Black pigskin tab by *Aurich etc..1942*. Black leather belt, tongue & riveted hook. About size 90. Avg. cond. $33.00

BELT BUCKLE ARMY EM WITH BELT: Stamped steel with gray paint. Brown tab with 1940/maker. Black leather belt, steel hook, leather tongue, size 90 & 1942/maker. Avg. cond. $58.00

BELT BUCKLE ARMY EM: Aluminum. Ink stamped *Panzer Abt 65* on leather tongue dated 37. Avg. cond. $76.00

BELT BUCKLE ARMY EM: Stamped pebbled alum. Brown tab with 1940 maker. Avg. cond. $27.00

BELT BUCKLE ARMY EM: Stamped pebbled alum. body. Brown leather tab with maker & clear unit stamp. Avg. cond. $34.00

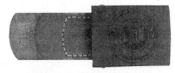

BELT BUCKLE ARMY EM

BELT BUCKLE ARMY EM: Stamped steel with gray paint, excellent details & *N&H 1941*. Brown tab with date/maker. Mint cond. $93.00

BELT BUCKLE ARMY EM: Stamped steel with gray paint. By *RS&S.* Brown leather tab with 1940/maker. Exc. cond. $36.00

BELT BUCKLE ARMY EM: Stamped steel with gray paint. By *SC 1940* with tree trademark. Avg. cond. $27.00

BELT BUCKLE ARMY EM: Stamped steel with gray/green paint. Brown leather tab by *B.Haarmann Ludenscheid 1940*. Mint cond. $48.00

BELT BUCKLE ARMY EM

BELT BUCKLE ARMY EM: Stamped steel with olive/gray paint & *R.S.&S.* Leather tab marked with 1940/maker. Near mint cond. $90.00

BELT BUCKLE ARMY EM: Stamped steel, gray paint & brown tab with 1942/maker. Avg. cond. $29.00

BELT BUCKLE ARMY EM: Stamped steel, olive/gray paint, *R.S.&S.* Brown tab 1942/maker. Mint cond. $69.00

BELT BUCKLE ARMY OFFICER
WITH BROCADE BELT

BELT BUCKLE ARMY OFFICER WITH
BROCADE BELT: Bright alum. facing with
green stripes, brocade loops, wool
backing, grommet size adjustment &
stamped alum. buckle. About size 95.
Exc. cond. $155.00
BELT BUCKLE ARMY OFFICER WITH
BROCADE BELT & LEATHER STORAGE
CASE: Bright alum. brocade facing with 2
green stripes. Gray wool backing, 2
brocade loops, leather tongue & about
size 110. Gray finished alum. buckle with
prongs to loop. 6" diam. brown leather
case with buckle-strap closure. Above
avg. cond. $200.00
BELT BUCKLE ARMY OFFICER WITH
BROCADE BELT" Alum brocade facing
with green strips. Gray wool backing.
Leather tongue. Stamped alum. buckle
with prongs to loop. Exc. cond. .. $66.00
BELT BUCKEL ARMY OFFICER WITH
BROCADE: Bright alum, facing with
strips, brocade loops, wol backing,
groomet size adjustment & stamped
alum, bickel. About size 95. Above avg.
cond. $155.00

BELT BUCKLE ARMY OFFICER

BELT BUCKLE ARMY OFFICER: Stamped
alum. disc with loop. Prongs to alum.
loop. Exc. cond. $76.00

BELT BUCKLE ARMY OFFICER: Stamped
gray alum. disc with same alum. loop to
both sides. Above avg. cond. $40.00

BELT BUCKLE ARMY TROPICAL
EM WITH WEB BELT

BELT BUCKLE ARMY TROPICAL EM
WITH WEB BELT: Olive/tan web body
with web tongue, steel hook, inked with
size 100 & 1942/maker. Stamped steel
buckle with olive paint & web tab. Mint
cond. $212.00
BELT BUCKLE ARMY TROPICAL EM WITH
WEB BELT: Stamped steel body with
gray paint & by *ESL 40*. Tan leather tab
with same maker/date. Olive web belt,
leather tongue, rust to steel hook & inked
RB#/size 85. Exc. cond. $95.00
BELT BUCKLE ARMY TROPICAL EM WITH
WEB BELT: Stamped steel by *ESL40*.
Same maker to leather tab. Olive web
belt, steel hook, leather tongue & inked
110. Avg. cond. $85.00
BELT BUCKLE ARMY TROPICAL EM WITH
WEB BELT: Tan web belt, steel hook,
olive tongue & inked 95. Stamped steel
buckle with gray paint & olive tab. Near
mint cond. $125.00
BELT BUCKLE ARMY TROPICAL EM:
Stamped steel body with *41* behind bar.
Olive web tab. Avg. cond. $90.00
BELT BUCKLE BAHNSCHUTZ POLIZEI
EM: Stamped pebbled steel body with
details & gray anodized finish. Above
avg. cond. $200.00

BELT BUCKLE BAHNSCHUTZ
POLIZEI OFFICER WITH BELT

BELT BUCKLE BAHNSCHUTZ POLIZEI OFFICER WITH BELT: Stamped alum. disc with excellent details & by *A DRGM 38* for Assmann maker. Black leather belt, tongue, loop, alum. pronged-loop, size 80 & stamped *R.B.D.MU*. Near mint cond. $486.00

BELT BUCKLE COASTAL ARTY EM: Stamped steel with blue/black paint. Above avg. cond. $50.00

BELT BUCKLE COASTAL ARTY EM: Stamped steel with dark gray paint. Exc. cond. $28.00

BELT BUCKLE DAF MEMBER

BELT BUCKLE DAF MEMBER: Stamped alum. by *RZM M4/24* with silver paint. With paper tag & same inked RZM maker. Near mint cond. $79.00

BELT BUCKLE DAF MEMBER: Stamped alum. with silver paint. By *RZM M4/28*. Above avg. cond. $55.00

BELT BUCKLE FIRE DEFENSE EM HAMBURG: Stamped pebbled steel with castle/shield center. Silver washed body. Avg. cond. $40.00

BELT BUCKLE FIRE DEFENSE OFFICER BAYERN WITH BELT: Stamped brass disc with nickel finish & 4 part divided shield. Black leather belt, 2 loops, tongue, 2 built-in D-rings, prongs to loop. Avg. cond. $125.00

BELT BUCKLE FIRE DEFENSE OFFICER BAYERN WITH BELT

BELT BUCKLE FIRE DEFENSE OFFICER PROV. SACHSEN WITH BELT: Stamped laurel leaf wreath with eagle to shield having crown to bars. Black leather body,

tongue stamped *Croupon*, prongs & inked size 98. Exc. cond. $28.00

BELT BUCKLE FIRE DEFENSE OFFICER RHEINLAND: Stamped brass disc with dark silver finish. Shield center & laurel leaf wreath border. Loop with prongs. Avg. cond. $32.00

BELT BUCKLE FORESTRY OFFICIAL WITH BELT: 45mm wide green leather belt is still owner tied with leather lace, 2 leather loops, green felt backing, leather tongue & black burnished finish to oval alum. buckle with eagle/wreath. Size 90. Mint cond. $140.00

BELT BUCKLE FORESTRY OFFICIAL WITH BELT: Bright alum. brocade facing with 2 green stripes. 2 brocade loops. Green twill wool backing with couple small moth holes. Leather tongue with pronged loop. Stamped alum. oval eagle buckle with oak leaf wreath. About 115. Near mint cond. $248.00

BELT BUCKLE FREIST HESSEN OFFICIAL BUCKLE WITH BELT: Stamped buckle with dark finish & crowned lion shield center. Black leather belt has tongue & size 93. Avg. cond. ... $125.00

BELT BUCKLE HITLER YOUTH MEMBER WITH BELT & CROSS-STRAP: Gray injected buckle with details & *RZM M4/ 72*. Black paper ersatz belt, riveted hook & leather tongue stamped *RZM DJ etc*. 2 imitation pigskin/paper belt loops & cross strap with nickel fittings. Both clips stamped *DRGM M5/8c RZM A*. Avg. cond. $120.00

BELT BUCKLE HITLER YOUTH MEMBER WITH BELT

BELT BUCKLE HITLER YOUTH MEMBER WITH BELT: Injected gray body with details & by *RZM M4/27*. Black belt with imitation pigskin look, riveted hook & leather tongue. About size 80. Above avg. cond. $50.00

BELT BUCKLE HITLER YOUTH MEMBER: Gray injected body. By *RZM M4/24*. Avg. cond. $26.00

BELT BUCKLE HITLER YOUTH MEMBER: Gray injection molded body by *RZM M4/ 38*. Above avg. cond. $30.00

BELT BUCKLE HITLER YOUTH MEMBER: Stamped steel with silver paint. Avg. cond. $20.00

BELT BUCKLE LUFTWAFFE
EM WITH BELT

BELT BUCKLE LUFTWAFFE EM WITH BELT: Stamped pebbled alum. body & 4 tab roundel with early down tailed eagle. Brown leather belt, leather tongue, riveted nickel, size 105 & blue felt backing. Above avg. cond. $75.00

BELT BUCKLE LUFTWAFFE EM WITH BELT: Stamped steel with blue-gray paint. Brown tab by *H. Aurich Dresden 1941*. Black combat belt with steel hook, about half of cut-down tongue, size 85 & added gull device from collar tab. Avg. cond. $37.00

BELT BUCKLE LUFTWAFFE EM: Stamped pebbled alum. body. Brown leather tab with 1939/maker. Avg. cond. $45.00

BELT BUCKLE LUFTWAFFE EM: Stamped pebbled alum. with 4 tab roundel. Avg. cond. $35.00

BELT BUCKLE LUFTWAFFE EM: Stamped pebbled alum. with wear to 2nd eagle. Avg. cond. $28.00

BELT BUCKLE LUFTWAFFE EM: Stamped steel buckle with tab marked *H.Aurich Dresden 1942*. Avg. cond. $50.00

BELT BUCKLE LUFTWAFFE EM: Stamped steel with paint. 1941/maker to leather tab. Near mint cond. $108.00

BELT BUCKLE LUFTWAFFE
OFFICER WITH BROCADE BELT

BELT BUCKLE LUFTWAFFE OFFICER WITH BROCADE BELT: Alum. brocade facing with 2 gray & 1 red stripe. 2 brocade loops, blue/gray wool backing with & grommets for size adjustments. Frosted silver finish to stamped buckle with 2 rivets holding gold down tailed eagle. Avg. cond. $325.00

BELT BUCKLE LUFTWAFFE OFFICER WITH BROCADE BELT: Alum. brocade facing with stripes. Blue-gray twill wool backing has grommet size adjustment & some moth holes. 2 brocade loops. Stamped buckle with silver frosted finish & affixed gold down tail eagle by 2 rivets. Large size. Avg. cond. $257.00

BELT BUCKLE NAVAL EM WITH BELT: Dark blue-gray paint to stamped steel buckle by *JFS*. Black leather belt & has rare Eagle-M. Size 96, leather tongue & steel hook. Near mint cond. $97.00

BELT BUCKLE NAVAL EM: Stamped alum. with gold wash. by *R.S.&S.* Brown tab with 1938/maker & Eagle-M stamp. Avg. cond. $124.00

BELT BUCKLE NAVAL OFFICER WITH BROCADE BELT: Beautiful die struck gilt anchor buckle with polished detail. Brocade with 2 black stripes. 2 brocade loops. Hidden loops for dagger. Adjustable size. Avg. cond. $135.00

BELT BUCKLE NAVAL OFFICER: 60mm. Solid heavy gray metal by *FLL* with gold finish. Avg. cond. $50.00

BELT BUCKLE NAVAL OFFICER

BELT BUCKLE NAVAL OFFICER: Brass. 60mm heavy cast body with gold finish to anchor & laurel leaf wreath. Fixed & loose loops. Above avg. cond. $50.00

BELT BUCKLE NAVAL OFFICER: Heavy stamped 60mm brass body with gold finish. Loop to back side & extra loop. Exc. cond. $70.00

BELT BUCKLE NAVAL OFFICER: Solid alum. body with gold finish at highlights of anchor & laurel leaf wreath. By *EJL*. Avg. cond. $23.00

BELT BUCKLE NSBO: Brass body, affixed roundel with logo center & oak leaf wreath border. 2 solder holes. Exc. cond. $50.00

BELT BUCKLE NSDAP JUGEND: 30mm oval swastika. Nickel plated body with affixed brass oval swastika to center. Slide bar & pronged keeper to back. Avg. cond. $36.00

BELT BUCKLE NSDAP OFFICIAL OPEN FACE WITH BELT: 55mm brown leather body & stamped *Croupon Herst.-NR.610*. Brown belt loop, nickel D-ring belt loop & brass pebbled buckle with claws. Avg. cond. $75.00

BELT BUCKLE NSDAP OFFICIAL WITH BELT: 60mm brown leather belt with 2 leather loops, Leather tongue, inked 95 & stamped *RZM Kernstuck L2/682/42*. Gold finished alum. buckle by *RZM M4/46* & loop by *RZM M4/77*. Above avg. cond. $177.00

BELT BUCKLE NSDAP OFFICIAL WITH BELT

BELT BUCKLE NSDAP OFFICIAL WITH BELT: 60mm gold finished solid alum. buckle *RZM M4/87* with prongs to loop. Pliable leather, 2 loops, tongue, RZM marked loop & stamped *Croupon RZM L2/600/42*. Inked size 100. Near mint cond. $282.00

BELT BUCKLE NSDAP OFFICIAL: 60mm diam. Heavy solid gray metal disc with gilt finish. By *RZM M4/77*. Prongs to loop. Late-war. Avg. cond. $40.00

BELT BUCKLE NSDAP OFFICIAL: 60mm. Solid alum. body with gold finished eagle & wreath by *RZM M4/24*. Oak leaves to prong-loop & to extra loop. Above avg. cond. $90.00

BELT BUCKLE NSDAP OFFICIAL: Solid alum. disc with gold finish. Oak leaves to loop with prongs. By *RZM M4/22*. Avg. cond. $35.00

BELT BUCKLE OFFICER OPEN FACE WITH BELT: 60mm wide brown leather belt with leather loop & stamped *Croupon Nr.6*. Silver finish to gray pebbled buckle with 22mm wide claws & stamped RZM. Exc. cond. $107.00

BELT BUCKLE OFFICER OPEN FACE WITH BELT: 60mm wide Havana-brown leather body by *Deutsches Leder Kernstuck 472*, leather belt loop & size 85. Silver finish to pebbled buckle by *A* for Assmann. Exc. cond. $87.00

BELT BUCKLE OFFICER OPEN FACE: 65mm wide pebbled gray body. 23mm wide prongs. By *RZM M5/140*. Avg. cond. $20.00

BELT BUCKLE OLYMPIC: Commercial. 30x43mm stamped rectangle is nickel plated. 5 rings to front panel with flaming background. Above avg. cond. $172.00

BELT BUCKLE OPEN-FACE WITH BELT & CROSS-STRAP

BELT BUCKLE OPEN-FACE WITH BELT & CROSS-STRAP: 45mm pliable dark brown leather body, loop & pebbled brass buckle. Dark brown cross strap *L2/2613*, pebbled brass fittings with clips by *A U RZM DRGM M5/289* 60mm size belt-loops with brass D-rings. Near mint cond. $345.00

BELT BUCKLE POLICE EM HANNOVER WITH BELT: Brown leather belt with pebbled aluminum buckle having running horse with *Gott Mit Uns* inscription. Two piece construction. Above avg. cond. $32.00

BELT BUCKLE POLICE EM HANNOVER:

BELT BUCKLE POLICE EM HANNOVER: stamped pebbled alum. body. 4 tab roundel with horse center etc. Avg. cond. $55.00

BELT BUCKLE POLICE EM WESTPHALIA:
Pebbled alum. with 4 tab roundel having
Gott Mit Uns, half oak-leaf wreath &
horse center. Avg. cond. $36.00

BELT BUCKLE POLICE OFFICER WITH
SS-STYLE BROCADE BELT

BELT BUCKLE POLICE OFFICER WITH
SS-STYLE BROCADE BELT: Stamped
alum. buckle with bright silver highlights,
pronged loop & *RZM M4/22 DRGM*.
Alum. brocade facing with SS runes,
oakleaves, black & silver borders. 2
brocade loops, dry leather tongue
stamped *Po 1939*, green twill wool
backing & paper RZM/SS tag. Exc.
cond. $578.00
BELT BUCKLE POSTSCHUTZ EM:
Stamped pebbled nickel body with title &
eagle details. Avg. cond. $368.00
BELT BUCKLE PRUSSIAN POLICE
OFFICER: 50mm diam. heavy cast or
stamped body with excellent details to
Prussian Eagle & *Freistaat Preussen*.
Gold finish with nickel highlights. By *LF
1931* with shield trademark. Prongs to
loop. Above avg. cond. $175.00
BELT BUCKLE RAD EM WITH BELT:
Stamped pebbled alum. body & maker
trade mark. Leather tab with 36 maker.
Black leather belt, tongue, alum. hook &
size 95. Stamped *B.A.Br. 9 38*. Avg.
cond. $60.00
BELT BUCKLE RAD EM: Stamped pebbled
alum. body. By *R.S.&S.* with gray-wash.
Exc. cond. $33.00
BELT BUCKLE RED CROSS EM M38: Gray
finished stamped pebbled alum. body
with eagle/wreath. By *olc ges.gesch*.
Near mint cond. $73.00
BELT BUCKLE RED CROSS EM M38:
Stamped pebbled gray alum. body with
eagle & wreath. *Ges.Gesch.1*. Avg.
cond. $135.00
BELT BUCKLE RED CROSS OFFICER
M38 WITH BELT: Alum. disc with eagle &
laurel leaf wreath. Marked *Ges.Gesch 2*.
Black leather belt with tongue & 2 sets of
factory added holes to body behind
tongue. Leather loop & alum. loop.

Tongue stamped *H* & about size 90.
Above avg. cond. $282.00
BELT BUCKLE REICHSWEHR EM:
Stamped pebbled nickel body &
affixed roundel by 2 solder holes. Avg.
cond. $20.00
BELT BUCKLE REICHWEHR EM: Pebbled
nickel body with roundel having 2 solder
holes. Avg. cond. $25.00
BELT BUCKLE REICHWEHR NAVAL EM:
Stamped brass body with eagle, Gott Mit
Uns & laurel half-wreath. Dark brown
leather tab with anchor-M stamp &
maker/date area. Avg. cond. $91.00
BELT BUCKLE RLB EM 2ND TYPE:
Stamped alum. with Luftschutz winged
swastika/wreath. Avg. cond. $30.00
BELT BUCKLE RLB EM 3RD TYPE:
Stamped steel with dark blue/gray paint.
Brown tab with 1941/maker. Above avg.
cond. $244.00

BELT BUCKLE SA MEMBER WITH BELT

BELT BUCKLE SA MEMBER WITH BELT:
Brass body with 2 solder holes to
common brass roundel. Black leather
belt with tongue, alum. hook, size 105
tagged & stamped *8./J.R.103.I*. Avg.
cond. $65.00
BELT BUCKLE SA MEMBER WITH BELT:
Brass body with 2 solder holes to
common brass roundel. Black leather is
pliable, leather tongue, steel hook & size
100. Above avg. cond. $45.00
BELT BUCKLE SA MEMBER WITH BELT:
Stamped brass body with common
eagle/swastika & bright nickel finish
overall. Black leather dress belt, tongue,
riveted hook & about size 95. Exc.
cond. $99.00
BELT BUCKLE SA MEMBER: Brass body, 2
solder holes, & common swastika to
brass roundel. Avg. cond. $28.00
BELT BUCKLE SA MEMBER: Bright plated
finish to smooth body & 2 solder holes to
roundel with common swastika. Above
avg. cond. $90.00

43

BELT BUCKLE SA-
WEHRMANNSCHAFTEN

BELT BUCKLE SA-
WEHRMANNSCHAFTEN: Stamped
alum. body with excellent details. By
RZM M4/22. Near mint cond. ... $480.00

BELT BUCKLE SS EM WITH BELT

BELT BUCKLE SS EM WITH BELT:
Stamped alum. marked *RZM 36/39 SS*.
Black leather belt, tongue, steel hook &
size 90. Above avg. cond. $250.00
BELT BUCKLE SS EM WITH BELT:
Stamped nickel body by *O&C
ges.gesch*. Black leather belt with
leather tongue & riveted nickel hook.
About size 95 & has stamped *RZM/SS*
in circles. Avg. cond. $293.00

BELT BUCKLE SS EM WITH BELT

BELT BUCKLE SS EM WITH BELT:
Stamped with silver paint. Unmarked.
Black leather body, steel hook, tongue,

stamped size 95 & 43-dated RB#. Above
avg. cond. $282.00
BELT BUCKLE SS EM WITH WHITE BELT:
Stamped nickel body by *O&C Ges.
Gesch*. White fiber belt by *A. Fischer
Berlin C.2 1937*, alum. hook, leather
tongue stamped *RZM 4/38 SS*. White
fiber covered leather bayonet frog made
by *A. Fischer Berlin C.2 1937*. Exc.
cond. $1,200.00

BELT BUCKLE SS EM WITH WHITE BELT

BELT BUCKLE SS EM: Stamped alum. with
silver paint. By *RZM 155/39 SS*. Above
avg. cond. $387.00
BELT BUCKLE SS EM: Stamped alum. with
silver paint. By *RZM 822/37 SS*. Near
mint cond. $349.00
BELT BUCKLE SS EM: Stamped nickel.
Above avg. cond. $170.00
BELT BUCKLE SS OFFICER WITH BELT &
CROSS-STRAP: Stamped alum. disc
with details. Back stamped *RZM SS 36/
38 OLC*. Prongs to fixed loop. Black
leather belt, leather tongue, leather loop,
alum. end loop. Black leather cross-strap,
nickel fittings & 1 clip stamped *A* for
Assmann. 2 black leather belt loops with
nickel D-rings. Near mint
cond. $906.00

BELT BUCKLE SS OFFICER WITH BELT &
CROSS-STRAP

BELT BUCKLE SS OFFICER: Stamped
non-magnetic metal disc with silver paint
& excellent details. Back stamped *RZM
SS 36/43 OLC*. With extra loop & black
printed paper maker's tag. Near mint
cond. $900.00
BELT BUCKLE SS OFFICER: Alum.
stamped with pressed in keeper bar.
Hmkd *OLC SS 36/39 RZM* on bar.
Alum. 2 pronged keeper attached &

unattached keeper bar with 2 prongs. Avg. cond. $339.00

BELT BUCKLE STAHLHELM
MEMBER FRONT HEIL

BELT BUCKLE STAHLHELM MEMBER FRONT HEIL: Brass body with nickel roundel having 3 solder holes. Above avg. cond. $56.00

BELT BUCKLE TURNVEREIN MEMBER

BELT BUCKLE TURNVEREIN MEMBER: Stamped pebbled body with 4 F center & dull-silver finish. Made by *Ideba*. Mint cond. $50.00

BELT BUCKLE TURNVEREIN MEMBER: Stamped pebbled nickel with 4 F center. By *ges.gesch* with trademark. Avg. cond. $45.00

BELT DAK WEB: Olive-green web belt, leather tongue, olive painted loop, inked size 98 & stamped *G.Reinhardt Berlin 1941*. Mint cond. $143.00

BELT DAK WEB: Olive-green web belt, olive painted hook, leather tongue inked 115 &

stamped *G.Reinhardt Berlin 1941*. Mint cond. $177.00

BELT HITLER YOUTH: Brown leather. 45mm body with riveted nickel hook & moved tongue. About size 85. Avg. cond. $23.00

BELT NSDAP OFFICIAL: 60mm. Brown leather, leather tongue, 2 belt loops & RZM M4/87 loop. Size 115. Above avg. cond. $60.00

BELT SS: Black leather. Leather tongue stamped *SS 1325/43 RZM*, gray painted steel hook by *SC 42* with tree trademark & size 100. 2 part black printed tag is glued to belt behind tongue. Exc. cond. $383.00

BELT SS: Black leather. Officer. 45mm wide body, tongue & 2 leather loops. Stamped *SS 1/40 RZM*. About size 100. Exc. cond. $227.00

CROSS-STRAP HITLER YOUTH

CROSS-STRAP HITLER YOUTH: With *HJ/DJ RZM* red printed triangular paper tag with rivet & inked price *1.90*. Mint condition leather strap stamped *RZM L2/699/39*. Nickel fittings with clips by *RZM M5c/93/16*. Mint belt loops. Mint cond. $75.00

CROSS-STRAP POLICE PARADE DRESS: 2" wide, with white finish to leather body & pebbled alum. fittings. Also has leather button hole end tabs. Avg. cond. $219.00

CHAPTER TWO: CLOTH INSIGNIA

IMPERIAL GERMAN CLOTH INSIGNIA

AIGUILLETTE BAVARIAN ADJUTANT: Double braided cords with shoulder loops, silver needles with open crown caps and blue and white coloration. Designed to secure to shoulder strap. Avg. cond. $72.00

AIGUILLETTE PRUSSIAN GENERAL: M1914. Double looped style. Gold bullion wire with gilt gold needles. Mint cond. $475.00

AIGUILLETTE PRUSSIAN GENERAL: Napoleonic era. Heavy gold double braided loops with shoulder woven planchet for securing on uniform. Cords have proper brass needles on ends. These were used for cleaning pistol vents in battle and also for the tradition of being impaled on your own aigulette should you fail the regimental honor. Poor cond. $59.00

AIGUILLETTE WURTTEMBERG ROYAL PALACE OFFICER: Worn by hofmeister or attendant to the royal castle. Massive gilt shoulder crest with crown shield and blackened silver deer with full antlers. Large gilt needles with crown caps. Silver braided double loop aiguillette with black flecking. Avg. cond. $108.00

CAP LINE & BREAST CORDS FOR UHLAN TSCHAPKA: Plaited pattern with tassels. Tan colored overall. Near mint cond. $384.00

CAP RIBBON NAVAL *1.IX.MATR.ARTILLERIE=ABTL.IX.1.:* 28" black ribbon with gold bevo Latin title. Above avg. cond. $59.00

CAP RIBBON NAVAL *4.I. MATR. ARTILLERIE=ABTL. I.4.:* Gilt wire block letters on black. Avg. cond. $45.00

CAP RIBBON NAVAL *4.II. MATROSEN=DIVISION. II.4.:* Gilt wire with block letters on black. Above avg. cond. $45.00

CAP RIBBON NAVAL *5.XV.SEEWEHR=ABTEILUNG.XV.5.:* 3.5' black ribbon with gold bevo block letters. Above avg. cond. $59.00

CAP RIBBON NAVAL *7.II. MATROSEN=DIVISION. II.7.:* Gilt wire style with block letters on black. Avg. cond. $45.00

CAP RIBBON NAVAL *A.1.II. WEFT=DIVISION. II.A.1.:* Silver wire with block letters on black. Near mint cond. $45.00

CAP RIBBON NAVAL *A.2. SCHIFFSSTAMMDIVISION DER*

NORDSEE. A.2.: Gilt wire block letters on black. Above avg. cond. $35.00

CAP RIBBON NAVAL *IV. HALBFLOTTILLE. IV.:* Gilt wire block letters on black. Avg. cond. $45.00

CAP RIBBON NAVAL *LINIENSCHIFF ELSASS:* 46" long black body with gold bevo Latin title. Avg. cond. $50.00

CAP RIBBON NAVAL *S.M.S. AEGIR:* 57" black body with gold Latin title. Avg. cond. $108.00

CAP RIBBON NAVAL *S.M.S. AEGIR*

CAP RIBBON NAVAL *S.M.S. BAYERN:* 45" black body style with silver Latin title. Above avg. cond. $75.00

CAP RIBBON NAVAL *S.M.S. BLUECHER:* 51" black body with gold Latin title. Above avg. cond. $118.00

CAP RIBBON NAVAL *S.M.S. DRESDEN:* 44" black body with silver Latin title. Avg. cond. $109.00

CAP RIBBON NAVAL *S.M.S. FREYA:* 46" black body with faint gold Latin title. Avg. cond. $75.00

CAP RIBBON NAVAL *S.M.S. FRIEDRICH CARL:* 45" black body with silver Latin title. Avg. cond. $75.00

CAP RIBBON NAVAL *S.M.S. FRIEDRICH DER GROSSE:* 47" black body with silver Latin title. Avg. cond. $93.00

CAP RIBBON NAVAL *S.M.S. FUERST BIKSMARCK:* 45" black body with silver Latin title. Exc. cond. $75.00

CAP RIBBON NAVAL *S.M.S. GRAUDENZ:* 27" black body with yellow cotton Latin title. Avg. cond. $75.00

CAP RIBBON NAVAL *S.M.S. HELGOLAND:* 36" black body with silver Latin title. Exc. cond. $75.00

CAP RIBBON NAVAL *S.M.S. HERTHA:* 43" black body with silver Latin title. Avg. cond. $75.00

CAP RIBBON NAVAL *S.M.S. KAISER WILHELM II:* 45" black body with gold Latin title. Exc. cond. $75.00

CAP RIBBON NAVAL *S.M.S. KAISER WILHELM II.:* 43" black body with silver Latin title. Exc. cond. $75.00

CAP RIBBON NAVAL *S.M.S. KAISERIN AUGUSTA:* 38" black body with silver Latin title. Above avg. cond. $75.00

CAP RIBBON NAVAL *S.M.S. KOENIG WILHELM*: 47" black body with dark gold Latin title. Avg. cond. $75.00

CAP RIBBON NAVAL *S.M.S. KOENIG*: About 4' black body with silver bevo Latin title. Above avg. cond. $45.00

CAP RIBBON NAVAL *S.M.S. KRONPRINZ*: 42" black body with silver Latin title. Above avg. cond. $75.00

CAP RIBBON NAVAL *S.M.S. LEIPZIG*: 39" black body with gold Latin title. Above avg. cond. $75.00

CAP RIBBON NAVAL *S.M.S. LEIPZIG*

CAP RIBBON NAVAL *S.M.S. LOTHRINGEN*: 45" black body with silver Latin title. Exc. cond. $75.00

CAP RIBBON NAVAL *S.M.S. MECKLENBURG*:47" black body with faint gold Latin title. Avg. cond. ... $75.00

CAP RIBBON NAVAL *S.M.S. NASSAU* : 56" black body with dark gold Latin title. Above avg. cond. $75.00

CAP RIBBON NAVAL *S.M.S. NUERNBERG*: 39" black body with gold Latin title. Above avg. cond. $93.00

CAP RIBBON NAVAL *S.M.S. POMMERN*: Gilt wire block letters on black. Above avg. cond. $75.00

CAP RIBBON NAVAL *S.M.S. RHEINLAND*: 47" black body with silver Latin title. Avg. cond. $75.00

CAP RIBBON NAVAL *S.M.S. STRALSUND*: Silver wire block letters on black. Avg. cond. $45.00

CAP RIBBON NAVAL *S.M.S. STRASSBURG*: 37" black body with silver Latin title. Avg. cond. $75.00

CAP RIBBON NAVAL *S.M.S. STUTTGART*: 38" black body with gold Latin title. Above avg. cond. $75.00

CAP RIBBON NAVAL *S.M.S. VICTORIA LOUISE*: 33" long black body with gold bevo Latin title. Avg. cond. $50.00

CAP RIBBON NAVAL RESERVEST REMEMBERANCE: 10' long with 1905-08 dates. Metal fouled anchors (one anchor lacks loop on top for rope). Silver block letter machine-sewn-inscription, *Volldampf Voraus, Jetz Gehts Nach Haus. Es Ist Erreicht, Es War Nicht Leight. Reserve SMS Vineta. Reserve Von Dem Ostseestrand Hat Treu Gedient Dem Vaterland.* Near mint cond. $75.00

EPAULETTES ARMY GENERAL IN CASE: Named. Custom deluxe figure-8 cardboard box with blue lining lid & yellow silk body. Fancy maker label to *Oekonomie*, Berlin, purveyors of gold & silver bullion. Shoulder boards have 2 stars for general rank with high silver half cresents, cloth of silver field with black and white necking & red wool backing. The boards have a leather reinforced frame for the massive silver bullion fronds. Both boards are named to *Brauer Nachf.* on the insides in old ink writing. Mint cond. $750.00

EPAULETTES ARTY LT: Single. Light blue wool body with silver braid border on tongue. Brass crescent border on body. With gilt metal flaming bomb over *23*. Red wool backing. Avg. cond. $26.00

EPAULETTES INFANTRY OFFICER

EPAULETTES INFANTRY OFFICER: Pair. Red wool backing. White wool field. Copper or brass half moons. Black and white tape necks. Gilt *55* and 2 rank pips. Near mint cond. $110.00

LANYARD VETERAN MARKSMANSHIP: Blue worsted cloth with brass detachable acorn. Mint cond. $100.00

NAVAL SPECIALIST SLEEVE RATE: Blue hand embr. crowned anchor with gear wheel & border on white. Near mint cond. $53.00

PLASTRON BAVARIAN CHEVAULEGE: Red wool with tan backing. No unit marks. Avg. cond. $40.00

SHOULDER BOARDS BAVARIAN ADMIN OFFICIAL: Single. Red wool backing, gold field, and blue flecking. Single gilt rank pip. Slip-on. Mint cond. $20.00

SHOULDER BOARDS BAVARIAN GENERAL: Pair. Red wool base with gold/silver with blue V's with gold wire braided cord tops with 2 silver metal pips & gilt ciphers & crown. Slip-on style. Above avg. cond. $1,100.00

SHOULDER BOARDS BAVARIAN LT: Pair. Sewn-in style. Silver field with blue flecking. White base. Mint cond. $30.00

SHOULDER BOARDS BAVARIAN LT: Wartime. Pair. White base, gray field, and blue flecking. Slip-on. Near mint cond. $25.00

SHOULDER BOARDS BAVARIAN OFFICIAL: Pair. On carmine back with blue undersides. Above avg. cond. $23.00

SHOULDER BOARDS DRAGOON RESERVIST LT: Pair. Pre-WWI. Sew-in pattern. White wool base, blue overlay with bright silver wire having black flecking. Above avg. cond. $40.00

SHOULDER BOARDS HESSEN CAPTAIN: Pre-WWI. Single. Red underlay. Silver field with red flecking. 2 gilt pips. Slip-on. Above avg. cond. $20.00

SHOULDER BOARDS MECKLENBURG OFFICER: Pair. 5" long narrow dark silver plaited bodies on blue wool. Sew-in style. Brass bull head buttons. Avg. cond. $28.00

SHOULDER BOARDS OFFICER: Pair. 4" long sew-in style with blue & yellow V cord bodies. Gold devices & small gray wool panel to back. Avg. cond. ... $85.00

SHOULDER BOARDS OFFICER

SHOULDER BOARDS OFFICER: Pair. Dark blue backing and two gilt pips on silver rope with black, red, white flecking. Avg. cond. $100.00

SHOULDER BOARDS OFFICER: Pair. Pre-WWI. White wool base with 8 silver wire cord tops with green V's & gilt *101* metal devices on each. Sew ins. Avg. cond. $50.00

SHOULDER BOARDS OFFICER: Pair. Sew-in with red wool bodies 4 large silver cord tops & black thread V's. Avg. cond. $20.00

SHOULDER BOARDS OFFICER: Pair. Silver cords with black & red V's on red & black wool backings. With gilt metal *13*. Sew-in. Above avg. cond. $40.00

SHOULDER BOARDS OFFICER: Pair. Silver cords with black V's on white surface. With gilt metal *84*. Removable. Above avg. cond. $41.00

SHOULDER BOARDS OFFICER: Pair. Twisted silver rope that has black flecking

and bright yellow slip-on backing. Above avg. cond. $59.00

SHOULDER BOARDS OFFICER: Pair. White wool base with rounded end & silver cord tops & black thread V's with gilt *33*. Sew-ins. Above avg. cond. $59.00

SHOULDER BOARDS POSENSCHES INF REGT #18 CAPTAIN: Pair. Yellow base. Subdued tops with black and white V's. Subdued rank stars and *18*. Sew-in pattern. Mint cond. $48.00

SHOULDER BOARDS PRUSSIAN ADMINISTRATIVE OFFICIAL: Pair. Wartime issue with blue velour base and gray tops with blue V's. Gray metal crowned shields with raised Prussian eagle. Slip-on pattern. Mint cond. $36.00

SHOULDER BOARDS PRUSSIAN INF LT

SHOULDER BOARDS PRUSSIAN INF LT: Pair. 4" long slip-on style. Gray cords with white & black V's. White wool bases. Near mint cond. $97.00

SHOULDER BOARDS PRUSSIAN KRANKENTRAGER LT: M1910. Single. Gray tops with black & white flecking. Bright carmine underlayment. Mint cond. $27.00

SHOULDER BOARDS PRUSSIAN LT.-COLONEL: Single. Pre-war style with white tab and white cloth underlay. Silver braid on top with black flecking. Gilt rank pip and the *5*. Above avg. cond. $20.00

SHOULDER BOARDS PRUSSIAN LT: Pair. Dark blue velveteen base with red upper layer. Gray field with black and white flecking. Grey metallic *4*. Unissued. Mint cond. $34.00

SHOULDER BOARDS PRUSSIAN LT: Pair. Gray cords with black & white V's on white cloth with gilt metal *33*. Have been sewn-in. Avg. cond. $45.00

SHOULDER BOARDS PRUSSIAN LT: Pair. Red wool base with silver wire field with single brass rank star. Black flecking. Avg. cond. $24.00

SHOULDER BOARDS PRUSSIAN LT: Pair. Sew-in style. Dark green base with silver field and black flecking. Above avg. cond. $25.00

SHOULDER BOARDS PRUSSIAN LT: Pair. Wartime subdued gray tops with black and white flecking and red bases. Near mint cond. $38.00

SHOULDER BOARDS PRUSSIAN LT: Wartime. Pair. Yellow base with gray field. Black and white flecking. Slip-on. Near mint cond. $25.00

SHOULDER BOARDS PRUSSIAN MAJOR: Pair. Pre-WWI. White wool base with Russian twist with black flecking. Above avg. cond. $40.00

SHOULDER BOARDS PRUSSIAN MEDICAL LT: Wartime. Pair. Medical service with subdued caduceus. Blue velveteen base with subdued tops. With black & white V's. Removable pattern. Near mint cond. $40.00

SHOULDER BOARDS PRUSSIAN
VETERINARIAN OFFICER

SHOULDER BOARDS PRUSSIAN VETERINARIAN OFFICER: Pair of sew-in boards with carmine backing. Tops have silver rope with black and white flecking also gilt snakes. Avg. cond. $76.00

SHOULDER BOARDS RESERVE LT: Single. Green base with red top. Silver field with black flecking. Gilt *15*. Avg. cond. $23.00

SHOULDER BOARDS SAXON CAPT: Single. Sew-in pattern. Red base with silver field with green flecking. Gilt double rank pips with *108*. Flat brass button. Avg. cond. $25.00

SHOULDER BOARDS SAXON OFFICER: Pair. Silver rope with green flecking and gilt crown with *FR* below and white slip-on backing. Above avg. cond. ... $177.00

SHOULDER BOARDS WURTTEMBERG ADMIN OFFICIAL: Pair. Blue wool base

with flat silver tops with gilt crowned shield with Wurt. coat of arms. Slip-on. Mint cond. $23.00

SHOULDER STRAPS 108TH
JAGER EM

SHOULDER STRAPS 108TH JAGER EM: Pair. Field gray with gilt metal *108*. Above avg. cond. $97.00

SHOULDER STRAPS 141ST INFANTRY 1 YEAR VOL EM: Pair. Large overcoat style. Black backing with yellow field. Also with red embroidered *141* and black and white alternating cord piping. Sew-in style. Avg. cond. $85.00

SHOULDER STRAPS 40TH FIELD ARTY EM: Wartime. Single. Gray wool body. Red piping with flaming bomb and #40. Sew-in style. Above avg. cond. $30.00

SHOULDER STRAPS 51ST FIELD ARTILLERY EM: Pair. Pre-WWI. Large overcoat size in red wool with yellow flaming bomb and *51*. Sew-in pattern. Avg. cond. $36.00

SHOULDER STRAPS 89TH MECKLENBURG GRENADIER EM: Pair. Overcoat style with white field, red embroidered crown and cipher. Near mint cond. $50.00

SHOULDER STRAPS 95TH INF REGT EM: Pre-WWI. Pair. Dark blue wool backed with red field with custom embr. crown & cipher. Sew-in. Avg. cond. $69.00

SHOULDER STRAPS AUSTRIAN BEAMTE OFFICIAL: Pair. Slip-on pattern. Orange wool backing with slip tabs. Gilt dbl. headed eagle buttons. Gold border. 3 gold bullion rank stars. Above avg. cond. $50.00

SHOULDER STRAPS EM: M1910. Pair. Field-gray with white piping and red crown with a *W* under it. Near mint cond. $229.00

SHOULDER STRAPS EM: M1915. White wool piping with field-gray bodies pointed ends & chain stitch *45* in red. Sew ins. Above avg. cond. $41.00

SHOULDER STRAPS EM: Pair. White wool with red chain stitched *5.* Dark blue wool backing. Avg. cond. $47.00

SHOULDER STRAPS EM: Single. 4.5" long gray wool pointed body, yellow wool piping & red crowned *FR III* cipher. Avg. cond. $40.00

SHOULDER STRAPS EM: Wartime. Pair. Dun colored wool bodies with white piping. Pink embr. crown, *W* cipher. Above avg. cond. $30.00

SHOULDER STRAPS EM: Wartime. Single. Sew-in style. Gray wool bodies. White piping with red embr. *142.* Above avg. cond. $25.00

SHOULDER STRAPS FIELD ARTY EM: M1915. Single. Red field, white piped. *FR* with crown above, bomb below. Avg. cond. $46.00

SHOULDER STRAPS FLIEGER EM: Pair. Field-gray wool bodies. Red embroidered winged propellers. Sew-ins with pointed ends. Avg. cond. $61.00

SHOULDER STRAPS FLIEGER EM: Wartime. Pair. 4.5" gray wool pointed body with red hand embr. wing/prop to each. Sew-in style. Avg. cond. $165.00

SHOULDER STRAPS FLIEGER EM

SHOULDER STRAPS FLIEGER EM: Wartime. Single. Gray wool with red embroidered winged propeller. Sew-in pattern. Above avg. cond. $55.00

SHOULDER STRAPS FOOT ARTY EM: M1915. Single. Yellow field with red crossed cannons with flames. Red embr. *16.* Includes single metallic flying AA bomb for board. Above avg. cond. $26.00

SHOULDER STRAPS INFANTRY EM: Single. Wartime. Field-gray wool field; red embr. *84.* Sew-in. Above avg. cond. $25.00

SHOULDER STRAPS NAVAL 2ND SEA BATL NCO: Pair. For large overcoat. Dark blue wool. Sew-in style. Yellow hand embroidered naval crown with banner above crossed anchors over Roman number *II.* Mint cond. ... $200.00

SHOULDER STRAPS TRANSPORT-RAIL EM: Wartime. Pair. Grey feldgrau wool bodies with yellow embr. spoked type wheel flanked by wings. Near mint cond. $126.00

SHOULDER STRAPS UHLAN EM: M1915. Pair. Red wool straps with yellow embroidered crown & cipher, white wool piping & field-gray backing, cipher is an *A* with a *II* below it. Above avg. cond. $112.00

SLEEVE CHEVRON NAVAL EM: Red, white & black double cord V's. Mint cond. $37.00

SLEEVE SPECIALIST PATCH NAVAL: Oval white cloth with blue border. Single Apprentice Engineer steering wheel in center. Near mint cond. $65.00

SLEEVE SPECIALIST RATE NAVAL ENGINEERING CPO: White cloth body. Blue sewn circle with crown, banner above anchor and steering wheel. Near mint cond. $63.00

SLEEVE SPECIALIST RATE NAVAL ENGINEERING: White cloth with blue cord style border: matching blue Imperial crown above anchor with cog wheel. Dated *Feb. 28, 1911* on reverse with *W* stamp for Wilhelmshaven issue. Above avg. cond. $85.00

SLEEVE SPECIALTY PATCH PIONEER: 4x4" black felt patch with crossed red embr. shovels. Exc. cond. $66.00

SLEEVE SPECIALIST PATCH NAVAL ANCHOR: 4" tall blue wool oval with yellow hand embr. crown over anchor. Avg. cond. $99.00

SWALLOW NEST BANDSMAN: Pair. Dark blue wool body with silver braid work and trim. Avg. cond. $35.00

SWALLOW NEST BANDSMAN: Pair. Olive drab field. Subdued white braid with red underlay. Above avg. cond. $45.00

SWALLOW NEST BANDSMAN: Pair. Subdued silver braid on tan cloth backing. Avg. cond. $25.00

SWALLOW NEST CAVALRY BANDSMAN: Golden-yellow wool body with seven diagonal bands of gold bullion (line cavalry unit), NCO tape (Tresse) & one horizontal bar. Yellow wool backing, all machine-sewn, sewn-in type. Above avg. cond. $25.00

SWALLOW NEST GARDE INFANTRY BANDSMAN: M1910. Pair. High quality thick white wool body with diamond pattern NCO tape in silver bullion with short (1") thin silver fringe, field-gray wool backing with five gray metal duck bill forged hooks. All machine-sewn construction. Above avg. cond. .. $25.00

SWALLOW NEST INFANTRY BANDSMAN: M1910. Pair. Field-gray body and backing, red wool piping, and gold bullion NCO tape. Exc. cond. $63.00

SWALLOW NEST INFANTRY BUGLER/ DRUMMER: M1910. Pair. Thick high quality enlisted field-gray wool body and backing with red wool piping and gold bullion NCO tape (Tresse). Reverse on each has seven forged (duckbill) flattened tip hooks of silver metal. Above avg. cond. $76.00

SWALLOW NEST MOUNTAIN TROOP BANDSMAN: Pair. Green wool body with diamond pattern silver bullion NCO tape (tresse), green wool piping, field-gray wool backing. Avg. cond. $45.00

VISOR CAP WREATH NAVAL OFFICER

VISOR CAP WREATH NAVAL OFFICER: Hand embr. gold crown over wreath with padded center having bullion cockade. Paper back type. Above avg. cond. $200.00

THIRD REICH SS, SA, NSKK & POLICE INSIGNIA

ARMBAND POLICE *HILFSPOLIZEI*: 3.5" tall white cotton twill body with black inked title & blue eagle stamp with faint wording. Blacked-out area to backside from early printed wording. Above avg. cond. $45.00

ARMBAND SA *SA GRUPPENVERPFLEGSFUHRER XXIII*: Three lines of black printed lettering on golden-yellow a cotton body. Avg. cond. $190.00

ARMBAND SA *SA VERPFLEGSFUHRER XXXIII/1*: 3 lines of black printed

lettering on golden-yellow. Above avg. cond. $190.00

ARMBAND SA SPORTS: Red cotton band with sewn-on white circle with gold embr. emblem. Has paper RZM tag inside. Above avg. cond. $30.00

ARMBAND SA SPORTS: Red cotton body. Bevo center disc sewn-on with sword & swastika in oak leaf wreath. Paper *RZM A4/308* tag. Near mint cond. $29.00

ARMBAND SS COTTON: 19" red body, black tape borders & composite center. Avg. cond. $96.00

ARMBAND SS WOOL

ARMBAND SS WOOL: 19" red wool body, black tape borders & composite center. Avg. cond. $132.00

ARMBAND SS WOOL: Early. Red wool body, black tape border & composite black swastika on sewn white center. Sewn back seam & has been on tunic. Avg. cond. $100.00

ARMBAND SS WOOL: Early. Red wool body, black tape border & composite black swastika on sewn white center. Sewn back seam & has been on tunic. Paper RZM/SS tag. Avg. cond. $116.00

BERET EAGLE SS: For panzer beret. About 4" wide gray machine embr. eagle on black felt. Avg. cond. $640.00

CAP DIAMOND SS FOREIGN VOL LITHUANIA: 50mm white diamond with embr. yellow with green and red embr. Avg. cond. $91.00

CAP EAGLE & SKULL SS: For visor cap. Heavy stamped bodies with silver paint & flat prongs. Skull marked *RZM SS475/ 43* & eagle *RZM SS373/43*. Near mint cond. $387.00

CAP EAGLE NSKK: Silver-gray bevo spread winged NSKK eagle on green triangle on black. Uncut. Above avg. cond. $20.00

CAP EAGLE NSKK: Flat-silver bevo on black. 3" wide wing-span. Eagle facing to viewers left. Has been sewn-on. Above avg. cond. $20.00

CAP EAGLE NSKK: Flat-silver bevo spread winged NSKK eagle on gray triangle on black. Above avg. cond. $30.00

CAP EAGLE POLICE BAHNSCHUTZ-POLIZEI EM: Stamped alum. with 2 prongs & by *CTD Ges Gesch*. Above avg. cond. $30.00

CAP EAGLE POLICE EM: For visor cap. Alum. stamped with 2 round brass prongs. Avg. cond. $20.00

CAP EAGLE POLICE EM: For visor cap. stamped alum. by *WH 40* & 2 prongs. Above avg. cond. $25.00

CAP EAGLE POLICE EM: Black uncut cloth with bevo wreath & eagle center. Near mint cond. $20.00

CAP EAGLE POLICE OFFICER: Flat-silver bevo on black. Mint cond. $50.00

CAP EAGLE POLICE OFFICER: For visor cap. High-relief alum. With prongs. Mint cond. $34.00

CAP EAGLE SA 1ST PATTERN: For coffee can cap. 35mm stamped metal pointed wing eagle, has 2 copper prongs. Nickel silver. *RZM 17*. Mint cond. $36.00

CAP EAGLE SA: Flat-silver bevo on blood-red on tan. Uncut. Mint cond. $51.00

CAP EAGLE SS

CAP EAGLE SS: For visor cap. Stamped alum., 2 prongs & *RZM SS 360/42*. Near mint cond. $124.00

CAP EAGLE SS: For visor cap. Stamped thick gray eagle with silver paint. By *RZM SS375/43*. Avg. cond. $32.00

CAP EAGLE/SKULL TRAPEZOID SS EM M43: Uncut field-gray cloth with silver and white bevo SS Nazi eagle & skull. Mint cond. $124.00

CAP EAGLE/SKULL TRAPEZOID SS EM: Bevo. Gray eagle over skull on uncut green. Exc. cond. $151.00

CAP EAGLE/SKULL TRAPEZOID SS EM: Machine embr. on black wool. Mint cond. $51.00

CAP EDELWEISS SS MT TROOP M43: Gray & yellow embr. flower on black wool. Above avg. cond. $37.00

CAP EDELWEISS SS: Silver metal, pin-on. Die struck 28.5mm silver finished

edelweiss with swastika in the center. Pb. Above avg. cond. $100.00

CAP EDELWEISS: SS officer size & made like the M43 cap style with silver bullion edelweiss with gold bullion stamens on blue-gray wool. Paper backed & very well made. Mint cond. $191.00

CAP INSIGNIA SS MT TROOP EM
(3 PIECES)

CAP INSIGNIA SS MT TROOP EM (3 PIECES): 3 piece set removed from cap. Bevo eagle, skull & embr. edelweiss. Avg. cond. $685.00

CAP SKULL SS TROPICAL: Bevo. Light tan on black. Uncut. Mint cond. $50.00

CAP SKULL SS: Early full jaw pattern of silvered brass, has *RZM M 1/52* hallmark on the forehead. Found on the black peaked & pillbox caps of early SS after 1936. Avg. cond. $135.00

CAP SKULL SS: For visor cap. Alum. Stamped skull with 2 prongs & RZM marked. Near mint cond. $160.00

CAPE EAGLE DISC SS OFFICER: Side with loop. 43mm disc, affixed eagle, and 4 bent prongs. Avg. cond. $150.00

COLLAR TAB POLICE (PAIR): Orange wool base with silver wire piping & sewn-on orange striped gray litzen centers. Avg. cond. $40.00

COLLAR TAB SA BRIGADEFUHRER (PAIR): Red wool bodies, twisted white celleon piping & hand embr. alum. 2 oak leaves, 3 acorns, pip. Paper RZM tag. Mint cond. $300.00

COLLAR TAB SA EM (PAIR): Blue wool with yellow cord piping. Unit side with white embr. *22/99*. Rank side blank. Paper RZM tag to each. Above avg. cond. $70.00

COLLAR TAB SA EM (PAIR): Both in yellow. Unit side with chain stitched *28/110*. Rank blank. Matted backs Above avg. cond. $118.00

COLLAR TAB SA EM (PAIR): matched set of pinkish red color & matted backs. Blank. 1 with paper RZM tag. Above avg. cond. $36.00

COLLAR TAB SA NAVAL (PAIR) WITH MATCHING SHOULDER STRAPS: *1* matched set with gilt metal fouled anchor & #18 & blank rank side on dark blue wool. Straps: 2 dark blue wool base with 8 brown cord tops with silver wire V's. Both with paper RZM tag on back. Mint cond. $126.00

COLLAR TAB SA
OBERGRUPPENFUHRER (PAIR)

COLLAR TAB SA OBERGRUPPENFUHRER (PAIR): Wine-red velvet bodies, twisted gray piping, affixed to silver metal. 3 oak leaves & pip to each. Near mint cond. $250.00

COLLAR TAB SA SACHSEN (PAIR) WITH SINGLE SHOULDER STRAP & WHISTLE: Green wool bodies, green & white twisted piping. Unit side with white chain stitched 178. Rank with 3 brass pips. Board 4 dark silver twisted cords on green wool sew-in strap. Black horn whistle with soiled yellow plaited cord lanyard with clip. Avg. cond. $176.00

COLLAR TAB SA UNIT (SINGLE): Blue-gray wool base with white chain stitched *21/26* with yellow braided piping. Avg. cond. $49.00

COLLAR TAB SA UNIT (SINGLE): Brown wool body, white cord piping & white embr. *6/105*. Paper RZM tag. Above avg. cond. $30.00

COLLAR TAB SA UNIT (SINGLE): Dark brown with white chain stitched *4/M58*. Above avg. cond. $72.00

COLLAR TAB SS CAMP GUARD (SINGLE): Silver-gray embr. double armed swastika on black wool. Near mint cond. .. $79.00

COLLAR TAB SS CAMP GUARD EM (SINGLE): Black wool body with gray embr. swastika. Mint cond. $50.00

COLLAR TAB SS EM (SINGLE): Black wool. Blank. Near mint cond. $50.00

COLLAR TAB SS EM (SINGLE): Black wool. Blank. Above avg. cond. $114.00

COLLAR TAB SS EM RUNIC (SINGLE): Gray bevo runes on black twill. Above avg. cond. $124.00

COLLAR TAB SS EM RUNIC (SINGLE): Gray runes on black twill with fiber-board backing. Mint cond. $223.00

COLLAR TAB SS EM TOTENKOPF (SINGLE): Horizontal pattern. Black wool body with embr. silver-gray deathhead. Paper RZM. Near mint cond. $250.00

COLLAR TAB SS EM TOTENKOPF (SINGLE): Horizontal pattern. Gray embr. deathhead on black wool. Mint cond. $202.00

COLLAR TAB SS EM TOTENKOPF
(SINGLE)

COLLAR TAB SS EM TOTENKOPF (SINGLE): Horizontal style, gray embr. death head on black wool & matte backing. Near mint cond. $276.00

COLLAR TAB SS FOREIGN VOL 29TH DIV ITALIAN (SINGLE): Black wool base with matted back & silver/white embr. of fasces (bundle of sticks & ax head). Mint cond. $45.00

COLLAR TAB SS FOREIGN VOL 5TH DIV VIKING (SINGLE): Black wool body, gray embr. Viking ship & paper RZM/SS tag. Near mint cond. $893.00

COLLAR TAB SS FOREIGN VOL 11TH DIV NORDLAND (SINGLE): Black wool body with gray embr. mobile swastika. Avg. cond. $115.00

COLLAR TAB SS FOREIGN VOL 15TH DIV LATVIAN (SINGLE): Silver-gray embr. sun & stars on black wool. Near mint cond. $125.00

COLLAR TAB SS FOREIGN VOL 18TH DIV HORST WESSEL (SINGLE): Silver-gray embr. SA logo on black wool. Near mint cond. $67.00

COLLAR TAB SS FOREIGN VOL 21ST DIV SKANDERBEG (SINGLE): Black wool body with gray embr. helmet. Avg. cond. $100.00

COLLAR TAB SS FOREIGN VOL 21ST DIV SKANDERBEG (SINGLE): Silver-gray embr. helmet on black wool. Near mint cond. $100.00

COLLAR TAB SS FOREIGN VOL 22ND DIV FLORIAN GEYER (SINGLE): Silver-gray embr. cornflower on black wool. Mint cond. $100.00

COLLAR TAB SS FOREIGN VOL 23RD DIV NEDERLAND (SINGLE): Black wool body with gray embr. wolfshook. Near mint cond. $135.00

COLLAR TAB SS FOREIGN VOL 25TH DIV HUNYADI (SINGLE): Silver-gray embr. H on black wool. Avg. cond. $125.00

COLLAR TAB SS FOREIGN VOL 27TH DIV LANGEMARCK (SINGLE): Black wool body with gray embr. 3 legged swastika. Mint cond. $79.00

COLLAR TAB SS FOREIGN VOL 29TH DIV ITALIENISCHE #1 (SINGLE): Black wool body with gray embr. fasces. Near mint cond. $65.00

COLLAR TAB SS FOREIGN VOL 29TH DIV RUSSISCHE #1 (SINGLE): Silver-gray embr. Maltese cross with swords on black wool. Avg. cond. $55.00

COLLAR TAB SS FOREIGN VOL 30TH DIV TARTARS (SINGLE): Silver-gray embr. wolf-head on black wool. Near mint cond. $80.00

COLLAR TAB SS FOREIGN VOL 30TH DIV. TARTARS (SINGLE): Silver-gray embr. wolf head on black wool. Near mint cond. $85.00

COLLAR TAB SS FOREIGN VOL 34TH DIV LANDSTORM NEDERLAND (SINGLE): Stamped silver metal flaming grenade having 4 prongs thru black wool tab. Near mint cond. $177.00

COLLAR TAB SS FOREIGN VOL 36TH DIV DIRLEWANGER (SINGLE): Black wool fabric body with field-gray embr. crossed rifles & stickgrenade. Avg. cond. $165.00

COLLAR TAB SS FOREIGN VOL HUNYADI (SINGLE): Gray embr. H on black wool. Exc. cond. $45.00

COLLAR TAB SS OFFICER ODALRUNE (SINGLE): Hand embr. alum. rune on black wool with twisted alum. piping. Above avg. cond. $381.00

COLLAR TAB SS SCHARFUHRER (PAIR): Gray embr. runes on black wool. Different maker to black wool rank tab with silver pip & black stripe to alum. tape. Avg. cond. $345.00

COLLAR TAB SS SCHOOL UNTERSCHARFUHRER (PAIR): Black wool bodies, gray embr. SS runes and Gothic B with paper RZM/SS tag & gray

pip to other. Near mint cond. $1,588.00

COLLAR TAB SS UNTERSTURMFUHRER RANK (SINGLE): Black wool body, twisted alum. piping & three silver finished pips. Exc. cond. $122.00

COLLAR TAB SS-ALLGEMEINE #9 SIGNAL UNIT (SINGLE)

COLLAR TAB SS-ALLGEMEINE #9 SIGNAL UNIT (SINGLE): Right hand black wool body with off-white embr. blitz & 9. Clean. Near mint cond. $748.00

COLLAR TAB SS-ALLGEMEINE RE-SERVE #26 SCHARFUHRER (PAIR): Light gray wool bodies, twisted black & alum. piping, black embr. 26 & 2 bronze pips. Black bevo RZM 38/38 SS cloth tag. Exc. cond. $790.00

CRASH HELMET EAGLE NSKK 1ST TYPE: 5" wide stamped nickel early party eagle holding wreath with peeled black swastika center. 6 prongs & has been on helmet. Avg. cond. $125.00

CRASH HELMET EAGLE POLICE: Silver finished eagle & wreath. 96mm wing span. 3 mount loops on back. Avg. cond. $75.00

CUFF TITLE POLICE FELDGENDARMERIE: 14" long. Gray bevo title & borders on brown. Near mint cond. $124.00

CUFF TITLE SA OBERSTE S.A.-FUHRUNG: Silver-gray machine embr. letters on red with silver wire borders. Sewn ends. Above avg. cond. .. $168.00

CUFF TITLE SA SCHLAGETER: Embr. 16.5" black body with gray Gothic title. Exc. cond. $550.00

CUFF TITLE SS ALLGEMEINE 2ND STURMBANN #5: 18.5" long black body with one end still sewn with bevo cloth tag RZM 1a/35 SS. Other end frayed. Dark blue borders & white embr. 5. Exc. cond. $275.00

CUFF TITLE SS EM *ADOLF HITLER*

CUFF TITLE SS EM *ADOLF HITLER*: 13.5"
long black body with frayed ends, 7
strand alum. borders & gray embr.
Sutterlin script title. Exc.
cond. $492.00

CUFF TITLE SS EM *ADOLF HITLER*: Bevo
pattern. 19" long black body with gray
title & borders. Salt & pepper back with
sewn ends & *Bevo-Wuppertal*. Near mint
cond. $748.00

CUFF TITLE SS EM *DAS REICH*: Bevo
pattern. 19" long black body with
frayed ends & *Bevo-Wuppertal*. Gray
borders & title. Salt & pepper back.
Avg. cond. $355.00

CUFF TITLE SS EM *DAS REICH*: RZM
pattern. 17" long black body with sewn
ends, 7 strand alum. borders & gray
embr. title. Mint cond. $397.00

CUFF TITLE SS EM *FRUNDSBERG*: Bevo
pattern. 18.5" long black body with sewn
ends. Gray borders & title. Salt & pepper
back. Near mint cond. $893.00

CUFF TITLE SS EM *GOTZ VON
BERLICHINGEN*: Bevo pattern. 19" long
black body with sewn ends & *Bevo
Wuppertal*. Gray borders & title. Salt &
pepper back. Mint cond. $643.00

CUFF TITLE SS EM *HOHENSTAUFEN*:
Bevo pattern. 17.5" long black body with
gray title & borders. Salt & pepper back
with sewn ends & *Bevo-Wuppertal*. Exc.
cond. $225.00

CUFF TITLE SS EM *HOHENSTAUFEN*:
Bevo pattern. 19" long black body with
sewn ends & *Bevo Wuppertal*. Gray
borders & title. Salt & pepper back. Near
mint cond. $796.00

CUFF TITLE SS EM *PRINZ EUGEN*: RZM
pattern. 15" long black body with frayed
ends, 7 strand alum. edges & gray title.
Avg. cond. $450.00

CUFF TITLE SS EM *REINHARD
HEYDRICH*: Bevo pattern. 19" long black
body, sewn ends & *Bevo Wuppertal*. Gray
title & borders. Salt & pepper back. Near
mint cond. $486.00

CUFF TITLE SS EM *SS-POLIZEI-DIVI-
SION*: RZM pattern. 19" long black body
with sewn ends, 7 strand alum. borders &
gray embr. title. Paper RZM/SS tag.
Above avg. cond. $301.00

CUFF TITLE SS EM TOTENKOPF SKULL:
16" black bevo base with tight silver wire
border & hand embr. skull. Has partial
remains of cloth RZM tag on back. Avg.
cond. $350.00

CUFF TITLE SS OFFICER *SS POLIZEI-
DIVISION*: 18" long black body still has
sewn ends & has been on tunic. 7 strand
alum. borders & same alum. strands to
twisted hand embr. title. Highlights show
wear with some white threads showing.
Avg. cond. $700.00

CUFF TITLE SS OFFICER *THURINGEN*:
RZM. Full length uncut black cloth with
correct silver wire thread border & silver
bullion lettering. Has folded ends & RZM
paper tag. Near mint cond. $542.00

CUFF TITLE SS OFFICER TOTENKOPF:
Alum. hand embr. skull to 13.5" long
black band with 7 strand alum. borders.
Shows tunic use. Avg.
cond. $1,200.00

RZM MAKER TAG SS

RZM MAKER TAG SS: 2 3/4" wide off-white
body with black *SS DIENSTMUTZE RZM*
printed details & tag was never filled out.
Near mint cond. $118.00

SHAKO EAGLE POLICE EM: Alum.
stamped front plate with nuts & washers
to both threaded posts. *A* for Assmann.
Near mint cond. $40.00

SHAKO EAGLE PRUSSIAN POLICE: 4"
wide stamped Prussian style eagle with
swastika to chest & frosted silver finish.
Avg. cond. $145.00

SHAKO EAGLE WATERPOLICE EM: Gilt
finish. Stamped & concave single piece
eagle. Pressed in screw mounts. Above
avg. cond. $185.00

SHOULDER STRAP CIPHER SS NCO *D*
(PAIR): For *Deutschland*. Stamped silver
Latin *D* & 2 prongs each. 10x12mm. Mint
cond. $219.00

SHOULDER STRAP CIPHER SS NCO *G*
(PAIR): For *Germania*. Stamped alum.
Latin *G* & 2 prongs each. 14x18mm. Mint
cond. $244.00

SHOULDER STRAP FEUERWEHR (PAIR):
Crimson red wool base with slip-on

tongues & black metal prongs. 8 cord top with silver wire with faded red centers. Avg. cond. $23.00

SHOULDER STRAP FIRE POLICE (PAIR): Crimson wool base piping with 2 outer silver wire cord with black V's & 4 black thread inner cords & single white metal pips. Sew ins. Avg. cond. $25.00

SHOULDER STRAP NSKK MAN (SINGLE): Black & alum. alternating cords to body, black wool material base. Above avg. cond. $40.00

SHOULDER STRAP NSKK MANN (SINGLE): black wool narrow board with dark green braid piping, 4 cord alternating black thread & silver wire tops & sew-in. Near mint cond. $40.00

SHOULDER STRAP POLICE (PAIR): Green fabric base with 2 outer silver cords with dark brown Vs & center cords. Slip-ons. In original paper wrap. Mint cond. $27.00

SHOULDER STRAP POLICE NCO-MEISTER (PAIR): Brown & silver plaited inner cords with silver outer cords with brown V's on orange cloth. Removable. Near mint cond. $20.00

SHOULDER STRAP POLICE OBERWACHTMEISTER (PAIR): Brown inner cords with silver outer cords with brown V's on orange cloth. Removable. Near mint cond. $20.00

SHOULDER STRAP SA (PAIR): 2nd pattern. golden-yellow wool bases with 4 light brown with silver V's tops. Sew-ins & both with paper RAM tags. Mint cond. $45.00

SHOULDER STRAP SA (SINGLE): Pre-war. Black wool base narrow 1st pattern style & 3 twisted double silver wire cord braided top with metal grommet & field-gray painted pebbled button. Sew-in Above avg. cond. $30.00

SHOULDER STRAP SA GRUPPE SUDETENLAND (SINGLE): Gray wool base with 4 cord top of twisted gray cord & black cord. Sew on. Near mint cond. $50.00

SHOULDER STRAP SA MANN (SINGLE): Pre-war. B&W silk thread twisted cord on carmine wool. Paper RZM tag. Avg. cond. $160.00

SHOULDER STRAP SA MANN (SINGLE): Pre-war. B&W twisted cord body, dark green wool base & nickel button. Avg. cond. $40.00

SHOULDER STRAP SS ALLGEMEINE EM (SINGLE): Sew-in black wool base with B/W twisted cord body. Above avg. cond. $143.00

SHOULDER STRAP SS ALLGEMEINE MANN (SINGLE): Black & silver twisted

cords on black wool. Sew-in. Above avg. cond. $45.00

SHOULDER STRAP SS ARTILLERY EM (PAIR): Slip-on style. Black wool body, red wool piping, gray wool back & tongue. Exc. cond. $160.00

SHOULDER STRAP SS EM (PAIR): Slip-on, black wool bodies & light green cord piping. Mint cond. $125.00

SHOULDER STRAP SS FACHFURER OFFICER-OBERSTURMFUHRER (SINGLE): Sew-in gray cord body, 3:3 red & gray piping, black wool base & large pip. Avg. cond. $87.00

SHOULDER STRAP SS INFANTRY NCO (SINGLE): Slip-on black wool body with tongue, white cord piping & gray tape stripe. Above avg. cond. $79.00

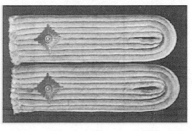

SHOULDER STRAP SS INFANTRY OFFICER-OBERSTURMFUHRER (PAIR)

SHOULDER STRAP SS INFANTRY OFFICER-OBERSTURMFUHRER (PAIR): Sew-in style. Gray-alum. cords, white wool piping, black wool bases & gold pip to each. Near mint cond. $174.00

SHOULDER STRAP SS INFANTRY OFFICER-UNTERSTURMFUHRER (PAIR): Black wool bases with white wool piping & 8 rows of silver wire tops & slip-on tongues. Avg. cond. $279.00

SHOULDER STRAP SS MEDICAL NCO (PAIR): Slip-on black wool bodies with tongues, blue cord piping & tan tape stripe. Near mint cond. $125.00

SHOULDER STRAP SS MOTOR TECH. OFFICER-LT (SINGLE): Sew-in black wool base, orange cord piping, gray cord body & bronze *L* device. Above avg. cond. $160.00

SHOULDER STRAP SS OBERBAYERN OFFICER: Pre-1936. For *Oberbayern*. Sew-in style 5" long twisted alum. cord body on black wool. Affixed dark silver *O* with 2 prongs. Grommet to hole with pebbled alum. button marked *Extra Fein 17mm* with sew on socket. Near mint cond. $450.00

SHOULDER STRAP SS PANZER OFFICER-LT (SINGLE): Slip-on black wool base, pink cord piping & gray body. Shows use. Avg. cond. $124.00

SHOULDER STRAP SS PANZER-GRENADIER OFFICER-LT (PAIR): Black wool base with light green braid piping with 8 silver wire cords & are sew ins. Above avg. cond. $255.00

SHOULDER STRAP SS SD STURMANN (PAIR)

SHOULDER STRAP SS SD STURMANN (PAIR): Sew-in style. Black cord body with silver V's to outer cord & green wool bases. Near mint cond. $250.00

SHOULDER STRAP SS SIGNAL EM (PAIR): Sew-in black wool bodies, yellow cord piping & still tied with original string. Mint cond. $100.00

SHOULDER STRAP SS SPECIAL SERVICE OFFICER-HAUPTSTURMFUHRER (SINGLE): Sew-in gray body, green piping, black wool base & 2 alum. pips. Above avg. cond. $23.00

SHOULDER STRAP SS SPECIAL SERVICE OFFICER-HAUPTSTURMFUHRER (SINGLE): Sew-in style gray cord body, green wool piping & black wool base. 2 alum. pips. Exc. cond. $100.00

SHOULDER STRAP SS TRANSPORT EM (PAIR): Slip-on style. Black wool bodies, light blue cord piping & gray wool backs. Exc. cond. $244.00

SLEEVE CHEVRON SA OLD-FIGHTER: brownish/gray wool with silver bevo stripe with 2 brown center stripes sewn-on. Has blue paper RZM tag on back. Near mint cond. $50.00

SLEEVE CHEVRON SS OLD FIGHTER: Bevo alum. with black stripes with black borders. Mint cond. $160.00

SLEEVE CHEVRON SS: Black wool with 2 silver braid V's. Near mint cond $33.00

SLEEVE CHEVRON SS: Black wool with silver braid V. Near mint cond. $27.00

SLEEVE DIAMOND NSKK OFFICER: Hand embr. silver bullion eagle to 6 spoke wheel on black wool diamond. Above avg. cond. $60.00

SLEEVE DIAMOND NSKK: Flat-silver bevo pointed/winged eagle superimposed on spoked wheel on black. Padded. Avg. cond. $50.00

SLEEVE DIAMOND SS *SD*: Silver-gray embr. SD to black wool diamond. Paper RZM/SS tag. Mint cond. $247.00

SLEEVE DIAMOND SS MEDICAL EM: Black wool base black snake with silver white outline. Mint cond. $35.00

SLEEVE DIAMOND SS MOTORIZED UNIT OFFICER

SLEEVE DIAMOND SS MOTORIZED UNIT OFFICER: Alum. hand embr. spoked wheel on black wool. Bevo cloth tag *St.159/35 SS*. Avg. cond. $175.00

SLEEVE DIAMOND SS NSKK-FORMER-MEMBER: Black fabric with silver wire bevo Nazi eagle center of a spoked wheel. Avg. cond. $40.00

SLEEVE DIAMOND SS NSKK-FORMER-MEMBER: Black fabric with silver wire bevo Nazi eagle center of a spoked wheel. Avg. cond. $40.00

SLEEVE DIAMOND SS ORDNANCE NCO: black wool with silver/gray embr. of crossed rifle & MG, cut & folded on mat back. Mint cond. $90.00

SLEEVE DIAMOND SS REICH SECURITY OFFICE SS & POLICE MATTERS ASSIGNMENT: Silver-gray machine embr. *SS* runes over Police eagle on black wool diamond. Backed. Near mint cond. $203.00

SLEEVE DIAMOND SS RF-SS PERSONAL STAFF: For "Press & War Economy Group" use. 3" tall black wool diamond with nicely gray & black embr. eagle. Exc. cond. $360.00

SLEEVE DIAMOND SS SIGNAL: Black wool diamond with silver/white embr. blitz. Backed. Mint cond. $32.00

SLEEVE DIAMOND SS VETERINARIAN EM: Black wool base with silver white snake embr. Mint cond. $28.00

SLEEVE EAGLE FIRE POLICE *SECHSHELDEN*: Carmine embr. eagle/ wreath & title on blue felt oval. Avg. cond. $50.00

SLEEVE EAGLE FIRE POLICE EM *REICHSBAUERNSTADT GOSLAR*: Carmine machine embr. on dark blue wool oval. Avg. cond. $76.00

SLEEVE EAGLE FIRE POLICE EM *ZELLSTOFFFABRIK WALDHOF WERK MANNHEIM*

SLEEVE EAGLE FIRE POLICE EM *ZELLSTOFFFABRIK WALDHOF WERK MANNHEIM*: Carmine machine embr. on dark blue wool oval. Avg. cond. $76.00

SLEEVE EAGLE POLICE EM *HAMBURG*: Blue/gray wool oval base with green embr. Nazi eagle in wreath & lettering Above avg. cond. $27.00

SLEEVE EAGLE POLICE EM *KOBLENZ*: Orange machine embr. on police-green summer weight oval. Avg. cond. $50.00

SLEEVE EAGLE POLICE EM *OBERHAUSEN*: Light green machine embr. police eagle & name on police-green wool oval. Avg. cond. $48.00

SLEEVE EAGLE POLICE EM *REGENSBURG*: Red embr. on white oval with reinforced border. Near mint cond. $91.00

SLEEVE EAGLE POLICE EM *STRASSBURG*: Orange embr. on wool oval. Near mint cond. $34.00

SLEEVE EAGLE POLICE POSTSCHUTZ: Gray wool oval with silver bullion hand embr. eagle with lightning bolts. Avg. cond. $177.00

SLEEVE EAGLE SS CAMO

SLEEVE EAGLE SS CAMO: Bevo. Tan on black. Uncut. Mint cond. $72.00

SLEEVE EAGLE SS EM 1ST TYPE: Gray embr. *dipped-wing tips* eagle on gray wool. Exc. cond. $250.00

SLEEVE EAGLE SS EM: Bevo. Gray eagle on black is zigzag machine-sewn to gray wool. Cut from tunic & trimmed close. Avg. cond. $91.00

SLEEVE EAGLE SS EM: Machine embr. Above avg. cond. $80.00

SLEEVE EAGLE SS OFFICER: 3 tone silver bullion hand embr. details with black highlights, black wool & black paper backing. Above avg. cond. $412.00

SLEEVE EDELWEISS SA MT TROOP: Embr. 2.75" tall brown wool oval with green border, gold seeds & white flower/stem center. Late-war item. Mint cond. $342.00

SLEEVE EDELWEISS SS MT TROOP: Black oval, gray embr. edelweiss with gold seeds & gray border. Mint cond. $50.00

SLEEVE OVAL SS AUX. RUSSIAN POLICE OFFICER: 3.5" tall black oval with flat-silver bevo *Treu Tapfer Gehorsam* title, swastika & laurel leaf wreath. Above avg. cond. $28.00

SLEEVE PIP SS PRIVATE: Silver-gray machine embr. on black wool. Mint cond. $20.00

SLEEVE RANK BAR SS GENERAL-OBERGRUPPENFUHRER: 2.5x4" black wool body with yellow embr. oak leaves/acorns over 3 bevo bars. Near mint cond. $200.00

SLEEVE RANK BAR SS GENERAL-OBERGRUPPENFUHRER: About 2.5x4" black wool rectangle with yellow embr. oak leaves & acorns over 3 bevo tape bars. Near mint cond. $93.00

SLEEVE RANK BAR SS GENERALLT: Black felt rectangular with yellow embr.

oak leaves & acorns & 2 yellow tape stripes. Near mint cond. $139.00

SLEEVE RANK BAR SS OBERFUHRER: Embr. Black wool rectangular, double green embr. oak leaves/ acorns & 4 green tape stripes. Mint cond. $79.00

SLEEVE RANK BAR SS OFFICER-MAJOR: Black wool base with 2 dark green embr. oak leave bars with sewn 4 celleon bar tress with 3 bars of black separating bars, bevo constr. 90x100mm. Mint cond. $190.00

SLEEVE RANK BAR SS OFFICER-OBERFUHRER: 3.5x4" black wool body with double green embr. oakleaves/acorns over 4 green bevo bars. Above avg. cond. $150.00

SLEEVE SHIELD SS FOREIGN VOL LATVIA: Red embr. shield with white title & diagonal stripe on black wool. Near mint cond. $75.00

SLEEVE SHIELD POLICE RUSSIAN FOREIGN VOL. EM: Orange bevo laurel leaf wreath, swastika & title to uncut gray. Mint cond. $50.00

SLEEVE SHIELD SS FOREIGN VOL ALBANIA: Black embr. Albanian eagle to red shield on black wool. Above avg. cond. $75.00

SLEEVE SHIELD SS FOREIGN VOL ALBANIAN

SLEEVE SHIELD SS FOREIGN VOL ALBANIAN: Black wool body, red embr. shield & black double headed eagle. Mint cond. $50.00

SLEEVE SHIELD SS FOREIGN VOL CROATIA: Red & white machine embr. checkerboard shield on black wool. Above avg. cond. $20.00

SLEEVE SHIELD SS FOREIGN VOL CROATIA: Black wool base with scrolled top red & white checkerboard shield Mint cond. $25.00

SLEEVE SHIELD SS FOREIGN VOL DANISH: Black wool base with red shield with white cross center. Embr. Mint cond. $44.00

SLEEVE SHIELD SS FOREIGN VOL ESTONIA: Light blue, dark blue & white barred, machine embr. shield on black wool. Near mint cond. $35.00

SLEEVE SHIELD SS FOREIGN VOL ITALIAN: Black wool with yellow machine embr. fasces with red high lights in yellow outlined shield. Near mint cond. $45.00

SLEEVE SHIELD SS FOREIGN VOL ITALIAN: Embr. yellow fasces with red highlights, yellow shield outline & on black wool. Near mint cond. $50.00

SLEEVE SHIELD SS FOREIGN VOL NORWAY

SLEEVE SHIELD SS FOREIGN VOL NORWAY: Black wool body, red embr. shield with blue & white cross. Mint cond. $105.00

SLEEVE SHIELD SS FOREIGN VOL FRANCE: Horizontal embr. red, white & blue shield on black wool. Above avg. cond. $237.00

SLEEVE TRIANGLE DUTCH NSB: Black wool triangle with gold bullion border & black/red field with bullion wolf angle, paper backed. Above avg. cond. $30.00

SPORT SHIRT INSIGNIA SA *KP*: 5.5" dia. green & white logo with blue printed RZM tag. Near mint cond. $70.00

SPORT SHIRT INSIGNIA SA *SU*: Light blue backing with white SA symbol & SU, has been cut & folded. Above avg. cond. $41.00

SPORT SHIRT SHIELD SA *KP*: White & dark green bevo SA logo with letters *KP*. Avg. cond. $50.00

THIRD REICH NSDAP, DAF, HJ, RAD, NSFK & DLV INSIGNIA

ARMBAND *BETRIEBSFUHRER*: 4" tall white cotton body with black printed title. Exc. cond. $65.00
ARMBAND DAF *WERKSCHAR*: 15" x 2" wide black cloth with printed cog with swastikas on either side of wording in white. Near mint cond. $65.00
ARMBAND HITLER YOUTH: Bevo body & sewn center with bevo swastika. Red printed paper tag. Exc. cond. ..$26.00
ARMBAND HITLER YOUTH: Red cotton body with white bevo center band. Bevo swastika diamond center sewn-on. Avg. cond. $20.00
ARMBAND HITLER YOUTH: Sewn together red cotton body with sewn-on bevo black swastika over sewn-on center stripe. Has 2 black snaps male sides on top of the back & front on the back. Avg. cond. $35.00
ARMBAND NSDAP NSDAP *KREISLEITUNG MUNSTER-STADT*: 5" tall white cotton body, black printed title & inked eagle stamp. Exc. cond. $100.00
ARMBAND NSDAP *NSDAP PARTEI-BEREITSCHAFT*: 2.5" tall red cotton body with black swastika to white center. Black title. Avg. cond. ..$40.00
ARMBAND NSDAP *ORGANISATIONSLEITUNG DER P.O.*:5" tall white cotton body, black printed title & inked eagle stamp. Near mint cond. $90.00
ARMBAND NSDAP *PARTEI-BEREITSCHAF*: 2" wide red cotton body with printed swastika in white circle & black inked titled. Avg. cond. $35.00
ARMBAND NSDAP MEMBER: Cotton. Bevo center sewn-on. Inked *MSA Sch Ha* on back. Avg. cond. $20.00
ARMBAND NSDAP MEMBER: Cotton. Bevo. Near mint cond. $21.00
ARMBAND NSDAP MEMBER: Wool. Bevo center sewn-on. Paper *RZM TA 260 Serie I* tag. Above avg. cond. $25.00
ARMBAND NSDAP MEMBER: Wool. Composite. Paper *RZM A4/10* tag. White *NSDAP* stamping on back. Avg. cond. $30.00
ARMBAND NSDAP ORTSGRUPPE HIGH LEADER: Red wool body with blue braid piping & 18mm gilt wire oak leaf tress strip across center. Satin center with gold twisted wire cord piping around them. Not sewn together. Has 6

gold wire 1mm border tresses at top, bottom & 2 both sides of center tress. Paper RZM tag. Avg. cond. $160.00

ARMBAND NSDAP ORTSGRUPPE
LEADER CANDIDATE

ARMBAND NSDAP ORTSGRUPPE LEADER CANDIDATE: 21" red wool body, blue cord piping & bevo swastika center with yellow outline. Paper RZM tag. Near mint cond. $90.00
ARMBAND ORG. TODT MEMBER: Red cotton body with print on white circle & black swastika with olive wool strip & white fabric with bevo *Org. Todt* sewn-on. Avg. cond. $63.00
ARMBAND RAD: 4" tall brown cotton twill body has flat-silver bevo borders & large eagle holding wreath with swastika/spade center. Near mint cond. $276.00
ARMBAND STUDENTENBUND: Composite cotton body with bevo swastika. Avg. cond. $35.00
BREAST RANK EAGLE BDM GRUPPENFUHRERIN: White wool shield with multi-tone silver bullion hand embr. flared winged eagle under *219*. Matte backing with paper *RZM A4/426 HJ tag*. Near mint cond. $400.00
CAP DEVICE RAD TRADITION *OST-NIEDERSACHSEN*: 36x42mm solid alum. crossed horseheads with swastika & traces of bronze finish. 4 prongs on back. Avg. cond. $70.00
CAP DIAMOND HITLER YOUTH: Bevo. Uncut. Mint cond. $36.00
CAP EAGLE NSFK MEMBER: Alum. Near mint cond. $48.00
CAP EAGLE POLITICAL 1ST TYPE: Silver finish. 37mm wing span. With prongs. Above avg. cond. $28.00
CAP EAGLE POLITICAL 2ND TYPE: Silver finish. 66mm stamped body with head facing left wing. 3 flat prongs & *RZM M1/8*. Near mint cond. $23.00
CAP INSIGNIA DLV MEMBER: 43x120mm on tan twill with color bevo blue backing with red circle & blue center with stylized wing prop & black swastika center. Mint cond. $50.00

CAPE CLASP RAD OFFICER (PAIR) WITH CHAIN: Silver-gray alum. Set with chain & alum. backing plates. Near mint cond. $248.00

COLLAR TAB NSDAP GAULEITER (SINGLE): 2nd type, left hand side. Red velvet body, dark red piping & large gold finished party eagle on 2 oak leaves. Above avg. cond. $310.00

COLLAR TAB NSDAP GAULEITUNG MAIN DEPT LEADER (PAIR): Brown wool, blue cord piping, 2 yellow tape L with swastikas & paper RZM tag. Near mint cond. $28.00

COLLAR TAB NSDAP GAULEITUNG SECTION LEADER (SINGLE): Right hand red velvet, red cord piping, gold eagle & oak leaf with 2 acorns. RZM tag. Above avg. cond. $50.00

COLLAR TAB NSDAP ORTSGRUPPE (single): 3rd pattern. Light blue braid piping with tan wool base with gold bullion litzen center. Right side. Avg. cond. $20.00

COLLAR TAB NSDAP ORTSGRUPPE MAIN DEPT. LEADER (PAIR): Brown felt body, blue cord piping & 2 silver swastika L-ape bars. Above avg. cond. $35.00

COLLAR TAB NSDAP REICHSLEITUNG SECTION LEADER (PAIR): Crimson velvet bodies, yellow cord piping, gold affixed eagle & oak leaf with 2 acorns. Paper RZM tag. Mint cond. $77.00

COLLAR TAB NSFK MEMBER (PAIR): Blue/gray wool twill. Unit with silver painted 6/23. Rank blank. Matted backs Mint cond. $81.00

COLLAR TAB RAD MEDICAL (PAIR): Bright alum. litzen on blue tabs. Exc. cond. $40.00

COLLAR TAB RAD OFFICER (SINGLE): Black velvet with silver bullion embr. wheat head & sawtooth border. Near mint cond. $66.00

COLLAR TAB RAD OFFICER 2ND TYPE (PAIR): Black velvet base with silver wire bar with braided wire center. Matted back. Avg. cond. $27.00

CUFF TITLE HITLER YOUTH LEADER AUSLANDEREINSATZ: 1.5x6" dark blue wool rectangle, machine-sewn edges & yellow embr. Gothic title. Near mint cond. $282.00

CUFF TITLE HITLER YOUTH SPORTS H.J.=SCHIESSWART: Green bevo on black. Near mint cond. $20.00

CUFF TITLE RAD EMSLAND 20: 16" black body with flat-silver bevo title & maker. Near mint cond. $139.00

CUFF TITLE RAD W: Hmkd Ges. Gesh. RADJ 44 G.e.W. 16" black body with Gothic W & white bar to each side. Near mint cond. $99.00

SHOULDER STRAP DEUTSCHES JUNGVOLK (PAIR): Narrow black cloth bodies with bevo white 565, black cord piping & black wool backing. Sew-in style. Avg. cond. $20.00

SHOULDER STRAP HITLER YOUTH LANDJAHR (PAIR): Removable black bodies with 2 snaps sewn at each end, green bevo L, green cord piping, worn silver pip & alum. tape loop to each. Above avg. cond. $145.00

SHOULDER STRAP HITLER YOUTH MEMBER (PAIR): Dark blue with light blue piping & light blue bevo 663. Removable. Above avg. cond. $36.00

SHOULDER STRAP HITLER YOUTH MEMBER (PAIR): Early. Tan twill with light blue piping & light blue chain stitched 92. Above avg. cond. .. $105.00

SHOULDER STRAP HITLER YOUTH MEMBER (PAIR): Tan twill material with dark blue piping & chain stitched 116 IV. Sew-in. Above avg. cond. $145.00

SHOULDER STRAP HITLER YOUTH MEMBER-SCHARFUHRER (PAIR)

SHOULDER STRAP HITLER YOUTH MEMBER-SCHARFUHRER (PAIR): Sew-in tan bodies, red cord piping, chain stitched 412 & 2 faded gray pips to each. Avg. cond. $105.00

SHOULDER STRAP HITLER YOUTH OFFICER (SINGLE): Sew-in black wool body, twisted alum. piping, hand embr. alum. 325. Alum. tape strip & 4 alum. pips. Above avg. cond. $100.00

SHOULDER STRAP HITLER YOUTH SCHOOL AHS (SINGLE): Slip-on style black body with red cord piping & red embr. AHS. Avg. cond. $100.00

SHOULDER STRAP RAD ADMIN ARBEITSFUHRER (PAIR): Silver-gray plaited cords with black V's on green velvet. Avg. cond. $20.00

SLEEVE DIAMOND DAF: Black wool body with alum. cogwheel with swastika device. Matte backing with paper *RZM A4/27* tag. Near mint cond. $22.00

SLEEVE DIAMOND HITLER YOUTH FIRE DEFENSE: Color bevo diamond with carmine eagle/wreath & border. Exc. cond. $54.00

SLEEVE DIAMOND HITLER YOUTH: 90mm bevo diamond on white uncut cloth & hmkd. Mint cond. $24.00

SLEEVE DIAMOND NSDAP DAF SER-VICE: Black wool diamond with white metal cog with swastika center. Has early paper RZM tag. Avg. cond. $20.00

SLEEVE DIAMOND NSDAP PROTESTANT-CHAPLAIN: 2.75" tall black wool diamond has violet cord piping & silver Protestant style cross affixed to center by 2 prongs. Mint cond. $360.00

SLEEVE RANK DISC DEUTSCHES JUNGVOLK: Blue wool disc with single silver and white embr. chevron. Near mint cond. $20.00

SLEEVE SHIELD HITLER YOUTH NAVAL SPECIALIST: 50mm tall blue wool oval with 6 embr. yellow arrows at center. Above avg. cond. $27.00

SLEEVE SHIELD HITLER YOUTH STANDARD BEARER: Off-white stylized eagle holds HJ diamond, black cloth shield & off-white border. Avg. cond. $115.00

SLEEVE SHIELD NSDAP
REICHSAUTOZUG

SLEEVE SHIELD NSDAP *REICHSAUTOZUG*: Tan uncut cloth base with bevo design of white eagle with red field. RZM tag. Above avg. cond. $381.00

SLEEVE SHIELD RAD EM: Bevo. Uncut black body with maker & red *271 9* to white spade. Mint cond. $55.00

SLEEVE TRIANGLE BDM *NORD NIEDERSACHSEN*: Cut & folded black cloth with bevo white lettering. Sewn down edges Above avg. cond. $28.00

SLEEVE TRIANGLE BDM *SUDOST KARNTEN*: Off-white bevo letters on black triangle. Above avg. cond. $24.00

SLEEVE TRIANGLE BDM *SUDOST STEIERMARK*: Off-white bevo on black triangle. Paper *RZM A4/213 HJ* tag. Exc. cond. $61.00

SLEEVE TRIANGLE BDM *WEST HEFFEN NASSAU*: Cut & folded black artificial silk with white bevo lettering. Avg. cond. $48.00

SLEEVE TRIANGLE BDM *WEST MOSELLAND*: Off-white bevo letters on black triangle. Near mint cond. ... $76.00

SLEEVE TRIANGLE BDM *WEST WESTFALEN*: White on black with silver tradition tape stripe & 3 metal snaps. Above avg. cond. $60.00

SLEEVE TRIANGLE HITLER YOUTH *MITTE THURINGEN*: Cut & folded black cloth base with golden yellow bevo border & letters. Avg. cond. $39.00

SLEEVE TRIANGLE HITLER YOUTH *OST SUDETENLAND*: Bevo yellow on black. Near mint cond. $35.00

SLEEVE TRIANGLE HITLER YOUTH *RUND-FUNKSPIELSCHAR MUNCHEN*: Yellow bevo on black. Mint cond. $537.00

SLEEVE TRIANGLE HITLER YOUTH *SUD FRANKEN*: Bevo. Yellow on black with gold machine-sewn-on tradition litzen. Above avg. cond. $75.00

SLEEVE TRIANGLE HITLER YOUTH *SUD HOCHLAND*: Yellow bevo on black cloth. Avg. cond. $65.00

SLEEVE TRIANGLE HITLER YOUTH *WEST SAARPFALZ*: Bevo yellow on black. Avg. cond. $37.00

SLEEVE TRIANGLE HITLER YOUTH SCHOOL *AHS TILSIT*: Yellow bevo on black. RZM tag. Mint cond. $485.00

SPEC PATCH DLV FLYING PERSONNEL: Blue-gray wool disc with gray hand-embr. winged prop. Avg. cond. $45.00

SPORT SHIRT EAGLE STUDENTBUND: White bevo spread winged eagle clutching swastika diamond on black. Uncut. Near mint cond. $65.00

SWALLOW NEST NSDAP GAULEITUNG MUSICIAN (PAIR): Red velvet bodies have 7 vertical gold celleon tape stripes with swastikas & 1 stripe below with 3cm long fringe. 5 hooks to each tan twill backing with blue printed paper RZM tag to each. Exc. cond. $270.00

TRADE PATCH RAD OFFICER PLANNING PERSONNEL: Flat-silver bevo wrench style design with arrow at one end on olive-green. Removed from sleeve. Hmkd *RADJ G&W*. Avg. cond. $20.00

WHISTLE LANYARD HITLER YOUTH WITH BAKELITE WHISTLE: 2.5" long black body whistle with gray plaited lanyard, 10" long. Above avg. cond. $35.00

WHISTLE LANYARD HITLER YOUTH: 2 white cords & 2 red cords twisted & knotted at both ends. Paper RZM tag. Mint cond. $65.00

THIRD REICH VETERAN, FREI-KORP, LUFTSCHUTZ & OTHER INSIGNIA

ARMBAND *DAOV*: Red cloth band with sewn-on black circle & hand embr. cog with hammer & swastika center & oak leaf wreath above lettering at base. Above avg. cond. $108.00

ARMBAND *DDAC*: 3.5" tall bevo tri-color oval machine-sewn to white twill armband with buckle strap to back. Variation style. Near mint cond. $213.00

ARMBAND *DEUTSCHE WEHRMACHT*: Cotton. Bevo. Black on golden-yellow. Above avg. cond. $24.00

ARMBAND *FRONT-SAMMELSTELLE*: 2 lines of golden-yellow bevo letters on light blue. Near mint cond. $53.00

ARMBAND *STADTFUHRER N.S.G KRAFTDURSCHFREUDE*: Blue cotton body with white printed lettering with swastika in cog with sunwheel swastika in center, has 2 white borders sewn-on & sewn together in back Above avg. cond. $55.00

ARMBAND KDF *REISELEITER GAU BADEN*

ARMBAND KDF *REISELEITER GAU BADEN*: 3" tall dark red wool body with red cloth lining. Gold bullion hand embr. title & silver KDF-logo background. Avg. cond. $177.00

ARMBAND KYFFHAUSERBUND: Blue wool body with bevo Nazi kyffhauserbund shield sewn-on & over it is 38x50mm bronze wreath & rayed oval badge with monument center attached by 1 prong. Avg. cond. $60.00

ARMBAND NSKOV LEADER: Dark blue wool body with sewn-on red bevo shield with black Maltese cross & swastika

center & silver rank tress bar center strip. Above avg. cond. $35.00

ARMBAND NSKOV LEADER: Dark blue wool body with sewn-on red bevo shield with black Maltese cross & swastika center & silver rank tress bar center strip. Above avg. cond. $45.00

ARMBAND ORG. TODT *O.T.11630*: 3" tall gray cotton body with red printed title. Near mint cond. $50.00

ARMBAND RED CROSS: White cotton body with red cotton cross sewn-on. Avg. cond. $45.00

ARMBAND RLB LEADER 1ST TYPE

ARMBAND RLB LEADER 1ST TYPE: Blue cotton body with blue & white bevo starburst. Hmkd *Bevo-Barmen Ges.Gesch*. Dark silver tape stripe sewn to each border. Exc. cond. $80.00

CAP EAGLE CUSTOM OFFICIAL: Visor cap. Gray metal. 3 flat prongs. Hmkd *RZM M1/53*. Above avg. cond. ... $40.00

CAP EAGLE FOREIGN OFFICE: 5" wide hand embr. 4 tone silver bullion eagle on gray wool. Avg. cond. $327.00

CAP EAGLE FORESTRY OFFICIAL: Visor cap. Alum. 55mm stamped body, *RZM M1/45* & 2 brass prongs. Above avg. cond. $28.00

CAP EAGLE TENO: M43 cap. Gray eagle & cockade on gray and brown twill trapezoid. Avg. cond. $50.00

CAP INSIGNIA LUFTSCHUTZ OFFICER: Flat-silver bevo winged swastika with Luftschutz scroll on dark blue on gray. Uncut. Above avg. cond. $20.00

COLLAR TAB CUSTOM OFFICIAL (PAIR): Both match green bevo with silver wire shark tooth border & cardboard back Near mint cond. $20.00

CUFF TITLE *PROPAGANDAKOMPANIE* SLEEVEBAND: 16" long black with flat-silver bevo title. Avg. cond. $95.00

CUFF TITLE CUSTOM OFFICIAL: Green cloth with silver bevo borders & eagle. Near mint cond. $50.00

CUFF TITLE KREIGERBUND *NORDWEST*: Silver-gray bevo letters on dark blue with

silver-gray crossed swords & borders.
Avg. cond. $38.00

CUFF TITLE KREIGERBUND *WEST*:
Silver-gray bevo letters, crossed swords
& borders on black. Sewn ends. Avg.
cond. $26.00

CUFF TITLE STAHLHELM *GAU
GELSENKIRCHEN*: 14" blue narrow
band with yellow bevo title. Near mint
cond. $75.00

CUFF TITLE STAHLHELM *L.V.GROSS-
HAMBURG*: 14" blue narrow band with
yellow title. Exc. cond. $75.00

CUFF TITLE TENO *TECHNISCHE
NOTHILFE*: 16" long black body with gray
bevo Gothic title & borders. Exc.
cond. $37.00

SHOULDER STRAP FORESTRY OFFICIAL
(PAIR): Prussian 1929-34. Sew-in style.
Gold centers to green plaited cords,
green velvet bases, gold pip & green
plastic eagle button to each. Comes with
original inked paper tag with script use/
dates. Above avg. cond. $150.00

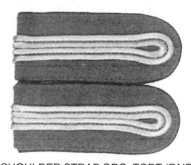

SHOULDER STRAP ORG. TODT (PAIR)

SHOULDER STRAP ORG. TODT (PAIR):
Slip-on style. Gray and brown wool
bodies, black cord piping & alum. cord
sewn to centers. Not standard style.
Near mint cond. $50.00

SLEEVE BADGE FREI-KORP 5 ARMEE
KORP: 37mm diam. Traces of silver
finish remain. Oak & laurel leave wreath
border with open center and with Roman
numeral *V*. Thin pin also. Avg.
cond. $120.00

SLEEVE DIAMOND DAF: Black wool
diamond with affixed alum. cogged
wheel swastika. Blue printed paper tag.
Mint cond. $20.00

SLEEVE DIAMOND NSKOV: Silver-gray
bevo logo on black diamond with thin
burlap backing. Near mint
cond. $81.00

SLEEVE DIAMOND
VOLKSSTURM *STANDSCHUTZEN
BATTALION BRUNECK*

SLEEVE DIAMOND VOLKSSTURM
*STANDSCHUTZEN BATTALION
BRUNECK*: Green wool diamond with
color embr. Tirol eagle & title. Avg.
cond. $61.00

SLEEVE EAGLE RAILWAY *HVD BRUSSEL*:
Golden bevo eagle over title on trimmed
black. Avg. cond. $20.00

SLEEVE EAGLE RAILWAY *RBD ESSEN*:
Golden-yellow bevo spread winged eagle
& name on black. Uncut. Exc.
cond. $54.00

SLEEVE EAGLE RAILWAY *RBD
NURNBERG*: Golden-yellow bevo spread
winged eagle & name on black. Uncut.
Mint cond. $40.00

SLEEVE EAGLE RAILWAY *WVD
BRUSSEL*: Golden bevo eagle & title on
black. Uncut. Mint cond. $27.00

SLEEVE SHIELD FACTORY PROTECTION
POLICE: 3.25" oval shield with silver wire
piping with embr. swastika shield over
factory & cog. Avg. cond. $22.00

SLEEVE SHIELD LETTLAND: White
vertical stripe to red shield with black
border & black title below. Uncut. Above
avg. cond. $91.00

SLEEVE SHIELD STAHLHELM *L.V.
BADEN*: Bevo. Yellow griffin on red with
red *Baden* to yellow top. Sewn-back
edges. Near mint cond. $40.00

SLEEVE SHIELD STAHLHELM *L.V. GAU
BREMEN*: Bevo. Blue shield, black title,
eagle, crossed horse-heads & 3 red/white
mini shields to center. Green felt backed.
Above avg. cond. $40.00

SLEEVE SHIELD STAHLHELM *L.V. SAAR*:
Bevo. Tri-color shield, white title, gray
helmet center & 2 colored small shields
below. Uncut. Above avg. cond. . $40.00

SLEEVE SHIELD STAHLHELM
L.V.GROSS-HESSEN SLEEVE PATCH:
Bevo. Large black oval with gray title,
steel helmet & color 3 part divided shield.
Above avg. cond. $45.00
SLEEVE SHIELD STAHLHELM
L.V.MECKLENBURG: Bevo. Crowned
black bull head on yellow with black title.
Exc. cond. $40.00
SLEEVE SHIELD STAHLHELM
L.V.NIEDERRHEIN: Bevo. Black cross to
green shield with white diagonal line &
white title. Machine-sewn back & has
been on tunic. Above avg.
cond. $35.00
SLEEVE SHIELD STAHLHELM *SAAR*:
Bevo with tri-color shield with helmet over
2 shields with lettering "Saar" at top. On
white. Above avg. cond. $40.00

SLEEVE SHIELD TENO OFFICER

SLEEVE SHIELD TENO OFFICER: Black
cloth with silver wire bevo cog wheel &
TD in center. Padded & hmkd *Ges.
Gesch G & W* on back in yellow. Above
avg. cond. $65.00
SWALLOW NEST BANDSMAN (PAIR):
Black twill bodies, 7 gold vertical tape
stripes & lower border strip. Brown twill
backs with 5 hooks. Exc. cond. .. $72.00
SWALLOW NEST BANDSMAN (PAIR):
Sew-in style green wool bodies, dark
silver vertical tape stripes & lower strip.
Avg. cond. $65.00

THIRD REICH AIR FORCE
(LUFTWAFFE) INSIGNIA

BREAST EAGLE LUFTWAFFE EM: Bevo.
Gray on dark blue. Mint cond. $30.00
BREAST EAGLE LUFTWAFFE EM: Bevo.
White on dark blue. Uncut. Near mint
cond. $71.00

BREAST EAGLE LUFTWAFFE EM:
Machine embr. Silver-gray on blue-gray
wool. Near mint cond. $20.00

BREAST EAGLE LUFTWAFFE EM

BREAST EAGLE LUFTWAFFE EM:
Machine embr. Silver-gray on dark blue
felt. Mint cond. $50.00
BREAST EAGLE LUFTWAFFE OFFICER
SUMMER PIN-ON: Solid alum. body with
A for Assmann. Pb. Near mint
cond. $90.00
BREAST EAGLE LUFTWAFFE OFFICER: 3
different kinds of silver bullion wire, hand
embr. on blue-gray wool. Above avg.
cond. $65.00
BREAST EAGLE LUFTWAFFE OFFICER: 3
tone silver bullion hand embr. on blue-
gray twill. Avg. cond. $85.00

BREAST EAGLE LUFTWAFFE OFFICER

BREAST EAGLE LUFTWAFFE OFFICER: 3
tone silver bullion hand embr. on blue-
gray wool. Avg. cond. $91.00
BREAST EAGLE LUFTWAFFE OFFICER: 3
styles of hand embr. alum. bullion on
blue-gray wool. Avg. cond. $139.00
BREAST EAGLE LUFTWAFFE OFFICER:
Hand embr. alum. down tail eagle on
blue-gray wool. Avg. cond. $75.00
BREAST EAGLE LUFTWAFFE TROPICAL:
Embr. gray eagle on tan twill cotton. Avg.
cond. $82.00
BREAST EAGLE LUFTWAFFE TROPICAL:
Silver-gray machine embr. on tan cloth
triangle. Avg. cond. $51.00
CAP EAGLE LUFTWAFFE HERMAN
GORING DIV: black wool with white
embr. eagle. Avg. cond. $35.00
CAP EAGLE LUFTWAFFE HERMANN
GORING PANZER DIV: Overseas cap.

black wool base with silver and white embr. eagle Mint cond. $32.00

CAP EAGLE LUFTWAFFE OFFICER SUMMER

CAP EAGLE LUFTWAFFE OFFICER SUMMER: White top visor cap. Hand embr. Three tone silver bullion eagle on white wool with brass backing and having two loops 27mm apart. Near mint cond. $292.00
CAP EAGLE LUFTWAFFE TROPICAL: 45x85mm tan cloth triangle with silver-gray embr. eagle. Avg. cond. $55.00
CAP WREATH LUFTWAFFE OFFICER: Visor cap. Silver bullion hand embr. on black wool. Avg. cond. $30.00
CAP WREATH LUFTWAFFE OFFICER: Visor cap. Silver-bullion hand embr. on black wool. Above avg. cond. $50.00
COLLAR TAB LUFTWAFFE ADMIN OFFICIAL (PAIR): Green body, bullion embr. half-wreath, pip & twisted alum. piping. Near mint cond. $30.00
COLLAR TAB LUFTWAFFE ADMIN OFFICIAL (PAIR): Green wool body, twisted alum. piping, bullion wreath & pip. Mint cond. $55.00
COLLAR TAB LUFTWAFFE ENGINEER OFFICER-HAUPTMANN (PAIR): Black bodies with twisted alum. piping, hand embr. half-wreath & 3 gulls. Near mint cond. $38.00
COLLAR TAB LUFTWAFFE ENGINEER OFFICER-LT (PAIR): Black bodies with twisted alum. piping, hand embr. half-wreath & gull. Near mint cond. ... $30.00
COLLAR TAB LUFTWAFFE ENGINEER OFFICER-MAJOR (PAIR): Black wool bodies, twisted alum. piping, alum. wreath & gull. Mint cond. $97.00
COLLAR TAB LUFTWAFFE ENGINEER OFFICER-OBERSTLT (PAIR): Black wool bodies, twisted alum. piping, alum. wreath & 2 gulls. Mint cond. $50.00
COLLAR TAB LUFTWAFFE ENGINEER-CORP OFFICER (PAIR): Pink wool bodies, alum. twisted piping & alum. wreath. Mint cond. $160.00

COLLAR TAB LUFTWAFFE FLAK OFFICER-LT (PAIR): Alum. embr. gull over half-wreath on red wool with gray piping. Near mint cond. $40.00
COLLAR TAB LUFTWAFFE FLAK OFFICER-MAJOR (PAIR): Hand embr. alum. bullion on red felt. Mint cond. $50.00
COLLAR TAB LUFTWAFFE FLAK OFFICER-MAJOR (PAIR): Red wool base & silver bullion full wreath with 1 gull center. Matted backs. Above avg. cond. $40.00
COLLAR TAB LUFTWAFFE FLAK OFFICER-OBERLT (PAIR): Red felt bodies, twisted alum. piping, hand embr. half-wreath & two gulls. Is late-war style. Above avg. cond. $20.00
COLLAR TAB LUFTWAFFE FLAK OFFICER-OBERST (PAIR): Red wool bodies, twisted alum. piping, alum. wreath & 3 gulls. Near mint cond. $65.00
COLLAR TAB LUFTWAFFE FLAK RESERVE OFFICER-LT (PAIR): Red body, blue border, twisted alum. piping, hand embr. alum. half-wreath & one gull to each. Avg. cond. $36.00
COLLAR TAB LUFTWAFFE FLIGHT EM (SINGLE): Golden-yellow wool with 2 gray metal gulls. Matte backing. Avg. cond. $24.00
COLLAR TAB LUFTWAFFE FLIGHT OFFICER-OBERLT (PAIR): Golden-yellow with silver piping & silver bullion details. Near mint cond. $39.00

COLLAR TAB LUFTWAFFE FLIGHT OFFICER-OBERST (PAIR)

COLLAR TAB LUFTWAFFE FLIGHT OFFICER-OBERST (PAIR): Yellow wool bases with silver bullion details. Avg. cond. $139.00
COLLAR TAB LUFTWAFFE FLIGHT OFFICER-OBERSTLT (SINGLE): Right hand side. Yellow wool body, twisted alum. piping, hand embr. alum. wreath & 2 gulls. Avg. cond. $27.00

COLLAR TAB LUFTWAFFE FLIGHT RESERVE OFFICER-HAUPTMANN (SINGLE): Left hand side. Yellow body, blue border, twisted alum. piping, hand embr. alum. half-wreath & 3 gulls. Above avg. cond. $23.00

COLLAR TAB LUFTWAFFE GENERAL-STAFF OFFICER-MAJOR (SINGLE): Left hand side. Crimson wool body, twisted alum. piping, alum. hand embr. wreath & 1 gull. Near mint cond. $68.00

COLLAR TAB LUFTWAFFE HERMAN GORING DIV EM (SINGLE): Right hand side. White wool body, red wool piping & 2 affixed alum. gulls. Above avg. cond. $56.00

COLLAR TAB LUFTWAFFE HERMANN GORING DIV EM (SINGLE)

COLLAR TAB LUFTWAFFE HERMANN GORING DIV EM (SINGLE): Right hand side only. White wool body with green cord piping. Affixed alum. gull. Avg. cond. $76.00

COLLAR TAB LUFTWAFFE HERMANN GORING DIV FLAK EM (SINGLE): Left hand side. White wool body with red wool piping. Affixed 2 alum. gulls. Avg. cond. $50.00

COLLAR TAB LUFTWAFFE HERMANN GORING DIV OFFICER-OBERLT (SINGLE): Left hand side. Hand embr. alum. bullion work on white wool. Avg. cond. $75.00

COLLAR TAB LUFTWAFFE HERMANN GORING DIV PANZER: For wrap-around tunic. Black wool twill with white piping & matted backing, gray metal skulls with two folding prongs each. Avg. cond. $559.00

COLLAR TAB LUFTWAFFE HERMANN GORING DIV OFFICER-LT (PAIR): White wool with silver bullion hand embr. single gull & oakleave half-wreath. Silver-gray twisted piping. Matte backings. Avg. cond. $385.00

COLLAR TAB LUFTWAFFE JUDICIAL OFFICIAL (SINGLE): Left hand side. Bordeaux red wool body, twisted gold piping, alum. hand embr. half-wreath & 3 pips. Above avg. cond. $113.00

COLLAR TAB LUFTWAFFE MEDICAL OFFICER-HAUPTMANN (PAIR): Blue wool body, twisted alum. piping, hand embr. alum. half-wreath & 3 gulls. Near mint cond. $34.00

COLLAR TAB LUFTWAFFE MEDICAL OFFICER-MAJOR (PAIR): Blue wool body, twisted alum. piping, hand embr. alum. wreath & gull. Mint cond. .. $59.00

COLLAR TAB LUFTWAFFE MEDICAL OFFICER-OBERSLT (PAIR): Blue wool bodies, twisted alum. piping, alum. wreath & 2 gulls. Mint cond. $55.00

COLLAR TAB LUFTWAFFE SIGNAL OFFICER-HAUPTMANN (PAIR): Brown wool body, twisted alum. piping, hand embr. alum. half-wreath & 3 gulls. Above avg. cond. $32.00

COLLAR TAB LUFTWAFFE SIGNAL OFFICER-LT (PAIR): Brown wool body, twisted alum. piping, hand embr. alum. half-wreath & gull. Mint cond. $40.00

COLLAR TAB LUFTWAFFE SIGNAL OFFICER-MAJOR (PAIR): Hand embr. alum. bullion work on brown felt. Mint cond. $50.00

COLLAR TAB LUFTWAFFE SIGNAL OFFICER-OBERLT (PAIR): Brown wool body, twisted celleon piping, hand embr. alum. half-wreath & 2 gulls. Near mint cond. $34.00

COLLAR TAB LUFTWAFFE SIGNAL OFFICER-OBERST (PAIR): Brown wool bodies, twisted alum. piping, alum. wreath & 3 gulls. Mint cond. $82.00

COLLAR TAB LUFTWAFFE SONDERFUHRER (SINGLE): Right hand side. Green wool body, twisted gray piping & alum. bullion wreath. Near mint cond. $45.00

CUFF TITLE LUFTWAFFE EM GESCHWADER GENERAL WEVER: 20" long blue wool body with gray embr. title. Above avg. cond. $300.00

CUFF TITLE LUFTWAFFE EM LEGION CONDOR: 12" blue felt body with gray embr. title. Above avg. cond. $374.00

CUFF TITLE LUFTWAFFE OFFICER GESCHWADER BOELCKE: 15" long dark blue wool. Hand embr. alum. title. Avg. cond. $400.00

CUFF TITLE LUFTWAFFE OFFICER GESCHWADER GENERAL WEVER: 15" long. Blue wool with silver bullion hand embr. lettering. Avg. cond. $550.00

CUFF TITLE LUFTWAFFE OFFICER JAGDGESCHWADER RICHTOHOFEN:

10" long blue wool body. Silver hand embr. title. Avg. cond. $480.00

CUFF TITLE LUFTWAFFE PARATROOPER EM *FALLSCHIRM-DIVISION* CUFF-TITLE

CUFF TITLE LUFTWAFFE PARATROOPER EM *FALLSCHIRM-DIVISION* CUFF-TITLE: 19" long dark green doeskin body with gray embr. title. Paper tag with inked RB# & 1944. Near mint cond. $1,319.00

CUFF TITLE LUFTWAFFE PARATROOPER EM *FALLSCHIRM-JAGER RGT 2*: White embr. on green velveteen. Orig. makers paper tag on back from Kargl & Sohne. Avg. cond. $1,605.00

CUFF TITLE LUFTWAFFE PARATROOPER EM *FALLSCHIRM-JAGER RGT.2*: 19" long green body with gray embr. title. Paper tag inked *L.Kargl & Sohne mechan.Seidenbandwiberei etc.* Exc. cond. $750.00

CUFF TITLE LUFTWAFFE PARATROOPER EM *FALLSCHIRM-JAGER RGT.2*: 19" long green doeskin body with gray embr. title. Inked paper tag *L.Kargl & Sohne etc.* Exc. cond. $826.00

SHOULDER STRAP LUFTWAFFE ADMIN OFFICIAL *GFP* (SINGLE): Sew-in style bright alum. body, wine-red piping & green base. 1 silver pip & *GFP* devices. Near mint cond. $185.00

SHOULDER STRAP LUFTWAFFE ADMIN OFFICIAL (PAIR): Sew-in style. Blue-gray plaited bodies with gray center stripes, 2 gray pips each, pink piping & green bases. Exc. cond. $80.00

SHOULDER STRAP LUFTWAFFE ADMIN OFFICIAL (PAIR): Silver cords on red & dark green wool underlay. With 2 gilt metal pips. Above avg. cond. $21.00

SHOULDER STRAP LUFTWAFFE AIR SIGNAL SCHOOL NCO (PAIR): Blue-gray wool with silver braid border & copper-brown piping. With alum. *NS* cipher & 2 alum. pips. Avg. cond. $59.00

SHOULDER STRAP LUFTWAFFE AIR TRAFFIC CONTROL NCO (PAIR): Slip-

on style. Blue-gray wool body, gray tape stripe & light green cord piping. Above avg. cond. $75.00

SHOULDER STRAP LUFTWAFFE EM (PAIR): Blue-gray wool with pink piping. Field-gray wool backing. Removable. Near mint cond. $255.00

SHOULDER STRAP LUFTWAFFE ENGINEER EM (PAIR): Blue-gray wool with black braided piping & lined slip-on tongues. Unissued. Mint cond. ... $40.00

SHOULDER STRAP LUFTWAFFE ENGINEER NCO (PAIR): Blue-gray wool with black piping & silver tress. Above avg. cond. $59.00

SHOULDER STRAP LUFTWAFFE ENGINEER OFFICER-LT (PAIR): Black wool base & 8 silver cord tops. Sew-ins. Near mint cond. $36.00

SHOULDER STRAP LUFTWAFFE FLAK NCO (PAIR): Slip-on blue-gray wool body, red cord piping & alum. tape. Above avg. cond. $55.00

SHOULDER STRAP LUFTWAFFE FLAK OFFICER-MAJOR (PAIR): Red wool base & 4 silver cord braided tops & sew-ins. Above avg. cond. $35.00

SHOULDER STRAP LUFTWAFFE FLAK OFFICER-OBERLT (SINGLE): Silver cords on red wool with gilt metal single pip. Removable. Above avg. cond. $20.00

SHOULDER STRAP LUFTWAFFE FLAK RESERVE OFFICER-LT (PAIR): Sew-in style bright alum. body, blue piping, red bases & gold #29 devices. Near mint cond. $55.00

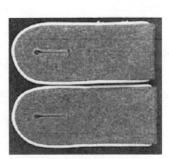

SHOULDER STRAP LUFTWAFFE FLIGHT EM (PAIR)

SHOULDER STRAP LUFTWAFFE FLIGHT EM (PAIR): Slip-on blue gray wool bodies & yellow cord piping. Near mint cond. $55.00

SHOULDER STRAP LUFTWAFFE FLIGHT EM (PAIR): Blue-gray wool slip-on bodies with yellow cord piping. Near mint cond. $45.00

SHOULDER STRAP LUFTWAFFE FLIGHT EM (PAIR): Slip-on blue-gray wool with yellow cord piping. Mint cond. .. $140.00

SHOULDER STRAP LUFTWAFFE FLIGHT KRAFTFAHRSCULE NCO (PAIR): Blue-gray twill wool bodies, yellow wool piping, dark silver tape strip & affixed frosted silver *KRS* device to each. Exc. cond. $113.00

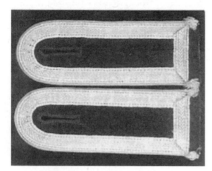

SHOULDER STRAP LUFTWAFFE FLIGHT NCO (PAIR)

SHOULDER STRAP LUFTWAFFE FLIGHT NCO (PAIR): Sew-in style blue-gray twill body, yellow cord piping & alum. tape. Avg. cond. $66.00

SHOULDER STRAP LUFTWAFFE FLIGHT OFFICER-HAUPTMANN (PAIR): Sew-in style bright alum. body on yellow with 2 gold pips. Above avg. cond. $93.00

SHOULDER STRAP LUFTWAFFE FLIGHT OFFICER-LT (SINGLE): Golden-yellow doeskin wool with 8 silver wire tops & slip-on. Above avg. cond. $23.00

SHOULDER STRAP LUFTWAFFE FLIGHT OFFICER-MAJOR (PAIR): Bright silver plaited cords on golden-yellow wool. Avg. cond. $55.00

SHOULDER STRAP LUFTWAFFE FLIGHT OFFICER-OBERST (PAIR): Bright silver plaited cords on golden-yellow wool. With 2 gilt metal pips. Sew-in. Avg. cond. $50.00

SHOULDER STRAP LUFTWAFFE FLIGHT OFFICER-OBERSTLT (PAIR): Bright alum. plaited body on yellow wool. Gold pip to each. Avg. cond. $97.00

SHOULDER STRAP LUFTWAFFE FORTRESS ANTI-AIRCRAFT NCO-CANDIDATE (PAIR): 3.75" long blue-gray wool bodies. Red wool piping & chain-stitched *F33*. Alum. tape loop sewn to each end for NCO candidate. Avg. cond. $90.00

SHOULDER STRAP LUFTWAFFE GENERALLT (PAIR) WITH PAIR OF COLLAR TABS: Tabs: Gold bullion hand embr. details to white wool tabs with gold piping. Boards: 4.5" long sew-in boards on white wool material. Avg. cond. $949.00

SHOULDER STRAP LUFTWAFFE GENERALMAJOR (SINGLE): Shirt size. 3 3/8" long gold & alum. plaited body. Slip-on style with small white felt base & tongue. Avg. cond. $149.00

SHOULDER STRAP LUFTWAFFE MEDICAL EM (PAIR): Blue-gray wool with blue braided piping & lined slip-on tongues. Unissued. Mint cond. ... $40.00

SHOULDER STRAP LUFTWAFFE SIGNAL NCO (PAIR): Slip-on style. Blue-gray wool body, brown cord piping, alum. tape stripe & alum. pip. Above avg. cond. $65.00

SHOULDER STRAP LUFTWAFFE SIGNAL OFFICER-HAUPTMANN (PAIR): Brown wool base & 8 silver cord tops with 2 gilt alum pips. Above avg. cond. $27.00

SLEEVE RANK BAR LUFTWAFFE OFFICER (PAIR): Dark blue wool with 2 white gulls over 2 white bars. Still stapled together & with original price tag. Mint cond. $34.00

SLEEVE RANK BAR LUFTWAFFE: Flight suit. Blue-gray wool with white wool gull wing & single bar sewn-on. Above avg. cond. $28.00

SLEEVE TRIANGLE LUFTWAFFE CIVILIAN TECH *GL*: 4.5" wide. Black machine embr. on golden-yellow. Above avg. cond. $20.00

SPEC PATCH LUFTWAFFE OFFICER FLIGHTING TECHNICAL PERSONNEL: 3 tone hand embr. bullion work on blue-gray wool with paper price tag at back. Above avg. cond. $165.00

SPORT SHIRT EAGLE LUFTWAFFE: Large size. Black bevo on white. Above avg. cond. $20.00

THIRD REICH ARMY (HEER) INSIGNIA

ARMBAND *DEUTSCHE WEHRMACHT*: Bevo. Black on golden-yellow. Eagle ink stamp. Above avg. cond. $28.00

ARMBAND *DEUTSCHE WEHRMACHT*: Bevo. Black on golden-yellow. Near mint cond. $20.00

ARMBAND *DEUTSCHE WEHRMACHT*: Bevo. Black on golden-yellow. Above avg. cond. $35.00

ARMBAND *DEUTSCHER VOLKSSTURM WEHRMACHT*: Red, white & black printed. Avg. cond. $72.00

ARMBAND *DEUTSCHER VOLKSSTURM WEHRMACHT*: Variation. Orange body with black printed wording & Nazi eagle ink stamp. Above avg. cond. $25.00

ARMBAND *HILFS=KRANKENTRAGER*: Black bevo title in rectangle on white. Avg. cond. $25.00

ARMBAND *IM DIENST DER DEUTSCHEN WEHRMACHT*: Black printed on white. Eagle ink stamp. Avg. cond. $25.00

ARMBAND *VERKEHRS-AUFSICHT*: 2 lines of black printed letters on orange. Near mint cond. $37.00

ARMBAND ARMY CIVILIAN EMPLOYEE: Yellow body with black eagle & eagle inked stamp *Heeresdienststelle 11*. Avg. cond. $55.00

ARMBAND ARMY RECRUITING OFFICE: Black bevo stylized eagle on white cotton. Avg. cond. $56.00

ARMBAND NON-MEMBER OF THE ARMED FORCES: Golden-yellow cotton body with black printed spread winged eagle. Above avg. cond. $23.00

BERET WREATH ARMY PANZER: Gray bevo wreath & tri-color pip on black. Uncut. Near mint cond. $27.00

BREAST EAGLE ARMY DAK EM: Light tan base with bevo bluish eagle with tan border. Above avg. cond. $108.00

BREAST EAGLE ARMY EM M44: Bevo. Gray on field-gray triangle. Uncut. Mint cond. $21.00

BREAST EAGLE ARMY EM M44: Bevo. Gray on field-gray triangle. Uncut. Near mint cond. $22.00

BREAST EAGLE ARMY EM: 1934 1st pattern with head facing left. Bevo. White on field-gray. Avg. cond. $320.00

BREAST EAGLE ARMY OFFICER

BREAST EAGLE ARMY OFFICER: 3 tone hand embr. alum. on dark green felt. Above avg. cond. $85.00

BREAST EAGLE ARMY OFFICER: 3 tone hand embr. alum. on green wool. Paper backed & has been on tunic. Above avg. cond. $61.00

BREAST EAGLE ARMY OFFICER: 4 tone hand embr. alum. on dark green felt. Paper backed. Mint cond. $93.00

BREAST EAGLE ARMY OFFICER: Flat-silver bevo on dark green on dark green. Avg. cond. $36.00

BREAST EAGLE ARMY OFFICER: Flat-silver bevo on gray on field-gray wool. Avg. cond. $27.00

BREAST EAGLE ARMY OFFICER: Multi-tone silver bullion hand embr. on dark green wool. With price tag. Above avg. cond. $65.00

BREAST EAGLE ARMY PANZER EM M44: Gray bevo on black triangle. Near mint cond. $22.00

BREAST EAGLE ARMY PANZER EM

BREAST EAGLE ARMY PANZER EM: M1944. White bevo eagle on uncut black triangle. Avg. cond. $50.00

BREAST EAGLE ARMY PANZER EM: White bevo on black. Uncut. Above avg. cond. $34.00

BREAST INSIGNIA ARMY FOREIGN VOL RUSSIAN: On uncut field gray cloth with gray & dark green 3 bar wings with slanted swastika in diamond center. Mint cond. $30.00

CAP EAGLE ARMY EM: Bevo. Gray on dark green. Uncut. Mint cond. $25.00

CAP EAGLE ARMY GENERAL: For visor cap. Hand embr. 3 tone gold eagle on dark green wool. Avg. cond. $185.00

CAP EAGLE ARMY OFFICER: Overseas cap. Flat-silver bevo on gray. Near mint cond. $29.00

CAP EAGLE ARMY OFFICER: Silver bullion hand embr. on dark green wool. Avg. cond. $48.00

CAP EAGLE ARMY OFFICER: Visor cap. Multi-tone silver bullion hand embr. on blue-gray wool. Avg. cond. $65.00

CAP EAGLE ARMY: 1st pattern. Visor cap. Stamped nickel silver. 2 copper prongs on back. Near mint cond. $24.00

CAP EDELWEISS ARMY MT TROOP. Gray metal. By *G.B.42*. 5 holes. Above avg. cond. $28.00

CAP SKULL ARMY INFANTRY REGT #17: For visor cap. Stamped gray metal skull with cross-bones. Avg. cond. $76.00

CAP SKULL ARMY INFANTRY REGT #17

CAP SKULL ARMY INFANTRY REGT #17: WWI style stamped skull with worn silver finish showing copper base. Avg. cond. $70.00

CAP WREATH ARMY GENERAL: For visor cap. Gold metal struck with polished highlights & all prongs. Also a high relief cockade with red wool center & prongs. Above avg. cond. $45.00

CAP WREATH ARMY GENERAL: Visor cap. Dark green wool padded base with gold celleon wreath & wire national color cockade. Avg. cond. $160.00

CAP WREATH ARMY: 1st pattern. Visor cap. Frosted silver with all prongs. Near mint cond. $40.00

CAP WREATH ARMY: Visor caps stamped alum. Hmkd & with prongs & separate attached cockade with red wool center. Near mint cond. $21.00

COLLAR TAB ARMY ADMIN OFFICIAL (PAIR): Dark green cloth base, black piping, woven wire litzen & dark green cord centers. Matted with DRGM num. Above avg. cond. $29.00

COLLAR TAB ARMY ADMIN OFFICIAL (PAIR): Green cord piping to 3 sides of light gray felt body having gray bevo bar & green center. Moth tracks. Above avg. cond. $25.00

COLLAR TAB ARMY ADMIN OFFICIAL HIGH GRADE CAREER (PAIR): Dark gold hand embr. bullion serrated bars on dark green felt with lighter green felt to 3 sides. Above avg. cond. $68.00

COLLAR TAB ARMY ARTILLERY EM (PAIR) WITH CUFF BAR SET: Parade dress. Alum. bevo tape litzen to red wool tabs. Mint cond. $60.00

COLLAR TAB ARMY ARTILLERY OFFICER (PAIR): Dark green wool base with bullion wire litzen & red braided centers. Matted back. Avg. cond. $29.00

COLLAR TAB ARMY ARTILLERY OFFICER (PAIR): Gray embr. litzen with twisted red centers & green wool bases. Avg. cond. $58.00

COLLAR TAB ARMY ARTILLERY OFFICER (PAIR): Parade dress. Silver bullion hand embr. bars on red wool. Matte backings. Avg. cond. $50.00

COLLAR TAB ARMY CAVALRY EM (PAIR) WITH CUFF BAR SET: Parade dress. Bevo alum. litzen on yellow wool. Mint cond. $60.00

COLLAR TAB ARMY CAVALRY EM (PAIR): Parade dress. Alum. tape litzen on yellow wool. Near mint cond. $20.00

COLLAR TAB ARMY CAVALRY OFFICER (PAIR)

COLLAR TAB ARMY CAVALRY OFFICER (PAIR): Green wool bases, gray litzen & twisted yellow cords. Exc. cond. . $77.50

COLLAR TAB ARMY CAVALRY OFFICER (PAIR): Parade dress. Bright silver bullion hand embr. bars on golden-yellow wool. Matte backings. Mint cond. $39.00

COLLAR TAB ARMY DAK EM (PAIR): Copper brown strips on power-blue. Mint cond. $66.00

COLLAR TAB ARMY EM (PAIR): Dark green wool base with sewn-on folded gray bars with dark green centers. Matted backs. Avg. cond. $36.00

COLLAR TAB ARMY FOREIGN VOL RUSSIAN (PAIR): cut & folded with bevo dark green centers & light green border & sewn-on white bevo tress border for NCO. Mint cond. $37.00

COLLAR TAB ARMY GENERAL (PAIR): Red wool bodies with yellow celleon embr. designs & matte backings. Above avg. cond. $197.00

COLLAR TAB ARMY GENERAL-STAFF OFFICER (SINGLE): Carmine wool body with gold bullion hand embr. litzen with sawtooth edges. Avg. cond. $72.00

COLLAR TAB ARMY INFANTRY OFFICER (PAIR): Alum. litzen with faded gray bullion centers & green wool bases. Avg. cond. $35.00

COLLAR TAB ARMY INFANTRY OFFICER (PAIR): Green cloth bases, gray bevo litzen & twisted white cords. Still sewn together & inked DRGM, etc. Near mint cond. $55.00

COLLAR TAB ARMY JAGER OFFICER (PAIR): Gray litzen with green twisted cord centers & green wool bases. Avg. cond. $41.00

COLLAR TAB ARMY JUDICIAL OFFICER (PAIR): Dark green felt bodies. Gray hand embr. bars with twisted wine-red cord centers. Above avg. cond. $55.00

COLLAR TAB ARMY MEDICAL EM (PAIR): dark green twill with gray bevo bars with cornflower-blue bevo litzen. Matte backings. Near mint cond. $55.00

COLLAR TAB ARMY MEDICAL OFFICER (PAIR): Alum. litzen with blue twisted cord centers & green wool bases. Near mint cond. $35.00

COLLAR TAB ARMY MT. TROOP EM (PAIR): Parade dress. Green wool with gray thread litzen & with gray color centers. Avg. cond. $66.00

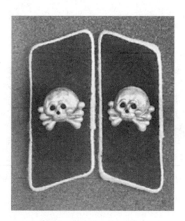

COLLAR TAB ARMY PANZER EM (PAIR)

COLLAR TAB ARMY PANZER EM (PAIR): For the wrap-around style tunic. Black felt material bodies with pinkinsh felt piping & affixed aluminum skulls. Exc. cond. $181.00

COLLAR TAB ARMY PANZER EM (PAIR) WITH CUFF BAR SET: Parade dress. Pink wool bases with silver wire bevo litzen. Sew on. Mint cond. $76.00

COLLAR TAB ARMY PANZER EM (PAIR): Dark green wool with gray tape bars with pink bevo litzen. Matte backings. Above avg. cond. $23.00

COLLAR TAB ARMY PANZER OFFICER (PAIR): Embr. gray litzen with twisted pink centers & green cloth bases. Still tied together. Inked DRGM 1477996. Mint cond. $80.00

COLLAR TAB ARMY PIONEER OFFICER (PAIR): Dark green wool base with silver bullion litzen with black cord centers. Avg. cond. $41.00

COLLAR TAB ARMY PIONEER OFFICER (PAIR): Thick alum. litzen with black centers & dark green backing. Near mint cond. $45.00

COLLAR TAB ARMY PROPAGANDA OFFICER (SINGLE): Parade dress. Alum. litzen on gray wool. Exc. cond. $38.00

COLLAR TAB ARMY RECON OFFICER (PAIR): Parade dress. Bright silver bullion hand embr. bars on brown wool. Matte backings. Mint cond. $101.00

COLLAR TAB ARMY SIGNAL EM (PAIR) WITH CUFF BAR SET: Parade dress. Bevo alum. litzen on yellow wool. Mint cond. $60.00

COLLAR TAB ARMY SIGNAL OFFICER (PAIR) WITH CUFF BAR SET: Parade dress. Lemon-yellow wool base & all with matted backs. Collar tabs are hand embr. bullion litzen & 4 cuff litzen are sewn-on silver wire bevo litzens. Avg. cond. $30.00

COLLAR TAB ARMY SIGNAL OFFICER (PAIR): Parade dress. Bright silver bullion hand embr. bars on lemon-yellow wool. Matte backings. Above avg. cond. $38.00

COLLAR TAB ARMY SMOKE TROOP OFFICER (PAIR): Dark green wool with silver-gray hand embr. bars with Bordeaux-red cord litzen. Matte backings. Above avg. cond. $82.00

COLLAR TAB ARMY SMOKE TROOP OFFICER (PAIR): Parade dress. Bright silver bullion hand embr. bars on Bordeaux-red wool. Matte backings. Mint cond. $42.00

COLLAR TAB ARMY WARTIME OFFICIAL (PAIR): Gold bullion hand embr. bars with 7 serrated teeth on each side of bars. On dark green wool with pink piping on 3 sides. Cardboard backing. Above avg. cond. $45.00

COLLAR TAB ARMY WARTIME OFFICIAL (PAIR): Gold nylon hand embr. bars with 7 serrated teeth on each side of bars. On dark green wool with light blue piping on

3 sides. Matte backings. Near mint cond. $20.00

COLLAR TAB ARMY WARTIME OFFICIAL (PAIR): Gold nylon head embr. bars with 7 serrated teeth on each side of bars. On dark green wool with light green piping on 3 sides. Matte backings. Near mint cond. $28.00

CUFF BAR ARMY GENERAL (SINGLE): Embr. on red wool & has been sewn-on. Above avg. cond. $80.00

CUFF TITLE ARMY *GROSSDEUTSCHLAND*: 14" dark green fabric with silver wire bevo border & lettering. Avg. cond. $585.00

CUFF TITLE ARMY *UNTEROFFIZERVORSCHULE*: Flat-silver bevo on green. Mint cond. . $55.00

CUFF TITLE ARMY *UNTEROFFIZERVORSCHULE*: Uncut field-gray base with silver wire bevo border & lettering. Sewn edges. Above avg. cond. $54.00

CUFF TITLE ARMY DAK *AFRIKA*

CUFF TITLE ARMY DAK *AFRIKA*: 18" long tan body, gray cord piping, gray embr. title & palm trees. Inked RB num. Near mint cond. $370.00

CUFF TITLE ARMY DAK *AFRIKAKORPS*: 16.5" long tan & green body with flat-silver bevo details. Avg. cond. .. $143.00

CUFF TITLE ARMY DAK *AFRIKAKORPS*: Flat-silver bevo on tan & dark green. Mint cond. $97.00

CUFF TITLE ARMY *OFFICER FUHRERHAUPTQUARTIER* 2ND MODEL: 16" black doeskin body with alum. piping borders & alum. hand embr. Sutterlin script title. Exc. cond. . $600.00

CUFF TITLE ARMY OFFICER *GROSSDEUTSCHLAND*: 15" black doeskin base with silver wire script lettering & silver wire cord borders. Avg. cond. $750.00

PITH HELMET SHIELD ARMY EAGLE: Alumn. by *G.B.41*. Mint cond. $20.00

PITH HELMET SHIELDS ARMY (PAIR): Eagle & Tri-color. Stamped gray metal with painted details. Avg. cond. .. $20.00

SHOULDER STRAP ARMY ADMIN OFFICIAL (PAIR): Dark green plaited inner cords with silver stripe & straight green outer cords with silver stripe on

gray & dark green wool backings. Sew-in. Near mint cond. $25.00

SHOULDER STRAP ARMY ADMIN OFFICIAL (PAIR): Green plaited inner cords with silver stripe & straight green outer cord with silver stripe on black & dark green wool backings. Sew-in. Above avg. cond. $30.00

SHOULDER STRAP ARMY ADMIN OFFICIAL (PAIR): Sew-in style. Gray cords with green stripe, gray wool piping, green wool bases, alum. *HV* & 2 pip devices. Exc. cond. $35.00

SHOULDER STRAP ARMY ADMIN OFFICIAL (PAIR): Dark green wool base, grass-green wool piping with 8 silver wire tops & single dark green cord center & gilt *HV* devices with slip-ons. Mint cond. $48.00

SHOULDER STRAP ARMY ANTI-AIRCRAFT RESERVE OFFICER-HAUPTMANN (SINGLE): Sew-in style. Gray cords, white wool piping, gray wool base & gilt *FL 46* cipher & 2 pips. Avg. cond. $100.00

SHOULDER STRAP ARMY ANTI-AIRCRAFT-SCHOOL OFFICER-OBERSLT (SINGLE): Sew-in style. Gray plaited cords, white wool base & gilt *S FL* cipher & single pip. Avg. cond. ... $80.00

SHOULDER STRAP ARMY ANTI-TANK EM (SINGLE): Sew-in green wool body, pink wool piping & chain-stitched *P*. Above avg. cond. $60.00

SHOULDER STRAP ARMY ANTI-TANK OFFICER-HAUPTMANN (PAIR)

SHOULDER STRAP ARMY ANTI-TANK OFFICER-HAUPTMANN (PAIR): Sew-in pink wool bases, gray cords, gold *P* & 2 gray pips each. Avg. cond. $105.00

SHOULDER STRAP ARMY ARTILLERY NCO (PAIR): Sew-in dark green wool bodies, red wool piping, red chain-stitched *60* & alum. tape stripe border. Avg. cond. $59.00

SHOULDER STRAP ARMY ARTILLERY NCO (SINGLE): Slip-on green felt body, red felt piping, alum. tape, silver frosted *20* & 2 pips. Exc. cond. $25.00

SHOULDER STRAP ARMY ARTILLERY OFFICER-HAUPTMANN (PAIR): Slip-on style. Gray cord bodies, red wool bases & gilt *39*. Above avg. cond. $61.00

SHOULDER STRAP ARMY ARTILLERY OFFICER-LT (PAIR): Silver-gray cords on red wool. Sew-in. Avg. cond. $25.00

SHOULDER STRAP ARMY ARTILLERY OFFICER-MAJOR (PAIR): 3.5" long slip-on gray plaited bodies on red wool. Avg. cond. $35.00

SHOULDER STRAP ARMY ARTILLERY OFFICER-OBERLT (PAIR): Red wool base with 8 silver wire tops & silver wash Gothic *S* cipher & 1 bronze pip. Slip-on Above avg. cond. $34.00

SHOULDER STRAP ARMY ARTILLERY RESERVE OFFICER-HAUPTMANN (PAIR): Gray wool bodies. Red wool piped with 8 silver wire cord & 2 gilt pips & silver X on each. Sew ins. Above avg. cond. $45.00

SHOULDER STRAP ARMY ARTILLERY RESERVE OFFICER-HAUPTMANN (SINGLE): Gray cords, red wool piping, gray wool base, gold 7 & 2 pip devices. Avg. cond. $35.00

SHOULDER STRAP ARMY ARTILLERY RESERVE OFFICER-OBERST (PAIR)

SHOULDER STRAP ARMY ARTILLERY RESERVE OFFICER-OBERST (PAIR): Sew-In gray wool bases, red wool underlay to gray plated bodies & 2 gold pips each. Avg. cond. $55.00

SHOULDER STRAP ARMY ARTILLERY-HQ OFFICER-HAUPTMANN (SINGLE): Sew-in style. Gray cords, red wool base, gold *XIII* & 2 pip devices. Avg. cond. $25.00

SHOULDER STRAP ARMY ARTILLERY-HQ OFFICER-OBERLT (SINGLE): Slip-on style. Alum. cords, red wool piping, gray wool base, silver *III* & gold pip devices. Above avg. cond. $37.00

SHOULDER STRAP ARMY ARTILLERY-NCO-SCHOOL OFFICER-MAJOR (SINGLE): Sew-in style. Gray plaited

cords, red wool base & gold *US 2* cipher. Avg. cond. $50.00

SHOULDER STRAP ARMY ARTILLERY-OBSERVATION OFFICER-HAUPTMANN (PAIR): Sew-in silver-gray body on red wool. Gold *B 20* & 2 pips affixed to each. Avg. cond. $77.00

SHOULDER STRAP ARMY ARTILLERY-OBSERVATION OFFICER-OBERLT (PAIR): Sew-in gray cord bodies on red wool. Gold pip, #7 & Gothic *B* cipher. Above avg. cond. $68.00

SHOULDER STRAP ARMY ARTILLERY-OBSERVATION-TRAINING OFFICER-OBERSTLT (SINGLE): Slip-on style. Gray plaited cords, red wool base & gold *BL* cipher. Above avg. cond. $107.00

SHOULDER STRAP ARMY ARTILLERY-TRAINING OFFICER-OBERSTLT (SINGLE): Slip-on style. Gray plaited cords, red wool base, gold *L* & silver pip devices. Avg. cond. $25.00

SHOULDER STRAP ARMY BICYCLE-BN OFFICER-LT (PAIR): Silver-gray cords with white wool backing. With gilt metal Gothic *R* cipher. Removable. Avg. cond. $115.00

SHOULDER STRAP ARMY CAVALRY EM (SINGLE): Sew-in style. Green wool body, yellow cord piping & hand embr. yellow *15*. Avg. cond. $20.00

SHOULDER STRAP ARMY CAVALRY NCO (SINGLE): Dark green wool with silver braid & golden-yellow piping. Silver alum. *18* & 2 pips. Field-gray wool backing. Removable. Avg. cond. $25.00

SHOULDER STRAP ARMY CAVALRY OFFICER-LT (PAIR): Golden-yellow wool base & 8 silver cord tops. Sew-ins Above avg. cond. $72.00

SHOULDER STRAP ARMY CAVALRY OFFICER-LT (SINGLE): Sew-In style. Alum. cords, yellow wool base & *D 4* cipher. Above avg. cond. $118.00

SHOULDER STRAP ARMY CAVALRY OFFICER-OBERLT (SINGLE): Silver-gray cords on golden-yellow wool. Gilt metal *17* & single pip. Has been sewn-in. Avg. cond. $23.00

SHOULDER STRAP ARMY CAVALRY OFFICER-OBERST (SINGLE): Slip-on. Gray cords, yellow wool, gold *15* & 2 pip devices. Above avg. cond. $20.00

SHOULDER STRAP ARMY CAVALRY-RECON OFFICER-LT (SINGLE): Slip-on style. Gray cords, yellow wool base & *A* cipher. Avg. cond. $50.00

SHOULDER STRAP ARMY CAVALRY EM (SINGLE): Dark green wool with golden-yellow piping. Field-gray wool backing. Removable. Mint cond. $23.00

74

SHOULDER STRAP ARMY CAVALRY NCO (SINGLE): Dark green wool with silver braid & golden-yellow piping. With silver alum. Roman numeral *VII* & single pip. Gray wool backing material. Above avg. cond. $20.00

SHOULDER STRAP ARMY CAVALRY OFFICER-MAJOR (PAIR): Silver-gray plaited cords on golden-yellow wool. Removable. Above avg. cond. .. $139.00

SHOULDER STRAP ARMY
CAVALRY-CORP-HQ EM (SINGLE)

SHOULDER STRAP ARMY CAVALRY-CORP-HQ EM (SINGLE): Dark green wool with golden-yellow piping & golden-yellow chain stitched roman numeral *XI*. Field-gray wool backing. Sew-in. Near mint cond. $50.00

SHOULDER STRAP ARMY DAK-INFANTRY EM (PAIR): Olive-green twill with white piping. Above avg. cond. $250.00

SHOULDER STRAP ARMY DAK-PANZER NCO (SINGLE): Slip-on style. Faded olive twill cotton body, variation design to tan tape, pink cord piping & police wool backside. Odd combination. Avg. cond. $48.00

SHOULDER STRAP ARMY EARLY ARTILLERY-OBSERVATION NCO (SINGLE): Early pointed style. Slip-on green wool pointed body, alum. tape & red chain-stitched *B 19*. Avg. cond. $50.00

SHOULDER STRAP ARMY EARLY EM (PAIR): Early pointed style. Dark green wool pointed style with white chain stitched *115* & white cloth loops at base. Removable. Gray wool backing. Avg. cond. $51.00

SHOULDER STRAP ARMY EARLY EM (SINGLE): Early pointed style. Slip-on pointed green wool body & white chain-stitched *L*. Near mint cond. $139.00

SHOULDER STRAP ARMY EARLY EM (SINGLE): Early pointed style. Slip-on style. Green wool pointed body with white chain-stitched *73*. Above avg. cond. $35.00

SHOULDER STRAP ARMY EARLY MACHINE-GUN-BN NCO (PAIR): Early pointed style. Pointed dark green wool body, alum. tape stripe, alum. *M 11* cipher & pip to each. Avg. cond. $82.00

SHOULDER STRAP ARMY EARLY NCO (PAIR): Early pointed style. Slip-on pointed dark green wool bodies, alum. tape stripe & affixed alum. *86*. 2 pips each. Avg. cond. $68.00

SHOULDER STRAP ARMY EARLY NCO (PAIR): Early pointed style. Slip-on style. Pointed green wool bodies, alum. tape & gray pip to each. Avg. cond. $60.00

SHOULDER STRAP ARMY EARLY NCO (PAIR): Early pointed style. Slip-on style. Pointed green wool body, alum. tape, alum. *31* & 2 pip devices. Above avg. cond. $20.00

SHOULDER STRAP ARMY EARLY NCO (SINGLE): Early pointed style. Slip-on green wool pointed body, alum. tape & alum. *S* cipher. Exc. cond. $40.00

SHOULDER STRAP ARMY EARLY NCO (SINGLE): Early pointed style. Slip-on green wool pointed body, alum. tape, frosted silver *S 4* cipher & pip. Exc. cond. $25.00

SHOULDER STRAP ARMY
EARLY NCO (SINGLE)

SHOULDER STRAP ARMY EARLY NCO (SINGLE): Slip-on pointed green wool body, alum. tape & silver *E 4* cipher. Near mint cond. $50.00

SHOULDER STRAP ARMY EARLY NCO CANDIDATE (PAIR): Early pointed style. Slip-on pointed gray wool bodies. White chain-stitched nos. Alum. tape stripe loops. Above avg. cond. $68.00

SHOULDER STRAP ARMY ENGINEER-CORP OFFICER-HAUPTMANN (SINGLE): Sew-in style. Gray cords, orange-red wool base, gilt cog wheel device & 2 pips. Avg. cond. $50.00

SHOULDER STRAP ARMY FORTRESS-SHOP-FOREMAN (PAIR): Sew-in style. Orange & alum. plaited bodies on black wool bases. Alum. *Fp* & gray pip to each. Near mint cond. $280.00

SHOULDER STRAP ARMY INFANTRY EM (PAIR): Sew-in. Dark green wool bodies, white wool piping, white chain-stitched *87*

& stone-gray backs. Above avg. cond. $77.00
SHOULDER STRAP ARMY INFANTRY EM (SINGLE): Sew-in style. Green wool body, white wool piping & white hand embr. *132.* Exc. cond. $25.00
SHOULDER STRAP ARMY INFANTRY NCO (SINGLE): Dark green wool top & white wool piping with silver wire bevo tress. Slip-on. Field-gray wool backing. Avg. cond. $34.00
SHOULDER STRAP ARMY INFANTRY NCO (SINGLE): Sew-in green wool body, white wool piping, alum. tape, alum. *513* & 2 pips. Exc. cond. $35.00
SHOULDER STRAP ARMY INFANTRY NCO (SINGLE): Slip-on gray wool body, soiled white cord piping & gray tape strip. Avg. cond. $25.00
SHOULDER STRAP ARMY INFANTRY OFFICER-HAUPTMANN (PAIR): Sew-in gray cord bodies on white felt. Gold pips & *67.* Avg. cond. $59.00
SHOULDER STRAP ARMY INFANTRY OFFICER-HAUPTMANN (PAIR): Silver-gray cords on white wool with gilt metal *33* & 2 pips. Sew-in. Avg. cond. $35.00
SHOULDER STRAP ARMY INFANTRY OFFICER-LT (PAIR): Sew-in style. Gray cords on thin white twill cloth bases. Paper loop *Schutz Marke RWB* printed with trademark. Near mint cond $23.00
SHOULDER STRAP ARMY INFANTRY OFFICER-LT (SINGLE): Parade dress. Sew-in style. Alum. cords, white wool & gold *40* with mis-matched 4's. Avg. cond. $65.00
SHOULDER STRAP ARMY INFANTRY OFFICER-MAJOR (PAIR): Sew-in style. Gray plaited bodies on white with gilt *6.* Above avg. cond. $135.00
SHOULDER STRAP ARMY INFANTRY OFFICER-MAJOR (PAIR): Silver-gray plaited cords on white wool. Sew-in. Above avg. cond. $28.00
SHOULDER STRAP ARMY INFANTRY OFFICER-MAJOR (SINGLE): Slip-on style. Gray plaited cords on white wool with gold *81.* Exc. cond. $40.00
SHOULDER STRAP ARMY INFANTRY OFFICER-OBERLT (PAIR): Sew-in gray cord bodies on white felt. Gold pip & *13.* Avg. cond. $50.00
SHOULDER STRAP ARMY INFANTRY RESERVE OFFICER-OBERLT (PAIR): Sew-in style. Gray cords, white wool piping, gray wool base, gold *45* & pip devices. Avg. cond. $36.00
SHOULDER STRAP ARMY INFANTRY-BANDSMAN OFFICER-OBERLT (PAIR):

Slip-on style gray & red bodies with white bases. Dark pip & alum. lyre to each. Avg. cond. $139.00
SHOULDER STRAP ARMY INFANTRY-BANDSMAN OFFICER-OBERLT (SINGLE): Slip-on. Alum. & red cords, white wool base & 3 gold devices. Above avg. cond. $100.00
SHOULDER STRAP ARMY INFANTRY-GUARD-TROOP OFFICER-LT (SINGLE): Sew-in style. Gray cords on white felt with gold *W* device. Avg. cond. $25.00

SHOULDER STRAP ARMY
INFANTRY-HQ EM (SINGLE)

SHOULDER STRAP ARMY INFANTRY-HQ EM (SINGLE): Sew-in style green wool body, white wool piping & white chain-stitched *D 22.* Near mint cond. ... $71.00
SHOULDER STRAP ARMY INFANTRY-HQ OFFICER-OBERLT(SINGLE): Slip-on style. Alum. cords, white felt, gold *G6* & pip devices. Exc. cond. $30.00
SHOULDER STRAP ARMY INFANTRY-HQ OFFICER-OBERSTLT (SINGLE): Sew-in style. Alum. plaited cords on white wool with gold *D* cipher & pip. Above avg. cond. $40.00
SHOULDER STRAP ARMY INFANTRY-INSTRUCTION OFFICER-MAJOR (SINGLE): Slip-on style. Gray plaited cords on white wool with tarnished gold *L* device. Above avg. cond $65.00
SHOULDER STRAP ARMY INFANTRY-NCO-SCHOOL EM (SINGLE): Sew-in style green wool body, white wool piping & white chain-stitched *UV XI.* Above avg. cond. $50.00
SHOULDER STRAP ARMY INFANTRY-NCO-SCHOOL-EUTIN EM (SINGLE): Slip-on style green wool body, white wool piping & white chain-stitched *US E.* Avg. cond. $80.00
SHOULDER STRAP ARMY INFANTRY-REGT-FELDHERRNHALLE OFFICER-OBERLT (SINGLE): Slip-on style. Gray cords, white wool base & gold devices. Silver pebbled button with sew on base. Avg. cond. $75.00
SHOULDER STRAP ARMY INFANTRY-REGT-GROSSDEUTSCHLAND EM (PAIR): Slip-on green wool bodies, white

wool piping & white embr. *GD*. Exc. cond. $212.00

SHOULDER STRAP ARMY INFANTRY-SCHOOL EM (SINGLE): Slip-on style. Gray wool body, white cord piping & white chain-stitched *US*. Near mint cond. $49.00

SHOULDER STRAP ARMY INFANTRY-SCHOOL NCO (SINGLE): Slip-on green wool body, white wool piping, alum. tape, alum. *AS*, frosted-silver *S* & 2 alum. pips. Near mint cond. $35.00

SHOULDER STRAP ARMY INFANTRY-SCHOOL OFFICER-LT (SINGLE): Wingtip removable. Alum. cords on white felt with wing-tips, fading gray *WS 2* & pip devices. Avg. cond. $30.00

SHOULDER STRAP ARMY INFANTRY-SCHOOL OFFICER-OBERSTLT (SINGLE): Sew-in style. Gray plaited cords on white wool with dark gold *S* & silver pip. Avg. cond. $45.00

SHOULDER STRAP ARMY INFANTRY-WAR-SCHOOL-POTSDAM NCO (SINGLE)

SHOULDER STRAP ARMY INFANTRY-WAR-SCHOOL-POTSDAM NCO (SINGLE): Slip-on style. Green wool body, white wool piping, gray tape, alum. *KS P* cipher & *3* pebbled button. Exc. cond. $50.00

SHOULDER STRAP ARMY JAEGER NCO: Slip-on green wool body, green wool piping, alum. tape, silver *100* & alum. pip. Above avg. cond. $46.00

SHOULDER STRAP ARMY JAGER-SCHOOL OFFICER-OBERSTLT (SINGLE): Sew-in style. Gray plaited cords, light green wool base & gilt *S* cipher & 2 pips. Avg. cond. $70.00

SHOULDER STRAP ARMY JUDICIAL OFFICER-MAJOR (PAIR): Silver-gray plaited cords on wine-red wool. Sew-in. Above avg. cond. $55.00

SHOULDER STRAP ARMY JUDICIAL OFFICER-OBERST (SINGLE): Slip-on style. Alum. plaited cords, wine-red wool base with gray tongue, gold sword & 2 pips. Avg. cond. $145.00

SHOULDER STRAP ARMY MACHINE-GUN-BN EM (SINGLE)

SHOULDER STRAP ARMY MACHINE-GUN-BN EM (SINGLE): Sew-in green wool material body, with white cord piping, with white hand embr. *M 66*. Exc. cond. $50.00

SHOULDER STRAP ARMY MEDICAL NCO (PAIR): Dark green wool with silver braid, cornflower-blue piping & single alum. pip. Field-gray wool backing. Removable. Above avg. cond. $77.00

SHOULDER STRAP ARMY MEDICAL NCO (PAIR): Slip-on style. Gray wool body, darkening to silver tape stripe, blue wool piping, blue chain-stitched *3* & snake/staff. Near mint cond. $150.00

SHOULDER STRAP ARMY MEDICAL NCO (SINGLE): Sew-in green wool body, blue felt piping, alum. tape, frosted silver snake/staff, gray *Z* & 2 pips. Above avg. cond. $40.00

SHOULDER STRAP ARMY MEDICAL OFFICER-HAUPTMANN (PAIR): Bright silver cords on cornflower-blue wool. With 2 gilt metal pips & snake/staff device. Above avg. cond. $45.00

SHOULDER STRAP ARMY MEDICAL OFFICER-LT (PAIR): Silver-gray cords on cornflower-blue wool. With gilt metal snake/staff device. Removable. Above avg. cond. $28.00

SHOULDER STRAP ARMY MEDICAL OFFICER-OBERLT (PAIR): Sew-in style. Bright alum. cords on blue wool, gold snake/staff & pip to each. Above avg. cond. $50.00

SHOULDER STRAP ARMY MEDICAL OFFICER-OBERLT (SINGLE): Sew-in style. Alum. cords, blue wool, gold snake/staff & 1 pip devices. Above avg. cond. $25.00

SHOULDER STRAP ARMY MEDICAL OFFICER-OBERST (SINGLE): Sew-in style. Gray plaited cords, blue wool base, gold Caduceus & 2 pips. Avg. cond. $30.00

SHOULDER STRAP ARMY MEDICAL OFFICER-OBERSTLT (SINGLE): Sew-in style. Alum. plaited cords, blue wool, gold snake/staff & pip devices. Avg. cond. $25.00

SHOULDER STRAP ARMY MEDICAL-ACADEMY NCO (SINGLE): Dark green wool with silver braid & cornflower-blue piping. With silver alum. Gothic *A* cipher & gray metal pip. Field-gray wool backing material. Removable. Above avg. cond. $25.00

SHOULDER STRAP ARMY MOTORCYCLE NCO (SINGLE): Field-gray wool with gray tape border & copper-brown piping. With silver alum. *52* & single pip. Removable. Near mint cond. $35.00

SHOULDER STRAP ARMY MOTORCYCLE OFFICER-HAUPTMANN (SINGLE): Slip-on style. Gray cords, white felt, gold *K* & 2 pip devices. Avg. cond. $35.00

SHOULDER STRAP ARMY MT. TROOP NCO (SINGLE): Slip-on green felt body, grass-green wool piping & gray tape strip. Near mint cond. $25.00

SHOULDER STRAP ARMY MT. TROOP OFFICER-HAUPTMANN (PAIR): Sew-in gray body on green wool. Gilt *138* & 2 pips affixed. to each. Avg. cond. . $86.00

SHOULDER STRAP ARMY OFFICER-CANDIDATE-SCHOOL NCO (SINGLE): Field-gray wool with silver braid & white piping. Silver alum. Gothic *KS* cipher & single pip. Sew-in. Avg. cond. $30.00

SHOULDER STRAP ARMY ORDNANCE OFFICER-LT (PAIR): Silver-gray cords on red wool with gilt metal crossed cannon barrel device. Above avg. cond. . $70.00

SHOULDER STRAP ARMY ORDNANCE OFFICER-LT (SINGLE): Slip-on style. Gray cords, orange-red wool, gold *Fz* device & silver pebbled button with sew-on base. Near mint cond. $80.00

SHOULDER STRAP ARMY PANZER EM (SINGLE): Leather. 4.5" long black slip-on body. Pink and red leather piping. Style used on leather greatcoat. Above avg. cond. $150.00

SHOULDER STRAP ARMY PANZER NCO (PAIR): Dark green wool with silver braid & pink piping. With silver finished single pip. Sew-in. Field-gray wool backing. Above avg. cond. $61.00

SHOULDER STRAP ARMY PANZER NCO (PAIR): Slip-on type with field-gray wool bases & pink braid piping with silver wire bevo tress borders. Near mint cond. $166.00

SHOULDER STRAP ARMY PANZER NCO (SINGLE): Sew-in green wool body, pink wool piping, alum. tape & pink embr. *1*. Near mint cond. $101.00

SHOULDER STRAP ARMY PANZER OFFICER-LT (PAIR): Sew-in silver-gray

body on pink wool. Dark tarnished 7. Affixed to each. Exc. cond. $77.00

SHOULDER STRAP ARMY
PANZER OFFICER-MAJOR (PAIR)

SHOULDER STRAP ARMY PANZER OFFICER-MAJOR (PAIR): Sew-in pink wool bases with gray plated bodies. Above avg. cond. $75.00

SHOULDER STRAP ARMY PANZER OFFICER-OBERLT (SINGLE): Sew-on style. Alum. cords, pink felt base & gold pip. Avg. cond. $50.00

SHOULDER STRAP ARMY PANZER RESERVE OFFICER-HAUPTMANN (SINGLE): Sew-in style. Gray cords, pink wool piping, gray base, silver *III* & 2 gold pips. Above avg. cond. $75.00

SHOULDER STRAP ARMY PANZER-RECON OFFICER-OBERLT (PAIR): Sew-in style. Gray cords on pink wool bases. Gold pip & *A* device to each. Above avg. cond. $90.00

SHOULDER STRAP ARMY PANZER-REGT-GROSSDEUTSCHLAND OFFICER-LT (PAIR): Sew-In style. Gray cords on pink wool bases with dark silver *GD* ciphers. Exc. cond. $374.00

SHOULDER STRAP ARMY PANZER-SCHOOL EM (SINGLE): Sew-in green wool body, pink wool piping & embr. pink *S 3*. Avg. cond. $87.00

SHOULDER STRAP ARMY PANZER-SCHOOL NCO (PAIR): Sew-in style. Gray wool bodies, pink wool piping, alum. tape, silver *S 2* & pip devices. Exc. cond. $100.00

SHOULDER STRAP ARMY PANZER-SCHOOL NCO (SINGLE): Slip-on green wool body, pink wool piping, alum. tape & pink chain-stitched *S 12*. Near mint cond. $116.00

SHOULDER STRAP ARMY PANZER-SCHOOL OFFICER-LT (SINGLE): Sew-in style. Alum. cords, pink wool base, gold *S* & *13*. Avg. cond. $50.00

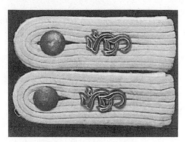

SHOULDER STRAP ARMY PARA-
TROOPER OFFICER-LT (PAIR)

SHOULDER STRAP ARMY PARA-
TROOPER OFFICER-LT (PAIR): Slip-on
white felt bases, gray cordoroy body,
brass *FI* devices & gray pebbled buttons.
Exc. cond. $793.00
SHOULDER STRAP ARMY PARA-
TROOPER OFFICER-OBERLT
(SINGLE): Sew-in style. Gray cords,
white wool base & worn gold paint to FL
& pip devices. Above avg.
cond. $500.00
SHOULDER STRAP ARMY PIONEER NCO
(PAIR): Dark green wool with silver braid
borders & black piping. Field-gray wool
backings. Removable style. Avg.
cond. $53.00
SHOULDER STRAP ARMY PIONEER NCO
(SINGLE): Slip-on green felt body, black
cord piping, alum. pip & tape strip. Above
avg. cond. $25.00
SHOULDER STRAP ARMY PIONEER NCO
(SINGLE): Slip-on style. Gray wool body,
black cord piping, alum. tape & silver *V*
device. Above avg. cond. $25.00
SHOULDER STRAP ARMY PIONEER
OFFICER-HAUPTMANN (SINGLE): Sew-
in style. Alum. cords, black wool base & 2
gold pips. Above avg. cond. $25.00
SHOULDER STRAP ARMY PIONEER
OFFICER-LT (PAIR): Slip-ons with black
wool base & 8 silver wire tops. Above
avg. cond. $50.00
SHOULDER STRAP ARMY PIONEER
OFFICER-OBERLT (PAIR): Slip-on style.
Gray cord bodies, black wool bases &
gold devices to each. Avg.
cond. $50.00
SHOULDER STRAP ARMY PIONEER
OFFICER-OBERLT (SINGLE): Sew-in
style. Gray cords, black wool base & gold
pip. Above avg. cond. $25.00
SHOULDER STRAP ARMY PIONEER
OFFICER-OBERST (PAIR): Silver-gray
plaited cords on black wool. With gilt
metal *9* & 2 pips. Avg. cond. $66.00

SHOULDER STRAP ARMY PIONEER
OFFICER-OBERST (PAIR): Slip-on black
felt bases, gray plated bodies & 2 gray
pips each. Avg. cond. $75.00
SHOULDER STRAP ARMY PIONEER
OFFICER-OBERSTLT (PAIR): Black wool
base & 4 silver cord braided tops & gilt
pip. Sew-in type. Avg. cond. $35.00

SHOULDER STRAP ARMY PIONEER-
INSTRUCTION NCO (SINGLE)

SHOULDER STRAP ARMY PIONEER-
INSTRUCTION NCO (SINGLE): Slip-on
green wool body, black wool piping, alum.
tape & chain-stitched *L 1* in B&W. Above
avg. cond. $112.00
SHOULDER STRAP ARMY PIONEER-
INSTRUCTION OFFICER-OBERST
(SINGLE): Slip-on style. Alum. plaited
cords, black wool base, gold *L* & 2 pip
devices. Above avg. cond. $40.00
SHOULDER STRAP ARMY PROPAGANDA
OFFICER-OBERLT (SINGLE): Sew-in
style. Gray cords, gray velvet base & gold
pip. Near mint cond. $75.00
SHOULDER STRAP ARMY RAILWAY-
ENGINEER NCO (SINGLE): Slip-on gray
wool body, black wool piping, alum. tape
& silver *E2* devices. Above avg.
cond. $50.00
SHOULDER STRAP ARMY RECON
OFFICER-HAUPTMANN (SINGLE): Slip-
on. Gray cords, brown wool base & gilt
pip. Avg. cond. $66.00
SHOULDER STRAP ARMY RECRUITING
NCO (SINGLE): Dark green wool with
orange piping & silver wire tress border,
with alum. *XIII* metal device on top. Sew-
in. Avg. cond. $26.00
SHOULDER STRAP ARMY RECRUITING
OFFICER-HAUPTMANN (SINGLE): Sew-
in style. Gray cords, orange-red wool
base, gold *17* & 2 pip devices. Near mint
cond. $40.00
SHOULDER STRAP ARMY RECRUITING
OFFICER-OBERST (SINGLE): Sew-in
style. Gray plaited cords, orange-red wool
base & 2 gold pips faded gray. Above
avg. cond. $40.00
SHOULDER STRAP ARMY REGIONAL-
DEFENSE-BN NCO (SINGLE): Dark
green wool with silver braid & white

piping. Silver alum. Gothic *L* cipher over *604* with 2 gray metal pips. Field-gray wool backing. Sew-in. Avg. cond. $85.00

SHOULDER STRAP ARMY RIFLE-REGT EM (PAIR): Dark green wool with pink piping & pink hand embr. Gothic *S* over *6*. Dark green wool backing. Sew-in. Mint cond. $300.00

SHOULDER STRAP ARMY SIGNAL EM (PAIR): Late-war bluish-gray wool bodies with slip-on tongues & lemon yellow braid piping. Mint cond. $33.00

SHOULDER STRAP ARMY SIGNAL NCO (PAIR): Slip-ons with field gray wool base & silver tress & yellow piping. Avg. cond. $50.00

SHOULDER STRAP ARMY SIGNAL OFFICER-HAUPTMANN (PAIR): Silver-gray cords on lemon-yellow wool with gilt metal *7* & 2 pips. Avg. cond. $35.00

SHOULDER STRAP ARMY SIGNAL OFFICER-LT (PAIR): Sew-in style. Alum. cords on bright yellow wool bases. Above avg. cond. $28.00

SHOULDER STRAP ARMY SIGNAL OFFICER-MAJOR (PAIR): Silver-gray plaited cords on lemon-yellow wool. Removable. Above avg. cond. $48.00

SHOULDER STRAP ARMY SIGNAL OFFICER-OBERSTLT (SINGLE): Sew-in style. Gray plaited cords, yellow wool base, gold *56* & pip device. Above avg. cond. $40.00

SHOULDER STRAP ARMY SIGNAL-SCHOOL NCO (SINGLE): Dark green wool with silver braid & lemon-yellow piping. With Gothic *S* cipher & 2 pips. Removable. Near mint cond. $25.00

SHOULDER STRAP ARMY SIGNAL-SCHOOL NCO (SINGLE): Dark green wool with silver braid & lemon-yellow piping. With silver alum. Gothic *S* cipher & 3 silver finished pips. Gray wool backing. Avg. cond. $35.00

SHOULDER STRAP ARMY SMOKE-TROOP NCO (SINGLE): Dark green wool with silver braid & Bordeaux-red piping. Removable. Above avg. cond. $33.00

SHOULDER STRAP ARMY SUPPLY OFFICER-HAUPTMANN (PAIR): Silver-gray cords on light blue wool with gilt metal *X* over *1* & 2 single pips. Removable. Above avg. cond. $38.00

SHOULDER STRAP ARMY SMOKE-TROOP OFFICER-HAUPTMANN (SINGLE): Sew-in style. Gray cords, Bordeaux wool & 2 gold pips. Above avg. cond. $50.00

SHOULDER STRAP ARMY SUPPLY EM (SINGLE): Sew-in style. Gray wool body,

blue wool piping & chain-stitched blue *6*. Near mint cond. $49.00

SHOULDER STRAP ARMY SUPPLY NCO (PAIR): Slip-on gray wool bodies, light blue piping, gray tape, alum. *2* & 3 pips each. Avg. cond. $54.00

SHOULDER STRAP ARMY SUPPLY OFFICER-LT (PAIR): Silver-gray cords on light blue wool. Gilt metal winged staff with intertwined snakes device. Sew-in. Above avg. cond. $30.00

SHOULDER STRAP ARMY SUPPLY OFFICER-MAJOR (PAIR): Powder-blue base & 4 silver braided cord tops & slip-ons with field-gray buttons. Above avg. cond. $35.00

SHOULDER STRAP ARMY SUPPLY OFFICER-OBERLT (PAIR): Slip-on style. Gray cords, light blue wool bases & gold pips. Above avg. cond. $40.00

SHOULDER STRAP ARMY SUPPLY OFFICER-OBERSTLT (PAIR): Silver-gray plaited cords on light blue wool with gilt metal *4* & single pip. Sew-in. Above avg. cond. $70.00

SHOULDER STRAP ARMY SUPPLY RESERVE OFFICER-HAUPTMANN (PAIR): Gray wool base with light blue piping & with 8 silver wire tops & gilt *6* & 2 gilt pips on each. Sew-ins. Above avg. cond. $35.00

SHOULDER STRAP ARMY SUPPLY-SCHOOL OFFICER-MAJOR (SINGLE): Sew-in style. Gray plaited cords, light blue felt base & worn gold *S* device. Avg. cond. $50.00

SHOULDER STRAP ARMY VETERINAR-IAN NCO (SINGLE): Dark green wool with silver braid & crimson piping. Silver finished snake device. Removable. Avg. cond. $25.00

SHOULDER STRAP ARMY VETERINAR-IAN OFFICER-LT (PAIR): Silver-gray cords on crimson with snake over roman numeral *VIII*. Avg. cond. $50.00

SHOULDER STRAP ARMY VETERINAR-IAN-TROOPS NCO (PAIR): Dark green wool with silver braid borders & carmine piping. With silver finished *17* & single pip. Field-gray wool backings. Remov-able. Above avg. cond. $77.00

SLEEVE CHEVRON ARMY: Large black wool field with double silver taped V's. Near mint cond. $22.00

SLEEVE EDELWEISS ARMY MT TROOP OFFICER: Silver bullion hand embr. edelweiss with gold bullion seeds on dark green wool with silver twisted cord and rope border. Avg. cond. $142.00

SLEEVE RANK PIP ARMY PRIVATE: Bullion. Dark green wool with hand embr.

silver bullion pip. Above avg.
cond. $23.00

SLEEVE SHIELD ARMY
DAK SONDERVERBAND
287 FREE ARABIC LEGION

SLEEVE SHIELD ARMY DAK
SONDERVERBAND 287 FREE ARABIC
LEGION: Bevo. Off-white swastika-
wreath, palm-tree, yellow sun & uncut
blue-green body. Mint cond. $267.00
SLEEVE SHIELD ARMY FOREIGN VOL
*ASERBAIDSCHA*N: Bevo. Field-gray
cloth with bevo design of black border
with red lettering over blue/red/green
shield. Above avg. cond. $35.00
SLEEVE SHIELD ARMY FOREIGN VOL
BA: Printed. Mint cond. $75.00
SLEEVE SHIELD ARMY FOREIGN VOL
BERGKAUKASIEN: Bevo. Black border
shield with all bevo 3 stylized horse
heads on wheel. Uncut field-gray cloth.
Mint cond. $61.00
SLEEVE SHIELD ARMY FOREIGN VOL
GEORGIEN: Bevo. Uncut field gray cloth
with black border & white lettering over
red field with black & white corner. Near
mint cond. $50.00
SLEEVE SHIELD ARMY FOREIGN VOL
HRVATSKA: Bevo. Mint cond. ... $100.00
SLEEVE SHIELD ARMY FOREIGN VOL
HUNGARIAN: Bevo. Hmkd *Bevo
Wuppertal*. Near mint cond. $50.00
SLEEVE SHIELD ARMY FOREIGN VOL
IDEL URAL: Bevo. Color bevo shield on
uncut gray with *Bevo Wuppertal*. Mint
cond. $55.00
SLEEVE SHIELD ARMY FOREIGN VOL
KB: Printed. Dark green cloth shield with
white *KB* over red & black divided shield
with white cloth back uncut cloth. Mint
cond. $37.00
SLEEVE SHIELD ARMY FOREIGN VOL
LETTLAND: Bevo. Avg. cond. $37.00

SLEEVE SHIELD ARMY
FOREIGN VOL *POA*

SLEEVE SHIELD ARMY FOREIGN VOL
POA: Bevo. Dark green cloth with yellow
bevo *POA* over bevo red border shield
with white field & blue cross center.
Above avg. cond. $55.00
SLEEVE SHIELD ARMY FOREIGN VOL
TURKISTAN: Bevo with pink & blue
shield with white bow & arrow. Dark
green border with blue lettering. Field-
gray background. Uncut. Near mint
cond. $58.00
SLEEVE SHIELD ARMY FOREIGN VOL
TURKISTAN: Printed. Black border shield
with divide center of pink & blue with bow
& arrow center & *Turkistan* at top. Above
avg. cond. $55.00
SLEEVE SHIELD ARMY JAGER: Dark
green wool oval with white embr. rope &
green embr. sprig of 3 oak leaves &
acorn. Mint cond. $29.00
SLEEVE SHIELD ARMY
STANDARDBEARER JAGER: Bevo.
alum. details, green standards, B&W
eagle & uncut green backing. Near mint
cond. $641.00
SLEEVE SHIELD ARMY
STANDARDBEARER PIONEER: Bevo.
Alum. details, black standards, B&W
eagle & uncut green backing. Near mint
cond. $391.00
SLEEVE SHIELD ARMY
STANDARDBEARER RECON: Bevo.
Alum. details, copper-brown standards,
B&W eagle & uncut green backing. Near
mint cond. $496.00
SLEEVE SHIELD ARMY
STANDARDBEARER SIGNAL: Bevo.
With flat-silver, bright yellow & white
details. Above avg. cond. $295.00
SPEC PATCH ARMY ARMOR MECHANIC
1ST CLASS: Pink machine embr.
cogwheel on field-gray wool with pink
twisted cord piping. Mint cond. ... $30.00
SPEC PATCH ARMY BOATSWAIN: Bulllon.
Dark green wool oval with hand embr.

anchor with boat wheel in center. Avg. cond. $40.00
SPEC PATCH ARMY PIGEON-POSTMAS-TER: Hand embr. Yellow Gothic *B* on dark green wool. Paper backed. Above avg. cond. $33.00
SPEC PATCH ARMY TECHNICAL ARTI-SAN: Pink machine embr. cogwheel on field-gray wool with silver twisted piping. Near mint cond. $36.00

THIRD REICH NAVAL (KRIEGSMARINE) INSIGNIA

ARMBAND SHIP DAMAGE SERVICE: Bevo. White body with blue borders, yellow & black anchor center. Near mint cond. $133.00

BREAST EAGLE COASTAL
ARTILLERY EM

BREAST EAGLE COASTAL ARTILLERY EM: Golden bevo on tan background. Avg. cond. $88.00
BREAST EAGLE COASTAL ARTILLERY EM: Golden-yellow bevo on dark green. Uncut. Mint cond. $23.00
BREAST EAGLE COASTAL ARTILLERY EM: Golden-yellow machine embr. on field-gray wool. Mint cond. $37.00
BREAST EAGLE COASTAL ARTILLERY EM: Golden-yellow machine embr. on field-gray wool background. Above avg. cond. $42.00
BREAST EAGLE COASTAL ARTILLERY OFFICER: 3 tone hand embr. with gold bullion on a green wool background. Avg. cond. $97.00

BREAST EAGLE COASTAL
ARTILLERY OFFICER

BREAST EAGLE NAVAL EM: Blue bevo on white. Uncut. Mint cond. $20.00
BREAST EAGLE NAVAL EM: Golden-yellow machine embr. on dark blue wool. Near mint cond. $37.00
BREAST EAGLE NAVAL OFFICER: Excellent 3 tone gold bullion hand embr. details on white wool. Metal backing has 4 affixed threaded studs, loose metal backing plate, 3 nuts remain of 4. Penciled name to plate *H.Watzmen.* Near mint cond. $590.00
BREAST EAGLE NAVAL OFFICER: Gold bullion hand embr. on dark blue wool. Avg. cond. $86.00

BREAST EAGLE NAVAL OFFICER

BREAST EAGLE NAVAL OFFICER: Hand embr. 3 tone celleon details on blue wool. Avg. cond. $66.00
BREAST EAGLE NAVAL OFFICER: Hand embr. thick yellow eagle on blue wool. Avg. cond. $85.00
CAP EAGLE NAVAL EM: Blue machine embr. on white. Near mint cond. $37.00
CAP EAGLE NAVAL EM: Donald duck cap. 50mm stamped alum. with gold finish by *R.S. and S. 40.* Knurled pin. Above avg. cond. $20.00
CAP EAGLE NAVAL OFFICER: Visor cap. Direct hand embr. celleon eagle on blue wool background cut from cap. Avg. cond. $59.00
CAP EAGLE NAVAL OFFICER: Visor cap. Hand embr. three tone celleon details on a blue wool backing material. Avg. cond. $66.00
CAP RIBBON NAVAL *1. MARINEUNTEROFFIZIERLEHRABTEILUNG. 1.:* Gilt wire Gothic letters on black. Above avg. cond. $35.00
CAP RIBBON NAVAL *1. SCHIFFSSTAMMABTEILUNG 1.:* Gilt wire Gothic letters on black. Above avg. cond. $35.00
CAP RIBBON NAVAL *1. SCHIFFSSTAMMABTEILUNG DER NORDSEE.1:* 39" uncut black silk-like with gilt wire bevo lettering. Darkening to letters. Above avg. cond. $55.00

CAP RIBBON NAVAL
1.MARINEUNTEROFFIZIERLEHRABTEILUNG1.:
38" long black body with bevo Gothic title
in yellow. Near mint cond. $35.00
CAP RIBBON NAVAL *1.MINENSUCH-
HALBFLOTTILLE.1.*: 60" black body with
gold Gothic title. Exc. cond. $65.00
CAP RIBBON NAVAL *2 ZERSTORER 2*:
52" black body with gold bevo Latin title.
Above avg. cond. $36.00
CAP RIBBON NAVAL *2. MARINEUNTER-
OFFIZIERLEHRABTEILUNG 2.*: Gilt wire
Gothic letters on black. Above avg.
cond. $35.00
CAP RIBBON NAVAL *2.A.
SCHIFFSSTAMMDIVISION DER
NORDSEE. 2.A.*: Gilt wire Gothic letters
on black. Above avg. cond. $35.00
CAP RIBBON NAVAL
*2.A.SCHIFFSSTAMMDIVISION DER
OSTSEE.2.A.*: 54" black body with gold
bevo title. Exc. cond. $50.00

CAP RIBBON NAVAL
2.GELEITFLOTTILLE.2.

CAP RIBBON NAVAL
2.GELEITFLOTTILLE.2.: 56" black fabric
body with dark gold Gothic title. Avg.
cond. $75.00
CAP RIBBON *NAVAL 2.MARINEUNTER-
OFFIZIERLEHRABTEILUNG.2.*: 58"
black body with gold Bevo title. Exc.
cond. $50.00
CAP RIBBON NAVAL *3. MARINEUNTER-
OFFIZIERLEHRABTEILUNG 3.*: Gilt
wire Gothic letters on black. Above avg.
cond. $35.00
CAP RIBBON NAVAL *3.
SCHIFFSSTAMMABTEILUNG 3.*:
Golden-yellow cotton Gothic letters on
black. Near mint cond. $35.00
CAP RIBBON NAVAL
3.SCHIFFSSTAMMABTEILUNG 3.: 43"
long black body with bevo Gothic title in
yellow. Exc. cond. $35.00
CAP RIBBON NAVAL *4.
MARINEARTILLERIEABTEILUNG. 4.*:
Gilt wire Gothic letters on black body.
Avg. cond. $45.00
CAP RIBBON NAVAL *4.
SCHIFFSSTAMMABTEILUNG DER
OSTSEE. 4.*: Golden-yellow cotton
Gothic letters on black. Above avg.
cond. $35.00

CAP RIBBON NAVAL
4.ZERSTORERDIVISION 4.

CAP RIBBON NAVAL
4.ZERSTORERDIVISION 4.: 53"
black body with dark gold Gothic title.
Avg. cond. $145.00
CAP RIBBON NAVAL
4.ZERSTORERDIVISION 4.: 56"
black body with dark gold Gothic title.
Avg. cond. $155.00
CAP RIBBON NAVAL *6.
SCHIFFSSTAMMABTEILUNG 6.*: Gilt
wire Gothic letters on black fabric. Avg.
cond. $35.00
CAP RIBBON NAVAL
7.SCHNELLBOOTGESCHWADER 7.:
54" black body with gold bevo Latin title.
Avg. cond. $37.00
CAP RIBBON NAVAL
I.TORPEDOBOOTS=HALBFLOTTILLE.I.:
46" black body with silver Latin title. Avg.
cond. $55.00
CAP RIBBON *NAVAL
II.MINENSUCH=DIVISION.II* 22" black
body with dark gold Latin title. Avg.
cond. $50.00
CAP RIBBON NAVAL
II.TORPEDOBOOTS=HALBFLOTTILLE.II.:
45" black body with silver Latin title. Avg.
cond. $55.00
CAP RIBBON NAVAL *KREUZER EMDEN*:
46" black body with dark gold Gothic title.
Avg. cond. $95.00
CAP RIBBON NAVAL *KREUZER EMDEN*:
Black *59* ribbon with gold bevo lettering.
Avg. cond. $35.00
CAP RIBBON NAVAL *KREUZER HAM-
BURG*: 50" black body with dark gold
Latin title. Avg. cond. $85.00
CAP RIBBON NAVAL *KREUZER KOLN*:
Black 45" ribbon with gold bevo lettering.
Avg. cond. $55.00
CAP RIBBON NAVAL *KREUZER LEIPZIG*:
58" long black ribbon with gold title.
Above avg. cond. $265.00

CAP RIBBON NAVAL *KREUZER LEIPZIG*

CAP RIBBON NAVAL *KREUZER LEIPZIG*:
58" black fabric body with yellow bevo

title tag. 3" tear to black. Above avg. cond. $61.00
CAP RIBBON NAVAL *KREUZER NYMPHE*: 57" black ribbon with dark gold bevo Latin title. Avg. cond. $27.00
CAP RIBBON NAVAL *KRIEGSMARINE*: 41" black body with yellow cotton Gothic title. Avg. cond. $55.00
CAP RIBBON NAVAL *KRIEGSMARINE*: 42" black silk-like base with golden-yellow bevo lettering. Near mint cond. $24.00

CAP RIBBON NAVAL *KRIEGSMARINE*

CAP RIBBON NAVAL *KRIEGSMARINE*: 56" black body with dark gold Gothic title. Above avg. cond. $55.00
CAP RIBBON NAVAL *KRIEGSMARINE*: Black 44" ribbon with gold bevo lettering. Above avg. cond. $25.00
CAP RIBBON NAVAL *KRIEGSMARINEDIENSTSTELLE BREMEN*: 44" black body with yellow cotton Gothic title. Exc. cond. ... $120.00
CAP RIBBON NAVAL *LINIENSCHIFF BRAUNSCHWEIG*: 46" black body with dark gold Latin title. Avg. cond. .. $75.00
CAP RIBBON NAVAL *LINIENSCHIFF SCHLESIEN*: 46" black body with yellow cotton Gothic title. Above avg. cond. $65.00
CAP RIBBON NAVAL *LINIENSCHIFF SCHLESIEN*: 57" black body with dark gold Gothic title. Avg. cond. $75.00
CAP RIBBON NAVAL *LINIENSCHIFF SCHLESWIG-HOLSTEIN*: 45" black fabric body with gold Latin title. Above avg. cond. $85.00
CAP RIBBON NAVAL *MARINENACHRICHTENSCHULE*: 4 black body with bevo Gothic title in gold. Above avg. cond. $35.00
CAP RIBBON NAVAL *MARINESCHULE FRIEDRICHSORT*: Gilt wire Gothic letters on black fabric body. Above avg. cond. $45.00
CAP RIBBON NAVAL *MARINESCHULE KIEL*: 38" long black fabric body with bevo Gothic lettering in yellow. Exc. cond. $35.00

CAP RIBBON NAVAL *MARINESCHULE WESERMUNDE*

CAP RIBBON NAVAL *MARINESCHULE WESERMUNDE*: 47" black fabric body with dark gold Gothic lettering. Avg. cond. $55.00
CAP RIBBON NAVAL *NORDD. LLYOD D. KAISER WILHELM DER GROSSE*: 37" uncut black silk with golden-yellow bevo lettering & fouled anchors on either end. Above avg. cond. $59.00

CAP RIBBON NAVAL *PANZERSCHIFF ADMIRAL SCHEER*

CAP RIBBON NAVAL *PANZERSCHIFF ADMIRAL SCHEER*: 55" black fabric body with dark gold small Gothic title. Avg. cond. $210.00
CAP RIBBON NAVAL *PANZERSCHIFF ADMIRAL SCHEER*: 55" black body with small dark gold Gothic title. Avg. cond. $220.00
CAP RIBBON NAVAL *PANZERSCHIFF DEUTSCHLAND*: 57" black fabric body with gold bevo lettering. Above avg. cond. $155.00
CAP RIBBON NAVAL *PANZERSCHIFF DEUTSCHLAND*: 69" black fabric body with yellow cotton Gothic title. Exc. cond. $170.00
CAP RIBBON NAVAL *SCHIFFSARTILLERIESCHULE*: 58" black body with gold bevo title. Above avg. cond. $50.00
CAP RIBBON NAVAL *SCHLACHTSCHIFF GNEISENAU*: 30" black body with yellow bevo Latin title. Tape scum to ends from display. Avg. cond. $50.00
CAP RIBBON NAVAL *SCHLACHTSCHIFF SCHARNHORST*: 30" black body with yellow bevo Latin title. Tape scum to ends from display. Avg. cond. $50.00

CAP RIBBON NAVAL *SCHLACHTSCHIFF SCHARNHORST*

CAP RIBBON NAVAL *SCHLACHTSCHIFF SCHARNHORST*: 43" black body with yellow cloth bevo Gothic title. Near mint cond. $185.00
CAP RIBBON NAVAL *SCHNELLBOOTSBEGLEITSCHIFF TANGA*: 42" black body with yellow cotton Gothic title. Avg. cond. $125.00

CAP RIBBON NAVAL *SCHULSCHIFF DEUTSCHLAND*: Golden-yellow bevo block letters on black ribbon with white & red borders. Near mint cond. $45.00

CAP RIBBON NAVAL *SEGELSCHULSCHIFF GORCH FOCK*: 56" black fabric body with dark gold Gothic lettering. Avg. cond. $110.00

CAP RIBBON NAVAL *SEGELSCHULSCHIFF GORCH FOCK*: 57" black fabric body with dark gold Gothic lettering. Avg. cond. $110.00

CAP RIBBON NAVAL *SEGELSCHULSCHIFF HORST WESSEL*: 47" long black fabric body with darkening to gold title. Avg. cond. $135.00

CAP RIBBON NAVAL *SMS KRONPRINZ*: 40" uncut black silk with silver bevo lettering Above avg. cond. $51.00

CAP RIBBON NAVAL *SPERRVERSUCHSKOMMANDO*: 45" black fabric body with gold Latin title. Above avg. cond. $70.00

CAP RIBBON NAVAL *TECHNISCHE MARINESCHULE*: Gilt wire Gothic letters on black fabric body. Above avg. cond. $20.00

CAP RIBBON NAVAL *TORPEDOSCHULE*: Black body with bevo Gothic title in gold. Exc. cond. $55.00

CAP RIBBON NAVAL *UNTERSEEBOOTS=FLOTTILLE MITTELMEER*: 42" black fabric body with faded silver/gray Latin title. Avg. cond. $177.00

CAP RIBBON NAVAL *UNTERSEEBOOTSSCHULE*: 57" long black ribbon with dark gold title. Avg. cond. $422.00

CAP RIBBON NAVAL *VERMESSUNGSSCHIFF METEOR*: 57" black body with dark gold Latin title. Avg. cond. $200.00

CAP RIBBON NAVAL *VORPOSTENFLOTTILLE*: 52" black body with gold Gothic lettering. Above avg. cond. $65.00

CAP RIBBON NAVAL *ZERSTORER ERICH STEINBRINCK*: 69" black fabric body with yellow cotton Gothic lettering. Exc. cond. $282.00

CAP RIBBON NAVAL *ZERSTORER HANS LODY*: 66" black fabric body with yellow cotton Gothic lettering. Exc. cond. $180.00

CAP WREATH NAVAL OFFICER: Visor cap. Dark blue wool fabric with embr. yellow celluloid wreath & bullion cockade. Padded & backed. Above avg. cond. $45.00

COLLAR TAB NAVAL CHAPLAIN

COLLAR TAB NAVAL CHAPLAIN (SINGLE): Dark blue wool body, alum. bullion hand embr. wreath, cross center & twisted alum. piping. Above avg. cond. $100.00

PITH HELMET EAGLE NAVAL ADMIN: Stamped silver eagle with frosted silver finish showing use. 3 loops lack pins. Above avg. cond. $112.00

SHOULDER STRAP COASTAL ARTILLERY EM (SINGLE): 4.5" long gray wool pointed body with yellow embr. winged-shell-anchor. Slip-on with scrap-book glue to back. Above avg. cond. .. $20.00

SHOULDER STRAP COASTAL ARTILLERY NCO (SINGLE): Field-gray wool 4.5" pointed body with gilt tress border and slip-on tongue Above avg. cond. $24.00

SHOULDER STRAP COASTAL ARTILLERY OFFICER-HAUPTMANN (PAIR): Removable wing-tip style. Gray cords, green wool bases, gold devices & 2 brown painted anchor buttons. Avg. cond. $70.00

SHOULDER STRAP NAVAL ADMIN OFFICER-CAPT (SINGLE): Blue twill cloth base with subdued silver cord tops & 2 gilt pips with gray metal snakes on a winged pole. Avg. cond. $25.00

SHOULDER STRAP NAVAL CIVILIAN OFFICIAL

SHOULDER STRAP NAVAL CIVILIAN OFFICIAL (SINGLE): Blue plaited inner cords with silver stripe with straight blue outer cord with silver stripe on dark blue wool. With 2 silver finished pips & stylized eagle device. Avg. cond. $50.00

SHOULDER STRAP NAVAL CPO (PAIR): Dark Navy blue wool with golden yellow tape border & gilt metal crossed anchors & silver gray metal rank star. Sew-in pattern. Near mint cond. $45.00

SHOULDER STRAP NAVAL OFFICER-LT (PAIR): 3.5" long bright alum. boards with black felt backing & straps. Above avg. cond. $27.00

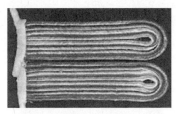

SHOULDER STRAP NAVAL OFFICER-LT (PAIR)

SHOULDER STRAP NAVAL OFFICER-LT (PAIR): Removable wing-tip style. Early silver cords show darkening & white felt bases. Grommet to button holes. Above avg. cond. $65.00

SHOULDER STRAP NAVAL OFFICER-LT (SINGLE): Slip-on style bright alum. cords on blue wool. Paper band by *Schutz Marke RWB*. Mint cond. .. $30.00

SPEC PATCH NAVAL DIVER: Hand embr. Red & blue hand embr. diver helmet on dark blue wool oval. Rare to find these hand embr. Above avg. cond. $65.00

THIRD REICH GORGETS & AIGULETTES

AIGUILLETTE: 2 plaited alum. bodies with 2 cords & silver painted metal tips. Near mint cond. $124.00

AIGUILLETTE: 2 plaited alum. bodies with 2 cords. Near mint cond. $85.00

AIGUILLETTE: 2 alum. plaited bodies with silver painted metal end-tips, 2 loops, button-hole, braided slide & end loops. Avg. cond. $87.00

AIGUILLETTE: Age yellowed body & 2 looped cords. Unsewn twisted bullion end loop. Avg. cond. $92.00

AIGUILLETTE: Clean plaited body with 2 cord loops. Lacks plaited slide. Above avg. cond. $106.00

AIGUILLETTE: Double plaited alum. bodies with both cords & silver painted metal tips. Near mint cond. $125.00

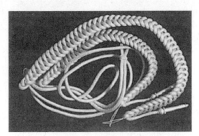

AIGUILLETTE

AIGUILLETTE: Double plaited body with silver painted metal tips & 2 loops. Complete. Near mint cond. $125.00

AIGUILLETTE: Double plaited body with silver painted metal tips & 2 loops. Complete. Near mint cond. $125.00

AIGUILLETTE: Early alum. bullion plaited body with cords & 2 dark silver tips. Exc. cond. $117.00

AIGUILLETTE: Heavy gold plaited body with 2 loops, braided slide, end loop & brass swivel fitting instead of button-hole. Exc. cond. $76.00

AIGUILLETTE: Variation gray and silver bullion plaited body with loop cord. Faded dark gold finish to 2 metal tips. Above avg. cond. $103.00

GORGET *BREMEN CITY STADTWEHR 968* WITH CHAIN. RARE: 6" wide stamped nickel half-moon body with raised title over crowned key-shield center being held by 2 lions and *968* below. Hole at each corner for wire loop. Original steel style link chain present. Above avg. cond. $275.00

GORGET *FELDGENDARMERIE* WITH CHAIN: Silver painted magnetic body & chain links. Clean luminous paint to eagle, title-scroll & corner buttons. Gray wool backing & center hook stamped with *M* in diamond. Only 1 prong loose at eagle wing. Near mint cond. $306.00

GORGET NSKK TRAFFIC DIRECTION: 7" wide stamped alum. half-moon. Raised details to eagle, *928* & *NSKK Verkehrs-Erziehungsdienst*. Near mint cond. $243.00

GORGET REICHS-LUFT-AUFSICHT 1ST MODEL WITH CHAIN: 6" wide half-moon body shows worn frosted-silver finish. Heavy brass winged swastika affixed over brass title. Green leatherette covered back with center hook stamped *C.E.Juncker Berlin*. Corner loops to silver linked chain. Above avg. cond. $675.00

CLOTH INSIGNIA

GORGET REICHS-LUFT-AUFSICHT
2ND MODEL WITH CHAIN

GORGET REICHS-LUFT-AUFSICHT 2ND
MODEL WITH CHAIN: Alum. half-moon
body with affixed gold finished title &
winged swastika. Green leatherette
backing, center hook & alum. chain. Near
mint cond. $616.00

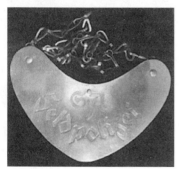

GORGET SA FELDPOLIZEI
WITH CHAIN

GORGET SA FELDPOLIZEI WITH CHAIN:
High quality locally made gorget. 6.5"
alum. half-moon body with ornate
stamped Gothic title. Rivet at each corner

for loop & center hook. Never had
backing. Interesting stamped steel chain
links with 1 side end loop having clip.
Exc. cond. $343.00
GORGET SA: Bright nickel heart-shaped
body with wear to silver finished brass
roundel having early mobile-swastika.
Gold finished brass starburst backing to
roundel. Brass corner domes with design
to each. Blue wool backing has large
metal RZM disc affixed. 2 hooks & 1
corner loop. Exc. cond. $248.00

GORGET SA

GORGET STAHLHELM FLAG BEARER
WITH CHAIN: Silver frosted body &
heavy cast eagle details over helmet etc.
3 nuts to threaded studs. Wear to frosted
finish chain. Avg. cond. $325.00
GORGET STAHLHELM WITH CHAIN:
Heavy non-magnetic shield backing,
cast-brass affixed crowned eagle over
wreath with M16 helmet & 4 standards.
Traces of silver finish to shield & 3 nuts
hold center. Dark non-magnetic chain.
Avg. cond. $435.00

CHAPTER THREE: METAL INSIGNIA, BADGES & TINNIES

IMPERIAL GERMAN METAL INSIGNIA

BUSBY FRONTPLATE HUSSAR SKULL:
80x100mm silvered stamped metal with
2 loop attachment on back. Avg.
cond. $158.00

BUSBY FRONTPLATE HUSSAR SKULL:
80x95mm stamped silvered metal with 3
sets of copper prongs & metal attachment slides on back. Above avg.
cond. $385.00

CAP COCKADE SAXON EM: 20mm size.
White with green ring. Two holed for
sewing. Avg. cond. $20.00

CAP CROSS RESERVIST: Brass 1914
Reservist Cross for Leather Visor Cap.
Avg. cond. $28.00

CAVALRY SADDLE BLANKET STAR
SAXON: Pre-war. 4.5" diam. 8 pointed
silver rayed metallic star with red cloth
center having large frosted silver royal
crown. Looped back for securing through
cloth of blanket or shabraque. Mint
cond. $252.00

DOG TAG AUSTRIAN WITH PAPER

DOG TAG AUSTRIAN WITH PAPER:
Hinged brass case missing one loop.
Printed paper with inked information:
Inf. Rgt. 102, Alois Kocab, 1914 etc.
Avg. cond. $124.00

DOG TAG WWI : 2.75" oval metal disc with
three holes & perforations for easy
breaking. Marked *KAISERS 240
LAUTERN* on each half & other info. Avg.
cond. $34.00

DOG TAG WWI: Gray oval with 2 holes &
stamped *Bruno Gregor Berlin etc.* &
Fuss-Artl.Batl. Nr. 406. Above avg.
cond. $40.00

GORGET MECKLENBURG NAPOLEONIC
WAR: 5.5" wide nickel/silver crescent-
moon body with 2 hanger holes. Affixed
gold crown over crossed standards with
steer-head shield & eagle-shield. Exc.
cond. $250.00

ID TAG: Gray zinc with 2 hanger holes &
stamped *I.E.B.J.R.81. 2.K. 1830
Wilh.Bernhardt.* Exc. cond. $44.00

ID TAG: M1915. Gray zinc oval with 2
hanger holes & stamped *Georg
Anielsperger Bring. 15.3.80.
Brs.Abt.bay.7.Fd.Autl.K.Nr.4 etc.* Above
avg. cond. $37.00

ID TAG: M1916. Gray zinc oval with 3
divider slots & stamped *Thomas
Owzarcak Wattenscheid Westf. 12.11.81.*,
crossed out units & added to reverse *1
LST J B Weimar 4 K etc.* Above avg.
cond. $66.00

SHAKO FRONTPLATE PRUSSIAN JAGER
EM: Stamped dark brass with 2 loops.
Above avg. cond. $72.00

SLEEVE SPECIALIST BADGE
MACHINE GUNNER

SLEEVE SPECIALIST BADGE MACHINE
GUNNER: Field gray cloth body: metal
backing. Gilt row of MG bullets with gilt
08/15 Spandau on mount. Backplate
bears 1918 date & Berlin maker name.
Mint cond. $185.00

SPIKED HELMET CHINSCALES INFAN-
TRY OFFICER

SPIKED HELMET CHINSCALES INFAN-
TRY OFFICER: Dark brass flat scales,
black leather backings. Avg.
cond. $145.00

SPIKED HELMET CHINSCALES INFAN-
TRY OFFICER: Brass. Avg.
cond. $158.00

SPIKED HELMET EAGLE CROWN GARDE
DU CORPS EM: Beautifully made with
open vaulting & cross on top. Metric
threaded. Designed for M89 pattern. In
brass. Near mint cond. $82.00

SPIKED HELMET FRONTPLATE BADEN EM GRIFFIN: Steel with gray finish. 5.5" wide griffin with scroll below. 2 loops. Avg. cond. $145.00

SPIKED HELMET FRONTPLATE BAVARIAN INFANTRY ONE YEAR VOLUNTEER: Pierced central crown: brass. Lug back. Mint cond. $66.00

SPIKED HELMET FRONTPLATE
HESSE LEIBGARDE

SPIKED HELMET FRONTPLATE HESSE LEIBGARDE: Silver. Full oak & laurel leaves: lion with silver & *Gott Ehre Vaterland* star. Loop back style. Mint cond. $345.00

SPIKED HELMET FRONTPLATE HUNGARIAN LIFE GUARDS: Pre-WWI. 75x40mm. Brass Hungarian shield with crown of St. Stephen above. Finely detailed. Prong back for attachment to helmet body. Near mint cond. ... $166.00

SPIKED HELMET FRONTPLATE PRUSSIAN EM: Brass. Pre-war. Loop back. Mint cond. $33.00

SPIKED HELMET FRONTPLATE PRUSSIAN EM: Loop back. Near mint cond. $45.00

SPIKED HELMET FRONTPLATE PRUSSIAN EM: Stamped steel with gray finish. Loop back. Near mint cond. $69.00

SPIKED HELMET FRONTPLATE PRUSSIAN GARDE EM: Dark stamped brass body, 2 prongs added to back instead of studs & 2 oval slots for missing star. Avg. cond. $77.00

SPIKED HELMET FRONTPLATE PRUSSIAN GUARD DRAGOON OFFICER: Stamped brass body with pierced crown, 2 threaded studs with fittings & affixed silver starburst. Avg. cond. $282.00

SPIKED HELMET FRONTPLATE PRUSSIAN GUARD GRENADIER EM: Brass eagle with silver Garde star on breast. Loop back. Mint cond. $135.00

SPIKED HELMET FRONTPLATE PRUSSIAN LANDWEHR EM: Stamped brass body with 4 solder holes to nickel cross & 2 threaded studs. Avg. cond. $66.00

SPIKED HELMET FRONTPLATE
PRUSSIAN LANDWEHR EM

SPIKED HELMET FRONTPLATE PRUSSIAN LINE INFANTRY OFFICER: Pierced crown with a gilt finish. Above avg. cond. $134.00

SPIKED HELMET KOKARDE PRUSSIAN EM: Near mint cond. $20.00

SPIKED HELMET KOKARDE PRUSSIAN OFFICER: 50mm black with white metal ring & black center, small hole in center. Near mint cond. $45.00

SPIKED HELMET KOKARDE WURTTEMBERG EM: Small hole pattern with silver round retainer. Above avg. cond. $40.00

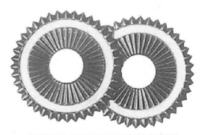

SPIKED HELMET KOKARDES
JAGER ZU PFERDE EM

SPIKED HELMET KOKARDES JAGER ZU PFERDE EM: Pre-war large size with Prussian & Reichs colors. Type worn with all Jager zu Pferde, Kurassier enlisted formations. Exc. cond. $50.00

SPIKED HELMET KOKARDES JAGER ZU PFERDE PRUSSIAN & REICHS EM: Near mint cond. $73.00

SPIKED HELMET KOKARDES PRUSSIAN & REICHS EM: Exc. cond. $59.00

SPIKED HELMET KOKARDES SAXON & REICHS EM: Serrated wartime patterns with Reichs kokarde plus serrated Saxon green white kokarde. Wartime issue. Near mint cond. $25.00

SPIKED HELMET KOKARDES WURTTEMBERG & REICHS EM: Above avg. cond. $25.00

SPIKED HELMET SIDE BOSSES OFFICER: Set of 2. Above avg. cond. $80.00

SPIKED HELMET SPIKE BASE EM: Brass. Round with mounting holes. Above avg. cond. $51.00

SPIKED HELMET SPIKE BASE INFANTRY OFFICER: Bras. 3" diam. base, 4 mounting holes, pearlband & threaded hole. Exc. cond. $45.00

SPIKED HELMET SPIKE BASE NCO: Pearlring pattern. Round. Near mint cond. $69.00

SPIKED HELMET SPIKE OFFICER: Nickel. 3.5" tall, 1 7/8" diam. & threaded stud. Avg. cond. $79.00

SPIKED HELMET SPINE OFFICER: Brass. Above avg. cond. $66.00

SPIKED HELMET TRICHTER EM/NCO WITH FULL BLACK HORSE HAIR PLUME: Brass. Trichter intact with cap, neck & thread hole. Plume is in very fine, soft & supple condition. All hair appears to be intact. Worn for dress parade by garde & line infantry units. Near mint cond. $643.00

SPIKED HELMET TRICHTER OFFICER: with round base. Exc. cond. $271.00

SPIKED HELMET VISOR TRIM OFFICER: Above avg. cond. $55.00

THIRD REICH MEMBER BADGES & MINIATURE INSIGNIA/BADGES

CIVIL BADGE LUFTWAFFE: 30mm wingspan to solid eagle, good finish & knurled pin. Near mint cond. $50.00

CIVIL BADGE LUFTWAFFE: 30mm wingspan to solid eagle, good finish & knurled pin. Near mint cond. $59.00

DONATION BADGE OPFER RING: 23mm white enamel body, black swastika & red backing to title. Pb & only marked *NSDAP*. Above avg. cond. $58.00

DONATION BADGE OPFER-RING: 23mm diam. with tricolor enamel work. Pb & *Gauleitung Baden NSDAP Ges. Gesch*. Near mint cond. $35.00

DONATION BADGE OPFERRING ELSASS: 23mm gray disc with title border & swastika center. Pb with maker & some silver finish. Avg. cond. $61.00

HITLER YOUTH BADGE HOCHLAND LAGER 1936: 35x45mm brass shield with

gold finish. Green & black enamel title. Enamel HJ diamond affixed to edelweiss. Pb with maker. Near mint cond. $82.00

HITLER YOUTH BADGE MARKSMANSHIP: 25mm silver oakleave wreath, black enamel target, affixed crossed rifles & enamel HJ diamond. Pb & *RZM M1/102*. Exc. cond. $49.00

HITLER YOUTH BADGE MEMBER GOLDEN HONOR

HITLER YOUTH BADGE MEMBER GOLDEN HONOR: Gold border to clean enamel center. By *RZM M1/120 B* & Pb. No serial num. & lacks lock to catch. Avg. cond. $150.00

HITLER YOUTH BADGE MEMBER GOLDEN HONOR: Good enamel diamond with gold border, stamped *86xx, RZM M1/70 Ges.Gesch*. & pin is coming unsoldered. Avg. cond. $165.00

HITLER YOUTH BADGE MEMBER: 25mm tall with unmarked back & variation pin. Avg. cond. $20.00

HUNTING ASSOC HANGER CHAIN: 40mm gold finished alum. disc with hunting badge front & reverse *Internationale Jagdausstellung Berlin 1937 Lander Pramierung Deutschland*. Hangerchain with catch. Avg. cond. $239.00

LAPEL CHAIN 5 PLACE: 16mm size to 1914 EK, Mecklenburg 1914 cross, Prussian 14 year long service cross, 12 & 4 year Wehrmacht long service medals. Chain has stickpin ends. Above avg. cond. $131.00

MARKSMANSHIP BADGE KREISSIEGER DEUTSCHER SCHUTZENBUND 1936: 53mm tall, gold wreath, black enamel eagle with affixed white target having gold swastika, title to green & red panels. Pb with maker. Above avg. cond. $63.00

MARKSMANSHIP BADGE TIROL KK-GEWEHR 1943: 40mm gold disc with red eagle, date, white swastika target & gold

title. Pb with maker. Near mint
cond. $40.00

MEMBER BADGE AIRCRAFT
REPORTING SERVICE

MEMBER BADGE AIRCRAFT REPORTING
SERVICE: 27mm size blue enamel body
with party flag & black plane. Pb, *ES* &
stamped *102390*. Exc. cond. $97.00
MEMBER BADGE COLONIAL BUND:
20mm tall shield, tricolor, Pb & maker.
Near mint cond. $45.00
MEMBER BADGE CZECH PRO-NAZI
VLASTI ZDAR NS: 15mm tall 4 color
divided enamel shield with title & 33mm
wide gold brooch pin. Maker marked.
Near mint cond. $150.00
MEMBER BADGE D.V.G. WESTMARK
(LOTHR.): 23mm size, tricolor, Pb & *M9/
312*. Above avg. cond. $28.00
MEMBER BADGE D.V.G. WESTMARK
(LOTHR.): 24mm black border with silver
title, red swastika to white center, Pb &
W.Redo Saarlautern. Above avg.
cond. $22.00
MEMBER BADGE DAF: 18mm nickel/silver
metal cog with swastika with etched pin
Avg. cond. $25.00
MEMBER BADGE DANZIGER
LUFTSCHUTZBUND: 22mm round with
white border & wording with DLB in 8
pointed rayed star center. Pb. Hmkd.
Above avg. cond. $55.00
MEMBER BADGE DDAC 1934: 17mm tall
tricolor oval with dated laurel leaf wreath
below. Marked. Above avg.
cond. $51.00
MEMBER BADGE DEUTSCHER
FRAUENHILFSDIENST: 40mm black
enamel disc with silver title, swastika &
life rune. Pb with maker. Above avg.
cond. $135.00
MEMBER BADGE DRL: 20mm tall bronze
eagle with 2 wide prongs holding broken
black leather strap. Above avg.
cond. $120.00
MEMBER BADGE DRV BICYCLISTS:
18mm silvered metal round with red
spoked wheel field/black swastika & DRV
across face. Machined pin & hmkd. Avg.
cond. $47.00

MEMBER BADGE FRAUENHILFSDIENST:
40mm silver border with black enameled
field & wording around runic life symbol.
Pb. Above avg. cond. $81.00

MEMBER BADGE FRAUENSCHAFT
LEADER TYPE III

MEMBER BADGE FRAUENSCHAFT
LEADER TYPE III: 36x36.5mm dark
silver triangular oak leaf wreath, blue
enamel border & black center with dark
silver title, eagle & rune. Pb & *RZM M1/
24*. Above avg. cond. $75.00
MEMBER BADGE FRAUENSCHAFT TYPE
II: 30mm size black enameled triangle
with white cross & red swastika center &
Gothic letters on each arm *G H L* & blue
border. Pb & hallmarked. Avg.
cond. $25.00
MEMBER BADGE FRAUENSCHAFT TYPE
II: 44mm tall triangular body with tricolor
enamel. Pb & stamped *Ges.Gesch.*
Above avg. cond. $80.00
MEMBER BADGE FRAUENSCHAFT TYPE
III: 22x24mm triangle with black field &
wording in red over sunwheel over life
rune. Pb & hmkd. Avg. cond. $23.00
MEMBER BADGE FREIE
SCHWESTERNSCHAFT: 32mm round
with thin black border & white field, silver
lettering & red runic symbol center. Hmkd
& very good condition. Near mint
cond. $150.00
MEMBER BADGE FUHRER WIENER
AERO CLUB LEADER: 30mm with gold
title to red enamel rim having large chip,
small chip to domed blue enamel center
with affixed brass balloon. Button hole
mount with stamped maker *J.Blacinchic
Wien*. Avg. cond. $140.00
MEMBER BADGE GERMANS IN FOREIGN
LANDS: Maker marked New York City,
22mm red enameled oval with swastika
above the rayed letters of *AV*. Machined
pin. Members held meeting in pre-WW II
Madison Square Garden. Above avg.
cond. $82.00
MEMBER BADGE
GROSSDEUTSCHLAND: 16mm tall gold
oak leaf wreath with open center having

GD. Knurled pin shows use. Above avg. cond. $130.00

MEMBER BADGE *KDF GAU KOLN AACHEN*: Multicolored enameled. Pb. Maker *Hoffstatter Bonn*. Mint. Mint cond. $34.00

MEMBER BADGE *KRIEGERBUND* 25 YEAR: 22mm with red enameled shield with black cross with swastika. Silver finished oak leaf wreath border with *25* at top. Pb. Hmkd *9 ges gesch*. Above avg. cond. $20.00

MEMBER BADGE KRIEGERBUND
THURINGEN 25 YEAR

MEMBER BADGE *KRIEGERBUND THURINGEN* 25 YEAR: 32x64mm divided shield with red & white enamel sides. White side has color enamel lion-shield holding swastika & *Thuringen* below. Silver title above. Badge style pin & maker marked. Well done. Near mint cond. $160.00

MEMBER BADGE LUFTSCHUTZ: Eagle with rayed star & swastika center Pb hmkd Avg. cond. $21.00

MEMBER BADGE LUFTWAFFE LH: 27x40mm gray metal with luft eagle & *L H* in center. Pb. Avg. cond. $29.00

MEMBER BADGE MEMEL POLICE: 70mm. Silver finish with upper half having rising sun, lower section has oak, laurel leaves with horizontal swastika. Phoenician style border. Simple Pb construction. Above avg. cond. $196.00

MEMBER BADGE NSFK: 25mm wide silver finished Icarus, title to border-ring with oak leaves & marked back. Near mint cond. $24.00

MEMBER BADGE NSKK FEMALE *KRIEGSKRAFTFAHRERIN:* 28mm disc with steering wheel outline, swastika to hub, title scroll & red painted background. Pb & by *RZM M1/35*. Avg. cond. $25.00

MEMBER BADGE NSKK: 20mm alum stamped with NSKK ribbon above eagle & Pb. Hmkd. Above avg. cond. ... $25.00

MEMBER BADGE NSKOV
GOLDEN HONOR

MEMBER BADGE NSKOV GOLDEN HONOR: Gold oakleave wreath diamond border, blue enamel border to white center & gold NSKOV logo center. Pb. Near mint cond. $220.00

MEMBER BADGE ORDER OF ST SEBASTIANUS: 22mm enameled oval with the martyred saint in center, tied to a tree with arrow in body & wording around border. Hmkd & etched pin. Above avg. cond. $27.00

MEMBER BADGE *PFALZISCHEN WIRTSCHAFT IM DIENSTE 25 JAHRE:* 31mm frosted silver disc with title border, swastika & 3 figure center. Pb. Avg. cond. $150.00

MEMBER BADGE POLICE *FELD & FORST HUTER:* 60mm stamped nickel starburst with eagle center & affixed bronze title scroll. Pb. Exc. cond. $150.00

MEMBER BADGE RD FU TR: Red, white & black enameled with microscope superimposed on crossed knives with swastika at top. Maker *Hartmann Hanover*. Knurled stickpin mount. No enamel damage. Near mint cond. $30.00

MEMBER BADGE RED CROSS HELPER TYPE II: About 30mm diam. Black border with silver *Deutsches Rotes Kreuz Helferin*, 2 swastikas & Red-Cross to white center. Pb & *Ges.Gesch*. Above avg. cond. $40.00

MEMBER BADGE RED CROSS: 20mm winged black enameled eagle with swastika center & red cross at base. Pb & hmkd. Avg. cond. $32.00

MEMBER BADGE *REICHSLANDBUND*: 15x17mm shield shaped with green background & 3 gold wheatheads over wording Hmkd & etched pin. Near mint cond. $24.00

MEMBER BADGE *REICHSNAHRSTAND LANDESBAUERNSCHAFT BAYERN 30 YEAR:* About 40x45mm gray metal oval with stamped details. Some corrosion to finish. Horizontal pin for brooch use. Avg. cond. $55.00

MEMBER BADGE *REICHSNAHRSTAND LANDESBAUERNSCHAFT KURHESSEN* WITH CASE BADGE: Black leatherette case with white satin lid lining & blue velvet base. 33mm diam. silver frosted body with *Blut und Boden* eagle center, title border & back has *25* in center of oak leaf wreath. Horizontal pin. Above avg. cond. $106.00

MEMBER BADGE SA: 16mm steel framed round with black border & intertwined SA on off white field insert. First of this style of lapel pin I have ever seen. Avg. cond. $59.00

MEMBER BADGE SA: Silver finished cutout SA logo. Knurled stickpin mount. Near mint cond. $33.00

MEMBER BADGE SS

MEMBER BADGE SS: 13mm disc with darkening to silver runes, good black enamel, stamped maker & *213xx* Knurled pin comes with spring lock. Above avg. cond. $229.00

MEMBER BADGE SS: 14mm diam. black enamel, dark silver SS-runes & border rings. Stamped *1385* & raised *Hoffstatter/ Bonn.* Knurled pin. Early one. Exc. cond. $65.00

MEMBER BADGE *STAHLHELM 1923:* Good black enamel, silver finished oak leaves, 1923 & affixed helmet. Pb, *sth* maker & engraved *IV.Mi.7778 15.10.1923.* Above avg. cond. .. $135.00

MEMBER BADGE *STAHLHELM 1924:* Good black enamel, silver oak leaves/ date & loose helmet from rivet shows past glue-repair attempts. Pb & engraved *VI.Ns.1396 1.5.24.* Easy repair. Avg. cond. $100.00

MEMBER BADGE *STAHLHELM 1926:* Good black enamel, dark silver oak leaves/date & helmet. Pb & engraved *V.Ba.106 15.7.26.* Exc. cond. ... $135.00

MEMBER BADGE *STAHLHELM 1930:* Good black enamel, silver oak leaves/ date & helmet. Pb, engraved *Wm.2687*

26.10.30 & maker *sth 935 ges.gesch.* Exc. cond. $108.00

MEMBER BADGE STAHLHELM 1931

MEMBER BADGE *STAHLHELM 1931:* 31mm black enamel body with silver finished details. Wide pin & by *STH 935 Ges.Gesch.* Exc. cond. $93.00

MEMBER BADGE *STUDENTEN KAMPFHILFE:* 23mm diam. B&W enamel with gold title & details. Pb with RZM M1/ 63. Near mint cond. $55.00

MEMBER BADGE STUDENTENBUND: 24mm gray metal diamond with painted red & white fields between the arms of black swastika. Pb & hmkd. Mint cond. $27.00

MEMBER BADGE U-BOAT LABORER: 22x33mm bronze Nazi eagle over oval cog with sub through center. Pin. Avg. cond. $159.00

MEMBER BADGE *VDK* DISABLED WAR VETERAN WITH CASE: Brown leatherette case with *VDK* embossed in gold, button catch & satin with brown velvet inners. Pin is 17mm oak leaf wreath with attached black enameled VDK over Deutschland, machined pin & hard to find. Nice together. Above avg. cond. $49.00

MINIATURE BADGE CAMPAIGN SHIELD LAPPLAND: 9mm tall bronze shield with knurled pin. Near mint cond. $24.00

MINIATURE BADGE CAMPAIGN SHIELD NARVIK: 17mm shield with eagle over crossed prop & anchor with edelweiss. Machined pin Avg. cond. $30.00

MINIATURE BADGE HITLER YOUTH PROFICIENCY SILVER: 22mm tall, Pb & RZM M1/72. Above avg. cond. ... $25.00

MINIATURE BADGE NAVAL DESTROYER: 18mm gilt gray metal with machined pin. Above avg. cond. $75.00

MINIATURE BADGE PANZER ASSAULT: gray 15mm oval with Nazi eagle over tank center. Machined pin style. Avg. cond. $20.00

MINIATURE BADGE SA SPORTS
BRONZE: Bronze round wreath with
sword over swastika center, machined pin
& hmkd. Above avg. cond. $20.00
MINIATURE MEDAL IRON CROSS 1939:
11mm with fair details & knurled pin.
Above avg. cond. $27.00
MINIATURE MEDAL LIFE SAVING MEDAL
SILVER: 25mm round .835 silver & Hmkd
on rim, has faded orange ribbon with 2
white stripes, full size but unmounted.
Above avg. cond. $263.00
MINIATURE MEDAL MOTHER CROSS
BRONZE: 21mm tall with good enamel &
bowtie ribbon with pin. Above avg.
cond. $30.00
MINIATURE MEDAL OCCUPATION
CZECH: 16mm bronze medal with
ribbon. Near mint cond. $28.00
MINIATURE MEDAL SS SERVICE 8 YEAR:
10mm dark brown metal with knurled pin.
Near mint cond. $145.00

NSDAP BADGE GAU BADEN
COMMEMORATIVE SILVER

NSDAP BADGE *GAU BADEN* COMMEMO-
RATIVE SILVER: 35x45mm silver finished
heavy oval oak leaf wreath, open center
with party eagle & black title below. Pb &
stamped *Pr.Klett Karlsruhe*. Near mint
cond. $350.00
NSDAP BADGE GAU ESSEN COMMEMO-
RATIVE: Wear to gold finished alum.
sword with crossed *1925/1935* hammers.
Bent spring to pin. By *Hoffstatter Bonn*.
Avg. cond. $69.00
NSDAP BADGE MEMBER GOLDEN
HONOR: 25mm. About 24mm badge has
small oak leave border. Enamel shows
use with scuffs. Pb with maker *Jos.Fuess
Munchen*, no vent & stamped *6648*. Avg.
cond. $340.00

NSDAP BADGE MEMBER
GOLDEN HONOR

NSDAP BADGE MEMBER GOLDEN
HONOR: 25mm. Dark gold wreath,
enamel shows wear, vent hole to back,
stamped *28672* & Pb. Early civilian dress
badge. Above avg. cond. $538.00
NSDAP BADGE MEMBER GOLDEN
HONOR: 30mm. Bright gold finish to
wreath, good enamel center, vent hole,
Ges.Gesch. Pb & owner name is
removed number was 5 digits. Avg.
cond. $895.00
NSDAP BADGE MEMBER PARTY EAGLE:
38mm wide eagle with darkening,
stamped with number 800, knurled pin &
tricolor ribbon rosette backing. Avg.
cond. $249.00
NSDAP BADGE MEMBER: 18mm size
tricolor with small chip to red. Pb &
Ges.Gesch. Avg. cond. $34.00
NSDAP BADGE MEMBER: 23mm with
good enamel. Pb & *RZM M1.25*. Above
avg. cond. $29.00
OLYMPIC BADGE: 30mm. Brandenburg
Gate over the 5 rings, all white field, gold
lettering Pb & hmkd. Above avg.
cond. $50.00
OLYMPIC BADGE: About 70mm diam. Dark
blue bakelite body has silver inset rings
over Brandenburg Gate engraved
XI.Olympiade Berlin 1936. Affixed alum.
num. band with black *3612*. Pb with
maker *Walgo Kierspe-Bhf.Westf.* Mint
cond. $252.00
OLYMPIC BADGE: Multicolored rings.
32mm wide with chips to blue & red rings.
Pb & maker name marked. Avg.
cond. $20.00

THIRD REICH TINNIES

TINNIE "1922 GEDENKTAG EHEM SCHW
ARTILLERISTEN NURNBERG": Dark
silver finish with field gun scene. Pb.
Maker marked. Near mint cond. . . $30.00
TINNIE "1924 BAYERISCHER
KRIEGSERBUND": Stamped antique

bronze colored sheet metal design, Pb. 29mm by 29mm size. Nice Bavarian Lion detail. Mint cond. $20.00

TINNIE "1925 1935 NSDAP THURINGEN": Fading to bronze finish. In form of stylized eagle with swastika on chest & shield between legs. Pb. Above avg. cond. $50.00

TINNIE "1925 SCHUTZVEREINS TAGUNG KUFSTEIN": 55.86x40.39mm. Stamped tin with litho. design. Has imperial style eagle in center. Small hole at top center. Above avg. cond. $20.00

TINNIE "1926 KREIS TURN U SPORTFEST KAISERSLAUTERN": Bronze finish with large *S* superimposed on cross made of 4 F's. Pb. Above avg. cond. $30.00

TINNIE "1927 LANDVOLKSTAG ALSFELD HESSISCHER": 37.58x30.35mm. Stamped metal with gilted finish has age darkened. Has likeness of building in center with coat of arms below. Above avg. cond. $20.00

TINNIE "1927 REICHSKRIEGERTAG BERLIN": Stamped bronze, Pb, 38mm diam., has holes for sewing on, has been crudely converted to safety pin back. Has profile of President Paul von Hindenburg in uniform. Above avg. cond. $20.00

TINNIE "1928 THURINGEN KATHOLIKENTAG WEIMAR": Bronze finish with church scene. Pb. Above avg. cond. $30.00

TINNIE "1929 REICHSFRONTSOLDATENTAG MUNCHEN": Edelweiss designed flower with raised steel helmet in center having *Der Stahlhlem* lettering on helmet. Circular lettering about helmet. Pb. 40x40mm. Near mint cond. $40.00

TINNIE "1929 REICHSFRONTSOLDATENTAG MUNCHEN": Silver finish with *Der Stahlhem* helmet superimposed on an edelweiss. Pb. Above avg. cond. $49.00

TINNIE "1929 REICHSFRONTSOLDATENTAG MUNCHEN": Silver metal Edelweiss with raised Stahlhelm style helmet in center. Black work lettering, *10 Reichsfrontsoldatentag Munchen 1929*. 35mm. Pb. Mint cond. $82.00

TINNIE "1930 DEUTSCHER TURNERBUND BUNDESTURNFEST INNSBRUCK": Large brass badge with mobile swastika & large shield having crowned Prussian style eagle. Ornate oak leave design to bottom left. Open work disc with incised lettering. Early *Kampfzeit* badge in superb condition. Pb.

Approx. 65mm size. Mint cond. $100.00

TINNIE "1930 NSDAP PFALZ-GAUTAG KAISERSLAUTERN": 35x25mm. Pb. Stamped metal with bronzed finish. Has sunset in center with swastika above. Above avg. cond. $50.00

"1930 NSDAP SCHLAGETER DUSSELDORF AM REIN"

TINNIE "1930 NSDAP SCHLAGETER DUSSELDORF AM REIN": 40x30mm. Pb. Stamped metal with gilded finish. Has likeness of man kneeling in front of post with hands tied. Has early party eagle design. Above avg. cond. $85.00

TINNIE "1930 STAFFELSTEIN 800 JAHRFEIER": Dark silver finish. Pb. Above avg. cond. $30.00

TINNIE "1931 NSDAP GAUTAG SUD HANNOVER BRAUNSCHWEIG": Stamped metal rectangular construction. Bronze finish. 30x50mm. Stylized lion standing in profile on two columns with horizontal swastika below. Full inscription *Gautag 21.22 Februar 1931. Sud Hannover Braunschweig NSDAP*. Mint cond. $118.00

TINNIE "1931 SALZBURG JUGENDTREFFEN DES DEUTSCHEN TURNERBUNDES": 30x60mm stamped brass/bronze rectangle with moble 4F logo over castle & wording to border. Flag-bearer center with youth behind & title below. Pb & well done with faint maker. Exc. cond. $139.00

TINNIE "1931/32 FRAUENSCHAFT GAU HESSEN-NASSAU": Stamped nonmagnetic disc with silver finish, mobile swastika & Pb. Near mint cond. .. $55.00

TINNIE "1932 BRAUNSCHWEIG REICHS TAGS WAHL": 50x35mm. Stamped metal with bronzed finish. Pb. Has likeness of lion with buildings in background with Swastika & wolves hook below. Above avg. cond. $100.00

TINNIE "1932 FLUGTAG
BRAUNSCHWEIG": Rectangular
stamped metal with matte silver finish.
Flying style eagle with swastika & view of
factories in background. *NS Flugtag
1932. Braunschweig*. 30x35mm. Mint
cond. $40.00

"1932 HITLER-WOCHE OSTPREUSSEN"

TINNIE "1932 HITLER-WOCHE
OSTPREUSSEN": 40x30mm. Pb.
Stamped metal style with gilded finish.
Has the likeness of a sword & swastika
with a rayed background. Above avg.
cond. $65.00

TINNIE "1932 HJ SACHSISCHEN
FRUHJAHRS-OFFENSIVE": 24x39mm
stamped magnetic gray rectangle. Hand-
held swastika flag over title. Pb has been
resoldered. Avg. cond. $59.00

TINNIE "1932 JW V GOETHE": Gilt finish
with profile bust of man. Pb. Above avg.
cond. $30.00

TINNIE "1932 KREISTURNFEST
PFALZISCHES NEUSTADT AD HDT":
Bronze finish with *DT* sun over building
scene. Pb. Near mint cond. $30.00

TINNIE "1932 NS TREFFEN
MITTELDEUTSCHES DESSAU":
42x42mm. Pb. Stamped. Cross shaped
with party eagle & statue of Frederick the
Great. Above avg. cond. $50.00

TINNIE "1932 SA TREFFEN
DUSSELDORF": Silver finish with
Schlageter cross superimposed on
swastika sun. Pb. Rare early tinnie.
Fading. Above avg. cond. $90.00

TINNIE "1933 BRAUNE MESS TRIER":
Diamond pattern. Brass finish. View of
exhibition hall. Swastika at bottom.
Braune Messe 1933 Trier. Pb. 25x40mm.
Mint cond. $40.00

TINNIE "1933 BRAUNE MESSE SCHAFT
ARBEIT": 30x30mm brown bakelite body
with raised yellow Hitler head profile
center & title border. Pb with maker

Bakelite Berlin & stamped *019960*. Near
mint cond. $70.00

TINNIE "1933 BRAUNE MESSE
WIESBADEN": Party pattern political
eagle in half wreath with raised lineal
inscription. Good details to body, wreath
& swastika. Raised inscription *Braune
Messe Wiesbaden 1933*. Pb. 35x38mm.
Mint cond. $40.00

TINNIE "1933 ERNTEDANKFEST
ORTSGRUPPE BILLSTEDT": Stamped
metal. Triangular with red, black, silver
finish. Rising swastika with barley
extending from body. Silvered border with
raised inscription. *Erntedankfest 1 Okt.
1933. Ortsgruppe Billstedt*. Pb.
45x45mm. Near mint cond. $40.00

TINNIE "1933 FLUGWOCHE FURTH
PFINGSTEN": Silver finish with plane
superimposed on a swastika. Pb. Maker
marked. Above avg. cond. $43.00

TINNIE "1933 FUR FRIEDE UND
GLEICHBERECHTIGUNG ICH STIMME
MIT": 35x35mm. Stamped. Pb. Bronzed
finish with red painted details. Has
likeness of swastika with JA! superimposed. Above avg. cond. $50.00

"1933 GAUTREFFEN ERFURT"

TINNIE "1933 GAUTREFFEN ERFURT":
42x50mm stamped dark silver eagle
holding swastika with title. Pb. Some age
darkening. Near mint cond. $50.00

TINNIE "1933 GIETS-AUFMARSCH
BRAUNE MESSE OSNABRUCK":
40x30mm. Pb. Stamped metal type with a
silvered finish. Hmkd. Above avg.
cond. $66.00

TINNIE "1933 GRENZLAND TREFFEN
KARLSRUHE": 26x50mm stamped brass
rectangle with party eagle to top. Title
center with griffen. Pb with maker. Near
mint cond. $50.00

TINNIE "1933 HITLER QUOTE": Gilt finish
with NSBO insignia & 1st type Political
eagle. Reads *Es Wird Kunftig Nur Noch
Einen Adel Geben Adel Der Arbeit Adolf
Hitler 1933*. Gilt finish. Pb. Near mint
cond. $40.00

TINNIE "1933 HITLERTAG BERSENBRUCK": Interesting badge issued for a visit of Hitler to the town. Metallic badge with free standing political eagle at top, gray finish. Shield with oak leaf border & raised lettering, *Hitler Tag. Bersenbruck. 24.9.1933.* Pb. 40x45mm. Mint cond. $68.00

TINNIE "1933 HJ FEST DER JUGEND" 30x48mm stamped metal, Pb. Reads *1. Fest der Jugend 24. Juni 1933* with likeness of camp fire below the party eagle. Near mint cond. $40.00

TINNIE "1933 HJ FRANKEN OSTMARK TREFFEN NUERNBERG": 26x45mm solid metal, Pb, hallmarked, reads *1. Franken Ostmark Treffen Nuernberg 22-23 7. 1933* with likeness of half eagle under banner depicting swastika & *H J* design. Near mint cond. $40.00

"1933 HJ GEBIETS JUGEND-TAG DUSSELDORF SCHLAGETER"

TINNIE "1933 HJ GEBIETS JUGEND-TAG DUSSELDORF SCHLAGETER": Stamped brass rectangle 30x50mm. Traces of gold finish to eagle swastika, cross & title. Pb with maker name. Above avg. cond. $50.00

TINNIE "1933 HJ MUNCHEN": 28x51mm heavy bronze shield. Raised party-eagle over monument with title below. Pb with maker. High quality badge. Near mint cond. $65.00

TINNIE "1933 HJ NORDSEE GEBIETSTREFFEN BREMEN 1933": Stamped brass oval with silver finish showing light wear. Galleon center with swastika sail & title below. Pb. Above avg. cond. $29.00

TINNIE "1933 HJ THURINGEN RUDOLSTADT": 30x40mm stamped brass shield with eagle holding HJ-diamond center & title below. Dark finish. Pb. Avg. cond. $65.00

TINNIE "1933 HJ WIR SIND DIE BAUHERRN D.3.REICHES UNTERBONN VII STUTTGART": 40x20mm. Stamped. Pb. Bronzed finish. Shield shaped. Has HJ flag flying over town. Above avg. cond. $136.00

"1933 HUYSBURG-TREFFEN"

TINNIE "1933 HUYSBURG-TREFFEN": 35x30mm. Pb. Stamped metal. Finish has turned gray. In shape of early party eagle. Above avg. cond. $50.00

TINNIE "1933 JUGENDTREFFEN WILHELMSHAVEN L.V.WESEREMS V.D.A.": 34x50mm stamped brass oval. Swastika center with flag & oath hand. Title border. Pb. Avg. cond. $56.00

TINNIE "1933 KREIS TREFFEN MITTWEIDA": Beautiful metallic badge in matte & subdued silver with free standing eagle clasping large swastika in right talon. Fine details to body with good clear head profile. Raised lettering on bottom, *Kreis Treffen Mittweida. 21. 22. Okt. 1933.* Pb. 35x50mm. Mint cond. $42.00

TINNIE "1933 KREISPARTEITAG BERGHEIM": Shield shaped in silvered finish with large radiant swastika: double side columns: view of factory & power lines at bottom. Full inscription, *Kreisparteitag Bergheim 1933.* 30x40mm. Pb. Mild age darkening only. Avg. cond. $36.00

TINNIE "1933 NS-BEAMTEN TREFFEN GAU WESTFALEN SUD HANNOVER": Antique bronze finish. Free standing Party eagle at top with swastika. Rampant horse at bottom. *NS Beamten Treffen. Gau Westfalen Sud. Hannover. 8 Okt. 1933.* 30x55mm. No pin. Near mint cond. $36.00

TINNIE "1933 NS-HAGO GAUTAGUN ESSEN": Brass pentagon badge with nicely detailed swastika on bottom. Latter has devices representing labor on its body. *Sept. 1933* lettering in art deco style. Raised lettering above swastika,

NS Hago. Gautagung Essen. 48x50mm. Pb. Mint cond. $42.00
TINNIE "1933 NSBD": 35mm x 55mm. bronze metal. Pb. With wreath & labor logo in center. Exc. cond. $50.00
TINNIE "1933 NSBO KREIS ISERLOHN TAG": Pb. stamped brass with reich eagle over wreath & reich labor emblem. Near mint cond. $36.00

"1933 NSDAP GAUTAGUN BEAMTEN WEIMAR"

TINNIE "1933 NSDAP GAUTAGUN BEAMTEN WEIMAR": Stamped brass shield 35x58mm. Raised shield with crowned lion holding swastika, title below & swastika/wreath. Pb. Near mint cond. $50.00
TINNIE "1933 NSDAP KREISTAG KREISSCHULE SEESEN": Large tan oval with blue background to school/building at center, swastika to wreath border & title. *Kreis Gandersheim 17.-18. Juni 1939.* RZM & maker marked. Pb. Nice one. Mint cond. $32.00
TINNIE "1933 NSDAP REICHSPARTEITAG NURNBERG": 30x50mm solid metal, bronze, Pb rewelded, reads *N.S.D.A.P. Reichsparteitag Nuernberg 1933* Winged party eagle with swastika design. Exc. cond. $20.00
TINNIE "1933 NSDAP REICHSPARTEITAG NURNBERG": 3x5" solid brass, Pb, party eagle with swastika/wreath in center, Above avg. cond. $66.00
TINNIE "1933 NSDAP REICHSPARTEITAG NURNBERG": Solid bronze/brass eagle over town with title. Traces of bronze wash. Pb. Above avg. cond. $77.00
TINNIE "1933 NSDAP SACHSENTREFFEN": Gilt finish with monument over swastika. Cut-out detail. Pb. Near mint cond. $50.00

TINNIE "1933 NSKK NSKOV TAG DER PFALZ KRIEGSBESCHADIGTEN": 41x54mm stamped nonmagnetic shield with silver finish. NSKK eagle holding NSKOV logo with title to shield. Pb. Near mint cond. $50.00
TINNIE "1933 NSKOV FAHNENWEIHE KREIS JSERLOHN": 43x30mm. Pb. Stamped metal with bronzed finish. Shield shaped with NSKOV emblem in center. Above avg. cond. $55.00
TINNIE "1933 PIONIERTAG BAD. KONSTANZ": Paper tagged to maker on verso. Flat dull silvered style metallic shield with anchor having oar & bill hook design. *43. Bad. Pionier Tag. Konstanz. 26-28 8 1933.* 30x45mm. Pb. Above avg. cond. $40.00
TINNIE "1933 SA AUF MARSCH LUDENSCHEID": 50x28mm. Pb. Stamped metal with bronzed finish. Has clasping hands & helmet in center of wreath with eagle above. Above avg. cond. $93.00
TINNIE "1933 SA AUF MARSCH LUDENSCHEID": 50x28mm. Pb, Stamped metal with bronzed finish. Has clasping hands & helmet in center of wreath with eagle perched above. Above avg. cond. $55.00
TINNIE "1933 SA BRIGADE APPELL 1933": Metallic body with eagle standing with spread wings at top: double chained swords with SA, Stahlhelm designs on sword guards. Fine deep details. The uppermost circle is inscribed *Leipzig Brigade Appell 19.11. 1933.* Pb. 25x70mm. Mint cond. $43.00
TINNIE "1933 SA BRIGADE AUFMARSCH HANN. OSTIN UELZEN": 28x52mm stamped brass eagle/shield. SA logo to swastika center & title below. Pb. Above avg. cond. $102.00
TINNIE "1933 SA GRUPPE NORDMARK AUFMARSCH KIEL": Silvered shield shaped badge with design of battleship on the ocean in center. Large swastika at bottom of shield. Inscribed *SA Aufmarsch Gruppe Nordmark. 7 Mai 1933. Kiel.* Pb. 35x45mm. Near mint cond. $36.00
TINNIE "1933 SONNWEND PLAUKN": 50mm diam. Bronze finish with gymnastic cross at bottom made of 4 F's. Has swastika around border with center having flames & monument design. Pb. Maker marked. Rare. Near mint cond. $59.00
TINNIE "1933 TAG DES DEUTSCHEN MADELS KOLN": Silver finish. In the form of a runic symbol. Pb. Maker marked. Exc. cond. $40.00

TINNIE "1933 TDDH BRAUNSCHWEIG": 55mm tall red enamel lion with silver title & details. Pb with *C.Poellath,* etc. disc coming loose. Avg. cond. $55.00

TINNIE "1933 TRIER": Stamped metal round circle with 4 corners, reads *Trier 1933*. Exc. cond. $20.00

TINNIE "1933 WERBUNG DEUTSCHE BUHNE KASSEL : Pb. 38mm diam. stamped bronze with laughing mask & lyre In center with swastikas on the border. Mint cond. $20.00

TINNIE "1933 WESTFALEN-TREFFEN DORTMUND": 46x30mm stamped brass. With shield, party eagle, swastika, prancing horse, SA logo & title. Pb. Exc. cond. $30.00

TINNIE "1933/34 DSV REICHS-JUGEND SKI TAG": 40x40mm stamped brass upside-down shield with swastika center, title border & *DSV* logo with ski. Pb with maker. Traces of gold finish to dark brass. Avg. cond. $93.00

"1933/34 WHW HITLER'S DANK GAU WESTFALEN-NORD"

TINNIE "1933/34 WHW HITLER'S DANK GAU WESTFALEN-NORD": 36mm disc with gold finished Hitler profile, title & *Winter-Hilfe 1933-34*. Pb with maker & shows wear. Avg. cond. $55.00

TINNIE "1934 ADOLF HITLER BRUCKE KOBLENZ": 45x30mm. Pb. Stamped metal with bronzed finish. Has likeness of bridge & party eagle above. Above avg. cond. $50.00

TINNIE "1934 AMBERG 900 JAHRE": Stamped silver rectangle with raised details of miner holding pick & lantern. Title above & below with faint Party Eagle design. Maker to back. Tricolor ribbon with silver crown *W* affixed & Pb. Frosted silver finish shows wear. Above avg. cond. $45.00

TINNIE "1934 AUFWARTS AUS EIGENER KRAFT": 25.71mm. Pb. Stamped metal with silver finish. Red & black painted details. Has stylized eagle with rayed sun behind. Near mint cond. $20.00

TINNIE "1934 BEFREITE PFALZ 10 JAHRE": 30x25mm. Pb. Stamped metal with gilded finish shows wear. Avg. cond. $55.00

TINNIE "1934 BNSDJ GAUTAGUNG MUNCHEN": Gilt finish with open center with lawyer assoc eagle. Pb. Rare. Above avg. cond. $145.00

TINNIE "1934 DAF DR LEY DOBELIN": 34x52mm stamped magnetic eagle holding large cogged wheel swastika with title. Bronze finished. Pb. Near mint cond. $90.00

TINNIE "1934 FLIEGER TREFFEN BERLIN": 75mm silvered nickel stamped beautiful full winged eagle with swastika in wreath on chest & 1 Flieger Treffen Berlin 1934 across chest Pb & very early. Above avg. cond. $50.00

TINNIE "1934 FLIGER-TREFFEN BERLIN": 25x73mm stamped nonmagnetic eagle design with bright silver finish. Swastika/ wreath center & title scroll to wings. Pb. Exc. cond. $50.00

TINNIE "1934 FLUGZEUGTAUFE OTTOBEUREN": 38x52mm stamped brass oval with bronze finish. Flight-badge styled with swastika to oak & laurel leaf wreath with glider at top, title center & eagle holding swastika. Pb with maker. Near mint cond. $145.00

TINNIE "1934 FREIKORPS EHREN MALWEIHE DORSTEN": 25x36mm stamped dark brass body. Large swastika to helmeted profile head, oak leaves & title below with *Lichtschlag u.Loewenfeld*. Pb. Exc. cond. $66.00

TINNIE "1934 GAU HALLE MERSEBURG MEIN SCHWUR DEM FUHRER": Stamped brass/bronze shield with title border & swastika center with hand held sword. Pb. Avg. cond. $45.00

TINNIE "1934 GAUPARTEITAG WURTTENBERG HOHENZOLLEN STUTTGARD": Pb. 29mm stamped brass disk with Nazi flag & raised right hand in center. Mint cond. $20.00

TINNIE "1934 GRENZLAND KUNDGEBUNG": Diamond pattern with stylized eagle standing on vertical swastika. Brass metallic finish. Raised lettering on border *Grenzland Kundgebung. Weil am Rhein. 3 Mai 1934*. Pb 36x36mm. Mint cond. $40.00

TINNIE "1934 HEIMATWOCHE STEGLIRER": 38.73x23.89mm. Stamped metal with bronzed finish. Has tower & building in center with swastika at bottom. Pb. Mint cond. $36.00

TINNIE "1934 HJ AUFMARSCH HAM-BURG": 35x45mm stamped metal, Pb, design. *H.J. Aufmarsch Hamburg*

Einweihung der Jug. Herberge Hein Godenwind 8 April 1934 with likeness of Viking ship on royal-blue background. Exc. cond. $40.00

"1934 HJ BLUT UND EHRE LOBERBANNAUFMARSCH HAGEN"

TINNIE "1934 HJ BLUT UND EHRE LOBERBANNAUFMARSCH HAGEN": 33x55mm stamped brass shield. HJ-diamond to oak tree, title border & *Oberbann Sauerland* below. Pb. Nice early quality. Near mint cond. ... $145.00

TINNIE "1934 HJ BURG NAMSTEIN": 25x51mm stamped brass metal shield with knight helmet over crossed swords with single rune at base. Pb. Above avg. cond. $74.00

TINNIE "1934 HJ DAF REICHS BERUFS WETTKAMPF DER DEUTSCHEN JUNGEND": 27x37mm solid bronze shield, HJ-diamond center & title border. Pb & maker. Above avg. cond. ... $50.00

TINNIE "1934 HJ GEBIET 13 AUFMARSCH": 20x69mm stamped metal, Pb, reads *Tag der Hunderttausend Aufmarch der HJ Gebiet 13, 25/26 8. 1934.* Near mint cond. $30.00

TINNIE "1934 HJ SAAR WESTMARK KOBLENZ 1934": 35x25mm. Pb. Stamped metal with bronzed finish. Above avg. cond. $20.00

TINNIE "1934 HJ TREFFEN": 32x49mm stamped nonmagnetic shield with frosted silver finish. Title over castle with HJ diamond & lion shield to gateway. Pb. Near mint cond. $145.00

TINNIE "1934 HJ": 20x30mm diamond shape, white plastic, Pb, *21 Juni 1934* in red fields. Black swastika in center. Near mint cond. $20.00

TINNIE "1934 KDF SEEFAHRT MONTE OLIVIA": 35mm round stamped metal with ocean liner center & wording. Pb. Hmkd. Avg. cond. $23.00

TINNIE "1934 KULTUR-WOCHE ROSTOCKER": Pb. 45 x 33mm rectangu-

lar stamped brass dated at top *10-17 Juni 1934*. Viking ship theme. Above avg. cond. $44.00

TINNIE "1934 KURHESSISCHER-KRIEGSOPFERTAG KASSEL": Stamped white sheet metal design with antique finish. 38mm diam. Pb. Has NSKOV sword & Iron Cross with swastika & buildings. Near mint cond. $20.00

"1934 NIEDERSACHSEN-TAG BRAUNSCHWEIG

TINNIE "1934 NIEDERSACHSEN-TAG BRAUNSCHWEIG": Worn silver finish to stamped lion with Party flag & title. Pb. Above avg. cond. $29.00

TINNIE "1934 NSDAP PARTEITAG HANNOVER": Stamped shield with bronze finish, horse to top, title center, swastika below & border *Gau Sud Hannover Braunschweig.* Pb. Above avg. cond. $27.00

TINNIE "1934 NSDFBST LUNEN": 40x30mm. Pb. Stamped metal with gilded finish. Emblem in center on shield with oak leaf. Above avg. cond. $55.00

TINNIE "1934 NSKK AUFMARSCH NIENBURG": 38x45mm stamped metal tinnie, Pb, *2 u. 3. Juni Aufmarsch 1934 Nienburg W.* with likeness of Party eagle, swastika over city. Near mint cond. $72.00

TINNIE "1934 REICHSKRIEGERTAG KASSEL": 25x35mm silvered brass oval with crossed flags, Nazi & other over building Pb Near mint cond. $20.00

TINNIE "1934 REICHSTAGUNG DEUTSCHE CHRISTEN": 45x30mm. Pb. Stamped metal with bronzed finish. Above avg. cond. $95.00

TINNIE "1934 SA BRIGADE 35 AUFMARSCH LEIPZIG": 50x40mm. Pb. Stamped metal with bronzed finish. Has SA emblem in center with oak leaves. Above avg. cond. $50.00

TINNIE "1934 SA BRIGADE 35 AUFMARSCH LEIPZIG": Large stamped disc with point to lower edge. SA logo center with oak & laurel leaves. Title border & at point. Copper finish shows age. Pb. Above avg. cond. $40.00

"1934 SA BRIGADE TREFFEN ERFURT OSTERN"

TINNIE "1934 SA BRIGADE TREFFEN ERFURT OSTERN": 4x7mm stamped brass, pb, sword design with SA logo. *Brigadetreffen Erfurt Ostern 34.* Exc. cond. $75.00

TINNIE "1934 SA BRIGADE TREFFEN ERFURT OSTERN": Stamped 70mm tall sword with age to frosted silver finish. Title to blade, SA logo to crossguard with oak leaves & swastika background. Pb. Above avg. cond. $49.00

TINNIE "1934 SA BRIGADE TREFFEN RUDOLSTADT": 51x62mm stamped brass with frosted silver finish showing wear. SA logo to oak leaf wreath with large swastika center having title to arms. Pb. Avg. cond. $65.00

TINNIE "1934 SA SACHSEN": Dark silver finish with large SA logo in oak leaf wreath over Saxon shield. Pb. Above avg. cond. $30.00

TINNIE "1934 SA SPORTFEST NURNBERG ALLES FUR DEUTSCHLAND BRIGADE 78": 40x25mm. Stamped. Pb. Silvered finish. Has likeness of SA dagger, town & SA emblem. Above avg. cond. $59.00

TINNIE "1934 SA STANDARTE 89 AUFMARSCH SCHWERIN": 28x48mm stamped brass shield with frosted-silver finish. Eagle holding SA logo, title center & knight shield below. Pb. Above avg. cond. $72.00

TINNIE "1934 SA STURMBANN VI STANDARTE R63 BAD HOMBURG SPORTFEST": Silver finish with spread winged eagle & SA logo. Pb. Above avg. cond. $90.00

"1934 SAARKUNDEBUNG KARLSRUBE"

TINNIE "1934 SAARKUNDEBUNG KARLSRUBE": 35x40mm. Pb. Stamped metal with bronzed finish. Above avg. cond. $55.00

TINNIE "1934 TAG DER ARBEIT": Bronze finish. Pb. Maker marked. Near mint cond. $20.00

TINNIE "1934 TREUEKUNGEBUND BEAMTEN RHINELAND WESTFALEN DORTMUND": Pb. 45 x 27mm stamped brass shield with swastika imposed on reich eagle. Above avg. cond. $36.00

TINNIE "1934 TREUESCHWUR GAU MAINFRANKEN": Gilt finish with hand holding 2 fingers up superimposed on a swastika. Pb. Maker marked. Above avg. cond. $50.00

TINNIE "1934 WESTMARK HJ SAAR KOBLENZ": Fading to bronze finish. In the form of a runic symbol. Pb. Avg. cond. $20.00

TINNIE "1934 WURZBURG": 20x75mm stamped brass wing design with HJ diamond to eagle-head center & title below. Pb. Above avg. cond. $50.00

TINNIE "1935 ARNSBERG DEUTSCHLAND ERWACHE": 31x51mm stamped magnetic shield with bronze finish. Standard center with title. Pb. Near mint cond. $76.00

TINNIE "1935 DRL BEFREIUNGS GAUFEST SAARBRUCKEN": Solid alum. oval with knight slaying dragon & title around border. Pb with maker. Above avg. cond. $24.00

TINNIE "1935 GAU TAG HESSEN-NASSAU DARMSTADT": 58mm oval with laced leather trim, embossed title & stylized eagle. Pb. Mint cond. $50.00

TINNIE "1935 GAU THING KOBLENZ TRIER": Silver finish with spread winged eagle at top. Pb. Maker marked. Above avg. cond. $20.00

TINNIE "1935 GAUTAG GAU OSTHANNOVER": Plastic. Red & silver finish with nude man on horseback. Pb. Above avg. cond. $20.00

TINNIE "1935 GAUTAG HANNOVER SUD HANNOVER BRAUNSCHWEIG: 1.75" diam. Pb. Stamped metal with silvered finish. Has crossed horses heads in center with swastika in center. Above avg. cond. $20.00

TINNIE "1935 GAUTAG HESSEN-NASSAU DARMSTADT": Leather. 60mm oval with laced border & stamped Nazi eagle center. Pb. Above avg. cond. $27.00

TINNIE "1935 GAUTAG SUD HANNOVER BRAUNSCHWEIG": 42.93mm diam. Stamped metal with silvered finish-has turned gray. Pb. Half of pin has broken off. Has likeness of crossed stylized horses heads with swastika above. Mint cond $20.00

TINNIE "1935 GROSSFLUGTAG DRESDEN-HELLER": Clay. 36mm diam. body with raised title border & planes in flight over town scene. Pb mount with 3 rim prongs covers most of reverse with wording & maker trademark crossed-swords. Near mint cond. $55.00

TINNIE "1935 HANS SCHEMM HALTETEINAN DER DIE TREUE", PLASTIC: Wear to silver finish. Pb. Avg. cond. $30.00

TINNIE "1935 HEIMATFEST SCHLESSBUSCH": Stamped shield shaped badge with antique matte gold finish. Wreath, swastika & heraldic design in center: Raised border lettering reads *July, 1935*. Some wear to finish on highlights only. Pb. 40x30mm. One small hook to retainer spring broken. Avg. cond. $36.00

TINNIE "1935 HJ DAF 1935 REICHS BERUFS WETTKAMPF DER DEUTSCHEN JUGEND": Stamped bronze/brass shield with title, HJ diamond & hammer with leaves. Pb with maker. Above avg. cond. $50.00

TINNIE "1935 HJ NORDSEE GEBIELSTREFFEN BREMAN": 43mm stamped oval with sailing ship with 3 sails & center has a swastika. Pb. Avg. cond. $40.00

TINNIE "1935 HJ NORDSEE GEBIETSTREFFEN BREMEN": Gilt finish with sailing ship with swastika on main sail. Pb. Above avg. cond. $50.00

TINNIE "1935 HJ SPORTFEST": 26x56mm solid alum. HJ diamond & title to proficiency-badge design. Pb with maker. No traces of colored-finish. Above avg. cond. $76.00

TINNIE "1935 HJ SPORTFEST": 26x56mm solid alum. HJ diamond & title to proficiency-badge design. Pb with maker. Worn red & black paint to diamond. Exc. cond. $59.00

TINNIE "1935 HJ SPORTFEST": 26x56mm solid alum. with large diamond to proficiency badge with title. Pb with maker. Near mint cond. $50.00

TINNIE "1935 HJ ZELTLAGER GEBIET 13": Silver finish with eagle head over HJ armband design. Pb. Maker marked. Exc. cond. $28.00

TINNIE "1935 JIK BERLIN": Silver finish. Pb. Above avg. cond. $20.00

TINNIE "1935 KIEL NORDMARK VORAN": 45x35mm. Pb. Stamped. Bronzed finish. In shape of swastika & sword in side of wreath. Party eagle at top. Above avg. cond. $50.00

TINNIE "1935 KREISBAUERNTAG GERA": Gilt finish with Reichsnarstand insignia (barley shaft & sword superimposed on a swastika). Pb. Near mint cond. ... $20.00

TINNIE "1935 KREISPARTEITAG SPATENSTICK 3. THING PLAT 3 P.R. HOLLAND": Silver finish with spread winged eagle superimposed on building scene. Pb. Maker marked. Above avg. cond. $25.00

TINNIE "1935 MUNSTER WESTFALENHALLE REGIMENTS APPELL": 31x44mm silver painted shield shaped with *13* in center. Pb. Mint cond. $35.00

TINNIE "1935 NORDMARK VORAN KIEL": 45x35mm. Pb. Stamped. Silvered finish. Pb. Swastika & sword inside of wreath with spread winged Eagle above. Above avg. cond. $50.00

TINNIE "1935 NORMARK VORAN KIEL": Stamped gray metal Nazi eagle on wreath & swastika. Pb. Some light wear to the finish. 35mm wide & 47mm high. Near mint cond. $36.00

TINNIE "1935 NSDAP 10 JAHR NAUNHOF": Stamped metal with bronze applied finish. Semi-rectangular with view of medieval wall & tower, swastika below. Wreathed at top. Raised inscription, *10 Jahre NSDAP Naunhof. 9-10 Marz 1935*. Pb. 30x44mm. Mint cond. $42.00

TINNIE "1935 NSDAP GAU BADEN 10 JAHRE KAMPF": Stamped bronze finished shield with Party Eagle, title & sword running through back. Pb. Near mint cond. $32.00

TINNIE "1935 NSDAP GAU BADEN 10 JAHRE": 30x59mm bronze shield shaped with Sword & center Nazi eagle. Pb with some patina. Avg. cond. $32.00

TINNIE "1935 NSDAP GAUTAG WESTFALEN SUD BOCHUM": 45x30mm. Pb. Stamped. Bronzed finish. Shield shaped with spread winged eagle perches on swastika. Above avg. cond. $58.00

TINNIE "1935 NSDAP GAUTAG WESTFALLEN SUD BOCHUM": Stamped brass colored metal design wire. Pd. No maker mark, 32mm wide & 45mm hIgh. PatIna highlight to the metal. Mint cond. $35.00

TINNIE "1935 NSDAP KREISTAG BONN": Stamped one piece gray metal with hallmarks. Rectangular badge with free standing Party eagle at top: View of medieval bridge in center. Raised lettering, *3 u. 4. 8. 1935. Kreistag der NSDAP Bonn.* Pb. 25x48mm. Mint cond. $36.00

TINNIE "1935 NSDAP TAG DER NSDAP KREIS GROSS=FRANKFURT": Stamped steel oval with faded copper finish to Party eagle center, town scene & title. Pb. Avg. cond. $32.00

TINNIE "1935 NSDAP THURINGEN": 2" size. Stamped metal with silvered finish, turned to gray. Pb. In shape of eagle with swastika, shield & wreath. Above avg. cond. $27.00

TINNIE "1935 RDR RUND FUNKTAGUNG BERLIN": This is the 1935 Radio Asso. Annual meeting in Berlin. Gold eagles on red 57x35 mm. Pb. Above avg. cond. $45.00

TINNIE "1935 SA BRIGADE 57 APPELL GOTTINGEN": Silver finish with spread winged eagle perched on a dagger superimposed on an SA logo in oak leaf wreath. Pb. Above avg. cond. $40.00

TINNIE "1935 SA GRUPPE NIEDERRHEIN REICHS WETTKAMPFTAGE": Stamped metal with gold applied finish. SA logo & sports badge design at top: Raised righting on lower section writing reads *Reichs Wettkampftage der SA Gruppe Niederrhein. 28-30 Aug. 1935.* 55x35mm. Pb. Near mint cond. $36.00

TINNIE "1935 SA GRUPPE NIEDERSACHSEN WETTKAMPFTAGE HANNOVER": *Wettkampftage der SA Gruppe Niedersachsen 6-8 Sept. 1935 Hannover* 35x48mm gray metal. Pb. With likeness of crossed sea horses on top. Exc. cond. $40.00

TINNIE "1935 SA STANDART WIESBADEN FUR ERHOLUNGSBEDURFTIGE VOLKSGENASSEN": Darkening to silver finish. In the form of an SA logo disc. Pb. Above avg. cond $68.00

TINNIE "1935 SA STANDARTE R.131 SPORTFEST LUDENSCHEID": 40x30mm. Pb. Stamped metal with dark bronzed finish. Has SA emblem in center

with swastika on either side. Above avg. cond. $164.00

TINNIE "1935 SAAR": Stamped metal. Rectangular. Dark antique red bronze finish. Raised design of man raising Nazi national flag with motto *Frei ist die Saar, 3/35.* Very well made. 30x43mm. Pb. Mint cond. $36.00

"1935 SEEFAHRT 1ST NOT TAG DER DEUTSCHEN SEEFAHRT"

TINNIE "1935 SEEFAHRT 1ST NOT TAG DER DEUTSCHEN SEEFAHRT": 42x46mm alum. oval with the party eagle at top, sailing ship center & title border. Pb with maker. Above avg. cond. $50.00

TINNIE "1935 SEEFAHRT IST NOT": Silver finish. Pb. Maker marked. Near mint cond. $20.00

TINNIE "1935 SOLDATENTAG DETROIT USA": 40x20mm. Pb. Stamped metal with a silvered finish. Has bust of soldier wearing helmet. Above avg. cond. $150.00

TINNIE "1935 STAHLHELM GAU TREFFEN DORTMUND": White metal rectangular badge with high silver finish. 30x50mm. Pb. Slight vaulting. Oak leaf & laurel flanking Stalhelm crest with helmet & swastika. Upper & lower bars inscribed *Gau Treffen Dortmund 6-7 April 1935.* Mint cond. $90.00

TINNIE "1935 TAG DER ARBEIT": Silver finish. Pb. Maker marked. Above avg. cond. $20.00

TINNIE "1935 TREUE UM TREUE SAAR": Gilt finish. Pb. Above avg. cond. . $20.00

TINNIE "1935 WIEDERSEHENSFEIER DER ALTEN PARTEIGENOSSEN GAU WESTFALENSUD": 45x30mm. Alum. Pb. Hmkd. Has spread winged eagle perched on wreathed swastika. Above avg. cond. $68.00

TINNIE "1935/36 KDF GAU FRANKEN"

TINNIE "1935/36 KDF GAU FRANKEN":
White metal badge with matte finish.
30x50mm. Pb. Design of man in walking
outfit standing above NSG swastika pin
wheel. Lower raised inscription *NSG
Kraft durch Freude. Gau Franken. Winter.
1935/36.* Tietse, Franken 34-02. Mint
cond. $50.00

TINNIE "1935/36 WHW DANK DEM
HELFER GAU ESSEN": Silver-gray finish
with sword superimposed on crossed
hammers. Pb. Near mint cond. ... $25.00

TINNIE "1935/36 WHW GAU ESSEN":
Silver-gray finish with factory scene. Pb.
Near mint cond. $20.00

TINNIE "1936 DEUTSCHES
JUGENDFEST": Bronze finish. Pb. Above
avg. cond. $20.00

TINNIE "1936 DEUTSCHES
JUGENDFEST": Copper finish. Pb.
Above avg. cond. $40.00

TINNIE "1936 DEUTSCHLAND ERWACHE
STANDARTENTAG OLDENBURG":
32x50mm stamped metal, standard
design with swastika. Red on gray color.
Pb. Reads *Oldenburg Deutschland
Erwache Standartentag 1936.* Near mint
cond. $49.00

TINNIE "1936 DJH RHEINLAND 25
AHLECK 25 JAHRE": Alum. shield with
nice castle details over title. Pb with
maker. Near mint cond. $27.00

TINNIE "1936 FRANKENTAG": Alum. eagle
shield 32x45mm, Pb, maker, Above avg.
cond. $50.00

TINNIE "1936 FREIHEIT UND BROT": Gilt
finish. Stickpin mount. Above avg.
cond. $20.00

TINNIE "1936 FRONTSOLDATEN UND
KRIEGSOPFER EHRENTAG
HEILBRONN": 30x40mm octagonal gray
metal, Pb. Marked design. *4.Schabischer
Frontsoldaten und Kriegsopfer Ehrentag
Heilbronn 1936* around border with town
& mountains in center. Exc.
cond. $50.00

TINNIE "1936 FUNKAUSSTELLUNG
BERLIN MENDE RADIO"

TINNIE "1936 FUNKAUSSTELLUNG
BERLIN MENDE RADIO": 35mm diam.
Pb. Grey plastic. Has likeness of radio in
center. Above avg. cond. $50.00

TINNIE "1936 GAU APPELL SACHSEN":
Large aluminum badge with hallmarks.
Mobile sun swastika design in center with
upright Viking short sword. Pseudo runic
lettering on edge, Gau Appell Sachsen
1936. Pb. 40x58mm. Near mint
cond. $36.00

TINNIE "1936 GAUAPPELL SACHSEN":
Aluminum 40x60mm. Sunwheel swastika
in center & Viking sword design. Pseudo-
runic lettering on rim. Reads *Gau Appel
Sachsen 1936.* Hallmarked. Pb. Unusual
design. Mint cond. $36.00

TINNIE "1936 GAUTAG HESSEN NASSAU
FRANKFURT AM MAIN": Silver finish.
Pb. Maker marked. Avg. cond. ... $20.00

TINNIE "1936 GAUTAG HILDESHEIM SUD
HANNOVER BRAUNSCHWEIG": Dark
silver finish. Knight with shield with
crossed stylized horse heads superimposed on a mobile swastika. Pb. Near
mint cond. $50.00

TINNIE "1936 GAUTAG HILDESHEIM":
42x60mm. Large shield shaped badge.
Finish shows age darkness. Mobile
swastika with armored knight & lance
standing with shield having Hannoverian
design. Incised lettering. *Gautag 1936
Hildesheim. Sud Hannover
Braunschweig. 12/14 Juni.* Pb. Avg.
cond. $40.00

TINNIE "1936 GAUTAG KOBLENZ TRIER":
Silver finish with some pitting. Pb. Avg.
cond. $50.00

TINNIE "1936 GAUTAG KURMARK
POTSDAM": Matte silver finish in form of
Tirol eagle with swastika on chest. Pb.
Above avg. cond. $50.00

TINNIE "1936 GAUTREFFEN DER
BAYRISCHEN OSTMARK": Porcelain.
White shield with raised eagle center
holding swastika/wreath & gold title
border. Pb shows glue repair & maker

LHS Bavaria etc. with lion. Above avg. cond. $46.00

"1936 HEIMATFEST STOTERITZ"

TINNIE "1936 HEIMATFEST STOTERITZ": 50x32mm. Pb. Stamped metal with gilded finish. Has likeness of clock tower with swastika in background. Above avg. cond. $55.00

TINNIE "1936 HJ GEBIET 7 NORDSEE SPORTTAG JADESTAEDTE": 30x50mm stamped bronze like metal design, Pb reads *Sporttage Gebiet 7 Nordsee Jadestaedte 29-30 Aug. 1936* with likeness of HJ diamond over ship in center. Near mint cond. $40.00

TINNIE "1936 HJ HOCHLAND LAGER": 30x37mm solid shield with copper finish. Tents with mountains at top, title center & HJ diamond to edelweiss at point. Pb. Near mint cond. $55.00

TINNIE "1936 HOMBURG PFALZ SAAR": 31x41mm stamped shield, bronzed finish of Nazi eagle over a tree & 2 hands clasp at bottom. January 18,1936. Pb Near mint cond. $32.00

TINNIE "1936 KDF URLAUBREISE GAU WESTFALLEN": Bevo tinnie design with metal frame. Wire Pd. Has some patina to the metal frame Above avg. cond. $36.00

TINNIE "1936 KREIS APPELL DER NSDAP MOERS": Fading to bronze finish. Pb. Avg. cond. $20.00

TINNIE "1936 KYFFHAUSERBUND FUHRER-TAG LANDESVERBAND WESTFALEN": Brass finish. Rectangular. 25x50mm. Inverted sword with Kyffhauser Monument logo on blade & heraldic shields of Westphalia. Radiant sunburst behind sword. Inscribed *Landesverband Westfalen. Fuhrer Tag 65. 13-15.6. 1936. Bottrop.* Pb. Mint cond. $55.00

TINNIE "1936 LANDESBUND THURINGEN KAMERADSCHAFTSBUND DEUTSCHER": 55x35mm. Stamped. Pb. Bronzed finish. Has polize insignia.

Reads *Polizeibeamten Arnstadt.* Above avg. cond. $85.00

TINNIE "1936 MIT KRAFT DURCH FREUDE IN OBERBAYERN": Gilt finish with man & woman with cogwheel with swastika. Pb. Near mint cond. $25.00

TINNIE "1936 NORDMARK-TREFFEN": 45x35mm. Pb. Alum. Hmkd. Has likeness of flying eagle perched on wreathed swastika, NSKK & SA man. Above avg. cond. $50.00

TINNIE "1936 NSDAP REICHSPARTEITAG": 40mm diam. gray metal, Pb. *W.Redo Saarlautern* maker marked. Avg. cond. $50.00

TINNIE "1936 NSKK TAGDES MOTORGR.HESSEN": 40x35mm. Stamped. Pb. Bronzed finish. Has NSKK emblem with three buildings above. Above avg. cond. $55.00

TINNIE "1936 PASSAU KREISBAUERNTAG": 40x30mm. Stamped. Pb. Gilted finish. Shield shaped. Above avg. cond. $50.00

TINNIE "1936 RDB BEAMTEN KUNDGEBUNG HERMANN NEEF KASSEL": Large green plastic shield with raised title & RDB eagle. *R.D.B Gau Kurhessen* below eagle. Pb with maker. Exc. cond. $27.00

TINNIE "1936 REICHS KRIEGER TAG KASSEL": Pb. 35mm diam. stamped & silvered with Reich eagle over shield & Kyfhauser bund emblem. Near mint cond. $20.00

TINNIE "1936 REICHSAUTOBAHN 1000KM": Stamped silver winged/wheel with title & party eagle at top. Resoldered stickpin instead of normal pin. Avg. cond. $22.00

TINNIE "1936 REICHSKRIEGER-KYFFHAUSERBUND LANDESVERVAND WESTFALEN": 50x25mm. Pb. Stamped metal with bronzed finish. Above avg. cond. $50.00

TINNIE "1936 REICHSPARTEITAGES WEIMAR": 49mm magnetic disc with bronze finish, raised title & *Thuringen Deutschland Erwache* standard. Pb with faint maker. Avg. cond. $60.00

TINNIE "1936 SA BRIGADE 49 SPORTTAG": 30mm stamped metal, Pb. SA logo on black background. Exc. cond. $82.00

TINNIE "1936 SA GRUPPE MITTE MAGDEBURG EINWEIHUNG EHRENMAL": 50mm diam. stamped bronze-like metal, Pb, reads *Einweihung SA Ehrenmahl der Gruppe Mitte Magdeburg 23.2.36* with likeness of three workers supporting party eagle. Near mint cond. $40.00

TINNIE "1936 SA GRUPPE NIEDERSACHSEN WETTKAMPFTAGE BRAUNSCHWEIG": 40mm diam. round, alum. design. Pb. Maker marked *Lehmann & Wundenberg Hannover.* Erected sword with oakleaves & SA logo in center. Border reads *Wettkampftage der SA Gruppe Niedersachsen 26.-27.9.1936 Braunschweig.* Near mint cond. $60.00

"1936 SA GRUPPE NORDSEE TAG BREMEN"

TINNIE "1936 SA GRUPPE NORDSEE TAG BREMEN": 32x45mm oval brass design, pb, maker marked, Lighthouse & SA logo in center. *Tag der SA Gruppe-Nordsee in Bremen 1936* around border. Exc. cond. $70.00

TINNIE "1936 SA GRUPPE NORDSEE TAG BREMEN": 34x45mm solid oval with frosted-silver finish. Title border, SA logo, SA trooper head with kepi & castle/tower at sea. Pb with maker. Near mint cond. $87.00

TINNIE "1936 SA GRUPPE NORDSEE TAG BREMEN": 43x32mm. Oval. Silvered finish. Hmkd. Pb. Design of profile of SA man with lighthouse in sea. SA logo below. Linear inscription, *Tag der SA Gruppe Nordsee in Bremen. 6-7 Juni 1936.* Mint cond. $45.00

TINNIE "1936 SA GRUPPE NORDSEE TAG BREMEN": 45mm tall solid oval with raised details of lighthouse, water, SA trooper head with kepi, SA logo & title border. Darkening to silver finish. Pb with maker. Avg. cond. $25.00

TINNIE "1936 SCHLAGETERTAG": Stamped steel rectangular design with black finish to swastika with sword-hilt, oak leave branch & title. Pb. Above avg. cond. $50.00

TINNIE "1936 TAG DER NATIONALEN SOLIDARITAT NEULAND HALLE ADOLF HITLER KOOG": 40x35mm. Pressed paper. Has printed design. Pb. Above avg. cond. $30.00

TINNIE "1936 TAG DER WEHRMACHT": 35mmx37mm, solid alum. with gold finish & helmeted patriotic soldier head. Pb. Above avg. cond. $47.00

TINNIE "1936 TAUSENDJAHRFEIER STADT CALBE/SAALE": Stamped white metal large badge. 40x55mm. Oak wreath rim with medieval statue & city having radiant swastika in background. Pb. Avg. cond. $45.00

TINNIE "1936 WIR GEHOREN ZUSAMNEN, DANNSRD MIR ALLIC GAUL KURHESSER": 40.68mm diam. Pb. Brown bakelite. Has party eagle in center with shield below that has rampant lion. Reads *1936-37 WHW.* Mint cond. $20.00

"1936/37 KDF GAU FRANKEN"

TINNIE "1936/37 KDF GAU FRANKEN": 20mm diam. alum. disc with *Kraft durch Freude* around border & person on skies in center. Below on scroll *Gau Franken 1936 1937* & swastika in center. Exc. cond. $51.00

TINNIE "1936/37 WHW GAU ESSEN": Silver-gray finish in form of a worker. Pb. Above avg. cond. $20.00

TINNIE "1937 BDM OBERGAU WURTTBG SPORTTAG": Stamped steel rectangle 30x44mm. Bronze finished front & silver back. Pb. Near mint cond. $65.00

TINNIE "1937 BRAUNSCHWEIGER HEIMATFEST": 30x40mm shield design, pb, silver frosted finish with black title marks. Has standing lion over oakleaves in center. Pb. Above avg. cond. .. $50.00

TINNIE "1937 DJH": Silver finish. Pb. In the form of a stylized eagle. Near mint cond. $20.00

TINNIE "1937 GAUTAG SCHLESWIG HOLSTEIN KIEL": Matte-silver finish with spread winged eagle & shield. Pb. Above avg. cond. $50.00

TINNIE "1937 GAUTAG SCHLESWIG-HOLSTEIN KIEL": Stamped shield with large Party Eagle to top, title border &

METAL INSIGNIA

divided shield below. Pb. Above avg.
cond. $32.00
TINNIE "1937 GAUTREFFEN WESTFALEN
NORD:" Plastic. Brown finish with
crossed hammers & crossed sword/
barley shaft superimposed on a swastika.
Pb. Near mint cond. $20.00
TINNIE "1937 HEILIGTUMSFAHRT
AACHEN": Bronze finish. Pb. Above avg.
cond. $20.00

"1937 HJ FEST DER
LEIBESUBUNGEN SAARLAUTERN"

TINNIE "1937 HJ FEST DER
LEIBESUBUNGEN SAARLAUTERN":
40mm diam. Pb. Stamped metal with
bronzed finish. Has early HJ eagle in
center. Above avg. cond. $129.00
TINNIE "1937 KREISTAG AACHEN STADT
LAND": Gilt finish with spread winged
eagle over building scene. Pb. Above
avg. cond. $25.00
TINNIE "1937 KREISTAG MAYEN":
40x30mm. Stamped. Pb. Bronzed finish.
Shield shaped with party eagle. Above
avg. cond. $50.00
TINNIE "1937 KREISTREFFEN
HOLZMINDEN": 60x40mm. Pb. Porcelain
with white glazed finish & painted details.
Has likeness of 3 buildings in center with
mountains in background. Above avg.
cond. $58.00
TINNIE "1937 NSDAP GAUTAG
WURTTEMBERG HOHENZOLLERN
STUTTGART": Mint silver finish with
large stylized eagle & swastika disc over
columns of marching soldiers. Pb. Maker
marked. Mint cond. $50.00
TINNIE "1937 NSDAP HESSENTAG": Red
plastic shield design, 40x45mm, Pb.
spread eagle on top. *Gau Kurhessen 28-
30 Mai Kassel.* Near mint cond. . $30.00
TINNIE "1937 NSDAP KREISTAG BONN":
Complete with old period pin, cord
suspension. Domed pattern with heraldic
shields of Bonn flanking upright sword
with swastika. 50mm size. Raised
Inscription, *Kreistag NSDAP Bonn 1937.*
Mint cond. $55.00

"1937 NSDAP KREISTAG
OBERBERGISCHEN KREISES"

TINNIE "1937 NSDAP KREISTAG
OBERBERGISCHEN KREISES": 41mm
stamped magnetic disc with bronze
finish. Title border, eagle head center,
swastika background & 3 small shields
below. Pb. Near mint cond. $50.00
TINNIE "1937 NSDAP KREISTAG
OBERHAUSEN/RHLD": 50x35mm.
Stamped. Pb. Silvered finish. In shape of
eagle with factory, swastika & crest.
Above avg. cond. $50.00
TINNIE "1937 NSKOV REICHSTREFFEN
BERLIN": Gray. Pb. Maker marked. Avg.
cond. $20.00
TINNIE "1937 NSKOV REICHSTREFFEN
BERLIN": Silver finish with NSKOV
insignia & scene of Brandenburg gate.
Pb. Near mint cond. $50.00
TINNIE "1937 NSKOV REICHSTREFFEN
BERLIN": Stamped light weight metal,
dark gray in color with oxide patina from
age. Wire pin, maker marked *Deschleru
S Munchen* on back. Avg.
cond. $20.00
TINNIE "1937 REICHSAUSSTELLUNG
DUSSELDORF SCHLAGETERSTADT":
Silver finish with hand with hammer
superimposed on a swastika. Pb. Near
mint cond. $20.00
TINNIE "1937 REICHSPARTEITAG": Gray.
Pb. Avg. cond. $20.00
TINNIE "1937 REICHSTREFFEN FRANK-
FURTER": 28x40mm gray metal.
*Reichstreffen der Ehem. Flakwaffe u. des
Luftschutzes* depicts athlete with bow &
arrow over title. Pb. Maker marked.
Above avg. cond. $50.00
TINNIE "1937 SA GRUPPE NIEDERRHEIN
SPORT U. WEHRWETTKAMPFE": 65mm
stamped silvered steel of SA symbol over
sword & in wreath with skyline of city. Pb.
& very impressive SA tinnie. Avg.
cond. $30.00
TINNIE "1937 SA GRUPPE NIEDERRHEIN
SPORT-U.WEHR WETTKAMPFE":

60x45mm. Stamped. Pb. Silvered finish. In shape of SA emblem, sword & wreath. Above avg. cond. $68.00

"1937 SA GRUPPE WESTFALEN SPORTKAMPFTAGE DORTMUND"

TINNIE "1937 SA GRUPPE WESTFALEN SPORTKAMPFTAGE DORTMUND": 46x57mm. Stamped. Nonmagnetic Sports Badge design with title, SA logo & horse to center. Pb. Frosted-silver finish. Exc. cond. $50.00

TINNIE "1937 SA KAMPFSPIELE GERA": 40x27mm. Pb. Brown leather. Hmkd. Has SA emblem & stylized flying eagle. Above avg. cond. $55.00

TINNIE "1937 SA KAMPFSPIELE GERA": Ink hallmarked. Rectangular. Green field with brown flying eagle & SA sports badge. Raised lettering, *SA Kampfspiele. Gera. 1937.* No pin. 28x40mm. Near mint cond. $36.00

TINNIE "1937 SA KAMPSPIELE GERA": Gray rectangle with raised high speed eagle holding SA sports badge & title below. Pb with maker. Above avg. cond. $27.00

TINNIE "1937 SANGERBUNDESFEST BRESLAU": 45.16x29.25 mm Black finish as above with lyre & wording rectangle pin. Pb. & hmkd. Near mint cond. $20.00

TINNIE "1937 SCHAFBERG": 50x30mm. Cutout piece of flat tin with silvered finish & red painted details. Pb. Pb. Above avg. cond. $58.00

TINNIE "1937 STADTISCHE RIEMERSCHMID HANDELSCHULE MUNCHEN": 34x115mm. Orange satin with brown bevo title & Munchen shield with party eagle. Pin & maker at top. Near mint cond. $35.00

TINNIE "1938 BRANDISER HEIMATFEST": Silver-gray finish with town scene. Pb. Maker marked. Near mint cond. ....:......... $20.00

TINNIE "1938 DESSAU GAUTAG MAGDEBURG-ANHALT": 50x35mm. Pb. Alum. Hmkd. Has likeness of party eagle, sword & building. Above avg. cond. $50.00

TINNIE "1938 GAUTAG ESSEN": 30x40mm tin frame with bevo center. Likeness of crossed hammer under sword. Exc. cond. $40.00

TINNIE "1938 GAUTAG LEIPZIG": 40x60mm solid metal, Pb, reads *Gautag 21-22 Mai 1938 Leipzig* with likeness of three sword reading *Ein Volk, Ein Fuehrer, Ein Reich.* Exc. cond. ... $40.00

TINNIE "1938 GROSSDEUTSCHER GAST STATTENTAG WIEN": Dark silver finish with church superimposed on map. Pb. Near mint cond. $40.00

TINNIE "1938 NORDMARK TREFFEN": 45mm diam. Stamped alum. Pb. Has likeness of three flags. Above avg. cond. $50.00

TINNIE "1938 NSDAP ANSBACH 15 JAHRE": Gray. Town scene over mobile swastika. Pb. Avg. cond. $40.00

TINNIE "1938 NSDAP KREISPARTEITAG OFFENBACH": 30x38mm. Pressed russet brown leather shield with party eagle & swastika above sprig of oak leaves. Sides of shield have raised inscription, *Kreis Parteitag der NSDAP. Kreis Offenbach. 14/15 Mai 1938.* Pb. Mint cond. $36.00

TINNIE "1938 NSDAP KREISTAG MECKLENBURG": 30x40mm alum. design. *NSDAP Gau Mecklenburg Kreistag 1938.* Party eagle/swastika over 2 eternal flames. Pb. Maker marked. Near mint cond. $61.00

TINNIE "1938 NSDAP KREISTAG ODENWALD": Gray plastic. 35mm diam. with Nazi eagle in wreath. Pb & hmkd. Mint cond. $36.00

TINNIE "1938 NSDAP KREISTAG": Gray. Pb. Avg. cond. $20.00

TINNIE "1938 NSDAP REICHSPARTEITAG": 40mm diam. bronze, Pb. *Brehmer Markneunkirchen RZM M9/4.* Exc. cond. $50.00

TINNIE "1938 NSKOV REICHSARBEITSTAGUNG NORTHEIM": Gray plastic shield with good details to raised castle, lion, NSKOV logo & title. Pb. Near mint cond. $27.00

TINNIE "1938 REICHSPARTEITAG": Large metallic round badge with copper colored finish. Raised design of two nude men above eagle with swastika & party flag. Hallmarked. Inscribed *1938 Reichsparteitag.* Pb. 40mm. Near mint cond. $37.00

TINNIE "1938 SA GRUPPE FRANKEN KAMPFTAGE": 42mm diam. Alum. Pb. Hmkd. Has swastika, sword & wreath in center. Above avg. cond. $50.00

TINNIE "1938 SA GRUPPE FRANKEN KAMPFTAGE": 43mm solid alum. disc, SA sports badge center & title border. Pb with maker. Near mint cond. $50.00

TINNIE "1938 SA GRUPPE FRANKEN KAMPFTAGE": Silver finish with facsimile SA sports badge in center. Pb. Maker marked. Near mint cond. $25.00

TINNIE "1938 SA GRUPPE HANSA GRUPPENWETTKAMPFE": Gilt finish with SA logo superimposed on sailing ship. Pb. Near mint cond. $59.00

TINNIE "1938 SA GRUPPE HOCHLAND WETTKAMPFE": 40x52mm solid alum. body, SA logo to sword pommel, oak leaf wreath & title border. Pb with maker & RZM. Near mint cond. $50.00

TINNIE "1938 SA GRUPPE KURPFALZ SPORT WETTKAMPF": Plastic. SA logo & oakleaves behind sword in hand. 36mm diam. Pb. Maker marked to *Richard Siepert u. Sohne Ludenscheid*. 36mm diam. Mint cond. $20.00

TINNIE "1938 SA GRUPPE KURPFALZ SPORT WETTKAMPFE": 36mm diam. round stamped metal design, Pb, reads *SA Gruppen Sport Wettkaempfe 1938 Gruppe Kurpfalz* with likeness of SA emblem & handheld sword in center. Near mint cond. $35.00

TINNIE "1938 SA GRUPPE KURPFALZ SPORT WETTKAMPFE": Plastic. Silver gray with hand holding sword superimposed on oak branch & SA logo. Pb. Maker marked. Mint cond. $20.00

TINNIE "1938 SA GRUPPE NIEDERRHEIN WETTKAMPFTAGE DUISBURG": Gray. Cutout detail. Pb. Avg. cond. $25.00

TINNIE "1938 SA GRUPPE NIEDERRHEIN WETTKAMPFTAGE DUISBURG": Stamped steel oak leaf oval wreath with open center having SA trooper holding title shield. No finish & some rust patina. Bent pin. Avg. cond. $32.00

TINNIE "1938 SA GRUPPE NORDSEE SPORTWETTKAMPFE": Grey plastic rectangle with nicely struck design of Viking ship with Hamburg key device in sail above SA logo with circular banner. 25x40mm. Hallmarked. Pb. Inscribed *Sportwettkampfe SA Nordsee 1938*. Mint cond. $45.00

TINNIE "1938 SA GRUPPE SUDWEST WETTKAMPFE KARLSRUHE": Gray lightweight metal disc with frosted silver recesses. SA sports badge center with title border *& 2.u.3.Juli 38. Karlsruhe*. Pb with maker & RZM. Avg. cond. $26.00

TINNIE "1938 SA GRUPPE WESTFALEN SPORT U. WEHRWETTKAMPFE DORTMUND": Multicolored plastic with spread winged eagle, SA logo & industrial agricultural motif. Pb. Maker marked. Mint cond. $113.00

TINNIE "1938 SA GRUPPE WESTMARK WETTKAMPFTAGE": Gilt finish with pointed winged eagle over man holding shield with SA logo. Cutout detail. Pb. Above avg. cond. $20.00

TINNIE "1938 SA GRUPPE WESTMARK WETTKAMPFTAGE": Gilt finish with political eagle perched on oak leaf wreath with man holding SA logo shield in center. Cutout detail. Pb. Above avg. cond. $50.00

TINNIE "1938 SA GRUPPEN SPORT WETTKAMPFE GRUPPE KURPFALZ:" plastic: Silver-gray finish with hand holding sword superimposed on oak leaves & SA logo. Pb. Maker marked. Near mint cond. $50.00

TINNIE "1938 SA GRUPPEN WETTKAMPFE GRUPPE HOCHLAND": 40x50mm alum. body with erected sword in oak wreath. Title below. Pb & maker marked *Lauer Nurnberg RZM M9/3*. Near mint cond. $55.00

TINNIE "1938 SA SPORT U. WETTKAMPFE DORTMUND": 35x50mm cream plastic, Pb. Hall-marked. *SA Sport U. Wettkampfe 1.2.3. Juli 1938 Dortmund* SA logo in lower center, brown, red, & green color finish. Near mint cond. $40.00

TINNIE "1938 SA SPORTWETTKAMPFE NORDSEE": 25x40mm. Plastic mold. Reads *Sportwettkaempfe Nordsee 1938*. SA insignia over Viking ship. Pb. Maker marked. Near mint cond. $38.00

TINNIE "1938 SCHWABISCHES LIEDERFEST STUTTGART": Has sailing ship over musical note. Stamped solid gilt metal. Pb. Maker marked *Adolf Besson, G Mund*. SG Exc. cond. $20.00

TINNIE "1938 TURN-U.SPORTFEST BRESLAU": 41mm diam. with sports eagle & swastika on chest. Pb. Hmkd. Near mint cond. $20.00

TINNIE "1939 GAUTAG OST HANNOVER": 35x62mm stamped alum. oval design, Pb. *Gautag Ost Hannover 1939*. A three tier arrangement depict likeness of KdF Volkswagen, banner, likeness of Viking ship, banner, & rock formation. All topped by the party eagle. Near mint cond. $45.00

"1939 GAUTAG OST-HANNOVER"

TINNIE "1939 GAUTAG OST-HANNOVER": 36x64mm stamped alum. ovak, party eagle top, *Kdf-Wagen* to VW, ship & title. Open center with paper backing having Pb. Above avg. cond. $87.00

TINNIE "1939 GILLER-BERGFEST": Carmine red ribbon with gold printed 1.5"x6" ettering & design. Some light age. No fastening device. SG Exc. cond. $20.00

TINNIE "1939 HJ GEBIETS JUGEND TAGE DUSSELDORF SCHLAGETER": 30x50mm stamped bronze metal. Pb. reads *HJ Gebiets Jugend Tage Duesseldorf 28.5.1939 Schlageter* with swastika & sword in center. Near mint cond. $40.00

TINNIE "1939 HJ GEBIETSTREFFEN FRANKISCHEN": 46mm diam. round, cream colored plastic, Pb. Hallmarked. Spread winged party eagle in center. Near mint cond. $40.00

TINNIE "1939 HJ LEISTUNGSSCHAU THURIGEN RUDOLSTADT": 30x50mm silver frosted gray metal. Pb. Maker marked. *Leistungsschau d.Thur. Hitler Jugend Rudolstadt Juli 1939* Shield design with HJ diamond in eagle center. Finish worn off front. Avg. cond. . $55.00

TINNIE "1939 HJ SPORTSTAG KARNTEN": 35mm round white plastic with scenes of the mountains over eagle HJ diamond in wreath. Pb & hmkd. Above avg. cond. $55.00

TINNIE "1939 KREIS OBERLAHN USINGEN": Pressed paper shield in light rose color with large Nazi eagle & swastika in center. Raised lettering. *Kreis Oberlahn Usingen. Der Kampf Geht Weiter 1939.* Pb. 38x50mm. Mint cond. $43.00

TINNIE "1939 KREISTAG BERHEIM": Matte gray plastic round badge with eagle having swastika on chest standing behind two medieval towers. Pb. Hmkd. 40mm. Mint cond. $28.00

TINNIE "1939 KREISTAG DUREN": Bronze finish. Pb. With large swastika with spread winged eagle, barley shaft, cog wheel, eagle/lion between arms. Above avg. cond. $40.00

TINNIE "1939 KREISTAG GROSS FRANK-FURT": 35.24mm diam. Die struck alum. Gray finish. Pb. Hmkd. Has party eagle mounted on pillar with road in back-ground. Near mint cond. $20.00

TINNIE "1939 KREISTAG": Gray. With pin. Avg. cond. $20.00

TINNIE "1939 NSDAP GAUTAG STEIEMARCK": 53mm red plastic with gilt painted eagle over crowned raging lion. Pb & hmkd. Not common. Above avg. cond. $20.00

TINNIE "1939 NSDAP GAUTAG STEIERMARK": 50x40mm. Molded red plastic with gold painted details. In shape of city crest with party eagle above. Pb. Hmkd. Above avg. cond. $30.00

TINNIE "1939 NSDAP GAUTAG STEIRMARK": 50x30mm. Shield design. Cream plastic. Gold tone lettering *Steirmark 1939* with lion in center, party eagle resting on top of shield. Maker marked. Exc. cond. $35.00

TINNIE "1939 NSDAP KIESTAG NORDENKRUMMHORN": 35x50mm stamped rectangle. Bronzed finish of the skyline of town's famous center point with a swastika in a wreath. Has oxidation to the finish & some pitting to finish. Avg. cond. $32.00

TINNIE "1939 NSDAP KREISTAG GRAFSCH.HOYA": 35x50mm solid alum. oval with party eagle at top, 3 trooper heads to center for NSKK, SS & SA. Title below with oak leaves & shield with 2 arms. Front has been painted copper. Pb with maker & *RZM M9/60*. Avg. cond. $81.00

TINNIE "1939 NSDAP KREISTAG HILDESHEIM EIN VOLK REICH FUHRER": 40mm diam. Pb. Pressed paper with silver-gray finish. Hmkd. Has party eagle with outline of country. Above avg. cond. $55.00

TINNIE "1939 NSDAP KREISTAG UNTERWESTERWALD": Interesting brown & light brown glazed ceramic design of raised eagle head flanked by swastikas. Thick style body. Raised lettering, *Kriestag NSDAP Unterwesterwald. 1939*. Top has keystone area with hole for loop for cord. Verso has clutch back pin which is a replacement. No damage. 40mm size. Near mint cond. $49.00

TINNIE "1939 NSDAP KREISTAG WOLFENBUTTEL": Plastic with hallmarked verso. Matte gold color with large free standing eagle at top with swastika & flanked by factory & crossed quills. Raised edge to shield. Lower field has raised lettering, *Kreistag NSDAP Wolfenbuttel 1939*. Pb. 46x50mm. Mint cond. $60.00

TINNIE "1939 NSDAP KREISTREFFEN BIELEFELD-HALLE": Plastic. Silver finish with spread winged eagle, farmer & laborer. Maker marked & RZM hmkd. Mint cond. $20.00

"1939 NSFK GROSSFLUGTAG GRUPE 11 FRANKFURT"

TINNIE "1939 NSFK GROSSFLUGTAG GRUPE 11 FRANKFURT": 42x51mm stamped steel oval with copper/bronze finish showing age. Icarus at top, speeding plane across center, title border & *Geschicklichkeitsflug Grossflugtag NSFK-Gruppe 11 Frankfurt a.M. Hessen-Westmark 28.-30. 7. 1939*. Pb. Avg. cond. $50.00

TINNIE "1939 NSKK MOTORGR HOCHLAND GRUPPENWETTKAMPFE": Hallmarked on verso. Brown, blue, burgundy colors. NSKK eagle at top: Edelweiss in center of shield. Brown lettered inscription, *Motorgr. Hochland. Gruppenwettkampfe 1939*. Pb. Pin is original but has been remounted. 32x45mm. Near mint cond. $82.00

TINNIE "1939 NSKK REICHS SPORTWETTKAMPFE": 40mm diam. Pb. Stamped metal with bronzed finish. Has likeness of NSKK motorcycle rider & man in sports shirt with emblem above. Above avg. cond. $90.00

"1939 NSRL SKI MEISTERSCHERTEN GAU XVI RUHPOLDING"

TINNIE "1939 NSRL SKI MEISTERSCHERTEN GAU XVI RUHPOLDING": 40x25mm. Pb. Stamped metal with painted details. Has NSRL emblem & mountains in background. Above avg. cond. $50.00

TINNIE "1939 REICHSKOLONIAL TAGUNG WIEN": 40x50mm oval design, stamped metal. Pb. Reads *Reichskolonial Tagung Wien 16/18 Mai 1939*. Near mint cond. $20.00

TINNIE "1939 REICHSKOLONIALBUND": Silver finish with African native scene with assoc. insignia at top. Pb. Hmkd *HA*. Solid. Rare. Mint cond. $32.00

TINNIE "1939 REICHSKOLONIALTAGUNG WIEN": Silver-gray finish with assoc insignia over spread winged eagle superimposed on sun & map of Africa. Pb. Above avg. cond. $25.00

TINNIE "1939 REICHSKOLONIALTAGUNG WIEN": Silver-gray finish. Pb. Avg. cond. $30.00

TINNIE "1939 REICHSNAEHRSTAND AUSSTELLUNG LEIPZIG": 40mm diam. round, alum. Pb. Hallmarked with likeness of winged eagle over swastika in center. Near mint cond. $40.00

TINNIE "1939 SA BRIGADE 94 WEHRWETTKAMPFE LINZ": 43x56mm stamped nonmagnetic oval with copper finish. SA Sports Badge center, 2 edelweiss flowers & title border. Pb. Near mint cond. $75.00

TINNIE "1939 SA GRUPPE DONAU GRUPPEN WETTKAMPFE DEM SIEGER": 80x60mm. White plastic. In shape of wreath with sword & banner. Appears to have had painted details at one time. No pin. Above avg. cond. $59.00

TINNIE "1939 SA GRUPPE HANSA WETTKAMPFSTAGE HAMBURG": White plastic disc with gold SA logo on galleon with castle gate background. Title to border. Pb with RZM & maker. Avg. cond. $45.00

TINNIE "1939 SA GRUPPE HOCHLAND WETTKAMPFE": 45mm diam. Stamped. Pb. Bronzed finish. Has edelweiss with sword superimposed & SA insignia on grip. Hmkd. Above avg. cond. $68.00

TINNIE "1939 SA GRUPPE HOCHLAND WETTKAMPFE": 45mm diam. Pb. Stamped. Bronzed finish. Has edelweiss flower with sword & SA emblem. Hmkd. Above avg. cond. $77.00

TINNIE "1939 SA GRUPPE HOCHLAND WETTKAMPFE": Large circular badge in bronze metallic finish. Upright dagger with SA logo on pommel cap: Edelweiss design at center with 1939 on dagger blade. Raised circular inscription, *SA Gruppe Hochland. Gruppen Wettkampfe*. Pb. Mint cond. $72.00

TINNIE "1939 SA GRUPPE HOCHLAND WETTKAMPFE": Open disc with laurel leaf cluster, upright sword with SA logo on handle. Antique bronze finish. Metallic. *Sa Gruppe Hochland. SA Gruppen Wettkampfe 1939* on sword blade in raised letters. Pb. 48x55mm. Mint cond. $30.00

TINNIE "1939 SA GRUPPE HOCHLAND WETTKAMPFE": Stamped bronze disc with SA dagger having date to blade. Edelweiss backing to open center & title border. Pb with RZM & maker. Near mint cond. $63.00

TINNIE "1939 SA GRUPPE KURPFALZ WETTKAMPFTAGE": Round. Gray plastic. Hmkd. 40mm. Design of two SA men throwing hand grenades with circular inscription, *SA Gruppe Kurpfalz. Gruppen Wettkampfentage 1939*. Pb. Mint cond. $30.00

TINNIE "1939 SA GRUPPE SACHSEN WETTKAMPFTAGE CHMNITZ": Leather. 70mm tall tan sword with title to blade, crossguard *Chemnitz 30.Juni 2.Juli 1939* & SA logo to hilt with oak leaves. RZM & maker marked back lacks pin. Above avg. cond. $33.00

TINNIE "1939 SA GRUPPE WESTMARK WEHRKAMPFETAG": 30x35mm gray metal shield with SA sport badge center wreath swastika & sword. Some finish remains. Pb. Hmkd. Avg. cond. $20.00

TINNIE "1939 SA HOCHLAND": 48mm round bronzed badge with 1939 sword over a edelweiss & SA emblem at hilt. With wording on the border. Pb. Near mint cond. $27.00

"1939 SS GAUTAG MUNCHEN"

TINNIE "1939 SS GAUTAG MUNCHEN": 45mm diam. round stamped gray metal design, pb, with party eagle, swastika over standard *Deutschland Erwache* reads: *SS Gautag Munchen 1939*. Pb. Above avg. cond. $139.00

TINNIE "1939 WHW TAG DER WEHRMACHT": Stamped metal disc with bronze finish showing age, title border & soldier center. Pin at top. Avg. cond. $40.00

TINNIE "1940 HJ": Plastic. Silver-gray. Pb. Near mint cond. $20.00

TINNIE "1940 RKB MITTELDEUTSCHE KOLONIALSCHAU WIEN": Large stamped shield of gray nonmagnetic metal. Excellent raised details to eagle on African map. R.K.B. shield to sun & oak wreath border has title. Pb. Mint cond. $32.00

TINNIE "1940 SA WEHRKAMPFE": 46x50mm. Stamped gray metal with silver finish. Pb. Party eagle with SA logo in center with title marks. Shows slight wear to highlights. Above avg. cond. $50.00

TINNIE "1941 HJ SPORTTAGE DER JUGEND OBER DONAU STEYR": 40x58mm stamped gray metal shield. Silver finish to raised details, eagle, HJ diamond, lion shield & title. Pb. Avg. cond. $129.00

TINNIE "1942 ERSTER KREISTAG LUXEMBURG": Gray. Pb. Hmkd *M9/62*. Avg. cond. $25.00

TINNIE "1942 hj": Plastic. Pb. Silver finish. Above avg. cond. $20.00

TINNIE "ALTMARK": 35mm diam. stamped metal, round design, Pb, reads *Altmark 16/17 10. 1937* with likeness of two swastikas on waving banners. With a black background. Near mint cond. $20.00

TINNIE "AN DER SCHONEN HESS BERGSTRASSE BENSHEIM": Dark silver finish with scene of warrior slaying a dragon. Pb. Near mint cond. $20.00

TINNIE "ARBEITSSCHLACHT GAU BAYR OSTMARK": Silver finish. Pb. Above avg. cond. $40.00

TINNIE "ARBEITSSCHLACT GAU BAYR OSTMARK": Bronze finish. Pb. Near mint cond. $40.00

TINNIE "BERKENHOFF & DREBES AG 50 JAHRE": White cloth center with printed DAF flag superimposed on oak branch over black lettering over blue logo *Bedea 1889*. Gilt metal frame. Pb. Rare. Near mint cond. $45.00

TINNIE "DEINE HAND DEM HANDWERK": Enameled red rectangle with hands shaking across swastika. Near mint cond. $34.00

TINNIE "DEUTSCH DIE SAAR": Heavy solid copper body with silver finish. Design of three hands making pledge. Chain logo with lettering. Pb. Rare early propaganda tinnie. Above avg. cond. $20.00

TINNIE "DLV SAARBRUCKEN BALLON ABTLG": 25x38mm stamped metal, silver finish, Pb. Shield design with likeness of hot air balloon with DLV logo & title border. Above avg. cond. $70.00

"EIN VOLK EIN REICH EIN FUHRER"

TINNIE "EIN VOLK EIN REICH EIN FUHRER": 40x30mm in size. Porcelain with blue glazed finish. Has outline of country. Pb. Mint cond. $50.00

TINNIE "FUR HEIMAT UND VOLKSTUM 1934": 32x50mm stamped brass. Pb. With eagle & *RV* in center chest. Exc. cond. $55.00

TINNIE "GAU AUFMARSCH DER P.O. MECKLBG.-LUBECK": 37x52mm gray metal finish. Pb. maker marked. Avg. cond. $55.00

TINNIE "GAU KOBLENZ": 30mm white plastic body with bronze medallion in center having grape arbor & inscription. Pb. Unusual variation. Appears to be of all plastic construction. Near mint cond. $40.00

TINNIE "GAUAPPELL HALLE-MERSEBURG": Silver finish with spread winged eagle superimposed on DAF cogwheel & swastika, Reichsnarstand insignia & factory smoke stacks. Pb. Above avg. cond. $25.00

TINNIE "GEJUNDE FRAUEN DURCH LEIBESUBUNGEN": 12x80mm stamped brass with silvering & black swastika on the end. Pb. Avg. cond. $23.00

TINNIE "HELFT UNS HELFEN!": 24x15mm. Pb. Plastic with red painted details. Above avg. cond. $20.00

TINNIE "HERMAN GORING QUOTE": Silver finish. In the form of a plane. Pb. Above avg. cond. $35.00

"HITLER DANK GAU SUD HANNOVER BRAUNSCHWEIG"

TINNIE "HITLER DANK GAU SUD HANNOVER BRAUNSCHWEIG": 35mm diam. Silver metal. Pb. High quality tinnie with Hitler head to center & reads *Hitler's Dank fur den Dienst am Volke Gau Sud Hannover Braunschweig*. Marked on reverse *Paulmann & Crone Luedenscheid Ges.Gesch*. Near mint cond. $80.00

TINNIE "HITLER JUGENDHERBERGE": 38mm diam. round, plastic design. Pb. With likeness of building in center. Exc. cond. $20.00

TINNIE "HITLER'S DANK FUR DEN DIENST AM VOLKE": 35mm diam. Solid. Silvered finish. Hmkd. Has bust of Hitler in center. Lacks pin. Above avg. cond. $50.00

TINNIE "HJ AUS WENIGEN WURDEN VIELE": 45mm shield shaped stylized eagle with swastika on chest & holding HJ diamond silvered steel with Pb. Not a common pin. Avg. cond. $40.00

TINNIE "HJ BANN 30 WERBE-WOCHE WIESBADEN": 25x56mm stamped brass shield with gold-wash. Gull flying near swastika/sun. Title below & HJ youth holding flag. Pb with maker. Above avg. cond. $50.00

TINNIE "HJ BANN 80 WERBE-WOCHE WIESBADEN": Stamped brass shield 25x57mm. Gull flying near swastika/sun, title center & HJ youth with flag below. Pb & gold finish shows use. Above avg. cond. $91.00

"HJ FUR BESONDERE LEISTUNG SAAR"

TINNIE "HJ FUR BESONDERE LEISTUNG SAAR": 45x30mm. Pb. Stamped metal with silvered finish. In shape of a diamond with a wreath around. Above avg. cond. $145.00

TINNIE "HJ FUR DES FUHRERS JUGEND": 50x27mm. Stamped. Pb. Silvered finish has turned gray. Has likeness of of Hitler Youth holding flag with tents in background. Above avg. cond. $50.00

TINNIE "HJ FUR DES FUHRERS JUGEND": Stamped steel shield 31x51mm with frosted silver finish. Eagle design to top, HJ youth holding flag at center, tents, title & HJ diamond below. Pb. Near mint cond. $65.00

TINNIE "HJ WIDUKIND": 40x30mm. Stamped. Pb. Silvered finish. Has likeness of horses heads, HJ insignia & sword. For Niedersachsen. Hmkd. Above avg. cond. $40.00

TINNIE "JOSEF GOEBBELS JUGENDHERBERGE": 20x50mm metal, Pb, spread eagle design, hallmarked. Exc. cond. $35.00

TINNIE "JUNGSTAHLHELM": 38mm stamped silver tone metal, sword design, Pb. With inscription on blade. Near mint cond. $35.00

TINNIE "KAMPFT GEGEN DIE NOT SCHUTZT MUTTER U KIND": Plastic. White. Stickpin mount. Above avg. cond. $20.00

TINNIE "KDF BAU HESSEN-NASSAU": 30x45mm alum. Pb. Maker marked tinnie *NSG Kraft durch Freude Urlaub am Rhein Gau Hessen-Nassau* around border with tourist boot in water along mountain range. Exc. cond. $50.00

TINNIE "KDF GAU HAMBURG HUMMEL-HUMMEL!": Bronze finish with the scene of a man carrying water. Pb. Mint cond. $20.00

TINNIE "KDF SONNIGES MAINFRANKEN": Gilt & red finish with KdF insignia over grapes. Pb. Above avg. cond. $28.00

TINNIE "LUFT SCHUTZ TUT NOT": 20x34mm pierced design, stamped tin, title to border, RLB star to house with plane above. Pb. Avg. cond. $20.00

TINNIE "LUFTSCHUTZ IST SELBSTSCHUTZ REICHLUFTSCHUTZBUND": 2.5x3.5mm stamped gray metal, pb, reads *Luftschutz ist Selbstschutz Reichluftschutzbund* with likeness of athlete with bow & arrow. Above avg. cond. $50.00

TINNIE "LUFTSPORT HILFT DEUTSCHLAND": Silver finish with plastic center with plane silhouette affixed. Pb. Near mint cond. $20.00

TINNIE "LUTHER BIBEL 100 JAHRE DEUTSCHE SCHRISTSRACHE": Silver finish with bust of man. Pb. Maker marked. Avg. cond. $24.00

TINNIE "MIT DER NS GEM KRAFT D FREUDE AN DIE MOSEL GAU KOBLENZ TRIER": Silver finish with a mountain scene. Pb. Maker name marked. Mint cond. $40.00

TINNIE "NSDAP KREISTAG INSTERBURG": 45x32mm. Pb. Stamped metal with bronzed finish. Has likeness of farmer & factory worker shaking hands with swastika & sun in background. Above avg. cond. $30.00

TINNIE "NSFK GROSSFLUGTAG GRUPPE 8 MITTE": 40x30mm. Stamped. Pb. Bronzed finish. Has NSFK emblem in center. Above avg. cond. $77.00

TINNIE "NSFK GRUPPE 8 MITTE GROSSFLUGTAG": 40x30mm. Pb. Stamped metal with bronzed finish. Has NSFK emblem in center. Above avg. cond. $50.00

TINNIE "NSKK 2000 KILOMETER DURCH DEUTSCHLAND AVD": Stamped dark brass oval with NSKK eagle top, map-route center, title border & AVD bottom. Pb. Exc. cond. $53.00

TINNIE "RAD REICHSTREFFEN GESUNDHEITSBEWEGUNG": 38x54mm. Dusseldorf tinnie. Stamped sheet metal design with antique silver finish showing some wear. 38mm wide & 54mm high. Wire pin backed. Lion with anchor on shield. Above avg. cond. $40.00

TINNIE "RHEINLAND 25 JAHRE": 20x45mm silver frosted finish, Pb, maker marked. Shield design with castle above title. Above avg. cond. $50.00

TINNIE "RLB LUFTSCHUTZ TUT NOT": Black & silver finish. Cut-out detail. Pb. Near mint cond. $30.00

TINNIE "RLB LUFTSCHUTZ TUT NOT": Silver & black finish. Pb. Near mint cond. $25.00

TINNIE "SA GRUPPE SACHSEN
WETTKAMPFTAGE CHEMNITZ":
30x70mm. Pressed leather construction
with nice design of vertical SA style
dagger. Grip is enclosed by oak leaves &
has an SA logo displayed on grip.
Impressed lettering, *Wettkampftage der
SA Gruppe Sachsen. Chemnitz. 30 Juni -
2 Juli 1939*. Pb. Near mint
cond. $80.00

TINNIE "SA STANDARTE 143 SPORTFEST
SPORTPLAZEINWEIH
RECKLINGHAUSEN": 45x35mm.
Stamped. Bronzed finish. Has likeness of
SA soldier jumping over hurdle & SA
emblem above. Pb. Above avg.
cond. $95.00

TINNIE "SAARBRUCKEN
SAARBEFREIUNG": 28x34mm alum. Pb.
Maker marked design with monument in
center & border line *Saarbrucken
Saarbefreiung*. Above avg.
cond. $50.00

TINNIE "SANGERGAU KURHESSEN 100
JAHRFEIER": Red plastic shield with a
gold background & the Nazi eagle. Pb.
Hmkd *Walgo Kierspe W*. 31x44mm high.
Near mint cond. $40.00

TINNIE "SS BLAST ZUM SAMMELN
GEGEN HUNGER U.KALTE" 26mm
stamped brass disc with worn silver
highlights, SS runes center, title border &
black background. Pb. Above avg.
cond. $177.00

TINNIE "SS BLAST ZUM SAMMELN
GEGENHUNGER KALTE"

TINNIE "SS BLAST ZUM SAMMELN
GEGENHUNGER KALTE": 25mm diam.
Pb. Stamped metal with black painted
background. Silvered finish has worn to
brass. Reads *SS Blast Zum Sammeln
Gegenhunger Kalte*. Has runic symbols in
center. Above avg. cond. $97.00

TINNIE "SS SPORTTREFFEN": 25x44mm
stamped nonmagnetic rectangle with
bronze finish. SS runes in wreath on
swastika background. Title shown over
building design below. Pb. Near mint
cond. $276.00

TINNIE "SS SPORTTREFFEN"

TINNIE "SS STANDARTE 57
SPORTSCHIESS IN SCHMALKEN
THUR. WETTHEWERB": SS shooting
tinnie. 42.56 mm diam., Pb. Silvered
finish. Very rare. Mint cond. $184.00

TINNIE "SS STANDARTE
SCHMALKALDEN THUR.
SPORTSCHIESS WETTBEWERB":
42mm stamped brass disc with frosted-
silver finish. SS runes shield to center
with target & castle. Title border &
Sportschiess-Wettbewerb der. Pb has
maker. Exc. cond. $240.00

TINNIE "TAG DER NATIO NALEN ARBEIT":
35mm diam. Pressed paper with printed
design. Has swastika in center. Pb.
Above avg. cond. $50.00

TINNIE "VDA FEST DER DEUTSCHEN
SCHULE": Stamped silver disc with oak
leave wreath border & title to swastika
center. Pb. Near mint cond. $22.00

TINNIE "VDA FEST DER DEUTSCHEN
SCHULE": Bright finished stamped sheet
metal disk, broken wire pin to back.
35mm diam. Has swastika in wreath.
Avg. cond. $20.00

TINNIE "VOLKSBUND DEUTSCHE
KRIEGSGRABERFURSORGE":
25x18mm. Stamped metal with silvered
finish & black painted details. Has
likeness of 5 crosses in 3 different sizes.
Stick Pb. Above avg.
cond. $30.00

IMPERIAL GERMAN SPIKED HELMETS & ASSOCIATED HEADGEAR

AUSTRIAN DRAGOON OFFICER HELMET: Pre-WWI. Black lacquered metal body with full tall gilt comb having raised design of lion in battle with serpent. Officer double headed eagle frontplate. Full scale chinstraps with lion head bosses. Calfskin and white silk deluxe liner. Very rare. Exc. cond. $3,061.00

AUSTRIAN M16 CAMO COMBAT HELMET: Shell 68. Brown painted inside & 10 stripe camo design with black & brown brush strokes, watermelon design. Steel band with 3 pads. Web chinstrap. Avg. cond. $218.00

AUSTRIAN M16 COMBAT HELMET

AUSTRIAN M16 COMBAT HELMET: Shell CAS66 with brown paint inside & out, 85%. 3 pad leather liner, grommets & cushions intact. Faint inked owner name to pads on steel band. Web chinstrap with grommets & roller buckles. Exc. cond. $378.00

AUSTRIAN M16 COMBAT HELMET: Steel band with 3 pad liner. Brown leather chinstrap. No size. Tan/brown paint inside & out. Above avg. cond. $210.00

AUSTRIAN M16 COMBAT HELMET: Variation. German shell ET64 has Austrian loops riveted in German locations. Brown painted inside & out. Steel liner band with light brown 3 leather pads with grommets. Above avg. cond. $155.00

AUSTRIAN M16 COMBAT HELMET: White 3 pad leather. Grommets & 2 cushions intact. Gray cloth chinstrap with gripper buckle. Brown paint inside & out. Above avg. cond. $210.00

BAVARIAN EM SPIKED HELMET: Ersatz gray felt body & visors. Brass trim to front, spine, spike & front plate. Reichs & Bavarian kokardes. Leather chinstrap. 9 finger black leather liner. Inked size 54. Avg. cond. $296.00

BAVARIAN OFFICER SPIKED HELMET: Black leather body & visors with red finished underside to back. Brass trim, fittings, removable fluted spike, front-plate with pierced crown & chinscales. Reichs & Bavarian kokardes. Leather sweatband & satin lining. Above avg. cond. $807.00

CAMO SPIKED HELMET COVER: Rush-green. 2 parts sewn body with affixed spiked cover held by 4 cloth straps. 5 brass hooks to rim. Exc. cond. $210.00

CAMO TSCHAPKA COMBAT COVER: Gray cloth multi-piece construction with 2 slots, 2 steel rim hooks & 6 hooks/loops at back closure-slash. Black inked *B.A.VI 1914*. Exc. cond. $200.00

COLONIAL AFRICA SERVICE TROPENHELM MADE FROM CAPTURED BRIT PITH HELMET: Helmet body has broad arrow marks and 1907 date. Frontplate is German colonial forces eagle with 'wrap around' style large Reichs kokarde on right band. Complete with liner and chinstrap. Khaki stiff body. Helmet captured in early battles in 1914 by Von Lettow-Vorbeck's forces and converted for German use when German supplies ran out. Isolated in Africa, the German Schutztruppe found they had to convert enemy stocks to their own use as they could not be supplied. The last attempt to supply colonial forces came with the zeppelin L-59 but it had to turn back before supplies could be dumped. A very rare and unusual helmet. Near mint cond. $600.00

COLONIAL EAST AFRICA OFFICER HUT OR DIGGER CAP FOR SCHUTZTRUPPE: Gray pressed felt construction. Tan band and puggree for East Africa with officer two piece Reichs kokarde on side. Silver roundel. Leather sweatband with the original maker label is still intact. Approx. size 57/58. Near mint cond. $456.00

HANNOVERIAN 10TH JAEGER BATL OFFICER SHAKO: Last pattern, circa 1912. Black cloth body, black leather visors, and top. Gilt officer eagle with silver Reservist cross on tail. Full battle honor bandeau with *Waterloo Peninsula Venta del Pozo*. Officer silver wire field badge with black velvet center. Flat style chinscales. Officer Reichs kokarde. With a full silk and calfskin liner. Avg. cond. $1,494.00

HESSE BEAMTE MILITARY OFFICER SPIKED HELMET: Hesse spiked helmets are rare, but officers' Beamtes are almost impossible to find. Fluted spike with cross base and plain stud mounts. Convex chinscales with Reichs and Hesse rosettes. Helmet has gilt pierced crown Hesse frontplate with miniature silver Hesse lion at base. Type used by Zahlmeister & military admin. officers. Avg. cond. $950.00

HUSSAR OFFICER BUSBY: Brown opossum fur body with red kolpak and large silver wire cap lines with black Prussian flecking. Gilt chinscales with officer silver wire field badge having black velvet center. Officer kokarde present. Deluxe calfskin liner with top inscribed *56 20/1/1911* indicating size and date. Frosted silver officer cross. Black leather form fitted case with padded liner. Near mint cond. $2,100.00

M16 CAMO COMBAT HELMET: Dark leather liner band has folded cloth cushions tied to band behind each black oil cloth pad. Leather chinstrap has steel end lugs & both buckles are nickel plated brass. Shell has thick green painted inside. Size 64 by vents. Camo design has 13 geometric panels with narrow black divider lines. Colors in red, green, yellow, brown, white & black. Avg. cond. $160.00

M16 CAMO HELMET: Thick green brush stroked rim & body. Avg. cond. $140.00

M16 COMBAT HELMET WITH GARDEKORPS INSIGNIA: Shell size 66. Green inside & out. Hand painted B&W 4 part divided hohenzollern crest to left side. Leather liner band with 3 pad liner. White painted *Dohms.* to rim. Avg. cond. $387.00

M16 COMBAT HELMET: Shell BF64 with green paint. String plugs to each grommet vent. Steel liner band with 2 leather pads. Avg. cond. $100.00

M16 COMBAT HELMET: Shell ET64. Green paint, 70%. Steel liner band has 3 pad liner. Avg. cond. $131.00

M16 COMBAT HELMET: Shell G62 with green paint. Dark leather liner band with 3 pads. Avg. cond. $238.00

M16 COMBAT HELMET: Shell Si66. Green paint inside & out with remains of paper USA address label at top. Steelband with 3 pad liner. Avg. cond. $111.00

M16 COMBAT HELMET: Shell by BF64. Dull gray period repaint inside & out. Avg. cond. $32.00

M16 CAMO COMBAT HELMET

M16 CAMO COMBAT HELMET: Shell ET64 with green inside. Dark leather band & 3 pad liner with cushions intact. Large geometric camo design with black divider lines. Green, brown & reddish brown. Avg. cond. $279.00

M16 CAMO COMBAT HELMET: Steel liner band with 3 pad liner. Shell ET64. Geometric camo design with black divider lines. 3 brown panels, 3 darker brown & 4 of a grayish green. Avg. cond. $177.00

MACEDONIAN FRONT PROTOTYPE ARMORED SPIKE HELMET

MACEDONIAN FRONT PROTOTYPE ARMORED SPIKE HELMET: M1915. Issued as a test for only three months by the German Army to reduce head wounds. Considered the transitional spike before the introduction of the M16 steel helmet. Armored body covered with dark OD linen material and having leather reinforced visor. Made without rear visor but complete with neck flap, liner. Double heavy leather chinstrap with chemically darkened frontplate which lacks crown, orb and scepter. Cloth covered bayonet mount for spike. An exceptionally rare helmet Avg. cond. $875.00

OFFICER YAK HAIR PLUME FOR TRICHTER: White soft yak hair with leather center for mounting on trichter. Mint cond. $164.00

PRUSSIAN ARTY EM SPIKED HELMET: Large black leather body & visors. Gray line eagle, visor trim & spine. Brass base & ball top. Leather liner. Below avg. cond. $235.00

PRUSSIAN BUSBY

PRUSSIAN BUSBY: Seal skin busby with complete liner and faint maker marks. Red kolpak with original cord retainers. Silvered frontplate with old black/white field badge. Original chinstraps (tongue broken but present. Male & female lugs gone. Reichs kokarde present. Replaced cap lines. Has 3 punched holes in front to make it into a Death Head Hussar busby. Skull and crossbones replaced post-war. Avg. cond. $683.00

PRUSSIAN DRAGOON NCO M1857 SPIKE HELMET: Tall black leather body with cruciform base spike having NCO pearlring. Large eagle frontplate with FWR device. Single large Prusssian kokarde (the Reichs one was not introduced until Dec. 1898). No extra holes. Large convex dragoon chinscales. Partial lining. Exc. cond. $1,210.00

PRUSSIAN DRAGOON NCO M1857 SPIKED HELMET: Tall solid black leather body & visors. Brass trim, spike with pearl band & cruciform base. FWR to eagle front plate & flat chinscales with Prussian kokarde. 9 finger black leather liner. Exc. cond. $1,000.00

PRUSSIAN EM SPIKED HELMET: Black leather body & visors. Gray metal trim, spine, side posts & base. 9 finger leather liner. Inked *1916*/maker & size *57*. Avg. cond. $137.00

PRUSSIAN EM SPIKED HELMET: Black leather body & visors with black inked *B.A.IV*. Gray metal trim, spine, removable spike & eagle frontplate. 9 finger leather liner. Inked *55* & *B4*. Below avg. cond. $237.00

PRUSSIAN EM SPIKED HELMET: Black leather body & visors. Gray metal trim, spine, removable spike & line eagle. 8 finger black leather original liner. Avg. cond. $176.00

PRUSSIAN EM SPIKE HELMET

PRUSSIAN EM SPIKE HELMET: Black leather body & visors. Dark brass trim, spine, spike & line eagle frontplate. 10 finger brown leather liner with felt pad to top. Reichs kokarde. Couple inked names to liner & stenciled front visor underside *R.v.d.H Berlin-Sch No.7 ???* Exc. cond. $538.00

PRUSSIAN DRAGOON NCO M1857 SPIKED HELMET

PRUSSIAN GARDE DU KORPS EM SPIKED HELMET: Inside stamped *CE Juncker 1915*. Tombak body, matching chinscales, silvered garde star & black eagle with motto *Suum Cuique* (To each his own). Silver trim, large kokardes. Avg. cond. $2,785.00

PRUSSIAN GARDE DU KORPS EM
SPIKED HELMET

PRUSSIAN GARDE DU KORPS OFFICER SPIKED HELMET: GKR.3E. Body, ridged visor & tail have silver trim. Stamped title to tail with black leather to underside. Front visor trim stamped *Wilh. Jaeger*. Below avg. cond. $825.00

PRUSSIAN GARDE JAEGER OFFICER SHAKO: Black leather top & visors with black wool covered body. Brass chinscales with buckle & strap. Reichs kokarde & silver bullion field badge. Dark silver Garde star with black enamel eagle & other enamel details. Leather sweatband with silk liner having inked owner *Schick*. Exc. cond. $2,296.00

PRUSSIAN GRENADIER OFFICER SPIKED HELMET: *L.G.1890*. Black leather visors to body with stamped title inside. Brass trim, spine, pearl ring to spike & eagle plate. Prussian kokarde with silver ring. 9 finger original leather liner inside. Avg. cond. $550.00

PRUSSIAN HUSSAR EM BUSBY: Ersatz body is composed of a black coarse cloth stretched over reed and sailcloth style inner liner. Flat-silver metal banner with convex scaled chinstraps. Helmet has white-black field badge with large brass *8* on center field. No bag or cap line holders. Remains of old paper label inside top. Avg. cond. $500.00

PRUSSIAN HUSSAR EM BUSBY: Field-gray pattern. Busby is of black seal skin with gray bandeau. Prussian black-white field badge; chinstrap and proper Reichs kokarde on the right side. Maker marked inside and 1916 dated. The busby has the white cord loops for the 'schnuren' or cap cords. Mint cond. $850.00

PRUSSIAN INFANTRY RESERVE OFFICER SPIKED HELMET: Black leather body & visors. Brass trim, spine, spike with pearl ring, 4 star bolts, chinscales & line eagle with nickel cross to chest. Prussian & Reichs kokardes. Below avg. cond. $350.00

PRUSSIAN JAEGER EM SHAKO: Black leather body & visors. 7 hole metal vents & gray side posts. Variation black leather chinstrap with roller buckle & gray metal end loops. Gray Jaeger eagle frontplate. 9 finger leather liner. Avg. cond. $231.00

PRUSSIAN JAGER ZU PFERDE EM
SPIKED HELMET

PRUSSIAN JAGER ZU PFERDE EM SPIKED HELMET: Blued steel body & lobster tail. Silver trim & rivets with backrim stamped *56 7.J.z.P. 1913 3.I.* Silver spike with fittings. Nickel eagle with affixed nickel star. 8 finger black leather liner. Stamped top *C.E.Juncker 1913*. Avg. cond. $559.00

PRUSSIAN KURASSIER EM SPIKED HELMET: Wartime. Steel body, lobster tail, rivets, trim & spike. Steel line eagle with loops. Below avg. cond. $292.00

PRUSSIAN KURASSIER OFFICER M1867 SPIKED HELMET: Steel shell with step visor and deep lobster tail. Silvered spread winged early 1860 Garde eagle on front having officer Garde star. Interior enamel ring missing, area has been painted blue. Convex chinscales, clover leaf base on spike, and ventilator in cross pattern with fluted steel spike. Single Landes kokarde present. Kreeblatten or side lugs appear to be 1897 issue. Screw mounts proper for M67. Below avg. cond. $1,440.00

PRUSSIAN UHLAN OFFICER TSCHAPKA: Black leather body. Silver front visor trim & line eagle plate with pierced crown. Brass chinscales with buckle/strap & Reichs kokarde. Silver bullion top field badge. Leather sweatband & satin lining with faint gold maker trademark. Above avg. cond. $1,500.00

IMPERIAL GERMAN VISOR HATS, CLOTH CAPS & FIELD COVERS

BAVARIAN CHEVAULEGER NCO VISOR CAP: Dark green with burgundy band and piping. Deluxe NCO kokarden. Fancy leather liner. Blue silken top with silver eagle maker logo, Nurnburg address. Near mint cond. $326.00

BAVARIAN DIPLOMATIC OFFICER FORE AND AFT HAT: Black pressed wool with white feather plumes along leading edges. Bare silver braid on right side with large Bavarian crown button. Leather and brown silk liner with gold Munich maker label. Mint cond. $205.00

BAVARIAN EM PILL BOX HAT

BAVARIAN EM PILL BOX HAT: Gray wool with red piping and band. Interior marked *BAXV JR138*. Reichs & also with 2 Bavarian rosettes. Near mint cond. $145.00

BAVARIAN OFFICER VISOR CAP: 1910 era. Quality gray wool body. Red piping and band. Two piece Reichs & Bavarian rosettes. Leather and cloth style liner. Approx. size 59. Owner initials marked in

the sweatband - *FH*. Above avg. cond. $229.00

BAVARIAN OFFICER VISOR CAP

BAVARIAN POLICE OFFICER VISOR CAP: White twill crown with black band & metal Bavarian shield in white sunburst on center. Blue enameled metal badge on white above band. Double strand woven silver cord chin strap & black visor. Lined interior. Avg. cond. $45.00

NAVAL ADMIRAL FORE & AFT FORMAL DRESS HAT: Fore & aft pattern with black leather sweatband, refolded style white silk liner. Size 59. Black stiff fur covered body with 1.75" of gold braid work. Heavy gold wire rope over national color cockade with large gold high relief naval button. Case is of black patent leather with carrying handle, side straps & black japanned tin lock. Yellow padded silk interior. Mint cond. $855.00

PILOT FUR CAP OF *LT. VON CONTA*

PILOT FUR CAP OF *LT. VON CONTA*: 8 black leather panels to body with earflaps & dark brown fleece covering. Reichs cockade to front & black quilted lining. No named paper work included. Exc. cond. $275.00

PRUSSIAN HUSSAR OFFICER VISOR CAP: Black wool with white piping. Officer Reichs and Prussian rosettes. Silvered skull and bones between rosettes. Custom purchase silk and leather liner. Near mint cond. ... $225.00

PRUSSIAN HUSSAR
OFFICER VISOR CAP

PRUSSIAN INFANTRY OFFICER VISOR CAP: Stiff tall saddle body with stone-gray wool body, red piping and band. Complete with officer Reichs, Prussian rosettes. Leather visor. Made without a chinstrap. Full deluxe lining with a celluloid moisture shield. Near mint cond. $334.00

PRUSSIAN INFANTRY
OFFICER VISOR CAP

PRUSSIAN RESERVIST EM PILLBOX FIELD CAP: Field-gray body with red wool piping on crown & red band around base. Off-white lining with well marked maker stamps & size *53*. National colors cockade over reservist with IC center. Avg. cond. $177.00

THIRD REICH HELMETS

CAMO HELMET COVER ITALIAN CAMO: 3 part sewn body, 7 sewn loops & drawstring on the edge. Above avg. cond. $55.00

CAMO HELMET COVER WAFFEN SS 2ND TYPE WITH LOOPS: Summer & fall oak leave pattern to 3 part sewn body with 6 loops. Black painted alum. 3 rocker clip. 3 hidden springs are intact. Exc. cond. $853.00

CIVIC HELMET BAHNSCHUTZ POLIZEI STUB BILL DOUBLE DECAL: Heavy steel shell with black paint. Winged wheel decal. 8 finger gray leather liner, top pad, 5 flap tabs & chinstrap. Avg. cond. $347.00

CIVIC HELMET FIRE POLICE CURVED DIP NO DECAL: Double 7 hole vents to black painted body with affixed alum. comb. 9 finger leather liner inked *54*. Black leather chinstrap, 5 flap tabs & black leather flap. Brown leatherette pad to top. Avg. cond. $115.00

CIVIC HELMET FIRE POLICE SQUARE DIP DOUBLE DECAL: Black paint. Bordered eagle & party decals. 3 plugs to holes from removed comb. 8 finger leather liner is combat style & has inked *L+E* etc. maker. Pad to top, & 5 flap tabs. Rim of shell stamped *Edelstahl*. Avg. cond. $75.00

CIVIC HELMET FIRE POLICE SQUARE DIP DOUBLE DECAL: Black painted steel shell. Bordered police & party decals. Leather 9 finger liner inked *57-61 63*. Black leather chinstrap. Pad to top. Exc. cond. $240.00

CIVIC HELMET FIRE POLICE SQUARE
DIP DOUBLE DECAL

CIVIC HELMET FIRE POLICE SQUARE DIP DOUBLE DECAL: Steel shell stamped *Edelstahl*. Black paint. Bordered eagle decal & party decal. 8 finger leather liner inked *57* & maker. Leather chinstrap, 5 tabs for flap & top pad. Above avg. cond. $110.00

CIVIC HELMET HITLER YOUTH GLADIA-TOR STYLE 1-PIECE: Has red, white, & black Hitler Youth diamond insignia on the left side. 9 finger white cloth liner. Black plastic chinstrap. Steel shell stamped *R.L.239/25* & blue painted. Used by the HJ with the Luftschutz. Near mint cond. $433.00

CIVIC HELMET LUFSCHUTZ GLADIATOR STYLE 3-PIECE: 9 finger leather liner. Black leather chinstrap. Inked wording to rim with size *56*. Dark blue paint. Decal. Near mint cond. $100.00

CIVIC HELMET LUFTSCHUTZ GLADIA-TOR-STYLE 1-PIECE: Brush stroked blue paint. 9 finger off-white cloth liner. Clear plastic chinstrap. Above avg. cond. $134.00

CIVIC HELMET LUFTSCHUTZ M42-BEADED-COMBAT

CIVIC HELMET LUFTSCHUTZ GLADIA-TOR-STYLE 2-PIECE

CIVIC HELMET LUFTSCHUTZ GLADIA-TOR-STYLE 2-PIECE: Steel shell with decals to rim, size *59*. Blue paint. Decal. 10 finger leather liner inked *59* & faint owner. Black leather chinstrap. Near mint cond. $188.00

CIVIC HELMET LUFTSCHUTZ GLADIA-TOR-STYLE 3-PIECE: 9 finger off-white cloth liner. Clear plastic chinstrap. Blue paint. Luftschutz decal. Above avg. cond. $64.00

CIVIC HELMET LUFTSCHUTZ M40-BEADED-COMBAT REISSUE WITH PAINTED *W*: Shell Q64 has dark blue repaint. 1" tall silver painted *W* to front shows painted over luftschutz decal below, period done. 6 finger off-white leatherette liner. Leather chinstrap. White handpainted *51* to inside top. Avg. cond. $80.00

CIVIC HELMET LUFTSCHUTZ M40-BEADED-COMBAT: Dark blue painted shell Q64. Traces of removed Luftwaffe eagle decal to left side with outline only. 7 finger off-white cloth liner & black leather chinstrap. Above avg. cond. $120.00

CIVIC HELMET LUFTSCHUTZ M40-BEADED-COMBAT: Shell Q64. Blue paint. Decal. 7 finger brown leatherette liner. Avg. cond. $125.00

CIVIC HELMET LUFTSCHUTZ M42-BEADED-COMBAT: Shell NS62. Dark blue paint. Decal. 9 finger white cloth liner & clear plastic chinstrap. Near mint cond. $110.00

CIVIC HELMET LUFTSCHUTZ M42-BEADED-COMBAT: Shell 64 with black paint inside & out. Decal at front. 8 finger off-white burlap liner. Leather chinstrap with a roller buckle. Avg. cond. $189.00

CIVIC HELMET POLICE CURVED-DIP DOUBLE-DECAL: Black painted steel body. Bordered eagle decal & party decal. 9 finger leather liner, top pad, 5 flap tabs & pigskin chinstrap. Above avg. cond. $117.00

CIVIC HELMET POLICE SQUARE-DIP DOUBLE-DECAL: Alum. shell with double 7 hole vents & black paint. Bordered eagle decal & party decal. Stamped rim *BBF* etc..*3.5.34* with trademark. 8 finger leather liner inked *58*, pad top, 5 flap tabs. Above avg. cond. $160.00

CIVIC HELMET RED CROSS M42-BEADED-COMBAT SINGLE-DECAL: Shell ckl64 with battleship-gray paint. Eagle decal. 7 finger off-white cloth liner inked *56*. Black leather chinstrap. Near mint cond. $393.00

CIVIC HELMET SA GLADIATOR-STYLE 1-PIECE DOUBLE-DECAL: Tan & brown paint over base blue. Political eagle decal to left side. SA logo decal to right. 10 finger off-white cloth liner. Clear plastic chinstrap. Blue paint to inside top of the steel shell. Rare style. Above avg. cond. $587.00

CIVIC HELMET SS-LAH M18-STYLE DOUBLE-DECAL: Early. Black finish. Unique steel shell is WWI M18 size but has stamped 7 hole vents & 4 liner rivets. Inside rim stamped with *RZM*, *SS* & *LAH* cipher. White stenciled *Warnung Dieser SS Helm ist etc.* property mark rim. Green paint to inside top, black rim & body. 1st SS runes decal. National decal. 3 pad leather liner on cardboard band has 2 intact finger tips with hole not torn.

No cushions & each pad has stamped different SS mark *Verkaufs Abteilung der W-ss 4.11.36* & *Karl Schmidt* etc. & *Dieser SS Helm* etc. Black leather chinstrap. Green inside black stenciled *SS IV.Wach-Bataillon* etc. & faint owner name *Carl Sattler SS-Oberfuhrer*? Exc. cond. $3,415.00

CIVIC HELMET SS-LAH M18-STYLE
DOUBLE-DECAL

CIVIC SHAKO POLICE EM: Black top & visors. Double screened vents to green wool body. Alum. eagle/wreath & cockade. Black leather chinstrap with alum. fittings. 8 finger tan leather liner. Maker decal in top *H.Becker & Co. Berlin etc..58*. Avg. cond. $257.00
CIVIC SHAKO POLICE OFFICER: Police green wool covered body with screen vents. Black top & 2 visors. EM thin stamped alum. eagle/wreath. Officer alum. chinscales. Leather sweatband inked *55*, off-white satin lining & maker decal at top. Avg. cond. $400.00
COMBAT HELMET ARMY M16-AUSTRIAN-TRANSITIONAL DOUBLE-DECAL: Riveted chinstrap loops. M31 liner inked *59*. Alum. 1939 liner band *66n.A.59*. Thin gray brush stroked paint shows green base. Eagle & national decals. Avg. cond. $495.00
COMBAT HELMET ARMY M16-AUSTRIAN-TRANSITIONAL NO-DECAL: Original brown paint to shell with chinstrap loops, steel liner band & 3 pad liner. Cloth red/yellow maneuver band with buckle & 3 hook straps. Early. Above avg. cond. $252.00
COMBAT HELMET ARMY M16-TRANSITIONAL DOUBLE-DECAL: Shell Q62 with green paint inside & out. Eagle & National decals. 1939 alum. liner band. Tan leather liner inked *54* & owner *Heinlin*. Variation black leather chinstrap with roller buckle. Exc. cond. $1,326.00
COMBAT HELMET ARMY M16-TRANSITIONAL DOUBLE-DECAL: Shell Si66 with green rim stenciled in black *66 57-*

58. M18 steel liner band, 3 pad leather liner, chinstrap loops & chinstrap with clip has 1918/maker. Green brush stroked paint. Eagle & national decals. Early. Avg. cond. $200.00
COMBAT HELMET ARMY M16-TRANSITIONAL DOUBLE-DECAL: Variant with black finish. Shell by Si66 with original vent lugs & chinstrap lugs. Black painted inside & out. Eagle & national decals. WWI leather 3 pad liner on leather band has 1939 dated. Avg. cond. $585.00

COMBAT HELMET ARMY M16-TRANSITIONAL SINGLE-DECAL

COMBAT HELMET ARMY M16-TRANSITIONAL SINGLE-DECAL: Shell Si66. Green painted inside & outside. Eagle decal. 1940 steel band, 58/66 & leather liner. Avg. cond. $322.00
COMBAT HELMET ARMY M16-TRANSITIONAL SINGLE-DECAL: Shell shows removed vent lugs & chinstrap lugs. Thick rough texture paint inside & out. Eagle decal. Steel band with leather liner inked *56*. Avg. cond. $282.00
COMBAT HELMET ARMY M18-TRANSITIONAL DOUBLE-DECAL: Steel shell with vent lugs shows brush stroked gray rim & outside. Eagle & national decals. White painted rim *Uffz.Jung 8/13*. 1939 alum. band, *66 n.A. 59* & leather liner. Complete chinstrap. Avg. cond. $403.00
COMBAT HELMET ARMY M18-TRANSITIONAL SINGLE-DECAL: M31 liner on 1939 alum. band, size 60/68. Full chinstrap. Gray rough texture painted rim & body. Eagle decal to left side. Avg. cond. $683.00
COMBAT HELMET ARMY M18-TRANSITIONAL SINGLE-DECAL: Gray rough texture paint inside & out. Size 62. Eagle decal. Bullet hole to right side. Steel liner band, 62/55 & pigskin liner. Avg. cond. $138.00
COMBAT HELMET ARMY M35 CAMO DOUBLE-DECAL REISSUE: Shell 62. Thick brush stroked green finish. Both

decals painted over. Brush stroked rim has white painted *Feldw. Berger*. Steel liner band 62/65 with tan leather. Chinstrap is shortened. Above avg. cond. $175.00

COMBAT HELMET ARMY M35 CAMO DOUBLE-DECAL WITH CAMO NET

COMBAT HELMET ARMY M35 CAMO DOUBLE-DECAL WITH CAMO NET: Shell ET64 with green inside & gray brush stroked outside. Eagle decal affixed over gray paint. National decal palnted over. 1938 alum. Ilner band with leather liner with name *Kolbe*. String net covering with union ring at top. 75" net spacing & attached around liner band. Above avg. cond. $454.00

COMBAT HELMET ARMY M35 DOUBLE-DECAL: Shell ET62 with gray rough texture paint inside & out. Both decals are painted over. Steel liner band. Leather liner inked size *54*. Full chinstrap. Avg. cond. $196.00

COMBAT HELMET ARMY M35 DOUBLE-DECAL: Shell Q64 with green paint. Eagle & national decals. Inked 1939 oval to inside top. 1937 alum. band with leather liner inked *57*. Full chinstrap with a 1938 date and maker. Exc. cond. $1,750.00

COMBAT HELMET ARMY M35 DOUBLE-DECAL: Shell Q66. Green period repaint. Eagle & national decals. 1939 alum. band 66/58. Leather liner. Above avg. cond. $375.00

COMBAT HELMET ARMY M35 DOUBLE-DECAL: Shell Q68 with thin gray brush stroked over base green. Eagle decal, painted over national has been uncovered. Leather liner. 1937 band & 58/61. Full chinstrap has RB# marked. Avg. cond. $433.00

COMBAT HELMET ARMY M35 DOUBLE-DECAL: Shell SE62 with green paint. Eagle & national decals. Rim painted in white *S.Schenk*. 1937 alum. band with leather liner. Full chinstrap by *gxy 42*. Avg. cond. $662.00

COMBAT HELMET ARMY M35 DOUBLE-DECAL

COMBAT HELMET ARMY M35 DOUBLE-DECAL: Shell by NS64. Green paint. Eagle & national decals. 1938 alum. band 64/57. Leather liner. 1938 date inked oval to the inside top. Above avg. cond. $1,210.00

COMBAT HELMET ARMY M35 NO-DECAL: Shell ET62 with green paint inside & out. Removed double decals. 1940 alum. band. Leather liner. Shortened chinstrap with alum. fittings fits over visor. Avg. cond. $93.00

COMBAT HELMET ARMY M35 SINGLE-DECAL REISSUE: Leather liner. 1939 band 66/58. Gray repainted rim & body over base green. Eagle decal. Avg. cond. $160.00

COMBAT HELMET ARMY M35 SINGLE-DECAL REISSUE: Shell ET62 with gray rough texture paint inside & out. Eagle decal. 1943 steel liner band 62/54 with leather liner. Above avg. cond. $440.00

COMBAT HELMET ARMY M35 SINGLE-DECAL REISSUE: Shell NS64 with gray rough texture paint. Eagle painted around. Smooth gray inside paint. 1940 steel liner band with leather liner & inked *57*. Full chinstrap with 1940 date and maker. Avg. cond. $267.00

COMBAT HELMET ARMY M35 SINGLE-DECAL REISSUE: Shell SE64 with gray rough texture paint. Eagle decal. Gray brush stroked rim. 1943 steel band, 64/56 & leather liner. Avg. cond. $199.00

COMBAT HELMET ARMY M40 CAMO SINGLE-DECAL: Shell EF64 with pea-green brushed camo over base gray. Eagle decal painted over but visible. Leather liner. Avg. cond. $237.00

COMBAT HELMET ARMY M40 CAMO SINGLE-DECAL: Shell ET62 with gray rough texture base paint covered with off-white wash that lets some gray show thru. Eagle decal painted around. Leather liner, SS teal band 62/55. Avg. cond. $250.00

COMBAT HELMET ARMY M40 CAMO SINGLE-DECAL: Shell Q64 with gray brushstroked period done finish, painted around eagle decal. Scratched out white painted rim name *Bink R*. & scratched *Kaiser* to side rim. Leather liner. Shortened chinstrap fits visor. Avg. cond. $170.00

COMBAT HELMET ARMY M40 CAMO
SINGLE-DECAL

COMBAT HELMET ARMY M40 CAMO SINGLE-DECAL: Shell size painted over with white. Gray to inside top. Good dull white paint to body. Eagle decal painted around. 1943 steel liner band 64/56. leather liner. Avg. cond. $565.00

COMBAT HELMET ARMY M40 CAMO: Leather liner with inked *57*. Shell EF64. Gray rough texture brush stroked finish is over decal & base paint with 5 green brushed splotches. Avg. cond. $310.00

COMBAT HELMET ARMY M40 CAMO: Shell EF64 with gray rough texture base painted over with tan, green & reddish camo. Decal removed before camo paint over. Leather liner. Steel liner band 64/56. Avg. cond. ..$502.00

COMBAT HELMET ARMY M40 NO-DECAL REISSUE: Q64 shell shows removed double decals from base rough texture gray. Reissue dark green paint inside & out. 1943 steel liner band, 57/64. Pigskin liner. Avg. cond. $80.00

COMBAT HELMET ARMY M40 SINGLE-DECAL REISSUE: Shell NS66 with white painted rim *Uffz.Meyer*. Gray rough texture paint. Repainted & covered eagle decal. Steel liner band. Leather liner. Avg. cond. $145.00

COMBAT HELMET ARMY M40 SINGLE-DECAL: Shell EF64. Gray rough texture paint. Eagle decal. 1941 steel band, 64/57 & leather liner. Full 1939 chinstrap with alum. fittings. Avg. cond. $328.00

COMBAT HELMET ARMY M40 SINGLE-DECAL: Shell ET64 with gray rough texture paint. Eagle decal. Leather liner size 56. Full pigskin chinstrap with faint 1941/maker. Avg. cond. $350.00

COMBAT HELMET ARMY M40 SINGLE-DECAL: Shell ET64 with gray rough texture paint. Eagle decal. White painted name to rim *Herkenrath*. Leather liner. Shortened chinstrap fits over visor. Avg. cond. $250.00

COMBAT HELMET ARMY M40
SINGLE-DECAL

COMBAT HELMET ARMY M40 SINGLE-DECAL: Shell ET66 with gray rough texture paint. Eagle decal. Steel liner band with a liner inked with a *58*. Avg. cond. $317.00

COMBAT HELMET ARMY M40 SINGLE-DECAL: Shell NS62. Gray rough texture paint. Eagle decal. Leather liner. Avg. cond. $211.00

COMBAT HELMET ARMY M40 SINGLE-DECAL: Shell Q62 with gray rough texture paint. Eagle decal. 1940 steel band 54/62. Leather liner, inked *54*. Avg. cond. $229.00

COMBAT HELMET ARMY M40 SINGLE-DECAL: Shell hkp60 with gray rough texture paint. Eagle decal. Pigskin liner inked *53*. 1942 steel band. Above avg. cond. $279.00

COMBAT HELMET ARMY M42 CAMO SINGLE-DECAL: Shell EF66 with base gray paint covered by green, splotches of tan & brown. Eagle decal mostly painted over. Leather liner. Below avg. cond. $175.00

COMBAT HELMET ARMY M42 CAMO

COMBAT HELMET ARMY M42 CAMO:
Shell 64 with gray inside. Thick rough
texture painted over decal area & sprayed
tan overall with green & reddish
splotches. Leather liner inked *57*. Full
chinstrap. Above avg. cond. $712.00

COMBAT HELMET ARMY M42 DOUBLE-
DECAL: Shell ckl66 with gray inside
having inked wording to top. Gray rough
texture paint. Eagle & national decals.
1943 steel liner band 58/66 & leather
liner. Early full chinstrap has alum.
fittings. Avg. cond. $608.00

COMBAT HELMET ARMY M42 NO-DECAL:
Shell hkp66. Gray rough texture paint.
Steel band 66/59. Tan pigskin liner with
inked *59* & owner *Kan. Schwarzmueller*.
Full chinstrap with stamped *44*. Exc.
cond. $282.00

COMBAT HELMET ARMY M42
SINGLE-DECAL

COMBAT HELMET ARMY M42 SINGLE-
DECAL: Shell ckl64 with gray rough
texture paint. Eagle decal. Liner size 56.
Inked procurement stamp to shell. Nice
full chinstrap with 1942/maker. Avg.
cond. $177.00

COMBAT HELMET ARMY M42 SINGLE-
DECAL: Shell ckl64 with gray rough
texture paint. Bullet dent to top left side.
Eagle decal. Inked procurement to top.
Dark liner from use & inked *56*.
Chinstrap has been shortened. Avg.
cond. $250.00

COMBAT HELMET BAHNSCHUTZ-
POLIZEI M42 SINGLE DEVICE: Shell
size 66 with gray painted inside & faint
inked wording to top. Dark blue-gray
rough texture outside. 3" wide stamped
brass winged wheel with lightning bolts &
cogged wheel swastika is affixed to left
side with 2 prongs thru vent hole and a
small added hole. 1943 steel liner band
with inked *58* to tan leather with scuffed
rim. Full black leather chinstrap with RB#.
Exc. cond. $893.00

COMBAT HELMET HUNGARIAN M35:
Same maker style as German M35
except has riveted loop to back rim.
Green painted inside top with gray rim &
outside. Leatherette covered steelband
with leather 3 pad liner with black rubber
pads. Leather chinstrap. Avg.
cond. $126.00

COMBAT HELMET HUNGARIAN M35:
Shell DE66 has riveted loop to back.
Thick green brush stroked inside has
leather liner band, 3 pads, cushions &
leather chinstrap. Thick green brush
stroked outside surface shows faint
airbrushed brown camo design. Above
avg. cond. $95.00

COMBAT HELMET HUNGARIAN-
NAZI M16-AUSTRIAN-
TRANSITIONAL DOUBLE-DECAL

COMBAT HELMET HUNGARIAN-NAZI
M16-AUSTRIAN-TRANSITIONAL
DOUBLE-DECAL: Larger shell with
original chinstrap loops & vents intact.
Black painted inside top, green rim &
green outside. Left side has white *Arrow
Cross* decal. Tricolor shield decal to right.
Avg. cond. $391.00

COMBAT HELMET LUFTWAFFE M18-
TRANSITIONAL DOUBLE-DECAL: Shell
L64 with bell trademark. Variation
battleship-gray paint inside & out. 1st
straight-leg eagle decal & national. M31
liner. Inked *56* & named *Markert*. 1939
alum. band & inked procurement oval to
inside top. Above avg.
cond. $1,200.00

COMBAT HELMET LUFTWAFFE M18-TRANSITIONAL DOUBLE-DECAL: Steel shell with vent lugs being size 64. Thick gray repaints over base green. Shows 2 sets of Luffwaffe double decals affixed with painted over eagles & last national left unpainted. 1931 alum. band with leather liner. Early loop chinstrap with clip to roller buckle end. Early. Avg. cond. $451.00

COMBAT HELMET LUFTWAFFE M35 CAMO DOUBLE-DECAL: 1936 alum. band size 66. Smooth gray finish shows traces of tan camo finish. 2nd type eagle decal & national decal. Below avg. cond. $118.00

COMBAT HELMET LUFTWAFFE M35 CAMO: Shell Q66 with blue gray inside. Thick camo repaint with sprayed green & tan design. Faint traces of painted over eagle decal. 1939 alum. 66/58 band. Leather liner. Full chinstrap. Avg. cond. $370.00

COMBAT HELMET LUFTWAFFE M35 DOUBLE-DECAL REISSUE: Pigskin liner inked 57. 1943 steel band. 1930s/maker chinstrap. Shell Q64. Smooth gray paint. Eagle & national decals. Avg. cond. $313.00

COMBAT HELMET LUFTWAFFE M35 DOUBLE-DECAL REISSUE: Q68 shell with blue-gray inside & white painted rim 1400 with triangle over bar. Smooth blue-gray paint. Painted over national decal, eagle decal on left. Below avg. cond. $165.00

COMBAT HELMET LUFTWAFFE M35 DOUBLE-DECAL REISSUE: Shell Q66 with rough texture blue-gray paint. Appears both decal were painted around, 2nd eagle & national. 1943 steel band, tan liner inked 58 & light brown chinstrap with RB#. Unique reissue. Above avg. cond. $308.00

COMBAT HELMET LUFTWAFFE M35 DOUBLE-DECAL: 1938 alum. band 64/57. Shell EF64. Blue-gray paint. 2nd style eagle decal & national decal. Leather liner. Avg. cond. $337.00

COMBAT HELMET LUFTWAFFE M35 DOUBLE-DECAL: Dark combat finish. Eagle & national decals. Alum framed leather liner. Avg. cond. $210.00

COMBAT HELMET LUFTWAFFE M35 DOUBLE-DECAL

COMBAT HELMET LUFTWAFFE M35 DOUBLE-DECAL: Shell EF64 with black inked name inside top, not oval. Blue-gray paint. Eagle and national decals. Shortened chinstrap fits visor. 1939 alum. band with leather inked 57 & owner Uffz. Bohler #. Back seam unsewn. Above avg. cond. $779.00

COMBAT HELMET LUFTWAFFE M35 DOUBLE-DECAL: Shell EF64 with smooth blue-gray paint. Early 'snake-leg' down tail eagle & national decals. National inked rectangle wording to inside top. 1935 alum. liner band. Leather liner. Leather chinstrap with alum. fittings & 1936 date with maker. Avg. cond. $399.00

COMBAT HELMET LUFTWAFFE M35 DOUBLE-DECAL: Shell ET64 with blue-gray paint. 1st eagle & national decals. Leather liner. 1936 alum. band 64. Avg. cond. $300.00

COMBAT HELMET LUFTWAFFE M35 DOUBLE-DECAL: Shell Q62 with brushstroked blue-gray paint. 2nd pattern eagle decal. National decal. Red painted name Frowen Kron to rim with white 5/26. Alum. 1937 band with leather liner. Below avg. cond. $220.00

COMBAT HELMET LUFTWAFFE M40 CAMO: Africa camo helmet with pinkish tan paint. Camo paint was applied over base blue-gray rough texture. Eagle decal painted over. Dark-blue gray inside to shell, SE62. Full leather liner. Avg. cond. $643.00

COMBAT HELMET LUFTWAFFE M40 CAMO: Shell ET68 with blue-gray repainted rim & body with brush strokes. Painted over eagle decal with traces scratched out. 1939 dated alum. liner band 60/68. Has full leather liner. Avg. cond. $147.00

COMBAT HELMET LUFTWAFFE M40 SINGLE-DECAL: Shell EF62 with blue-gray rough texture paint. Eagle decal. Tan leather liner inked 55. Near mint cond. $709.00

COMBAT HELMET LUFTWAFFE M40 SINGLE-DECAL: Shell ET64. Blue/gray rough texture paint. Eagle decal. Tan leather liner inked *56*. Full chinstrap. Avg. cond. $245.00

COMBAT HELMET LUFTWAFFE M40
SINGLE-DECAL

COMBAT HELMET LUFTWAFFE M40 SINGLE-DECAL: Shell NS62. Blue-gray rough texture paint. Eagle decal. Liner inked 54. Full pigskin chinstrap. Above avg. cond. $225.00

COMBAT HELMET LUFTWAFFE M40 SINGLE-DECAL: Shell Q66 with blue-gray paint. Eagle decal. Leather liner. Above avg. cond. $374.00

COMBAT HELMET LUFTWAFFE M40 SINGLE-DECAL: Shell Q66, blue-gray rough texture finish. Eagle decal. Pigskin liner. Avg. cond. $165.00

COMBAT HELMET LUFTWAFFE M40 SINGLE-DECAL: Shell Q66. Blue-gray rough texture paint. Eagle decal. 1941 alum. band 66/58 & leather liner. Below avg. cond. $113.00

COMBAT HELMET LUFTWAFFE M40 SINGLE-DECAL: Shell SE64 with blue-gray rough texture paint. Eagle decal. Size 57 liner. White handpainted name to rim *E. Becker*. Avg. cond. $180.00

COMBAT HELMET LUFTWAFFE M40 SINGLE-DECAL: Shell SE66 with white handpainted owner to rim *Schauffele*. Blue-gray rough texture paint. Eagle decal. Leather liner Full chinstrap. Avg. cond. $145.00

COMBAT HELMET LUFTWAFFE M40 SINGLE-DECAL: Shell hkp64 with rough texture blue-gray paint. Eagle decal. 1943 steel band with 64/57 size, leather liner inked *54*. Chinstrap by *dla 43*. Avg. cond. $223.00

COMBAT HELMET LUFTWAFFE M42 SINGLE-DECAL: Leather liner inked *56*. Shell NS64. Blue-gray rough texture paint. Eagle decal. Avg. cond. .. $214.00

COMBAT HELMET LUFTWAFFE M42 SINGLE-DECAL: Light use to liner with inked *55* & inked out block, owner name? Shell NS62. Blue-gray rough texture paint Eagle. Avg. cond. $190.00

COMBAT HELMET LUFTWAFFE M42 SINGLE-DECAL: Shell ET64 with blue-gray rough texture paint. Eagle decal. Steel liner band, 57 & leather liner. Avg. cond. $150.00

COMBAT HELMET LUFTWAFFE M42
SINGLE-DECAL

COMBAT HELMET LUFTWAFFE M42 SINGLE-DECAL: Shell NS64. Blue-gray rough texture paint. Eagle decal. Tan liner inked *57*. Exc. cond. $361.00

COMBAT HELMET LUFTWAFFE M42 SINGLE-DECAL: Shell NS64 with blue gray rough texture paint. Eagle decal. Tan liner inked *57*. Avg. cond. $183.00

COMBAT HELMET LUFTWAFFE M42 SINGLE-DECAL: Shell ckl64 with blue-gray rough texture paint. Blue eagle decal. Leather liner inked *57*. Avg. cond. $292.00

COMBAT HELMET LUFTWAFFE M42 SINGLE-DECAL: Shell hkp62 with blue-gray rough texture paint. Eagle decal. Tan liner inked *55* & owner named twice *Ogefr.Endler*. Full chinstrap with RB#. Above avg. cond. $183.00

COMBAT HELMET NAVAL M16-TRANSI-TIONAL DOUBLE-DECAL: Shell W66 has original green painted inside, lugs for chinstrap, 3 pad leather liner & band. Original green outside paint. Nice gold eagle & national decals. Unique transitional that didn't get M31 liner. Above avg. cond. $600.00

COMBAT HELMET NAVAL M35 DOUBLE-DECAL: Leather liner with inked *58*. Shell ET66 with painted white owner to top

Bruhn. Smooth green paint. Gold eagle decal shows gold & black painted touch-up. Oversize painted tri-color national side. Avg. cond. $298.00

COMBAT HELMET NAVAL M42 CAMO: 2 part liner is half pigskin. Shell NS66. Light gray brush stroked rim & body. Avg. cond. $205.00

COMBAT HELMET NAVY M40 SINGLE-DECAL: Shell Q66 with gray rough texture paint. Gold eagle decal. Leather liner. Size 66/58 on 1941 steel band. Full chinstrap with 1941/maker. Avg. cond. $331.00

COMBAT HELMET NAVY M42
SINGLE-DECAL

COMBAT HELMET NAVY M42 SINGLE-DECAL: Shell ET62 with gray rough texture paint. Gold eagle decal. Tan liner inked *55*. Full chinstrap by *gfg42*. Exc. cond. $544.00

COMBAT HELMET POLICE M16-AUS-TRIAN-TRANSITIONAL DOUBLE-DECAL: Style used from 1934 thru 1936 & steel shell appears to be special made for the police using Austrian style riveted chinstrap loops that swivel. Nice black paint. Swastika decal & national decal is tilted. Leather liner band with 3 pads having connecting leather straps & cushions at back. Leather chinstrap. Exc. cond. $1,000.00

COMBAT HELMET POLICE M35 DOUBLE-DECAL: Liner with inked owner name. 1939 alum. band 53/60. Pigskin chinstrap with 1940/maker. Shell ET60 with green inside having inked 1939 oval to top. Age patina to green outside. Eagle decal without border. Party decal. Avg. cond. $316.00

COMBAT HELMET POLICE M35 DOUBLE-DECAL: Shell ET62 with smooth gray paint. Unbordered eagle/wreath decal & party decal. 1940 alum. band. Leather liner inked *55*. Full chinstrap with RB num. Avg. cond. $400.00

COMBAT HELMET POLICE M40 DOUBLE-DECAL: Black patent leather chinstrap

with maker/44. Shell ET64. Dark gray rough texture finish. Unbordered eagle decal & party decals. Leather liner. Avg. cond. $412.00

COMBAT HELMET
SA-FELDHERRNHALLE M40
DOUBLE-DECA

COMBAT HELMET SA-FELDHERRNHALLE M40 DOUBLE-DECAL: Shell EF64 with brown paint inside & out. Monument decal to left side. Swastika decal. Steel liner band 57/64. Leather liner. Exc. cond. $2,691.00

COMBAT HELMET SS M35
DOUBLE-DECAL

COMBAT HELMET SS M35 DOUBLE-DECAL: Shell Q62 has original green top, sprayed gloss back rim & body. 1st SS runes decal & party decal. 1937 alum. liner band 54/62. Leather liner. Short-ened chinstrap fits over visor. Above avg. cond. $3,150.00

COMBAT HELMET SS-ALLGEMEINE M18-TRANSITIONAL DOUBLE-DECAL: Black painted over WWI combat green finish. 30x40mm decal of 3 silver oak leafs on black field with silver border on left side & other is same size decal of first pattern SS runes with silver border. Has original 3 pads liner with metal band ring. Marked inside *Zurn* & *Gann 9/111* on leather liner band, WWI unit markings. The oak leaf decal is unreferenced in any book &

matches the manufacture of the SS runes. Avg. cond. $3,500.00

COMBAT HELMET SS-ALLGEMEINE M35 DOUBLE-DECAL: Shell EF64. Original green top with inked oval mark, black painted rim & body. 1st runes decal & party decal. 1939 alum. band to liner inked *57*. Cut-down chinstrap fits over visor. Near mint cond. $2,369.00

COMBAT HELMET
SS-ALLGEMEINE
M35 DOUBLE-DECAL

COMBAT HELMET SS-ALLGEMEINE M35 DOUBLE-DECAL: Shell Q64 with black painted rim & original green to top. Nice black finish. 1st runes decal & party decal. White painted Gothic owner name to rim *Hefer*. Helmet was redone in 1939 using an Army combat helmet, green. 1939 alum. band. Leather liner. Above avg. cond. $2,300.00

COMBAT HELMET SS-LAH M18-TRANSI-TIONAL DOUBLE-DECAL: Black painted. 60x67mm right decal of black & silver field shield with silver SS runes with black border. Left decal of black shield & silver script LAH on other side. 1933 dated replacement leather liner & rivets. Has large oval white ink stamp at back rim with NSDAP SS stamp dated 1933 & owners ID & no num. on side, inked in. Liner & chinstrap. Avg. cond. $4,500.00

COMBAT HELMET SS-SD M16-AUS-TRIAN-TRANSITIONAL DOUBLE-DECAL: Replacement liner inked *56*. Shortened black chinstrap fits over visor. Original green to top with dark green rim & body. Reversed decals with 1st runes to left side, Party to right side with traces of decal behind. Avg. cond. $480.00

COMBAT HELMET SS-WAFFEN M40 DOUBLE-DECAL REISSUE: With SS reissue decal. Shell Q62 with gray rough texture paint. Combat issued as police double decal, 1st SS runes decal covers eagle/wreath decal. Original party to right side. Leather liner, inked with *55* & faint owner name. Avg. cond. $750.00

COMBAT HELMET SS-WAFFEN M40 DOUBLE-DECAL: Leather liner inked *56*. Full chinstrap. Shell Q64. Gray rough texture finish. SS runic decal & party decal. Avg. cond. $716.00

COMBAT HELMET SS-WAFFEN M42 SINGLE-DECAL: Shell EF68 with gray rough texture paint. 2nd runes decal. Dark pigskin liner has 1943 steel band, size 60. Avg. cond. $643.00

COMBAT HELMET SS-WAFFEN M42 SINGLE-DECAL: Shell CKL68 with gray rough texture paint. 2nd runes decal. Leather liner. 1944 steel band & 68/61. Full chinstrap. Avg. cond. $1,735.00

COMBAT HELMET SS-WAFFEN M42 SINGLE-DECAL: Shell EF64 with gray rough texture paint. 2nd runes decal. Traces of twine netting cover still stuck in steel band with inked *55* tan liner. Cut-down chinstrap fits over visor. Avg. cond. $1,300.00

COMBAT HELMET
SS-WAFFEN M42 SINGLE-DECAL

COMBAT HELMET SS-WAFFEN M42 SINGLE-DECAL: Shell hkp66 with gray rough texture paint. 2nd runes decal. Leather liner. 1940 steel band 64/56. Full chinstrap. Avg. cond. $626.00

COMBAT HELMET WAR-ART ARMY M40: Liner inked 56. Full chinstrap with 1941/maker. Shell EF64 has original Army-gray inside. Outside handpainted in WWI camo style with B&W swastika to top. Geometric design in red, white, gray, brown & wide black divider lines. Avg. cond. $230.00

FLIGHT HELMET LUFTWAFFE
SUMMER-PATTERN LKP N101

FLIGHT HELMET LUFTWAFFE SUMMER-
PATTERN LKP N101: Brown mesh body
is style with out top fittings. Dark brown
leather ear cups with fleece lining. Oval
bakelite throat mikes. Bevo label by *hdc
etc.* & size *58*. Below avg.
cond. $111.00

FLIGHT HELMET LUFTWAFFE SUMMER-
PATTERN LKP S101

FLIGHT HELMET LUFTWAFFE SUMMER-
PATTERN LKP S101: Flightsuit style tan/
brown cloth body, brown leather fittings,
green satin & fleece lining. Oval throat
mikes & long cord with plug. Bevo label
by *Siemens etc.* & size *58*. Exc.
cond. $328.00
FLIGHT HELMET LUFTWAFFE SUMMER-
PATTERN LKP S101: Tan cloth body.
Brown satin lining with fleece ear cups
sewn shut. Bevo maker label *Deutsche
Telephonwerke etc.* with inked size *57*.
Below avg. cond. $85.00
FLIGHT HELMET LUFTWAFFE WINTER-
PATTERN CREWMAN: Brown leather
body is style with out radio gear. Fleece
lining. Bevo maker tag *Striegel & Wagner
etc.* Avg. cond. $80.00

FLIGHT HELMET LUFTWAFFE WINTER-
PATTERN LKP W101: Brown leather
body & fleece lining. Radio gear intact
with oval bakelite throat mikes, long cord
& bakelite plug. 1 broken plastic ear
cover. Bevo maker tag by Siemens with
inked *57* size & *19.Nov.1939*. Above avg.
cond. $226.00

FLIGHT HELMET LUFTWAFFE WINTER-
PATTERN LKP W101

FLIGHT HELMET LUFTWAFFE WINTER-
PATTERN LKP W101: Brown leather
body with fleece lining. Oval bakelite
throat mikes & long cord with plug. Bevo
maker label *Siemens etc.* Above avg.
cond. $250.00
FLIGHT HELMET LUFTWAFFE WINTER-
PATTERN LKP W101: Brown leather
body & fleece lining. Speakers to ear
cups with plastic covers. Bevo *Siemens
etc.* label with inked size *58*. Below avg.
cond. $107.00
FLIGHT HELMET LUFTWAFFE WINTER-
PATTERN LKP W101: Brown leather
body with fittings intact, oval bakelite
throat mikes & long cord with plug.
Fleece inside with bevo tag *Siemens etc.*
& inked *55*. Exc. cond. $200.00
FLIGHT HELMET LUFTWAFFE WINTER-
PATTERN LKP W101: Brown leather
body with fleece lining. Oval bakelite
throat mikes & short cord with plug. Bevo
maker label by Siemens. Below avg.
cond. $108.00
MOTORCYCLE HELMET NSKK 1ST
PATTERN: Black leather with padded
ridges. Nickel 1st type eagle. Brown
leather neck flap & ear covers with roller
buckle chinstrap. 10 finger leather liner
inked 57. Avg. cond. $280.00

MOTORCYCLE HELMET NSKK 1ST TYPE

MOTORCYCLE HELMET NSKK 1ST
TYPE: Black leather body with ridged
pads, metal grommet vents, brass
affixed eagle, neckflap & ear flaps with
roller buckle strap. 9 Finger leather
liner with oil cloth RZM tag & inked *55*.
Leather pad at top has inked NSKK
unit & *Berolina* color maker decal.
Above avg. cond. $436.00

PARADE HELMET ARMY CIVIC-
POLICE-STYLE DOUBLE-DECAL:
Steel shell with black paint inside.
Green painted outside. Eagle &
national decals. 8 finger leather liner
inked *59*. Black leather chinstrap with
roller buckle. Near mint
cond. $355.00

PARADE HELMET ARMY OFFICER
ALUMINUM DOUBLE-DECAL: Nice
alum. shell with rolled rim, civic 'curved
dip' style & double 7 hole vents. Apple-
green paint inside & out. Eagle &
National decals. 10 finger leather liner,
pad at top & chinstrap with clip end.
Above avg. cond. $450.00

PARADE HELMET ARMY OFFICER M35
DOUBLE-DECAL: 9 finger tan leather
liner & brown leather chinstrap with
alum. clip. Green/gray paint inside &
out with penciled *57 1/2* to inside top.
Alum. shell with rolled rim, large
grommet vents & 4 liner rivets. Eagle &
national decals. Mint cond. $2,000.00

PARADE HELMET SA-
FELDHERRNHALLE SINGLE-DECAL:
Steel. Rolled rim to body with
screened vent to each side, 3 liner
rivets & 2 chinstrap loop rivets. Gray
paint. Tri-color monument decal to left

side. Leather band with 3 pad liner.
Variation shell. Avg. cond. $955.00

PARATROOPER HELMET LUFTWAFFE
CAMO:

PARATROOPER HELMET LUFTWAFFE
CAMO: Shell ET68 with gray rough
texture base paint, eagle decal
appears painted over with gray & 11
brushed tan splotches. 2 wire lengths
are wrapped over helmet with 4
hooked ends at rim. Leather liner with
inked maker *Heisler/Muller etc.. 57/68*.
Gray chinstrap/harness has friction clip
with strap. 4 spanner bolts. Above avg.
cond. $4,187.00

PARATROOPER HELMET LUFTWAFFE
CAMO SINGLE-DECAL: Shell ET68
with gray base showing thick sawdust
camo repaint. Tan & green sprayed
design. Painted over eagle decal &
spanner bolts, eagle is slightly visible.
Alum. liner band to leather with faint
maker & size *57/68*. Gray leather
chinstrap/harness & friction clip with
strap. Italian front camo. Avg.
cond. $3,161.00

PARATROOPER HELMET LUFTWAFFE
DOUBLE-DECAL 1ST MODEL: Steel
shell by *ET71*. Grommet vents. Gray
paint inside & out. Eagle & national
decals. Avg. cond. $2,785.00

PARATROOPER HELMET LUFTWAFFE
NO-DECAL: Shell ET68. Gray rough
texture paint. 3 solid & 1 vented alum.
liner bolts. Liner with inked RB num.
& size *56/58*. Couple inked owner
initials to liner. Chinstrap/harness
still intact. Avg. cond. $1,600.00

PARATROOPER HELMET LUFTWAFFE
SINGLE-DECAL WITH METAL CAMO
BAND: Shell ET66. Gray rough t
exture paint. Eagle decal. Leather
liner & gray leather chinstrap/harness
withfriction clip & strap. Half inch wide
steel band riveted into cross with
wavy band around body. Unique
camo style. Avg.cond. $2,634.00

PARATROOPER HELMET LUFTWAFFE
SINGLE-DECAL

PARATROOPER HELMET LUFTWAFFE
SINGLE-DECAL: Shell by ET71 with
blue-gray rough texture paint. Eagle
decal. Variation steel liner bolts are
vented & slotted. Early tan leather liner
with maker & 60/71. Leather chinstrap/
harness with friction clip & strap.
Above avg. cond. $2,700.00

PITH HELMET ARMY

PITH HELMET ARMY: Canvas model.
Tan canvas body, green leather trim &
chinstrap. Painted gray metal side
shields. Leather sweatband is inked *53*
& red lined across the top. Above avg.
cond. $175.00
PITH HELMET ARMY: Felt model.
Green body with green leather trim &
chinstrap. Brass eagle shield & alum.
National shield. Leather sweatband
with underside inked *APN 1942 56*.
Above avg.
cond. $181.00
PITH HELMET ARMY: Felt model.
Green felt body with early dark
brass shields. Leather sweatband.
Red felt liner. Below avg.
cond. $81.00

PITH HELMET NAVY

PITH HELMET NAVY: Canvas model. White
canvas covered cork body with white
leather trim & brown chinstrap. Gold
finished gray metal eagle to front. Green
canvas lining with leather sweatband.
Embossed *Erel* maker & is inked with
1941 date and size *58*. Above avg.
cond. $1,096.00

**THIRD REICH VISOR CAPS & FIELD
CAPS**

CAMO FIELD CAP SS-WAFFEN 2ND
MODEL: M43 styled with center seam.
Reversible with spring oak leave design
to outside & fall inside with small
sweatband. 2 grommet vents per side.
Exc. cond. $788.00

CAMO FIELD CAP SS-WAFFEN
2ND MODEL

COFFEE CAN CAP NSFK: Blue-gray wool
covered body has stiff shape. Yellow wool
piping to top & sides with double
grommet vents. Alum. eagle & black
leather chinstrap. Brown leather
sweatband. Purple satin lining. Above
avg. cond. $491.00

COFFEE CAN CAP SA

FEZ SS-WAFFEN

COFFEE CAN CAP SA: Entire cap has same brown wool construction, 2 grommet vents per side, twisted B&W piping around sides & dark silver twisted piping around top. Silver eagle, pebbled button & black leather chinstrap. Leather sweatband & orange waterproof full lining with inked *30.B.245*. Avg. cond. $1,350.00

COFFEE CAN CAP SA: Tan twill body. Double grommet vents to yellow wool sides. Gray wartime eagle, nickel button & brown chinstrap. Leatherette sweatband with oilcloth RZM tag. Orange waterproof top lining with inked size *57*. Above avg. cond. $550.00

DONALD DUCK CAP NAVAL EM: Removable blue wool top has blue satin lining sewn inside. Blue wool band with leather sweatband & front stiffener inked *56 HFT*. Gold bevo Kriegsmarine tally. Gold painted eagle pin lacks cockade. Avg. cond. $365.00

FEZ SS-WAFFEN: Maroon. Black tassel to back & bevo gray eagle over skull to front. Leather sweatband & inked 57 size. Above avg. cond. $588.00

FEZ SS-WAFFEN: Maroon. Black tassel. Bevo eagle over skull with both machine- sewn. Leather sweatband. Avg. cond. $387.00

FIELD CAP ARMY M43 EM: Good gray wool body, 2 gray pebbled buttons & bevo trapezoid is machine sewn on. Gray twill cotton lining. Unmarked & fair size. Above avg. cond. $437.00

FIELD CAP ARMY M43 EM: Gray wool body with single gray pebbled button & embr. thin gray trapezoid is machine zig-zag-sewn. Gray satin lining inked *58*. Avg. cond. $215.00

FIELD CAP ARMY M43 EM: Gray wool body, 2 gray pebbled buttons & bevo trapezoid is hand-sewn. Gray satin lining with inked with RB# *58 44*. Avg. cond. $328.00

FIELD CAP ARMY M43 EM

FIELD CAP ARMY M43 EM: Gray wool body, 2 gray pebbled buttons & embr. trapezoid is hand-sewn. Gray satin lining. Below avg. cond. $73.00

FIELD CAP ARMY MT TROOP OFFICER: Custom made. Gray doeskin body, alum. piped top, 2 alum. buttons, metal Edelweiss to side & flat-silver bevo T-form eagle/cockade is machine-sewn. Leather sweatband & gray satin lining. Above avg. cond. $486.00

FIELD CAP ARMY M43 MT TROOP OFFICER: Gray felt body with alum. piping around top, 2 pebbled alum. buttons, metal Edelweiss sewn to side & bevo T-form eagle/cockade hand-sewn.

Tan canvas lining & sweatband. Avg. cond. $685.00

FIELD CAP ARMY M43 MT TROOP OFFICER

FIELD CAP ARMY TROPICAL DAK EM: Olive twill body with double grommet vents. Hand-sewn blue bevo eagle & cockade both on tan. Red lining inked *RF#* & *60*. Above avg. cond. $425.00

FIELD CAP COASTAL ARTY M43 OF-FICER: Variation. Tan twill cotton body with double grommet vents & bevo insignia machine-sewn. Alum. piping sewn around sides to give scalloped look, no side scallops to cap construction. Green twill cotton lining inked *HPC 57*. Exc. cond. $600.00

FIELD CAP HITLER YOUTH M43 FLAK-HELPER: Blue-gray wool body, gray pebbled button & bevo HJ diamond machine-sewn. Gray satin lining with quilted top inked *RB# 57 44*. Near mint cond. $135.00

FIELD CAP LUFTWAFFE M43 EM

FIELD CAP LUFTWAFFE M43 EM: Blue/gray wool body, 2 pebbled gray buttons, embr. eagle is zigzag-sewn & bevo cockade is machine-sewn. Purple satin lining inked *RB#, 1944* & *57*. Exc. cond. $370.00

FIELD CAP LUFTWAFFE M43 EM: Thin blue-gray twill wool body with 2 gray pebbled buttons. Gray satin lining & inked *57*. Avg. cond. $129.00

FIELD CAP LUFTWAFFE M43 OFFICER: Blue-gray twill wool body, alum. piped top, 2 silver painted pebbled buttons, hand embr. alum. bullion eagle & cockade both hand-sewn. Blue satin lining. Exc. cond. $525.00

FIELD CAP LUFTWAFFE TROPICAL EM: Variation. Heavy tan twill body with double grommet vents. Heavy red twill lining. Gray embr. eagle on tan twill is hand-sewn. Variation heavy construction for a tropical cap. Below avg. cond. $270.00

FIELD CAP ORG. TODT M43 OFFICER: Brown twill wool body with dark tarnished silver piped top. 2 gray pebbled button front & machine-sewn bevo trapezoid on green/brown. Leather sweatband. Green twill satin lining with inked size *57*. Below avg. cond. $350.00

FIELD CAP ORG. TODT M43 OFFICER: Green/brown twill wool body with alum. piping at top & front scallop. White bevo eagle on green & cockade. Gray satin lining. Avg. cond. $155.00

FIELD CAP POLICE M43 OFFICER: Police wool body, alum. piped top, 2 silver pebbled button front, 2 part metal edelweiss sewn to side & 6 sided EM bevo eagle/wreath with cockade machine-sewn. Green satin lining inked *57*. Exc. cond. $625.00

FIELD CAP POLICE M43 OFFICER: Blue/green twill body with silver wire piping around crown & 2 silver pebbled button front, has high relief alum. police eagle in wreath badge on front & 2 vent holes on either side. Leather sweatband with original paper price tag still stapled to back, green twill satin lining with beautiful Hamburg makers emblem of ships wheel/arrow with lion & size 54. Mint cond. $329.00

FIELD CAP SA: Brown/green wool body with rose-pink wool sides & left side patch with metal affixed edelweiss. 2 brown pebbled button front & faded gold eagle. Brown twill lining inked *57*. Above avg. cond. $662.00

FIELD CAP SA: Gray/brown wool body with 2 brown plastic button front. Hand-sewn flat-silver bevo eagle on blue triangle. Tan twill lining with inked size *56* and oilcloth title RZM tag. Exc. cond. $388.00

FIELD CAP SS-ALLGEMEINE EM: Black twill wool body is combination styled after kepi & mt. troop caps. Tall body & flaps with 2 black resin button front. Early jawless skull to front & early party eagle to left side with both showing gray corrosion to silver finishes. Leather forehead sweatband to black twill satin lining with bevo *Vom Reichsfuhrer SS etc* tag. Near mint cond. $2,000.00

FIELD CAP SS-WAFFEN M43 EM: Gray twill wool body with black resin button to front. Traces of stitches from removed embr. eagle & skull. Gray satin lining is inked *57 SS-BW 1944*. Above avg. cond. $591.00

FIELD CAP SS-WAFFEN M43 EM: black wool body with 2 pebbled buttons to front. No traces of insignia. Gray satin lining has inked *RB# E43 59*. Above avg. cond. $429.00

FIELD CAP SS-WAFFEN M43 MT TROOP EM: Gray twill wool body with 2 gray pebbled button front. Machine-sewn green trapezoid with gray bevo eagle/ skull. Zigzag sewn embr. edelweiss on black wool to left side. Green cloth lining inked *57*. Late-war example. Near mint cond. $1,500.00

FIELD CAP SS-WAFFEN M43 MT. TROOP EM: Gray wool body, 2 pebbled buttons, gray bevo trapezoid on green & embr. edelweiss on black wool are both machine-sewn. Gray twill lining is inked *57 RB#*. Light age only. Exc. cond. $1,000.00

FIELD CAP SS-WAFFEN M43 OFFICER

FIELD CAP SS-WAFFEN M43 OFFICER: Gray twill wool body with alum. piping around top. Single brown plastic button to front. Zigzag stitches remain from cut off gray embr. eagle & skull. Gray satin lining with inked size *5*. Avg. cond. $400.00

FIELD CAP SS-WAFFEN M43 OFFICER: Gray/green twill wool, alum. piped top, & lacks both gray bevo insignia with zig-zag stitches intact. Gray satin lining has inked

out areas & large Russian museum *#722*. Avg. cond. $375.00

FOUL-WEATHER CAP NAVAL: Gray/brown rubberized cloth body, off-white tie strings & white inked *Willy Sprengpfeil etc...U29*. Early U-Boat item. Near mint cond $90.00

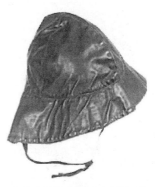

FOUL-WEATHER CAP NAVAL

FOUL-WEATHER CAP NAVAL: 4 part main body with 2 part large rim. Gray cloth lining & neck flap with tie strings. Inked RB#, maker name & 1943 date. Exc. cond. $199.00

OVERSEAS CAP ARMY DAK EM: Olive twill cotton body with grommet side vents. Correct bevo eagle & cockade are both machine-sewn. Red lining inked *54 RB# etc*. Exc. cond. $154.00

OVERSEAS CAP ARMY DAK PANZER OFFICER: Clean olive twill body with machine-sewn alum. piping to top & front before cap was finished. Grommet vent to each side. Blue bevo eagle & cockade on tan are both hand-sewn. Pink soutache is machine sewn on. Red lining inked *58 Robert Feldstein Berlin NO55 1941*. Exc. cond. $1,641.00

OVERSEAS CAP ARMY EM: M34. Gray wool body & grommet side vents. Bevo eagle & cockade both machine-sewn with eagle done as triangle. Gray lining. Avg. cond. $120.00

OVERSEAS CAP ARMY EM: M34. Gray wool body, grommet vent per side & removed soutache. Poor hand-sewn bevo eagle & cockade. Gray lining. Avg. cond. $68.00

OVERSEAS CAP ARMY EM: Gray wool body, grommet vent per side, bevo gray eagle is hand-sewn & bevo cockade machine-sewn. Gray satin lining is inked *CKE 1943* size *55*. Shows light use. Avg. cond. $150.00

OVERSEAS CAP ARMY INF EM: Gray wool body. Bevo eagle & cockade hand-sewn. White soutache machine-sewn. Lacks both grommet vents. Gray lining inked with size 57. Below avg. cond. $110.00

OVERSEAS CAP ARMY PANZER EM WITH SOUTACHE

OVERSEAS CAP ARMY PANZER EM WITH SOUTACHE: Gray wool body, grommet side vents, bevo insignia & machine-sewn soutache. Gray eagle on green is hand-sewn & machine-sewn cockade. Off-white lining with inked 60 P.We????bach Glauchau 1941. Avg. cond. $275.00

OVERSEAS CAP ARMY PANZER EM: Black wool body with grommet vent per side. Gray bevo eagle on black is hand-sewn as is bevo cockade on green. Pink soutache is machine-sewn. Gray lining inked with Lago Berlin 1941 56 B.II.40 & Russian museum marks. Exc. cond. $1,052.00

OVERSEAS CAP ARMY PANZER OFFICER WITH SOUTACHE

OVERSEAS CAP ARMY PANZER OFFICER WITH SOUTACHE: Doeskin body with alum. piping to top & front. Grommet vent per side, flat-silver bevo eagle is hand-sewn, bullion cockade & a pink

soutache. Full gray satin lining with leather forehead sweatband having an embossed stamp. Medium size. Avg. cond. $395.00

OVERSEAS CAP ARMY PIONEER EM: M34. gray wool body, grommet vents & bevo insignia hand-sewn as is black soutache. Gray twill cotton lining inked size 60 & M1935 with maker. Near mint cond. $212.00

OVERSEAS CAP BDM: Cotton body with white cord side piping is hand-stitched. Inked size 56 to full lining with oilcloth RZM BDM-Mutze etc tag. Avg. cond. $125.00

OVERSEAS CAP COASTAL ARTY EM WITH SIGNAL SOUTACHE: Gray wool body, yellow bevo eagle hand-sewn, embr. cockade is machine-sewn as is yellow soutache. Gray lining French maker ink stamped & size 57. Near mint cond. $200.00

OVERSEAS CAP COASTAL ARTY EM: Gray wool body with owner sewn closed top. Yellow bevo eagle & cockade both hand-sewn. Gray lining inked with Hannover/maker 56 1941. Above avg. cond. $100.00

OVERSEAS CAP DAF OFFICER

OVERSEAS CAP DAF OFFICER: Blue wool body with light blue silk piping on brim & top. Has silver wire bevo eagle with 2 small alum pebbled buttons on front. Has original DAF RZM oilcloth tag, black interior cloth & half leather sweatband. Above avg. cond. $200.00

OVERSEAS CAP DAF: Blue wool body with blue piping & lacks insignia. Black cloth lining, leather forehead sweatband, inked 54 & oilcloth RZM/DAF tag. Avg. cond. $55.00

OVERSEAS CAP HITLER YOUTH MEMBER: Tan twill body with red cord piping around sides. Lacks bevo diamond to front with stitch outline visible. Leather sweatband to gray lining with oilcloth tag. Avg. cond. $97.00

OVERSEAS CAP HITLER YOUTH: Tan brown body with red silk piping around fold & hand-sewn bevo HJ diamond on front. Light tan lining with brown oilcloth RZM tag & size 55. Above avg. cond. $125.00

OVERSEAS CAP LUFTWAFFE EM: Blue-gray wool body with embr. eagle & cockade both hand-sewn. Gray cloth two tone lining with inked *55*. Above avg. cond. $100.00

OVERSEAS CAP LUFTWAFFE EM: Blue-gray wool body with gray embr. eagle & cockade both zigzag-stitched. Gray lining. Avg. cond. $65.00

OVERSEAS CAP LUFTWAFFE EM

OVERSEAS CAP LUFTWAFFE EM: Blue-gray wool body with hand-sewn gray embr. eagle & cockade. Gray lining with inked maker name & size *53*. Avg. cond. $75.00

OVERSEAS CAP LUFTWAFFE EM: Blue-gray wool body, embr. eagle & cockade both hand-sewn. Gray lining. Avg. cond. $76.00

OVERSEAS CAP LUFTWAFFE EM: Blue-gray wool body. Embr. eagle & cockade both hand-sewn. Gray lining. Avg. cond. $90.00

OVERSEAS CAP LUFTWAFFE EM: Blue-gray wool body. Gray embr. eagle & thick cockade both hand-sewn. Gray lining. Avg. cond. $86.00

OVERSEAS CAP LUFTWAFFE EM: Blue-gray wool body. Gray embr. eagle on wool is hand-sewn. Machine-sewn cockade. Tan cloth lining inked *54*. Near mint cond. $110.00

OVERSEAS CAP LUFTWAFFE EM: Blue-gray wool body. Thick cockade is hand-sewn & lacks eagle. Gray lining shows use & inked size *54 70*. Avg. cond. $55.00

OVERSEAS CAP LUFTWAFFE PANZER DIV GORING EM: Black wool body. Insignia both hand-sewn, embr. gray eagle on black wool & embr. cockade on blue-gray wool. Black satin lining. Avg. cond. $340.00

OVERSEAS CAP NAVAL EM: Black wool body, yellow bevo eagle & bevo cockade. Black lining inked 60. Avg. cond. $125.00

OVERSEAS CAP NAVAL EM: Paris made. Blue wool body, yellow embr. eagle is hand sewn on, embr. cockade is machine-sewn & black lining is Paris maker ink stamped & size *54*. Above avg. cond. $244.00

OVERSEAS CAP NAVAL FEMALE AUX

OVERSEAS CAP NAVAL FEMALE AUX: Dark blue wool body with yellow wool piping to sides. Lacks eagle triangle cut from front. Black lining inked RB#, *1944* date & size *54*. restoration body. Avg. cond. $45.00

OVERSEAS CAP NAVAL FEMALE AUX: Dark blue wool body, yellow wool side piping & yellow bevo eagle on blue is hand-sewn. Black lining inked RB# & size *54*. Above avg. cond. $139.00

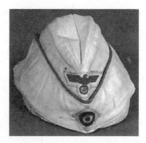

OVERSEAS CAP NAVAL OBERFAHNRICH

OVERSEAS CAP NAVAL OBERFAHNRICH: Summer pattern.

White twill cotton body with gold celleon piping to sides. Blue embr. eagle & cockade are both on white material & zigzag-sewn. White cloth full lining with inked size 59. Exc. cond. $906.00

OVERSEAS CAP NSKK: Black wool body has 2 alum. eagle/spoked wheel buttons & flat-silver bevo eagle scroll on yellow triangle. Black lining has RZM oilcloth tag. Avg. cond. $125.00

OVERSEAS CAP OLYMPIC HOSTESS

OVERSEAS CAP OLYMPIC HOSTESS: White wool overseas cap style with 5 color plastic rings. Inked word inside. Avg. cond. $148.00

OVERSEAS CAP ORG. TODT EM: Brown wool body with hand-sewn bevo eagle & cockade both on brown. Tan cloth lining with inked *Karl Kubach* etc..*54 1940*. Avg. cond. $225.00

OVERSEAS CAP RED CROSS EM: Dark gray wool body with grommet vent per side. Bevo eagle oval is hand-sewn to left side. White soutache is machine-sewn. Gray lining & inked *56*. Avg. cond. $72.00

OVERSEAS CAP SLOVAKIAN CAPTURED WITH ARMY EM INSIGNIA: Gray wool body. Low scallop to front of cap with bevo T-form insignia hand-sewn. Tan HBT lining with leather sweatband. Avg. cond. $96.00

OVERSEAS CAP SS-WAFFEN EM: Gray wool body. Both gray bevo insignia are hand sewn on. Gray satin lining. Avg. cond. $492.00

VISOR CAP ARMY ARTY EM: Gray wool body, red wool piping & green band. Alum. eagle, wreath & 3 part cockade. Black chinstrap & visor. Leatherette sweatband. Satin lining with diamond by *Deutsche Wert Arbeit*. Below avg. cond. $126.00

VISOR CAP ARMY ARTY EM: Gray twill wool body, red wool piping & green band. Alum. eagle, wreath & 3 part cockade. Black chinstrap & visor. Leather sweat-

band inked *1937/maker* & unit *11./(E) A.R.27 I.* Orange lining with diamond & inked size *60*. Below avg. cond. $83.00

VISOR CAP ARMY ARTY EM

VISOR CAP ARMY ARTY OFFICER: Gray felt/wool body. Red wool piping. Green wool band. Alum. eagle, wreath & 3 part cockade. Alum. chincord & black visor. Leather sweatband. Gold satin lining with diamond inked *Stirndruckfrei Deutsches Reichspatent*. Below avg. cond. $208.00

VISOR CAP ARMY ARTY OFFICER: Old style crush. Gray wool body. Red wool piping. Green wool band. Flat-silver bevo wreath & cockade on green. Eagle on tan/gray. Black leather visor is pliable & folded. Brown leather sweatband embossed *Deutsches Leder*. Gold lining. Avg. cond. $450.00

VISOR CAP ARMY CAV EM: Smooth gray wool body, yellow piping & green band. Alum. eagle, wreath & 3 part cockade. Black chinstrap & visor. Leather sweatband embossed *Deutsches Leder*. Satin lining with gold *Anton Baumgart Bad Kissingen*. Saddle shape. Above avg. cond. $280.00

VISOR CAP ARMY CAV OFFICER

VISOR CAP ARMY CAV OFFICER: Gray doeskin saddle shaped body, yellow wool piping & green band. Frosted silver finish to eagle & wreath. 3 part cockade, alum. chincord & black visor. Leather sweatband inked size *58*, gold satin lining, diamond & *Pekuro Stirndurckfrei etc.* Early quality. Above avg. cond. $795.00

VISOR CAP ARMY GENERAL-STAFF OFFICER: Saddle shape to gray wool body with thick crimson wool piping & green band. Alum. eagle, bullion wreath & 3 part cockade. Alum. chincord & black visor. Gray leather sweatband embossed *Kaps.* Gray satin lining with diamond having maker *Paul Kaps etc.* Above avg. cond. $765.00

VISOR CAP ARMY INF EM: Gray twill wool body, white wool piping & green band. Alum. wreath, 3 part cockade & lacks eagle. Black chinstrap & visor. Leatherette sweatband, brown lining & diamond. Avg. cond. $139.00

VISOR CAP ARMY INF EM: Gray twill wool body, white wool piping & green band. Alum. eagle, wreath & 3 part cockade. Black chinstrap & visor. Brown leather sweatband with inked 1937/maker. Brown lining with diamond & size 58. Avg. cond. $165.00

VISOR CAP ARMY INF OFFICER: Gray doeskin body with padded sides, white wool piping & green band. Alum. eagle, hand embr. bullion wreath & 3 part cockade on padded green wool. Alum. chincord & black visor. Leather sweat-band on velvet rim. Satin lining with diamond by *Pekuro Stirndruckfrei etc.* About size 59. Exc. cond. $538.00

VISOR CAP ARMY INF OFFICER: Light gray twill wool body, white wool piping & green band. Alum. hand embr. bullion eagle, wreath & cockade. Alum. chincord & black visor. Leatherette sweatband. Satin lining with diamond. Late-war. Avg. cond. $191.00

VISOR CAP ARMY INF OFFICER: Gray doeskin body with padded sides, white wool piping & green band. Silver painted gray metal eagle, wreath & 3 part cockade. Black visor. Orange satin lining with diamond by *Seit 1890 Konietzko Lotzen/Ostpr.* Below avg. cond. $225.00

VISOR CAP ARMY MEDICAL OFFICER: Old style crush. Gray twill wool body, blue wool piping & green band. Flat silver bevo eagle, wreath & cockade. Variation black fiber visor instead of normal leather. Gray leatherette sweatband, tan satin lining & diamond with maker *Karl Schmult etc.* Above avg. cond. . $500.00

VISOR CAP ARMY MEDICAL OFFICER: Old style crush. Soft gray wool body. Blue wool piping & green band. Flat-silver

bevo eagle & wreath/cockade both hand sewn on. Black leather visor. Brown leatherette sweatband. 2 shades of green cloth lining with *Wilh. Kern Freiburg.* Avg. cond. $340.00

VISOR CAP ARMY MEDICAL OFFICER

VISOR CAP ARMY MEDICAL OFFICER: Gray twill wool body with nice saddle shape, blue wool piping & green band. Nice alum. bullion eagle & wreath with 3 part cockade. Alum. chincord & black visor. Leatherette sweatband. Full black satin lining & diamond maker mark by *Max Teuscher, Halle/Saale etc.* Avg. cond. $310.00

VISOR CAP ARMY MOTORCYCLE RECON EM: Gray twill wool body with green band & golden-yellow wool piping like cavalry color. Alum. eagle & wreath with 3 part cockade. Black chinstrap & visor. Leather sweatband inked *HB 37.* Orange lining inked *54* & *1.(Pz.Sp.) Kompanie Krad.Schutz ????.9.* Avg. cond. $316.00

VISOR CAP ARMY PANZER EM: Gray twill wool body, pink wool piping & green band. Silver eagle, alum. wreath & 3 part cockade. Black visor & side buttons with alum. chincord. Leather sweatband with 1937/maker marks. Tan lining. Avg. cond. $276.00

VSOR CAP ARMY PIONEER EM: Early. Flat top to gray twill wool body, black wool piping & green band. Alum. eagle, wreath & 3 part cockade. Black chinstrap & visor. Brown leatherette sweatband, orange lining & diamond. Avg. cond. $150.00

VISOR CAP ARMY PIONEER EM: Gray twill wool body has soft crush cap look, black wool piping & green band. Alum. eagle, wreath & 3 part cockade. Black visor & chinstrap. Leather sweatband 38 dated & maker marked. Orange water-proof lining with diamond. Inked inside with size *56* & a paper name label marked *Pz.Pi.W.Rode.* Above avg. cond. $100.00

VISOR CAP ARMY PIONEER OFFICER: Gray doeskin body has nice saddle shape, black wool piping, green band, alum. eagle, wreath & cockade. Silver celleon chincord. Black visor. Leather sweatband with *A B* owner initial discs affixed. Gold satin lining with maker trademark diamond with silver lettering. Avg. cond. $318.00

VISOR CAP ARMY PIONEER OFFICER: Gray doeskin body. Black wool piping & green band. Bullion eagle & wreath. Alum. chincord & black visor. Leather sweatband. Satin lining with diamond & inked *Deutsche Arbeit* with eagle trademark. Avg. cond. $187.00

VISOR CAP ARMY RECRUITING OF-FICER: Gray doeskin saddle shaped body, orange red wool piping & green band. Frosted silver finish to wreath, alum. eagle & 3 part cockade. Alum. chincord & black visor. Leather sweatband, gold satin lining lacks the maker diamond & has faint *Erel etc.* maker. Early. Avg. cond. $645.00

VISOR CAP ARMY SIGNAL EM: Early. Flat top to gray twill wool body, yellow cord piping & green band. Gray eagle, alum. wreath & 3 part cockade. Black chinstrap & visor. Leatherette sweatband, orange lining & diamond with inked *57*. Avg. cond. $160.00

VISOR CAP ARMY SMOKE TROOP OFFICER: Gray doeskin body with saddle shape, bordeaux piping & green band. Alum. eagle, wreath & 3 part cockade. Alum. chincord & black visor. Leather sweatband, gold satin lining, diamond with *Deutsche Arbeit* & printed cloth tag *Wendt 2.Battr.Nebel=Abt.2.* Above avg. cond. $651.00

VISOR CAP CUSTOM OFFICIAL: Saddle shaped gray wool body, green wool piping & band. Alum. eagle, wreath & 3 part cockade. Alum. & green twisted chincord. Black visor, leather sweatband, copper satin lining with diamond & *Aug. Schellenberg Berlin etc.. 55*. Avg. cond. $385.00

VISOR CAP DAF: Dark blue wool body with double grommet vents. Oak leaves & acorns bevo black band. Bevo oval insignia with gold frame. Black visor with trim. Leather sweatband with owner metal initials *HN*. Full blue lining with oilcloth RZM/DAF tag. Above avg. cond. $120.00

VISOR CAP FIRE POLICE EM: Dark blue wool body, carmine piping & black velvet band. Alum. eagle/wreath & 3 part cockade. Black chinstrap & visor. Leatherette sweatband, brown lining inked *W. Langner etc..Neuwied*. Avg. cond. $114.00

VISOR CAP FIRE POLICE OFFICER: Blue wool body, carmine piping & double grommet vents. Silver eagle/wreath, 3 part cockade, alum. chin cord & black visor. Leather sweatband, satin lining & diamond with paper maker *Heinrich Steiner etc..Koln*. Avg. cond. $125.00

VISOR CAP FORESTRY OFFICIAL: Top quality manufacture & materials. Saddle shape to green twill wool body with green wool piping & band to back of headband. Alum. eagle & hand embr. alum. wreath with 3 part cockade. Alum. chincord & black visor. Leather sweatband & gray satin lining with diamond by *Kasp.Luther Regensburg etc*. Near mint cond. $664.00

VISOR CAP KYFFHAUSERBUND MEMBER

VISOR CAP KYFFHAUSERBUND MEM-BER: Early 1935/1936 style blue wool body, black bevo band with alternating swastika & monument shield. Gold wreath with bevo EK monument & cockade above. Black chinstrap & visor with trim. Leather sweatband, blue satin lining & diamond with title monument shield etc. Above avg. cond. $100.00

VISOR CAP LUFTWAFFE DIV GORING EM: Smooth gray wool body with nice saddle shape. White wool piping & black mohair band. Alum. 1st eagle & alum. wreath/cockade below. Black chinstrap & visor with trim. Brown leatherette sweatband & blue satin lining with diamond. Exc. cond. $588.00

VISOR CAP LUFTWAFFE FLAK EM SUMMER-PATTERN: White removable twill top has snap, cloth pocket & gray eagle. No lining. Black mohair band with red wool piping & white frame with front stiffener. Alum. wreath/cockade. Black chinstrap & visor with trim. Leather sweatband & punched owner *GJ*. Above avg. cond. $329.00

VISOR CAP LUFTWAFFE FLAK EM: Blue-gray twill wool body, red wool piping & black band. Gray eagle, alum. wreath & cockade. Black chinstrap & visor with trim. Leather sweatband, orange lining & diamond with maker *Franz Ritter etc...1938 55 1/2*. Avg. cond. $225.00

VISOR CAP LUFTWAFFE FLAK EM: Saddle shape to blue-gray twill wool body, red wool piping & black band. Alum. eagle & wreath/cockade. Black chinstrap & visor with trim. Leather sweatband, orange lining & diamond by *Kurschner etc..Berlin 1939 58*. Exc. cond. $300.00

VISOR CAP LUFTWAFFE FLIGHT EM SUMMER-PATTERN

VISOR CAP LUFTWAFFE FLIGHT EM SUMMER-PATTERN: White twill cloth cover. Early alum. eagle with 2 prongs. Black mohair band with yellow wool piping, black chinstap & visor with trim. Affixed alum. winged/wreath/cockade. Leather sweatband. White satin lining with Koln/maker to diamond. Below avg. cond. $244.00

VISOR CAP LUFTWAFFE FLIGHT EM: Blue-gray twill wool body. Yellow wool piping & black band. Alum. insignia, black chinstrap & visor with trim. Brown lining with diamond by *Robert Lubstein etc..1939 56*. Avg. cond. $200.00

VISOR CAP LUFTWAFFE FLIGHT EM: Blue/gray twill wool body, yellow wool piping & black mohair band. Early alum. eagle & wreath/cockade. Black chinstrap & visor with trim. Leather sweatband, brown lining, diamond maker mark & *Kurschner-u. Mutzenmacher Berlin etc 1939 57-1/2*. Above avg. cond. $200.00

VISOR CAP LUFTWAFFE FLIGHT EM: Blue/gray wool body, yellow wool piping & black band. Early alum. eagle & wreath/cockade. Black chinstrap & visor with

trim. Leather sweatband is unit inked *Fl. Ausb.Rgt.23 Horst Komp*. Brown lining with maker diamond. Avg. cond. $175.00

VISOR CAP LUFTWAFFE FLIGHT EM: Saddle shape to blue-gray twill wool body. Yellow wool piping. Black mohair band, chinstrap & visor with trim. Alum. eagle & winged/wreath/cockade. Leather sweatband *Erel etc.* marked. Light blue satin lining with maker diamond & *Sonderklasse Privat etc.* Avg. cond. $419.00

VISOR CAP LUFTWAFFE FLIGHT EM

VISOR CAP LUFTWAFFE OFFICER SUMMER-PATTERN: Removable twill linen top with affixed gray metal eagle. Black mohair band with alum. piping & alum. wreath/cockade. Alum. chincord & black visor with trim. Leather sweatband embossed *Deutsches Leder*. White satin lining with diamond embossed *Deutsche Arbeit* & size *57*. Complete cap that will improve with care. Avg. cond. $410.00

VISOR CAP LUFTWAFFE OFFICER SUMMER-PATTERN

VISOR CAP LUFTWAFFE OFFICER SUMMER-PATTERN: Removable white linen top, gray metal eagle, black mohair band with alum. piping & bullion wreath/cockade hand embr. Black visor with trim, leather sweatband with CW maker, white satin lining still intact & diamond has gold *Verkaufsabteilung der Luftwaffe etc.* Leather sweatband. Exc. cond. $1,011.00

VISOR CAP LUFTWAFFE OFFICER: Soft saddle shape to blue-gray twill wool body with alum. cord piping & black band. Bullion hand embr. eagle, wreath & cockade. Alum. chincord. Black visor with trim. Title inked leather sweatband, gold satin lining, silver title maker. Avg. cond. $550.00

VISOR CAP LUFTWAFFE OFFICER

VISOR CAP LUFTWAFFE OFFICER: Blue-gray twill wool body. Alum. piping. Black mohair band with bullion wreath & cockade. Bullion eagle on wool & sewn through lining. Black visor is style without trim. Leatherette sweatband & silver satin lining. Avg. cond. $350.00

VISOR CAP LUFTWAFFE OFFICER: Saddle shape to blue-gray twill wool body. Alum. piping & black mohair band. hand embr. bullion insignia & eagle. Alum. chincord. Black visor with trim. Gray sweatband embossed *Deutsches Leder*. Green satin lining by *Dalluge Hannover etc.* Above avg. cond. $401.00

VISOR CAP LUFTWAFFE SIGNAL EM: Blue/gray wool body, brown wool piping & black mohair band. Early alum. eagle & wreath/cockade. Black chinstrap & visor without trim. Leather sweatband, brown lining with maker diamond by *Gebr. Alm etc. Berlin 1937 54-1/2.* Avg. cond. $175.00

VISOR CAP MINING OFFICIAL: Saddle shape to black wool body, red wool piping & black velvet band. 67mm alum. eagle, gold crossed hammer & 3 part cockade. Black visor, leather sweatband inked *Stirndruckfrei D.R.P.* & paper size tag *55.* Waterproof lining with maker diamond *Hut Allstadt etc.* & typed paper owner *Willi Dippel Velmeden.* Mint cond. $210.00

VISOR CAP NAVAL VETERAN MEMBER: Soft blue wool body, black bevo band with

oak leaves & acorns. Anchor buttons for blue braided chincord, wool covered visor, leather sweatband, gold satin lining & inked *K* maker trademark. Alum. veteran eagle is style without anchor. Avg. cond. $87.00

VISOR CAP NSDAP KREISLEITUNG

VISOR CAP NSDAP KREISLEITUNG: Tan twill wool body, thick white wool piping & brown velvet band. Gold eagle, wreath & chincord. 3 part cockade & brown visor. Brown leather sweatband, oilcloth RZM tag, satin lining with maker diamond & paper size tag *57.* Saddle shape. Exc. cond. $597.00

VISOR CAP NSDAP ORTSGRUPPE: Light brown twill body with saddle shape, blue cord piping, brown velvet band & gold insignia with 3 part cockade. Yellow celleon & brown visor. Owner name to leather sweatband, gold satin lining & inked paper name tag. Above avg. cond. $219.00

VISOR CAP NSDAP REICHSLEITUNG

VISOR CAP NSDAP REICHSLEITUNG: Saddle shape to tan twill wool body, gold piping & brown velvet band with direct hand embr. dark gold wreath. Gold metal eagle, 3 part cockade, gold chincord & brown visor. Brown leather sweatband, oilcloth RZM tag, satin lining with maker trademark diamond & silver embossed party eagle. Near mint cond. . $3,505.00

VISOR CAP NSKK OFFICER: Saddle shape to gray/brown twill wool body. Brown wool piping & band. Alum. eagle/scroll, 3 part cockade, alum. chincord & black visor. Inside with leather sweatband, gold satin lining & maker diamond by *Otto Zillmann Schweinfurt etc.* Avg. cond. $875.00

VISOR CAP POLICE EM: Variation. Dark green wool body, carmine piping & band. Alum. eagle wreath & 3 part cockade. Black chin strap & visor. Leather sweatband. Satin lining inked *VPS.* Below avg. cond. $98.00

VISOR CAP POLICE OFFICER: Municipal. Twill wool, saddle shaped body, green wool piping & brown band. Gray eagle/wreath, 3 part cockade, alum. chincord & black visor. Gray satin lining. Below avg. cond. $181.00

VISOR CAP POLICE OFFICER: Rural. Saddle shaped wool body, orange piping & brown band. Screened vents, alum. eagle/wreath, 3 part cockade, alum. chincord & black visor. Leatherette sweatband, orange waterproof lining, inked *S.P? 1943* many owner inked stamps. Avg. cond. $250.00

VISOR CAP RAILWAY: Dark blue wool to saddle shaped body with red wool piping & black velvet band. Gray eagle, 3 part cockade, blue & gold twisted chincord. Black visor, tattered leatherette sweatband & diamond to orange waterproof lining. Maker *Peter Kupper W.-Ronsdorf 54 1/2 etc.* Below avg. cond. $93.00

VISOR CAP RED CROSS EM: Gray wool body, piping & band. Lacks enamel eagle. Alum. wreath & 3 part cockade. Black leather chinstrap & early visor. Leather sweatband. Satin lining with diamond by *Gustav Terhritz Falkenstein.* Below avg. cond. $82.00

VISOR CAP REICHSWEHR CAVALRY: Gray wool body with light yellow wool piping & gray band. Direct hand embr. silver wreath to band with 3 part cockade. Gold & red wool cockade above. Black visor & leather sweatband. White satin lining inked *Crown-U.C.* Avg. cond. $160.00

VISOR CAP RLB EM: Blue/gray twill wool body, black wool band & lilac wool piping. Alum. winged wreath with 3 part cockade & dark silver eagle above. Black chinstrap & visor. Leather sweatband, gray lining & diamond. Avg. cond. $284.00

VISOR CAP RLB OFFICER: WWI style dark blue wool body, gray wool piping, black velvet band, variation 48mm alum. eagle & 3 part cockade. Black visor.

Leatherette sweatband, gold satin lining & maker diamond by *Carl Isken Koln etc.* Typed owner tag *Bauerfeind 56.* Avg. cond. $600.00

VISOR CAP RLB OFFICER

VISOR CAP SS-ALLGEMEINE EM: Black twill wool body, white wool piping & black twill band. Frosted silver eagle & skull. Black leather chinstrap & visor with underside inked *RZM SS.* Leatherette sweatband with oilcloth RZM/SS tag behind. Off-white satin lining with diamond having gold SS runes & size *53.* Avg. cond. $1,054.00

VISOR CAP SS-ALLGEMEINE EM: Early style. Black twill wool body & band with white wool piping. Early brass eagle & silver jawless skull. Black leather chinstrap with nickel loop & buckles. Black leather visor. Leather sweatband. Full brown cloth lining. Above avg. cond. $1,945.00

VISOR CAP SS-ALLGEMEINE OFFICER SUMMER-PATTERN: White top with black piping & black velvet band with black piping, silver SS eagle & skull with antique finish, silver chin cord. SS runes in gold in gold circle on top inside with Black cloth RZM tag. White satin lining & sweatband. Marked size *58.* Near mint cond. $6,000.00

VISOR CAP SS-ALLGEMEINE OFFICER: Black twill wool body, alum. piping, black velvet band, frosted silver finish to eagle & skull. Alum. chincord & black visor. 3 SS marks inside, inked *RZM/SS* to underside of visor, gold SS disc behind diamond & oilcloth tag behind leather sweatband. Typed paper tag and maker trademark diamond *SS Obergruppenfuhrer u.Gauleiter A.Eigruber.* Near mint cond. .. $3,000.00

VISOR CAP SS-ALLGEMEINE OFFICER: Saddle shape to black doeskin body, white wool piping & black velvet band. Frosted silver finish to eagle. Dark tarnish to silver skull. Alum. chincord & black visor with underside inked *RZM/SS.* Leather sweatband with oilcloth RZM/SS tag behind. White satin lining with diamond having bevo RZM/SS tag behind, peeled gold SS runes/disc, size *59* & paper label inked *Sonder-Anfertigung*. Exc. cond. $2,610.00

VISOR CAP SS-WAFFEN INF OFFICER: Saddle shape to gray wool body, white wool piping & black velvet band. Alum. chincord & black visor. Silver painted gray metal eagle & skull. Grommet vent behind skull is *Erel* feature. Embossed *Erel etc..* to leather sweatband. Gold satin lining with diamond & faint *Erel etc..* marks. Exc. cond. $1,750.00

VISOR CAP SS-WAFFEN PANZER OFFICER

VISOR CAP SS-WAFFEN PANZER OFFICER:·Gray twill wool body with nice saddle shape, pink wool piping, black velvet band, gray eagle & skull devices. Alum. chincord & black visor. Leather sweatband embossed *Deusches Leder*, gray satin lining, diamond, ornate maker trademark *Xaver Heinzmann Muenchen etc*. & typed paper tag *Ustuf. Karl Wolters 1./SS-Pz.Rgt.TK*. Near mint cond. $3,285.00

VISOR CAP STAHLHELM MEMBER: Gray wool body with green wool top piping & band. Blue & yellow piping over band. Black leather visor & chinstrap. Affixed *Der Stahlhelm* helmet badge, 3 part cockade & 2 part cockade with blue backing. Leatherette sweatband with owner affixed initial ovals *RL*. Tan lining. Avg. cond. $327.00

WINTER CAP ARMY: Gray wool body with gray rabbit fur flaps & tie strings at top. Gray quilted satin lining inked *1943/ maker* & *56*. Exc. cond. $124.00

WINTER CAP ARMY: Gray wool body with natural gray rabbit fur flaps & tie strings at top. Gray quilted lining inked *M43/ maker* & *56*. Exc. cond. $88.00

WINTER CAP ARMY

WINTER CAP ARMY: Gray wool body & white fur flaps. Gray metal eagle with prongs & sewn on. Gray satin lining inked *RB# 43 61*. Large size. Near mint cond. $198.00

WINTER CAP ARMY: Gray wool body, natural rabbit fur flaps with strings & button. Alum. eagle at front flap, gray stain quilted lining & inked maker etc. Exc. cond. $98.00

WINTER CAP LUFTWAFFE

WINTER CAP LUFTWAFFE: Natural suede body with thick white fleece inside. Gray embr. eagle & thick cockade. Snap flaps to ear openings on flaps. *57* size tag. Above avg. cond. $301.00

WINTER CAP RMBO OFFICER: Brown wool body with fold down side flaps & alum. piping around top. Brown satin quilted lining inked in red *1944 57 G.A.Hoffmann Berlin SW 29*. Hand-sewn green and brown twill wool trapezoid with gray embr. eagle & cockade. Not standard RMBO eagle insignia & looks to be period altered for Org. Todt use. Avg. cond. $435.00

IMPERIAL GERMAN FIELD GEAR

AMMO BELT MG08: Off-white body with brass fittings & unmarked starter tab ends. 1 end inked in red *Top*. Above avg. cond. $100.00

AMMO MAGAZINE
MG08 BASKET STYLE

AMMO MAGAZINE MG08 BASKET STYLE: Hinged steel body stamped with maker *Feuer! Kurbelhoch*. Crank handle to one side with the drum inside. Avg. cond. $207.00

AMMO POUCH WITH GARDE STAR: 2x4x5" black leather body with belt loop & large flap having affixed brass Garde star with 4 flaming cannon balls. Divided inside & maker stamped *Loh Sohne Berlin*. Near mint cond. $538.00

AMMO POUCH: 1870 Saxon cavalry. Large black leather body, 4x6x2.5" with nickel large crowned cipher in front. Two interior compartments. Maker name marked. Straps on the box to hook the cross belt. Above avg. cond. $295.00

AMMO POUCH: 1874. Black leather. Belt loops, straps & brass studs intact. Leather loops inside for 20 rounds & Inked *FB 3GRzF*. Exc. cond. $35.00

AMMO POUCH: 3 pocket. Clip pockets stamped *LZA J.Breslau* with crowned eagle holding lightning bolts. 1917/maker to back. Avg. cond. $23.00

AMMO POUCH: 3 pocket. Narrow brown leather body with black polished front. 1916/maker. Above avg. cond. ... $30.00

AMMO POUCH: M1850. Black leather body, belt loops & brass stud. Stamped *2P.9.C.5*. Above avg. cond. $93.00

AMMO POUCH: M1874. Black leather body, belt loops & brass studs. Leather loops inside, paper name label with unit *1.Comp.28.Inf.Regt. etc.* & same unit to leather. Above avg. cond. $55.00

AMMO POUCH: M1887 unteroffiziere. Black leather body with brass fittings & stamped *1888 121.R. etc*. Above avg. cond. $35.00

AMMO POUCHES: 3 pocket. Pair. 2" thick style in brown leather & black dyed front to brown leather. 1 maker marked. Above avg. cond. $90.00

AMMO POUCHES

AMMO POUCHES: 3 pocket. Pair. Standard large size ammo pouches. Both pouches have a similar look & appearance. Both have all brass fittings & pebbled leather finish. Maker marked & dated *BENNY SPIRO HAMBURG 1914/15* & *HCH. GRETSCH GMBH OFFENBACH/M 1914* Unit marked inside. Avg. cond. $139.00

AMMO POUCHES: 3 pocket. Pair. Standard large size ammo pouches. Both pouches have a similar look & appearance. Both have all brass fittings & pebbled leather finish. Maker marked & dated *WALLA SPRUNG DRESDEN 1915 & SATTLEN GENOSSRCOFT AACHEN 1915*. Unit marked inside. Avg. cond. $97.00

AMMO POUCHES: Pair. Styled after 1880 pouch with 2x3.5x7.5" size in black polished leather. Nickel metal rack fitted inside with stamped 1915/maker to lid. 1 inked *Wurtt. Staales etc*. Above avg. cond. $113.00

AMMO POUCHES: Pair. Styled after 1880 pouch with 2x3.5x7.5" size in black polished leather. Nickel metal rack fitted inside with stamped 1915/maker to lid. Above avg. cond. $165.00

ANTI-AIRCRAFT ROUND: 1918 20MM BECKER. 2 3/4" tall brass case & 3" tall metal projectile. Faint head-stamps. Avg. cond. $82.00

ANTI-TANK RIFLE ROUND: 13mm. Brass case had stamped *PM*. FMJ projectile. Above avg. cond. $110.00

ARMOR BACK PLATE FOR TRENCH WARFARE: Experimental. Iron. Form fitted. Heavy plate is of one piece & weighing approx. 20 lbs. Field gray painted. Unknown small 5mm hole in rear made with plate. Designed for Stosstruppen or Assault units. Avg. cond. $950.00

ARMOR PLATE BREAST: Gray paint to all 6 metal fittings with both shoulder. 3 lower plates are intact with cushions & woven straps. 4 large bullet holes to main body. Avg. cond. $588.00

ARMOR PRUSSIAN KURASSIER LIGHT WEIGHT PARADE CHEST: Light steel body with brass banding & studs: front & back plate. No shoulder straps. Leather trim remains. Frontplate has two small holes from test. Avg. cond. $425.00

ARTY GUNNER QUADRANT IN CASE: 10". Brass with eye adjuster for setting range. Cassel maker marks. In water-proof carrier. Mint cond. $131.00

ARTY PANORAMIC SIGHT: 4.5x5.5x6" black painted steel box, hinged lid with rivets, handle & front latch. Rubber sealed lid, wood block & leather inside fittings. 6" tall blued metal body, 3 scale dials, black rubber eye cup, optics oil-fogged & maker marked *Nedinsco s Gravenhage Systeem Carl Zeiss Jena*. Exc. cond. $110.00

ARTY PANORAMIC TELESCOPE

ARTY PANORAMIC TELESCOPE: *1917 C.P. GOERZ.* 10" tall blued metal body with 3 dial scales. By title maker *Berlin Rundblick Fernrohr Nr114798 DRP & Gesichtsfeld 10 Vergr.4x IX.17.* Above avg. cond. $65.00

ARTY SHELL 1918 BRASS 15CM: 19 3/4" tall body with head stamped *Aug.1918 Polte Karth 538 Magdeburg Sp406.* Above avg. cond. $87.00

ARTY SHELL CASE 1917 BRASS: Cut down. 8.5" diam. to 9" tall dark body. Head stamped *Juni 1917 Patronenfabrik Karlsruhe 90 Sp255.* No primer. Above avg. cond. $75.00

ARTY SHELL CASE 1918 BRASS 8CM M16: 9" tall dark body with title head-stamp & *Berndorf 411 W-n18v.* Avg. cond. $20.00

AVIATION BOMB: 7" long overall, 3.5" cast body with green paint. Gray fuse & sheet metal 4 fintail. Avg. cond. $35.00

BACKPACK ERSATZ: 13x15". 1915 dated. Maker marked. Complete with straps &

roller buckles. Cloth compartments. Dark olive gray ersatz pebbled leather body. All loops present. Avg. cond. $60.00

BANDSMAN FIFE NAVAL: In black wood, marked *Sonora* with maker mark on body: silvered fittings. Complete with a black leather & brass carrying case having a belt loop with crown & *M* mark for the Imperial navy. Above avg. cond. $115.00

BAYONET KNOT: Gray cloth strap with gray acorn, yellow neck & red base. Avg. cond. $20.00

BELT PRUSSIAN HUSSAR OFFICER DRESS *SCHARPE*: Silver wire with black flecking; full cording with tassels & hangers. Worn with dress attila by officers of all Prussian hussar regiments. Near mint cond. $270.00

BINOCULARS 08 WITH CASE

BINOCULARS 08 WITH CASE: Black leather case by *Emil Busch etc.* with brass fittings & straps intact. Smooth green/gray painted bodies by same maker as case. Avg. cond. $50.00

BINOCULARS 08 WITH CASE: Green/gray covered bodies. Stiff black cloth covered case with metal cover to base & loose lid. Paper instruction label with GI inked name. Avg. cond. $38.00

BINOCULARS 08: By *Carl Zeiss Jena etc.* to green rough textured covered bodies. Heavy leather neck strap & optics are clear. Avg. cond. $66.00

BINOCULARS

BINOCULARS: 1870s. 6" extended blacken brass body, with black pebbled leather cover on body & pull out sun shades.

Hmkd *C. Linsenbarth -Eisenach* on both
eye lenses & *5 Mal Vergross*. Above avg.
cond. $145.00
BREAD BAG: Gray canvas body with inked
Army issue to inside. Avg. cond. $21.00

BREAD BAG

BREAD BAG: Reddish brown canvas body
with brown leather & gray metal fittings.
Inked *B.A.XV.1913*. Shoulder strap.
Above avg. cond. $75.00
CALTROP DEVICE: Twisted 2 strands of
wire with barb to pointed ends. 1 barb
always points up for use against cavalry
or the tires of vehicles. Above avg.
cond. $32.00
CANTEEN DRINKING CUP AUSTRIAN:
Thick green porcelain outside with 2
loops & white 1917/maker name disc.
Blue & white swirl inside. Above avg.
cond. $30.00
CANTEEN DRINKING CUP: Porcelanized.
Oval shape with handle in gray. Above
avg. cond. $20.00
CANTEEN MEDIC: Gray painted steel body
& cup. Cup by *Mussbach 1915*. Gray
padded twill cloth cover. Brown leather
skeleton harness with shoulder strap
having red web body. Cover inked *JR 18.
EF 17*. Avg. cond. $63.00

CANTEEN TRENCH ART *LANDW.J.
REGT. NO.13* ALUM. CANTEEN

CANTEEN TRENCH ART *LANDW.J. REGT.
NO.13* ALUM. CANTEEN: Body by
Basse&Fischer Ludenscheid & unit
stamped *R84.9.C.* Large EK engraved to
front with scroll *Zur Erinnerung an den
Feldzug 1914/16*. Oakleave branch &
laurel leaves to sides. Title unit to back
with owner"s name removed. Avg.
cond. $108.00
CANTEEN: Gray painted metal body, gray
corduroy cover, clip to leather strap &
cork stopper with leather strap. 1917/
maker. Avg. cond. $40.00
CANTEEN: Gray porcelanized body with
gray corduroy cover sewn on at rusted
snaps. Cork stopper has leather loop &
clip. Avg. cond. $26.00

CANTEEN

CANTEEN: Gray painted steel body 1915/
maker tag. Cork stopper with leather
strap & clip. Avg. cond. $50.00
CASH BOX WITH 1914 EK PAINTED ON
THE LID: With key. 4x7x9.5" gray painted
body with a handle on the lid & tri-color
border. EK center with ribbon & wreath.
With change drawer inside. Heavy duty.
Exc. cond. $158.00
CAVALRY SADDLE: Dark brown leather
body with the rear edge stamped *4B
1.Esk.1908* & *5.Ch.R.1908*. Avg.
cond. $321.00
CAVALRY SABRETACHE PRUSSIAN
HUSSAR OFFICER: Red leather with flat
silver tressing: blue wool field with silver
FWR cipher under crown. Rings present.
Avg. cond. $430.00
CAVALRY SADDLE BAGS JAGER ZU
PFERDE: Pair. Half size sabretaches
worn by the 8th Jaeger zu Pferde
Regiment. Red Moroccan leather
backing. Two buckles each. Stone-gray
field with double yellow borders. Near
mint cond. $360.00
CAVALRY SADDLE BAGS: Pair. 1870.
Brown leather with full flaps, double

tongues. Roller buckles. Each approx.
12x15" in size. Avg. cond. $68.00
CAVALRY SADDLE BAGS: Pair. Russet
leather with full flaps & side pockets.
Pack horse style with connected leather
pouches being 6x13x16" size. 2 roller
buckle straps to each flap & small pouch
located at 1 end of each larger pouch.
Exc. cond. $230.00
CLEANING ROD GEW-88 BREECH: 14.5"
long wood body with cut to tip for cloth.
Near mint cond. $20.00
COMPASS WITH GRAY METAL CASE:
1.75" diam. Crystal top with functional
compass & stop. Complete with carrying
ring & a hook for attachment to other
equipment or a belt. Near mint
cond. $41.00
DRUM HANGER PRUSSIAN EAGLE:
Brass. 1/2 size. Possibly for a cadet
formation. Above avg. cond. $20.00
DRUM HANGER PRUSSIAN EAGLE: Brass
crowned eagle with 2 hooks, has brown
leather belt loop. Avg. cond. $51.00
DUFFEL BAG NAVAL: About 3' tall black
finished outside to off-white woven cloth/
canvas body. 2 shoulder straps with
leather & steel fittings. Inside inked
B.A.K. 7.11.14. Large white painted
owner to side *Scheffler 1579D.* Avg.
cond. $66.00
EATING UTENSILS OFFICER STYLE
FOLDING: Fork, knife & a large spoon,
all having folding wire handles. Stamped
DRGM & knife blade stamped *Solingen
Stahl.* With nickel plated ends. Avg.
cond. $37.00
EXPLOSIVE BOX *200GR. WESTFALIT
ETC.*: 1.5x2x3.5" size wax paper covered
with title & more wording to 3 sides.
Above avg. cond. $32.00
EXPLOSIVE BOX *200GR. WESTFALIT
ETC.*: Wax sealed cardboard box with
printed title etc. 1.5x2x3.5". Empty. Avg.
cond. $40.00
FIELD GUN 7.7CM *SCHLAGBOLZEN*
FIRING PIN: 5" tall 2 part steel body with
threaded pin & title marked tube-body.
Matching serial #*1530 A.* Exc.
cond. $40.00
FIELD PHONE AUSTRO-HUNGARIAN:
About 4.5x8x11" oak hinged case that
folds open. Side loops for missing
shoulder strap. Ground stack stored
inside front door with metal maker plate
Ericsson Budapest etc. Works intact with
4 line hook-ups, alum. & black leather
receiver with same maker. Exc.
cond. $487.00

FLARE PISTOL

FLARE PISTOL: 15" long steel body by
Gebr.R. Wood grips & lanyard rings. Avg.
cond. $112.00

FLIGHT GOGGLES

FLIGHT GOGGLES: Brown leather body,
round steel frames, clear glass lenses &
elastic band. Above avg. cond. ... $78.00

GASMASK WITH CANISTER

GASMASK WITH CANISTER: Dark leather
body is pliable & straps intact, 1917
dated filter. About 7" tall metal body with
gray paint. 4 extra lens packets. Avg.
cond. $93.00
GASMASK WITH CANISTER: Stiff gray
mask with straps having inked owner tag
W.Siegert. Gray metal filter by *M2 AGFA
11.Apr.18 etc.* Loose paper instructions in
gray painted metal can with woven
straps. Avg. cond. $100.00
GASMASK: Pliable brown leather body with
all straps & strings intact. Clear glass
lenses & metal base made by *M2.* Metal
filter inked *1.Feb.18.* Near mint
cond. $110.00
GRENADE ANTI-TANK RIFLE STYLE:
13mm. About 5.5" tall with slug. Brass

case head stamped *18 T67 P 6*. Above avg. cond. $39.00

GRENADE ANTI-TANK RIFLE STYLE: 13mm. Dark brass case with primer intact, slug shows pulled marks & no powder. Head stamped *T67 P 4 18*. Above avg. cond. $34.00

GRENADE ANTI-TANK

GRENADE ANTI-TANK: 2' long overall with wood nose & tail. 10.5" sheet metal body with 4 wire rod framework. Avg. cond. $100.00

GRENADE BALL STYLE

GRENADE BALL STYLE: Cast iron ball with 3 ridges upper & lower around center serrated band. Fuse is inserted. Above avg. cond. $90.00

GRENADE DISC STYLE

GRENADE DISC STYLE: Pancake shaped with safing pin in fuse & threaded accesses around the perimeter. Avg. cond. $139.00

GRENADE EGG STYLE WITH FUSE: Black finished cast-iron body with segmented

center ridge & by *WFR*. Crimped metal fuse. Above avg. cond. $85.00

GRENADE EGG STYLE WITH FUSE: Safed weapon. Remains of red finish on egg portion & serrated band around middle. Above avg. cond. $42.00

GRENADE EGG STYLE: Cast body with serrated band & maker marked *HE H*. Above avg. cond. $27.00

GRENADE RIFLE STYLE: Designed for Gewehr-98 cup grenade launcher. Cast metal with threaded fixtures. Above avg. cond. $135.00

HOLSTER P08: Brown leather body. Stamped *B.A.VII 1913* & inked *J.R.???*. Avg. cond. $84.00

HOLSTER P08: Brown leather. Maker *Rudolf Wiemer & Co. Mulbein Rhur 1916*. Comes with plastic display tag with maker/date. Avg. cond. $79.00

LICE POWDER CAN *TRIKRESOL STREUPUDER*: Gray & black finished oval shaped can with contents. Above avg. cond. $28.00

LIGHT PERSONAL BATTERY STYLE: *Perlux*. 4" dia. with gray green paint, has belt clips on back, lid covers front. Avg. cond. $90.00

MAP CASE WITH GEO. TOPO. CLOTH BACKED DRESDEN MAP: Map case & map is the type used by WWI Pilots. 7x9.5" black leatherette body with clear front & 2 snap flap. String at back for neck/shoulder use. 26x30" B&W topographic paper map mounted to gray oilcloth. *#101 Dresden-Bischofswrda etc*. area. Above avg. cond. $50.00

MAP CASE: 3 color camo design inside. About 2.5x8x11" size. 2 gray leather roller-buckle straps at back D-rings. Gray canvas body has latch closure to flap. Avg. cond. $75.00

MAP CASE: Half-flap with roller buckle & tool pouches. Divided pouch. Stamped *A.R.5* to under-side of flap with owner inked lettering *Stabsbatterie, etc*. 2 roller buckle loops to back. Avg. cond. $25.00

MAP POUCH: 1x7x8.5" dark-brown body with half-flap, 2 roller buckle belt loops & tool pockets inside. Inked eagle stamp disc to flap & paper owner label *Chevauleger Philipp 5.Eskadron k.b.3.Chevauleger-Regiment*. Above avg. cond. $76.00

MAP POUCH

MEDICAL BELT POUCH: 3.5x5x8" brown leather body with 2 belt loops, swivel latch to strap, fold-out pocket with roller-buckle strap & inked *1917 etc.* Above avg. cond. $24.00

MESS KIT: Porcelainized steel. Blue-gray finish to body & lid. Wire handle. Avg. cond. $36.00

MESS KIT: 7.5" tall body & lid with handle. With leather strap. Both marked to *Ed.Sommerfeld Berlin.S.O. 11.* Wire handle. Above avg. cond. $87.00

MG SPARE BARREL CONTAINER

MG SPARE BARREL CONTAINER: 2x4x32" gray painted steel covered wood body with hinged end caps. Has attached burlap shoulder strap. Avg. cond. $165.00

MG08 ARMOR-SHIELD TO WATER-JACKET: 6" tall green painted heavy metal fitting with barrel hole. Near mint cond. $145.00

MG08 SOAKING/CLEANING CONTAINER FOR BLANK FIRING DEVICE: 6" tall by 2.5" diam. gray painted container with threaded lid. Unmarked. Above avg. cond. $34.00

MORTAR ROUND MINENWERFER: 11" long overall with fuse & threaded 4 fin tail to cast-iron segmented body. Above avg. cond. $265.00

PICK AX WITH CARRIER: Heavy combat ready weapon with 18.5" wavy wood handle. 10.5" long gray painted ax-head with pick. Affixed to wood by 2 metal straps & band. Brown leather carrier with 2 belt loops, roller buckle strap, handle

loop with extra loop & stamped *II.Grt.* Above avg. cond. $221.00

PICK AX WITH CARRIER

PICK AX WITH CARRIER: 9.5" long steel head & 18" wood handle. Black leather carrier with roller buckle loop, snap strap & elastic. Avg. cond. $107.00

POUCH: 2x10.5x13" red/brown canvas body has leather trim to flap with 2 roller buckle straps. Inked *1887 76R etc.* & sewn tag *Freyholdt I.Komp.Inf.=Rgt. Hamburg etc.* 5 small leather loops at back top-edge, 2 added belt loops with brass buttons & missing 1 corner hook. Avg. cond. $82.00

PROPELLER AIRCRAFT *MERCEDES*: About 103" long & 8" wide. Light & dark wood laminated construction. Center hub has 6 mounting holes & 2 metal wall hangers. Marked *100 PS, Mercedes, D270, St175.* Above avg. cond. $800.00

PROPELLER WWI FIGHTER AIRCRAFT: 59" tall-1 blade on hub with opposite side blade cut away-leaving flat side that allows remaining blade to stand upright off hub on the floor. Laminated wood construction, Hub is impressed *Nofan Propeller / Berlin O / 100P Mercedes / 27000143S / Zug / No. 2411 & Stand 13300 Geppert P&W.* Avg. cond. $288.00

RATION BAG NAVAL MARINE ARSENAL WILHELMSHAVEN: 2x4' tan woven body with a black printed title. Avg. cond. $25.00

TELEGRAPH BATTERY TESTER: 4x6x6.5" wood box with mortise/tenon corners. Leather handle. Glass viewing port at top with needle, scale & title marked. 3 wire hook-ups *0,1,2.* Canvas pouch shows black waterproofing, felt pad to lid & 2 roller buckle straps. Above avg. cond. $68.00

TENT POLES/STAKES WITH POUCH: Gray canvas body with brown leather straps, 2 brass buttons & flap inked *1915 Elberfeld etc.* 3 wood stakes & poles with steel fittings. Exc. cond. $80.00

TRENCH MACE

TRENCH MACE: 22" OA with 3" iron warhead having conical/triangular spikes. Knob at end of handle. Avg. cond. $139.00

TRENCH SHIELD SNIPER

TRENCH SHIELD SNIPER: Size 18x23.5". 3/16" thick steel plate with rolled ends. Oval shaped cover to rifle port & pivot leg to back. Avg. cond. $193.00

WEHRPASS POUCH GARDE FIELD ART. REMEMBRANCE CHRISTMAS 1915: 4x5" white Ersatz cloth pouch with open top for slipping pass into it. Black printed lettering, *Zur Erinnerung an Weihnachten 1915. Proville. Frankreich. 3. Batterie. Ersatz Garde Res.-Feldart Reg.* Near mint cond. $20.00

THIRD REICH FIELD GEAR

A-FRAME BATTLE PACK: Olive web body inked *epf1944*, 4 steel hooks & three black leather straps. Variation style. Exc. cond. $271.00

A-FRAME BATTLE PACK: Olive-green web with inked *Willy etc.Berlin* maker. Shows use & rust stain to strap. Hooks for Y-strap use. Avg. cond. $300.00

ARTILLERY CARRIAGE SEAT: Rubber bike-style with metal mount. 2.5x12x15" black rubber seat is mounted to tan painted metal base with spring fitting. Avg. cond. .. $59.00

ASSAULT PACK PIONEER

ASSAULT PACK PIONEER: Center. Green canvas body with 2 side openings & mess kit pocket to top flap. Web fittings & hooks for use with Y-straps. Avg. cond. $117.00

ASSAULT PACK POUCH TROPICAL: For A-frame use. Small olive canvas body with black leather & web fittings. Inked maker. Above avg. cond. $141.00

BACKPACK ARMY CABLE-LAYER: Field gray Metal tube-frame & reel. Chain drive reel with wire-guide. Crank handle is stored in brown leather pouch with leather pad to back, canvas back-panel, brown leather shoulder straps & leather brake-strap. alum. maker tag *IBB Berlin 1940*. Above avg. cond. $264.00

BACKPACK CAMO COVER WINTER: 22" long white cotton body resembles large helmet cover. Double tiestrings to one end & other end has single tiestring. Covers compelte backpack. Near mint cond. $38.00

BACKPACK PONY-FUR: Model *07/13*. Gray canvas body, wood frame & reddish fur back. Black leather fittings & gray web shoulder straps. By *RZM L3/160/41*. Ollcloth RZM tag inside & inked *NPEA Achern?* Avg. cond. $38.00

BACKPACK PONY-FUR: 2 tone brown fur flap & green canvas body. Black leather shoulder straps with stamped unit *10./ J.R.115 I.* 2 leather equipment straps to sides. Dated 1940/maker. Above avg. cond. $54.00

BACKPACK PONY-FUR: Dark brown flap, green canvas body, brown leather & alum. fittings. 1940/maker & black leather straps. Even has belt hook strap & short black roller buckle strap. Avg. cond. $30.00

BACKPACK PONY-FUR: Green canvas body, brown fur & brown leather fittings. Maker *Gebruder Klinge Dresden 1940*. Black straps. Avg. cond. $40.00

BACKPACK PONY-FUR

BACKPACK PONY-FUR: Brown fur flap & sides. Olive canvas body, wood frame, alum. fittings with roller buckle missing prong & inked *RAD etc.* Black leather shoulder straps & 1937/maker. Avg. cond. $65.00

BACKPACK PONY-FUR: RZM TAG *RZM Tornister*, oil cloth. Reddish-brown fur flap, gray canvas body, wood frame & black leather shoulder straps. Avg. cond. $65.00

BACKPACK SIGNALMAN PONY-FUR

BACKPACK SIGNALMAN PONY-FUR: Brown fur to all sides & leather *1* to front. Brown leather fittings. Gray canvas inside with dividers. Stamped *fft/41 WaA136.* Avg. cond. $66.00

BACKPACK: Tan/brown canvas body with wood frame & brown leather fittings. Owner inked inside *M.Schiller etc.* Above avg. cond. $50.00

BACKPACK: Wood frame to brown canvas body with brown & black leather fittings. Inked owner to wood *K.Ulex HBG.- Osdorf.* Avg. cond. $59.00

BANDSMAN DRUM-STICK FROG: 6.5" tall dark-brown leather body. Holds 2 sticks. Avg. cond. $20.00

BATTERY CHARGER *PHILIPS TYPE 368*: 4.5x6.5x12" blue-gray painted metal body with handle to top. Grill to top & front with large light-bulb inside. +- hook-ups to front with title plate & diagram for *6amp* & *4.5amp* battery use. Cord with 2 prong plug. Ground hook-up to back with hole for wall mount. As used on the Russian Front. Above avg. cond. $176.00

BELT LOOP DAK: Olive-green web with gray painted ring. Inked 1941/maker. Near mint cond. $82.00

BELT LOOPS WITH D-RINGS: Lot of 4. 3 brown leather & other black with pebbled rings. Same 1938/maker to each. Above avg. cond. $30.00

BINOCULARS *6X30 DIENSTGLAS*

BINOCULARS *6X30 DIENSTGLAS*: Black rough texture paint to body by *ddx Dienstglas etc.* Scale to right side. Leather neck strap. Avg. cond. ... $54.00

BINOCULARS *6X30 DIENSTGLAS*: Late-war. Tan finish. 4.5" tall body by *Dienstglas 6x30 ddx etc.* No scale. Black leather neck strap, black rubber eye cup cover. Avg. cond. $185.00

BINOCULARS *7X56 NACHT-DIALYT* WITH CASE: 9" tall bodies, rough black texture & trim turning gray. By *Hensoldt-Wetzlar Nacht-Dialyt.* Optics clear & black leather neckstrap. Black leatherette case. Avg. cond. $286.00

BINOCULARS *8X ZEISS* WITH CASE: Black leather case with shoulder strap is for 6x30 style binoculars. Stamped edge *Hensoldt Wetzlar 1938* & police eagle proof. *Carl Zeiss Jena* binoculars. Avg. cond. $131.00

BINOCULARS *8X24 HENSOLDT* WITH CASE: 4.5" tall black leather covered body with stamped title, etc., single adjustment knob & leather neck strap. Lacks 1 eye cup & optics are clear. Brown leather case with shoulder strap & closure strap. Avg. cond. $32.00

BINOCULARS ARTILLERY *10X80 D.F.*

BINOCULARS NAVAL *7X50 ZEISS*
WITH CASE

BINOCULARS ARTILLERY *10X80 D.F.*:
11" long, gray painted, title marked &
dkl maker. No sun shields but has both
dovetails & top fitting for missing
headpad. Optics are clear with
crosshair & 4 position filter knob
works. Exc.cond. $292.00

BINOCULARS ARTILLERY *10X80 D.F.*:
15" long gray painted 45 degree bodies
with sun shields to ends. By *beh
D.F.10x80 etc.* Dove-tail mount to base
& gray rubber head pad. Optics clear
with cross-hair & filter knob stuck.
Above avg. cond. $281.00

BINOCULARS ARTILLERY RABBIT-EAR
CAPTURED FRENCH: 10.5" tall tan
painted bodies with pivot hinge & small
movable handle. Marked *8x24
Decigrades M.G. S.R.P.1 etc.* Avg.
cond. $100.00

BINOCULARS COASTAL ARTY *7X50
ZEISS FLAK.(KUSTE)* WITH CASE:
Excellent complete cased set for
Coastal Flak use with 2 sets of
lenses tint/filters still intact. 8.5" tall
black leatherette case with all fittings
intact except for shoulder strap.
Stamped *blc* & Eagle-M IV/1. 7" tall
binoculars with black rough texture
finish, brown rubber eye cups,
leather neck strap with leather
cover & marked *Carl Zeiss Jena
Flak.(Kuste) etc.* with Eagle-M IV/1.
Optics clear with crosshair scale
reading *10-20 thru 50.* Exc.
cond. $500.00

BINOCULARS DAK *6X30*: Tan painted
body with alum. ends by *cag 6x30 etc.*
Scale to right side. Leather neck strap.
Avg. cond. $100.00

BINOCULARS FLAK *12X60 FLA-
LAEITER-F ZEISS*: 11.5" long green
painted body. Optics appear clear
with scale. Rubber face pads to
hinged assembly. Metal cover to
eye-cups on leather strap with
spring-latch. Filter knob *Farbglaser* ,
title plate & scale-use plate. Avg.
cond. $160.00

BINOCULARS NAVAL *7X50 ZEISS* WITH
CASE: 7" tall bodies show remains of
leatherette covering & black rough texture
paint. by *Carl Zeiss Jena D.F.7x50 etc.* &
Eagle-M IV/1. Optics are a little fogged,
leather neck strap & leather eye cup
cover. Commercial brown leather case
with shoulder strap. Avg.
cond. $250.00

BOOT-JACK: Officer folding. 5/8x4x13.5"
body has 2 metal hinges at center seam.
2 wood pivot legs. Inked anchor trademark *George Hartmann Arfeldeder.*
Above avg. cond. $23.00

BREAD-BAG ARMY: Late-war olive canvas
body with black leather & steel fittings.
98k cleaning kit pocket has canvas
closure strap. Exc. cond. $75.00

BREAD-BAG ARMY: Gray canvas with
black leather & alum. fittings. Inked inside
flap *1942 Ferdinand Brenner etc.* Divided
pouch. Near mint cond. $35.00

BREAD-BAG ARMY: With cleaning-kit
pocket. Green canvas body with 3 sewn
loops at top. Black leather & steel fittings.
Canvas pocket for cleaning-kit. Near mint
cond. $177.00

BREAD-BAG HITLER YOUTH WITH
CANTEEN: Gray canvas body, black
leather & alum. fittings. Large oil cloth
HJ/RZM *Brotbeutel etc.* tag. Alum. body
canteen & cap *RZM M6/2/40* , brown
corduroy cover, brown leather strap &
alum. clip. Above avg. cond. $276.00

BREAD-BAG HITLER YOUTH
WITH CANTEEN

BREAD-BAG HITLER YOUTH: Tan colored
cotton bag that has ink stamp on inside

flap to HJ. Bag has all hooks, snaps, & straps. Above avg. cond. $52.00

BREAD-BAG LARD-CONTAINER: Tan bakelite. Near mint cond. $40.00

BREAD-BAG LUFTWAFFE: Blue-gray body with minor wear to flap. Leather, alum. & steel fittings. Avg. cond. $20.00

BREAD-BAG LUFTWAFFE: Blue-gray canvas with gray leather & alum. fittings. Inked inside flap *WL 41 etc.* & LW eagle. Near mint cond. $35.00

BREAD-BAG LUFTWAFFE

BREAD-BAG LUFTWAFFE: Blue/gray canvas body, black leather & steel fittings. Inside flap inked black *B.B.1648.2.* Avg. cond. $50.00

BREAD-BAG SA: Commercial style canvas body with divided pouch, green leather & alum. fittings. Gray strap with buckle. Bevo owner name tag *U.Enders.* Type bought by Party from commercial companies before RZM style used. Above avg. cond. $20.00

BREAD-BAG SA: Dark brown bag. Early. Near mint cond. $203.00

BRIEFCASE SS CORT: Black leather. 6x13x16" body with handle to top, 2 straps to flap with roller-buckles & latch. Inside inked *R.Larsen Berlin 1942.* B&W painted panel to flap *SS IIIA 97 Hauptamt SS Gericht (B) Sturmbannfuhrer D.Muller.* Above avg. cond. $244.00

CANTEEN COMBAT TROPICAL: Alum. body by *KCL 42* , padded olive felt cover, olive web strap with clip, black cap & bakelite cup. Mint cond. $155.00

CANTEEN COMBAT: 1942 alum. body, felt cover, black leather strap & green steel 1943 cup. Avg. cond. ......:.......... $40.00

CANTEEN COMBAT: Alum. body & cap by *ESB 40.* Gray felt cover, black leather strap, alum. clip & black painted alum. cup by same maker. Exc. cond.$139.00

CANTEEN COMBAT

CANTEEN COMBAT: Alum. body & cup by *CFL43.* Black cap, gray felt cover & black leather strap. Mint cond. $196.00

CANTEEN COMBAT: Alum. body by *G&CL39* , black cap & green painted steel cup. Gray felt cover & olive web strap. Near mint cond. $90.00

CANTEEN COMBAT: Alum. body, black cap, gray cover & web strap. Above avg. cond. $28.00

CANTEEN COMBAT: Alum. body, cap & cup all by *HRE35.* Gray wool cover. Black leather strap with alum clip. Avg. cond. $50.00

CANTEEN COMBAT: RZM. Alum. body & cap by *RZM M6/2/40.* Gray felt cover with alum. snaps & inked RZM. Black leather strap with alum. clip is style with o cup. Avg. cond. $20.00

CANTEEN COMBAT: Red steel body & black cap. Gray cloth cover & black leather strap with clip. 1940 cup with black paint. Avg. cond. $30.00

CANTEEN COMBAT: Red steel body & cap. Gray cloth cover, black leather strap & gray painted *CFL44* steel cup. Mint cond. $243.00

CANTEEN COMBAT: Red steel body, black plastic cap, gray cover, pigskin strap & black painted alum. cup by *FWBN42.* Avg. cond. $66.00

CANTEEN COMBAT: Variation. 1942 alum. body is bulging & has light bulb shape. Gray wool cover with 4 snaps & only 2 close. Black strap & green painted alum. cup. Avg. cond. $40.00

CANTEEN COMBAT

CANTEEN COMBAT: Alum. body, black plastic cap, padded gray cover, pigskin strap & 1944 dated black cup. Avg. cond. $50.00

CANTEEN DAK: Bakelite covered body by *HRE 43*. Web skeleton strap & green steel cup. Avg. cond. $40.00

CANTEEN DAK

CANTEEN DAK: Bakelite/wood covered body by *HRE 41*. Olive web skeleton strap with clip & roller buckle. Black bakelite cup. Exc. cond. $60.00

CANTEEN DAK: Bakelite/wood covered body by *HRE 42*. Olive web skeleton strap with cut-strap to alum. cap with 43 date. Avg. cond. $50.00

CANTEEN OFFICER: Alum. body & cap by *HRE 40*. Gray felt cover, brown leather shoulder strap with roller-buckle. Black finished alum. cup by *HRE 40* & color decal to side *F.Haberkorn Bregenz etc.* Above avg. cond. $50.00

CANTEEN OFFICER: Alum. body & cup by *HRE41*. Padded gray cover, black leather skeleton strap with shoulder strap & black alum. cup *HRE40*. Exc. cond. $85.00

CANTEEN OFFICER: Alum. body by *CFL 38* with 37 dated cap. Padded gray felt cover. Leather skeleton strap is missing shoulder strap. Avg. cond. $20.00

CANTEEN OFFICER: In cloth cover with black leather skeleton straps & rings for shoulder straps. Black bakelite cup. Mint cond. $36.00

CANTEEN RZM: Alum. body & cap stamped *RZM M6/43/39*. Gray wool cover, black leather strap & steel clip. Used by SS, NSDAP, SA etc. Above avg. cond. $74.00

CAVALRY SADDLE BAGS: Brown leather. by *dkk 43*. Avg. cond. $79.00

CAVALRY SADDLE: Dark brown leather body by *eqr 43 WaA750* & size-5. Green canvas covered cushions to underside. Metal stirrup to both leather straps. Near mint cond. $650.00

CLOTHING BAG: 3x12x15" green canvas body with flap with leather handle & 2 closure straps with roller buckles. Avg. cond. $20.00

CLOTHING PACK TROPICAL: Type that the clothing is folded over & can be carried like a suit case or like a shoulder pack. Olive canvas body with grommet adjustment & closure front. Web fittings & shoulder straps. Avg. cond. $32.00

CLOTHING WHIP RAD: 12" long wood handle with hole for hanger string, stamped *RAD* & 7 leather laces to end. Above avg. cond. $40.00

CLOTHING WHIP RAD: 12" wood handle with stamped title, inked maker & GI name/address. 8 leather laces. Near mint cond. $40.00

CLOTHING WHIP: 10" long wood turned handle has purple finish. Leather laces. Avg. cond. $20.00

COME-ALONG WRIST-CHAIN POLICE: 13" long nickel chain & T-ends. Near mint cond. $50.00

COME-ALONG WRIST-CHAIN POLICE: Nickel. Figure 8 shaped with pivot hinge at center. Spring loaded latch/ lock to hand-loop. Exc. cond. $40.00

COMPASS LUFTWAFFE PILOT FLUID-FILLED WRIST-STYLE: Bakelite body

stamped *Armbandkompass AK39 etc.*
FL#ed. Dark dial/scale still works. Gray
leather wrist strap. Avg.
cond $78.00

COMPASS LUFTWAFFE PILOT
FLUID-FILLED WRIST-STYLE

COMPASS LUFTWAFFE PILOT FLUID-
FILLED WRIST-STYLE: Bakelite body
stamped *Armbandkompass AK39 etc.*
FL#ed. Dark dial/scale still works. 2 part
gray leather wrist strap. Near mint
cond. $134.00

COMPASS LUFTWAFFE PILOT FLUID-
FILLED WRIST-STYLE: Clear dial with
bakelite body & black numbered inside.
Bakelite by *AK39 Fl. 23235
Armbandkompass etc.* Fluid filled. 3
leather straps for wrist or leg use. Near
mint cond. $112.00

COMPASS LUFTWAFFE PILOT FLUID-
FILLED WRIST-STYLE: Hmkd *AK39*.
Bakelite body with back
Armbandkompass etc.Fl.23235. Black
leather straps. All fluid present. Mint
cond. $181.00

COMPASS MARCH: Bakelite body by *cxn*
with scale, black lid with mirror & works.
String & leather neck strap. Above avg.
cond $40.00

COMPASS MARCH: Bakelite body with
hinged brass cover. Berlin maker marked.
Avg. cond. $25.00

COMPASS MARCH: Bakelite body with
scale, white *A* stenciled to black lid with
mirror & black neck string. Exc.
cond. $40.00

DUFFEL BAG: Olive canvas body has 10
alum. grommets at opening with rope.
Olive canvas shoulder strap with black
leather fittings & alum. roller buckles.
Wood name tag marked *Obergefreiter
Heinz Schiffer Nr.679956*. Above avg.
cond. $30.00

DUFFEL-BAG: Olive-green canvas. GI style
bag. Canvas straps with black leather
fittings. Grommet closure with rope. Avg.
cond. $22.00

EQUIPMENT CASE SS: Galvanized metal.
13.5x16x29" body with gray paint.
Stamped metal body has stiffener ridges,
hinged lid with 2 latches & wire handle to
each side. Inside of lid has sprayed
stencil *Eigentum der Waffen-SS* in tan.
Above avg. cond. $158.00

EQUIPMENT POUCH: 3.5x10x14.5" blue-
gray canvas covered body with brown
leather trim & shoulder strap with roller
buckle. 2 closure straps to flap & inside
edge inked *hla/1940 WaA???*. Pocket
inside & couple empty tool pockets. Near
mint cond. $90.00

EQUIPMENT POUCH: Black leather.
3x7.5x7.5" body with hinged lid at end
with roller buckle strap. Belt loops & D-
ring to back. Inside lid stamped *gmn
1941 WaA136* & has 2 snap leather loop.
Avg. cond. $37.00

FLASHLIGHT HITLER YOUTH *PICK*: 4.5"
long tube body with worn brown paint.
Title marked end with clip to side. On-off
switch & rotating lens lacks bulb. Above
avg. cond. $41.00

FLASHLIGHT PERSONAL-SIZE *ARTAS*:
Black painted metal body with raised title,
glass lens & 3 slides for green, red, blue.
2 leather button-hole tabs. Avg.
cond. $44.00

FLASHLIGHT PERSONAL-SIZE *DAIMON
FOCUS*: 4" tall brown painted metal tube-
body with glass lens. End cap title
marked. Clip to side with switch. Avg.
cond. $37.00

FLASHLIGHT PERSONAL-SIZE *DAIMON
TELKO 4*: Black sheet metal body with
flip cover for lens. Leather straps. Tri-
color filters. Avg. cond. $25.00

FLASHLIGHT PERSONAL-SIZE: Gray
painted body & hood to domed glass lens
with slides for green & red. Metal belt
loop lacks 1 wire button fitting. Party
eagle marked *Wehrmacht-Eigentum*
battery. Avg. cond. $126.00

FLIGHT COMPUTER LUFTWAFFE PILOT
HAND-HELD WITH HOLDER: It is Fl.
marked & is specially made to fit. 6"
diam. black alum. rim to B&W plastic
body with scales to both sides. Maker,
date & *Fl.23825*. 1x7x8" tan painted
alum. holder has indented side with clips
to hold computer. Other side has 6" diam.
movable scale with plastic lens over
paper grid, adjustment wheel. 6 screws to
cover for adjusting paper. Near mint
cond. $271.00

FLIGHT COMPUTER LUFTWAFFE PILOT
HAND-HELD: 6" diam. black finished
alum. rim. B&W plastic centers with
scales to each side. Maker, date &
Fl.23825. Above avg. cond. $72.00

FLIGHT COMPUTER LUFTWAFFE PILOT HAND-HELD

FLIGHT COMPUTER LUFTWAFFE PILOT HAND-HELD: 6" diam. Maker marked & dated 1941. Avg. cond. $79.00

GAS-BOOTS/LEGGINGS WITH CARRY-ING BAG: Black rubber soles & lowers to boots with gray leggings having tie-strings. Above avg. cond. $82.00

GAS-MASK COMBAT WITH CANISTER: M30 mask with straps & *Auer* filter with paper Luftschutz label. Dated & eagle proofed fluted canister with gray paint. Extra lens packet. Above avg. cond. $74.00

GAS-MASK COMBAT WITH CANISTER: Fluted metal canister with all straps, 1940/maker & extra lens packet. White painted *Schubert* to bottom, to filter/FE37 & Bevo name tag to strap of M30 mask. 1940 dates overall. Above avg. cond. $127.00

GAS-MASK COMBAT WITH CANISTER: Gray paint to fluted body with shoulder strap & pivot lid latch. Stamped 36 maker to inside lid with inked WaA & extra lens packet. M30 mask with straps & *S-filter Luftschutz etc.* filter. Exc. cond. .. $93.00

GAS-MASK COMBAT WITH CANISTER: M30 mask with straps & *FE41* filter with plug. *Auer* stamped name to lid *Luftschutzgesetz etc.* Gray paint & thin shoulder strap with hook-strap. Avg. cond. $61.00

GAS-MASK COMBAT WITH CANISTER: M30 mask with straps, *44 btc* nose & *FE41* filter. Gray D-canister with empty extra lens holder stamped *eph 44* & inked *WaA*??. With shoulder strap. Above avg. cond. $135.00

GAS-MASK COMBAT WITH CANISTER: M38 mask with straps, *FE37R* filter & cap to filter. Green painted D-canister lacks rubber seal & straps. Inked *WaA145* to lid of holder with 1943 date. Above avg. cond. $50.00

GAS-MASK COMBAT WITH CANISTER: dark gray rubber mask with FE37 filter & 1940 date. Canister with straps. Avg. cond. $45.00

GAS-MASK COMBAT WITH CANISTER

GAS-MASK COMBAT WITH CANISTER: M30 mask with 44 dated blue metal fittings. *FE41* filter. 1942 fluted D-canister with gray paint & lacks straps. Extra lens packet. Avg. cond. $50.00

GAS-MASK GLASSES *MASKEN-BRILLE* WITH CASE: Gray metal box with black title. Lenses to nickel frames with cloth ear loops. Avg. cond. $30.00

GAS-MASK GLASSES *MASKEN-BRILLE* WITH CASE: Gray metal case stamped *hce 1944 WaA?? 60*. Frames with cloth straps. Near mint cond. $22.00

GAS-MASK LUFTSCHUTZ WITH CANISTER

GAS-MASK LUFTSCHUTZ WITH CANIS-TER: Fluted body with gray paint, stamped *Auer* to lid. M30 mask with straps & 41 date. 41 Auer filter with paper tag & cap. Exc. cond. $60.00

GAS-MASK LUFTSCHUTZ WITH CANIS-TER: Full head green rubber mask in original cardboard case. Alum. filter. Rare ersatz version that is very difficult to find. Inked instructions inside. Avg. cond. $48.00

GAS-SHEET POUCH: Gray rubberized cloth. 2 snaps to flap inked *gdv 251/ 1940*. No sheet. Avg. cond. $34.00

GAS-SHEET POUCH: Gray rubberized. 2 gray glass buttons to flap inked *apn 1942*. No sheet. Avg. cond. $20.00

GAS-WARNING FLAG SET CASE: Black leatherette. 22" long with no contents. inked maker, date & *WaA*?? Gray web shoulder strap. Avg. cond. $30.00

GOGGLE CASE: *Deyea*. Aluminum. About 3x4x9" hinged case with large maker plate to lid dated *13.11.1936*. Avg. cond. $85.00

GOGGLES AVIATION *AUER 295* WITH BOX

GOGGLES AVIATION *AUER 295* WITH BOX: Tan cardboard box with maker label to lid & inked *4.Apr.1940*. Contents label to underside listing 6 items. Full gray rubber face pad with maker, gray finished oval alum. frames with stamped numbers & tinted lenses. Green elastic head-band & extra band. *Auer* suede cleaning section & 2 sets extra lenses, clear & tinted. Near mint cond. $250.00

GOGGLES AVIATION-STYLE WITH CASE: About 2.5x2.5x4.5" metal case with area inside for extra gray elastic headband. 4 clear plastic lenses in gray pouch. Rectangular brown painted brass frames with brown leather pads, tinted plastic lenses & elastic headband. Above avg. cond. $212.00

GOGGLES AVIATION-STYLE WITH CASE: Clean white rubber pads with nickel frames & bridge with screw. Tint to plastic oval lenses. Gray elastic band with hook. Gray tin can inked *RB number 1943*. Captured Italian & German issued. Near mint cond. $88.00

GOGGLES AVIATION-STYLE WITH CASE: Coated finish to tin storage case. Gray rubber pads & oval gray frames with clear glass lenses. Gray elastic headband & extra clear lenses in felt pouch. Near mint cond. $219.00

GOGGLES AVIATION-STYLE WITH CASE

GOGGLES AVIATION-STYLE WITH CASE: White rubber pads to nickel oval frames with plastic lenses & elastic headband. Green painted case. Near mint cond. $170.00

GOGGLES DUST THROW-AWAY STYLE WITH POUCH: Gray cloth pouch with 4 pockets is inked *ang WaA??* Holds 2 clear & 2 tinted goggles. Near mint cond. $46.00

GOGGLES DUST THROW-AWAY WITH POUCH: Variation. Green cloth pouch with *Prym* snap to flap. Orange tint to lenses, screen to sides, brown velvet frames & elastic headband. Near mint cond. $20.00

GOGGLES GENERAL-PURPOSE WITH POUCH: Black rubber body with round red lenses, gray elastic & cloth straps. *Auer* marked & *Neophan* above nose area. Gray canvas pouch with button. Near mint cond. $55.00

GOGGLES GENERAL-PURPOSE WITH POUCH: Rubber body by *Auer Neophan* round lenses & elastic headband. Gray cloth pouch with metal button closure. Avg. cond. $37.00

GOGGLES MT TROOP WITH CASE

GOGGLES MT TROOP WITH CASE: Yellow tinted oval glass lenses to gray metal frames with vent holes. Leather nose bridge, gray velvet padding to frames & white elastic band. Green painted metal can with bottom inked *8/44*. Exc. cond. $61.00

GOGGLES MT TROOP: Variation. Stamped deep alum. ovals with 4 slashes for viewing, leather padded rims & elastic headband. Above avg. cond. $25.00

GREATCOAT STRAPS: Lot of 3. Black leather, 17 holes, roller-buckle & strap with stud. 3 different maker marks & 2 dated. Avg. cond. $28.00

GREATCOAT STRAPS: Lot of 3. Black leather. Roller buckles, 17 holes & short strap with stud. By *erg 3/42*. Matched set. Near mint cond. $72.00

LANTERN ARMY CARBIDE: Bakelite. 11" tall body with handle & alum. hook chain. Stamped *WaA38* to alum. hook, 3 clear lenses with side covers. Above avg. cond. $100.00

LANTERN ARMY CARBIDE

LANTERN ARMY CARBIDE: Bakelite. Makers military secret code *efv*. Redish-brown bakelite was developed during the 1930s & used by the German military as replacement for much needed war materials. This form of plastic is strong & easy to work with. 9" tall 4x4.5" body with 3 clear lenses. Alum. hook to back. Avg. cond. $75.00

LIFE PRESERVER VEST MAY-WEST STYLE: Yellow rubberized canvas body & neck area. Manual inflation hose. Rubberized strap across back with buckle. Vertical back strap with owner inked on a label. Avg. cond. $318.00

MAP CASE LUFTWAFFE: Brown leather. Full flap, empty tool pockets, divided pouch, inked maker & stamped *LBA (s)*. Above avg. cond. $50.00

MAP CASE LUFTWAFFE: Dark brown leather body with alum. roller buckle straps. Maker/1940 marked & *LBA*. Avg. cond. $55.00

MAP CASE LUFTWAFFE: Dark brown pebbled body, half flap with roller-buckle strap, tool pouches & divided main pouch. Stamped *LBA(S)* with inked maker. Comes with eraser & color map paper packet showing *Die Westfront* & *African Kolonien*. Avg. cond. $108.00

MAP CASE WITH CONTENTS: Black leather. Pebbled body with full flap having US style *Tuck-Tite* closure missing loop. Tool pouches to front & folds open to reveal 2 clear grid panels. Inked German Owner name to flap with snap pouch to back & 2 RZM D-rings. Large color map of French coast *Strassenkarte von Sudwestfrankreich Blatt 29 La Rochelle-Bordeaux.* 1938/40 dated. Avg. cond. $36.00

MAP CASE: Black leather. Dark pebbled body. Half flap with roller buckle strap & tool pouches at front. Divided main body. 2 roller buckle straps at back. Avg. cond. $35.00

MAP CASE: Black leather. Pebbled body, half flap, tool pockets, inked RB number, etc. Near mint cond. $50.00

MAP CASE: Black leather. Pebbled body, half flap, tool pockets, roller-buckle strap & 2 back roller-buckle straps. Avg. cond. $45.00

MAP CASE

MAP CASE: Brown leather, pebbled body, half flap, roller-buckle & tool pouches. Stamped 1938/maker & inked owner *Oblt. Wehner*. 2 belt straps with alum. roller-buckles. Exc. cond. $66.00

MAP CASE: Brown leather. Pebbled body with half flap & roller-buckle strap. Tool pouches with wood ruler. Inked maker *Anton Schnell Dresden etc.* 2 roller buckle straps to back. LW-style but not marked. Avg. cond. $69.00

MAP CASE: Brown leather. Pebbled body. Long leather straps on back. Roller buckles. Two compartments. Pencil holders. Avg. cond. $30.00

MAP CASE: Brown leather. Variation. 7x9.5" body with 2 D-rings, empty snap tool pouch at back & fold open front with grid/celluloid panels. Avg. cond. $50.00

MAP CASE: Brown leather. With snap pouch side & fold open side to reveal clear plastic to one side of map viewing area. Has carry strap with rivets. Avg. cond. $26.00

MAP CASE: Dark brown leather body, full flap, alum. closure adjustment & empty tool fittings. Nice 1936/maker stamp & inked owner 3 times. Avg. cond. $40.00

MAP CASE

MAP CASE: Variation. 1x7.5x9" brown leather body, half flap with roller buckle strap, fold open front with grid pocket having scales & divided main pouch with wood ruler & US ruler. Leather shoulder strap attached with hooks. Avg. cond. $50.00

MAP CASE: Variation. 1x8x11" green leatherette body, brown leather trim, full flap with closure strap. Divided inside pouch & empty tool pockets at front. 2 belt loops with D-rings & a leather & lace shoulder strap. Avg. cond. $65.00

MAP COLORING PENCILS WITH CASE: *Johann Faber.* 2 part cardboard cigar-style case with color map legend listing 10 colors. 4" long title marked pencils. Above avg. cond. $23.00

MAP RULER: 20cm. 8.5" long natural wood body with hanger hole & black scale. Avg. cond. $20.00

MEDICAL BELT POUCH HITLER YOUTH: Dark brown leather, 2.5x3.5x6", stamped diamond to lid with empty tool fittings inside. *Reichsjugendfuhrung Berlin etc.* near the belt loops. Avg. cond. $47.00

MEDICAL BELT POUCH LUFTSCHUTZ: Brown leather. 4x4.5x8" body with straps & loops. Inked contents label & inked title. Avg. cond. $26.00

MEDICAL BELT POUCH RED CROSS: 3x4x6.5" black leather body stamped *DRK Sanitatslager Babelsberg 10.* Above avg. cond. $30.00

MEDICAL BELT POUCH RED CROSS: Black leather. 3x4x6.5" body stamped *DRK Sanitatslager Babelsberg 10.* Near mint cond. $50.00

MEDICAL BELT POUCH SS *HAGEDA*

MEDICAL BELT POUCH SS *HAGEDA*: Brown leather. 4x4.5x8" body with belt loops & alum. rivets. Nice stamped title maker mark & smaller SS-runes in circles above, looks to be added later. Same inked maker to inside of lid with leather fitting for missing equipment. 1930s. Above avg. cond. $85.00

MEDICAL BELT POUCH WITH CONTENTS: Brown leather. 3x4x6.5" size by *dny 1941 R.* Large paper wrapped bundles *Zellstoffwatte* & *Dreieck=Tuch.* Avg. cond. $36.00

MEDICAL BELT POUCH: 2x8x8.5" brown leather body with fold open front. Alum. tray inside. 2 belt loops. Inked maker. Avg. cond. $45.00

MEDICAL BELT POUCH: 3x3.5x6.5" brown leather body by *dny 1942* & R-side. Avg. cond. $25.00

MEDICAL BELT POUCH: 3x4x6.5" brown leather body with maker, *K* & L-side. Lacks label & has eagle ink stamp inside. Above avg. cond. $25.00

MEDICAL BELT POUCH: Black leather. 3x4x6.5" size. Inked *WaA65* inside lid. Exc. cond. $20.00

MEDICAL BELT POUCH: Brown leather. 3x3.5x6.5" body by *dny 1942* & R-side. Alum. fittings. 1940 dated paper contents label. Avg. cond. $23.00

MEDICAL BELT POUCH: Brown leather. 3x4x6.5". Stamped *Karl Barth Waldbrol 1939 WaA145* & R-side. No contents label but has 5 tubes with *Rapex Rot Gaspatrone.* Avg. cond. $20.00

MEDICAL BELT POUCH: Early. Black leather body 3x4.5x7" with brass studs. Avg. cond. $35.00

MEDICAL BELT POUCHES: 2 different sizes. Brown leather. 3x4x6.5" with 1936 maker & R-side. 1940 contents label & divider inside. 4x4.5x8" size. Luftschutz contents label & inked 1939 etc. Above avg. cond. $36.00

MEDICAL BOX DEUTSCHES JUNGVOLK WITH CONTENTS

MEDICAL BOX DEUTSCHES JUNGVOLK WITH CONTENTS: 4x7x9.5" green painted cardboard body with reinforced corners & stenciled red cross to lid. Inked paper label inside *NSDAP Deutsches Jungvolk Jungstamm VIII/110 Ziegelhausen a.N. etc.* 8 contents, 1937 bandage, 1944 bandage, Verbandpackchen Typ 3, Kameradenhilfe pouch, pins, etc. Avg. cond. $219.00

MEDICAL EQUIPMENT *RIECHMITTEL* AMPULES IN BOX: Title to white cardboard box with Berlin maker. Holds 5 white cloth covered tubes/ampules. Exc. cond. $27.00

MEDICAL PACK: Brown leather. 4.5x8.5x10.5" body with top flap having 2 stud straps & fold open back. Leather handle at top, shoulder strap & belt loops. Cardboard divided tray inside. Avg. cond. $60.00

MEDICAL POUCH RED CROSS WITH CONTENTS: Brown leather. 2.5x7x8.5" body, fold open front, handle at top, D-rings at back & stamped *DRK Sanitatslager Babelsberg 19.* Contains 8 items, a gray cloth sling, Sulfapyridin, Wiesbasan, & more items. Above avg. cond. $100.00

MEDICAL POUCH RED CROSS: Brown leather. 2.5x7x8" body with fold open front, handle at top & 2 D rings at back. Stamped *D.R.K.Sanitatslager etc.* Typed property marks inside & paper owner tag

DRK=Helferin Weissmantel, R. Leipzig. Exc. cond. $25.00

MESS HALL TOWELS NAVAL: 3 different. 21x39" woven off-white body with 2 loops at center/ends. Inked party eagle *H U.* Same size with 4 end loops & inked party eagle *H.U.1937* & 23x27" off-white with 2 red stripes, 1 corner loop & inked Naval Eagle M *MWA 1944.* Above avg. cond. $85.00

MESS-KIT SS: 7" tall alum. body & lid with black paint. Stamped *RZM FA.1/34.* With a wire handle. Above avg. cond. $50.00

MESS-KIT UTENSILS 3 PIECE SET *BIWAK* WITH POUCH

MESS-KIT UTENSILS 3 PIECE SET *BIWAK* WITH POUCH: Large alum. spoon stamped Germany & has riveted holder. Alum. fork, alum. handle to knife with title & Rostfrei blade with opener. Felt pouch with title to snap torn from flap. Avg. cond. $61.00

MESS-KIT UTENSILS 4 PIECE SET *BIWAK* WITH POUCH

MESS-KIT UTENSILS 4 PIECE SET *BIWAK* WITH POUCH: Large alum. spoon & fork. Gusstahl knife & holder/opener has Eagle stamp/5266. Felt pouch with *Biwak* snap. Near mint cond. $108.00

MESS-KIT UTENSILS 4 PIECE SET: All clean Rostfrei parts with eagle stamp to each. Star-A *Rostfrei* to knife, *GAG* fork & *C&C.W.* spoon/holder. Above avg. cond. $93.00

MESS-KIT UTENSILS 4 PIECE SET: All stamped *WSM 42 Rostfrei* & eagle. Above avg. cond. $44.00

MESS-KIT UTENSILS 4 PIECE SET: All stamped except for knife with *FBCM 43* & eagle. With plated nickel finish. Avg. cond. $28.00

MESS-KIT UTENSILS 4 PIECE SET: Eagle stamp only to silver plated holder/opener & date to rest. Plated knife, alum. fork & spoon. Avg. cond. $59.00

MESS-KIT UTENSILS 4 PIECE SET: Eagle stamp only to silver plated holder/opener, plated knife, alum. fork & spoon. Avg. cond. $25.00

MESS-KIT UTENSILS 4 PIECE SET: Opener/holder with knife, fork & spoon. Silver finish. Above avg. cond. ... $20.00

MESS-KIT

MESS-KIT: Steel. Green painted outside & red inside. Wire to body by *OHW 42* & lid *OHW 43*. Leather strap, 14 adjust-ment holes & roller-buckle. Near mint cond. $139.00

MESS-KIT UTENSILS 4 PIECE SET: Rostfrei *WSM 41* & party eagle to 3 pieces except for knife. Above avg. cond. $25.00

MESS-KIT UTENSILS FORK & SPOON: Aluminum. Pivoting handle. *O.H.W.38 WaA??*. Avg. cond. $20.00

MESS-KIT UTENSILS FORK & SPOON: Hmkd WJS 3. Pre-war. Pivot at handles. Avg. cond. $30.00

MESS-KIT UTENSILS FORK & SPOON: Avg. cond. $20.00

MESS-KIT UTENSILS FORK & SPOON: Pivot rivet to handles by *OSW 38* & has owner's initials. Avg. cond. $28.00

MESS-KIT WITH SOLDIER ART *1941 45*: 7" tall alum. body & lid with gray paint. Lid by *GNL 38* with body by *MG 41*. Wire handle to body with back having scratched-out owner name with *1941 45* - shield below. Avg. cond. $33.00

MESS-KIT: 2.5 liter. Black leather strap. Maker code *B&FL 28*. Lid has owner's name engraved, *IBRAHIMDV*. Avg. cond. $24.00

MESS-KIT: 2.5 liter. Matching black leather strap. Avg. cond. $25.00

MESS-KIT: Alum. Green paint. Handle stamped *FWBN 44*. Wire hanger. Avg. cond. $20.00

MESS-KIT: Aluminum. Gray paint. Lid by *HRE 44*. Has wire handle. Above avg. cond. $23.00

MESS-KIT: Black painted 6" tall alum. body with stamped hinge *RZM M6/35*. Wire handle. Above avg. cond. $55.00

MESS-KIT: Gray finish. Unit marked *I. 3./ A.R.36*. Canvas with 1934/maker to leather strap. Mint cond. $58.00

MESS-KIT: Green painted alum. body by *MN44*. Exc. cond. $40.00

MESS-KIT: Green painted alum. body by *SMM 44*. Wire handle & shows use. Avg. cond. $28.00

MESS-KIT: Porcelanized. Early. 6" tall body & lid with black finish by *AWC*. Wire handle. Avg. cond. $25.00

MESSAGE CONTAINER AIRCRAFT DROPS TO GROUND TROOPS: 2" diam. by 14.5" long red painted metal tube. Removable end cap & other end has grenade style blue cap ignitor. Above avg. cond. $124.00

MITTENS 3 FINGER CAMO

MITTENS 3 FINGER CAMO: Late-war. Reversible. Water pattern camo to winter white. Style used with 4 part outfit. 16" long bodies with different maker camo print to each. Trigger finger, long cloth connector strap & reversible to white. Exc. cond. $160.00

MITTENS 3 FINGER: 12.5" long bodies with leather covered 3 finger area. Adjustment buckle belt at wrist & elastic opening. Inked numbers. Above avg. cond. $23.00

MITTENS 3 FINGER: 13" long gray canvas body with gray leather hand area & 2 snap straps along back. Inked RB #. Above avg. cond. $50.00

MITTENS 3 FINGER: 14" green canvas bodies with gray leather palms/fingers. 2 gray leather snap straps to gauntlets. Inked *A.Brilling 1940 7 1/2*. Above avg. cond. $72.00

MITTENS 3 FINGER

MITTENS 3 FINGER: 14" long green
canvass bodies, gray leather hand area
with trigger finger & 2 leather snap straps
at back. inked 1941/maker. Above avg.
cond. $50.00
MITTENS 3 FINGER: 14" long green
canvas bodies with gray leather palm/
finger area & 2 snap straps each. Inked
1941 date & maker name. Size 8. Avg.
cond. $90.00
MITTENS 3 FINGER: 14.5" long bodies
with leather covered palm, finger &
thumb. Two gray leather adjustment
straps with snaps marked *JRE*. Inked
size 10. Lined hand area. Above avg.
cond. $20.00
MITTENS 3 FINGER: 14.5" long green &
gray canvas bodies with gray leather
hand area. 2 leather snap-straps to each.
Inked RB number & size 10. Avg.
cond. $28.00
MITTENS 3 FINGER: 14.5" long green
canvas bodies with gray leather palms &
2 snap straps. Partial felt lined. Inked RB
number & size 9. Above avg.
cond. $43.00
MITTENS 3 FINGER: 15" long olive cloth
bodies, green leather hand area & 2 snap
straps to each. Inked *Hugo Weigel
etc.1942 10.* Near mint cond. $34.00
MITTENS 3 FINGER: Chemical protection.
Heavy rubber. 14" long dark-green
pebbled rubber bodies. Above avg.
cond. $20.00
MITTENS 3 FINGER: French made. 13.5"
green canvas bodies, brown leather palm
area & 1 snapstrap each. Inked with
maker, size 2, & date. Above avg.
cond. $35.00
MITTENS 3 FINGER: Gray wool. 12" long
bodies with darker wool lining. Wood
toggle & loop to openings. Paper tag has
inked maker. Exc. cond. $32.00
MITTENS 3 FINGER: Rabbit fur lined. 10.5"
reed-green HBT bodies & wrist straps
with snaps. Avg. cond. $40.00

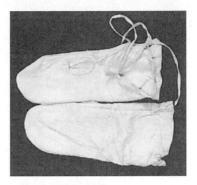

MITTENS WINTER LUFTWAFFE

MITTENS WINTER LUFTWAFFE: Off-white
canvas exterior with padded interior & tie
cuffs. Exc. cond. $135.00

MITTENS WINTER REVERSIBLE

MITTENS WINTER REVERSIBLE: 15.5"
green/gray wool side & white cotton side.
Connecting strap also is gauntlet closure.
Above avg. cond. $66.00
MITTENS WINTER: Gray canvas. 12" long
with elastic around cuffs. Fleece lined
hand areas with the right side having
trigger finger. Inked size *3*. Near mint
cond. $45.00
MITTENS: 11.5" tan canvas bodies & have
wrist buckle straps. White felt lined &
bevo maker tag *Engelhardt Erzeugnis 11.*
Avg. cond. $25.00
MITTENS: 15" long gray canvas bodies with
brown leather at each thumb area. Elastic
to wrist area & belt closure to opening.
Exc. cond. $23.00
MITTENS: Gray canvas. 15.5" long canvas
with gray leather to thumb area. Elastic
band at wrist. Buckle/strap at cuffs with
wood toggle & loop to other side. Exc.
cond. $45.00
MOSQUITO HEAD NETS: Lot of 2. Green
with drawstring opening. Above avg.
cond. $37.00

MOSQUITO NET BED-ROLL COVER: About 3x7' size with white mesh upper body in rectangular shape & gray cloth lower sides. 3 tie-strings at each end. Inked maker to blue-gray cloth. Above avg. cond. $110.00

MOUNTAIN CRAMPONS ARMY MT. TROOP *STUBAI 43*

MOUNTAIN CRAMPONS ARMY MT. TROOP *STUBAI 43*: 10 point steel bodies, title stamped & *Eckenstein Made in Austria*. Metal toe loop & rings for straps. Above avg. cond. $165.00

MOUNTAIN PICK/HAMMER ARMY MT. TROOPER: 11" long wood handle stamped *G.J.R.137* & *WaA*?? Leather wrist loop. Steel head by *WG* in crown. Avg. cond. $53.00

MOUNTAIN SKI SET *SCHAFER SKI SPLITKEIN* WITH POLES: 2 tone wood bodies have title maker decals & stamped *2331 205*. Boot fittings are intact. Blue handled poles with black plastic grips made by *Eckel*. Above avg. cond. $223.00

MOUNTAIN SKI STRAPS: Fur covered white canvas straps with buckle & strap fittings. Pair. Exc. cond. $55.00

MOUNTAIN SKI STRAPS: Imitation fur for up-hill use. Black & gray spotted design with web straps & 1 leather strap each. Above avg. cond. $20.00

MUSICIAN POUCH ARMY: Black leather. 3x8x8.5" body with half flap & roller buckle. Stamped 1939/maker & *WaA389*. 2 belt loops & D-rings to back. Avg. cond. $32.00

NIGHT-STICK POLICE WITH SCABBARD: 15.5" long overall in scabbard. Grooved black rubber handle with hole for wrist strap. 10.5" long white body. Brown leather scabbard with belt loop having stamp. Avg. cond. $40.00

PARACHUTE EQUIPMENT DROP: 8' orange silk body with riser lines attached to braided static line. Above avg. cond. $21.00

PARACHUTE HARNESS PARATROOPER WITH CHUTE STORAGE BAG: *17.Dez.1942 etc.* printed maker tag to off-white web shoulder strap with buckle. Harness has waist fittings & leg buckles.

Green canvas pack has printed maker label with same date & titled *Sprungschirm fur Fallschirmtruppen*. Loose green canvas 1942 *Packhulle Innen etc.* Green woven storage bag, inked *Fl.30220*. Avg. cond. $475.00

PARACHUTE LUFTWAFFE PARA-TROOPER CAMO: This is the packed chute with riser lines & 2 connector lines with clips. Lacks harness & back pack. Inked 1941 date & other maker marks. No static line. Above avg. cond. $683.00

PARACHUTE PRE-CHUTE: 3' diam. to white body with riser lines & cable with threaded loop. Inked *amy etc.* Above avg. cond. $20.00

PARACHUTE STORAGE BAG PARA-TROOPER: Brown burlap body with green cloth trim & handles. Snap fittings to flap. Avg. cond. $40.00

PARACHUTE STORAGE BAG PARA-TROOPER: Green burlap body with green woven straps & all snaps intact. Near mint cond. $263.00

PARACHUTE STORAGE BAG PARA-TROOPER: Green woven body with 2 web handles & flap closure with snaps intact. Avg. cond. $50.00

PARATROOPER GLOVES: Brown leather. 13.5" long bodies. Elastic cuffs with 3 elastic/spring fittings sewn-in to gauntlets. Inked *LBA37*. Other unit inked in white *I/Fallsch.-Jager Rgt.1*. Avg. cond. $2,258.00

PERISCOPE *SFL.Z.F.1*

PERISCOPE *SFL.Z.F.1*: 14" tall, 2 part body & tan painted. Title marked & *beh etc.* Optics clear & fitting for night use. Avg. cond. $200.00

PERISCOPE TRENCH: 21" overall 7/8" diam. tan painted metal tube. Optics clear with rubber eye cup & by *dow*. Above avg. cond. $80.00

PIONEER AX/TAPE MEASURE CARRIER ARMY: Quality construction. 18.5" long body having pouch for 8" wide ax head & about 4" diam. tape measure fitting with roller-buckle. Belt loop to back. Stamped *Frost & Jahnel Breslau 1939 WaA182*. Near mint cond. $122.00

RADIO HEADSET PANZER: Black leather covered steel band, black rubber earcups & brown cloth covered cord with 2 prong plug. Avg. cond. $345.00

RADIO HEADSET PANZER

RADIO HEADSET PANZER: Black rubber earcups to 1943 dated speakers. Black leather covered steel headband. Brown cloth covered cord with 2 prong plug. Exc. cond. $683.00

RADIO LUFTWAFFE MULTI-BAND *SIEMENS K32 GWB*: 7.5x12x18" blue-gray painted wood case with large white stenciled eagle to back & 2 smaller eagles to front doors. Handle to top, speaker & multi-band adjustments to front. Shows some tube rework inside with paper parts illustration with couple extra tubes/fittings. Above avg. cond. $464.00

RADIO LUFTWAFFE MULTI-BAND
K42 NORA

RADIO LUFTWAFFE MULTI-BAND *K42 NORA*: 4.5x11x19" blue-gray painted wood body with handle to top & hinged door in front. 2 stenciled white LW eagles. Paper instruction sheet to door, multi-band adjustment knob & works appear intact with some extra tubes. Exc. cond. $227.00

RADIO THROAT-MIKE SET PANZER: Black leather covered steel band with bakelite mikes, cloth covered cord, bakelite switch with clip & 2 prong plug. Above avg. cond. $184.00

RADIO THROAT-MIKE SET: For normal radio set. Bakelite switch box having added words *Trvale zapnuto Vypnuto etc.* Bakelite plug has 1944 date & 5 prongs. Leather covered band to bakelite throat mikes. Cloth covered cords. Avg. cond. $140.00

RAILWAY BOXCAR EAGLE: Aluminum body. Nicely hmkd on back. Metric threaded. 28" wing spread. 15.5" tall with eagle standing on swastika. Exc. cond. $277.00

RAILWAY BOXCAR EAGLE: Hmkd with maker marks, etc. Metric threaded bolt holes. Large spread winged eagle on wreath & swastika. Wing span approx. 28". Height 15.5". Above avg. cond. $300.00

RANGE-FINDER LUFTWAFFE *1M A-INSTR M/43* WITH CASE: 3 part. Blue-gray painted metal case is 6x8x46.5" with handle at each end, 2 latches to rubber-sealed lid & title plate. Tan painted inside has illustrated picture of contents but lacks listing side. Gray repaint over base tan to 45" long body by *fwq etc.* Only few loose contents remain with Dutch *Materiel-Kontrollbok etc.* with matching Serial#. Shoulder harness of gray leatherette construction by *fwq 1943* with shoulder straps & waist strap. Gray painted aluminum storage can for tan metal clamp fittings. Exc. cond. $695.00

RANGE-FINDER LUFTWAFFE *1M A-INSTR M/43* WITH CASE

RATION BAG: 2.5x3.5' white body with 2 blue stripes. Black inked party eagle & *H.Vpfl. 1943*. Avg. cond. $20.00

RATION BAG: 26x41" off-white woven body with 2 blue stripes. Black inked eagle side & *H.Vpfl. 1941* side. Avg. cond. $20.00

RATION BAG: 27x44" woven off-white body, 2 blue stripes & inked eagle *H.Vpfl.1941*. Above avg. cond. $28.00

RATION BAG: 28x46" brown woven body with black inked eagle & *H.Vpfl. 1943*. Avg. cond. $25.00

RATION BAG: Off-white woven body with 2 blue stripes. Black inked eagle & *H. Vpfl. 1936.* Above avg. cond. $27.00

RATION HEATER *ESBIT-KOCHER MOD9*: Gray metal folding body with stamped title & illustrated instructions. With fuel tablet. Avg. cond. $66.00

RATION HEATER *ESBIT-KOCHER MOD.9*: Folding gray metal body with stamped title & illustrated instructions. Above avg. cond. $26.00

RUCKSACK ARMY: Green canvas body with 2 pocket front, grommet closure & rope. Black leather shoulder straps. Avg. cond. $55.00

RUCKSACK ARMY: Green canvas body, 2 pockets, black leather fittings, grommet closure & rope. Inked RB number inside with cloth pocket. Hooks for Y-strap use. Near mint cond. $46.00

RUCKSACK ARMY: Green canvas body, 2 pockets, black leather fittings, grommet closure & rope. Tan web shoulder straps. Above avg. cond. $37.00

RUCKSACK CAMO SPLINTER-PATTERN: Full size. 1 pouch to front with leather roller-buckle closure, grommet closure flap-strap, shoulder straps of camo & woven material with leather buckle ends. Above avg. cond. $114.00

RUCKSACK DAK: Canvas body, 2 pocket front, alum. grommet closure with string, 3 cloth pouches inside with torn flap & metal hooks for Y-strap use. Avg. cond. $40.00

RUCKSACK DAK: Olive canvas body shows with web fittings. 2 pocket front. Avg. cond. $45.00

RUCKSACK DAK: Olive canvas body with 2 pocket front & web fittings overall. Grommet closure & 3 cloth pockets inside. Removed 3 hooks to back for Y-strap use & brown leather straps added to large D-ring at center. 1 original hook strap remains with leather roller-buckle added to other side. Avg. cond. $113.00

RUCKSACK DAK

RUCKSACK ARMY

RUCKSACK ARMY: Green canvas body, large front pocket, smaller side pockets, large flap with 3 closure straps, grommet closure with string & 2 inside pockets. Black leather straps. 1942/maker. Avg. cond. $53.00

RUCKSACK ARMY: Large green canvas body, front pocket & flap with 3 closure straps. Alum. & brown leather fittings. 1939/maker stamped inside. Side pockets & brown shoulder straps. Avg. cond. $62.00

RUCKSACK ARTILLERY: Green canvas body has moved 2 front leather straps to each side & sewn on. Leather RB numbered. Avg. cond. $37.00

RUCKSACK ARTILLERY: Green canvas body, black leather fittings, grommet closure & string. Black leather straps & RB number to back. Avg. cond. .. $25.00

RUCKSACK DAK: Olive canvas body, 2 pocket front, grommet closure with string & 2 cloth pouches inside. Web & steel fittings. Web shoulder straps. Above avg. cond. $65.00

RUCKSACK LUFTWAFFE

RUCKSACK LUFTWAFFE: Blue/gray canvas body, drawstring closure with grommets, black leather strap to flap & hooks for Y-strap use. Near mint cond. $70.00

RUCKSACK LUFTWAFFE: Blue-gray canvas body with 2 pocket front. Black leather fittings, grommet closure & string. Stamped 1942/maker name & black leather shoulder straps. Avg. cond. $90.00

RUCKSACK LUFTWAFFE: Blue-gray canvas body, 2 pocket front, black leather fittings, grommet closure & rope. Stamped RB number & black leather shoulder straps. Above avg. cond. $50.00

RUCKSACK LUFTWAFFE: Blue-gray canvas body, black leather fittings, 2 pocket front & rope to grommet closure. Black leather shoulder straps. 1943/ maker. Above avg. cond. $49.00

RUCKSACK LUFTWAFFE: Blue/gray canvas, black leather & steel fittings. 2 pockets, grommet closure with rope & shoulder straps. 1940/maker stamp. Avg. cond. $40.00

RUCKSACK SS ARTILLERY-STYLE: Olive canvas body, grommet closure with rope, top flap, 2 black leather straps to front, 4 hooks for Y-strap use & leather stamped *SS L3/46 1940*. Above avg. cond. $265.00

RUCKSACK: Field made. Splinter pattern camo shelter quarter material is nicely sewn up as rucksack with 2 pocket front. Grommet closure with rope. Web & leather shoulder straps. Above avg. cond. $125.00

RUCKSACK: Green burlap body with front pocket. Brown leather roller/buckle straps. Small flap & grommet closure with rope. Avg. cond. $30.00

RUCKSACK: Tan burlap, ration bag style, body has 2 small pouches to front with steel button flaps. Small flap top, rope closure & small pocket inside. Maker marked & dated brown leather fitting for removable straps. Straps dated 1937 with alum. fittings. Avg. cond. $45.00

SEXTANT LUFTWAFFE NAVIGATOR HAND-HELD WITH CASE: 12" long, tan crinkle paint finish metal unit with large rotating dials on each side. Precision optics with flip-in filters, etc. In a fitted wooden storage case. Above avg. cond. $315.00

SEXTANT LUFTWAFFE NAVIGATOR HAND-HELD WITH CASE: 5.5x9x13" blue-gray painted alum. storage box with handle to each end, 2 part lid with alum. operating instructions & contents list.

About 12" long main body with tan crinkle paint, aluminum tag *Libellen-Oktant etc.Fl.23750*. Maker *De Te We*. Comes with couple extra fittings. Exc. cond. $347.00

SHELTER QUARTER CAMO ITALIAN: 3 color camo print to one side, head slash at center, alum. buttons & sewn corner grommets. Exc. cond. $195.00

SHELTER QUARTER CAMO SPLINTER PATTERN: 1941 dated with maker name. Avg. cond. $80.00

SHELTER QUARTER CAMO SPLINTER-PATTERN: Light & dark printed sides, gray grommets & buttons. 1941 maker. Avg. cond. $75.00

SHELTER QUARTER CAMO
SPLINTER-PATTERN

SHELTER QUARTER CAMO SPLINTER-PATTERN WITH POLE & STAKE: Light & dark printed sides, gray grommets & buttons. Wood pole with steel fittings. Heavy steel stake by *S&C40*. Above avg. cond. $80.00

SHELTER QUARTER CAMO SPLINTER-PATTERN WITH POLE & STAKE: Light & dark printed sides, gray grommets & steel buttons. inked 1944/RB number. Wood stake & pole with steel fittings. Avg. cond. $91.00

SHELTER QUARTER CAMO SPLINTER-PATTERN: 1935 dated. Named. Above avg. cond. $125.00

SHELTER QUARTER CAMO SPLINTER-PATTERN: Light & dark print sides, alum. grommets & buttons with some missing. Avg. cond. $58.00

SHELTER QUARTER CAMO SPLINTER-PATTERN: Light & dark sides about same shade with grommets & most buttons. Avg. cond. $67.00

SHELTER QUARTER NSDAP GAU SCHWABEN: Square tan/brown canvas body with alum. buttons & corner grommets. Head slash at center has bevo maker tag *Wesa-Zeltbahn DRP.ang.*

Nr.3784. Inked title to corner with *189.* Above avg. cond. $117.00

SHELTER QUARTER RAD: Tan/gray triangular body with alum. grommets & stamped gray metal buttons. Inked *Weber A.G. Wuppertal 1939.* Above avg. cond. $53.00

SHELTER QUARTER SA: Brown canvas. Alum. grommets & all buttons. Ink stamped to SA unit— *SA Sturm 34/95* ?. Owner name inked at other corner. Near mint cond. $120.00

SHELTER QUARTER SS CAMO

SHELTER QUARTER SS CAMO: Late-war HBT, burred edge camo. Spring & fall sides are burred-style with half of quarter being made of HBT material. Avg. cond. $350.00

SHELTER QUARTER SS CAMO: Oak leaf camo pattern. Spring & fall sides with inked RB number. Gray grommets & buttons. Avg. cond. $450.00

SHOVEL CARRIER: Black paper/cardboard body for rectangular blade. Stamped *WaA 392 194??* Black leather belt loops & roller buckle closure strap. Above avg. cond. $166.00

SHOVEL FOLDING WITH CARRIER

SHOVEL FOLDING WITH CARRIER: Black painted steel blade stamped *VBW WaA727,* bakelite nut & wood handle. Black leather carrier by *cgn41 WaA47.* Above avg. cond. $342.00

SHOVEL FOLDING WITH CARRIER: Black steel blade, bakelite nut & wood handle. Black leatherette carrier stamped *ggu 1942.* Avg. cond. $140.00

SHOVEL FOLDING WITH CARRIER: The carrier is marked *Berlin 1940* & *WaA286.* Black painted pointed steel folding shovel with large bakelite tightening nut & nice wooden knobbed handle. Avg. cond. $196.00

SHOVEL WITH CARRIER: 45" long body with rounded steel blade. Trademarked with stick-man holding shovel & *H 1944.* Ball tip to end of wood handle. Brown leather pouch/carrier having 2 closure straps. Stamped maker & unit *4.P.B.* Avg. cond. $360.00

SHOVEL WITH CARRIER

SHOVEL WITH CARRIER: Rectangular steel blade. Trademark stamped with Maltese cross. Wood handle varnished. Black leatherette carrier by *jvf1943 WaA204,* brown leather belt loops & closure strap. Avg. cond. $195.00

SIREN HAND-POWERED: *1940 Jurk.* 12" tall brown painted metal body with title & stamped *WaA??* Bakelite handle to crank, grill & back fitting. Lever to change pitch. Exc. cond. $154.00

SLEEPING-BAG ARMY: About 6' long body is 29" wide. Gray cloth exterior & gray felt interior. Bakelite buttons at open end & side slash. 2 storage bands at end. Exc. cond. $124.00

SLIDE RULER ARTILLERY: With field made splinter pattern camo pouch sewn from shelter-quarter material. 9" long wood rule with alum. scale facing & clear slide. Above avg. cond. $43.00

SOCK SUPPORTERS ARMY: Gray woven cloth strap with black rubber fitting with metal loop. Adjustment buckle to cloth-strap. Near mint cond. $20.00

STOP WATCH: Nickel plated. Maker name is *Hankart.* 7 jewels. White face. Sweep second hand, small minute hand. Needs some interior adjustment for running. Above avg. cond. $30.00

TELEGRAPH KEY: For field radio. Black rubber cover to bakelite base with body having hinged cover *vor dem Offnen Stecker herausziehen* & signal. 2 prong plug to cord. Above avg. cond. . $114.00

TELEGRAPH KEY: Bakelite base & finger fitting. Nickel plated metal fittings. Above avg. cond. $280.00

TELEPHONE DESK M38: Bakelite. Complete body with alum. maker plate

Heliwatt AC 1940. Stamped WaA??
Receiver stamped *1941 WaA618.* Exc.
cond. $56.00

TELEPHONE DESK WITH SWITCH
BOARD ARMY: For desk. Bakelite body
with stamped *WaA304* , metal maker
plate *1940 Heliowatt AG* & alphabet
chart. Handcrank to side & bakelite
receiver. Wired bakelite switchbox with 5
lines & empty battery area. Near mint
cond. $114.00

TELEPHONE FIELD

TELEPHONE FIELD: Tan painted works,
crank, receiver, battery box & 8 extra
speakers from receiver. 1 drilled hole to
bakelite front. Above avg. cond. . $76.00

TELEPHONE FIELD: Bakelite. 1937 dated
works & broken black receiver. Crank
intact. Avg. cond. $40.00

TELEPHONE FIELD: Bakelite. Dark case
with dated works. 44 dated receiver. Avg.
cond. $50.00

TELEPHONE-CABLE REEL HAND-
CRANK: 10" diam. gray spool with wood
grip to side crank handle. Frame stamped
D.Z.43 WaA5 with large wood handle.
Exc. cond. $150.00

TELEPHONE-CABLE REEL HAND-
CRANK: 6" long black painted metal body
with wood handle & bar socket with lock.
Stamped metal *Heimschutz Berlin 36
WaA315.* Above avg. cond. $50.00

TELEPHONE-CABLE REEL WITH
BACKPACK FRAME: 11" diam. green
painted metal ends to 10" wide reel
having old cloth covered wire to center.
Center shaft has affixed cogged wheel to
1 side with square end for crank. Riveted
alum. frame with canvas covered pad &
web shoulder straps with wool pads on
leather. Avg. cond. $200.00

TELESCOPE *4X20* MULTI-PURPOSE:
Prismatic lens, brass frame with gray
finish. Mountable by screws thru bottom.
Hmkd *C.P. GOERTZ, BERLIN.* Leather
case Above avg. cond. $25.00

TENT POLE POUCH WITH POLES &
STAKES: Splinter pattern camo. 2 leather
loops & alum. buttons to camo pouch.
Inked 1942 date & maker to flap with
cross in shield. 3 white painted wood
poles, alum. sockets & gray galvanized
stamped stakes. Above avg.
cond. $145.00

TENT POLE POUCH WITH POLES: 3
Swiss-style white painted wood poles
with alum. cups. Gray canvas pouch with
2 alum. buttons & 2 leather loops. Avg.
cond. $36.00

TENT STAKES WITH POUCH

TENT STAKES WITH POUCH: RZM. Gray
canvas body, 2 black leather roller buckle
straps, 2 alum. buttons & oilcloth
Zeltbahn-Zubehor Beutel. Has 2 alum.
stakes by *L&E 38* & 1 *RZM SS39/36*
stake. Above avg. cond. $285.00

TRAINING PISTOL: All metal. 1930s. 8"
long with 4" grip & simulated trigger. Cast
black iron in pistol configuration. Above
avg. cond. $50.00

TYPEWRITER *OLYMPIA* WITH SS RUNIC
KEY, CASED: 7x14x15" hinged wood
case with metal reinforced corners, 2
latches & metal handle to end. Most
green paint has peeled-off wood. Gray
finished body has SS runes on #5 key.
Paper illustrated instruction sheet inside
lid *Kurze Erklarung Der Olympia Robust
etc.* Avg. cond. $300.00

TYPEWRITER *OLYMPIA* WITH SS RUNIC
KEY: Gray finished body with metal cover
to keys/works & SS runes on #5 key. Avg.
cond. $350.00

WHISTLE WITH LANYARD: About 2.5" long
plastic body & plaited black lanyard.
Above avg. cond. $30.00

WHISTLE: Bakelite with leather strap.
80mm black tube & ball hanging loop.
Has extra hole in body for control. 4"
leather strap loop. Avg. cond. $20.00

WHISTLE: Nickel. Heavy drum body with
mouth piece stamped *Germany.* Fitting
for lanyard ring. Near mint cond. $20.00

WIRE-CUTTER POUCH: Black leather. 16"
tall body. Roller buckle closure to flap.
maker *hjh 41.* Avg. cond. $46.00

WIRE-SIZE TOOL: 9" long with wood
handle & steel fitting for 5 mm sizes, 1
thru 3. Screw toggle closure. Stamped
1934/maker & WaA134. Above avg.
cond. $40.00

Y-STRAPS COMBAT: Black leather. Steel D-rings & fittings. Avg. cond. $100.00

Y-STRAPS COMBAT: Black leather. Steel D-rings & fittings. Avg. cond. $120.00

Y-STRAPS COMBAT: Variation. Brown leather straps, variation D-rings & steel fittings. Above avg. cond. $125.00

Y-STRAPS TROPICAL DAK: Canvas & leather. Back hook strap is leather & marked. Front straps are canvas. Avg. cond. $400.00

THIRD REICH HOLSTERS, CLEANING KITS & AMMO MAGAZINES

AMMO BANDOLEER MG13: 1 side only. Gray canvas body with canvas handle & dry brown leather fittings. Held 4 magazines. Eagle proof & 1936 maker to belt loop. Variation brown leather straps with roller buckle & swivel clip ends. Avg. cond. $40.00

AMMO BASKET DRUM MG34 CAMO

AMMO BASKET DRUM MG34 CAMO: Brush stroked tan base with sprayed green & red splotches. Blue gray inside. Above avg. cond. $139.00

AMMO BELT MG08 250 ROUND: White web belt with brass fittings & leather endtabs. Inked numbers up to *250* & stamped brass *1932* with maker trademark. Near mint cond. $105.00

AMMO CAN MG 300 ROUND: Heavy steel body with stamped lid *1942 ??? WaA???* Avg. cond. $27.00

AMMO CANS MG 300 ROUND: Lot of 2. Both repainted gray with some leather loops remaining to handles. Stamped out maker marks & 1 *SA* -Finnish stamped. Avg. cond. $20.00

AMMO LOADING TOOL MP38/40: Black finished body by *kur 43 WaA815*. Avg. cond. $45.00

AMMO LOADING TOOL MP38/40: Blued body by *agp 40 WaA708*. Above avg. cond. $66.00

AMMO LOADING TOOL MP38/40: Blued body by *kur 42 WaA815*. Above avg. cond. $55.00

AMMO LOADING TOOL P08: Blued finish. Avg. cond. $26.00

AMMO MAGAZINE BB-TRAINING RIFLE 6 SHOT *ANSCHUTZ*: 1920s. 1.5" tall gray body with title & numbered side showing shots left. Pre-.22 training rifle used. Near mint cond. $33.00

AMMO MAGAZINE K43 10 ROUND: Black painted body by *aye WaAB43*. Avg. cond. $37.00

AMMO MAGAZINE MP38 32 ROUND: 1940 dated. Above avg. cond. $55.00

AMMO MAGAZINE MP43 32 ROUND

AMMO MAGAZINE MP43 32 ROUND: Blued curved metal body with a stamped title & *fxo* /eagle 37 proof. Avg. cond. $128.00

AMMO MAGAZINE P38: Eagle proof & blued finish. Avg. cond. $55.00

AMMO POUCH 3 POCKET NAVAL: Black dyed brown leather sewn body with 1938/maker & stamped eagle M. Avg. cond. $23.00

AMMO POUCH 3 POCKET SS: Black leather. Alum. fittings, 1939/ maker. Center lid inked inside *SS-Verfugungstruppe*. Avg. cond. $40.00

AMMO POUCH 3 POCKET SS: Waffen SS owner named. Riveted construc- tion to black pebbled leather body with RB number. Inked name to inside of lid *SS-W.Specht*. Avg. cond. $50.00

AMMO POUCH 3 POCKET: Black leather sewn body with RB number & 1944. Above avg. cond. $20.00

AMMO POUCH 3 POCKET: Black leather. Avg. cond. $37.00

AMMO POUCH 3 POCKET: Black leather. Pebbled body with RB number & riveted construction. Above avg. cond. $24.00

AMMO POUCH 3 POCKET: Black leather. Riveted construction. RB number. Avg. cond. $37.00

AMMO POUCH 3 POCKET: Black leather. Sewn flaps & riveted back. Printed cloth *Garber* tag affixed over RB number. Exc. cond. $21.00

AMMO POUCH 3 POCKET: Black polished front with brown back stamped *1937 Stecher Freiberg*. Avg. cond. $20.00

AMMO POUCH 3 POCKET: Brown back, black polished front & alum. fittings. 1934/maker. Printed cloth tag to center lid *Lurz Rudolf 5./Pz.=Regt.4.* Avg. cond. $25.00

AMMO POUCH 3 POCKET: Brown leather. Sewn const. Avg. cond. $34.00

AMMO POUCH 3 POCKET: Riveted construction & RB number. Near mint cond. $40.00

AMMO POUCH MP 38/40 3 POCKET: Left hand side. Leather tabs. D ring with belt loops. Leather tabs. Avg. cond. $165.00

AMMO POUCH MP 38/40 3 POCKET: Right hand side. Feldgrau cloth with brown leather tabs. D-ring & belt loops present. Avg. cond. $196.00

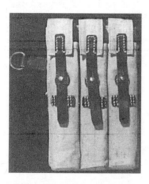

AMMO POUCH MP38/40 3 POCKET
WITH AMMO MAGAZINES

AMMO POUCH MP38/40 3 POCKET WITH AMMO MAGAZINES: Right hand. Beige-canvas body with black leather closure fittings, D-ring & belt loops stamped *MP38u.40 WaAB66 43*. 3 blued magazines. By *98E 40* plus *kur 43* plus *bte 43*. Above avg. cond. $370.00

AMMO POUCH MP38/40 3 POCKET: Left side. Field gray canvas with black leather taps. Loops & D-ring on back. Avg. cond. $282.00

AMMO POUCH MP38/40 3 POCKET: Right hand. Dark green canvas body with brown leather fittings, belt loops & D-ring strap. White inked *MP.38u40*. Above avg. cond. $265.00

AMMO POUCH MP38/40 LUFTWAFFE 3 POCKET: Right hand. Blue-gray canvas body, brown leather closure fittings, gray web belt loops & D-ring fitting. Avg. cond. $191.00

AMMO POUCH POLICE: Black leather. 1.5x3x5.5" body with affixed 4" alum. eagle wreath to large flap. 3 loops at back. Exc. cond. $90.00

AMMO POUCHES 3 POCKET

AMMO POUCHES 3 POCKET: Lot of 2. 1 marked with 43 date. Sewn construction, steel fittings. Avg. cond. $60.00

AMMO POUCHES 3 POCKET: Lot of 2. Black leather both front & back. Both 1938 dated with different makers. Avg. cond. $76.00

AMMO POUCHES MP34 WITH 6
AMMO MAGAZINES

AMMO POUCHES MP34 WITH 6 AMMO MAGAZINES: Matched pair pouches with leather straps, brass stud & party eagle stamped at back. 6 Steyr/MP34 magazines - dull blued/black finish to each 32 round body with bullseye trademark & eagle 189. Police, SS & garrison troops used. *WaA24* stamp to inside of both flaps. Exc. cond. $290.00

AMMUNITION BAGS RIFLE GRENADE: Pair. Brown canvas. Both bags have roller-buckle closure belts to flaps & connected by web neck strap. Inked maker from *Remse 1940* inside & three small inside pockets. Above avg. cond. $160.00

CLEANING KIT 98K: *Tobacco Can* style canister. Stamped *arr41*. Contains: bakelite oiler, both brushes & odd cleaning string with metal loop & rod at ends. Avg. cond. $20.00

CLEANING KIT 98K: Gray finish to *Tobacco-Tin* style canister by 'arr 43 WaA20. Includes chain, 2 brushes & bakelite oiler. Avg. cond. $20.00

CLEANING KIT 98K: Gray finished *Tobacco-Tin* style canister by *ab41*. Incl. bakelite oiler, chain, 2 brushes. Avg. cond. $30.00

CLEANING KIT MG: Blue-gray finish to *Tobacco-Tin* style canister with lid stamped *64 WaA20*. Contains: metal oiler, both brushes, larger brush with string pull-thru, drift pin, *WaA* to extractor & *64 WaA20* to spring-tool. Above avg. cond. $145.00

CLEANING KIT MG: Dark gray painted tin with stamped lid *64 WaA20*. Contains metal oiler both brushes, chain & spring loaded tool. Near mint cond. $101.00

FLARE PISTOL *WALTHER*
WITH HOLSTER

FLARE PISTOL *WALTHER* WITH HOLSTER: Early blued steel body/ barrel with stamped maker & scroll. Crown proofs & eagle 4. Wood grips. Black paper holster has leather closure strap stamped *dla 44*. Avg. cond. $207.00

FLARE PISTOL WITH HOLSTER: Black finished alum. alloy body by *ac 1940*. Bakelite grips & clean bore. Black leatherette holster by *fsx 41 WaA445*. Avg. cond. $180.00

FLARE PISTOL: Black finish to alum./ alloy body with bakelite grips. By *ayf 43* with proofs. Near mint cond. $200.00

FLARE PISTOL: Black finished alum. body by *ac 42*. Bakelite grips & lanyard ring. Avg. cond. $101.00

FLARE PISTOL

FLARE PISTOL: Black finished alum. body by *ayf 42* & large *Z* to barrel. Bakelite grips, lanyard ring. Avg. cond. $475.00

FLARE PISTOL: Black finished alum. body with bakelite grips. By *43 duv* & eagle proofs. Above avg. cond. $101.00

FLARE PISTOL: Black finished alum./ alloy body by *duv 42* with eagle proofs. Bakelite grips, lanyard ring. Near mint cond. $161.00

FLARE PISTOL: Worn black finish to alum./alloy body. Stamped *S/237 1938* & many eagle proofs. Bakelite grips. Lanyard ring. Avg. cond. $91.00

FLARE PISTOL

FLARE PISTOL: Zinc. Gray finished body with bakelite grips. Stamped *106511 euh WaA??*. Above avg. cond. $100.00

FLARE PISTOL: Black finished alum. body by *ac 41*. Bakelite grips & lanyard ring. Avg. cond. $150.00

FLARE PISTOL: Black finished alum. body by *ayf 42*. Bakelite grips & lanyard ring. Above avg. cond. $145.00

GRIPS MP38/40: Bakelite. Well marked. Matched. Avg. cond. $25.00

GRIPS P38: Bakelite. Dark brown bodies with owner scratched initials to each *J.G.* Original screw with worn head. Avg. cond. $26.00

HOLSTER FLARE PISTOL: Black leatherette with cleaning rod. Stiff body with flap stamped *gxy 1944*. Belt loops with D-rings. Steel cleaning rod with clip to leather tab on loop. Near mint cond. $659.00

HOLSTER HI-POWER BREAK-AWAY: Body has been black polished over brown base leather. Fittings intact. Flap stamped *hlv 43 WaA668*. Above avg. cond. ... $90.00

HOLSTER LUGAR LUFTWAFFE PILOT SHOULDER-STYLE

HOLSTER LUGAR LUFTWAFFE PILOT SHOULDER-STYLE: Russet leather shoulder holster with clip pocket to front. Marked *RSK* on front. Above avg. cond. $177.00

HOLSTER P08: Hardshell body appears black polished to original brown leather. Police style holes to body & flap from removed fittings with added roller-buckle strap. Rest fittings intact with 1 belt loop coming unsewn. Early large eagle stamp to back. 1920s/30s era. Avg. cond. $69.00

MG SPARE PARTS POUCH LUFTWAFFE: Brown leather. 1.5x6x7.5" size with flap stamped *FL45966 fzs* & eagle 2 proof. 2 belt loops & D-ring. Above avg. cond. $35.00

OPTICAL SIGHT *10X80* FLAK: 11" tall wire & metal body with dove-tail mount. Blue-gray painted & some luminous paint remains. Avg. cond. $144.00

OPTICAL SIGHT *2CM Z.F.3X8 FLAK*: About 10.5" long turned metal body with dove-tail mount having title marks & maker *jve etc*. Fitting for battery light use. Optics clear with a scale. Avg. cond. $93.00

OPTICAL SIGHT ARTY AIMING-CIRCLE: Styled like a *M31 aiming circle* with some variations. About 6.5" tall blue-gray painted alum. body by *cme etc*. Socket mount to round base with scale to side. Various adjustment knobs & scales. Optics clear with scale & cross-hair. Avg. cond. $145.00

OPTICAL SIGHT ARTY. *4X* PANORAMIC: 9" tall M16. Blued body with brass adjustment scales & red painted center. Optics are good. Maker *A.-G. Hahn Cassel Rundblick etc*. Avg. cond. $90.00

OPTICAL SIGHT MG-08/15 WITH CASE: Heavy dark brown leather body with brass fittings & 2 belt loops. Stamped *Hensoldt Wetzlar 1936 WaA112*. 1 yellow tinted filter to lid. Felt lining. Green textured body by *G.Rodenstock Munchen* with brass end cap on a leather strap. Dove-tail mount. Mint cond. $165.00

PERISCOPE ARTY M31 AIMING-CIRCLE WITH CASE: 9.5" tall reddish-brown leatherette case by *ddx WaA380 1943*, 3 leather loops to back & lid has metal spring-latch closure. 9" tall green painted periscope by *ddx etc.*, clear optics & dovetail mount at lower lens for mounting on an M31 device. Exc. cond. $75.00

SIGHT MOUNT *K98K ZF.41* SNIPER SCOPE: Blued finish to casting with stamped title & *duv 214 eagle proof*. Caps & screws intact. Near mint cond. $101.00

SIGHT MOUNT *K98K ZF.41* SNIPER SCOPE: Blued finish to casting with stamped title & *duv 214 eagle proof*. Caps & screws intact. Near mint cond. $124.00

SIGHT RING MG34 ANTI-AIRCRAFT: About 4.5" diam. metal ring with cross-hair & mounting stud. Eagle 4 stamped proof. Near mint cond. $145.00

SIGHT RING MG34 ANTI-AIRCRAFT: 4 1/4" diam. to gray metal sight with large spring-loaded base mount. Eagle 4 proof stamp. Exc. cond. $145.00

SIGHT RING MG34 ANTI-AIRCRAFT

SIGHTING DEVICE 98K TRAINING MIRROR: Blued metal fitting stamped

DRGM. Mirror at top & spring for looping around stock. Instructor can see how shooter is using sights. Near mint cond. $82.00

SPARE BARREL CARRIER MG: Blue-gray painted body. Gray web strap. End stamped *Laufschutzer brc 43 etc.* Avg. cond. $48.00

SPARE BARREL CARRIER MG: Chocolate-brown painted metal body with web strap. Stamped *bpr43 Laufschutzer 42.* Avg. cond. $90.00

SPARE BARREL CARRIER MG

SPARE BARREL CARRIER MG: dark gray painted body with web shoulder strap. By *bpr43* & *Laufschutzer 42.* Avg. cond. $76.00

TAKE-DOWN TOOL P-08: Blued finish with stamped *III/19.26.* Other side with crowned-cipher & stamped-out unit *??J.R.19.31.* Avg. cond. $36.00

IMPERIAL GERMAN EDGED WEAPONS

BAYONET CHASEPOT CONVERSION:
Conversion of French bayonet received
after Franco-Prussian War. Hmkd with an
S on ricasso. Wooden grip. Below avg.
cond. $48.00

BAYONET DRESS WITH FROG: Carbine
blade. Black painted steel fittings with
solid hilt having fixed button. Checkered
wood grips. Thick black painted scabbard. Brown leather frog. Avg.
cond. $33.00

BAYONET DRESS WITH FROG

BAYONET DRESS WITH FROG: Carbine
nickel blade. Black painted hilt with solid
hilt having button. Black wood grips with
brass crowned cipher. Black painted
scabbard. Black leather frog. Above avg.
cond. $280.00

BAYONET DRESS: Bright carbine blade
with faint *E. Pack* trademark man. Wood
grips. Nickel fittings & scabbard. Solid
button to hilt slot. Above avg.
cond. $55.00

BAYONET DRESS: Nickel carbine blade. By
Eickhorn with trademark *C.E.* with back-
to-back squirrels. Black painted steel
fittings with checkered wood grips. With a
black scabbard. Above avg.
cond. $66.00

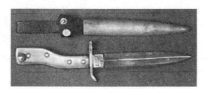

BAYONET ERSATZ CRANK HANDLE

BAYONET ERSATZ CRANK HANDLE:
Demag. Has scabbard with original
leather belt loop. 6" blade & 4" handle,
well hmkd on both sides of blade. All
steel construction. Avg. cond. ... $175.00

BAYONET ERSATZ: 11.5" flat steel blade
with crown proof to spine. 3/4 muzzle ring
to cross guard stamped *1143* & steel hilt.
Blued steel scabbard. Above avg.
cond. $30.00

BAYONET ERSATZ: 12.25" steel blade with
wide fuller & Crown proof to spine. 3/4"
muzzle ring to crossguard stamped *1371*.
Metal hill stamped *3134*. Steel scabbard.
Avg. cond. $24.00

BAYONET ERSATZ: 16" long overall & 9.5"
polished steel blade with fuller. Heavy
cast hilt with 3/4 muzzle ring, green paint
& double stamped crossguard numbers.
Green painted steel scabbard with
rounded frog stud. Avg.
cond. $27.00

BAYONET ERSATZ: Dark sheet steel hilt
with 3 rivets & vent hole. Crossguard with
3/4 ring. Steel blade with a fuller & 2
proofs. Steel scabbard style. Avg.
cond. $40.00

BAYONET FROG: Brown leather. Larger
style with 4 rivet const. Stamps to back.
Stitches loose to center. Avg.
cond. $37.00

BAYONET FROG: M98/05 style black
leather body, 4 rivets of copper & brass.
Avg. cond. $25.00

BAYONET KNOT: Original tiestring to white
cloth strap, blue slide, blue painted stem,
blue fuzz ball & white tassels. Exc.
cond. $25.00

BAYONET KNOT: Original tiestring to white
cloth strap, blue slide, yellow stem, blue
fuzz ball & white tassels. Exc.
cond. $42.00

BAYONET KNOT: Original tiestring to white
cloth strap, yellow slide, blue painted
stem, yellow fuzz ball & white tassels.
Exc. cond. $25.00

BAYONET KS98 DRESS: Nickel carbine
blade, black painted hilt & 3 rivets to
black grips. Black scabbard. Below avg.
cond. $20.00

BAYONET KS98 SAWTOOTH DRESS
WITH FROG: 10" bright nickel blade with
spine teeth & by *A.Wingen Jr. Solingen*.
Nickel fittings with working slot, 2 rivets to
black horn grips. Black scabbard. Avg.
cond. $101.00

BAYONET M71 DOUBLE ENGRAVED
DRESS

BAYONET M71 DOUBLE ENGRAVED
DRESS: By *W.K&C* with heads. Engraved
floral & military equipment. Nickel
crossguard & solid brass hilt with fitted

spring. Black leather scabbard. Avg.
cond. $139.00
BAYONET M71/84: Bright blade hmkd on
ricasso. Wood grips. Black leather
scabbard with metal tip & throat. Avg.
cond. $52.00
BAYONET M71: 18.5" long steel blade is
unmarked. Steel crossguard & brass hilt
with slot. Avg. cond. $69.00
BAYONET M71: Steel blade. Spine Crown
W, *74* & proof. Maker *P.D. Luneschloss
etc.* Steel crossguard *107.R.2.19.* Avg.
cond. $63.00
BAYONET M84/98 BAYONET: Nickel plated
blade by *Move-Werke etc.* & spine
stamped Crown W, *15* & proof. Wood
grips to nickel hilt. Black painted
scabbard. Avg. cond. $129.00
BAYONET M84/98 SAWTOOTH: By *Erfurt*
with crown & *Gebr.Heller Marienthal.*
Crossguard stamped *3620.* Wood grips.
Black leather scabbard with steel fittings
& stamped *B.8.R.R.9.176.* Below avg.
cond. $66.00
BAYONET M84/98 SAWTOOTH: Prussian
1915. by *Erfurt* & spine Crown W,*15* &
proof. Avg. cond. $95.00

BAYONET M84/98 WITH FROG

BAYONET M84/98 WITH FROG: Polished
bright steel blade & fittings. By
Rich.A.Herder etc., Crown W, *18* & proof.
Wood grips. Polished bright blued
scabbard. Small brown leather frog with 3
rivets. Near mint cond. $134.00
BAYONET M98 QUILLBACK DRESS:
Nickel blade by *C.E.* with squirrels. Good
wood grips to nickel hilt. Black leather
scabbard with nickel fittings. Avg.
cond. $87.00

BAYONET M98 QUILLBACK

BAYONET M98 QUILLBACK: Steel blade by
Simson&Co. Suhl. Crossguard stamped
6164. Black leather scabbard with steel
fittings. Avg. cond. $58.00
BAYONET M98/05 SAWTOOTH: By
Weyersberg etc. & Crown W, *16* &proof.
Wood grips. Blued scabbard. Above avg.
cond. $101.00

BAYONET M98/05 SAWTOOTH: Dark blued
blade by *Alex Coppel Solingen* with good
teeth to spine stamped Crown W, *15* &
proof. Steel fittings with wood grips & no
stamps to crossguard. Blued steel
scabbard with dents & stamped *2204
Mauser etc..* Avg. cond. $107.00

BAYONET M98/05 SAWTOOTH

BAYONET M98/05 SAWTOOTH: Saxon
1907 by *WK&C etc.*, Crown FA, *07* &
proof. Partial Muzzle Ring to crossguard
stamped *22.P.2.97.* Good wood grips
without flash guard. Black leather
scabbard with gray steel fittings &
stamped *PKP 225.* Exc.
cond. $478.00
BAYONET M98/05 SAWTOOTH: By *J.H.
Beckert etc.* & spine only stamped *3.*
Blued scabbard by *Mauser etc.* Avg.
cond. $99.00
BAYONET M98/05 SAWTOOTH: By
Deutsche Maschinenfabrik A-G Duisburg,
Crown W, *15* & proof. Blued steel
scabbard. Avg. cond. $82.00
BAYONET M98/05 WITH FROG: By *Rich.
A. Herder etc.* & just a proof to spine.
Wood grips. Blued scabbard. Black
leather frog. Avg. cond. $95.00
BAYONET M98/05: 1917 Bavarian. by
Fichtel & Sachs etc., Crown L, 17 &
proof. Crossguard stamped *1920.* Blued
scabbard. Above avg. cond. $65.00
BAYONET M98/05: By *Alex Coppel* , crown
proof marked & dated 16. Below avg.
cond. $20.00
BAYONET M98/05: Gray blade by *Deutsche
Maschinenfabrik etc.*, Crown W, 16 &
proof. Wood grips. Metal scabbard. Avg.
cond. $58.00
BAYONET M98/05: Reissued. Bright steel
blade by *Waffenfabrik Mauser etc.*, spine
Crown W, *18* & proof. Crossguard
stamped *6447.* Replaced smooth wood
grips & no flash guard. Olive painted
steel scabbard. Avg. cond. $80.00
BAYONET M98/05: Steel blade by
O.Dietrich Altenburg & spine Crown W,
15 & proof. Wood grips. Black finished
scabbard. Avg. cond. $53.00
BAYONET M98/05: Steel blade by
Weyersberg etc., Crown W & *17.* Steel
scabbard. Below avg. cond. $50.00

BAYONET M98/05: Blued blade by *Mauser etc.* & spine Crown W, *18* & proof. Crossguard & throat stamped *P.W.2862.* Wood grips & blued steel scabbard. Avg. cond. $139.00

BAYONET M98/05

BAYONET M98/05: By *P.D. Luneschloss etc.* & Crown W, *18* &proof. Wood grips. Avg. cond. $90.00

BAYONET M98/05: By *Pack Ohliger & Co. etc.*, Crown W, *17* & proof. Wood grips. Blued steel scabbard. Avg. cond. $58.00

BAYONET NAVAL CADET M1872 DOUBLE ENGRAVED: Eickhorn. About 13" nickel blade. Engraved Crowned fouled anchor, galleon, military & floral motif to both sides. Maker *C.E.* with back-to-back squirrels. All fittings are WWI era steel with gold finish. Folding clamshell with fouled anchor. Crown to crossguard. Black leather scabbard with gold fittings with back of throat engraved in script *Babin* -owner. Avg. cond. $1,210.00

DAGGER KNOT NAVAL: Silver cord with flecks, slide & stem also have flecks. Silver cap & ball with tri-color bullion to inset. Mint cond. $120.00

DAGGER NAVAL 1890 CADET DOUBLE ENGRAVED: 19" overall. 1912 *High-Neck* Knight head trademark. Gray blade with crowned fouled anchor, galleon & military equipment. Reverse has same except for different equipment. Ivory grip. Closed cadet crown pommel. Brass scabbard with lightning bolts, knot hanger bands & faint traces of engraved name at back of throat. Above avg. cond. $1,237.00

DAGGER NAVAL OFFICER DRESS: Dbl. engraved blade with knight head logo. White handle with gold gilt crown pommel cap. Lighting bolt scabbard. Complete with original silver wire dagger knot with marine colors. Weapon is approx. 19.25" OA length & is named on the throat to *Kayser, Karl.* A check of naval service records indicates that Kayser served on shipboard & at shore in several naval hospital installations & held the rank of Unteroffizier mit portepee. Blue cloth named dagger hanger belt with clips & straps. Avg. cond. $2,200.00

DAGGER NAVAL OFFICER DRESS

DAGGER NAVAL OFFICER DRESS: 11.5" fully engraved on both sides of blade, not hmkd. Gilded brass guard with naval emblems on each side & gilded crown pommel. Ivory grip. Brass scabbard with ritual engraved marks & emblems & 2 rings. Avg. cond. $850.00

FASCHINENMESSER SAXON M1845 WITH UNIT *12.R.310* : About 19" steel blade by *P.D.L.* & crowned *AR.* Solid brass hilt & crossguard with stamped title crown. Above avg. cond. $90.00

FASCHINENMESSER SAXON INF M1845

FASCHINENMESSER SAXON INF M1845: 18.75" steel blade with faint crown. Solid brass hilt & crossguard with stamped *103.R.8.171.* reissued. Black leather scabbard with mismatched stamped brass throat *104.R.10.229.* Avg. cond. $145.00

FIGHTING KNIFE: WWI folding style by Mercator. White metal frame with trademark of leaping cat & K55K lettering. Base of blade maker marked & also stamped *Solingen. Germany* for export purposes. 8" OA length when extended. Complete with lock for blade & metal lanyard. Avg. cond. $45.00

FIGHTING KNIFE AUSTRIAN: 8" modified dagger style blade with long false edge. Marked KH on ricasso. Steel diamond shaped guard loose. Two part wood grip held by 3 rivets. Metal scabbard. Avg. cond. $57.00

FIGHTING KNIFE AUSTRIAN: 8" steel blade with faint *R* to ricasso. Green paint to scabbard with 2 metal loops & web belt loop. Avg. cond. $87.00

FIGHTING KNIFE BAYONET VARIATION: Standard metal & black leather loop with straps to sheath. 6" single edge blade is steel wooled. Nickel finish is peeling on cast hilt with muzzle ring to crossguard. Wood grips with 2 rivets. Avg. cond. $45.00

FIGHTING KNIFE BAYONET: 6" hunting style blade with bent tip. Nickel plated finish to crossguard & solid hilt with fixed button. Wood grips. Black finished scabbard. Avg. cond. $64.00

FIGHTING KNIFE BAYONET: Eickhorn *C.E.* double squirrels trademark to steel blade. Steel hilt resembles bayonet with crossguard & non-functioning button to solid pommel, no slot. Black checkered wood grips. Metal scabbard with remains of leather loop. Below avg. cond. $80.00

FIGHTING KNIFE STAG HANDLE: 5" gray steel blade with finger guard at ricasso. Nice antler grip with silver pommel cap. Black leather sheath with silver metal fittings. Avg. cond. $103.00

FIGHTING KNIFE STAG HANDLE

FIGHTING KNIFE STAG HANDLE: 8.5" overall. 4.5" gray steel blade stamped *Fein Stahl*. Stag antler grip. Brown leather sheath with nickel throat. Avg. cond. $55.00

FIGHTING KNIFE: *Ern* style. Bright steel blade title stamped & *Rasiermesser Fabrik* Steel crossguard & 3 rivets to groove wood grips. Black finished scabbard. Above avg. cond. $75.00

FIGHTING KNIFE: *Ern* style. Steel blade with title maker. Steel crossguard & grooved wood grips. Black steel scabbard. Below avg. cond. $95.00

FIGHTING KNIFE: *Gottlieb.* Bright steel blade with maker, etc. & crown proof. Steel crossguard & wood grips. Avg. cond. $52.00

FIGHTING KNIFE: *NAHKAMPFER.* 5.5" steel blade, title stamped & faint engraved title. Bayonet style hilt with working slot, nickel finish & wood grips. Black scabbard with leather loop & straps. Below avg. cond. $65.00

FIGHTING KNIFE: 5" steel blade with faint *Anton Wingen etc.* Large stag grip with black steel fittings. Black steel scabbard. Below avg. cond. $95.00

FIGHTING KNIFE: Spear blade, nickel bayonet style fittings & stag grips. Metal scabbard, woven burlap belt loop & leather straps. Avg. cond. $81.00

FIGHTING KNIFE: Steel blade stamped *Demag, Germany* & crown proof. Steel crossguard & wood grips with grooves.

Black steel scabbard with leather belt loop & straps. Avg. cond. $72.00

FIGHTING KNIFE: Steel blade stamped *with Ern Wald,Rhein etc.* & crown proof. Steel crossguard & wood grips. Avg. cond. $68.00

FIGHTING KNIFE: Steel blade, steel crossguard & wood grips with grooves. Black paint to steel scabbard with leather loop and straps. Below avg. cond. $50.00

FIGHTING KNIFE

FIGHTING KNIFE: Weyersberg trade-marked with King & Knight heads. Wood grips. Black scabbard. Below avg. cond. $75.00

FOLDING BLADE KNIFE: Sheet metal. 4" blade shows use. Blued body with lanyard loop & lock loop release. Avg. cond. $30.00

HUNTING CUTLASS WITH GARDE STAR

HUNTING CUTLASS WITH GARDE STAR: 16.5" steel blade with engraved details. Knight head trade mark. Brass clam shell with affixed silver star having enamel disc. Deerfeet to brass crossguard, brass pommel & 3 brass ovals. Stag grip. Black leather scabbard with brass fittings. Avg. cond. $300.00

HUNTING CUTLASS: *WK&C.* Double engraved. About 15.5" steel blade with wide fuller, title maker & heads trade-marked. Engraved hunter, stag, doe & hunting equipment. Reverse stag, dog after 2 fox, hunting equipment & deer. Brass clamshell with stag resting. Stag feet to crossguard & acorn nut to pommel cap. Stag antler grip. Black leather scabbard with brass fittings. Avg. cond. $231.00

HUNTING CUTLASS: 14" nickel blade engraved with stag, doe & hunting equipment. Other has dog, fox, stag, doe & hunting equipment. Spine marked *Adolph Schwartz Hannover.* Brass clam shell with affixed silver horse, deer feet tips to crossguard & brass pommel. Stag grip with 3 brass acorns. Black leather scabbard with brass fittings. Avg. cond. $450.00

HUNTING CUTLASS: 16" blade with Eickhorn trademark of back-to-back squirrels. Faint stag, hunter & dog scene. Other side with deer, boar & grouse. Brass clamshell, deer foot crossguard, pommel & scabbard fittings. Stag antler grip with 3 dark acorns. Black leather scabbard with 4" blade to skinning knife with stag grips & 1 acorn. Above avg. cond. $339.00

HUNTING CUTLASS

HUNTING CUTLASS: 17" steel blade with wide fullers & faint traces of engraving. Brass clam shell with stag & 2 does. Deerfoot crossguard, stag grip & lacks pommel. Gray sharkskin covered scabbard with brass fittings having hanger ring. Avg. cond. $213.00

HUNTING CUTLASS: 1860-1880 period with engraved blade & Kings Head hmkd on ricasso. Steel guard with ball quillons in *S* position. Avg. cond. $82.00

HUNTING CUTLASS: 19" steel blade with military & floral engraved panel & front panel with crowned eagle over scroll *Mit Gott fur Kaiser und Reich*. Nickel clam shell, deer foot crossguard, stag grip & nickel pommel. Black leather scabbard with nickel fittings. Avg. cond. ... $300.00

HUNTING CUTLASS: 19" steel blade with military & floral engraved panels. Brass clam shell, deer foot crossguard, stag grip 3 brass acorns & brass pommel. Black leather scabbard with brass fittings & frog stud. Avg. cond. $250.00

HUNTING CUTLASS: 25.5" steel blade with wide fuller, 13" blued panels with gold crowned MK cipher, military & floral motifs. By *P.W.KNECHT SOHNE in Solingen*. Brass clam shell, cross guard with ornate oakleaves, boar & stag heads to lower band. Blackhorn grips. Black leather scabbard with brass fittings. Above avg. cond. $436.00

HUNTING CUTLASS: This is a very early example, approx. the 1870's. About 13" bright steel blade by *JV Garantiert Solingen*. Engraved military equipment motif. Other *Gott Mit Uns* with ornate border & oak leaves. Brass clamshell & D-guard with deer foot tips. Stag grips with 2 rivets. Black leather scabbard has brass fittings with raised sunburst design

to front & acorn frog stud at back. Avg. cond. $425.00

HUNTING KNIFE

HUNTING KNIFE: *TRESCH*. 8.5" folding nickel blade with title. Silver crossguard, stag grips with release button & nickel pommel. Black leather sheath with nickel fittings for tip cover when closed. Above avg. cond. $143.00

HUNTING KNIFE: Folding 6" steel blade with graying, brass crossguard & stag grips. With brass tip cover having lockspring. Above avg. cond. $125.00

MINIATURE BAYONET DRESS: About 9.5" overall. 5.5" steel wooled nickel blade with fuller. Black grips & polished bright steel fittings. Black scabbard with faint EK decal. Avg. cond. $44.00

MINIATURE SWORD HESSEN: 12" long overall. About 9" long nickel plated blade engraved *Hnasa Eisen* in script. Solid cast brass hilt with crowned lion holding sword on basket, black painted grip & crown pommel. Black painted brass scabbard. Avg. cond. $167.00

POCKET KNIFE: *MERCATOR K55*. 4.5" long stamped steel with cat trademark, title & Germany. 3" folding blade & *Mercator Solingen*. Avg. cond. ... $85.00

POCKET KNIFE: Sheet metal. Stamped body by *K55K Mercator Germany*. About 3.5" long blade shows sharpening. Export lock blade knife with lanyard ring & the cat trademark. Above avg. cond. $28.00

SHORT SWORD AUSTRIAN: 15.5" gray steel blade with stamped *R*. Steel S-crossguard. Wooden grips with 3 rivets and a green painted scabbard. Avg. cond. $104.00

SHORT SWORD

SHORT SWORD: 26" curved heavy steel blade with King head trademark. Brass P-guard & fittings, brass wrapped black leather grip & black leather scabbard with brass fittings having round frog stud. Avg. cond. $81.00

SWORD ARTY NCO DOUBLE ENGRAVED LOW PROFILE LION HEAD: 35" curved nickel blade by *WK&C* with heads. Engraved *Unteroffizier Dierkmann* with rose motif, horse head & military equipment. Reverse has rose motif with 5 ovals of military equipment. Gold finish to brass fittings with crossed cannons to rectangular langet. P-guard with Knight head & faces. Lion hilt with 2 paws behind. Wire wrapped black grip. Black finished scabbard. Avg. cond. .. $400.00

SWORD ARTY OFFICER DOUBLE ENGRAVED LOW PROFILE LION HEAD: 31.5" curved heavy steel blade with traces of floral engraving under dark patina. Dark brass fittings with crossed cannons to langet, military equipment to P-guard & lion head hilt with 2 paws behind. Sharkskin grip. Steel scabbard with 2 brass hanger rings. Below avg. cond. $148.00

SWORD AUSTRIAN OFFICER DOUBLE ENGRAVED: 29" nickel blade by *Weyersberg* etc. & distributor. Crown profile over crowned FA cipher & floral motif. Reverse has military equipment etc. Gold finished brass D-guard with pierced crowned double headed eagle & floral design. Wire wrapped sharkskin grip. Black leather scabbard with 3 ornate brass fittings, throat has crowned FA cipher. Avg. cond. $277.00

SWORD AUSTRIAN OFFICER: 25" nickel blade. Gold finished brass D-guard with pierced crowned double headed eagle & floral design. Wire wrapped sharkskin grip. Black leather scabbard with 3 ornate brass fittings, throat has crowned FA cipher. Avg. cond. $187.00

SWORD BAVARIAN ARTY DOUBLE ENGRAVED

SWORD BAVARIAN ARTY DOUBLE ENGRAVED: 32.5" very curved nickel blade by *C K Co* with crossed swords & crown trademark. *In Treue Fest*, flowers, shield & goddess. Nickel D-guard & fittings. Celluloid grip. Nickel scabbard. Avg. cond. $125.00

SWORD BAVARIAN ARTY OFFICER DOUBLE ENGRAVED: 32.5" curved

nickel blade with different engraved *In Treue Fest!* panels having blued backings. Scroll has oak & laurel leaves to each side plus extra Crowned shield with 5 panel Bavarian details to obverse. Nickel hilt fittings & black celluloid covered grip. Black scabbard. Avg. cond. $106.00

SWORD BAVARIAN CIVIL SERVICE DOUBLE ENGRAVED WITH KNOT: 34.5" straight nickel blade by *Chr.Block, Munchen* & Knight head trademark. *In Treue Fest* scroll & floral to each side. Gold finish to ornate brass fittings, lions to clamshell, D-guard, lion head hilt, mother-of-pearl grips with affixed gold crown to front. Black leather scabbard with brass fittings. Gold knot with bullion crowns to stem. Above avg. cond. $300.00

SWORD BAVARIAN CIVIL SERVICE DOUBLE ENGRAVED: 32" straight blade by *F.X.Gropper,Augsberg*, *In Treue Fest* scroll to each side. Dark brass fittings with affixed crown/wreath to clamshell. Wire wrapped sharkskin grip. Below avg. cond. $93.00

SWORD BAVARIAN CUIRASSIER OFFICER DOUBLE ENGRAVED: 33" straight nickel double fullered blade with Knight head trademark. Same *In Treue Fest* scroll & floral design to each side. Nickel hilt fittings. Wire wrapped sharkskin grip. Blued scabbard. Avg. cond. $145.00

SWORD BAVARIAN INF OFFICER DOUBLE ENGRAVED: 30.75" curved nickel blade by *C.E.* with squirrels. Engraved *In Treue Fest* scroll & Lion Shield with oak trees to both sides. Nickel B-guard & fittings. Wire wrapped blackgrip. Black scabbard. Avg. cond. $125.00

SWORD BAVARIAN INF OFFICER DOUBLE ENGRAVED

SWORD BAVARIAN INF OFFICER DOUBLE ENGRAVED: 33" curved nickel blade by *WK&C* with heads & 4 leaf clover with male head in center. *In Treue Fest* scroll to each side. Brass B-guard & fittings. Brass wrapped imitation sharkskin/bakelite grip. Avg. cond.. .... $57.00

SWORD BAVARIAN INF OFFICER DOUBLE ENGRAVED: About 30.5" nickel blade by *C.E.* with 2 squirrels. Engraved panel *In Treue Fest* with oak tree & lion/shield to both sides. Black painted steel fittings with B-guard & wire wrapped black grip. Black scabbard. Above avg. cond. $160.00

SWORD CHILD: About 28" overall with 22" nickel blade having blunt tip. Nickel hilt fittings. Sharkskin grip. Metal scabbard. Avg. cond. $145.00

SWORD FUSILIER STYLE: About 28.5" nickel blade. Dark brass fittings. Brass wire wrap to sharkskin grip. Black scabbard. Avg. cond. $65.50

SWORD KNOT BAVARIAN: Alum. brocade strap has double blue line borders. Silver cap & ball. Avg. cond. $27.00

SWORD KNOT NAVAL: Darkening to silver cord with black & red flecks. Same zigzag flecks to slide & stem. Dark silver cap & ball with bullion tricolor inset. Has been on sword. Avg. cond. $108.00

SWORD KNOT NAVAL: Very dark silver cord with black & red flecks. Same zigzag flecks to slide & stem. Very dark silver cap & ball with tricolor bullion inset. Avg. cond. $165.00

SWORD KNOT: Large silver cord acorn with black leather strap with silver wire striping. Avg. cond. $20.00

SWORD M89 *BOHER SEINEM BRUER 1902* ENGRAVED: 29.5" double fuller nickel blade, title engraved & distributor to spine *Otto Mertens Solingen*. Deluxe brass fittings with ornate engraved details & folding eagle guard. Wire wrapped black horn grip with brass cipher. Black scabbard. Below avg. cond. $238.00

SWORD M89 *HUSAREN=REGT. LANDGRAF ECT. 14* DOUBLE ENGRAVED

SWORD M89 *HUSAREN=REGT. LANDGRAF ECT. 14* DOUBLE ENGRAVED: 31.5" straight nickel blade with 3 blued panels & engraving with rose, horse, military equipment, etc. Title panel & *Friedrich II. von Hessen-Homburg (2.Kurhss.) No14*. Crowned cipher panel & mounted troopers panel. Eagle to folding nickel guard with tip stamped

14.H.3.127 & black grip. Below avg. cond. $162.00

SWORD MINING OFFICIAL: 30.5" quillback curved nickel blade with spine stamped *A-C*. Gold finished brass fittings with affixed crossed hammers & tongs to langet. Dark wire wrap to sharkskin grip. 3 gold finished brass fittings to black leather scabbard. Avg. cond. $300.00

SWORD NAVAL OFFICER DOUBLE ENGRAVED WITH KNOT: 29" nickel blade with crowned anchor having eagle, military equipment & sails. Reverse has fouled anchor, galleon & crossed cannons. Gold finished steel fittings, folding crowned anchorguard with oak leaves, D-guard with oak leaves & lionhead with green/red eyes. Ivory grip has dark wire wrap. Leather scabbard has hammered steel fittings with gold finish. Dark silver knot with red & black flecks. Avg. cond. $789.00

SWORD NAVAL OFFICER DOUBLE ENGRAVED WITH KNOT: Appears to be wartime made with gold finished steel fittings instead of brass. 29.5" nickel blade with Eickhorn trademark *C.E.* with 2 squirrels. Same engraved crowned anchor, floral & ship design to each side. Gold finished fittings, crowned anchor to folding guard, folding lock, oak leaves to D-guard, red & green eyes to tall lionhead. Wire wrapped off-white celluloid grip. Black leather scabbard with hammered design to 3 fittings. Avg. cond. $558.00

SWORD NCO DOUBLE ENGRAVED WITH CAVALRY BELT, HANGER & KNOT: 32" curved nickel blade with Knight head trademark. Floral & military equipment engraved motif. Nickel fittings. Sharkskin grip with wire wrap. Nickel scabbard. White buff leather belt with brass buckle, hanger strap tied to ring & regain chain. White cloth knot with red stem. Below avg. cond. $177.00

SWORD OFFICER: 31" curved nickel blade with Eickhorn back-to-back squirrels *C.E.* trademark. Gold finish to nickel fittings with bent P-guard, wear. Dark wire wrapped black grip. Black finished scabbard. Below avg. cond. $89.00

SWORD PRUSSIAN CIVIL SERVICE DOUBLE ENGRAVED: 32" nickel blade engraved floral design, military equipment & eagle. Reverse with crowned eagle & floral. Gold finished brass fittings, folding clamshell & wire grip. Nickel scabbard. Avg. cond. $145.00

SWORD PRUSSIAN COMBAT

SWORD PRUSSIAN COMBAT: 29.5" heavy curved steel blade by *Simson & Co. Suhl* & spine Crown W, *14* & proof. Steel P-guard & fittings show rust. Bakelite grip. Steel scabbard. Avg. cond. $145.00

SWORD PRUSSIAN COMBAT: 29.5" heavy curved steel blade by *Weyersburg etc.* & spine Crown W, *05* & proof. Steel P-guard, stamped *8.A.F.1.64.* Blued scabbard with matching unit. Above avg. cond. $193.00

SWORD PRUSSIAN CUIRASSIER OFFICER DOUBLE ENGRAVED: 32.5" curved steel blade, faint floral motif & spine *Gebr. Baus & Cie Fabrikanten in Solingen.* Dark brass 3 branch guard. Bullion wrap black leather grip. Below avg. cond. $98.00

SWORD PRUSSIAN INF OFFICER M89: 29" double fullered steel blade by *O.Pack* with trademark man. Brass fittings with traces of gold finish & eagle to folding guard. Wire wrapped sharkskin grip with brass cipher. Black scabbard. Avg. cond. $229.00

SWORD PRUSSIAN INF OFFICER M89: 32" nickel double fullered blade. Gilt finished brass fittings & folding eagle guard. Silver wire wrap to sharkskin grip with brass cipher. Nickel scabbard with 2 hanger rings. Avg. cond. $158.00

SWORD PRUSSIAN INF OFFICER M89: Wartime steel. 31.5" double fullered steel blade. Steel fittings with folding eagle guard. Dark wire wrap to black grip. Leather finger loop. Blued scabbard with unit number stamped *3.Div.21.* Avg. cond. $126.00

SWORD PRUSSIAN M89 CAVALRY

SWORD PRUSSIAN M89 CAVALRY: Straight blade, polished steel. Hmkd *Weyersberg & Co./Solingen.* Steel basket

with eagle crest & bow back to pommel. Notched, ribbed, contoured bakelite grip. Avg. cond. $80.00

SWORD PRUSSIAN M89 DOUBLE ENGRAVED *SCHUTZEN/MAJOR 1875-1900* SWORD: 34" nickel blade engraved *Dem Herrn Christian Tornay gewidmet von der St. Sebastianus Schutzen Gesellschaft zu Hahn zum 25. Jubilaum als Major 1875-1900* with floral motif. Other side has military equipment & floral motif. Maker *Weyersberg Kirschbaum & Co. Solingen.* Gold finished brass fittings & 3 branch guard with eagle. Leather finger loop. Imitation sharkskin grip with silver wire wrap & brass Crown WII. Bright nickel scabbard with 2 rings. Above avg. cond. $415.00

SWORD PRUSSIAN M89 INF OFFICER: 30.5" double fullered steel blade by *WK&C* with heads. Brass hilt fittings with folding eagle guard. Wire wrapped sharkskin grip with brass crown cipher. Nickel scabbard with 2 hanger rings. Avg. cond. $158.00

SWORD PRUSSIAN OD89 OFFICER DOUBLE ENGRAVED: Nickel steel fittings with matching single ring scabbard. Military martial floral arrangements. Pierced work Prussian eagle in guard with Hohenzollern cross on breast. Black composition grips. Avg. cond. $200.00

SWORD PRUSSIAN SUPPLY TRAIN BASKET HILT DAMASCUS: *EISENHAUER DAMASTSTAHL.* 33" quillback *maiden-hair* curved blade with excellent details & 5" long gold ricasso with title to both sides. Nickel basket with rust peeling to inside. Leather finger loop & wire wrapped sharkskin grip. Nickel scabbard with 2 hanger rings. Above avg. cond. $639.00

SWORD QUILLBACK: 32" steel blade with bent & by *F.&H.HEUHA??* Brass P-guard, fittings & langet stamped *L.G.* that matches throat. Wire wrapped sharkskin grip. Black leather scabbard with brass fittings & frog stud. Below avg. cond. $108.00

SWORD RAILWAY POLICE/ BAHNSCHUTZ: 30" straight nickel blade by *Julius Voos etc.* Gold finish to ornate cast brass hilt fittings & clamshell. Black leather scabbard with gilt finish fittings. Avg. cond. $269.00

SWORD RAILWAY: 1890 era. Bright blade with Weyersberg/solingen hmkd. Langet with transportation emblem & Winged helmet of Hermes in center of guard. Hilt all brass with knuckle bow to globe pommel. Metal scabbard with black finish, brass drag, band & throat have well done images of railway system. Avg. cond. $250.00

SWORD WURTTEMBERG DOUBLE ENGRAVED

SWORD WURTTEMBERG DOUBLE ENGRAVED: 30.5" steel blade with different military equipment to each side. Maker *WK&C* with heads. Gold finish to brass fittings, military equipment to P-guard, short lion head & langet has affixed silver star with enamel *Furchtlos und Trew*. Steel scabbard. Below avg. cond. $385.00
SWORD WURTTEMBERG TRAIN BATT. NO.13. DOUBLE ENGRAVED WITH KNOT: 32" nickel blade by *W.Baumeister etc.* & knighthead trademark. Title engraved with military equipment, mounted trooper & etc. Other *Zur Erinnerung on meine Dienstzeit* scroll with king profile & etc. Nickel basket guard. Wire wrapped sharkskin grip with fingerloop. Black scabbard. Avg. cond. $166.00
TRENCH KNIFE: *GOTTLIEB HAMMESFAHR*. Bright steel blade shows sharpening, title maker *Solingen-Foche* & *Germany* crown proof to other ricasso. Steel crossguard, wood grips, black scabbard & dry leather loop. Avg. cond. $81.00
TRENCH KNIFE: 6" spear point blade. Black painted steel crossguard. Wood grips with grooves. Black scabbard with leather belt loop & straps. Above avg. cond. $133.00

THIRD REICH DAGGERS

CUTLASS SHOOTING ASSOC DOUBLE ENGRAVED 1920s FINLAND: Maker *ACS*. 16" long blade with engraved hunter, stag, doe & hunting motif with floral, reverse with side stag, dog, foxes & hunting motif with floral. Cast brass clamshell guard with gold finish to hand detailed oakleaves, trees & 3 deer. Gold finished crossguard with oak leaves &

acorn tips. Oak leaves to pommel with acorn tang nut. Stag grip with 3 affixed acorns with oak leaves. Black leather scabbard with gold finished brass throat & tip. Engraved back of throat *Wanderpreis gestiftet von E.Verstege Helsingfors (Finnland)* & front of tip *Dem entgultigen Sidger Voigt 52 Ringe* with 8 names & ringe scores below. Above avg. cond. $2,400.00

DAGGER ARMY OFFICER ENGRAVED *DIE UFFZ.DER 2.KP.GRZ.I.R.128*

DAGGER ARMY OFFICER ENGRAVED *DIE UFFZ.DER 2.KP.GRZ.I.R.128*: Maker *J.A. Henckels Solingen*. Nickel blade. Nickel crossguard has back title engraved. Nickel pommel & scabbard. Yellow grip. Long alum. knot. Deluxe hangers with oak leaves to all fittings. Above avg. cond. $550.00
DAGGER ARMY OFFICER WITH OWNER INITIALS: Unmarked. Nickel fittings. Back of crossguard jeweler engraved *O.H.* Orange celluloid grip. Nickel scabbard. Above avg. cond. $399.00
DAGGER ARMY OFFICER: Maker *Alcoso ACS Solingen* with scales. De-Nazified. No swastika/wreath to eagle crossguard. Dark yellow grip. Avg. cond. $128.00
DAGGER ARMY OFFICER: Maker *Alcoso ACS Solingen*. Nickel fittings & scabbard. Orange celluloid grip. Above avg. cond. $327.00
DAGGER ARMY OFFICER: Maker *Alcoso ACS Solingen*. Nickel fittings & scabbard. Orange celluloid grip. With hanger. Avg. cond. $207.00

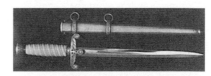

DAGGER ARMY OFFICER

DAGGER ARMY OFFICER: Maker *Alcoso ACS Solingen*. Nickel fittings. White celluloid grip. Nickel scabbard. Above avg. cond. $200.00
DAGGER ARMY OFFICER: Maker *E&F Horster Solingen*. Aluminum fittings.

Orange celluloid grip. Nickel scabbard. With hanger. Avg. cond. $185.00

DAGGER ARMY OFFICER: Maker *Eickhorn*. Nickel fittings. Orange celluloid grip. Long alum. knot. Hanger with alum. fittings & some with oak leaves. *Johnson* black suede zipper case. Exc. cond. $455.00

DAGGER ARMY OFFICER: Maker *Eickhorn*. Nickel hilt & scabbard. Orange celluloid grip. Early. Above avg. cond. $300.00

DAGGER ARMY OFFICER: Maker *Eickhorn*. Nickel hilt & scabbard. Yellow celluloid grip. Early. Above avg. cond. $275.00

DAGGER ARMY OFFICER: Maker *FW Holler*. Early. Nickel blade, fittings & scabbard. Dark yellow celluloid grip. Above avg. cond. $200.00

DAGGER ARMY OFFICER: Maker *Gustav Spitzer*. Silver finished fittings. White celluloid grip. Silver finished scabbard. Above avg. cond. ..$270.00

DAGGER ARMY OFFICER: Maker *Puma Solingen*. Nickel fittings. Orange celluloid grip. Nickel scabbard. Long silver cord knot. Avg. cond. ...$270.00

DAGGER ARMY OFFICER: Maker *Puma*. Nickel blade, fittings & scabbard. Yellow celluloid grip. Long alum. knot. Hangers with some oakleave fittings. Above avg. cond. $300.00

DAGGER ARMY OFFICER: Maker *SMF Solingen*. Nickel fittings & scabbard. Has white celluloid grip. Above avg. cond. $215.00

DAGGER ARMY OFFICER: Maker *SMF*. Aluminum hilt. Variation yellow celluloid grip with swirl. Nickel scabbard. Silver cord knot. Avg. cond. $330.00

DAGGER ARMY OFFICER: Maker *WKC*. Nickel blade, fittings & scabbard. Yellow celluloid grip. Above avg. cond. $219.00

DAGGER ARMY OFFICER: Maker *WKC*. Wartime gray metal fittings & scabbard. White celluloid grip. Avg. cond. $152.00

DAGGER ARMY OFFICER: Maker *WKC Solingen*. Nickel fittings & scabbard. Dark yellow celluloid grip. Long silver cord knot. Above avg. cond. ..$292.00

DAGGER ARMY OFFICER: Unmarked. Nickel hilt & scabbard. Orange celluloid grip. Avg. cond. $160.00

DAGGER ARMY OFFICER: Unmarked. Silver finished fittings. Orange celluloid grip. Silver finished scabbard. Avg. cond. $175.00

DAGGER ARMY OFFICER: Unmarked. Silver finished fittings. Orange celluloid grip. Silver finished scabbard. Long silver cord knot. Avg. cond. $250.00

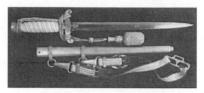

DAGGER ARMY OFFICER

DAGGER ARMY OFFICER: Unmarked. Silver finished fittings. White celluloid grip. Steel scabbard. Long silver cord knot. Deluxe pattern hanger with oak leaves on all of the metal fittings. Avg. cond. $268.00

DAGGER ARMY OFFICER: Unmarked. Nickel fittings. Orange celluloid grip. Nickel scabbard. Avg. cond. $212.00

DAGGER BAHNSCHUTZ LEADER M35: (Railway Protection Police) Maker *E.u.F.Horster Solingen* with trademark oval. Early nickel plated crossguard, pommel & scabbard. Black celluloid grip. Long alum. knot. Exc. cond. $1,116.00

DAGGER BOHEMIA & MORAVIA SENIOR YOUTH LEADER JUGENDERZIEHUNG IN BOHMEN & MAHREN: (Curatorship for Youth Training in Bohemia & Moravia) Non-German construction. 15" overall length. Cast alum. pommel has raised details of Duke Wencelas eagle, Bohemia lion shield & Moravia eagle shield below wings. Alum. wire wrapped grip & alum. crossguard. Unmarked nickel blade. Steel scabbard has 2 nickel plated brass hanger ring bands with raised swastika to upper fitting. Avg. cond. $2,500.00

DAGGER BULGARIAN ARMY OFFICER: Double engraved blade. Nickel crossguard with lion heads, lion shield & affixed cross. Nickel crown pommel. Dark wire wrap to orange grip with small chip. Army style scabbard has pebbled details. Hanger with brown straps, oakleaves on the buckles & slides, pebbled clips & top clip. Avg. cond. $950.00

DAGGER CUSTOM LAND OFFICIAL: Maker *WKC*. Aluminum fittings. Twisted brass wire wrap to leather grip. Green leather covered scabbard with 3 nickel plated fittings. Avg. cond. $901.00

DAGGER CUSTOM LAND OFFICIAL: Maker *WKC*. Aluminum fittings. Twisted brass wire wrap to green leather grip. No scabbard. Avg. cond. $492.00

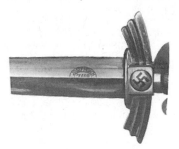

DAGGER DLV MEMBER

DAGGER DLV MEMBER: Maker *Eickhorn*. Silver finished fittings with enameled swastikas. Blue leather covered grip. Blue leather covered scabbard with nickel fittings with DLV winged prop stamped at throat. Brown leather hanger with nickel fittings. Below avg. cond. $450.00

DAGGER DLV MEMBER: Maker *JMB Joseph Munch Brotterode* in oval. Nickel/silver crossguard, pommel & scabbard fittings. Black enamel swastikas to crossguard. Dark blue leather to grip & scabbard. Stamped DLV logo to throat. Black leather hanger with nickel fittings. Exc. cond. $775.00

DAGGER HUNGARIAN AIR FORCE OFFICER: Lock button to back of brass eagle crossguard. Eagle head pommel. Black fluted grip. Brass scabbard with crest to front. Avg. cond. $270.00

DAGGER LUFTWAFFE OFFICER 1ST MODEL: Maker *Alcoso*. Nickel blade, crossguard & pommel. Dark wire wrap to blue leather grip. Blue leather scabbard with nickel fittings. Avg. cond. $375.00

DAGGER LUFTWAFFE OFFICER 1ST MODEL

DAGGER LUFTWAFFE OFFICER 1ST MODEL: Maker *E&F Horster*. Nickel blade. Alum. crossguard & pommel & gold swastikas. Alum. wire wrap to blue leather grip. Blue leather scabbard with alum. fittings. Chain hanger with clip. Avg. cond. $300.00

DAGGER LUFTWAFFE OFFICER 1ST MODEL: Maker *P.D.Luneschloss Solingen*. Silver finished fittings with copper & brass mobile swastikas. Wire wrapped blue leather covered grip. Blue leather covered scabbard with silver finished fittings. Aluminum chain hanger with clip. Avg. cond. $387.00

DAGGER LUFTWAFFE OFFICER 1ST MODEL: Maker *Tiger Solingen*. Aluminum fittings with gilt remaining on swastikas. Wire wrapped blue leather covered grip. Blue leather covered scabbard with aluminum fittings. Aluminum chain hanger with clip. Near mint cond. $538.00

DAGGER LUFTWAFFE OFFICER 1ST MODEL: Unmarked. Silver finished fittings. Wire wrapped blue leather covered grip. Blue leather covered scabbard with aluminum chain hanger. Avg. cond. $280.00

DAGGER LUFTWAFFE OFFICER 2ND MODEL DAMASCUS BLADE: Maker *Echt Damascener C.W.* Rose pattern Damascus blade. Aluminum fittings. Wire wrapped yellow celluloid grip. Steel scabbard with hanger. Near mint cond. $1,780.00

DAGGER LUFTWAFFE OFFICER 2ND MODEL DAMASCUS BLADE: Unmarked. Maidenhair Damascus Blade. Alum. fittings. Wire wrapped white celluloid grip. With steel scabbard. Near mint cond. $1,400.00

DAGGER LUFTWAFFE OFFICER 2ND MODEL WITH OWNER NAME: Maker *Eickhorn*. Back of blade & between scabbard hanger bands both hand engraved *Neubauer*. Dark aluminum fittings. Wire wrapped orange celluloid grip. With steel scabbard. Above avg. cond. $300.00

DAGGER LUFTWAFFE OFFICER 2ND MODEL: Maker *Alcoso ACS Solingen* with scale trademark. Gray alum. crossguard & pommel. Dark bullion wrap to orange grip. Gray steel scabbard. Exc. cond. $290.00

DAGGER LUFTWAFFE OFFICER 2ND MODEL: Maker *Alcoso ACS Solingen*. Gray aluminum hilt. Wire wrapped white celluloid grip. Steel scabbard. Above avg. cond. $250.00

DAGGER LUFTWAFFE OFFICER 2ND MODEL: Maker *Alcoso ACS Solingen*. Gray alum. fittings. Wire wrapped white celluloid grip. Steel scabbard. Below avg. cond. $140.00

DAGGER LUFTWAFFE OFFICER 2ND MODEL

DAGGER LUFTWAFFE OFFICER 2ND MODEL: Maker *Alcoso*. Nickel blade. Aluminum crossguard & pommel. Dark wire wrap to white grip. Dark steel scabbard. Aluminum knot. Above avg. cond. $244.00

DAGGER LUFTWAFFE OFFICER 2ND MODEL: Maker *Eickhorn*. Aluminum fittings. Silver wire wrapped yellow celluloid grip. Steel scabbard with hanger. Short silver cord knot. Avg. cond. $282.00

DAGGER LUFTWAFFE OFFICER 2ND MODEL: Maker *Eickhorn*. Eagle 5 issue marked. Aluminum fittings. Wire wrapped white celluloid grip. Steel scabbard. Avg. cond. $210.00

DAGGER LUFTWAFFE OFFICER 2ND MODEL: Maker *Ernst Pack & Sohne Siegfried*. Aluminum fittings. Wire wrapped white celluloid grip. Steel scabbard. Avg. cond. $225.00

DAGGER LUFTWAFFE OFFICER 2ND MODEL: Maker *F.W. Holler Solingen*. Gray alum. fittings. Wire wrapped white celluloid grip. Steel scabbard. Above avg. cond. $250.00

DAGGER LUFTWAFFE OFFICER 2ND MODEL: Maker *F.W.Holler Solingen*. Gray aluminum fittings. Wire wrapped orange celluloid grip. Gray steel scabbard. Avg. cond. $200.00

DAGGER LUFTWAFFE OFFICER 2ND MODEL

DAGGER LUFTWAFFE OFFICER 2ND MODEL: Maker *Puma*. Aluminum crossguard & pommel. Orange grip. With bright steel scabbard. Below avg. cond. $137.00

DAGGER LUFTWAFFE OFFICER 2ND MODEL: Maker *Rich. Abr. Herder Slingen*. Gray aluminum fittings. Wire wrapped white celluloid grip. Steel scabbard. Short silver cord knot. Exc. cond. $380.00

DAGGER LUFTWAFFE OFFICER 2ND MODEL: Maker *Rich.Abr.Herder*

Solingen. Alum. fittings. Wire wrapped orange celluloid grip. Steel scabbard. Silver cord knot. Army Deluxe Pattern Hanger. Avg. cond. $225.00

DAGGER LUFTWAFFE OFFICER 2ND MODEL: Maker *Rudolf Buchel etc*. Dull alum. fittings. Wire wrapped dark orange celluloid grip. Steel scabbard. Avg. cond. $216.00

DAGGER LUFTWAFFE OFFICER 2ND MODEL: Maker *SMF Solingen*. Eagle 5 issue marked. Aluminum fittings. Wire wrapped orange celluloid grip. Steel scabbard. Long silver cord knot. Avg. cond. $248.00

DAGGER LUFTWAFFE OFFICER 2ND MODEL: Maker *SMF*. Eagle proof marked. Aluminum fittings. Wire wrapped yellow celluloid grip. Silver finished scabbard. Early. Above avg. cond. $341.00

DAGGER LUFTWAFFE OFFICER 2ND MODEL: Maker *SMF*. Eagle 5 issue marked. Nickel blade by *SMF Solingen* with trademark & eagle 5 proof. Aluminum fittings. Silver wire wrapped orange celluloid grip. Steel scabbard with hanger. Short silver cord knot. Avg. cond. $315.00

DAGGER LUFTWAFFE OFFICER 2ND MODEL: Maker *WKC Solingen*. Alum. fittings. Wire wrapped white celluloid grip. Gray steel scabbard. Above avg. cond. $223.00

DAGGER LUFTWAFFE OFFICER 2ND MODEL: Maker *WKC*. Silver finished fittings. Yellow celluloid grip. Wire wrapped yellow celluloid grip. Steel scabbard. Short silver cord knot. Deluxe pattern hangers with oak leaves on fittings. Near mint cond. $467.00

DAGGER LUFTWAFFE OFFICER 2ND MODEL: Unmarked. Gray alum. crossguard & pommel. Wire wrap to off-white grip. Gray scabbard. Short aluminum knot. Deluxe hangers with oakleaves to all of the gray metal fittings. Avg. cond. $250.00

DAGGER LUFTWAFFE OFFICER 2ND MODEL: Unmarked. Gray aluminum fittings. Gray alum. crossguard & pommel. Wire wrap to white celluloid grip. No scabbard. Avg. cond. $116.00

DAGGER LUFTWAFFE OFFICER 2ND MODEL: Unmarked. Gray aluminum fittings. Wire wrapped orange celluloid grip. Gray steel scabbard. Below avg. cond. $190.00

DAGGER LUFTWAFFE OFFICER 2ND MODEL: Unmarked. Gray aluminum fittings. Wire wrapped white celluloid grip.

Gray steel scabbard. Below avg. cond. $196.00

DAGGER LUFTWAFFE OFFICER 2ND MODEL: Unmarked. Gray aluminum fittings. Wire wrapped white celluloid grip. Silver finished scabbard. Avg. cond. $190.00

DAGGER LUFTWAFFE OFFICER 2ND MODEL: Unmarked. Gray aluminum fittings. Wire wrapped yellow celluloid grip. Silver finished scabbard. Avg. cond. $211.00

DAGGER NAVAL CADET M1919: Unmarked. 8.5" double edged steel blade. Lock button to brass crossguard. Brass flaming ball pommel. Brass twisted wire wrap to black horn grip. Dark blued metal scabbard with brass tip, knot with ring & steel frog stud. 6.5" black hanger strap with brass lion heads buckle & 2 clips. 1st cadet dagger of the *Provisional Reich Navy*. Exc. cond. $1,584.00

DAGGER NAVAL OFFICER DAGGER: Bright nickel double fullered blade. Brass eagle pommel & crossguard with lock button. White grip with twisted brass wire. Brass lightning bolt scabbard with oak leaves to hanger bands. Clean one overall. Exc. cond. $403.00

DAGGER NAVAL OFFICER DOUBLE ENGRAVED

DAGGER NAVAL OFFICER DOUBLE ENGRAVED: Maker *ACS* with scale trademark. Looks to be a transitional dagger with added eagle pommel. Blade with fouled anchor, galleon & floral motif. Anchor to brass crossguard. Wire wrap to ivory grip. Hammered brass scabbard with knot hanger bands. With long tied aluminum knot. Below avg. cond. $538.00

DAGGER NAVAL OFFICER DOUBLE ENGRAVED: Maker *E&F Horster*. Double engraved blade with fouled anchor motif. Brass crossguard with lock button, eagle pommel & lightning bolt scabbard. Twisted brass wire to white celluloid grip. Avg. cond. $397.00

DAGGER NAVAL OFFICER DOUBLE ENGRAVED: Maker *Eickhorn*. Double engraved blade with Naval motif. Brass eagle pommel & crossguard with button

release. Twisted brass wire wrap to white grip. Lightning bolts to brass scabbard with oakleave hanger bands. Avg. cond. $401.00

DAGGER NAVAL OFFICER DOUBLE ENGRAVED: Maker *Eickhorn*. Double engraved blade with fouled anchor motif with Naval Eagle M issue stamp. Brass crossguard with lock button & eagle pommel. Twisted brass wire wrap to white celluloid grip. Brass lightning bolt scabbard with tied knot hanger ring bands & stamped throat *O.929*. The *O* stands for East sea Division. Above avg. cond. $978.00

DAGGER NAVAL OFFICER DOUBLE ENGRAVED: Maker *Eickhorn*. Double engraved blade with fouled anchor motif. Gold finish to brass crossguard, eagle pommel & lightning bolt scabbard. Wire wrapped white celluloid grip. Silver cord knot. Near mint cond. $802.00

DAGGER NAVAL OFFICER DOUBLE ENGRAVED: Maker *Eickhorn*. Double engraved blade with fouled anchor motif. Brass crossguard with lock & eagle pommel. Brass twisted wire wrap to off-white grip. Lightning bolts to brass scabbard. Alum. long knot. Avg. cond. $525.00

DAGGER NAVAL OFFICER DOUBLE ENGRAVED: Maker *WKC*. Gilt finished brass crossguard, eagle pommel & lightning bolt scabbard. Twisted brass wire to white celluloid grip. Silver cord knot. Above avg. cond. $545.00

DAGGER NAVAL OFFICER DOUBLE ENGRAVED

DAGGER NAVAL OFFICER DOUBLE ENGRAVED: Maker *WKC*. Transition dagger converted from WWI to 3rd Reich. 10" nickel blade with engraved crowned anchor, galleon & military motif with about the same to back. Lock button to crossguard. Wire wrapped ivory grip. Brass 3rd Reich eagle pommel. Brass scabbard started as normal lightning bolt design with custom hammered pebbled skin/leather look added, Oakleave hanger bands with design to rings. 3rd Reich knot. Above avg. cond. $2,000.00

DAGGER NAVAL OFFICER ENGRAVED DAMASCUS: Maker *WKC*. Transition dagger converted from WWI to 3rd Reich. 9" double fullered maidenhair Damascus blade, engraved 1914 at each end of initials *H.F. H.J. C.R.* Brass crossguard with lock button. Wire wrapped ivory grip. Gilt finished 3rd Reich eagle pommel. Hammered brass scabbard. Above avg. cond. $2,500.00

DAGGER NAVAL OFFICER M1929 DOUBLE ENGRAVED: Maker *WKC*. Double engraved nickel blade with fouled anchor motif. Lock button to gold finished brass crossguard. Twisted wire wrap to white grip. Brass flaming ball pommel. Gold finish to brass lightning bolt scabbard with oakleaf wreath bands. Above avg. cond. $600.00

DAGGER NAVAL OFFICER: Maker *ACS*. Hmkd with naval eagle M & *N738*. Double fullered blade. Gilt fittings. Wire wrapped white celluloid grip. Gilt lighting bolt scabbard with throat also stamped. Above avg. cond. $930.00

DAGGER NAVAL OFFICER: Maker *F.W.Holler*. Nickel double fullered blade. Brass fittings. Wire wrapped orange celluloid grip. Lighting bolt scabbard. Below avg. cond. $570.00

DAGGER NPEA STUDENT: Maker *Karl Burgsmuller Berlin*. Silver finished aluminum fittings. Dark wood grip. Olive painted scabbard with steel tip. Above avg. cond. $1,500.00

DAGGER NSFK MEMBER: Maker *David Malsch Steinbach(Thur.)* with *DM* oval. Nickel fittings. Blue leather cover grip. Blue leather covered scabbard with nickel fittings, throat stamped with NSFK winged man insignia. Below avg. cond. $342.00

DAGGER NSFK MEMBER: Maker *F.& A.Helbig*. Alum. fittings with black finished swastikas. Blue finished alum. grip. Blue finished scabbard with silver finished fittings. Exc. cond. $790.00

DAGGER NSKK MEMBER M33

DAGGER NSKK MEMBER M33: Maker *RZM M7/13*. Silver finished fittings. Black painted scabbard with silver finished fittings. Black leather hanger with silver

finished clip & buckle. Avg. cond. $223.00

DAGGER NSKK MEMBER M33: Maker *Wilh. Weltersbach*. Nickel crossguards *Wm*. Black painted scabbard with nickel fittings. Above avg. cond. $397.00

DAGGER NSKK MEMBER M36: Maker *Eickhorn* with double mark *RZM M7/66 1938*. Silver finished fittings. Painted scabbard with nickel chain hanger with clip & stamped *NSKK etc.* to back link. Above avg. cond. $1,526.00

DAGGER NSKK MEMBER M36: Maker *Haenel*. Nickel crossguards *Sa* stamped on lower. Black painted scabbard with silver finished chain hanger with clip. Stamped *NSKK etc.* & *RZM M3/23*. Above avg. cond. $1,400.00

DAGGER NSKK MEMBER M36: Maker *RZM M7/38*. Nickel crossguards. Black anodized scabbard with nickel fittings. Silver finished chain hanger with clip & black leather belt loop with *D* ring. Chain *RZM* hmkd & marked *Musterschutz NSKK Korpsfuhrer*. Above avg. cond. $1,200.00

DAGGER NSKK MEMBER M36: Maker *RZM M7/38*. Silver finished fittings. Anodized scabbard with steel linked chain hanger with runics & sunwheel swastikas. Hmkd *RZM 5/8* with NSKK markings on the different links. Avg. cond. $1,252.00

DAGGER POSTSCHUTZ LEADER: (Postal Protection Police). Maker *Weyersberg*. Underside of nickel crossguard stamped *DRP 836*. Black celluloid grip with affixed nickel eagle with lightning bolts. Black scabbard with 3 nickel fittings. Nickel chain hanger with plated clip marked *DRGM*. Exc. cond. $2,000.00

DAGGER RAD LEADER HEWER WITH OWNER NAME

DAGGER RAD LEADER HEWER WITH OWNER NAME: Maker *F&A Helbig*. Aluminum fittings. White celluloid grips. Silver finished scabbard with engraved owner name. Avg. cond. $850.00

DAGGER RAD LEADER HEWER: Maker *ACS Alcoso Solingen*. Aluminum fittings. White celluloid grip. With a silver finished scabbard. Above avg. cond. $878.00

DAGGER RAD LEADER HEWER: Maker *ACS*. Silver finished aluminum fittings. White celluloid grips. With a frosted silver finished scabbard. Above avg. cond. $765.00

DAGGER RAD LEADER HEWER: Maker *Alcoso ACS Solingen*. Polished alum. hilt fittings with white grips. Nickel scabbard. Avg. cond. $560.00

DAGGER RAD LEADER HEWER: Maker *Carl Julius Krebs*. Silver finished fittings. White celluloid grips. Nickel scabbard. Avg. cond. $813.00

DAGGER RAD SUBORDINATE HEWER: Maker *Carl Jul. Krebs*. Frosted silver finish to hilt. Stag grips. Black painted scabbard with frosted silver fittings. Avg. cond. $400.00

DAGGER RAD SUBORDINATE HEWER: Maker *Carl Jul. Krebs*. Nickel fittings. Stag grips. Black scabbard with nickel fittings. Above avg. cond. $479.00

DAGGER RAD SUBORDINATE HEWER: Maker *Carl Jul. Krebs*. Silver finished fittings. Stag grips. Black painted scabbard with nickel fittings. Avg. cond. $285.00

DAGGER RAD SUBORDINATE HEWER: Maker *Eickhorn*. Nickel hilt with nice stag antler grips. Black painted scabbard with nickel fittings. Exc. cond. $427.00

DAGGER RAD SUBORDINATE HEWER: Maker *Gottlieb Hammesfahr*. Nickel fittings. Black painted scabbard. Avg. cond. $291.00

DAGGER RAD SUBORDINATE HEWER WITH REVERSED MOTTO TO BLADE

DAGGER RAD SUBORDINATE HEWER WITH REVERSED MOTTO TO BLADE: Unmarked. Nickel blade has motto to left side instead of normal right side. Nickel fittings. Stag grips. Black painted scabbard with nickel fittings. Near mint cond. $750.00

DAGGER RED CROSS LEADER: Unmarked. Nickel blade. Nickel fittings. Orange celluloid grip. Silver finished scabbard with rectangular hanger loop. Avg. cond. $572.00

DAGGER RED CROSS LEADER: Unmarked. Nickel fittings. Has a yellow celluloid grip. With nickel scabbard. Near mint cond. $1,116.00

DAGGER RED CROSS SUBORDINATE HEWER

DAGGER RED CROSS SUBORDINATE HEWER: Unmarked. Bright sawtooth blade. Nickel fittings. Black grips. Black painted scabbard & nickel fittings. Black leather frog with alum. rivets. Exc. cond. $300.00

DAGGER RED CROSS SUBORDINATE HEWER: Unmarked. Sawtooth blade. Silver finished fittings. Black grips. Black painted scabbard with silver finished fittings. Avg. cond. $303.00

DAGGER SA HIGH LEADER DAMASCUS BLADE

DAGGER SA HIGH LEADER DAMASCUS BLADE: Maker *Eickhorn*. Missing leather scabbard covering, replacement wood grip & lacks top crossguard. Very dark blade from moisture exposure has blunt tip, no gold finish to motto or oak leaves & faint 1933-34 era maker mark. Age darkening to silver lower cross guard with oak leaves & acorns design. Replacement walnut grip has silver washer & pommel nut at top. 3 dark silver scabbard fittings with outline grooves are intact on steel body with ding to back. Dark patina to swastika linked chain with SA logo clip all missing gold & silver plated finishes. Below avg. cond. $5,515.00

DAGGER SA MARINE M36: Maker *GK Gebr.Krumm Solingen*. Nickel crossguards. Black wood grip with nickel eagle & SA logo. Black leatherette covered scabbard has nickel throat & tip with M36 plated center band. Nickel hanger rings have alum. LW style chains & clip by *OLC Ges.Gesch*. Back of upper throat fitting has jeweler engraved owner initials. Near mint cond. $2,200.00

DAGGER SA MARINE ROHM HONOR GROUND: Maker *Haenel*. This is the copper wash to nickel fittings style dagger. Blade is ground with no traces of dedication. Nickel crossguards *Th*. Brown anodized scabbard with nickel fittings. Above avg. cond $1,000.00

DAGGER SA MEMBER ROHM HONOR GROUND: Maker *E Pack & Sohne*. Factory ground off Rohm dedication. Nickel crossguards *Wf*. Brown anodized scabbard with nickel fittings. Below avg. cond. $150.00

DAGGER SA MEMBER ROHM HONOR GROUND: Maker *E. Pack & Sohne*. Factory ground blade shows no traces of lettering to Rohm dedication. Nickel crossguards *Th*. With anodized scabbard. Avg. cond. $219.00

DAGGER SA MEMBER ROHM HONOR GROUND: Maker *E. Pack & Sohne*. Ground blade reverse with traces of lettering to Rohm dedication. Nickel crossguards *He*. Anodized scabbard. Avg. cond. $348.00

DAGGER SA MEMBER ROHM HONOR GROUND: Maker *F.Dick*. Most of Rohm dedication remains on reverse of blade with Rohm name removed. Nickel crossguards *Wm*. Dark wood grip with nickel eagle & SA logo. Painted scabbard. Avg. cond. $520.00

DAGGER SA MEMBER ROHM HONOR

DAGGER SA MEMBER ROHM HONOR: Maker *E. Pack & Sohne*. Full Rohm inscription on blade without grinding. Nickel fittings. Brown anodized scabbard with nickel fittings. Brown leather hanger with nickel clip. Above avg. cond. $1,800.00

DAGGER SA MEMBER WITH RUNIC SYMBOLS TO SCABBARD: Maker *E&F Horster*. Nickel crossguards. Black painted steel scabbard has copper/ bronze details soldered to front with 3 runic symbols at center, lines & sun wheel at each end. Plated nickel fittings Brown leather hanger with nickel clip. Exc. cond. $2,000.00

DAGGER SA MEMBER: Maker *Aesculap Tuttlingen* with crowned staff snake.

Nickel crossguards *Sw*. Brown anodized scabbard with nickel fittings. Black leather hanger strap with nickel clip stamped *RZM M5/8 A DRGM*. Below avg. cond. $145.00

DAGGER SA MEMBER: Maker *Aesculap Tuttlingen*. Nickel crossguards *Sw*. Brown anodized scabbard with nickel fittings. Below avg. cond. $160.00

DAGGER SA MEMBER: Maker *Albert Dorschel Solingen*. Nickel crossguards *Ho*. Brown anodized scabbard with nickel fittings. 3 piece hanger with brown leather strap with nickel clip, brown leather handle loop & brown leather belt loop with *a D*-ring. Avg. cond. $400.00

DAGGER SA MEMBER: Maker *Aug.Merten Ww.Solingen-GR*. Nickel crossguards *S*. With anodized scabbard. Above avg. cond. $271.00

DAGGER SA MEMBER: Maker *Aug.Merten Ww.Solingen-Gr*. Nickel crossguards *Wm*. Brown anodized scabbard with nickel fittings. Avg. cond. $219.00

DAGGER SA MEMBER: Maker *Axt-Und Hauerfabrik Solingen* with horse head trademark in circle. Nickel crossguards *Wf*. Brown anodized scabbard with nickel fittings. Avg. cond. $290.00

DAGGER SA MEMBER: Maker *Carl Heidelberg C.H. Solingen*. Nickel crossguards *Wf*. Anodized scabbard. Avg. cond. $225.00

DAGGER SA MEMBER: Maker *Carl Wusthof* with trademark & *RZM M7/112* (Dual Mark). Silver finished fittings. Brown scabbard with silver finished fittings. Below avg. cond. $160.00

DAGGER SA MEMBER: Maker *Carl Wusthof*. Nickel crossguard *S*. Anodized scabbard. Avg. cond. $250.00

DAGGER SA MEMBER: Maker *Christianswerk Solingen*. Nickel crossguards *Nrh*. Anodized scabbard. Early. Avg. cond. $203.00

DAGGER SA MEMBER: Maker *Eickhorn*. Nickel fittings *Wf*. Brown anodized scabbard with nickel fittings. Below avg. cond. $240.00

DAGGER SA MEMBER: Maker *Fr.v.d.Kohlen Solingen*. Nickel crossguards *No*. Anodized scabbard. Brown leather hanger strap with narrow nickel clip. Early. Exc. cond. $435.00

DAGGER SA MEMBER: Maker *Gust.Weyersberg Solingen Nachf*. Nickel crossguards *Ns*. RZM brown painted scabbard with silver finished fittings. Avg. cond. $220.00

DAGGER SA MEMBER: Maker *Haco Berlin*. Nickel crossguards *B*. Brown anodized scabbard with nickel fittings. Avg. cond. $180.00

DAGGER SA MEMBER: Maker *Herm. Konejung* with eye glasses trademark in oval. Nickel crossguards *Nrh*. Brown anodized scabbard with nickel fittings. Early. Below avg. cond. $177.00

DAGGER SA MEMBER: Maker *J.A. Henckels*. Nickel crossguard *Wf*. Brown anodized scabbard with nickel fittings. Avg. cond. $300.00

DAGGER SA MEMBER: Maker *Klittermann & Moog*. Nickel crossguard *Nrh*. Brown anodized scabbard with nickel fittings. Avg. cond. $400.00

DAGGER SA MEMBER: Maker *RZM M7/ 104*. Double marked with shield with crossed hammers maker trademark. Silver finished fittings. Brown painted scabbard with silver finished fittings. Above avg. cond. $248.00

DAGGER SA MEMBER: Maker *RZM M7/19 1938*. Silver finished fittings. Brown painted scabbard with silver finished fittings. RZM stamped brown leather hanger with buckle & *RZM M6/71 olc*. Avg. cond. $215.00

DAGGER SA MEMBER

DAGGER SA MEMBER: Maker *RZM M7/2*. Silver finished fittings. Brown painted scabbard with silver finished fittings. Exc. cond. $257.00

DAGGER SA MEMBER: Maker *RZM M7/27*. Silver finished fittings. Brown painted scabbard with silver finished fittings. RZM stamped brown leather hanger strap with a RZM clip. Avg. cond. $171.00

DAGGER SA MEMBER: Maker *RZM M7/37*. Silver finished fittings. Brown painted scabbard with silver finished fittings. Avg. cond. $185.00

DAGGER SA MEMBER: Maker *RZM M7/42*. Silver finished fittings. Brown painted scabbard with silver finished fittings. Avg. cond. $196.00

DAGGER SA MEMBER: Maker *RZM M7/42*. Silver finished fittings. Brown painted scabbard with silver finished fittings. Below avg. cond. $140.00

DAGGER SA MEMBER: Maker *RZM M7/51 1939* with Knight trademark. Silver finished fittings. Brown painted scabbard with silver finished fittings. RZM brown

leather hanger strap with RZM clip. Below avg. cond. $165.00

DAGGER SA MEMBER: Maker *RZM M7/ 66 1941*. Silver finished fittings. Brown painted scabbard with silver finished fittings. Leather hanger with clip hmkd *RZM M5/71 OLC*. Exc. cond. . $300.00

DAGGER SA MEMBER: Maker *SMF* with trademark. Nickel crossguard *HO*. Brown anodized scabbard with nickel fittings. Below avg. cond. $175.00

DAGGER SA MEMBER: Maker *SMF*. Nickel crossguards *B*. Anodized scabbard. Above avg. cond. $291.00

DAGGER SA MEMBER: Maker *Wilh. Kober*. Nickel crossguards *Sa*. Anodized scabbard. Early. Exc. cond. $348.00

DAGGER SA MEMBER: Maker *Wilh.Kober & Co. Suhl Gegr.1874* with trademark. Early. Nickel crossguards *Th*. Brown anodized scabbard with nickel fittings. Above avg. cond. $275.00

DAGGER SA MEMBER: Maker *Wilh.Kober & Co.Suhl*. Nickel crossguards *Th*. Brown anodized scabbard with nickel fittings. Avg. cond. $287.00

DAGGER SS MEMBER M33 ROHM HONOR GROUND: Maker *Eickhorn*. Most of the Rohm dedication intact except for name area showing deep scratches with highlights remaining. Nickel crossguards with back *I* & *89041* added over earlier same smaller number. Anodized scabbard. Black leather hanger strap with narrow nickel clip. Belonged to *Josef Blasl Sturmbannfuhrer-1937 Stab SS=Hauptant etc*. Above avg. cond. $3,858.00

DAGGER SS MEMBER M33 ROHM HONOR GROUND: Maker *Hammesfahr*. Entire Rohm dedication factory ground off. Nickel crossguards *III*. Anodized scabbard. Avg. cond. $499.00

DAGGER SS MEMBER M33 STYLE WITH SA MOTTO: Maker *RZM M7/36*. Blade with *Alles fur Deutschland* motto. Aluminum fittings. Black wood grip with no insignia. Black painted scabbard with silver finished fittings. This wartime dagger is not referenced but the few that are in collections are all marked *RZM M7/36* for Horster. Never saw much distribution & possibly SS Veteran or SA Marine use. Avg. cond. $451.00

DAGGER SS MEMBER M33: Maker *Gottlieb Hammesfahr*. Nickel

crossguards *III*. Anodized scabbard with black leather vertical hanger with belt loop. Above avg. cond. $1,000.00

DAGGER SS MEMBER M33

DAGGER SS MEMBER M33: Maker *Herder*. Nickel crossguards *I*. Black anodized scabbard with nickel fittings. Above avg. cond. $1,257.00

DAGGER SS MEMBER M33: Maker *RZM 1052/38 SS*. Silver finished crossguards. Brown wood grip instead of black has nickel eagle, no SS logo. Black scabbard with silver finished fittings. Below avg. cond. $428.00

DAGGER SS MEMBER M33: Maker *RZM 1053/39 SS*. Nickel plated crossguards. Black painted scabbard with nickel fittings. Black leather hanger with nickel clip. Avg. cond. $607.00

DAGGER SS MEMBER M33: Maker *RZM 121/34 SS*. Nickel fittings. Anodized scabbard. Above avg. cond. $760.00

DAGGER SS MEMBER M33: Maker *Robert Klaas Solingen*. Nickel crossguards *III*. Anodized scabbard. Early style. Avg. cond. $632.00

DAGGER SS MEMBER M36 WITH ENGRAVED PRESENTATION: Maker *Robert Klaas Solingen*. Motto to blade obverse, reverse with factory engraved *Zur Erinnerung a. SS-Sportschule Furth II 15.7-25.8.34*. Nickel crossguards *III*. Anodized scabbard with Type I chain hanger with clip. Silver cord knot. Avg. cond. $1,628.00

DAGGER TENO SUBORDINATE HEWER: Maker *Eickhorn*. Blade hmkd with Teno eagle *Ges.Gesch.* & numbered *6340* that matches scabbard throat. Silver finished fittings. White celluloid grip. Black finished scabbard with silver finished fittings. With complete frog with alum. clip, leather flap & leather grip strap. Above avg. cond. $1,277.00

MINIATURE DAGGER ARMY OFFICER: Unmarked. 8" long overall. White celluloid grip. Below avg. cond. $200.00

MINIATURE DAGGER LUFTWAFFE OFFICER 2ND MODEL: Maker *E&F Horster*. Silver finished hilt & scabbard. Wire wrapped orange celluloid grip. Avg. cond. $285.00

MINIATURE DAGGER LUFTWAFFE OFFICER 2ND MODEL: Maker *Georg Maas, Nurnberg*. 9" long overall. Nickel blade. Aluminum fittings. Orange celluloid grip. Steel scabbard. Below avg. cond. $196.00

MINIATURE DAGGER LUFTWAFFE OFFICER 2ND MODEL: Maker *SMF SOLINGEN DRGM*. De-Nazified. 9.5" overall length. Nickel blade. Aluminum fittings with swastikas removed. Twisted wire wrap to orange celluloid grip. Gray steel scabbard. Below avg. cond. $88.00

MINIATURE DAGGER LUFTWAFFE OFFICER 2ND MODEL: Unmarked. 8" overall. Nickel blade. Gray fittings & scabbard. Wire wrapped yellow celluloid grip. Below avg. cond. $124.00

MINIATURE DAGGER RAD OFFICER HEWER: Maker *Alcoso*. 10.5" overall. Silver frosted fittings & scabbard. Above avg. cond. $250.00

THIRD REICH BAYONETS & FIGHTING KNIVES

BAYONET 98K: Maker *41 cvl* matching. Bakelite grips. Black leather frog. Avg. cond. $40.00

BAYONET 98K: Maker *Carl Eickhorn 1937*. Wood grips. Black leather frog with straps. Avg. cond. $45.00

BAYONET 98K: Maker *Carl Eickhorn 1939*. Bakelite grips. Avg. cond. $30.00

BAYONET 98K: Maker *Carl Eickhorn 1939*. Bakelite grips. Avg. cond. $36.50

BAYONET 98K: Maker *Carl Eickhorn 1940*. Bakelite grips. Avg. cond. $27.00

BAYONET 98K: Maker *Carl Eickhorn 1940*. Bakelite grips. Avg. cond. $29.50

BAYONET 98K: Maker *Coppel G.m.b.H. 38* matching. Wood grips. Black leather frog. Avg. cond. $48.00

BAYONET 98K

BAYONET 98K: Maker *Durkopp 1939*. Bakelite grips. Tropical olive-green web frog with straps. Avg. cond. $68.00

BAYONET 98K: Maker *EuF Horster 1938* matching. Bakelite grips. Below avg. cond. $20.00

BAYONET 98K: Maker *EuF Horster 1940* matching. Bakelite grips. Black leather frog. Avg. cond. $45.00

BAYONET 98K: Maker *F.Herder A.Sn 39*. Bakelite grips. Black leather frog. Avg. cond. $31.00

BAYONET 98K: Maker *FW Holler 37*. Wood grips. Avg. cond. $49.00

BAYONET 98K: Maker *FW Holler 38* matching. Bakelite grips. Black leather frog with straps. Avg. cond. $35.00

BAYONET 98K: Maker *FW Holler 38* matching. Bakelite grips. Black leather frog. Avg. cond. $45.00

BAYONET 98K: Maker *FW Holler 38*. Bakelite grips. Avg. cond. $28.00

BAYONET 98K: Maker *Mundlos 39* Bakelite grips. Avg. cond. $28.00

BAYONET 98K: Maker *Mundlos 40* matching. Bakelite grips. Brown leather frog unit marked *5./Flak Rgt.62*. Below avg. cond. $48.00

BAYONET 98K: Maker *S/172G*. Wood grips. Black leather frog with straps. Below avg. cond. $35.00

BAYONET 98K: Maker *S/174G*. Wood grips. Avg. cond. $30.00

BAYONET 98K: Maker *S/175G* matching. Wood grips. Brown leather frog. Avg. cond. $73.00

BAYONET 98K: Maker *S/175G*. Bakelite grips. Black leather frog with 1941 maker. Avg. cond. $31.00

BAYONET 98K

BAYONET 98K: Maker *S/176 37* matching. Wood grips. Black leather frog with strap. Avg. cond. $72.00

BAYONET 98K: Maker *S/178G*. Wood grips. Black leather frog. Below avg. cond. $26.00

BAYONET 98K: Maker *S/184G* matching. Wood grips. Below avg. cond. $36.00

BAYONET 98K: Maker *S/185 36*. Wood grips. Below avg. cond. $22.00

BAYONET 98K: Maker *S/244 36*. Wood grip. Above avg. cond. $33.00

BAYONET 98K: Maker *WKC 40* matching. Bakelite grips. Black leather frog with straps. Below avg. cond. $37.00

BAYONET 98K: Maker *asw 43*. Bakelite grips. Above avg. cond. $47.50

BAYONET 98K: Maker *asw 44* matching. Bakelite grips. Late-war variation. Above avg. cond. $105.00

BAYONET 98K: Maker *clc 41*. Bakelite grips. Black leather frog with 1940 maker. Avg. cond. $48.00

BAYONET 98K: Maker *cof 43*. Bakelite grips. Tropical tan web frog with straps. Avg. cond. $120.00

BAYONET 98K: Maker *cof 44* matching. Bakelite grips. SS style black leather narrow frog with straps, stamped with RB# & *EZGJ1944*. Exc. cond. .. $265.00

BAYONET 98K: Maker *cqh 43* matching. Bakelite grips. Black leather frog with straps. Avg. cond. $38.00

BAYONET 98K: Maker *crs 41*. Bakelite grips. Avg. cond. $207.00

BAYONET 98K: Maker *cve 42*. Wood grips. Below avg. cond. $24.00

BAYONET 98K: Maker *cvl 41* & matching. Bakelite grips. Avg. cond. $30.00

BAYONET 98K: Maker *cvl 43* matching. Wood grips. Above avg. cond. $50.00

BAYONET 98K: Maker *ffc 44*. Bakelite grips. Avg. cond. $40.00

BAYONET 98K: Maker *fnj 40* matching. Bakelite grips, Below avg. cond. . $40.00

BAYONET 98K: Maker *fnj 42* matching. Bakelite grips. Black leather frog. Avg. cond. $34.00

BAYONET 98K: Maker *fnj 43* matching. Clear Plexiglas grips added. Black leather frog. Below avg. cond. $25.00

BAYONET CUSTOM OFFICIAL KS98: Maker *Alexander Coppel ACS Solingen*. 10" gray steel blade. Steel fittings with crossguard stamped *R.F.V.* Checkered wooden grips with a groove cut to back. No scabbard. 1920s. Above avg. cond. $125.00

BAYONET CUSTOM OFFICIAL KS98: Maker *Paul Weyersberg & Co Solingen*. 10" bright steel blade Maker. Steel fittings with crossguard stamped *R.F.V.* Black grips. Slot in pommel. No scabbard. 1920s made. Above avg. cond. $157.00

BAYONET DRESS ENGRAVED: Maker *Eickhorn*. Distributor marked *Militarwarenhaus Durbeck Wien IX*. Short model. Single engraved with 2 engraved stylized eagles, scroll *Zur Erinnerung an meine Dienstzeit* with oak leaves. Avg. cond. $232.00

BAYONET 98K

BAYONET DRESS ENGRAVED

BAYONET DRESS ENGRAVED: Maker
Eickhorn. Long model. Double engraved.
Obverse with scroll with oak leaves *Zur
Erinnerung an meine Dienstzeit*, stylized
eagle end & crossed rifles with helmet/
oakleave wreath. Reverse marked
Infanterie-Regiment No.119 Stuttgart.
Avg. cond. $352.00
BAYONET DRESS ENGRAVED: Maker
Eickhorn. Short model. Single engraved
blade with scroll *Zur Erinnerung an
meine Dienstzeit* with oak leaves, stylized
eagle & wreath with crossed rifles and
steel helmet. Black patent leather frog.
Above avg. cond. $211.00
BAYONET DRESS ENGRAVED: Maker *FW
Holler*. Short model. Single engraved
blade with *Zur Erinnerung an meine
Dienstzeit* scroll, oak leaves & military
scene of MG crew, Arty. crew & tank. No
scabbard. Below avg. cond. $95.00
BAYONET DRESS ENGRAVED: Maker *FW
Holler*. Short model. Single engraved
blade with scroll with oak leaves *Zur
Erinnerung an meine Dienstzeit* with MG
crew, Arty. crew & small tank. Above avg.
cond. $238.00
BAYONET DRESS ENGRAVED: Maker *FW
Holler*. Single engraved blade with vines
to sides of *Zur Erinnerung an meine
Dienstzeit Inft.Rgt.3 Mohrungen/Ostpr*.
Exc. cond. $726.00
BAYONET DRESS VARIATION: Unmarked.
Short model with double edged nickel
blade with narrow center fuller. Avg.
cond. $93.00
BAYONET DRESS WITH IMITATION STAG
GRIP: Unmarked. Short model. Carved
wood grips simulating stag. Red wool
plug in slot. Black patent leather frog.
With knot gray cloth strap, blue slide, red
stem, blue cap & gray ball to knot. Avg.
cond. $133.00

BAYONET DRESS WITH SA FELDHERRNHALLE ENGRAVED MOTTO

BAYONET DRESS WITH SA
FELDHERRNHALLE ENGRAVED
MOTTO: Maker Eickhorn. Short model.
Carbine blade engraved *Ehre, Kraft,
Freiheit*. Below avg. cond. $400.00
BAYONET DRESS WITH STAG HANDLE:
Maker *WKC*. Long model. Stag grips.
Below avg. cond. $44.00

BAYONET DRESS WITH STAG HANDLE:
Unmarked. Long model. Stag grips. Black
patent leather frog. Below avg.
cond. $48.00
BAYONET DRESS: Maker *A.Evertz
Solingen*. Long model. Added laminated
wood grips. WWI black painted steel
scabbard. Avg. cond. $38.00

BAYONET DRESS

BAYONET DRESS: Maker *Alcoso ACS
Solingen*. Long model. Black leather frog.
With knot with Gray cloth strap, yellow
slide, white stem, yellow cap & gray ball.
Above avg. cond. $95.00
BAYONET DRESS: Maker *Alcoso ACS
Solingen*. Short model. Black patent
leather frog. With green & alum. Exc.
cond. $66.00
BAYONET DRESS: Maker *Anton Wingen Jr*.
Short model. Black patent leather frog.
Below avg. cond. $37.00
BAYONET DRESS: Maker *E&F Horster*.
Long model. Avg. cond. $48.00
BAYONET DRESS: Maker *E. Pack &
Sohne*. Long model. Avg.
cond. $40.00
BAYONET DRESS: Maker *Eickhorn*. Long
model. Black patent leather frog. Avg.
cond. $35.00
BAYONET DRESS: Maker *Eickhorn*. Long
model. Avg. cond. $33.00
BAYONET DRESS: Maker *Eickhorn*. Short
model. Brown leather Czech frog. Below
avg. cond. $49.00
BAYONET DRESS: Maker *Eickhorn*. Short
model. Red wool plug in slot. Brown
leather frog. Above avg.
cond. $73.00
BAYONET DRESS: Maker *Gustav Spitzer*.
Long model. With 98K Scabbard *S/173G*.
Avg. cond. $44.00
BAYONET DRESS: Maker *JA Henckels*.
Short model. Avg. cond. $35.00
BAYONET DRESS: Maker *Klittermann*.
Short model. Red wool plug in slot. Avg.
cond. $35.00
BAYONET DRESS: Maker *Puma*. Long
model. Above avg. cond. $37.00
BAYONET DRESS: Maker *Puma*. Short
model. Red wool plug in slot. Black
leather frog. Above avg. cond. $45.00
BAYONET DRESS: Maker *Robert Klaas*.
Long model. Avg. cond. $24.00
BAYONET DRESS: Maker *Robert Klaas*.
Long model. Avg. cond. $30.00

BAYONET DRESS: Maker *Robert Klaas*. Long model. Avg. cond. $48.00
BAYONET DRESS: Maker *Tiger*. Long model. Distributor marked *Georg Rieder Munchen*. Above avg. cond. $48.00
BAYONET DRESS: Maker *WKC*. Long model. Early. Avg. cond. $48.00
BAYONET DRESS: Maker *WKC*. Long model. Avg. cond. $32.00
BAYONET DRESS: Maker *WKC*. Long model. Avg. cond. $40.00
BAYONET DRESS: Maker *Wilh. Wagner*. Long model. Below avg. cond. ... $40.00

BAYONET DRESS

BAYONET DRESS: Maker *Anton Wingen Jr.* Short model. Early. Black leather frog. Avg. cond. $75.00
BAYONET DRESS: Unmarked. Long model. Avg. cond. $24.00
BAYONET DRESS: Unmarked. Long model. Avg. cond. $31.00
BAYONET DRESS: Unmarked. Short model. Below avg. cond. $49.00
BAYONET FIREMAN DRESS SAWTOOTH: Maker *Eickhorn*. Short model. Sawtooth blade. Black leather frog. Early. Exc. cond. $265.00
BAYONET FIREMAN DRESS: Maker *Johann Leupold*. Long model. Avg. cond. $30.00
BAYONET FIREMAN DRESS: Maker *Puma*. Long model. Black leather frog. Avg. cond. $91.00
BAYONET FIREMAN DRESS: Maker *Spitzer*. Long model. Black leather frog. Early. Above avg. cond. $54.00
BAYONET FIREMAN DRESS: Maker *Tiger*. Long model. Distributor marked *Georg Reider Munchen*. Avg. cond. $35.00
BAYONET FIREMAN DRESS: Unmarked. Long model. Brown leather scabbard. Above avg. cond. $61.00
BAYONET FIREMAN DRESS: Unmarked. Long model. Avg. cond. $71.00
BAYONET FIREMAN DRESS: Unmarked. Short model. Black patent leather frog. Exc. cond. $90.00
BAYONET NAVAL 98K: Maker *Elite Diamant 39* matching. Bakelite grips. Crossguard stamped *O.17983K*. Black leather frog eagle M issue proofed. Above avg. cond. $160.00
BAYONET POLICE 98K: Crossguard marked *P.R.8 8263* no Nazi military proof only the police & serial num. Wood grips have special police style bolts. Blued

scabbard. Black leather frog. Above avg. cond. $86.00
BAYONET POLICE 98K: Maker *ACS*. Spined eagle stamped with letter. Bakelite grips. No scabbard. Above avg. cond. $100.00
BAYONET POLICE DRESS CLAMSHELL: Maker *E&F Horster Solingen*. Weimar era. 16.5" long nickel blade. Brass eagle clamshell & solid eagle head hilt with oak leaves to crossguard. Stag grips with affixed nickel eagle star. Black leather scabbard with brass fittings. Avg. cond. $460.00
BAYONET POLICE DRESS CLAMSHELL: Unmarked. Short model. 9.75" nickel blade. Nickel clamshell with eagle. Nickel oakleave crossguard & eagle head pommel. Stag grips with brass rivets. Black painted scabbard. Brown leather frog. Avg. cond. $275.00

BAYONET POLICE DRESS
M98/05 PSS

BAYONET POLICE DRESS M98/05 PSS: Maker *Solingen*. Crown W 15 proofed. 14.25" long narrowed blade is nickel plated. Engraved oak leaves to crossguard & hilt. Stag grips with affixed nickel police eagle/wreath. Black painted scabbard. Black leather frog. Above avg. cond. $1,250.00
BAYONET POLICE DRESS TRANSITIONAL VARIATION: Maker *WKC*. 11.5" stiletto/carbine style nickel blade. Clamshell guard removed. Nickel hilt fittings. Stag grips having affixed bronze eagle/wreath. Black leather scabbard with nickel fittings. Avg. cond. ... $221.00
BAYONET POLICE DRESS TRANSITIONAL: Maker *ACS*. 13" cut down nickel blade. Nickel fittings with red wool to slot, crossguard stamped *S.M.IV.1386* that matches scabbard throat. Stag grips with aluminum eagle/wreath. Black leather scabbard. Avg. cond. $206.00
BAYONET POLICE DRESS TRANSITIONAL: Maker *Alexander Coppel Solingen ACS*. 13" cut down nickel blade. Solid nickel fittings with crossguard stamped *L.Lg.148* that matches scabbard throat. Stag grips with alum. eagle/wreath. Brown leather scabbard with nickel fittings. Above avg. cond. $280.00

BAYONET POLICE DRESS TRANSI-
TIONAL: Maker *Eickhorn*. 13" cut down
nickel blade. Heavy nickel eagle head hilt
with working slot. Stag grips with nickel
eagle/wreath. Brown leather scabbard
with nickel fittings has stamped *S.B.5320*.
Brown leather frog. Above avg.
cond. $352.00

BAYONET POLICE DRESS TRANSI-
TIONAL: Maker *Eickhorn*. Spine proofed.
Solid nickel fittings with oak leaves &
eagle head. Stag grips with plugged hole
& alum. eagle/wreath device. Stamped
crossguard & throat *S.Br.I.1921*. Black
leather scabbard with nickel fittings. Avg.
cond. $300.00

BAYONET POLICE DRESS
TRANSITIONAL

BAYONET POLICE DRESS TRANSI-
TIONAL: Maker *Weyersberg*. Cut down
13" blade. Crossguard stamped *S.Ko.I.*
Stag grips with eagle. Black leather
scabbard with nickel fittings. Avg.
cond. $221.00

BAYONET POLICE DRESS: Maker *Alcoso
ACS Solingen*. 9.5" nickel blade. Solid
alum. eagle hilt. Stag grips with alum.
eagle wreath. Black leather scabbard
with nickel fittings. Black leather frog.
Avg. cond. $275.00

BAYONET SG42 2ND MODEL
WITH 4 PART TOOL SET

BAYONET SG42 2ND MODEL WITH 4
PART TOOL SET: Maker *cof* &
waffenampt proofed. Fighting knife style
steel blade. Dark bakelite grips are
riveted & has steel hilt with slot for rifle
stud. Blued metal tools remove from grips
with pivot bar, *ltk* marked opener,
screwdriver & spike to end with corkscrew at other end. Bakelite covered
scabbard with blued steel belt loop. Exc.
cond. $3,703.00

DIVER KNIFE NAVAL: 14" long body. Loop
to side, rubber seal & grooved handle.
8.5" *M* marked steel blade. Marked with
an *M* on handle. Avg. cond. $520.00

DIVER KNIFE NAVAL: About 14" overall
heavy brass body. Threads located below
the handle with grooved grip, 6.5" plain
steel blade & scabbard. Avg.
cond. $339.00

DIVER KNIFE NAVAL

FIGHTING KNIFE LUFTWAFFE: Eagle 5
issue marked. Steel crossguard, 3 rivet
grips & 3 spring clip to black scabbard.
Above avg. cond. $110.00

FIGHTING KNIFE LUFTWAFFE: Eagle 5
issue marked. 6.5" long steel blade. 3
rivets to wood grips. Black scabbard has
3 spring clips. Avg. cond. $149.00

FIGHTING KNIFE LUFTWAFFE: Eagle 5
issue marked. Steel crossguard, 3 rivets
to wood grip & black scabbard with 3
spring clips. Near mint cond. $120.00

FIGHTING KNIFE LUFTWAFFE: Eagle 5
issue marked. Steel crossguard, 3 rivets
to wood grip & black painted scabbard
with 3 spring clips. Exc. cond. .. $116.00

FIGHTING KNIFE LUFTWAFFE: Eagle 5
issue marked. Steel crossguard, 3 rivets
to wood grip & black painted scabbard
with 3 spring clips. Exc. cond. .. $120.00

FIGHTING KNIFE LUFTWAFFE

FIGHTING KNIFE LUFTWAFFE: Eagle 5
issue marked. Steel crossguard, 3 rivets
to wood grip. Black scabbard with 3
spring clips. Near mint cond. $116.00

FIGHTING KNIFE LUFTWAFFE: Eagle 5
issue marked. Steel crossguard, 3 rivets
to wood grip. Black scabbard with 3
spring clips. Near mint cond. $116.00

FIGHTING KNIFE LUFTWAFFE: Eagle 5
issue marked. Steel crossguard, 3 rivet
grips & 3 spring clip to black scabbard.
Above avg. cond. $110.00

FIGHTING KNIFE LUFTWAFFE: Eagle 5
issue marked. Steel crossguard, 3 rivet
wood grips & 3 spring clip to black
scabbard, 90%. Exc. cond. $117.00

FIGHTING KNIFE LUFTWAFFE: Eagle 5
issue marked. Steel crossguard, 3 rivet

wood grips with owner carved *F* & 3 spring clip to black scabbard. Above avg. cond. $110.00

FIGHTING KNIFE LUFTWAFFE: Eagle 6 issue marked. Steel blade. Steel crossguard & 3 rivets to light wood grips. Black scabbard with 3 prong loop. Near mint cond. $125.00

FIGHTING KNIFE LUFTWAFFE: Eagle 6 issue marked. Steel cross guard & 3 rivet to wood grips. Black scabbard with 3 spring clips. Avg. cond. $79.00

FIGHTING KNIFE STAG HANDLE WWI STYLE: 6" nickel blade, steel crossguard, stag antler grip & black painted steel scabbard with long spring clip. Avg. cond. $85.00

FIGHTING KNIFE WITH 4 TOOL GRIP

FIGHTING KNIFE WITH 4 TOOL GRIP: 6" steel blade. Steel crossguard. Black composite grips, corkscrew, marlin spike, opener & screw driver. Black scabbard with metal belt loop. Avg. cond. $276.00

FIGHTING KNIFE WITH 4 TOOL GRIP: Maker *S.* 6" steel blade. Steel crossguard. Stag grips, corkscrew, marlin spike, opener & screw driver. Black scabbard with 3 spring/clips. Avg.cond. $408.00

FIGHTING KNIFE WITH 4 TOOL GRIP: Unmarked. 6" steel blade. Steel crossguard, 3 rivets to dark wood grips & 4 tools: corkscrew, spike, opener, screwdriver. Black metal scabbard with metal belt loop. Avg. cond. $195.00

FIGHTING KNIFE YOUTH STYLE: Unmarked. 9" long overall. 4.5" bright youth style blade & tang. Single wood wrap around grip with finger guard, 6 carved grooves per side & 2 rivets. Black youth style steel scabbard with large spring/belt loop to back. Exc. cond. $221.00

FIGHTING KNIFE: Maker *Puma*. Gray crossguard & bakelite grips. Black scabbard with one spring clip. Avg. cond. $125.00

FIGHTING KNIFE: Maker *Puma*. Bakelite grips. Black painted steel scabbard with spring clip. Avg. cond. $112.00

FIGHTING KNIFE: Maker *Puma*. Bakelite grips. Black painted scabbard with steel clip. Avg. cond. $107.00

FIGHTING KNIFE: Maker *cof.* Cast crossguard & tang. 3 rivets to wood grips having owner carved *K*. Black scabbard with long spring clip. Avg. cond. $125.00

FIGHTING KNIFE: Only 9" long overall, 4.5" bright steel blade & 2 rivets to wood grip with grooves. Black painted steel scabbard with long spring/clip. Mint cond. $319.00

FIGHTING KNIFE: Steel blade stamped *W*. Steel crossguard & 3 rivets to wood grips. Black scabbard with 3 prong loop. Exc. cond. $123.00

FIRE AX FIREMAN PARADE

FIRE AX FIREMAN PARADE: 13" long black painted wood handle with nickel end cap & 5.5" long head. Stamped *3* that matches frog stamp. Bayonet style black leather frog with added leather straps having brass & steel studs. Exc. cond. $375.00

FIRE AX: 18" long with black wood shaft & nickel silver plated metal parts. Ax Head with Curved spike at one end & ax at other. Plus flanges to attach to shaft. Two rings just below head. Unmarked presentation plates on each side nailed to wood. Metal ferrule & ball at other end. Above avg. cond. $425.00

GRAVITY KNIFE PARATROOPER TAKE DOWN MODEL: RARE TAKE DOWN LUFTWAFFE PARATROOPER KNIFE: RB numbered. Eagle 5 issue marked. Blued finish. Wood grips with owner initial. Operational. Avg. cond. .. $300.00

GRAVITY KNIFE PARATROOPER TAKE DOWN MODEL: Unmarked. Blued finish. RB numbered. Wood grips. Above avg. cond. $275.00

GRAVITY KNIFE PARATROOPER. Unmarked. Silver finish. Wood grips. Avg. cond. $135.00

GRAVITY KNIFE PARATROOPER: Maker *Paul Weyersberg*. Eagle 5 issue marked. Avg. cond. $195.00

GRAVITY KNIFE PARATROOPER: Maker *SMF* Eagle 5 issue marked. Silver finish. Wood grips. Avg. cond. $130.00

GRAVITY KNIFE PARATROOPER: Maker *SMF*. Eagle 5 issue proof. Silver finish. Wood grips. Operational. Above avg. cond. $300.00

GRAVITY KNIFE PARATROOPER
TAKE DOWN MODEL

GRAVITY KNIFE PARATROOPER TAKE DOWN MODEL: Maker *SMF Solingen*. Blued finish. Wood grips. With 58" long braided rope lanyard with sewn end loops having 2 steel clips. Near mint cond. $750.00

GRAVITY KNIFE PARATROOPER: Unmarked. Eagle 5 issue marked. Silver finish. Wood grips. Operational. Avg. cond. $175.00

KNIFE HJ MEMBER WITH MOTTO: Maker *F. Plucker Jr. Solingen-Gr* dual marked *RZM M7/62*. Avg. cond. $293.00

KNIFE HJ MEMBER WITH MOTTO: Maker *G. Felix Solingen* double marked *RZM M7/28*. Avg. cond. $295.00

KNIFE HJ MEMBER WITH MOTTO: Maker *Herm.Konejung A-G*. Early. Below avg. cond. $107.00

KNIFE HJ MEMBER WITH MOTTO: Maker *RZM M7/51 1937*. Avg. cond. ... $130.00

KNIFE HJ MEMBER WITH MOTTO

KNIFE HJ MEMBER WITH MOTTO: Maker marked *Robt.Klaas Solingen etc*. Avg. cond. $101.00

KNIFE HJ MEMBER: Maker *Eickhorn* dual marked *RZM M7/66 1942*. Below avg. cond. $85.00

KNIFE HJ MEMBER: Maker *Eickhorn* dual marked with *RZM M7/66*. Below avg. cond. $80.00

KNIFE HJ MEMBER: Maker *Puma*. Early. Avg. cond. $150.00

KNIFE HJ MEMBER: Maker *RZM M7/2 1940*. Black scabbard with plastic belt loop. Below avg. cond. $79.00

KNIFE HJ MEMBER: Maker *RZM M7/31*. Below avg. cond. $45.00

KNIFE HJ MEMBER: Maker *RZM M7/36*. Avg. cond. $112.00

MACHETE LUFTWAFFE SURVIVAL: Maker *Alcoso ACS Solingen*. 21.5" long overall. 16" steel blade. Brass crossguard & hilt with removable wood grips. Blued steel scabbard. Above avg. cond. $750.00

MINIATURE BAYONET DRESS: Maker *GG Leykauf Nurnberg*. 9.5" long overall. 5.5" nickel. Below avg. cond. $55.00

PRESENTATION KNIFE DEUTSCHLANDFLUG 1935: 5" steel blade on hunting style knife. Hmkd on ricasso & Presentation on side. *EHRENPREIS/DEUTCHLANDFLUG 1935* & makers name. Nickel silver guard with Ball quillons & two piece stag grip with nickel silver insert on one side. Avg. cond. $275.00

THIRD REICH SWORDS

MINIATURE SWORD LUFTWAFFE OFFICER MOUNTED ON MARBLE BASE: 1/2x3.5x6" black marble base with green felt. 9" overall affixed sword. About 8" long 1 piece cast sword with unmarked nickel plated blade. Desktop display. Above avg. cond. $395.00

SWORD ARMY NCO *ANTON WINGEN JR* : 33.5" nickel blade with maker & trademark. Nickel fittings. Wire wrapped black celluloid grip. Black painted scabbard. Avg. cond. $96.00

SWORD ARMY NCO *EICKHORN #40* : 32" bright nickel blade with title maker & squirrel sword. Gold finished alum. fittings. Brass wire wrap to black grip. Black scabbard. Avg. cond. $130.00

SWORD ARMY NCO *G. WEYERSBERG* : 33.5" nickel blade with maker. Silver finish plain fittings. Silver wire wrap to black grip. Black painted scabbard. Knot with green cloth strap with dark silver border stripes, green & silver slide, stem, cap & dark silver ball with green bullion insert. Avg. cond. $117.00

SWORD ARMY NCO *HORSTER* : 33" nickel blade with trademark. Nickel fittings. Dark wire wrap to black grip. Black painted scabbard. Above avg. cond. $127.00

SWORD ARMY OFFICER *ALCOSO*
#119 LION HEAD

SWORD ARMY OFFICER *ALCOSO #119*
LION HEAD: 32" nickel blade by *Alcoso
ACS* with scales. Gold finish brass
P-guard with oakleaves, Party Eagle
langet/ crossguard & ruby eyes to head.
Dark silver wrap to black grip. Black
scabbard. Above avg. cond. $292.00
SWORD ARMY OFFICER *ALCOSO
UNATTRIBUTED* DOVE HEAD DOUBLE
ENGRAVED: About 35.5" curved nickel
blade with trademark & maker. Engraved
floral motif with National eagle, crossed
rifles with Army helmet & blank center
panel showing factory removed owner
name. Nice mounted charge to other side
with stylized eagle & crossed swords with
Army helmet. Brass fittings with oak
leaves, P-guard & large eagle to langet/
crossguard. Wire wrapped black celluloid
grip. Black painted scabbard. Avg.
cond. $280.00
SWORD ARMY OFFICER *ALCOSO
UNATTRIBUTED* DOVE HEAD: 30.5"
steel blade by *Alcoso AWS Solingen* with
scales. Gold finished brass fittings, oak
leaves to P-guard, eagle to langet, oak
leaves to crossguard & backstrap. Dark
wire wrap to dark grip. Black scabbard.
Avg. cond. $178.00
SWORD ARMY OFFICER *ALCOSO
UNATTRIBUTED* DOVE HEAD: 31.5"
bright nickel blade with *ACS* with
scales. Dark brass fittings with laurel
leaf wreath to langet, oak leaves to
P-guard & backstrap. Dark wire wrap
to black grip. Leather finger loop. Black
scabbard. 1920s Reichsheer use?
Avg. cond. $177.00
SWORD ARMY OFFICER *EICKHORN
#1693 WRANGEL #1693* DOVE HEAD:
29.5" bright nickel blade with title maker
& squirrel sword. Bright gold finished
alum./alloy fittings with party eagle langet
crossguard. Black grip with wire wrap.
Black scabbard. Above avg.
cond. $190.00
SWORD ARMY OFFICER *EICKHORN
#1714 FREIHERR VON STEIN* DOVE
HEAD: 34" curved nickel blade with
trademark & maker. Dark copper finish to
all alum./alloy fittings with oak leaves &

stylized eagle langet. Black grip with wire
wrap. Black scabbard. Municipal Police
knot. Avg. cond. $210.00
SWORD ARMY OFFICER *EICKHORN
#1735 DERFFLINGER* DOVE HEAD: 31"
bright nickel blade with squirrel sword
trademark, etc. Gold finish to dark brass
hilt, stylized eagle to langet, flat P-guard,
dove head & design overall. Alum. wrap
to black grip. Black scabbard Knot with
gold cloth strap with silver border stripes,
alum. stem, cap & ball. Avg.
cond. $239.00
SWORD ARMY OFFICER *EICKHORN
#1765 PRINZ EUGEN* DOVE HEAD: 32"
nickel blade with title maker. Gold finish
fittings. Party eagle to langet &
crossguard. Back langet jeweler
engraved *KHG*. Stylized eagle to
pommel. Alum. wrap to black grip. Black
scabbard. Avg. cond. $430.00

SWORD ARMY OFFICER *EICKHORN*
#40 DOVE HEAD

SWORD ARMY OFFICER *EICKHORN #40*
DOVE HEAD: About 32" bright nickel
blade with squirrel sword & maker. Bright
gold finish to brass fittings. Alum. wrap to
black grip. Black scabbard. Near mint
cond. $158.00
SWORD ARMY OFFICER *EICKHORN*
LION HEAD: Gilded aluminum lion head
fittings with stylized eagle shield on
crossguard. Wire wrapped black celluloid
grip. Hmkd *Ges Gesch*. Black painted
scabbard. Avg. cond. $205.00
SWORD ARMY OFFICER *KREBS #3*
DOVE HEAD: 33" unmarked blade. Party
eagle to langet & crossguard. Oak leaves
to P-guard that is bent at top & more
leaves to back strap. Wire wrapped black
celluloid grips. Black painted scabbard.
Avg. cond. $131.00
SWORD ARMY OFFICER
RICH.A.HERDER DOVE HEAD: 32.5"
nickel blade with maker & trademark.
Gold finish to hilt fittings leaving copper
shade. Party eagle to langet &
crossguard. Oak leaves to backstrap & P-
guard. Wire wrap to black grip. Black
scabbard. With knot. Avg.
cond. $190.00

SWORD ARMY OFFICER UNMARKED DOVE HEAD: Gold finished brass fittings with stylized eagle shield on cross guard. Wire wrapped black celluloid grip. Black finished scabbard. Avg. cond. .. $175.00

SWORD ARMY OFFICER UNMARKED LEOPARD HEAD: 31.5" curved nickel blade is unmarked. Gold finished brass P-guard with oak leaves, party eagle to crossguard/langet & ruby eyes to head. Wire wrapped black celluloid grip. Black painted scabbard. Avg. cond. $178.00

SWORD CHILD'S ARMY OFFICER LION HEAD: Gold finished brass lion head backstrap, alum/alloy P-guard & crossguard with party eagle. Wire wrapped black grip. 27.5" overall & 19.5" blunt steel blade with fuller. Black repainted scabbard with side loop only. Above avg. cond. $240.00

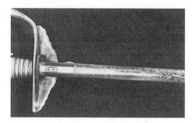

SWORD DIPLOMATIC OFFICIAL
DOUBLE ENGRAVED (DETAIL)

SWORD DIPLOMATIC OFFICIAL DOUBLE ENGRAVED: 32" bright nickel blade with engraved national eagle to floral design. Other has floral design. Excellent details to eagle head pommel with mother-of-pearl grips. Black leather scabbard with nickel fittings. Above avg. cond. $6,000.00

SWORD FIREMAN OFFICER DOVE HEAD: 32" curved nickel blade with distributor to spine *Hast & Uhthoff, Dresden* Gold finished brass P-guard. Wire wrapped black celluloid grip. Black finished scabbard. Avg. cond. $140.00

SWORD MINER DOUBLE ENGRAVED: Maker *ACS*. 28" steel blade engraved crossed hammers with *Gluck Auf* & floral motif. Reverse floral motif. Brass P-guard, fittings & affixed crossed hammers to langet. Black leather scabbard with 3 brass fittings, 2 hanger rings. Avg. cond. $265.00

SWORD NAVAL OFFICER LION HEAD: Maker *WKC*. 29.5" quillback steel blade with Knight head & title. Folding brass fouled anchor guard, D-guard, lionhead & back folding lock stamped eagle M *N2694* that matches throat num. Brass wire wrap to white grip. Black leather scabbard with 3 brass fittings. This sword is rare because most swords were private purchase & only a very few issued & have Nazi waffenamp proof marks. Avg. cond. $750.00

SWORD NAVAL OFFICER: 29.5" gray steel quillback blade by *Alcoso ACS* etc. with scales. Gold finished brass fittings, folding anchor guard & folding lock stamped *O.2488* as is throat. Wire wrapped white celluloid grip. Black leather scabbard with 3 gilded brass fittings, Eagle M issue stamped. Avg. cond. $495.00

SWORD ORDNANCE: Maker *EuF Horster*. 31.5" nickel blade. Brass P-guard & fittings with matching stamped marks *1682*. Wire wrapped black grip & lacks fingerloop. Blued scabbard. 1938. Avg. cond. $145.00

SWORD SS SENIOR NCO: 35" long steel blade. Nickel fittings with SS runes to pommel button. Black painted wool grip. Black painted scabbard with nickel fittings, throat stamped with *SS* runes. Avg. cond. $750.00

THIRD REICH EDGED WEAPON ACCOUTERMENTS

ADVERTISEMENT CALENDAR WKC: About 1x9.5x14" size with wood frame backing having 2 hanger loops. 2 dial adjustment knobs at each side day/month. Blue & silver *WKC* center with Knight head, 2 color swords & bayonet *Blanke Waffen Aller Art* with address below. Exc. cond. $240.00

ADVERTISEMENT CATALOG: *Paul Seilheimer* edged weapons. 8x12" gray paper cover with green printed title & maker trademarks. 8 pages of nicely illus. dress sidearms. Avg. cond. $20.00

ADVERTISEMENT CATALOG: *WKC* edged weapons. About 10x12.5" light blue paper cover with silver & blue details. 15 pages with illustrated examples of various edged weapons. Above avg. cond. $75.00

ADVERTISEMENT SIGN WKC: Self framing. Metal. 12.5x19" size. Still wrapped in original brown paper. Colorful. Has likeness of 2 swords & bayonet with trade mark. Above avg. cond. $150.00

ADVERTISEMENT SIGN WKC

ADVERTISEMENT SIGN WKC: Still has
original paper covering. 12.5x19" size
with silver Knight head & *WKC
Qualitatsmarke* on blue shield at
center. Color detailed swords,
bayonet & wording on white background. Hanger chain attached to
metal backing. Mint cond. $187.00
ADVERTISEMENT SIGN WKC: Tin.
BLANKE WAFFEN ALLER ART in the
upper right corner. celluloid over metal
sign with colorful design of the Co.
logo with 2 swords & a dress bayonet.
At bottom black lettering of Co. name
& location Solingen. 19" high, 12.5"
wide. Near mint cond. $301.00
BELT LOOP & D-RING: Brown leather
loop will fit 1 3/4" wide belt. Nickel D-
ring & rivet for release of loop. Below
avg. cond. $20.00
BELT SWORD UNDER THE TUNIC:
Blue web body with brown leather
loops, brass D-rings & roller buckle
strap. About 95. Near mint
cond. $50.00
BELT SWORD UNDER THE TUNIC:
Blue web body with brown leather
loops, nickel D-rings & roller buckle
strap. About 85. Above avg.
cond. $45.00
BELT SWORD UNDER THE TUNIC:
Blue web body with cord still strong.
Red Leather closure with brass
buckle. Brown leather loop with nickel
plated clip affixed *DRGM*. Belt about
size 90. Exc. cond. $34.00
BELT SWORD UNDER THE TUNIC:
Blue web body. Brown leather fittings
with sewn D-ring & movable D-ring.
Avg. cond. $20.00
BELT SWORD UNDER THE TUNIC:
Dark blue web body. Dark brown
leather fittings. D-rings are thin brass
wire. Avg. cond. $20.00

FROG 98K BAYONET
LATE-WAR SS STYLE

FROG 98K BAYONET LATE-WAR SS
STYLE: Back body with handle straps &
4 rivets. Above avg. cond. $66.00
FROG 98K BAYONET TROPICAL WEB:
Olive body with straps. Inked maker.
Above avg. cond. $76.00
FROG 98K BAYONET: Black leather with 2
broken alum. rivets. Faint 1937 maker.
Below avg. cond. $20.00
FROG 98K BAYONET: Black leather with
four steel rivets & stamped RB#. Avg.
cond. $25.00
FROG 98K BAYONET: Black leather with
four steel rivets. Maker and date marked,
Wittkop & Co BieleFeld 1942. Above avg.
cond. $25.00
FROG 98K BAYONET: Black leather with
handle straps. Faint 1940/maker. Above
avg. cond. $23.00
FROG 98K BAYONET: Black leather. Maker
Goch 1940. 4 steel rivets. Exc.
cond. $28.50
FROG AX: Black leather. 4x7.5" body
covers entire head. Flap closure with
strap hides fittings for missing pick. Steel
clip at back & maker stamped *Gebrueder
Ohliger Kaiserslautern*. Above avg.
cond. $25.00
FROG DRESS BAYONET: Black patent
leather. Avg. cond. $28.00
FROG LUFTWAFFE 98K BAYONET: 4
alum. rivets & sewn construction.
Stamped *Gebruder Klinge Dresden 1937
LBA(S)*. Exc. cond. $91.00
HANGER ARMY OFFICER DAGGER
DELUXE PATTERN: Alum. brocade
facings on green velvet straps. Oak
leaves to all gray metal fittings. Avg.
cond. $46.50
HANGER ARMY OFFICER DAGGER
DELUXE PATTERN: Bright alum.
brocade facings to green velvet straps.
Oak leaves to all frosted silver fittings.
Near mint cond. $115.00

HANGER ARMY OFFICER DAGGER
DELUXE PATTERN

HANGER ARMY OFFICER DAGGER DELUXE PATTERN: Alum. brocade facing to green velvet straps. Oak leaves to all gray metal fittings with silver frosted finish. Avg. cond. $82.00

HANGER ARMY OFFICER DAGGER: Alum. brocade facing on green velvet. Oak leaves to alum. buckles & slides. Gray pebbled clips & aluminum loop. Avg. cond $45.00

HANGER ARMY OFFICER DAGGER: Aluminum brocade facing to green velvet straps. Alum. buckles & slides with oak leaves. Gray pebbled clips. Above avg. cond. $65.00

HANGER ARMY OFFICER DAGGER: Aluminum brocade facing to green velvet straps. Silver paint to buckles, slides & clips of gray metal with oak leaves. Avg. cond. $75.00

HANGER ARMY OFFICER DAGGER: Alum. brocade facings on green velvet straps. Oak leaves to alum. buckles & slides. Pebbled gray clips & nickel top loop. Avg. cond. $45.00

HANGER ARMY OFFICER DAGGER: Alum. brocade facings on green velvet straps. Oak leaves to brass buckles & to gray slides. Pebbled gray clips & nickel top loop. Avg. cond. $45.00

HANGER ARMY OFFICER DAGGER: Alum. brocade facings to green velvet straps with oak leaves to clips, slides & buckles. Nickel plated clip Maker *A DRGM*. Avg. cond. $95.00

HANGER ARMY OFFICER DAGGER: Alum. brocade on brown velvet. Alum. buckles & slides with oak leaves. Silver painted gray pebbled clips & alum. loop. Early. Above avg. cond. $55.00

HANGER ARMY OFFICER DAGGER: Alum. brocade on green velvet. Gray oakleave buckles & slides. Gray pebbled hooks. Below avg. cond. $40.00

HANGER ARMY OFFICER DAGGER: Alum. brocade on green velvet. Oakleave buckles & slides. Gray pebbled hooks & plain loop. Below avg. cond. $40.00

HANGER ARMY OFFICER DAGGER: Oak leaves to alum. buckles & slides. Gray pebbled clips. Alum. brocade facing to green velvet straps. Avg. cond. .. $40.00

HANGER CUSTOM OFFICIAL DAGGER: Green velvet straps with alum. brocade facing having green borders. Oak leaves to round alum. buckles, slides, clips & to alum. loops at hanger loop. Avg. cond. $375.00

HANGER LUFTWAFFE OFFICER 2ND MODEL DAGGER DELUXE PATTERN: Facings on blue felt straps. Faint gold wash to gray metal fittings with oak leaves overall. Above avg. cond. $82.00

HANGER LUFTWAFFE OFFICER 2ND MODEL DAGGER DELUXE PATTERN: Facings on gray velvet straps. Oak leaves to all gray fittings with faint gold wash. Above avg. cond. $65.00

HANGER LUFTWAFFE OFFICER 2ND MODEL DAGGER DELUXE PATTERN: Facings on gray velvet straps. Oak leaves to all fittings. Avg. cond. $40.00

HANGER LUFTWAFFE OFFICER 2ND MODEL DAGGER DELUXE PATTERN: Facings on gray velvet straps. Oak leaves to all fittings. Avg. cond. $46.00

HANGER LUFTWAFFE OFFICER 2ND MODEL DAGGER: Brocade straps & velvet backing. Oakleaves to gray buckles & slides. Gray top loop & pebbled clips. Below avg. cond. $34.00

HANGER LUFTWAFFE OFFICER 2ND MODEL DAGGER: Gray velvet straps with facing having tear down center. Gray metal clip & 2 pebbled lower clips. Oakleaves to alum. buckles & slides. Below avg. cond. $60.00

HANGER LUFTWAFFE OFFICER SWORD: 5" tall blue leather teardrop, silver painted pebbled clip & adjustment rivet. Stamped 1936/maker. Lacks belt loop with D-ring. Avg. cond. $55.00

HANGER LUFTWAFFE OFFICER SWORD: Blue leather 4" tall teardrop with 2 position strap for rivet that lacks belt loop D-ring. Pebbled alum. clip. Stamped *1936 Paul Klopfer Berlin* & blurred inked unit. Avg. cond. $40.00

HANGER NAVAL ADMIN. DAGGER: Short black strap with alum. clips, buckle & chain. Long strap has early heavy nickel/silver finished clips & lion heads buckle. Exc. cond. $250.00

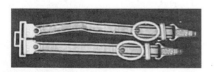

HANGER CUSTOM OFFICIAL DAGGER

HANGER NAVAL ADMIN. DAGGER

HANGER NAVAL OFFICER DAGGER: Black velvet backed water pattern artificial silk front straps, all gilded alum. lion face buckles/snaps & fitting. Avg. cond. $350.00

HANGER RAD SUBORDINATE HEWER VARIATION: 10.5" tall black leather body with spade design, leather loop with hook for scabbard & removable belt loop with nickel clip. Leather stamped *Otto Sinde Berlin 1937 etc.*Above avg. cond. $156.00

HANGER RAD SUBORDINATE HEWER: 10" tall black leather body with spade design & belt loop. Dull nickel clip. Stamped *A A&S 37 RADJ* & leather stamped 1937/maker *38 B.A.Fu.* Above avg. cond. $177.00

HANGER SA DAGGER: Brown leather strap with loop, dark nickel buckle & clip. Avg. cond. $37.00

HANGER SA DAGGER: Brown leather strap with stamped RZM, gray buckle & clip marked *RZM M5/71OLC* Avg. cond. $47.00

HANGER SA DAGGER: Brown leather with nickel clip & buckle. Leather loop. Avg. cond. $35.00

HANGER SS M33 DAGGER VERTICAL: Black leather body, loop & roller buckle strap. Nickel clip Maker *DRGMM5/8cRZM A.* Below avg. cond. $202.00

HANGER SWORD WITH SHOULDER HARNESS: White cloth shoulder strap with buckle, black leather tab & pebbled silver painted clip Maker *A DRGM* for Assmann. Above avg. cond. $30.00

HANGER SWORD WITH SHOULDER HARNESS: White cloth web harness with adjustment buckle. Brown leather tab with affixed nickel plated clip. Avg. cond. $28.00

HANGER SWORD: 6.5" long imitation pigskin body with gray pebbled clip, rivet & loop. Good wartime example. Avg. cond. $20.00

HANGER SWORD: Black leather. 7" tall teardrop body with nickel clip, rivet & loop. Avg. cond. $50.00

HANGER SWORD: Brown leather. 4" long teardrop with nickel clip & D-ring. Below avg. cond. $20.00

KNOT ARMY OFFICER SWORD: Black leather strap with silver stripes. Braided slide. Dark silver stem, cap & ball. Early. Avg. cond. $54.00

KNOT ARMY OFFICER SWORD: Green leather strap has silver stripes. Alum. to rest. Below avg. cond. $20.00

KNOT ARMY OFFICER SWORD: Below avg. cond. $20.00

KNOT ARMY OFFICER SWORD: Large size. Green leather strap with 3 double silver stripes, slide, stem, cap & ball. Exc. cond. $40.00

KNOT ARMY OFFICER SWORD: Silver cord acorn with green leather strap with silver wire striping. Avg. cond. $20.00

KNOT ARMY OFFICER SWORD: Tiestring to green leather strap with alum. stripes, slide, alum. stem, cap & ball. Mint cond. $33.00

KNOT BAYONET: Gray cloth strap, red slide, yellow stem, red cap & gray ball. Above avg. cond. $24.00

KNOT BAYONET: Green cord acorn with off-white cap & slider. Green cloth strap. Avg. cond. $24.00

KNOT BAYONET: Green strap with alum. stripes, alum. stem with green zig-zags, green cap with silver flecks & alum. ball. Above avg. cond. $26.00

KNOT FIREMAN SWORD: Black leather strap, darkening to silver stripes, silver & carmine to rest. Avg. cond. $20.00

KNOT LUFTWAFFE BAYONET: Gray leather strap with faint 1937 maker, white leather slide, red cap & gray ball. Above avg. cond. $24.00

KNOT LUFTWAFFE BAYONET: Gray pigskin strap, white slide, blue cap & gray ball. Near mint cond. $35.00

KNOT NAVAL OFFICER DAGGER: Gold cord. Long model. Avg. cond. $45.00

KNOT NCO SWORD: Green cloth strap, alum. border stripes, fixed slide to stem, green cap with silver flecks & alum. ball. Above avg. cond. $20.00

KNOT OFFICER DAGGER: Gold cord. Long model. Exc. cond. $37.00

KNOT OFFICER DAGGER: Silver cord. Long model. Exc. cond. $66.00

KNOT OFFICER DAGGER: Silver cord. Long model. Near mint cond $38.00

KNOT OFFICER DAGGER: Silver cord. Long model. Near mint cond. $51.00

KNOT OFFICER DAGGER: Silver cord. Long model. Avg. cond. $20.00

KNOT OFFICER DAGGER: Silver cord. Long model. Above avg. cond. ... $25.00

KNOT OFFICER DAGGER: Silver cord. Short model. Avg. cond. $35.00

KNOT OFFICER DAGGER: Silver cord. Short model. Below avg. cond. ... $27.00

KNOT POLICE SWORD KNOT: Municipal. Large. Black leatherette strap, alum. & red stripes. Rest alum. with tricolor bullion inset. Avg. cond. $20.00

KNOT POLICE SWORD: Municipal. Black cloth strap with alum. & red stripes is still tied with string. Mint cond. $45.00

KNOT POLICE SWORD: Municipal. Black cloth strap, alum. & red stripes. Rest alum. with tricolor bullion inset, still tied. Near mint cond. $40.00

KNOT POLICE SWORD: Municipal. Standard size with black cloth strap etc. Near mint cond. $37.00

KNOT SS NCO SWORD: 14" long overall with aluminum brocade strap having double black border stripes. Black & aluminum zigzag design to slide & stem. Black & aluminum cap & ball. Above avg. cond. $164.00

KNOT SS SWORD: Has 2 twisted silver wire & single black cord acorn & black top with silver wire braided top & 26" folded strap. Silver wire & black cord center slip. Strap silver wire with 2 black stripes. Avg. cond. $38.00

KNOT SWORD: Alum. brocade strap with black border stripes & is still tied. Alum. stem, alum. cap & ball with black cords. Mint cond. $35.00

KNOT SWORD: Alum. brocade strap with black border stripes & is still tied. Alum. stem, black cap & alum. ball with black cords. Mint cond. $20.00

KNOT SWORD: Alum. brocade strap with double black border stripes, braided slide, alum. stem, black cap, black & alum. ball. Near mint cond. $55.00

MINIATURE SWORD KNOT WITH CLIP: 5" long overall with clip to top, black cloth strap, dark age patina to all silver bullion work. Above avg. cond. $68.00

SWORD BAG: *FW Holler.* Paper. 40" long tan tapered body with flap & black inked title front etc. Unissued with blank #/ length. Near mint cond. $95.00

SWORD TAG: *Eickhorn.* 4" tall color printed shield design with maker, trademark & blank specification lines. Alum. grommet. Mint cond. $29.00

IMPERIAL GERMAN SERVICE MEDALS & DECORATIONS

AIR WAR HONOR GOBLET: About 8" tall, hammered steel body with stamped eagle in battle, *Dem Sieger im Luftkampfe* base & 4 ball mounts. Based stamped *Chef des Feldflugwesens* with Imperial eagle. Exc. cond. $3,500.00

AIR WAR HONOR GOBLET

ANHALT FIRE SERVICE HONOR MEDAL: Dark silver finish with fire helmet, equipment. White, green & red ribbon. Near mint cond. $126.00

ANHALT WAR VETERAN HONOR CROSS: Silvered cross pattee with white field. Red, green & silver center with walking bear. House order colored rb. Mint cond. $76.00

AUSTRIAN 1ST REPUBLIC PILOT BADGE: 60x65mm dark green enameled bronze wreath with bronze spread winged flying eagle. Creme colored shield below with national colors & propeller. Two piece construction with vertical pin. Mint cond. $79.00

AUSTRIAN 2ND REPUBLIC NATIONAL SERVICE ORDER IN SILVER: Large silvered medal with eagle, wreath & shields. Red & white trimmed mounted rb. Near mint cond. $45.00

AUSTRIAN AERO COMMISSION BADGE: 35mm oval. Enameled with yellow border with *Oesterreichische Aeronautische & Kommission* in black, sky blue center with

gilt eagle attached. Pb & well made & WWI. Above avg. cond. $150.00

AUSTRIAN ASSAULT (STURM) TROOP BADGE: 1.75x2" in size. Silver oval wreath with Austrian soldier throwing M-96 stick grenade with shrouded skeleton in cape embracing him. Hungarian inscription below. Pb. Mint cond. $48.00

AUSTRIAN FRANZ JOSEF BRAVERY MEDAL: 40mm. With mounted rb. Near mint cond. $95.00

AUSTRIAN LONG SERVICE CROSS 6 YEARS: Cross with roundel bearing VI in center. Yellow & black mounted rb. Near mint cond. $20.00

AUSTRIAN MILITARY SERVICE CROSS WITH CASE: Beautiful old red leatherette case with full inscription. Fancy gold *Rothe Jeweler* hallmark inside on upper silk lining. Black flocking. Full red, white enameled cross with wreath. Mounted proper rb. Mint cond. $145.00

AUSTRIAN MILITARY SILVER SERVICE CROSS: In form fitting red leatherette case with gold impressed title on lid, *Vom Offizierkorps der Luftschifferabteilung.* Medal is in wartime gray with red enamel arms. Mtd. red rb. Ornate *Rothe* maker hallmark in gold on white silk inner lid. Gray flocking. Unusual as badge was given to a member of an airship unit. Near mint cond. $350.00

AUSTRIAN SERVICE CROSS

AUSTRIAN SERVICE CROSS: Tri-fold red & white striped ribbon with Maltese 30mm enameled cross with round center red border & white inner surface *Ver Dienst* in center & white enameled on back. Red leatherette case named in gold & push button catch, black flocked fitted inner surface & white surface with gold embossed maker mark. Above avg. cond. $120.00

AUSTRO-HUNGARIAN FEMALE RED CROSS SERVICE MEDAL WITH BOX: White cardboard box with silver lettering. With red & white female broach mount. Includes miniature also. Above avg. cond. $135.00

AUSTRO-HUNGARIAN INF. SEARCH LIGHT UNIT BADGE: 45mm gold finished heavy brass disc with crown over lightening bolts & oakleave wreath border. Clip to back for right breast use. Near mint cond. $61.00

BALTIC CROSS 1ST CLASS: Silvered frame. Gilt brass cross with fleur-de-lis ends. Pb. Near mint cond. $95.00

BAVARIAN 1813/14 FATHERLAND CROSS: Issued for service against Napoleon. Finish of black worn from brass underlay. Avg. cond. $71.00

BAVARIAN 1916 CROSS: Light blue & white track style ribbon unmounted & bronze patee cross with profile in center of obv. & *7.1/1916* in center of reverse. Avg. cond. $37.00

BAVARIAN 1916 LUDWIG CROSS WITH MINIATURE: Dark wartime finish. Both with ribbons. Above avg. cond. ... $61.00

BAVARIAN 1918 GOLDEN JUBILEE MEDAL: Wartime gray. Blue, gold & white rb. Oval with busts of monarchs & full inscription. Mint cond. $65.00

BAVARIAN BRAVERY MEDAL FOR MEDICAL PERSONNEL: Silver strike. 1870 era. 40mm size with full bust, inscription. Black, white & blue ribbon. Mint cond. $1,299.00

BAVARIAN BRAVERY MEDAL: Formal dress. 35mm size with fine details & bust. Proper black, white & blue ribbon. Near mint cond. $97.00

BAVARIAN MILITARY MERIT CROSS 3RD CLASS WITH SWORDS: In issue box. Above avg. cond. $39.00

BAVARIAN MILITARY MERIT CROSS 4TH CLASS WITH SWORDS: Frosted silver finish. No rb. Above avg. cond. ... $25.00

BAVARIAN PILOT BADGE: Hollow constructed silver body with Bavarian crown to wreath & good details. Rayed reverse with vent hole shows. Stamped with maker *Karl Pollath*. Above avg. cond. $435.00

BAVARIAN RED CROSS ARMY ENAM-ELED IDENTIFICATION BADGE: 36mm. Domed. Hmkd. Pb. White & blue field with red cross. Gilt inscription, *Bayr. Rotes Kreuz Sanitatskolonne*. Near mint cond. $90.00

BRUNSWICK 1914 WAR MERIT CROSS 2ND CLASS: Near mint cond $39.00

CENTENNIAL MEDAL OF THE 16TH INF. REGT: Brass. Obv. with busts of Friedrich Wilhelm, Wilhelm II. Verso with wreath & regimental inscription. Avg. cond. $32.00

COLONIAL BADGE SUDSEE AFRIKA KIAUTSCHOU: 33x37mm solid silver badge with raised details, Pb & *Ges.Geschutzt Nr. 33992*. Near mint cond. $110.00

COLONIAL SERVICE MEDAL FOR BLACK TROOPER: Large silver medal with wreath & inscription. Black & white rb. Above avg. cond. $526.00

COLONIAL SOUTHWEST AFRICA 1884 COMMEMORATIVE MEDAL: 30mm brass. Obv. with view of the Nautiulus memorial. Verso with full inscription. National color rb. Mint cond. $65.00

COLONIAL SOUTHWEST AFRICA COMBAT MEDAL: For 1904-1906 combat service. Unmounted ribbon. Exc. cond. $59.00

COMMEMORATIVE MEDALLION ZEPPE-LIN L.Z 125 1924 AMERICA TRIP: 34mm round silvered brass with Dr. Hugo Eckener profile on 1 side & other is a Zeppelin over coast line & list of stop at base. *Made for export* & *Made in Germany* on back. Avg. cond. $64.00

DUPPEL 1864 WAR CROSS: Proper orange, blue, black & white rb. Above avg. cond. $65.00

EAST FRONT CROSS: Unmounted ribbon. Green enameled patee cross with dates 1914 1918 on horizontal arms. Avg. cond. $59.00

FIELD HONOR BADGE: Large silver starburst with affixed white enamel cross, gold cross swords & silver soldier profile center. Wide pin & 2 rivet construction. Hamburg marked back. Avg. cond. $50.00

FIELD HONOR BADGE: Large silver starburst with affixed white enamel cross, gold cross swords & soldier profile center. Pb & 2 rivet construction. Hamburg maker marked back. Avg. cond. $65.00

FRANKFURT 1815 WAR NAPOLEONIC PERIOD MEDAL: Large silvered badge with crowned eagle design. White & red rb. Near mint cond. $300.00

FREI KORP BERLIN SLEEVE BADGE: Rampant bear under Berlin crown. Bronze oak leaf trim. Oval shaped badge. Pierced for sleeve wear. Mint cond. $110.00

FREI KORP BREMEN IRON LEGION 1919 BADGE: Oval bronze finished with medieval knight, cathedral. Ancient style inscription. Pb. Mint cond. $90.00

FREI KORP HAMBURG SLEEVE BADGE: Silvered brass oval with three coats of arms, Hamburg logo. Wreath trim. Pierced for sewing on to sleeve. Mint cond. $110.00

FREI KORP HEUCHKEL MORTAR UNIT SLEEVE SHIELD: Oval wreath with skull at top resting on bones. Silvered raised *MWH* lettering for *Minen Werfer Heuchkel*. Pierced for sleeve wear. Near mint cond. $139.00

FREI KORP VON DIEBITSCH
NECK ORDER

FREI KORP VON DIEBITSCH NECK ORDER: Only 20 known to have been issued. 1st class. Pierced gilt crown suspension with gilt framed black Malta cross utilizing crossed swords. Stag head on center medallion. Yellow & black neck rb. Mint cond. $519.00

FREI KORP VON DIEBITSCH SILVER SERVICE MEDAL: Issued for exceptional horse training. Fancy Garde Star to center of medal with inscription. Yellow & black rb. Mint cond. $130.00

FREI KORPS BALTIC DIVISION BADGE: 1.5x2". Oval silver metal wreath with open work center showing inverted sword piercing silver shield with black Baltic cross. Pb. Mint cond. $155.00

FREI KORPS HAMBURG SLEEVE SHIELD: Oval, pebbled finish with wreath. 3 coats of arms in center. Designed to be sewn to sleeve. Mint cond. $117.00

FREI KORPS VON DIEBITSCH MERIT CROSS 1ST CLASS: Extremely rare. Gilt framed Malta cross with black enamel arms. Crossed swords with crest in center. Crown suspension with black & yellow rb. Mint cond. $410.00

FREI KORPS VON DIEBITSCH SERVICE ORDER 1ST CLASS: Only approx. 20 ever issued. Gilt framed black enamel Malta cross with crossed swords. Crown suspension. Black & yellow neck ribbon. Mint cond. $455.00

HANNOVER 2ND INF REGT #77 CENTENNIAL MEDAL: 1913. Silvered finish. Obv. with bust of Kaiser & Garde du Corps helmet. Verso with 1813-1913 dates & memorial. Proper ladder style rb. Avg. cond. $39.00

HANNOVER COMMEMORATIVE SERVICE MEDAL: Round bronze colored medal with wreath & inscription. Swords mounted on yellow & white rb. Above avg. cond. $47.00

HANSEATIC CROSS HAMBURG: Full enamel work. Above avg. cond. . $30.00

HANSEATIC CROSS HAMBURG: Red enameled with silver castle center. Avg. cond. $52.00

HESSE-CASSEL CIVIL SERVICE CROSS 1ST MODEL: Issued between 1832-47 & struck in silver. With ribbon. Mint cond. $1,299.00

HESSE-DARMSTADT LONG
SERVICE GOLDEN MEDAL

HESSE-DARMSTADT LONG SERVICE GOLDEN MEDAL: Silver gilt with exceptionally fine portrait of Ernst Ludwig. Burgundy & black rb. Mint cond. $162.00

HESSE-DARMSTADT LUDWIG LONG & LOYAL SERVICE ORDER: Gilt brass medal with bust of Ernst Ludwig & inscription. Burgundy & black rb. Mint cond. $195.00

HESSE-DARMSTADT WAR HONOR SERVICE MEDAL: White & red ribbon.

Bright brass body with cipher, crown & inscription. Mint cond. $65.00

HESSE-DARMSTADT WAR REMEM-BRANCE BADGE: Iron style. Black circular wreath with silvered Crown above & cipher in center. Shield with *25* below. Straight pin. Near mint cond. $65.00

HESSEN 1840-66 GENERAL CAMPAIGN MEDAL: Bronze finish. Unmounted ribbon. Avg. cond. $55.00

HESSEN SILVER LIFE SAVING MEDAL: With bust of Duke Ernst Ludwig. Blue, white, & red barred ribbon. Near mint cond. $234.00

HOHENZOLLERN HUNTER HONOR BADGE: Beautiful open work silver stag head with crowns enclosing crown & device. Vertical pin. Mint cond. . $130.00

HOHENZOLLERN PRINCE WILHELM GOLD BENE MERENTI MEDAL: Actual gold. Beautiful strike of bust of prince with inscription. Old & proper white & black Hohenzollern House Order ribbon. Near mint cond. $1,299.00

IRON CROSS 1813
2ND CLASS

IRON CROSS 1813 2ND CLASS: Magnetic black centers, blank front & 1813 reverse. Silver frame & ribbon ring. Above avg. cond. $492.00

IRON CROSS 1870
1ST CLASS

IRON CROSS 1870 1ST CLASS: By *J.WAGNER & S. 14 LOTIG.* Silver frame. Magnetic black center. Wide pin & stamped title maker to back. Above avg. cond. $900.00

IRON CROSS 1870 1ST CLASS: Magnetic black center. Silver frame. Wide pin. Exc. cond. $1,109.00

IRON CROSS 1870 2ND CLASS WITH OAK LEAVES: Silver frame with non-magnetic black centers. 24mm wide 3 silver oak leaves with *25* center, 2 round prongs & clean ribbon. Near mint cond. $345.00

IRON CROSS 1870 2ND CLASS WITH OAK LEAVES: magnetic black centers, silver frame, ribbon with affixed silver oak leaves & bar with enamel EK. Exc. cond. $950.00

IRON CROSS 1914 1ST CLASS WITH CASE & BOX: Maroon leatherette case with paper 1914 EK affixed. White satin & purple velvet lining. Magnetic black center, tarnished frame, swollen pin & stamped *KO*. 4 line title label to storage box. Above avg. cond. $200.00

IRON CROSS 1914 1ST CLASS WITH CASE & MINIATURE: Maroon leatherette case with paper 1914 EK affixed. White satin & purple velvet lining. Magnetic black center, swollen pin & stamped *KO*. 15mm Pb EK with fair details. Above avg. cond. $120.50

IRON CROSS 1914 1ST
CLASS WITH CASE

IRON CROSS 1914 1ST CLASS WITH CASE: Black leatherette body with checkered design & silver EK outline. White lid lining & purple velvet base. Magnetic black center. Pb. Stamped *KO*. Above avg. cond. $114.00

IRON CROSS 1914 1ST CLASS WITH CASE: Black leatherette case with EK outline to lid, white satin & velvet lined. Magnetic black vaulted body, bright silver frame, wide pin & stamped *950* with double headed eagle trademark. Exc. cond. $306.00

IRON CROSS 1914 1ST CLASS WITH CASE: Leatherette body with silver EK outline, white satin lid lining & purple velvet base. Magnetic black center, dark silver frame is vaulted. Pb & stamped 800. Avg. cond. $125.00

IRON CROSS 1914 1ST CLASS: Magnetic black center with darkening to silver frame that is vaulted. Wide Pb. Avg. cond. $72.00

IRON CROSS 1914 1ST CLASS: Magnetic black center with darkening to silver frame that is vaulted. Wire Pb. Avg. cond. $124.00

IRON CROSS 1914 1ST CLASS: Screw back. Magnetic black center, slightly vaulted bright silver frame, double screw posts with nuts & silver disc backing plate. Above avg. cond. $99.00

IRON CROSS 1914 1ST CLASS: Screw back. Magnetic black center, slightly vaulted silver frame, prong to top arm, threaded stud & winged nut & silver backing disc. Above avg. cond. $175.00

IRON CROSS 1914 1ST CLASS: Screw back. Magnetic black center, slightly vaulted silver frame, threaded stud & Polish brass disc *A.Nagalski etc. Warszawa*. Above avg. cond. ... $225.00

IRON CROSS 1914 1ST CLASS: Screw back. Magnetic black center, slightly vaulted silver frame, threaded stud & nut & gray metal backing disc. Avg. cond. $250.00

IRON CROSS 1914
1ST CLASS

IRON CROSS 1914 1ST CLASS: Screw back. Magnetic black center, slightly vaulted silver frame, threaded stud & stamped *J.H.Werner Berlin*. Silver backing disc & round nut with pivot loop. Exc. cond. $250.00

IRON CROSS 1914 1ST CLASS: Screw back. Magnetic center, vaulted silver frame, threaded stud & stamped 800. Small silver EK shape backing plate & disc with DRGM#. Exc. cond. ... $175.00

IRON CROSS 1914 1ST CLASS: Variation. Magnetic black center, dark silver frame with stamped *800*, slightly vaulted & 2 threaded posts with nuts. 2" diam. Gray metal backing disc with 12 sew-on holes. Avg. cond. $136.00

IRON CROSS 1914 2ND CLASS WITH CASE: Austrian issue. Gold title to maroon leatherette case with rounded

end. White satin lid lining has gold maker *Rothe & Neffe Wien etc.* with eagle trademark. White velvet fitted base. Magnetic EK, frosted silver frame & tri-fold ribbon. Mint cond. $370.00

IRON CROSS 1914 2ND CLASS WITH CASE: Black leather body, paper maker tag attached to back *Max Pinnow Duisburg*, white lid lining with elastic loops for ribbon & fitted white velvet base. Magnetic black center, bright silver frame & long ribbon. Near mint cond. $200.00

IRON CROSS 1914 2ND
CLASS WITH CASE

IRON CROSS 1914 2ND CLASS WITH CASE: Gray leatherette body with paper EK to lid, purple satin lining & velvet fitted base. Magnetic black center. Exc. cond. $269.00

IRON CROSS 1914 2ND CLASS WITH CASE: Red leatherette hinged lid box with form fitted dark green flocking liner for EK: white silk upper lid. Upper lid of box has gilt metallic pierced crown & cipher (double initials). EK has *w* hallmark on ring. Complete with compartment for ribbon. Near mint cond. $200.00

IRON CROSS 1914 2ND CLASS WITH RIBBON BAR: Magnetic black centers, dark frame & long ribbon. 1" wide ribbon bar with silver EK device & Pb. Avg. cond. $24.00

IRON CROSS 1914 2ND CLASS: Magnetic black centers. Avg. cond. $30.00

IRON CROSS 1914 2ND CLASS: Non-combatant. Magnetic black centers, darkening to frame & white ribbon with black stripes. Above avg. cond. .. $30.00

IRON CROSS 1914 2ND CLASS: On medal bar mount. Magnetic. Ring is hmkd *Z*. Bar hmkd *DRP*. Above avg. cond. $37.00

IRON CROSS 1914 2ND CLASS: Rb. Has patriotic national color bow mounted to it with celluloid picture of von Mackensen in hussar busby in center shield. Near mint cond. $65.00

IRON CROSS BAR 1914 FOR 1870 IRON CROSS 2ND CLASS: 13mm black enameled IC 1914 cross on 33mm silver metal slide bar. Not hmkd. Pebbled back bar with good detail. Avg. cond. $320.00

IRON CROSS OAK LEAVES FOR 1870 EK 2ND CLASS: 27mm wide. Has 3 dark silver oak leaves with *25* center, 2 flat prongs & 3.5" long ribbon. Near mint cond. $167.00

JEWISH RABBI MILITARY SERVICE NECK BADGE: 50x65mm flat style white enamel trimmed black Latin cross with separately affixed silver open work Star of David. Mounted on black Iron Cross ribbon. Above avg. cond. $1,948.00

KAISER COMMEMORATIVE COIN OF HIS 1912 VISIT TO ROME: 45mm round of silver white metal with high relief of Kaiser & wife & other side is of the trip & dated. Near mint cond. $54.00

KAISER WILHELM II 80TH BIRTHDAY HONOR BADGE: Gilt open wreath with crown, *W* cipher, dates & age in Roman numerals. Pb. Mint cond. $87.00

KAISER WILHELM SILVER
JUBILEE HONOR BADGE

KAISER WILHELM SILVER JUBILEE HONOR BADGE: Rb. is of the Black Eagle Order. Mtd. rb. with silver wreath, XXV numbers on front. 1913 25th ann. of reign. Near mint cond. $162.00

KONIGRATZ 1866 CROSS: Complete with original old ribbon. Avg. cond. $35.00

KYFFHAUSERBUND WWI VETERAN MEDAL: Oval. Brass. With ribbon. Exc. cond. $20.00

LAPEL CHAIN 6 PLACE: 4" double gold chain with stick pins to each side with 1914 EK, Friedrich August Konig von Sachsen medal, 1914 *FA* cross, silver 20 year cross, Kriegsmarine 1914/18 cross with swords & Schlesien eagle. Above avg. cond. $145.00

LAPEL CHAIN 7 PLACE: 4.5" chain with stick pins to each side. 15mm EK 1870 with 25 oakleaves, 2 Kriegsverdienst medal, 1870/1871 War medal 1863 Cross, 1897 Wilhelm der Grosse, *UTTA III* bar. Above avg. cond. $166.00

LAPEL CHAIN 7 PLACE

LIPPE-DETMOLD MILITARY SERVICE MEDAL: 1914 issue. Antique bronze finish with wreath, cipher & crossed swords. Red rb. with yellow border. Near mint cond. $97.00

LIPPE-PETNOLD ORDER OF THE CROSS OF HONOR NECK ORDER: WWI. 70x100mm gilt with hinged crown top on double sided white enameled Maltese cross with 8 rayed star centers on both sides, *Fur Treue Und Verdienst* & red flower center. Other crown over *L* on red, crossed sword. Multi-piece construction with hanging loop. Above avg. cond. $2,100.00

LUBECK 1914 WAR MERIT CROSS: In gilt & red enamel with black eagle. Red & white rb. Mint cond. $58.00

MACHINE GUNNER SLEEVE BADGE: Stamped steel oval with MG08 on sledge. Gold painted finish. Gray wool oval & gray backing plate stamped *C.E.Juncker etc.* Avg. cond. $136.00

MECKLENBURG-SCHWERIN 1849 MILITARY MERIT CROSS: Gilt plated bronze 40mm Maltese cross FF center, crown at top & date base on arms & wording on other side. Above avg. cond. $250.00

MECKLENBURG-SCHWERIN 1849 WAR SERVICE CROSS 2ND CLASS: Fine high gold gilt finish with yellow, blue & red barred ribbon. Mint cond. $325.00

MECKLENBURG-SCHWERIN 1870 SERVICE CROSS 2ND CLASS: Complete with original ribbon. Gilt finish. Avg. cond. $117.00

MECKLENBURG-SCHWERIN 1877 SERVICE CROSS 2ND CLASS:

Complete with rb. Very rare. Gilt remains. Near mint cond. $527.00

MECKLENBURG-SCHWERIN 1914 WAR SERVICE CROSS 2ND CLASS: 1914 issue. Fine gold finish with excellent details. Yellow, blue & red rb. Near mint cond. $52.00

MECKLENBURG-SCHWERIN FRIEDRICH FRANZ CROSS: Latin cross in gilt brass with wreath & ladder style ribbon. Above avg. cond. $105.00

MECKLENBURG-SCHWERIN LONG SERVICE CROSS: Gilt plated bronze 35 mm Maltese cross with round center/ crown over script letters & other side *XV*, has unmounted ribbon of light blue center with white red stripes border. Near mint cond. $50.00

MECKLENBURG-STRELITZ LIFE SAVING MEDAL: 1922-34. Large gilt brass medal showing two figures clasping hands. Yellow rb. with red & blue rb. 40mm size. Mint cond. $292.00

MECKLENBURG-STRELITZ NCO SERVICE CROSS 21 YEAR: Silver finish with cross pattee, cipher & crown. Multi-colored ribbon. Near mint cond. $195.00

MECKLENBURG-STRELITZ OFFICER LONG SERVICE CROSS 25 YEAR: Gilt cross pattee with cipher, inscription. Mint cond. $162.00

MECKLENBURG-STRELITZ PRINCE ADOLPH FRIEDRICH SERVICE MEDAL: Dull silver finish with bust of prince & inscription. Complete with multi-colored original ribbon. Near mint cond. $105.00

MECKLENBURG-STRELITZ SERVICE MEDAL: Bust of Prince Adolph Friedrich. Silver finish to medal with proper barred rb. Near mint cond. $130.00

MEDAL BAR 10 PLACE NAVY

MEDAL BAR 10 PLACE NAVY: 10.5" wide bar has angled tri-fold ribbons. 1914 EK, Saxon gold merit cross, Saxon bravery medal, Hindenburg cross with swords, Kaiser Cent., Saxon service silver medal, Saxon Landwehr service medal, Austrian silver bravery medal, Austrian bronze bravery medal & Hungarian WWI service. Brass pin. Above avg. cond. $850.00

MEDAL BAR 3 PLACE: 1914 Iron Cross 2nd class/1914 Hamburg Service Cross/ Hindenburg Cross with swords. Above avg. cond. $85.00

MEDAL BAR 3 PLACE: 1914 Iron Cross 2nd class/Hindenburg Cross with swords/ Red Cross Service medal. Large flat style ribbon mounts. Above avg. cond. $80.00

MEDAL BAR 3 PLACE: Bavarian 3rd class service cross with swords. 1914 EK 2nd & Bavarian 3rd Class Service Medal. Double wrapped ribbons & brass pin. Avg. cond. $150.00

MEDAL BAR 4 PLACE BAVARIAN: Group includes 1914 Iron Cross 2nd class. Bavarian Military Service Cross 4th class with swords. Hindenburg Cross with swords. Bavarian 9 Year Long Service medal. Pb. Exc. cond. $133.00

MEDAL BAR 4 PLACE SAXON

MEDAL BAR 4 PLACE SAXON: Bar consists of 1914 Iron Cross 2nd class/ General Saxon Honor Cross with swords for combatant/Friedrich August medal/ Hindenburg Cross with swords. Above avg. cond. $129.00

MEDAL BAR 4 PLACE: Hindenburg Cross with swords/Prussian 1916 War Service cross/1897 Centennial medal/9 Year Long Service medal. Avg. cond. $71.00

MEDAL BAR 6 PLACE DIPLOMAT: Reverse order medals with slanted angle to be worn on diplomatic frock coats. Medals, in order, consist of 9 Year Long Service medal/1897 Kaiser Wilhelm Centennial medal/Landwehr II class medal/Non-Combatant Hindenburg Cross/2nd Class Wesen Veteran Cross/Russian Order of St. Ann. Werner-Godet maker tag. Exc. cond. $150.00

MINIATURE BLUE MAX CROSS: 17mm blue enamel arms with gold letters & eagle between each arm. Button hole disc at back. Above avg. cond. . $225.00

MINIATURE JAEGER HONOR BADGE: 25x25mm. Open work design of stag skull with antlers. Crossed *L* ciphers below crown. Pb. Mint cond. $117.00

NAVAL 1914-18 CROSS WITH BAR *BELGIEN*: Above avg. cond. $90.00

NAVAL AIRSHIP PILOT COMMEMORA-
TIVE BADGE: 61x69mm silvered brass
with stamped oval wreath with crown at
top & with airship center. Avg.
cond. $855.00

NAVAL LAND PILOT BADGE PRINZEN
SIZE: High gilt finish. Fine details to
wreath, flying eagle & buildings. Pin back.
30x46.5mm in size. Near mint cond.
$350.00

NAVAL OBSERVER FLIGHT BADGE:
Hollow body with vent hole, Pb &
stamped *800* double headed eagle
trademark. Frosted gold finish. Near mint
cond. $1,441.00

NAVAL PILOT BADGE: Prinzen size.
Antique gilt gold finish with flying eagle &
sun burst. Vertical pin. Near mint
cond. $162.00

NAVAL U-BOAT BADGE: Thin stamped
bronze oval with crown over U-boat, Pb.
Gilt finish. Near mint cond. $93.00

OLDENBURG 1813 CIVIL SERVICE
MEDAL: Gold finish with early style
crown, inscription. Blue & red rb. Mint
cond. $1,753.00

OLDENBURG 1870/71 WAR MEDAL: Made
from melted down cannon bronze. With
ribbon. Mint cond $260.00

OLDENBURG 1871 WAR
SERVICE MEDAL

OLDENBURG 1871 WAR SERVICE
MEDAL: Silver finish. Complete with an
old multi-colored ribbon. Above avg.
cond. $325.00

OLDENBURG 1914 FREDREICH AUGUST
CROSS 2ND CLASS: Dark bronze pattee
cross with date. With ribbon. Above avg.
cond. $39.00

OLDENBURG 1914 WAR SERVICE
CROSS 1ST CLASS: Dark wartime
finish. Mint cond. $82.00

OLDENBURG 1914 WAR SERVICE
CROSS 2ND CLASS WITH BAR FOR
COURAGE BEFORE THE FOE: Red &
blue rb. Dark badge. Near mint
cond. $100.00

PILOT BADGE PRUSSIAN: Stamped.
Magnetic body with frosted silver finish.
Pb. Above avg. cond. $275.00

PRIZE MEDAL TURNVERIN 1924 5000
METER 2ND PLACE: 40mm bronze with
DT on front & engraved on back for
Hannover. Avg. cond. $53.00

PRUSSIA 1864 WAR MEDAL: War against
Schleswig-Holstein. Bright bronze finish.
Proper black rb. with yellow, white stripes.
Above avg. cond. $51.00

PRUSSIAN 1914/18
ORDER OF LUISE

PRUSSIAN 1914/18 ORDER OF LUISE:
32mm double sided Maltese cross with
black enameled arms & blue centers & L
& reverse is 1914/18. Has loop for
hanging. Above avg. cond. $900.00

PRUSSIAN AVIATION LAPEL PIN: 18mm
round brass with sky blue enameled field,
Prussian crown over black eagle on
shield with 4 white prop blades & letters
K C AE in between prop. Hmkd on
back. $167.00

PRUSSIAN KAISER WILHELM II 80TH
BIRTHDAY BADGE: 35mm stamped
bronze solid metal & over cut with crown
over *W* over *1859-1939 LXXX*. made.
Avg. cond. $93.00

PRUSSIAN LONG SERVICE CROSS 15
YEAR: Copper/bronze cross with crown
center, *XV* reverse & blue water pattern
ribbon. Avg. cond. $49.00

PRUSSIAN MAIN-ARMY WAR CROSS:
With proper rb. Near mint cond. . $52.00

PRUSSIAN OBSERVER BADGE: Hollow
silver body, vent hole, 2 enamel prongs
to square center. Pb. & stamped
C.E.Juncker Berlin 800 to rayed backing.
Near mint cond. $750.00

PRUSSIAN PILOT BADGE PRINZEN SIZE: 45mm stamped white metal with crown over cutout pilot badge. Well made & Pb. Above avg. cond. $50.00

PRUSSIAN PILOT BADGE: Hollow back pattern as used in the field. Drawn pin construction. Wartime piece. Near mint cond. $227.00

PRUSSIAN PILOT BADGE: Prinzen size. Finely detailed with open work center. Delicate construction with narrow straight pin. Near mint cond. $97.00

PRUSSIAN PILOT BADGE: Silver hollow body with ventholes & highlights show use. Pb & stamped 800. Above avg. cond. $575.00

PRUSSIAN PILOT
BADGE

PRUSSIAN PILOT COMMEMORATIVE BADGE: 46x73mm heavy body with dark patina. Excellent details to front. Wide pin. With stamped *925* & a double headed eagle shield proof. Mint cond. $801.00

PRUSSIAN PILOT REMEMBRANCE BADGE: Fine old period piece in silver. Drawn pin construction. Beautiful details. Near mint cond. $625.00

PRUSSIAN RED CROSS MEDAL: Dark bronze disc pendant with cross engraved. Bow style ribbon for presentation to women. Ribbon shows light soiling. Above avg. cond. $36.00

PRUSSIAN REGIMENTAL JUBILEE MEDAL OF THE 6TH KURASSIER REGIMENT: Issued for the 25th anniversary of Czar Nicholas I as Cheif of the regiment. Cyrillic device with fine silver body. Dark blue Russian mounted style rb. Near mint cond. $195.00

PRUSSIAN SERVICE CROSS: 1912 issue. Fine gold finish to cross pattee with cipher. Yellow & blue rb. Near mint cond. $97.00

PRUSSIAN ST. JOHN ORDER LUXURY GRADE: Heavy gilt gold body with full white enamel arm. Pb. Also known as the Malta Cross. Mint cond. $270.00

PRUSSIAN WAR SERVICE VETERAN HONOR CROSS: 1914-18 dated. Black & white enameled cross pattee with silver crossed swords. Black & white rb. Very similar to the Hohenzollern House Order design which was given to German Pour le Merite winners. Mint cond. $82.00

PRUSSIAN RED EAGLE ORDER MEDAL: Gilt plated bronze 25mm round with Maltese cross center & eagle & reverse is gothic letters, on unmounted white ribbon with golden yellow border stripes. Above avg. cond. $73.00

RED CROSS SERVICE MEDAL: Long unmounted ribbon red with 2 black & white stripes on either side, 32mm gray medal round. Avg. cond. $20.00

RIBBON BAR 7 PLACE: Ribbons are 1914 EK. Hindenburg cross with swords, Austrian War Service medal with swords, Long Service, Prussian Life Saving, Hungarian War Service with swords, Bulgarian War Service. Brass pin. Above avg. cond. $36.00

RIBBON BAR 9 PLACE

RIBBON BAR 9 PLACE: Pb. White metal backing. Medals include EK 1914, Bavarian Mil. Svc. order with swords, Hindenburg Cross with swords, 1939 War Service rb. with swords, Bulgarian Mil. Merit medal with swords, Turkish War Service with swords, etc. All Above avg. cond. $72.00

SAXE-ALTENBURG 1849 WAR MEDAL: Gilt brass with wreath, date. On dark green rb. with white stripes. Above avg. cond. $260.00

SAXE-ALTENBURG DUKE ERNST WAR CROSS 1ST CLASS: Large silver badge with cross pattee, swords & bust of duke. Pb. Very rare type. Near mint cond. $877.00

SAXE-COBURG-GOTHA 1914/18 WAR SERVICE MEDAL: In wartime gray finish with ribbon & rare unattached bar with crossed swords, 1914/18 dates. Mint cond. $49.00

SAXE-COBURG-GOTHA ARTS & SCIENE SERVICE MEDAL: Era of Duke Carl Eduard. Gold class with green & silver ribbon. Mint cond. $164.00

SAXE-COBURG-GOTHA DUKE CARD EDUARD JUBILEE MEDAL: In dark antique silver finish. Well detailed. Complete with multi-colored rb. Mint cond. $130.00

SAXE-MEININGEN 1914/15 WAR MEDAL: With beautiful dark bronze finish. Proper black, yellow, ribbed style ribbon. Near mint cond. $75.00

SAXE-WEIMAR 1914 WAR MERIT MEDAL: Gilt finish. Exc. cond. $98.00

SAXE-WEIMAR SERVICE MEDAL 9 YEAR: Silvered finish with cipher, crown & inscription. Green, yellow & black rb. Above avg. cond. $62.00

SAXON CAROLA MEDAL: Bronze. Nicely detailed bust & inscription. Complete with yellow, black & blue rb. Near mint cond. $78.00

SAXON KING FRIEDRICH AUGUST ROYAL LABOR MEDAL: Silver grade. Nicely struck with good details. Medium forest green rb. Near mint cond. . $58.00

SAXON SERVICE CROSS: In gold gilt finish with proper green & white banded ribbon. Near mint cond. $75.00

SCHAUMBERG-LIPPE MERIT MEDAL: Crown hanger with silver pendant. Exc. cond. $145.00

SCHAUMBURG-LIPPE JUBILEE MEDAL: In antique silver finish with heads of the monarchs. Proper white rb. with blue & red border. Near mint cond. $95.00

SCHWARZBURG-RUDOLSTADT 1870 WAR MEDAL: Large silver badge with cipher, crown, date. Blue & yellow rb. Above avg. cond. $584.00

SCHWARZBURG-RUDOLSTADT 1870 WAR MEDAL: Silver finish with ring. Wreath with inscription. No ribbon. Very rare as the principality was exceptionally small & few such medals were issued. Above avg. cond. $555.00

SCHWARZBURG-SONDERHAUSEN ART & SCIENCE SERVICE MEDAL: Antique silver with portrait of duke. Dark blue rb. Above avg. cond. $117.00

SCWARZBURG 1914 WAR MEDAL: Silvered finish. Large size with cipher, date & crown. Blue & yellow rb. Above avg. cond. $65.00

STICKPIN MINIATURE 1914 IRON CROSS: 18mm. Knurled stickpin mount. Near mint cond. $33.00

STICKPIN MINIATURE PRUSSIAN PILOT BADGE: About 20mm tall frosted silver badge with good details. Knurled pin. Near mint cond. $50.00

TANK BATTLE BADGE: Die struck hollow with back plate open throw the eyes of the skull to the back plate. One of the rarest of all German badges. 44x67mm in size. weight 19.7 grams. These badges were made after WWI for a very small group of men, tank crews. Long vertical flat sided pin. Near mint cond. .. $795.00

TANK BATTLE BADGE

TANK BATTLE BADGE: Hollow constructed silver body has vent hole & wide pin. Vent holes to eyes & nose of skull. Above avg. cond. $1,000.00

WALDECK 1814-15 NAPOLEONIC WAR MEDAL: Dark bronze finish. Very clean with gold, black & red rb. Near mint cond. $649.00

WALDECK FRIEDRICH-BATHILDES WAR MEDAL: Dark bronze finish. Complete with black orange, red ribbon. Mint cond. $204.00

WALDECK MILITARY SERVICE ORDER 3RD CLASS: Silvered cross pattee with gilt ring. Red enamel center with silver crowned cipher. Proper rb. Near mint cond. $292.00

WATERLOO MEDAL ISSUED TO GERMAN SOLDIERS WHO FOUGHT IN THE BATTLE: 35mm. Bronze. Obv. with bust of Friedrich Wilhelm. Verso with wreath, 1815 date & commemorative inscription. Rim named to Ernst Pabst, 3rd Line Battalion. 100% original with age wear. Highly collectable as few have survived the following years. Avg. cond. . $225.00

WESTPHALIA 1809 BRAVERY MEDAL: Oval medal with cipher, crown, design of 6 cannon balls. Early Napoleonic piece. Near mint cond. $555.00

WESTPHALIA NAPOLEONIC BRAVERY MEDAL 2ND PATTERN: Oval badge with arms trophy, 7 cannon balls. Old blue & white ribbon. Above avg. cond. $438.00

WOUND BADGE 1914 BLACK: Cutout.
Stamped. Pb. Above avg.
cond. $45.00
WOUND BADGE 1914 BLACK: Stamped
steel. Pb. Avg. cond. $20.00
WOUND BADGE 1914 BLACK: Stamped
steel. Pb. Above avg. cond. $20.00
WOUND BADGE 1914 GOLD: Pb. Mint
cond. $53.00
WOUND BADGE 1914 GOLD: Custom
made of high quality material with
beautiful toned gold finish for officer
tunic. Near mint cond. $38.00

WOUND BADGE 1914 GOLD

WOUND BADGE 1914 GOLD: Magnetic
stamped steel, gold finish. Pb. Above
avg. cond. $75.00
WOUND BADGE 1914 SILVER: Cutout.
Stamped brass with frosted silver finish.
Pb. Avg. cond. $55.00
WOUND BADGE 1914 SILVER: Screw
back. Stamped brass body with silver
finish worn at highlights. Threaded stud
at back & rayed disc with socket. Above
avg. cond. $135.00

WOUND BADGE NAVAL BLACK

WOUND BADGE NAVAL BLACK: Brass
body with subdued black finish. Pb. Near
mint cond. $80.00
WOUND BADGE NAVAL BLACK: Stamped
steel with black paint to chain wreath with
crossed swords to anchor center. Pb.
Above avg. cond. $42.00
WOUND BADGE NAVAL SILVER: Stamped
steel with silver paint to chain border,
anchor & crossed swords. Pb. Near mint
cond. $150.00
WURTTEMBERG 1914 BRAVERY MEDAL:
Silver. With black & yellow rb. Mint
cond. $39.00

WURTTEMBERG 1916
CHARLOTTEN CROSS

WURTTEMBERG 1916 CHARLOTTEN
CROSS: Silver finish. Black & yellow
ribbon. Near mint cond. $58.00
WURTTEMBERG WILHELM CROSS WITH
SWORDS: Dark bronze finish. Complete
with yellow & black striped rb. Above avg.
cond. $100.00

**IMPERIAL GERMAN HOUSE
ORDERS & BADGES**

ANHALT ALBRECHT THE BEAR ORDER
COMMANDER BADGE: Large oval silver
gilt badge with double loop ring. Fine

details to crowned bear, inscription. Mint cond. $714.00

ANHALT ORDER OF ALBERT THE BEAR KNIGHT CLASS: Crown suspension. Silver finish. Green & red ribbon. Near mint cond. $251.00

AUSTRIAN/BOURBON
GOLDEN FLEECE ORDER

AUSTRIAN/BOURBON GOLDEN FLEECE ORDER: One of Europe's oldest Orders, founded 1430 by the first Duke of Burgundy. Awarded only by the Bourbon courts of old Imperial Austria & royal Spain. The Spanish Order is very simple but the Austrian version reflects the ancient splendor of knightly Europe. This example has 4 separate elements all attached to a proper large red neck ribbon. Gold & blue oval pendant integral to ribbon. Matching gold & blue suspension mount with motto *Praeium Laborum Nonville*. Red flames below with dark oval center having white & black work. Actual gold hanging lamb of the Golden Fleece. Superb early construction, circa 1900 period. The only other Order of Europe that is older is that of the Gaiter, UK, founded 1340 by Edward III Plantagenet of England. The Austrian Order is no longer officially bestowed & only a few

examples such as this have been found. Mint cond. $3,650.00

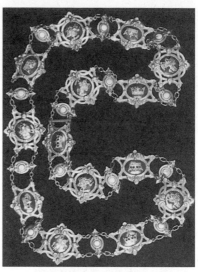

BADEN BERTHOLD I
ORDER NECK CHAIN

BADEN BERTHOLD I ORDER NECK CHAIN: 31" gilt silver necklace. Hmkd *900* & with a double clasp catch. Alternating links of crown & man with banner on horse on red enameled field & white stone center links. WWI era. Above avg. cond. $7,000.00

BADEN DUKEDOM HOUSE ORDER OF THE ZAHRINGEN LION: Large Commander neck order with heavy gold gilt field. Dark enamel cross with beautiful hand painted enamel order insignia in center. Mint cond. $527.00

BADEN FIDELITY HOUSE ORDER: Silver gilt pattern. 1900 issue with superb large 70mm cross pattee with silver gilt ciphers in vertices. Pierced & vaulted crown suspension. Yellow sash ribbon with silver wire. Mint cond. $2,273.00

BADEN FIDELITY ORDER BREAST STAR: Beautiful large sunburst breast badge. 80mm size. 1900 period production. Gilt ciphers on field with red enamel cross pattee having *Fidelitas* & cipher in center. Large vertical drawn flat style pin. Mint cond. $1,623.00

BADEN KARL FRIEDRICH MILITARY SERVICE ORDER KNIGHT CLASS: With green, white enamel. Full gilt gold crown. Mint cond. $650.00

BAVARIAN ST GEORGE ORDER JUBILEE ISSUE: 40mm. Silvered medal with bust of king. White, red & blue rb. Above avg. cond. $974.00

BRUNSWICK HENRY THE LION HOUSE ORDER 1ST CLASS BADGE: Silver gilt body. Large Malta design with blue enamel field, gold colored center. Double loop suspension ring. No ribbon. Mint cond. $585.00

BRUNSWICK HENRY THE LION HOUSE ORDER GENERAL SERVICE MEDAL: Silvered body with *Immota Fides* inscription. Orange & red ribbon. Near mint cond. $123.00

HOHENZOLLERN HOUSE ORDER 3RD CLASS IN BRONZE: Last model. With black & white rb. & golden-yellow border. Near mint cond. $195.00

HOHENZOLLERN HOUSE ORDER GOLD SERVICE CROSS: Last model. Beautifully made with open wreath & cross pattee. White & black ribbon. Mint cond. $260.00

MECKLENBURG-SCHWERIN GRIFFIN ORDER BREAST STAR: 52mm size. Large gilt & red enamel vaulted breast badge with gold griffin center. Verso nicely hallmarked. Group also includes knight miniature badge of the Order in blue & white enamel work on proper ribbon. Mint cond. $585.00

MECKLENBURG-SCHWERIN GRIFFIN ORDER COMMANDER GRADE: Gilt Malta cross body with gilt frame. Large gilt griffin in center. Full yellow & red ribbon. Large size. High quality. Mint cond. $411.00

MECKLENBURG-STRELITZ CROWN OF WENDEL HOUSE ORDER OFFICER BREAST STAR: Silver sunburst in diamond form with gilt rings. Blue & red enamel work with gold crown, motto *Avito viret honore* (I bask in the Glory of my Ancestors). Beautifully hallmarked by Godet of Berlin. Mint cond. $2,028.00

OLDENBURG HOUSE ORDER GOLD SERVICE CROSS: Well struck. With old original dark blue & red ribbon Near mint cond. $161.00

PERSONALITY ITEM BAVARIAN MILITARY ORDER OF MAX JOSEF GIVEN TO PAUL VON HINDENBURG: Large sash order with black, white & gray wide silk ribbon. Massive cross pattee in gold with white enamel body. Gold & blue roundel in center with device. Pierced Bavarian gold crown suspension. Order bears serial number 15. Mint cond. $12,987.00

PRUSSIAN BLACK EAGLE ORDER BREAST STAR: 80mm rayed silver white metal with raised high relief multi-piece construction of silvered brass & enameled black eagle center. Is named & dated 1934. 2 hook back & 6 piece pin & catch. Avg. cond. $670.00

PRUSSIAN BLACK EAGLE ORDER: Silver gilt 1916 issue. With *W* for Wagner maker mark. Bright yellow ribbon sash. Mint cond. $2,597.00

PRUSSIAN HOUSE MEDAL COMMEMORATING VISIT TO ROME: 45mm silvered table medal in formal case with royal purple velvet lining & royal cipher on case. Obv has profile of royal couple. Exc. cond. $150.00

PRUSSIAN POUR LE MERITE: Also known as the *Blue Max*. Silver gilt wartime piece, circa 1916. Full original old neck ribbon. Nicely toned finish to gilt with enamel Malta cross, gold lettering. Near mint cond. $1,994.00

PRUSSIAN RED EAGLE
ORDER 4TH CLASS
WITH SWORDS

PRUSSIAN RED EAGLE ORDER: First model. Issued between 1734-1767. 35mm white enamel vaulted cross pattee with white enamel center having red eagle with black & white shield on breast. Red & white enameled crown suspension. This item coincides with the reign of Frederick the Great. Near mint cond. $5,195.00

REUSS HOUSE ORDER SERVICE MEDAL WITH SWORDS FOR COMBATANT: Fine silver finish with full wreath & delicate crossed swords above. Proper rb. Near mint cond. $97.00

REUSS PRINCELY HONOR CROSS: 60mm size on 3" of dark violet ribbon. Pierced gold crown suspension with gold sunburst & white enamel cross pattee. Gold shield & crown in center on red enamel field. Mint cond. $459.00

SAXE-PRINCIPALITIES ERNESTINE HOUSE ORDER COMMANDER CLASS: Large pierced & gold crown suspension. White enamel cross with standing gold lions in vertices. Green, blue & gold center with bust. *25 Dec. 1833* founding date on verso with bar of rue, Saxon coat of arms. Violet & green neck ribbon. Very early, 1890 period. Mint cond. .. $756.00

SAXON ALBERT ORDER KNIGHT CROSS WITH SWORDS: 32x42mm white enameled cross with blue & white center with gilt bust of Albert affixed. Gilt crossed swords between arms. With ribbon. Hmkd *9* on rim of bottom arm. Avg. cond. $171.00

SAXON RAUTENKRONE
ROYAL HOUSE ORDER

SAXON RAUTENKRONE ROYAL HOUSE ORDER: 70x70mm with silver gilt frame to cross pattee in green & white enamel. Beautiful center with green wreath, gilt house motto. Large gilt ring. Fine gilt devices between arms. Mint cond. $1,623.00

WALDECK HOUSE ORDER SILVER SERVICE MEDAL: Fine silver finish with cipher, crown. 1.5" of old original rb. Near mint cond. $97.00

WALDECK MERIT ORDER WITH CROWN: Large 52mm neck order with gold trimmed cross in white enamel format. Large gold crown suspension. Blue enamel center with white backing, red cross & gold lettering. Full royal cipher to verso. Yellow large neck ribbon with a red & black border. Above avg. cond. $1,485.00

IMPERIAL GERMAN VETERAN BADGES & INSIGNIA

BUTTONNAIRE IRON CROSS 2ND CLASS & WOUND BADGE: Blue long svc. rb. Above avg. cond. $27.00

PATRIOTIC BADGE HUNGARIAN IRON CROSS 1914: Enameled 35mm diam.

with black EK center to white body with black border. Gold finished details & wording *Buszken Aldoztam A Hazaert*. Pb & stamped *Ges.Gesch*. Near mint cond. $52.00

PATRIOTIC BADGE KAISER PROFILE: Enameled 31mm round white metal with black enameled border & *Gotterhalte Unsern Kaiser* & separate attached round silver metal profile with *Durch Kampf zum Sieg* at left of bust. Pb. Avg. cond. $28.00

PATRIOTIC BADGE ROSEBACH CROSS: Pb. White enameled pattee cross with brass deer heads between each arm. Black enamel center with brass *R*. Exc. cond. $265.00

VETERAN BADGE BAVARIAN KRIEGER VEREIN: Triangular silver shield with lion, crown & shield. Blue & white ribbons. Pb. Mint cond. $23.00

VETERAN BADGE OLDENBURG: Stamped brass wreath with crown, *P* & crossed swords. Approx. 1x1" Above avg. cond. $20.00

VETERAN BADGE PRUSSIAN CAVALRY ASSOCIATION: 2x2". Silvered metal horseshoe with crossed sabers. Open center with horse head. Shoe bears inscription, *T.R. U. P.A. cu Sc. Hi. M. Bu. left*. Near mint cond. $45.00

VETERAN BADGE VON MACKENSEN CAVALRY ASSOCIATION: 45x45mm. White painted enamel cross pattee with inner blue enameled ring inscribed *Waffenring Deutscher Kavallerie*. Gilt full face portrait of von Mackensen in center. Coburg maker marked. Vertical pin. Mint cond. $99.00

VETERAN BADGE WURTTEMBERG: Silver & brass colored shield with heraldic crests. Black & red cloth pendants. Pb. Avg. cond. $22.00

VETERAN BREAST BADGE
WWI CAVALRY ASSOCIATION

VETERAN BREAST BADGE WWI CAV- ALRY ASSOCIATION: Large cross pattee with bust of Mackensen in center. Full inscription. Hallmarked. Pb. Above avg. cond. $65.00

VETERAN CROSS BAVARIAN LONG SERVICE 25 YEAR: Gilt & blue worked German cross with gilt shield, crown in center, white field & gilt *25*. Ring present but no ribbon. Avg. cond. $30.00

VETERAN CROSS BAVARIAN WAR SERVICE: Silver cross with raised lion & shield in center. Blue enamel band with lettering. Pb. Exc. cond. $61.00

VETERAN CROSS KYFFHAUSERBUND SERVICE TO THE ASSOCIATION: 43mm. Cross pattee in silver finish with center medallion having war memorial. Black & white ladder style rb. Near mint cond. $32.00

VETERAN CROSS PRUSSIAN 1914/1918 WELT KRIEG ETC WITH SWORDS: 38mm silver frame, black border & white enamel arms. Silver cross swords & affixed enamel center with title etc. Black & white tri-fold ribbon. Exc. cond. $95.00

THIRD REICH MEDALS

ARMED FORCES SERVICE MEDAL 12 YEAR: Gold medal with ring. Above avg. cond. $31.00

ARMY SERVICE CROSS 18 YEAR: Silver cross with National eagle affixed to blue ribbon. Avg. cond. $103.00

ARMY SERVICE MEDAL 4 YEAR WITH ENVELOPE: Frosted silver finish & blue ribbon with eagle. Envelope with 2 line title & maker. Exc. cond. $48.00

CROATIAN BRAVERY MEDAL: Gilt pendant with busy likeness of Pavelic on obverse. Mounted on tri-fold ribbon. Above avg. cond. $125.00

EASTERN PEOPLE MEDAL 1ST CLASS GOLD WITHOUT SWORDS WITH CASE: Black leatherette case with gold award to lid, white satin & black flock inside. Faded gray award with traces of gold & wide pin. Avg. cond. $133.00

Black leatherette case with faint award to lid, white satin & black velvet inside. Faded gray award with traces of silver wide pin. Avg. cond. $130.00

EASTERN PEOPLE MEDAL 2ND CLASS BRONZE WITHOUT SWORDS: Fading gray body with green ribbon & Pb. Avg. cond. $50.00

EASTERN PEOPLE MEDAL 2ND CLASS GOLD WITH SWORDS: Graying to gold finish. Red stripes on green ribbon with pin. Avg. cond. $77.00

EASTERN PEOPLE MEDAL 2ND CLASS SILVER WITHOUT SWORDS: Faded gray award with traces of silver finish & wide pin. Avg. cond. $50.00

EASTERN PEOPLE MEDAL 2ND CLASS SILVER WITHOUT SWORDS: Some darkening. Green ribbon with white stripes. Avg. cond. $40.00

EASTERN PEOPLE MEDAL 2ND CLASS SILVER WITH SWORDS: Light graying to silver finish. White stripes on green ribbon with pin. Avg. cond. $50.00

FAITHFUL SERVICE CROSS 25 YEAR WITH CASE: Red leatherette box with silver 25, maroon flock inside & printed maker tag. Black swastika to frosted silver cross, blue ribbon & pin back. Above avg. cond. $61.00

FAITHFUL SERVICE CROSS 25 YEAR: Bright silver finish, black enamel swastika & blue ribbon with pin. Near mint cond. $23.00

FAITHFUL SERVICE CROSS 25 YEAR: Silvered metal Maltese cross with wreath separating arms & black enameled swastika center & has a pin mounted blue ribbon with staining. Avg. cond. .. $20.00

EASTERN PEOPLE MEDAL 1ST CLASS SILVER WITH SWORDS WITH CASE

EASTERN PEOPLE MEDAL 1ST CLASS SILVER WITH SWORDS WITH CASE:

FAITHFUL SERVICE CROSS 40 YEAR WITH CASE

FAITHFUL SERVICE CROSS 40 YEAR WITH CASE: Red leatherette body with gold 40 wreath, white satin & red velvet interior. Black enamel swastika to frosted gold cross, blue ribbon & pin. Case shows most age with torn satin at hinge. Above avg. cond. $95.00

FINNISH CROSS 1941-43 PATTERN: Blue enamel cross, swastika arms *Petsamo, Litsa, Kiakkoniem& Liinahamari* & black enamel center with ornate details. Screw back with disc & 2 domed rivet construction. Exc. cond. $282.00

GERMAN CROSS IN GOLD
(CLOTH PATTERN) WITH
CELLOPHANE WRAPPER

GERMAN CROSS IN GOLD (CLOTH PATTERN) WITH CELLOPHANE WRAPPER: Still sealed in wrapper excellent embr. details on gray wool with a gold 1941 date/wreath. Near mint cond. $222.00

GERMAN CROSS IN GOLD (CLOTH PATTERN): Colored embr. work on gray felt star. Corrosion to alum. star details. Gold 1941 wreath. Paper backing has inked maker tag *C.A.Westmann Dresden*. Above avg. cond. $145.00

GERMAN CROSS IN GOLD (CLOTH PATTERN): Colored embr. work on gray felt star. Gold 1941 wreath. Black mesh cloth backing. Exc. cond. $137.00

GERMAN CROSS IN GOLD (CLOTH PATTERN): Embr. work on gray felt backing shows light corrosion to alum. Bright gold 1941/wreath. Paper backed. Above avg. cond. $200.00

GERMAN CROSS IN
GOLD (CLOTH PATTERN)

GERMAN CROSS IN GOLD (CLOTH PATTERN): Excellent embr. details on gray wool with gold 1941/wreath & paper backing. Near mint cond. $195.00

GERMAN CROSS IN SILVER: 4 hollow rivet constructed body. Black enamel swastika center with age darkening to silver background. Date to gold wreath with red enamel background. Black & silver star finishes show wear. Wide pin stamped *20*. Original showing Combat Use. Above avg. cond. $1,100.00

GERMAN CROSS IN SILVER: Black enamel swastika shows scuffs, worn silver finish to brass 1941 wreath, red enamel background & 2 part starburst backing has 4 hollow rivets. Pin stamped *20*. Avg. cond. $1,426.00

GERMAN EAGLE ORDER 1ST CLASS WITH SWORDS: About 50mm black enamel cross with gold border & gold oak leaf outline to each arm. Golden party badge center, gold eagle between each arm & crossed swords wreath above with oakleave ribbon loop having party eagle. Same design to reverse except for no oak leaves & center has facsimile gold Hitler signature. 10.5" tri-color 45mm wide neck ribbon with tie ribbon ends. Only 10 known presentations in 1942-45 of this cross. Mint cond. $8,475.00

GERMAN EAGLE ORDER CASE SERVICE CROSS 2ND CLASS: 1943/45 pattern. Red leather body with gold embossed eagle & border to lid with 2 latches. White satin lid lining with gold *Orden vom Deutschen Adler Verdienstkreuz mit Stern*. Fitted black velvet base. Near mint cond. $500.00

GERMAN EAGLE ORDER
MERIT MEDAL BRONZE
WITH SWORDS

GERMAN EAGLE ORDER MERIT MEDAL BRONZE WITH SWORDS: Dark finish,

Latin script, affixed swords, ring stamped *30* & pin to ribbon. Near mint cond. $650.00

GERMAN EAGLE ORDER MERIT MEDAL WITHOUT SWORDS: Good silver finish, Gothic script, *835 etc.* on rim & ribbon. Near mint cond. $400.00

GERMAN EAGLE ORDER MERIT MEDAL WITH SWORDS: Good silver finish, Gothic script, affixed swords & ribbon with pin. *835 etc.* to rim. Near mint cond. $600.00

GERMAN EAGLE ORDER SERVICE CROSS 3RD CLASS WITH SWORDS WITH CASE: Hmkd *900 21* on the ring, excellent example, Case is red leatherette covered with embossed gold party eagle. Super piece. Above avg. cond. $800.00

GERMAN/ITALIAN AFRICA CAMPAIGN MEDAL: Bronze body with maker & ribbon has added safety pin. Above avg. cond. $70.00

GRAND CROSS OF THE IRON CROSS 1939: 1x5.5x7" blue leatherette body with latch front to hinged lid, white satin lid lining & black velvet fitted base. 55mm wide tri-color ribbon is 16.5" long. 63mm heavy silver frame with magnetic black centers. Ribbon loop to ring with faint stamped *800* below. Mint cond. $4,200.00

HINDENBURG CROSS WITH SWORDS WITH CASE: Black 2 piece cardboard box with black velvet fitted compartment for medal & area for the folded ribbon, included both, ribbon has age stains & also has small ribbon bar with crossed gilt swords Avg. cond. $79.00

IRON CROSS 1914 1ST CLASS WITH 1939 SPANGE: Magnetic black center shows wear from use. Darkening to silver frame by *KO.* Slightly vaulted. Pb frosted silver spange by *L/56.* Avg. cond. $175.00

IRON CROSS 1914 1ST CLASS WITH 1939 SPANGE: Combined set with wide pin having hinge to spange & catch to EK. Magnetic black center with same silver finish to the frame & spange. Exc. cond. $675.00

IRON CROSS 1914 1ST
CLASS WITH 1939 SPANGE

IRON CROSS 1914 1ST CLASS WITH 1939 SPANGE: Screw back. Darkening to silver eagle with dated scroll. Threaded stud at back & rayed disc with socket. Above avg. cond. $164.00

IRON CROSS 1939 1ST CLASS WITH CASE & ISSUE BOX: Missing end flap & tear to top with 6 line title. Box has kept black leatherette case, with EK outline, very white. Satin lid lining & velvet base. Magnetic black center to bright silver frame. Wide pin. Above avg. cond. $225.00

IRON CROSS 1939 1ST CLASS WITH CASE: Black leatherette body with silver EK outline, white satin & velvet interior. Magnetic black center, silver frame & a wide pin which is stamped *L/56.* Exc. cond. $165.00

IRON CROSS 1939 1ST CLASS WITH CASE: Black leatherette body, silver EK outline, white satin & velvet interior. Magnetic black center, silver frame & wide pin. Avg. cond. $110.00

IRON CROSS 1939 1ST CLASS WITH CASE: Black leatherette case is style without latch, white flock inside & black stenciled *LDO* logo to lid flock. Magnetic black center, bright silver frame, wide pin & stamped *L/11.* Clean display. Near mint cond. $168.00

IRON CROSS 1939 1ST CLASS WITH CASE: Black leatherette case, domed lid with silver EK outline, white satin & velvet lined. Bright silver frame, magnetic black center & wide pin stamped *L15.* Near mint cond. $177.00

IRON CROSS 1939 1ST
CLASS WITH CASE

IRON CROSS 1939 1ST CLASS WITH CASE: Black leatherette case, domed lid with silver EK outline, white satin & velvet lined. Some tarnish to silver frame & black painted non-magnetic center appears to be brass. Wide pin. Early one. Above avg. cond. $160.00

IRON CROSS 1939 1ST CLASS WITH CASE: Black leatherette case, with silver EK outline, white satin & velvet lined. Magnetic black center, tarnished frame & wide pin stamped *L15*. Exc. cond. $123.00

IRON CROSS 1939 1ST CLASS WITH CASE: Black leatherette case, with silver EK outline, white satin & velvet lined. Magnetic black center, tarnished frame, Pb & stamped *L/19*. Above avg. cond. $155.00

IRON CROSS 1939 1ST CLASS: Dull silver frame & magnetic black center with some rust. Wide pin stamped *L15*. Avg. cond. $85.00

IRON CROSS 1939 1ST CLASS: Magnetic black center shows some rust & dull silver frame. Wide pin stamped *L15*. Avg. cond. $85.00

IRON CROSS 1939 1ST CLASS: Non-magnetic black center, dark silver frame & wide pin. Avg. cond. $120.00

IRON CROSS 1939 1ST CLASS:

IRON CROSS 1939 1ST CLASS: Screw back. Magnetic black center, dark silver frame, threaded socket & prong at back. *800* stamped EK shaped backing plate & disc with threaded stud. Exc. cond. $212.00

IRON CROSS 1939 2ND CLASS WITH CASE: Black leatherette body with inked *L/11* to back, yellow inside with printed *LDO* to lid with tape damage. Magnetic black center, silver frame & 4" ribbon. Exc. cond. $165.00

IRON CROSS 1939 2ND CLASS WITH CASE: Black leatherette body with tan bottom inked *EK.II. L/54. LDO* to tan lid inside with fitted flock base. Magnetic black centers, frosted ridge, bright silver frame, ring stamped *65* & clean loose ribbon. Near mint cond. $195.00

IRON CROSS 1939 2ND CLASS WITH ENVELOPE: Magnetic black center with darkening to bright silver frame. Clean ribbon & large blue envelope

with 3 line title & maker. Torn off top to envelope. Avg. cond. $59.00

IRON CROSS 1939 2ND CLASS WITH ENVELOPE: Magnetic black center, age darkening to silver frame & long ribbon. Small tan envelope with 3 line title & lacks flap. Above avg. cond. $56.00

IRON CROSS 1939 2ND CLASS
WITH ENVELOPE

IRON CROSS 1939 2ND CLASS WITH ENVELOPE: Magnetic black centers, frosted ridge, darkening to frame & clean ribbon. 3 line title to blue envelope with maker at back. Exc. cond. $76.00

IRON CROSS 1939 2ND CLASS WITH ENVELOPE: Magnetic. Darkening to frame. With ribbon. Large blue titled envelope. Hard to find with envelopes. Above avg. cond. $54.00

IRON CROSS 1939 2ND CLASS: Magnetic black centers, dark frame & long ribbon. Never cleaned. Avg. cond. $65.00

IRON CROSS 1939 2ND CLASS: Magnetic black centers, dark silver frame & long ribbon. Above avg. cond. $37.00

IRON CROSS 1939 2ND CLASS: Magnetic black centers, frosted silver ridge & mirror bright frame. Long ribbon. Rare. Mint cond. $95.00

IRON CROSS 1939 2ND CLASS: Magnetic centers, darkening to silver frame & long ribbon. Above avg. cond. $33.00

IRON CROSS 1939 2ND CLASS: Magnetic, bright frame, stamped *23* ring & clean ribbon. Exc. cond. $42.00

IRON CROSS 1939 2ND CLASS

IRON CROSS SPANGE 1939 2ND CLASS

IRON CROSS 1939 2ND CLASS: Medal bar mount. Magnetic black center with darkening to silver frame. Double wrapped ribbon, gray felt backing & brass Pb. Above avg. cond. $276.00

IRON CROSS SPANGE 1939 1ST CLASS WITH CASE: Black leatherette case with silver spange to top. White satin lid lining & black velvet base. Frosted silver 44mm wide eagle with bright silver highlights. Pb. Near mint cond. $200.00

IRON CROSS SPANGE 1939 1ST CLASS

IRON CROSS SPANGE 1939 1ST CLASS: Bright & frosted silver finish. Wlre Pb. Broken black leatherette case missing 4 sides. Near mint cond. $100.00

IRON CROSS SPANGE 1939 1ST CLASS: Early silver finish & Pb has faint maker. Exc. cond. $91.00

IRON CROSS SPANGE 1939 1ST CLASS: Frosted & bright silver finish. Pb. Mint cond. $105.00

IRON CROSS SPANGE 1939 1ST CLASS: Frosted finish & pin stamped *L/11* Exc. cond. $99.00

IRON CROSS SPANGE 1939 2ND CLASS: 25mm. Frosted silver finish with bright highlights, 2 flat prongs & 5" long ribbon. Near mint cond. $180.00

IRON CROSS SPANGE 1939 2ND CLASS: 25mm. Good frosted & bright silver finish to the eagle with 2 flat prongs thru the 2.5" long ribbon. Near mint cond. $150.00

IRON CROSS SPANGE 1939 2ND CLASS: 25mm. Good frosted & bright silver finish to eagle with 4 flat prongs thru 4" ribbon. Near mint cond. $180.00

KNIGHTS CROSS OF THE IRON CROSS 1939: Bright heavy silver frame is stamped *800* below ring. Magnetic centers have peeling to black paint. Silver loop has faint *65 800.* 12.5" long ribbon. Above avg. cond. $2,029.00

KNIGHTS CROSS OF THE WAR MERIT CROSS IN GOLD WITH SWORDS WITH CASE: Marked *900 20* on the edge of the lower arm, full neck ribbon with tie string, in large blue leatherette case with white velvet lining. Near mint cond. . $5,500.00

KNIGHTS CROSS OF THE WAR MERIT CROSS IN SILVER WITHOUT SWORDS: Nice details to 53mm cross with some age darkening. Stamped *900* to lower arm. Smooth ring mount & loop for 20" long ribbon with mini KVK ribbon tie strings. Only 137 awarded. Near mint cond. $1,700.00

KNIGHTS CROSS OF THE WAR MERIT CROSS IN SILVER WITH SWORDS WITH CASE

KNIGHTS CROSS OF THE WAR MERIT CROSS IN SILVER WITH SWORDS

WITH CASE: Blue leatherette case, white satin & black velvet fitted interior. 53mm frosted silver body with bright highlights, lower arm stamped *900 1* & ribbed loop. 20" ribbon with ribbon tie strings. Early original set. Near mint cond. .. $4,400.00

LEGION CONDOR SPANISH CAMPAIGN MEDAL WITH BOX (SPANISH ISSUE): Gold & gray 1936 medal with good details. Tri-color ribbon only has pin without rectangle. Blue printed maker to cardboard box. Near mint cond. $93.00

LEGION CONDOR SPANISH CAMPAIGN MEDAL: Gold & blued finish to medal with good details. Ribbon is age soiled, frayed & has Spanish style brass pin mount. Avg. cond. $55.00

LUFTSCHUTZ CROSS
2ND CLASS WITH CASE

LUFTSCHUTZ CROSS 2ND CLASS WITH CASE: Clean gray leatherette body, 3 line title & gray flock inside. Clean gray finished alum. medal, ribbon & pin. Near mint cond. $145.00

LUFTSCHUTZ CROSS 2ND CLASS WITH CASE: Gray paper covered cardboard with 3 line title. Paper hinge about torn. Gray 1938 medal & clean long ribbon. Avg. cond. $108.00

MEDAL BAR 2 PLACE: Clean double wrapped ribbons, bronze Hindenburg cross with swords & bronze NSDAP 10 year service cross. Gray felt backing & Pb. Exc. cond. $140.00

MEDAL BAR 2 PLACE: Double wrapped blue ribbons with eagle devices, gold 25 year cross & worn silver 18 year cross. Gray felt backing & brass Pb. Above avg. cond. $300.00

MEDAL BAR 2 PLACE: Double wrapped padded ribbons. Hindenburg cross with swords & Hungarian 1914/18 service. Black wool & Pb. Exc. cond. $27.00

MEDAL BAR 3 PLACE

MEDAL BAR 3 PLACE: 3.5" wide double wrapped ribbons. Starts 1914 EK 2nd, Hindenburg cross with swords & Prussian Reserve Landwehr 2nd service medal. Red felt backing & brass pin. Above avg. cond. $66.00

MEDAL BAR 3 PLACE: Double wrapped ribbons, 1914 EK, Hindenburg cross with swords & 1938 40-year gold faithful service cross. Gray wool & Pb. Above avg. cond. $93.00

MEDAL BAR 4 PLACE: About 4.5" long double wrapped ribbons. Starts Russian Front, Army 4-year service, Crown Order white enamel cross with real gold fittings & Valor cross. Red wool backing & brass pin. Above avg. cond. $450.00

MEDAL BAR 5 PLACE: Clean double wrapped ribbons. 1914 EK, 1939 KVK without swords, Pr. war service cross, Hindenburg cross without swords, & NSDAP 15 year service cross with good enamel. Blue wool backing & brass Pb. Exc. cond. $230.00

MEDAL BAR 6 PLACE: 7.5" long double-wrapped ribbon bar with green felt backing & brass pin. Starts 1939 KVK with swords, Eastern People gold & silver, WWI St. George cross, Rumanian 1941 medal with *Crimea* bar to ribbon & Italian campaign cross. George cross is unsewn. Avg. cond. $450.00

MEDAL BAR 6 PLACE: Double wrapped ribbons are padded. 1914 EK, Crowned Prussian gold WR medal, Hindenburg with swords, 18 year Army Service cross with eagle, Service Ribbon lacks medal & Turkish WWI service medal. Black wool back with bevo maker *Grabow & Matthes Kiel* & brass pin. Above avg. cond. $200.00

MEDAL BAR 8 PLACE

MEDAL BAR 8 PLACE: 9" long with double wrapped ribbons. Starts 1914 EK, Hamburg enamel merit cross with chipped-arm, Hindenburg with swords, 4-year Army service medal with eagle device, Austrian enamel merit cross with chips & missing center, Austrian WWI service medal, Hungarian WWI medal, Bulgarian WWI medal. Mothing to gray felt backing with brass pin. Avg. cond. $160.00

MOTHER CROSS BRONZE: Dark body, good enamel & full ribbon shows use. Above avg. cond. $45.00

MOTHER CROSS BRONZE: Dark finish & faint fracture cracks to enamel on long-arm. Avg. cond. $20.00

MOTHER CROSS BRONZE: Good enamel & dark bronze. Short ribbon. Above avg. cond. $25.00

MOTHER CROSS GOLD WITH CASE: Blue leatherette body with gold cross to lid, white satin lining with maker & flock base. Small chip to white enamel, gold finish & long ribbon. Avg. cond. $65.00

MOTHER CROSS GOLD
WITH CASE

MOTHER CROSS GOLD WITH CASE: Blue leatherette, gold cross design, white satin lid lining with maker & white velvet base. Clean gold finish, enamel & long ribbon with snaps sewn to ends. Near mint cond. $111.00

MOTHER CROSS GOLD: Mint enamel & finish. Ribbon still tied & wrapped with tissue. Mint cond. $82.00

MOTHER CROSS GOLD: Enamel & gold finish. Long ribbon with tied knot. Near mint cond. $47.00

MOTHER CROSS SILVER: Darkening to silver finish, good enamel & full ribbon. Avg. cond. $32.00

MOTHER CROSS SILVER: Frosted silver, good enamel & long sewn ribbon. Near mint cond. $45.00

MOTHER CROSS SILVER: Wear to silver finish, chip to enamel & soiled full ribbon. Avg. cond. $30.00

NSDAP BLOOD ORDER 2ND TYPE: 40.5mm size to tarnished silver medal stamped *800* & serial # *2344*. Above avg. cond. $2,974.00

NSDAP SERVICE CROSS 10 YEAR: Dark bronze finish with some corrosion. Clean ribbon. Avg. cond. $80.00

NSDAP SERVICE CROSS
15 YEAR

NSDAP SERVICE CROSS 15 YEAR: Good blue enamel & frosted silver finish. Medal lacks the ribbon ring. Above avg. cond. $120.00

OCCUPATION MEDAL AUSTRIAN WITH CASE: Red leatherette body with gold eagle, white satin lid lining & maroon velvet base. Darkening to silver medal with ribbon having pin. Above avg. cond. $69.00

OCCUPATION MEDAL CZECH WITH CASE: Maroon leatherette body with gold eagle, white satin lid lining & maroon velvet base. Bronze medal with ribbon & pin coming unsewn. Above avg. cond. $61.00

OCCUPATION MEDAL CZECH WITH CASE: With Prague Bar. Maroon leatherette body with gold eagle, white satin lid lining & maroon velvet base. Bronze medal with ribbon, pin & bronze bar with 2 wide prongs just tucked behind ribbon. Exc. cond $106.00

OCCUPATION MEDAL CZECH: On parade bar mount. Bronze medal & clean double wrapped ribbon, gray felt backing & Pb. Exc. cond. $55.00

OCCUPATION MEDAL CZECH: With Prague Bar. Dark bronze medal, clean long ribbon & bronze bar with 2 prongs. Near mint cond. $91.00

OCCUPATION MEDAL MEMEL

OCCUPATION MEDAL MEMEL: Dark
bronze with long ribbon. Near mint
cond. $129.00
OLYMPIC BREAST CROSS 1936 2ND
CLASS WITH CASE: White leatherette
case with gold rings & outline. Gray
satin & velvet lined. White enamel work
& gold finish. Pin to ribbon. Only
(3,364 awarded). Near mint
cond. $1,050.00

RED CROSS MEDAL

RED CROSS MEDAL: 1937-39 pattern.
Good white enamel disc, red cross center
& black affixed eagle center. Wording to
reverse. Exc. cond. $75.50
RED CROSS SISTER CROSS 10 YEAR:
49mm frosted silver cross with bright
silver border & clean enamel center. Ring
looks to be style for missing bowtie
ribbon. Exc. cond. $300.00
REICHSNAHRSTAND WESTFALEN
MEDAL: 39mm bronze disc with title
border & *Blut & Boden* eagle logo.
Wreath to reverse *Fur zuchteriche
Leistungen.* Exc. cond. $50.00

OLYMPIC CROSS CASE 2ND CLASS

OLYMPIC CROSS CASE 2ND CLASS:
White leatherette body with gold rings &
border to lid. Gray satin & velvet inside
for 65mm tall cross. Near mint
cond. $559.00
RAD SERVICE MEDAL 12 YEAR: Frosted
silver finish shows darkening & short
blue ribbon. Avg. cond. $100.00
RAD SERVICE MEDAL 18 YEAR FE-
MALE: Darkening to highlights of
frosted silver medal. Blue bowtie ribbon
with silver affixed eagle & Pb. Avg.
cond. $300.00

RUSSIAN FRONT MEDAL
WITH ENVELOPE

RUSSIAN FRONT MEDAL WITH ENVE-
LOPE: Faded gray rim, long ribbon, small
tan envelope, 4 line title, maker & tear to
back. Avg. cond. $61.00
RUSSIAN FRONT MEDAL WITH ENVE-
LOPE: Good silver rim to medal & ring
has faint stamp. Long ribbon & tan
envelope with 4 line title & maker. Exc.
cond. $72.00
RUSSIAN FRONT MEDAL: graying to rim &
long ribbon. Avg. cond. $27.00
SPANISH CROSS SILVER WITH
SWORDS: Frosted & bright silver
finish to cross. Affixed eagles to swords.
Stamped *L/11.* Above avg.
cond. $750.00

SPANISH RUSSIAN FRONT MEDAL
BLUE DIVISION WITH BOX: Silver/gray
finished eagle with black EK center.
Rusia 1941 to back. Clean ribbon with
gold rectangle Pb. Blue printed maker
to cardboard box. Near mint
cond. $158.00

SS SERVICE MEDAL 4 YEAR

SS SERVICE MEDAL 4 YEAR: Unmounted blue ribbon with tear drop
loop & ribbed hanging loop, 38mm
round bronze with black finish. Near
mint cond. $227.00
WAR MERIT CROSS 1939 1ST CLASS
WITHOUT SWORDS WITH CASE:
Black leatherette case, silver cross
outline, white satin & black flock
lined. Frosted silver finish to cross.
Wide pin stamped *L15*. Exc.
cond. $95.00
WAR MERIT CROSS 1939 1ST CLASS
WITHOUT SWORDS WITH CASE:
Black leatherette with silver cross to
lid, white satin & black velvet inside.
Frosted silver finish with bright
highlights showing some darkening.
Wide Pb stamped 56. Exc.
cond. $110.00
WAR MERIT CROSS 1939 1ST CLASS
WITH SWORDS WITH CASE: Black
leatherette body with silver KVK,
white satin & black flock inside.
Frosted silver cross with brighter
highlights showing darkening. Pb &
stamped *L/11*. Above avg.
cond. $100.00
WAR MERIT CROSS 1939 1ST CLASS
WITH SWORDS WITH CASE: Black
leatherette with silver cross to lid,
white satin & black velvet inside.
Frosted silver finish with bright
highlights showing some darkening.
Pb & stamped *L/12*. Exc.
cond. $125.00

WAR MERIT CROSS 1939
1ST CLASS WITH SWORDS WITH CASE

WAR MERIT CROSS 1939 1ST CLASS
WITH SWORDS: Early silver finish, Pb &
stamped *1*. Near mint cond. $60.00
WAR MERIT CROSS 1939 1ST CLASS
WITH SWORDS: Excellent silver finish &
details. Wide pin & stamped *3*. Mint
cond. $85.00
WAR MERIT CROSS 1939 1ST CLASS
WITH SWORDS: Good silver finish &
wide pin. Exc. cond. $85.00
WAR MERIT CROSS 1939 2ND CLASS
WITH SWORDS WITH ENVELOPE:
Faded bronze with ribbon & large tan
envelope with 4 line title for cross without
swords & scuffed *ohne*. Maker at back.
Late-war. Avg. cond. $20.00
WAR MERIT CROSS 1939 2ND CLASS
WITH SWORDS: Early bronze finish.
Clean ribbon. Above avg. cond. . $26.00
WAR MERIT CROSS CASE 1ST CLASS
WITH SWORDS: Black leatherette body
with silver cross & swords to lid. White
satin & black flock lined. Above avg.
cond. $60.00
WEST WALL MEDAL WITH ENVELOPE:
Early bronze, copy ribbon, small
envelope with 3 line title & maker. 16mm
tall bronze oval with ribbon. 1" wide
soiled ribbon bar, Pb. Above avg.
cond. $30.00
WEST WALL MEDAL WITH ENVELOPE:
Fair finish & tan envelope with 3 line title
& maker. Above avg. cond. $20.00

THIRD REICH AWARD BADGES

ANTI-PARTISAN BADGE BRONZE
(BULLION): Full size hand embr. 3 styles
of bronze bullion on black wool oval.
Shows age corrosion & yellow highlights
have some minor damage. Paper backing

& appears to have been on tunic. Above avg. cond. $1,500.00

ANTI-PARTISAN BADGE BRONZE: *Juncker* style construction with semi-hollow back. Good finish overall & cutout snake heads. Wide pin. Above avg. cond. $475.00

ANTI-PARTISAN BADGE BRONZE: *Juncker* style construction with semi-hollow back. Good finish overall & cutout snake heads. Wire style Pb. Above avg. cond. $450.00

ANTI-PARTISAN BADGE GOLD

ANTI-PARTISAN BADGE GOLD: *Juncker* style construction with semi-hollow back. Good finish overall & cutout snake heads. Wire style Pb. Above avg. cond. $906.00

ANTI-PARTISAN BADGE SILVER: *Juncker* style construction with semi-hollow back. Nice finish overall & cutout snake heads. Wire Pb. Exc. cond. $600.00

ARMY PARATROOPER BADGE (ALUMI-NUM): Deluxe quality gold finished eagle/wreath with bright alum. eagle affixed by domed alum. rivets. Pb, unmarked & appears unused. Near mint cond. $1,035.00

ASSAULT BADGE GENERAL #25: *JFS* Frosted silver wreath with affixed #25 plate. Black eagle with crossed bayonet & stick grenade have worn silver highlights & 4 domed rivets. Wide pin. Exc. cond. $473.00

ASSAULT BADGE GENERAL #25: Silver finished wreath with affixed #25 panel. Gray eagle with stick grenade & bayonet has 4 rivets. Wide pin & by *RK*. Above avg. cond. $454.00

ASSAULT BADGE GENERAL #50: Good silver finish to wreath with affixed gray #50 panel. Dark gray eagle has fracture crack to left wing & is held by 4 domed rivets. Wide pin & *RK* marked. Avg. cond. $399.00

ASSAULT BADGE GENERAL: Solid with frosted silver finish & Pb. Above avg. cond. $50.00

ASSAULT BADGE INFANTRY BRONZE WITH ENVELOPE: Solid with nice finish,

Pb & by *JFS*. Small envelope, 3 line title, same maker & torn top corner. Above avg. cond. $80.00

ASSAULT BADGE INFANTRY BRONZE: Solid body with wear to finish. Pb. Avg. cond. $70.00

ASSAULT BADGE INFANTRY SILVER

ASSAULT BADGE INFANTRY SILVER: Solid body with good details & Pb. Near mint cond. $76.00

ASSAULT BADGE INFANTRY SILVER: Solid body with wear to finish. Pb. Avg. cond. $72.00

ASSAULT BADGE INFANTRY SILVER: Solid body, finish fading gray & Pb. Avg. cond. $50.00

ASSAULT BADGE INFANTRY SILVER: Solid with age darkening & bubbled silver finish. Pb. Avg. cond. $32.00

ASSAULT BADGE INFANTRY SILVER: Solid with bright frosted silver finish. Near mint cond. $82.00

ASSAULT BADGE INFANTRY SILVER: Solid, Pb & *A* marked for Assmann. Exc. cond. $80.00

ASSAULT BADGE PANZER BRONZE: Solid body has very dark finish, Pb & by *L/5?* Exc. cond. $135.00

ASSAULT BADGE PANZER BRONZE: Solid with darkening to finish. Pb. Above avg. cond. $65.00

ASSAULT BADGE PANZER BRONZE: Solid, indented backside, finish fading, *L/53* & Pb. Avg. cond. $50.00

ASSAULT BADGE PANZER SILVER #100: Faded gray stamped eagle/wreath with indented back. #100 plate has rivet. Silver finished tank has 2 rivets that show thru to front. Late-war unmarked example. Avg. cond. $275.00

ASSAULT BADGE PANZER SILVER #50: Dull silver eagle wreath & affixed #50 plate by hollow rivet. 2 hollow rivets to gray tank with *GB* at back. Indented backside. Exc. cond. $550.00

ASSAULT BADGE PANZER SILVER #50: Graying to silver eagle/wreath & affixed

#50 plate. 2 domed rivets to gray/black tank. Wide pin & marked *JFS*. Above avg. cond. $300.00

ASSAULT BADGE PANZER SILVER #50

ASSAULT BADGE PANZER SILVER: Gray body with silver finish worn & indented back. By *RK* & Pb. Avg. cond. $87.00
ASSAULT BADGE PANZER SILVER: Solid, indented backside, finish fading gray & Pb. Avg. cond. $50.00
ASSAULT BADGE PANZER SILVER: Stamped with silver finish worn gray at highlights. Pb. Avg. cond. $55.00
BDM PROFICIENCY CLASP BRONZE: Dark finish to metal frame with back stamped *RZM M1/? 134377*. Pb & clean ribbon. Exc. cond. $175.00
BDM PROFICIENCY CLASP BRONZE: Good finish to metal frame with back stamped *RZM M1/15 B8257*. Pb & clean ribbon. Near mint cond. $276.00
BELGIAN REXIST BADGE *BLOOD ORDER*: 41mm solid silver disc with *Bravoure Honneur Fidelite* border, open center with crossed twigs & sword. Pb. Near mint cond. $325.00
BULGARIAN PILOT WING WITH ENAMELED SERVICE CROSS & ID: #1 61mm bronze crowned over eagle & B center, Pb. # 2 50mm red enameled Maltese cross with crossed swords & white border with 1941 date & crowned lion center, flat Pb. Comes with 1942 ID booklet with both German & Bulgarian language & wings embossed on front & signed. Also a presentation envelope for wings. Rare. Avg. cond. $369.00
CAMPAIGN SHIELD CRIMEA: Faded gray shield, gray wool backing & paper covered backing plate. Has been on tunic. Avg. cond. $87.00
CAMPAIGN SHIELD DEMJANSK: Magnetic shield, soiled gray wool oval & paper backed. Avg. cond. $218.00
CAMPAIGN SHIELD KUBAN: Bronze shield with darkening, blue-gray wool, paper

backing covers plate with 4 prongs. Above avg. cond. $164.00
CAMPAIGN SHIELD NARVIK: Gray non-magnetic shield on gray wool oval with paper backing over metal. Near mint cond. $196.00
CAMPAIGN SHIELD NARVIK: Gray shield on green wool oval & wool backed. Traces of silver finish. Wool shows tunic use. Avg. cond. $125.00

CAMPAIGN SHIELD NARVIK

CAMPAIGN SHIELD NARVIK: Gold non-magnetic shield with blue wool oval, wool oval backing, oval backing plate with cut corners & 4 flat prongs. Above avg. cond. $212.00
CAMPAIGN SHIELD NARVIK: Non-magnetic gray shield on gray wool overall with paper covered backing plate. Above avg. cond. $135.00
.CLOSE COMBAT CLASP BRONZE: 100mm bronze oakleave bar with Nazi eagle over crossed bayonet & stick grenade, has anodized steel backing plate & hmkd *JFS* & *Peekhaus Berlin* on back. Large flat pin with stamped in hinge & catch. Mint cond. $177.00
CLOSE COMBAT CLASP BRONZE: Dark finish, blued panel, wide pin & *JFS/ Peekhaus etc*. Exc. cond. $129.00
CLOSE COMBAT CLASP BRONZE: Early dark bronze body with faint graying to highlights. Patina to metal panel. Wide pin. By *Fec.W.E.Peekhaus etc*. Avg. cond. $125.00
CLOSE COMBAT CLASP BRONZE: Finish shows graying at highlights, blued panel, wide pin & *JFS Peekhaus etc*. Avg. cond. $165.00

CLOSE COMBAT CLASP BRONZE: Gray body shows remains of dark bronze finish. Blued panel, wide pin, stamped *Peekhaus etc.* & raised *JFS.* Avg. cond. $101.00

CLOSE COMBAT CLASP SILVER

CLOSE COMBAT CLASP SILVER: Faded gray body with worn bright highlights. Metal panel. Wide pin, hinge & catch all have the silver finish intact. Avg. cond. $150.00

CZECH HARVEST GUARD BADGE *BEEIDETE WACHE/PRISEZNA STRAZ*: Smaller variation badge shown. 67x76mm stamped silver metal oval with raised details of crowned lion to center & title wording at sides. Pb. Near mint cond. $200.00

DLV BALLOON PILOT BADGE 1ST TYPE: Dark blue wool oval has gray machine embr. 3/4 oakleave wreath. Stamped metal hot air balloon sewn to center shows graying to frosted silver finish. Near mint cond. $301.00

DR. FRITZ TODT HONOR BADGE GOLD: Private purchase style, heavy body with gold finish, plain grained reverse & wide pin. Mint cond. $800.00

DR. FRITZ TODT HONOR BADGE STEEL: Solid black eagle with title name, wide pin & catch. Near mint cond. $350.00

DRIVER BADGE BRONZE: Blue-gray wool disc with bronze badge & paper backing. Near mint cond. $23.00

DRIVER BADGE GOLD: Gray wool disc, gold badge & metal backing with prongs. Above avg. cond. $20.00

DRIVER BADGE SILVER: Stamped non-magnetic body, traces of silver finish, 2 prongs. Avg. cond. $20.00

HITLER YOUTH BADGE HAMBURG 1938 NATIONAL TRADE COMPETITION PARTICIPANT: Given to finalist. Dark silver finished solid body with party eagle holding enamel HJ diamond with chips, castle gate with ship in arch & *Reichskampf 1938 Hamburg.* Pb. Avg. cond. $180.00

HITLER YOUTH BADGE KREISSIEGER 1939 NATIONAL TRADE COMPETITION VICTOR: Beautiful bronze finish & white enamel, with red enameled HJ diamond & Bronze Nazi Eagle. Pb with maker *H.Aurich.* $170.00

HITLER YOUTH BADGE PROFICIENCY BADGE: Bright finish with dark spot to wording. Pb with maker & stamped *72xx* Avg. cond. $50.00

HITLER YOUTH BADGE REICHSSIEGER 1938 NATIONAL TRADE COMPETITION VICTOR: Bright gold eagle finish & wreath. Fracture cracks to enamel HJ diamond affixed to cogged wheel. Good white enamel backing with gold title. Pb & by *G.Brehmer Markneukirchen.* Hard to find style. Above avg. cond. $900.00

LUFTWAFFE BOMBER SQUAD OPERATIONAL FLIGHT CLASP BRONZE: Dark body with rivet to silver winged bomb. Wide pin. Above avg. cond. $175.00

LUFTWAFFE BOMBER SQUAD OPERATIONAL FLIGHT CLASP SILVER: Frosted silver finished shows light graying. Rivet to black winged bomb, wide pin & stamped *G.H.Osang Dresden.* Above avg. cond. $290.00

LUFTWAFFE DAY FIGHTER SQUAD OPERATIONAL FLIGHT CLASP GOLD

LUFTWAFFE DAY FIGHTER SQUAD OPERATIONAL FLIGHT CLASP GOLD: Bright gold finish to oak & laurel leaves. Domed rivet to dark winged arrow. Wide pin. Near mint cond. $550.00

LUFTWAFFE DUTY SERVICE LANYARD: Plaited cloth body with loops at each end & 2 short cords with silver painted tips. Exc. cond. $174.00

LUFTWAFFE FLAK BADGE: Early heavy example with good finish & affixed eagle. Pb. Exc. cond. $140.00

LUFTWAFFE FLAK BADGE: Early quality with dark silver finish, Pb & stamped *Brehmer etc.* Blue flock base removed from case. Exc. cond. $177.00

LUFTWAFFE FLAK BADGE: Faded gray wreath/gun & affixed eagle with traces of silver finish. Pb & *W* trademark. Avg. cond. $115.00

LUFTWAFFE FLAK BADGE: faded gray wreath/gun & affixed eagle. Pb & *WH.* Avg. cond. $125.00

LUFTWAFFE GLIDER PILOT BADGE: Excellent details to silver oakleave wreath with cutout swastika. 2 domed rivets to gray eagle stamped *C.E.Juncker Berlin SW* Pb. Near mint cond. $1,641.00

LUFTWAFFE GLIDER PILOT BADGE

LUFTWAFFE GROUND ASSAULT BADGE:
Solid one part body with graying to silver frosted eagle/wreath. Gray finished center. Pb. Avg. cond. $65.50

LUFTWAFFE GUNNER/ENGINEER BADGE WITH CASE: Blue leatherette case with 3 line silver title *Luftwaffen= Fliegerschutzen= Abzeichen.* Blue satin & velvet lined. Frosted silver finish to solid swastika/wreath, gray eagle & 2 domed rivets. Pb & eagle stamped *W.Deumer etc.* Light age graying only. Above avg. cond. $370.00

LUFTWAFFE HONOR GOBLET: Marked *935* silver crown & eagle *Jon Wagner & Sohn.* Has age patina, dated 16-3-42. Fighting eagles on the front & the 1939 Iron Cross on the back. Near mint cond. $3,375.00

LUFTWAFFE HONOR GOBLET: The document is Goring signed & is the formal version. Marked *ALPAKA Feinsilver Auflage Jon Wager & Sohn.* Has age patina, dated 16-8-42. Fighting eagles on the front & 1939 Iron cross on the back. Unteroffizier Gustav Klemme. Near mint cond. $3,950.00

LUFTWAFFE OBSERVER BADGE (CLOTH): 2 tone gray eagle, gray wreath, blue gray wool backing & padded backside. Early. Near mint cond. $79.00

LUFTWAFFE OBSERVER BADGE (CLOTH): Padded blue-gray wool oval with subdued gray wreath & eagle with swastika cloth backed & mint condition. Nice. Mint cond. $75.00

LUFTWAFFE OBSERVER BADGE CASE: Blue leatherette body with silver *Beobachterabz.* to lid. Blue satin & velvet lining. Near mint cond. $160.00

LUFTWAFFE PARATROOPER BADGE (CLOTH): Thick gold eagle, gray wreath, & blue gray wool oval. Near mint cond. $33.00

LUFTWAFFE PARATROOPER BADGE (CLOTH): Padded blue-gray wool oval with gray embr. wreath & golden-yellow eagle in center. Has been sewn-on but in good condition. Avg. cond. $96.00

LUFTWAFFE PARATROOPER BADGE

LUFTWAFFE PARATROOPER BADGE: *B&NL.* Late-war gray wreath with affixed gray eagle by 2 rivets. Faint traces of finish to each. Pb & eagle title stamped. Avg. cond. $150.00

LUFTWAFFE PARATROOPER BADGE: Gray wreath & faded gray eagle with traces of gold finish. Pb, 2 rivets & marked *A L/64* for Assmann. Never cleaned original. Avg. cond. $177.00

LUFTWAFFE PARATROOPER BADGE: Wartime faded gray wreath with 2 rivets holding gold finished eagle having worn gray highlights. Pb & stamped *G.H.Osang Dresden.* Combat Veteran. Avg. cond. $350.00

LUFTWAFFE PARATROOPER BADGE: Wartime gray wreath, wear to gold finished gray eagle, 2 rivets, stamped *B&N L* & Pb. Avg. cond. $225.00

LUFTWAFFE PILOT BADGE (BULLION): 3 tone alum. hand embr. eagle/wreath on blue-gray wool. Paper backed. Has been on tunic. Avg. cond. $356.00

LUFTWAFFE PILOT BADGE (BULLION): Oversized badge has 58x70mm alum. bullion hand embr. wreath & 70mm wide eagle. 3 tone alum. bullion details. Gray wool has been painted white at padded center & has been sewn on to something. Avg. cond. $225.00

LUFTWAFFE PILOT BADGE (CLOTH): Gray eagle/wreath on blue gray wool. Above avg. cond. $72.00

LUFTWAFFE PILOT BADGE (CLOTH): Blue-gray wool oval with white wreath & gray eagle with swastika cloth backed. Mint cond. $75.00

LUFTWAFFE PILOT BADGE: 43x54mm silver wreath, 62mm gray eagle with 2

domed rivets & stamped *C.E.Juncker etc.*
Pb. Exc. cond. $300.00

LUFTWAFFE PILOT BADGE

LUFTWAFFE PILOT BADGE: Heavy quality
frosted silver wreath with darkening to
highlights, 2 rivets to nickel silver eagle,
Pb & stamped *GWL*. Shows honest use.
Above avg. cond. $685.00

LUFTWAFFE PILOT BADGE: Age tarnish to
silver eagle & wreath. 43x53mm & 64mm
wingspan. Pb, 2 domed rivets & eagle
stamped *CEJ*. Exc. cond. $492.00

LUFTWAFFE PILOT COMMEMORATIVE
BADGE: 42x55mm heavy dark silver
oakleave wreath with cutout swastika
arm. Detailed eagle center with cutout
legs. Pb & stamped *CE Junker Berlin
SW68*. Near mint cond. $1,500.00

LUFTWAFFE PILOT/OBSERVER BADGE:
Eagle stamped *CE Juncker etc.*, 2 domed
rivets & faint gold wash to gray wreath.
Traces of silver finish to eagle. Pb &
wartime example shows age. Avg.
cond. $339.00

LUFTWAFFE PILOT/OBSERVER BADGE:
Heavy 43x53mm dark gold wreath.
65mm dark silver eagle with good details
& 2 domed rivets. Pb, maker stamped
C.E.Juncker Berlin SW68. Near mint
cond. $944.00

LUFTWAFFE RECON SQUAD OPERA-
TIONAL FLIGHT CLASP BRONZE: Dark
bronze body with riveted silver eagle
head center. Wide pin & stamped *BSW* in
clover leaf trademark. Above avg.
cond. $405.50

LUFTWAFFE SEA BATTLE BADGE:
44x57mm gold painted oakleave wreath
with affixed gray eagle by 2 rivets. Silver/
gray finish to ship center with details at
back giving stamped look. Pb with pliers
marked rivets/eagle & some pits to back.
Late-war quality. Above avg.
cond. $1,000.00

MARKSMANSHIP BADGE TYROL 1943
PISTOL: 52mm green enamel oakleaf
border, red eagle & date to gold center
with white swastika target. Pb. Near mint
cond. $73.00

MARKSMANSHIP BADGE VETERAN
ASSOC WETTKAMPFSIEGER 1941:
64mm tall dark bronze oakleave wreath
with swastikas, 1914 EK, monument
center, crossed rifles on target & title.
Blue wool oval & backing show some
moth holes. Avg. cond. $75.00

MARKSMANSHIP LANYARD ARMY WITH
1 ACORN: Plaited alum. body, gray satin
backing, gray wool backing, 1 alum.
acorn & alum. eagle shield. Clean
example. Exc. cond. $63.00

MARKSMANSHIP LANYARD ARMY
WITH 3 ACORNS

MARKSMANSHIP LANYARD ARMY WITH
3 ACORNS: Plaited alum. body has 3
acorns, gray satin backing, alum. eagle/
shield & gray wool backing. Shows age.
Avg. cond. $64.00

MARKSMANSHIP LANYARD ARMY WITH
ARTILLERY SHELL DEVICE: Alum.
plaited body, gray satin & felt backing.
Gray/alum. eagle/wreath with crossed
swords shield. Turned alum. shell. Near
mint cond. $68.00

MARKSMANSHIP LANYARD ARMY:
Plaited alum. body, gray satin backing,
alum. eagle/shield & gray wool backing.
Above avg. cond. $50.00

MARKSMANSHIP LANYARD ARMY:
Plaited alum. body, soiled gray satin
backing & moth hole to felt. Alum. eagle
wreath with crossed swords to shield.
Avg. cond. $32.00

MARKSMANSHIP LANYARD
LUFTWAFFE: Alum. zigzag to gray
plaited body, alum. eagle/wreath & moth
holes to wool backing. Avg. cond. $76.00

MARKSMANSHIP LANYARD
LUFTWAFFE: Blue-gray plaited body
with alum. zig-zags. Stamped gray eagle/
wreath & gray felt backing. Exc.
cond. $65.00

MARKSMANSHIP LANYARD NAVAL: Gold
plaited body shows age darkening. No
shield or cloth backings. Loop at each
end. Avg. cond. $29.00

NAVAL AUXILIARY CRUISER BADGE
(FRENCH MADE): Darkening to gold
finished eagle/wreath & Viking ship.
Silver globe & backing details with
wide horizontal pin & the top hook.
Avg. cond. $180.00

NAVAL AUXILIARY CRUISER BADGE:
Late-war gray eagle/wreath & Viking ship
on globe center. No rivet & Pb. Avg.
cond. $126.50

NAVAL AUXILIARY CRUISER BADGE

NAVAL AUXILIARY CRUISER BADGE:
Frosted gold eagle/wreath & Viking ship.
Domed rivet to silver globe. Wide silver
pin & unmarked early example. Near mint
cond. $450.00

NAVAL BLOCKADE RUNNER BADGE
WITH CASE: Blue leatherette body with
blue flock interior. Paper separated at
hinge. Wear to frosted silver eagle & gray
ship. Wide pin & maker *Otto Placzek etc*.
9mm mini badge/stickpin. Shows age.
Avg. cond. $275.00

NAVAL BLOCKADE RUNNER BADGE:
Early heavy gray body with silver finished
eagle. Wide pin & by *Fec. Otto etc*. Near
mint cond. $189.00

NAVAL BLOCKADE RUNNER BADGE:
Heavy brass/bronze body shows tunic use
with only faint traces of original finishes.
Wide pin & by *Fec.Otto Placzek etc*. No
doubt original. Avg. cond. $293.00

NAVAL BLOCKADE RUNNER BADGE:
Silver frosted eagle & silver ship show
graying. Wide pin & by *Fec.Otto Placzek
Berlin etc*. Avg. cond. $175.00

NAVAL COASTAL ARTILLERY BADGE
(FRENCH MADE): Gray body with gold
eagle/wreath showing wear, silver gun
center, indented details at back, wide
horizontal pin & lacks top hook. Avg.
cond. $150.00

NAVAL COASTAL ARTILLERY BADGE:
Gold finished eagle/wreath & gray gun.
Pb. Above avg. cond. $90.00

NAVAL COASTAL ARTILLERY BADGE:
Heavy quality, gold eagle/wreath & silver-
gray gun. Wide horizontal pin at top
& *Schwerin Berlin*. Exc. cond. .. $328.00

NAVAL DESTROYER BADGE: Gold
finished eagle/wreath & gray ship center.
Horizontal wire pin, top hook, maker *JFS*
& owner scratched *Rose*. Above avg.
cond. $131.00

NAVAL DESTROYER BADGE: Late-war
gray body with worn gold finish to eagle/
wreath & silver center. By *R.S* & Pb. Avg.
cond. $135.00

NAVAL DESTROYER BADGE: Gold eagle
wreath, silver ship/water, wide horizontal
pin, top hook & by *G.W.L.* Near mint
cond. $175.00

NAVAL DESTROYER BADGE

NAVAL DESTROYER BADGE: Silver gray
eagle/wreath & ship show no traces of
finish. By *S.H.u.Co.*, with horizontal pin &
hook at the top. Late-war style. Avg.
cond. $95.00

NAVAL HIGH SEAS FLEET BADGE: Good
gold finished eagle/wreath with white
corrosion to gray ship center. Wide pin &
stamped *L/18*. Variation maker mark.
Above avg. cond. $175.00

NAVAL HIGH SEAS FLEET BADGE

NAVAL HIGH SEAS FLEET BADGE: Late-
war gray body with about half of gold
finish to eagle/wreath & faded gray ship.
R.S. & Pb. Avg. cond. $125.00

NAVAL MINESWEEPER BADGE: Gold
finished eagle/wreath with highlights
worn gray. Faded gray silver water. Pb.
Avg. cond. $95.00

NAVAL MINESWEEPER BADGE: Heavy
quality with dark gold finish to eagle/
wreath. Silver water. Wide pin & by
*Fec.Otto Placzek Berlin Ausf.Schwerin
Berlin*. Near mint cond. $279.00

NAVAL U-BOAT BADGE (BEVO): Age
darkening to flat gold bevo badge on blue
& uncut black. Avg. cond. $85.00

NAVAL U-BOAT BADGE: Darkening to early brass/bronze body. Wide pin. Stamped *Frank & Reif Stuttgart*. Avg. cond. $135.00

NAVAL U-BOAT BADGE: Early brass body, gold finish worn at highlights, cutout swastika, wide pin & by *Frank & Reif etc*. Avg. cond. $145.00

NAVAL U-BOAT BADGE: Good gold finish to front with faded gray back. Solid swastika & horizontal wire Pb. Fair display for late-war badge. Above avg. cond. $84.00

NAVAL U-BOAT BADGE

NAVAL U-BOAT BADGE: Heavy body with gold wash worn at highlights showing brass base. Wide pin & stamped *Schwerin Berlin 68*. Exc. cond. $500.00

NAVAL U-BOAT BADGE: Heavy brass body with gold finish, cutout swastika, wide pin & stamped *Frank & Reif Stuttgart*. Highest quality. Near mint cond. $155.00

NAVAL U-BOAT BADGE: Heavy brass body with gold finish, solid swastika, wire pin & stamped *GWL*. Above avg. cond. $170.00

NAVAL U-BOAT BADGE: Wartime gray badge with gilt wash worn from highlights. Wire horizontal pin & by *f.o.* Avg. cond. $195.00

NAVAL U-BOAT BADGE: Wartime gray body with gold finish showing wear, solid swastika & wide pin. Above avg. cond. $171.00

NAVAL U-BOAT COMBAT CLASP SILVER: Frosted silver finish shows some light darkening. Fluted, wide pin & *Schwerin* & *Peekhaus are* marked. Above avg. cond. $545.00

NAVAL U-BOAT COMBAT CLASP SILVER

SINGLE HANDED TANK DESTRUCTION BADGE: Silver wire woven strip with 2 black stripe borders & blacken steel struck tank with 3 prong attachment to zinc

backing plate & field-gray cloth backing. Above avg. cond. $212.00

SLOVAKIAN BADGE OF HONOR FOR SERVICE ON THE EASTERN FRONT: 45mm silvered bronze oval wreath with sword through helmet & communist emblem dated *22 VI 1941* on helmet. Concave & red wool backing, Pb. A good original. Avg. cond. $72.00

SPORTS BADGE DRL SILVER: Frosted silver finish is worn dark at highlights. Swastika to wreath. Pb & maker. Avg. cond. $35.00

SPORTS BADGE HORSEMAN BRONZE: Dark finish, maker marked & Pb. Avg. cond. $65.00

SPORTS BADGE HORSEMAN SILVER: *R* logo to oakleaf wreath with horse rider center. Frosted silver finish shows graying. Pb & maker marked. Avg. cond. $105.00

SPORTS BADGE SA BRONZE: Bronze finish shows light age, 1st issue wording, maker, Pb & stamped *122132*. Above avg. cond. $50.00

SPORTS BADGE SA SILVER: Silver frosted finish shows light age, 3rd issue wording. Pb. Above avg. cond. $75.00

U-BOAT TEST OPERATOR BADGE *FRONTREIF* : 40x52mm solid metal body, gold painted Party Eagle to oakleave wreath, U-boot diving at center with title above. Unmarked. Wire pin & catch. Near mint cond. $880.00

WOUND BADGE 1936 BLACK CUTOUT: Stamped brass with worn paint to highlights. Cutout center design. Pb. Avg. cond. $223.00

WOUND BADGE 1936 BLACK: Stamped non-magnetic body with thick black paint. Pb. Above avg. cond. $80.00

WOUND BADGE 1939 GOLD WITH CASE: Black leatherette, white satin & flock lined. Solid with bright gold finish. Pb & stamped *30*. Early style. Near mint cond. ... $183.00

WOUND BADGE 1939 GOLD: Solid gray body with gold finish worn at swastika. Pb. Above avg. cond. $95.00

WOUND BADGE 1939 SILVER WITH CASE: Maroon leatherette body with maroon velvet base. Solid body with frosted finish fading gray. *65* & Pb. Avg. cond. .. $75.00

WOUND BADGE 1939 SILVER WITH CASE: Maroon leatherette body, red flock inside & lid needs glue repair corners. Solid body with frosted finish, Pb & *65*. Avg. cond. $100.00

WOUND BADGE 1939 SILVER WITH CASE: Frosted silvered metal oval wreath with swastika on helmet over crossed swords. Pb & solid back with Hmkd *65* on back. Dark red box with red flocked insert. Some wear to box. Above avg. cond. $85.00

IMPERIAL GERMAN PHOTOS & POSTCARDS

CDV HUSSAR NCO: Man shown in attila & breeches with visor cap resting on chair. He clutches his sword with both hands & also carries gloves. 1906 dated. NCO rank insignia on collar with lacing. Mint cond. $20.00

CDV PRUSSIAN ONE YEAR VOLUNTEER GROUP: 4.25x6.5" photo of 3 young Prussian 1 year volunteers in dress uniforms & swords. Sepia tone. Above avg. cond. $20.00

CDV UHLAN 9TH LT: Photo shows man standing with sword held in left hand. Full dress ulanka with banjo boards with 9. High polished tschaka worn with large Prussian eagle. Excellent details to uniform, headgear. Mint cond. $27.00

CDV WWI PRUSSIAN SOLDIER WITH HIS IRON CROSS: Bust & head. Man dressed in M15 tunic with crown buttons. EK mounted on 2nd button hole. Studio marked in gold lettering. Near mint cond. $20.00

PHOTO ALBUM NAVAL SAILOR TSING TAO, CHINA: 138 large captioned pictures showing sailor's voyage through Suez Canal through South Seas to Tsing Tao, the German protectorate. 1905 period. Excellent pictures of natives, German sailors on SMS Fuerst Bismarck, & other capital ships. Soldier went on leave to Japan & took pictures of temples & Russian troops. Album has large lacquered covers obviously made in China with delicate bird & foliage motifs. Above avg. cond. $301.00

PHOTO ALBUM WWI NAVAL

PHOTO ALBUM WWI NAVAL: Contains 63 photos of ships, U-boats, crashed German airplane in sea, Zeppelin, mine damage to ship, downed British airplane, portrait shots of officers & men, etc. most photos captioned. 1914 Iron Cross on the cover, red, white, black cored binding, 9x12" size. Exc. cond. $93.00

PHOTO ALBUM WWI SAXON SOLDIER: 9x12" album with black covers. Onion skin dividers. Early pictures all have captions. Owner apparently served with a Pioneer battalion & fought in Russia. Mixture of color cards of Eastern territories with postcard sized photos of soldiers. Superb details to equipment in transition from 1915-17 with good shots of assault soldiers with grenade bags, specialized equipment, etc. Above avg. cond. $114.00

PHOTO ALBUM WWI SOLDIER: 10x13" brown cover. Approx. 177 photos & 10 postcards. Various sizes with most 3x4". Uniforms, rest, war damage, trenches, map Cambrai 13C , 1917 parade with officers Falkenhausen. Most captioned. Avg. cond. $150.00

PHOTO ALBUM WWI SOLDIER: 1912-1938. About 7x9.5" plaid paper front to blue cover. Approx. 82 photos with most military shots postcard size. Captions to each page & starts with young man in 1912, 1915 in uniform, nice combat group shots with steel helmets, General, trenches, plane in flight, arty. bursts, 1925 motorcycle with side car, family 1930's, etc. Above avg. cond. $166.00

PHOTO ALBUM WWI SOLDIER: 5x7.5" black cover with EK, title & tri-color affixed ribbon. Approx. 73 postcards. Starts with Bismarck, etc., Kaiser Wilhelm II, Hindenburg, field troops with Red Cross wagon, kitchen, arty. & some post-war color shots of monuments or gravestones. Above avg. cond. $300.00

PHOTO ALBUM WWI SOLDIER: 7x9.5" black/red cover with 70 pictures. Photos cover soldiers in formation, in field exercises, artillery, family & friends. No captions. Neat & clean. Above avg. cond. $60.00

PHOTO ALBUM WWI VETERAN: 9x12" size, cloth covered album, string bound with approx. 140 photos. This professionally done b/w photo album illustrates the WWI battle entrenched locations throughout Europe. This album was put together to commemorate a 1933 visit by former German soldiers to WWI battle sites. Avg. cond. $50.00

PHOTOGRAPH ARTY NCO & FAMILY: 4x6.5" b/w matted photo shows man in NCO dress tunic with single military medal on chest posing with his little girl & wife. Soldier has a shooting cord & carries his custom purchase dress artillery saber with cannons on Target. Near mint cond. $20.00

PHOTOGRAPH GARDE OFFICER IN DRESS PARADE ATTIRE: Matted. Full dress uniform with white Sam Browne belt & overcoat. Man has on white plumed Garde officer helmet & carries dress saber. 4x6". Mint cond. $22.00

PHOTOGRAPH KAISER WILHELM AS COMMANDER OF THE GARDE DU CORPS: 2.5x4". Beautifully detailed picture showing Kaiser on horseback wearing the cuirass & helmet of the unit with ornate shabraque trimmed with Garde Du Corps star & all fittings. Large frosted silver eagle on top of helmet. Near mint cond. $32.00

PHOTOGRAPH NAVAL SHIP SMS DANZIG WITH CREW: Nice large 11x15" backed b/w photo of Officers & EM's on the Danzig. All Seamen are in either whites or blues with Donald Duck hats. One standing Officer has Naval dagger hanging on left side. Above avg. cond. $35.00

PHOTOGRAPH SAXON INF. OFFICER & WIFE: Man dressed in walking out tunic & breeches with white topped visor cap having both rosettes.: Complete with sword in hand. Excellent detail. 4x6". Mint cond. $20.00

PHOTOGRAPH WWI AERIAL PILOT: 7x11". Man dressed in visor cap & great coat. 2nd Lt. straps with winged propeller clearly evident. Nice early wartime picture. Avg. cond. $20.00

POSTCARD COLOR ART STYLE BLACK AFRICAN COLONIAL SOLDIER WITH NATIONAL COLOR FLAG: Unused with caption on back, has full standing black man in uniform with rifle & black with red flag. Above avg. cond. $24.00

POSTCARD PHOTO STYLE AERIAL ACE FLIEGERLT. WILHELM FRANK: Photo indicates he was deceased as of time of release. Nice studio shot showing Frank standing with army tunic, visor cap. Good details to Blue Max, EK1 & Prussian pilot badge. Mint cond. $36.00

POSTCARD PHOTO STYLE AERIAL ACE HAUPTMANN BUDDECKE: Man shown standing in dress tunic with Blue Max: large rb. bar with EK1 & Prussian 1913 pilot badge. Mint cond. $36.00

POSTCARD PHOTO STYLE AERIAL ACE LT. BOHME: Subject shown seated in dress tunic with EK1, Prussian pilot badge. 4 ribbon bar on chest. Mint cond. $36.00

POSTCARD PHOTO STYLE AERIAL ACE LT. FREIHERR VON ALTHAUS: Field shot showing man from waist to head. He wears a Blue Max on his army style tunic with EK1 & Prussian Pilot badge. Mint cond. $36.00

POSTCARD PHOTO STYLE AERIAL ACE LT. HOHNDORF: 3/4 studio shot with man in dress tunic of a garde regiment with full collar litzen. Blue Max visible as are EK1 & Pilot badge. Austrian pilot badge on right side of tunic. 2 rbs. in 2nd button hole. Mint cond. $36.00

POSTCARD PHOTO STYLE AERIAL ACE LT. LEFFERS: 3/4 standing studio pose showing leffers in dress tunic with Blue Max, EK 1, Pilot badge & medal bar with 3 orders. Mint cond. $36.00

POSTCARD PHOTO STYLE AERIAL ACE LT. SCHLEICH: Formal dress tunic with two button front. Blue Max clearly seen as are the EK1 & Pilot badge (Bavaria). EK 2 & Bav. Mil. Serv. rbs. in 2nd button hole. Sword seen to lower right. Mint cond. $43.00

POSTCARD PHOTO STYLE AERIAL ACE LT. WENDELMUTH: Photo shows him seated beside a table while holding cap in right hand. 2 medal bar with EK2 & unknown House Order. Man wears both Prussian & Turkish pilot badges, has on an EK1 & also a 1915 Gallipoli Star. Mint cond. $36.00

POSTCARD PHOTO STYLE AERIAL ACE LT. Z.S. L. BOENISCH

POSTCARD PHOTO STYLE AERIAL ACE LT. Z.S. L. BOENISCH: Card shows man in naval Lt. dress tunic with visor cap: EK1, Sea Pilot Observer badge on tunic with EK 2 rb. in button hole. Clear signature on front; verso dated in pilot's own handwriting, *Berlin July 30, 1934.*

Short handwritten message to admirer—
(trans.) *Thank you for your greetings.*
Herewith I am sending you a card in
friendly greetings with my signature. Heil
Hitler! followed by signature again. Mint
cond. $108.00
POSTCARD PHOTO STYLE HAUPTMANN
HANS HESSE: War Hero #599. Shown in
uniform from chest up with glasses. Near
mint cond. $25.00
POSTCARD PHOTO STYLE LT.
FRICKART: War Hero #598. This studio
photo postcard & most of the following
are by *W.Sanke Berlin* with number listed.
Shown in uniform from waist up with
medal bar, EK 1st & pilot badge. Near
mint cond. $25.00
POSTCARD PHOTO STYLE LT. PFEIFER:
War Hero #428. Shown in uniform from
knees up with EK & visor cap. Near mint
cond. $24.00
POSTCARD PHOTO STYLE NAVAL
AERIAL ACE LT. CHRISTIANSEN: Nicely
detailed with man in naval dress tunic
wearing 4 medal bar to include EK,
Hohenzollern Order, Hamburg Service
medal & EK1 on tunic with Naval Flying
badge. Blue Max at neck. Near mint
cond. $36.00
POSTCARD PHOTO STYLE NAVAL
AERIAL ACE OBERFLUGMEISTER
FABECK: War Hero #635. Shown from
waist up with Naval pilot badge, EK,
medal bar, leather belt with bayonet &
visor cap. Near mint cond. $25.00
POSTCARD PHOTO STYLE NAVAL
SAILOR IN DARK BLUE TUNIC WITH
BIB: Nice details to knot, bib & standard
jumper with large chevron & flaming shell
specialty patch with two small chevrons
below it. Near mint
cond. $20.00
POSTCARD PHOTO STYLE WWI BAVAR-
IAN MUSICIAN IN FIELD TUNIC: Taken
outdoors by barracks. Good details to
visor cap, swallows nests, wrap leggings,
breeches & shoes. Feldpost stamped to
unit on back. Above avg.
cond. $25.00
POSTCARD PHOTO STYLE WWI BAVAR-
IAN NCO: Subject shown wearing M15
tunic with lower slash pockets & crown
buttons. Subdued Garde litzen on collar
with NCO lace. NCO style visor cap
shown with both rosettes. Above avg.
cond. $20.00
POSTCARD PHOTO STYLE WWI BAVAR-
IAN SOLDIERS: Two older men shown
with beards. Figure on left wears a four
pocket style tunic with concealed buttons:
man on right dressed in M15 tunic with
concealed buttons & lower slash pockets.

Both shown wearing visor caps. Above
avg. cond. $20.00

IMPERIAL GERMAN MISC. CURRENCY & PAPER MATERIALS

COIN 1899 DREI MARK DEUTCHES
REICH: 33mm diam. with title side having
eagle. Kaiser profile with *A etc.* Rim has
oak leaves & *Gott Mit Uns.* Above avg.
cond. $20.00
COIN 1900 FUNF MARK DEUTSCHES
REICH: 38mm diam. with title side having
eagle. Kaiser profile with *A etc.* Rim has
oak leaves & *Gott Mit Uns.* Avg.
cond. $22.00
COIN 1923 1000 MARKS NOTGELD
WESTFALEN: Bronze. 46mm round with
horse & other side is profile of Von Stein
1757-1831, gold finish Avg.
cond. $20.00
MAP 1700s BATTLE OF HOCHSTET:
15x20" approx. size, *Plan of the Glorious*
Battle of Hochstet gained by the Allies on
August 13th 1704. Plan illustrates battle
positions with explanations. Above avg.
cond. $40.00
PAMPHLET FRIEDRICH AUGUST MEDAL:
8pg. With various emendations &
changes to the regulations 1905-1916.
Very nice list of changing regulations
allowing more people to win it. 7x9". This
was a very popular medal in the WWI
period & this data is officially issued by
the Orders Commission. Near mint
cond. $20.00

POSTER WWI AUSTRIAN WAR LOAN

POSTER WWI AUSTRIAN WAR LOAN:
About 27.5x41" rolled body. Nice

illustrated helmeted soldier about to throw stick-grenade & signed by *W.Kuhn 1917*. Color crowned double headed eagle shield below with *K. K. Priv. Allgemeine Verkehrsbank, Wien Zeichnet Die Siebente Osterr. Kriegsanleihe etc. By Wagnersche K.K. Universitats Buchdrunckerie, R.Kiesel, Innsbruck.* Exc. cond. $213.00

POSTER GERMAN OCCUPATION OF BELGIUM: 27x40" paper with German, French, Belgium language poster of Instructions on the General government. Yellowing paper with a fabric backing. Avg. cond. $90.00

POSTER WWI PATRIOTIC

POSTER WWI PATRIOTIC: 38x48" approx. size. Magnificent red gold crowned Imperial eagle depicted without spread wings on mountain top. Strong & powerful. Full lower lettering advertises the exploits of the Tyrolian heroes in the Galizien campaign. Avg. cond. . $135.00

IMPERIAL GERMAN ID BOOKLETS & PERSONAL PAPERS

DOCUMENT 1870/71 SERVICE GROUP: Set of 2. 1 for service in war & other 1870-71 medal. Has good graphics & named to same man. Folded & would look good framed. Avg. cond. ... $124.00

DOCUMENT NAPOLEONIC WAR LEAVE PASS FOR A LEIB GRENADIER IN THE KURHESSISCHES: Regiment Garde-Grenadier dated 12 January 1816 & signed by his Captain. Valid to 17 March 1817. Gives age & description of the Grenadier for identification. Presumably

for him to go home & tend the crops, family matters etc. Europe was still very unsettled as the battle of Waterloo was only 7 months past, June 1815. 7x9" document with emblem & handwritten info. Exc. cond. $101.00

DOG TAG M1916 *5.G.R.Z.F.4.K. NO.695*: Gray oval with title stamped side & other *Paul Gloddeck Dortmund etc.* Above avg. cond. $42.00

ID BOOKLET *MILITAIR PASS* 1865: 3.5x5.5" ID booklet to soldier with many entries where he served & when. All done in handwritting very neatly. Attached in back is a permit for leave from 3rd Com. des Koniglichen Landwehr Battalions dated 1867. 8.5x13" in size. With official stamp & signature. Above avg. cond. $20.00

ID BOOKLET *MILITAIR PASS*: Passport was issued in 1910 to a Marine in 5. Kompagnie IV Matr. Artl. Abt. with entries about his training, promotions, cruises, & others. Exc. cond. $40.00

ID BOOKLET COVER

ID BOOKLET COVER: 4x6" Blue fiber & cloth body with full color design of Prussian plumed dragoon helmet, cross lances, rifle & saber: Silvered lettering, *Dragoner-Regiment Freiherr v. Manteuffel. Rheinisches Nr. 5* with shoulder strap design. Cardboard interior with cloth straps & pocket to hold Militarpass & other personal papers. Pre-war. Above avg. cond. $59.00

IMPERIAL GERMAN PERIOD RELATED BOOKS & DOCUMENTS

BOOK *1900 PRUSSIAN-WURTTEMBERG ARMY RANK LIST 1900 FOR ALL OFFICERS*: Deluxe dark red stiff covers with gold embossed Iron Cross, Imperial eagle. Covers all active & reserve officers of both armies with service entry dates, awards, commands, etc. Near mint cond. $139.00

BOOK *AVIATION AWARDS OF IMPERIAL GERMANY IN WORLD WAR 1* VOL. 2: O'Connor, sb, large format. 285 pages with lots of period photos of the men in the flying units. This volume covers all Prussian awards including The Blue Max. Mint cond. $21.00

BOOK *AVIATION AWARDS OF IMPERIAL GERMANY IN WWI* VOL. #3 *KING. OF SAXONY*: O'Connor, 1993 sb, large format. 279 pages with period photos of the medals, pilots & planes of WWI. Covers Immelmann's awards & the medals. Mint cond. $26.00

BOOK *AVIATION AWARDS OF IMPERIAL GERMANY IN WWI* VOL. 2 PRUSSIA: O'Connor, 1990, sb, large format. 283 pages with period photos of the medals, pilots & planes of WWI. Covers Richthofen awards & the medal Blue Max. Mint cond. $26.00

BOOK *AYESHA*: (WWI GERMAN NAVAL HISTORY BOOK) by Captain v. Mucke. med./small format, 122 pages with war history & of the ship Ayesha. German text. Has photo of the captain in front. Above avg. cond. $32.00

BOOK *BISMARCK DENKMAL FUER DAS DEUTSCHE VOLK*

BOOK *BISMARCK DENKMAL FUER DAS DEUTSCHE VOLK*: 1895. large format with embr. hb cover, 390 pages. German text with many illus. & photos & some color lithographs. Avg. cond. $495.00

BOOK *DAS MARNE DRAMA*: 1926. Covers the battles from 5-8 Sept. 1914 of the Garde Corps on the right wing of the German Army. Excellent Order of battle.

275 pages with 10 maps & illustrations. Above avg. cond. $20.00

BOOK *DAS VOLK IN WAFFEN*: By Oberstlt. Hoppenstedt, by 160 photos of horses & troops in various war activities & German text. sb, dj, large format. Dj shows most age. Above avg. cond. $20.00

BOOK *DER DRAHTVERHAU*: 170 pages Amusing stories of the soldiers in the German Army with pen & ink illustrations of service life & personal memoirs. Above avg. cond. $20.00

BOOK *DER WELTBRAND*: 3 vol. set. Large format, hb cloth, 1919, approx. 300 pages each with color plates, maps & b/w photos relating to war activities. Avg. cond. $114.00

BOOK *DER WELTKRIEG IM BILD*: Hb, med. format, 1928, 350 photos, text & protecting thin paper between each photo. Dark blue cover with gold title print. Above avg. cond. $37.00

BOOK *DER WELTKRIEG*: By Karl Helfferich, hb, med. format, 1919, 428 pages, deals with beginning of war & U-boat battles. German text. Above avg. cond. $20.00

BOOK *DEUTSCHE HELMET 1897-1914*: 1978/79 edition, sb, small format, 270 pages with b/w photos with values of each & rarity. Good reference, all German text. Near mint cond. $33.00

BOOK *DIE DEUTSCHE ARMEE VOR DEM WELTKRIEGE*: By Moritz Ruhl. sb, med. format with complete list of regiments & battalions of the Imperial army. 12 fold-out color lithos of the uniforms of the Imperial army from all parts of Germany. Near mint cond. $130.00

BOOK *ERINNERUNGEN DES KRONPRINZEN WILHELM*: (Memoirs of the Crown Prince) 350 pages All text, no pictures. The Crown Prince as recalled through speeches, war dispatches & personal papers. Hard cover. Above avg. cond. $20.00

BOOK *FLUEZEUG-ABBILDUNGEN*: (Plane Pictures) WWI period. Excellent line drawings of major German fighters with data on them. Used for training & aid ID. Avg. cond. $183.00

BOOK *GEFSCHICHTE DES INFANTERIE REGIMENTS KAISER WILHELM*: (HESSIAN INFANTRY REG. 116 UNIT HISTORY) Filled with interesting info. with names of men & a map in the back plus picture of excellent picture of the KAISER. Small format, hb cardboard, 1913, 200 pages of German text. Above avg. cond. $45.00

BOOK *GERMAN IRON CROSS DOCU-MENTS OF WWI*: Sb, !arge format, 227 pages. 1990's printed, by William E. Hamelman. Many photos, illus. & documents. Signed copy by author. Near mint cond. $30.00

BOOK *GROSSER BILDER-ATLAS DES WELTKRIEGES*: (Great Photo Atlas of The World War). Complete with dust cover. 406 pages with superb shots of army, zeppelin, navy & air forces. Fine b/w shots of all fronts— covers battles, fortifications, propaganda of all sides, etc. 12x15". Exc. cond. $52.00

BOOK *HINDENBURG*: Medium format, hb cloth with gold embossed title, 1927, 287 pages. German text. Book dedicated to Hindenburg on his 80th birthday, it commemorates his years of faithful service & devotion to the Fatherland. Avg. cond. $20.00

BOOK *ILLUSTRIERTE GESCHICHTE DES WELTKRIEGES 1914-15*

BOOK *ILLUSTRIERTE GESCHICHTE DES WELTKRIEGES 1914-15*: 2 volume set. Hb with color illustrated soldiers to covers, large format & both have cardboard issue sleeves that have kept both. 500 pages & 504 pages. With many nice photos of WWI combat. Above avg. cond. $87.00

BOOK *IM TORPEDOBOOT GEGEN ENGLAND*: (WWI German Naval History) By von Fritz Graf. sb, med./small format, 101 pages with war history of German torpedo boats. German text. Has photo of the captain in front Above avg. cond. $32.00

BOOK IMPERIAL GERMAN EDGED WEAPON CATALOGUE & PRICE GUIDE: 1985. sb, large format, appears

to be a reprint of a Carl Eickhorn Catalog of period with a separate price guide attached. All turn of century art. Mint cond. $40.00

BOOK *KRIEGSLAGGE*: (The War Flag) 1900. 160 pages with 64 photos & illustrations of naval life in the Imperial Navy. Fine rare pictures of deck board life, sailor uniforms & equipment. Fancy stiff cover with sailor hoisting the famous battle flag. Avg. cond. $27.00

BOOK *PRUSSIAN-WURTTEMBERG OFFICIAL RANK LIST FOR 1900 FOR ALL OFFICERS*: Hard bound stiff covers with Imperial eagle, Iron Cross. Covers all officers, active/reserve of the Prussian & Wurt. Army as of 1900. Lists service entry, decorations, honors, units, etc. Avg. cond. ..$90.00

BOOK *SCHIESSVORSCHRIFT FUR DIE FEARTILLERIE*: (FIELD EXERCISES OF THE FIELD ARTILLERY). 1911. Berlin published. Stiff stock covers. 80 pages with fold-out maps, tables, etc. Avg. cond. $20.00

BOOK ANCIENT & MODERN HISTORY OF GERMANY: 1923. *Deutsche Gedenkhalle* (German Hall of Memory). Large format with stiff blue cover, gold embossed eagle with title. Approx. 440 pages of Gutenburg style text with deluxe end papers. No photos but two impressive gold style coats of arms of Hindenburg & Germania. Above avg. cond. $75.00

BOOK GERMAN ARMY RANK LIST 1896: Medium format, hb cardboard, 1299 pages. Superb listing of all active & reserve officers & all corps & units of the Imperial German army at the turn of the century. Minor wear to spine but not detractive. The standard work for looking up names of officers who appear on gift swords, presentation goblets, statues. Lists all medals, service patents & transfers. Avg. cond. $124.00

BOOKLET *WWI DEUTSCHE ARMEE MILITAR-ALBUM*: By Moritz Ruhl. 16 fold-out color lithos of the field gray uniforms of the imperial army from all parts of Germany. Period reference. Avg. cond. $135.00

CIGARETTE CARD ALBUM *DER WELT KRIEG*: Sb, large format, approx. 32 pages. Post WWI print. A color printed pictorial & historical account of WWI. No cards missing. Exc. cond. ..$35.00

CIGARETTE CARD ALBUM *DER WELTKRIEG*: On the cover is a sword stabbed into Mother Earth on Fire &

imprinted *Der Welkreig.* sb, large
format, 70 pages complete with all b/w
photo cards. Avg. cond. $82.00

CIGARETTE CARD ALBUM *ORDEN*

CIGARETTE CARD ALBUM *ORDEN*: Sb,
large format, album with color prints of
medals, a collection of the best known
German medals & awards. 58 pages
by Waldorf Astoria GmbH Muenchen.
Above avg. cond. $100.00
CIGARETTE CARD ALBUM *DER WELT
KRIEG*: 10x13" size album with color
printed photos of WWI. Sb, large
format, 71 pages. Post-war print.
Cover is flaming red with yellow print.
Exc. cond. $40.00
DOCUMENT IRON CROSS 1914 1ST
CLASS AWARD: 5x8" document dated
13 June 1915 with official Imperial
stamp & signature. Folded. Avg.
cond. $39.00
DOCUMENT IRON CROSS 1914 2ND
CLASS AWARD: 6.5x8" printed paper
with typed *Musk. Weiss, Phil. 3.
Kompagnie Infanterie- Regiment Nr. 87*
& issued 28.5.1917. Folded. Above
avg. cond. $61.00
DOCUMENT IRON CROSS 1914 2ND
CLASS AWARD: 7x8.75" ornate
printed paper typed to *Soldat Paul
Martin Dietze, 4.Kompagnie Infanterie
- Regiments Nr. 182* & issued *4.Juli
1918*. Folded. Above avg.
cond. $79.00
DOCUMENT IRON CROSS 1914 2ND
CLASS: 7x8.25" printed paper with
typed *Gefreiten Karl Rossler on 6.Juli
1917.* Folded. Above avg.
cond. $66.00
DOCUMENT WOUND BADGE 1914
BLACK: To telegraph operator in *6
Infanterie-Division, Koeniglich
Preussen.* Nov. 1918 dated. Exc.
cond. $35.00

DOCUMENT FIELD HONOR BADGE
AWARD WITH BADGE & MINIATURE

DOCUMENT FIELD HONOR BADGE
AWARD WITH BADGE & MINIATURE:
11.75x16.5" nicely printed b/w details
with green border, military branches near
1914/1918 EK, townshields to sides &
named to *Leutnant Walter Bauer etc.* Was
framed now rolled. Full size badge &
20mm badge stickpin. Above avg.
cond. $168.00
HANDBOOK *ANHANG ZUM EXERZIER-
REGLEMENT FUR DIE
FELDARTILLERIE*: (Official Field Artillery
Manual) Small format, hb, 1913, 250
pages with b/w graphics of equipment &
field related articles. Near mint
cond. $45.00
MANUAL GERMAN MILITARY AIRCRAFT
ID NOTEBOOK: 1920-30. Hb, large
format, 13 heavy cardboard pages with
silhouettes & profiles of military aircraft of
era before Germany rebuilt the Luftwaffe.
Has naval planes & others all labeled
with parts. Most pages shows the
formations of military flying. Steel binder
bound book. All are eagle ink stamp in
corner. Title in German Is *Tafeln fur den
Flugzeug-Erkennungsdienst* Avg.
cond. $149.00
MAP MILITARY TOPOGRAPHY
HOHENSTEIN-ERNSTTHAL AREA
1925: 20x22" gray fabric backed paper &
folded, color graphics & very detailed.
Has complete legend at base & dated.
Avg. cond. $36.00
MAP MILITARY TOPOGRAPHY MAP
SECTION DIPPOLDISWALDE AREA
1881: 19x20" gray fabric backed paper &
folded, color graphics & very detailed.
Has complete legend at base & dated
Dec. 1881 with embossed stamp at base
Avg. cond. $36.00

NEWSPAPER WWI *ILLUSTRIETE GESCHICHTE DES WELTKRIEGES*: 15 issues. With reports, photos & illus. of battles on land sea & air on all fronts during 1914-1916. Good reference. Exc. cond. $52.50

PERIODICAL *DAS BANERLAND* 1925: April-Sept. issue, 40 pages with all German text on the history & photos of the old trains models, cut aways, stamps, carriage models & other good reference photos. Avg. cond. $20.00

PERIODICAL *DER REITER VON SUDWEST* 1927: (MAGAZINE FOR SOLDIERS IN COLONIES OF AFRICA) Feb. issue, small magazine format, 44 pages with cover art of a colonial mounted soldier of period. All German text with news & articles & ads Avg. cond. $20.00

PERIODICAL *KAISERZEIT*: A total of 16 issues with binder. Holds various papers. This set includes the following issues: *Vol.I issues 1 thru 6, Vol.II issues 1 thru 6 & Vol. III issues 1 thru 4.* Near mint cond. $145.00

PERIODICAL *MITTEILUNGEN* 1925: (WWI Veteran Magazine for Reserve Infantry Regiment 27) sb, small magazine format, 48 pages with all German text articles on the meeting memorials, parades & other, has photos. Has cover art of helmeted soldier with pipe, stain on top half of cover. Avg. cond. $20.00

PERIODICAL *SKAGERRAT* 1931: (German Naval Veteran Magazine) med. magazine format, 14 pages with cover of the tattered WWI German battle flag & ships in distance. Printed for the men of Skagerraksclacht, has lots of WWI photos of damaged ships & sailors & leaders. Avg. cond. $20.00

PERSONALITY ITEM FRANZ JUSTUS JULIUS VON TRENK NOBILITY ENTITLEMENT: Comes with a photo copy military history of Trenk 10.5x14" 8 page parchment with ornate hand ink lettering overall & color illus. coat of arms. He was born in 1825, long military service with many awards, he retired as a Generallt. in 1887 & died in 1897. Near mint cond. $700.00

PHOTO ALBUM WWI SAILOR: Fully captioned. 26 photos. Covers 1913-17 period with early pictures of a squadron visit to the fjords of Norway. Later pictures show mine ship, submarines & battleships. Good pictures of officers & sailors in wartime uniforms. Captions all typed & easy to read. Avg. cond. $68.00

SHEET MUSIC GERMAN MILITARY BANDS: 10x13". 1900 period with beautiful color cover litho of red plumed bandsmen marching in Berlin with a bearded Kapelmeister at the fore. 4 music selections inside for piano & violin. Above avg. cond. $20.00

THIRD REICH POSTCARDS & SEALS

POSTCARD *DER BERGHOF OBERSALZBERG ARBEITSZIMMER DES FUHRERS*: By Hoffmann. Nr. 471. color photo of Hitler's desk & seating group. Unused. Above avg. cond. $34.00

POSTCARD *DER POTSDAMER KURS*

POSTCARD *DER POTSDAMER KURS*: Photo of Potsdam Garnison church with 3 German leaders below, Hitler, Frederick the Great & Hindenburg. 1934 mailed. Avg. cond. $50.00

POSTCARD *DEUTSCHE WEIHNACHT*: By Hoffmann. VDA print depicting profile of Hitler & a lightened Christmas tree. Unused. Above avg. cond. $40.00

POSTCARD *DIE KRIEGSORDEN DES GROSSDEUTSCHEN REICHS*: 4x5" color art of Iron Cross 1st class with 1939 eagle bar. Card unused but yellowing to writing side. Above avg. cond. $28.00

POSTCARD *DIE KRIEGSORDEN DES GROSSDEUTSCHEN REICHS*: 4x5" color art of Knight Cross War Merit cross with swords. Card unused but yellowing to writing side. Above avg. cond. $28.00

POSTCARD *EAS*: Showing Mt. trooper with rope, pick & rifle. Unused. Near mint cond. $25.00

POSTCARD *EIN VOLK EIN REICH EIN FUHRER 1938*: Hitler profile in center of map of Germany & Nazi eagle. Has 1 printed stamp & 2 others with no cancellation. Good condition. Near mint cond. $24.00

POSTCARD *GENERALFELDMARSCHALL HERMANN GORING 1938*: Used with 3 different cancellations, 2 Osterreich stamps & Nazi sports stamp & Wein Des Fuhrer birthday April 20 1938. Avg. cond. $30.00

POSTCARD *GROSSADMIRAL DONITZ*: By Hoffmann. Facsimile signature. Unused card R58a. Exc. cond. $38.00

POSTCARD *MAENNER UNSERER ZEIT*: Hitler as leader & father des Volkes. Unused. Has stamp & postmark 1943, Wien. Exc. cond. $40.00

POSTCARD
*REICHSFRONTSOLDATENTAG
3.-4.SEPT.1932 BERLIN*

POSTCARD *REICHSFRONTSOLDATENTAG 3.-4.SEPT.1932 BERLIN*: Illustrated combat soldier with Brandenburg gate in background. Title at back. Near mint cond. $50.00

POSTCARD *REICHSPARTEITAG NURNBERG 1937*: Color litho, unused but 1938 Nurnberg cancellation. Mint cond. $22.00

POSTCARD *TAG DER DEUTSCHEN KUNST 1938*: 2 tone card with sculpted king head, party eagle & title. Same details to ornate Munich postmark & used. Above avg. cond. $65.00

POSTCARD *UNSERE PANZERWAFFE, GENERALFEDMARSHALL ROMMEL*: W. Willrich color print, unused. Portrait of Rommel with goggles & cap. Dressed in coat & tunic. IC around his neck. Exc. cond. $25.00

POSTCARD *UNSERE WAFFEN SS*: Titled *Pak setzt uber einen Kanal*. Group of Waffen SS soldiers on rubber raft with PAK gun. Above avg. cond. $20.00

POSTCARD *VERLAG FUR TRADITIONSPFLEGE*

POSTCARD *VERLAG FUR TRADITIONSPFLEGE*: Color illustrated Panzer soldier with beret & shoulders. By *Verlag fur Traditionspflege etc.* Near mint ond $55.00

POSTCARD GENERALMAJOR RINGEL: By Hoffmann. With b/w photo of Ringel in uniform with EK & other medals & bars. Exc. cond. $34.00

POSTCARD HITLER: 1938. Has b/w drawing of chest up profile with overcoat & peaked hat. Unused Near mint cond. $28.00

POSTCARD HITLER: Photo illus. Hitler & has 5 colorful stamps on reverse commemorating Art Exhibit in Berlin 1938. Canceled. Exc. cond. $40.00

POSTCARD HITLER: Postcard illus. portrait of Hitler in his party uniform. Stamped & canceled 1939. Exc. cond. $40.00

POSTCARD HITLER: Postcard is a thank you note to birthday wishes received & is addressed to Ortsgruppe Sued der N.S.D.A.P. dated 5 May 1925. Postcard is typewritten but has original signature of Adolf Hitler as written in his earlier days. Also photocopy of excepts from Charles Hamilton's Leaders & Personalities of the Third Reich. Illustrated are signatures & excerpts written by Hitler while incarcerated in 1924 & 1925. A very rare item. Near mint cond. $895.00

POSTCARD HITLER: Unused but with Condor Legion cancellation of 1939 Berlin but no stamp. Has profile shot of Hitler face & surrounding with his conquests from 1933 to 1939. Very good quallty. Near mint cond. $20.00

POSTCARD KC WINNER WITH OAK
LEAVES: Army Hauptmann Schroer. By
Hoffmann. Portrait photo in full military
gear with personal ink signature at
bottom. & KC with oak leaves. unused.
Exc. cond. $45.00

POSTCARD KC WINNER: Army General
Guderian. With b/w litho of chest up of
the man in uniform with KC & facsimile
signature, some slight age staining,
unused. Avg. cond. $82.00

POSTCARD KC WINNER: Army General
Keitel. With b/w photo with chest up shot
of man with ink stamped signature on
front over facsimile signature, unused.
Above avg. cond. $91.00

POSTCARD KC WINNER: Army
Generalmajor Ringel. By Willrich. 2 tone
drawing of Ringel portrait with KC at
neck. Unused. Exc. cond. $45.00

POSTCARD KC WINNER: Naval U-Boat
Capt Schne. Different b/w shot with
portrait shot of man with facsimile
signature on front. Has caption back.
Unused. Mint cond. $72.00

SPECIAL 1936 MUNICH STAMP

SPECIAL 1936 MUNICH STAMP: Munich
brown band race stamp block wax seal
stamp *WAFFEN SS*. Brass head with
wood handle. Serial numbered on side &
waffemamt stamped. Clear Waffen SS
eagle, inscription. Approx. 5" tall. Above
avg. cond. $175.00

TRANSPARENCIES PARATROOPER WITH
STORAGE BOX: 5x6x6" wooden box with
metal hook catch & insert label
Fluzeugkunde/Flugzeugwartung 4x5"
clear celluloid photos, art & illus. on jump
training, packing chutes, other equipment, all in individual envelopes 220
different & all German text. Above avg.
cond. $375.00

WAX SEAL STAMP
GENERALFELDMARSCHALL V. KLEIST:
38mm bronze disc with raised title,
national eagle & 2 screws affixed to wood
handle. Exc. cond. $395.00

WAX SEAL STAMP *II. PZ. ART. RGT.
BRANDENBURG*: 38mm diam. brass
disc with Nazi eagle center & border
II.Pz.Art.Rgt. Brandenburg. Tall with
wood handle. Avg. cond. $263.00

WAX SEAL STAMP *ROHA AMT II OST*:
38mm diam. bronze disc with raised
eagle/title details & wood handle. Exc.
cond. $375.00

WAX SEAL STAMP *SS
TOTENKOPFSTANDARTE
BRANDENBURG*: 38mm bronze disc
with raised title & national eagle. Wood
handle. Exc. cond. $591.00

WAX SEAL STAMP *WAFFEN SS*

WAX SEAL STAMP *WAFFEN SS*: Brass
head with wood handle. Waffenamt
stamped, serial numbered. Large eagle
with Waffen SS & circular inscription.
Very clean. Approx. 5" tall. Near mint
cond. $328.00

WAX SEAL STAMP *POSTAMT AUGSBURG
II*: Hallmarked circular brass stamping
service with excellent details to eagle,
lettering. Tall walnut grip. 4.5" tall. Mint
cond. $150.00

THIRD REICH ID BOOKLETS

HISTORICAL GROUPING LUFTWAFFE
HONOR GOBLET WINNER: Consists of
Luftwaffe Pilot license with owner picture
in Luft NCO tunic, dated July 12, 1941 &
7 personal photos of owner in uniform
with all decorations. LW soldbuch with
Feldwebel rank in it (no picture) & entries
for EK 1st & 2nd, Bronze, Silver & Gold
LW close combat clasps, Honor Goblet
(1944). Man served with 5th Night Fighter
Squad & also received the German Cross
in gold. Avg.
cond. $729.00

ID BOOKLET *DEUTCHES REICH
KENNKARTE*: ID booklet was issued to
female worker in 1944. Has photo ID &
fingerprints. Kennkarte is made of oil
cloth & has party eagle on cover. Has
several official stamps & is signed by
mayor of city. Exc. cond. $24.00

ID BOOKLET *DEUTSCHES REICH
KENNKARTE*: Both are made from oil
cloth. Both were issued to females, one

was a student in 1945 & the other was a farm laborer in 1940. Both have id photos, & fingerprint. Shows some age. Above avg. cond. $22.00

ID BOOKLET *HEER WEHRPASS*: Owner was inducted in to army in 1944 after he was found fit for limited military duty before. Has owners photo in civilian clothes. Exc. cond. $30.00

ID BOOKLET *HEER WEHRPASS*: Owner was inducted into service in 1940 & served in Panzer Regiment. Many entries reveal his training & assignments. Last entry shows he was killed in Russia in 1943. Has photo ID. Above avg. cond. $50.00

ID BOOKLET *HJ LEITSUNGSBUCH*: DJ & HJ leistungsbuch with picture to youth in Jungbann 208. Was awarded HJ proficiency badge in bronze 1940. Lists all performances 1938-1940. Also has entry for Gelaendesportwart der HJ 1940. Incl. is the corresponding cuff title 5.5" long, gold lettering on black background. Above avg. cond. ... $75.00

ID BOOKLET *LUFTWAFFE SOLDBUCH*: With photo of owner in military attire in front. Man served with a Flak Battalion. Book well filled out with many entries. Man received the Luft Ground Contacts war badge. Avg. cond. $66.00

ID BOOKLET *LUFTWAFFE WEHRPASS*

ID BOOKLET *LUFTWAFFE WEHRPASS*: 2nd issue. 1944 issue shows youth in civilian dress. Martin Schulte-Heuthaus with 1936 volunteer service thru 1944 listing various flak assignments & ends with 1945 *Luftkriegsschule 8*. Weapons training included 2cm & 3. 7cm flak guns & awarded 3 medals incl. EK 2nd. Near mint cond. $160.00

ID BOOKLET *SOLDBUCH* & *FUHRERSCHEIN* TO SAME MAN: 1939 issue to same man *Peter Enderle* with photo as EM to drivers license from *IV.s.Geb.Art.Rgt.79*. Soldbuch from

3.Art.Abt.408. Service on Westfront & Africa with awarded KVK2nd with swords & Italian DAK medal. Last entry on 17. Marz 1942. 1992 letter from archives states no additional information available. Exc. cond. $282.00

ID BOOKLET *SOLDUBHC* KC WINNER: Book is noted as being a replacement for an earlier one. Inside front cover shows Kluge in Army captain tunic with EK around neck. Full signature. Book issued in 1944 with many entries to hospital & training service. Complete with personal purchase black leatherette carrier. One page loose but on it is clearly marked that he won the Knight's Cross on June 6, 1944. Above avg. cond. $608.00

ID BOOKLET *SS SOLDBUCH*

ID BOOKLET *SS SOLDBUCH*: Late-war issue with eagle stamp & inked wording to photo area. Issued *29 January 1945, 8/3/25.W.Gren.Div.Hunyadi SS* & few entries with couple nice SS officer signatures. Above avg. cond. $72.00

ID BOOKLET *SS WEHRPASS*: 1939 issued with photo in civilian dress of Wilhelm Rehsl. 1944 inducted 18./SS Flak A.u.e.Rgt. & ends with 1945 unit. Few entries. Near mint cond. $76.00

ID BOOKLET *SS WEHRPASS*: Issued with photo in civilian dress of Hans Werner Sparbeck. Volunteer with 4 unit entries & 2 rank entries. Exc. cond. $87.00

ID BOOKLET *SS WEHRPASS*: Issued with photo in civilian dress of Hugo Ristau. 9 army units from 1940 thru 1944 & ends with 1944 unit *9.SS Totenkopf Wachbatallion Sachsenhausen*. Many combat listings & only got Russian front medal. Near mint cond. $131.00

ID BOOKLET *SS WEHRPASS*

ID BOOKLET *SS WEHRPASS*: Issued with photo in civilian dress of Wernfried Theis. RAD service, 1944 SS Pz.Gren.Ausb.u.Ers.Btl.2 & 3 other SS units. Communications training & 45 rank Unterfuhrer Anwarter. Near mint cond. $87.00

ID BOOKLET *SS=AUSWEIS*: 1934 issue. Photo of man in civilian suit, *Adolf Pauly #147527* & tan card filled out. Exc. cond. $160.00

ID BOOKLET *SS=AUSWEIS*: 1934 issue. Photo of man in civilian suit, *Oskar Kelm #147036* & tan card filled out. Above avg. cond. $160.00

ID BOOKLET *SS=AUSWEIS*: 1934 issue. Photo of man in civilian suit, *Richard Will #153813* & tan card filled out. Binder holes. Above avg. cond. $100.00

ID BOOKLET *SS=AUSWEIS*: 1934 issue. Photo of young man in SA uniform *54* collar tab. *Kurt Leiding #213115* on tan card. Exc. cond. $100.00

ID BOOKLET *W H FESTUNGSBAU DIENSTBUCH*: Title to gray paper cover with national eagle. Rusted staples at binding with pages loose. Photo of man in suit with entries & 1939/40 work duty. Avg. cond. $139.00

ID BOOKLET *WEHRPASS*: 1937 issue with photo of man in suit. Kurt Heinen shows WWI service & EK 2nd. 39/41 military desk service & discharged in 1941. Avg. cond. $70.00

ID BOOKLET *WEHRPASS*: 1939 issued with photo of man in suit & has Hitler mustache. 3 infantry assignments with entries for France & Russia duty. Above avg. cond. $50.00

ID BOOKLET *WEHRPASS*: Issued to a man who served in Russia & won the Black Wound Badge & the Russian Front medal (1943). Promoted to rank of Gefreiter. Man served with several different grenadier regiments. Service postings cover period from 1941-43. Above avg. cond. $45.00

ID BOOKLET *WEHRPASS*: Issued to man in 1939, with photo in civilian attire. He served in an artillery regiment & was promoted to Gefreiten in 1941. He fought many battles on the Western Front in 1940. Further entries show he also served on the Eastern Front & was killed in Russia on 24.2.1942. Exc. cond. $46.00

ID BOOKLET *WEHRPASS*: Man served with the Pz. Gren. Ers. Batl. 3. 2 Feb. 1942. Photo shows him in civilian attire. Book notes he was killed in action, June, 1943. Man had training in the 98K MG34 & P-08 pistol. Above avg. cond. $49.00

ID BOOKLET *WEHRPASS*

ID BOOKLET *WEHRPASS*: Photo of man in suit Heinrich Robers, RAD service, 5 army units, 3 LW & ends in 1944 5.SS Pz.Div.Viking. Exc. cond. $177.00

ID BOOKLET COVER *DEUTSCHES REICH SOLDBUCH*: Cover is made from brown leatherette material with eagle design & title embossed on cover. Cover is size of Soldbuch. Inside is lined & has pockets. Exc. cond. $40.00

ID BOOKLETS *BDM AUSWEISS* & RED CROSS PERSONALAUSWEIS & AWARD DOCUMENT TO SAME GIRL: 6 page ID with added 4 page section, nice photo in uniform, 1934 issue & to *Elisabeth Siggelkow*. A 1941 issue Red Cross Personalausweis document & her 1943 issued War Merit medal document as a DRK Hilfsschwester. Above avg. cond. $200.00

ID BOOKLETS *BDM AUSWEISS* & RED CROSS PERSONALAUSWEIS & AWARD DOCUMENT TO SAME GIRL

ID BOOKLETS *DJ LEISTUNGSBUCH* & *GESUNDHEITSPASS*: Photo of DJ in uniform, *20.April.1939* & with *Jungbann 135 Mark*. Some entries, 1940 awarded DJ badge, etc. No HJ entries. 6 page pass with same name but different birth dates. 1st entries only & 38 dated. Exc. cond. $81.00

ID BOOKLETS *HJ AUSWEIS* & *DJ AUSWEIS* TO SAME BOY: Both named to Gunther Muller & photos show him in DJ uniform. 1933 issue 4 page DJ Stuttgart etc. 1937 issue 6 page from Stuttgart. Above avg. cond. $276.00

ID BOOKLETS *LUFTWAFFE WEHRPASS* & *SOLDBUCH* TO SAME MAN: Both to Harry Kruger with same photo in NCO flightblouse. 1938 Wehrpass by *Fliegerhorstkompanie Schweinfurt* with many entries, various units from 1936 thru 1944 for paratrooper ground unit. Vendor states aircraft & radio repairman with duty in Czech., France, Russia etc. Added typed page showing service & blue Soldbuch, 2nd issue with entries up to 1944. Above avg. cond. $300.00

THIRD REICH DOCUMENTS

AWARD DOCUMENT SS SERVICE MEDAL 12 YEAR: Approx. 14x20" black matte with document in center. Left side has stock paper cover with large SS runes in black circle. Document issued to SS Unterscharfuhrer Theodor Dietl of 2. SS Totenkopf Infanterie Regiment for 12 Years Long Service. Issues the man the 2nd class SS Long Service medal. Meissner signed with facsimile Hitler signature. Large Chancellery seal. Dated at Berlin, 12 July 1942. Very clean. Period item. Mint cond. $500.00

AWARD DOCUMENT *URKUNDE II.PREIS 1935*: 9.5x12.5" size color printed document with ornate laurel border, circle with stahlhelm soldier in upper part, title, competition, date & name in lower part. Inked signature & ink stamp. Above avg. cond. $40.00

AWARD DOCUMENT ASSAULT BADGE IN BRONZE: Document is 5.75x8.25" in size & was issued to a Hauptfeldwebel in *I. RGT, Panzergrenadier Div. Grossdeutschland in Warschau 8.9.44*. Has signature & party stamp. Slightly stained. Above avg. cond. $83.00

AWARD DOCUMENT BAVARIAN TRUE SERVICE MEDAL WITH MEDAL

AWARD DOCUMENT BAVARIAN TRUE SERVICE MEDAL WITH MEDAL: About 10x15" ornate color printed document hand inked to *Herrn Alois Ziszler Maschinenarbeiter etc.* Silver medal with Bavarian enamel shield & parade mount ribbon with pinback. Above avg. cond. $245.00

AWARD DOCUMENT BRONZE CLOSE COMBAT CLASP: 5.5X8" Dated 11.10.1944 & named to a man in a grenadier regiment. Holed & folded. Avg. cond. $77.00

AWARD DOCUMENT GOLD GERMAN CROSS: 1944 issue. About 6x8" printed sheet with typed *Oberstleutnant Strecker Kdr. Gr.Rgt.220* & dated 14 October 1944. Folded & binderholes. Avg. cond. $250.00

AWARD DOCUMENT GOLD GERMAN CROSS: 6x8" with illus. of cross at top. Named to NCO 7./Gr.Rgt.45 & dated May 44. Has been folded & has some small edge tears Avg. cond. $315.00

AWARD DOCUMENT IRON CROSS 2ND CLASS: 5.5x8" document awarded to Obergefreiten in Stab/PZ. Aufkl. Abt.

Grossdeutschland the Iron Cross 2. Class in May 1944. Official ink stamp depicting Panzer Gren Div. Grossdeutschland & signature of Generalleutnant & Divisionskommandeur. Document comes with gilded wooden period frame. Exc. cond. $387.00

AWARD DOCUMENT KNIGHTS CROSS
OF THE IRON CROSS

AWARD DOCUMENT KNIGHTS CROSS OF THE IRON CROSS: 14x16.5". Vellum style parchment with hand lettered gold name. Signed by Adolf Hitler at the Fuhrer Headquarters & dated 18 Sept. 1941. Full folio style as removed from award document holder. No rips or tears. Clear early war Hitler signature. Nice age mild yellowing to vellum as is proper. Near mint cond. $2,625.00

AWARD DOCUMENT NAVAL BLACK WOUND BADGE: Issued to Machinist Corporal Adolf Schneider on the *Muenster* & dated 25 April 1941. Signed by the senior surgeon of Reserve Hospt. 103. Ink stamped. Near mint cond. $65.00

AWARD DOCUMENT OLYMPIC COM-MEMORATIVE MEDAL: 8.5x12" original wood frame with glass & hanger. Clean 2 color printed document with embr. eagle. Hitler facsimile signature & typed to *Polizei=Revieroberwachtmeister Karl Leimbach*. Near mint cond. $105.00

AWARD DOCUMENT RUSSIAN FRONT MEDAL: Document 5.5x8" awards the Eastern badge to a Gefreiten for serving in Winterschlacht im Osten 1941/42. Sealed & signed by Commanding Officer. Above avg. cond. $26.00

AWARD DOCUMENT SS SERVICE MEDAL 4 YEAR: 8.5x12" awarded to SS Obersturmfuehrer Fritz Streipart dated September 1938. Has embossed Nazi Eagle stamp, facsimile signature of Hitler & other. Has been folded in center but in very good condition. Look good framed. Above avg. cond. $225.00

AWARD DOCUMENT WAR MERIT DOCUMENT GROUP NAVAL SCUBA DIVER (UDT): Group consists of field award document for *Armband Crete* issued on 1 Oct. 1943 to Funkgefreiten Herbert Preuse & signed by Vice Admiral Werner Lange, KC winner. Field issue Iron Cross document, 2nd class issued to same man on 28 June 1941 & signed by Admiral Schuster. Document for the War Service Cross 2nd class with swords issued to Preuss on 30 Jan. 1945 & signed by his commander, Vice Admiral Hellmuth Heye, commander of the Kleinkampfverbande or Scuba (UDT) units of the Kriegsmarine. These men manned two man torpedoes & were frogmen in the German navy. Rare to find such interesting documents to a UDT man. Above avg. cond. $1,200.00

DOCUMENT GROUPING HITLER YOUTH MEMBER: 1: small format, Black cover with gold imprint Motor HJ Prufungsabzeichen. Issued to Karsten Deudtler who was in technical & practical driving school from 1 May 1939 thru 12 Jun. 1940 in Rendsburg. No photo but official NSKK stamps. 2: small blue booklet to same person with Motorgefolgschaft 1/163 Rendsburg listing his achievements in 1941. Has due stamp. Near mint cond. $164.00

PERSONNEL FILE ARMY

PERSONNEL FILE ARMY: 6x8 file booklet filled in with information & also with medical file booklet & 11 other added pieces of separate documents & papers on man, has civilian photo ID size & lots of Nazi army ink stamps & entries. Avg. cond. $77.00

PERSONNEL FILE LUFTWAFFE LT: 11 pages on 6 sheets, official forms with ink stamps & original signatures. Material dated 1944-45 & consists of an assessment of the leadership qualities of Lt. Hans Amler of the III/Luftnachrichten Regt. (mot) 14. Man received the Iron Cross, Krim Shield & Luft Ground Contacts badge. Documents indicate man was being considered for a promotion to regimental adjutant. Near mint cond. $63.00

PERSONNEL FILE LUFTWAFFE LT: 4 pages on 3 sheets. Official forms with ink stamps & original signatures. 1944-45 dated. Documents are assessments of his character & a letter from his commanding officer on his good qualities. All refer to Lt. who won the War Service Cross 2nd class with swords on Jan. 3 1943. Near mint cond. $45.00

PLEDGE DOCUMENT HITLER
YOUTH FEMALE

PLEDGE DOCUMENT HITLER YOUTH FEMALE: About 6x8.5". 2 tone printed paper with eagle over wording. Inked female name & 2 signatures. Picture postcard of girls performing at Christmas dinner. Near mint cond. $145.00

PROMOTION DOCUMENT: Issued to Peter Bachmann & promoting him to rank of *Marinebbaumeister*. Dated Berlin, 21 August 1941 with clear Senior Commander of Naval Unit signature (man under Raeder). Raised Party eagle seal. Near mint cond. $90.00

SERVICE DOCUMENT FEMALE TREUE & TREUE 1ST PARACHUTE DIVISION & DEVICE: 8x11" 4 page white stock paper, black print *Treue um Treue* with wording having hearts instead of dots to *i, a, & j*. Typed name *Emmi Maschke*, inked signature Heidrich & dated 24.12.1944, with party eagle stamp *1.Fallschirmjager Division*. Embossed paratrooper badge to

cover. Inked out swastikas inside. Necklace device 12x20mm stamped silver mini paratrooper badge with back engraved *Treue um Treue* & hanger ring. Near mint cond. $2,500.00

SERVICE DOCUMENT HITLER YOUTH

SERVICE DOCUMENT HITLER YOUTH: 5.75x8.25" document of HJ committing to duty in 1943. Large eagle with sword & hammer in each claw illus. on top of document. Signatures of leaders of NSDAP & HJ. Never folded. Exc. cond. $90.00

SERVICE DOCUMENT SS DEATH: 8.25x11.75" gold eagle embossed white stock with black *Getreu seinem etc.* & hand inked *SS Sturmmann Eberhard Kling 9./SS-Pz.Gren.Rgt.7 etc.* Died 2.7.1944, ink signature & eagle stamp of *SS-Pol.Pz.Gren. Rgt.7 9.Kompanie*. Exc. cond. $76.00

SERVICE DOCUMENT SS DEATH: 8.25x11.75" gold eagle embossed white stock with black *Getreu seinem etc.* & typed *Kurt Seyfarth SS-Unterscharfuhrer in der 8.Kompanie SS-Polizei-Schutzen-Regiment 3*. Inked signature of *SS-Obersturmfuhrer etc.*, 2.August 1944 & eagle inked. Near mint cond. $50.00

SERVICE DOCUMENT SS LEIBSTANDARTET: 8x12" size typewritten document requires SS Schutze to denouce his church membership in 1942. Many official signatures & Nazi stamp. Document was of the Feldpost design & was canceled. Above avg. cond. $129.00

SERVICE DOCUMENT SS DEATH

SERVICE DOCUMENT SS DEATH:
8.25x11.75" gold eagle embossed white stock with black *Getreu seinem etc.* & hand inked *SS Unterscharfuhrer Willi Struch 9./SS-Pz.Gren.Rgt.7 etc.* Died 2.7.1944, ink signature & eagle stamp of *SS-Pol.Pz.Gren. Rgt.7 9.Kompanie.* Near mint cond. $381.00

SERVICE DOCUMENT SS MARRIAGE

SERVICE DOCUMENT SS MARRIAGE:
5.75"x8.25" size document granting permission to marry to SS officer. Large Nazi stamp & ink signature. Included is a postcard size photo of a young woman seated by table reading a book. Exc. cond. $145.00

THIRD REICH PHOTO ALBUMS

PHOTO ALBUM ARMY FRENCH CAM-PAIGN: 8x10". 137 photos. Album kept by a private soldier & contains photos he took of the campaign In France, 1940 with shots of black French troops, white soldiers, stops along road, traditional channel pictures, some leave, etc. Nice detail. Good shot of bicycle German troops & nice shots of officers. Above avg. cond. $85.00

PHOTO ALBUM ARMY INFANTRY REGT POTSDAM: 9x12" with silver airplane on tan cover. Album has hand lettered April 1934-October 1935 service time inscription on inside cover. 150 photos. Last part of album covers 1940 campaign in France with photos of dead Belgian, British soldiers, knocked out planes, tanks, cannons. Early shots show MG training, usual drill & dress photos with nice early uniforms & equipment. Some photos of Dunkirk. Above avg. cond. $159.00

PHOTO ALBUM ARMY MT. TROOPER: 9x12" size, brown cover, string bound, includes. 56 photos of mountain troops during training in snow covered mountains. Good detail shots. Cover Above avg. cond. $82.00

PHOTO ALBUM ARMY
PANZER/ARMORED CAR

PHOTO ALBUM ARMY PANZER/AR-MORED CAR: 9x12.5" brown cover with owner added silver painted metal likeness of panzer badge & national eagle. Approx. 194 shots in many various sizes. Starts with inspection in drill tunics, black wrap-around shots, early armored radio cars, 4 wheeled armored cars, garage maintenance, shots of cars stuck, few combat shots, scenic & early war Berlin parade with cars. Some removed shots. Above avg. cond. $355.00

PHOTO ALBUM ARMY RUSSIAN FRONT: *EHREN=CHRONIK.* 9x12" black leatherette cover with silver embossed EK & title. Printed war leaders at front, Hitler, combat & blank record pages. 1942 dated service document, NSKOV typed letter about WWI service. Approx. 41 photos 2.5x3.5" size. Equipment, trucks, bridges, Russian countryside. Blank family history pages at back. Above avg. cond. $165.00

PHOTO ALBUM ARMY RUSSIAN FRONT: 7x11" green cover, gray string bound, with IC, 1939 Erinnerungen embossed. Approx. 153 b/w photos of soldiers & equipment in ice, snow & mud. Photos of POW, dead, graves, destruction of tanks, vehicles & houses. Very graphic. Some loose pages. Exc. cond. $199.00

PHOTO ALBUM ARMY: *MEINE DIENSTZEIT.* 7.5x10.5" brown leatherette body with affixed silver metal helmet having eagle & silver embossed title below. Approx. 38 shots 2.5x3.5" size with some postcard uniform group shots at beginning. Troopers wear transition WWI ear cut out helmets, MG08's on carts, page dated *29.6.-8.1936 3.(M.G.) Kp. E.B.21 + April 1939 4./J.R.101. (MG)Kp.* & nice EM uniform shots showing HJ Golden Leaders 1937 Sports Badge. Exc. cond. $85.00

PHOTO ALBUM ARMY: 8x10" orange & white cloth cover. Approx. 102 photos with most 2.5x3.5", larger 1940 group shot. 2 large funeral at back. Training & off to France, equipment, fortifications, etc. Some good uniform shots. Above avg. cond. $95.00

PHOTO ALBUM ARMY: 9x12.5" brown leatherette album. Approx. 306 shots in various sizes. Starts with NCO wedding, uniform shots, groups, training, equipment, inf. standard, bridging equipment, France, officers meeting General at train, Russian Front, winter, etc. Above avg. cond. $175.00

PHOTO ALBUM HITLER YACHT: *AVISO GRILLE.* With 1937 Hitler Christmas card. 9.5x13" brown leatherette cover with galleon to front. Approx. 110 photos ranging in size 2.5x3.5" on up. Starts with a color illus. print of ship *Aviso Grille.* Most pages are captioned, excellent uniform shots & various shots of crew & ship. 3 shots of Hitler in Hamburg on board ship. Photo of map showing route of 1937 sea cruise with various stops. 3 shots in Hamburg dry dock & several 1938 shots & ends with 4 more shots of Hitler at dock. Exc. cond. $600.00

PHOTO ALBUM LUFTWAFFE GENERAL: 1930s. 9x12" white cloth with red design album. Approx. 209 family photos with 30 of military subjects. *D-LZ130* zeppelin in flight. 1937 4.5x7" General shot with officers on parade, named *Zenetti* with others & couple LW Admin. Large LW group. Above avg. cond. $100.00

PHOTO ALBUM LUFTWAFFE: *STAB 11/8 1940/42.* 9x13" gray paper cover with owner hand inked title & name *Uffz.Berle.* 63 photos 2.5x3.5" showing the staff occupation of Schloss Hartlieb & surrounding grounds. Excellent shots of castle, converted rooms for office use etc. & all pages are captioned. Uffz. Berle oversaw the motorpool with shots of office & vehicles. Female staff & photographer & medical area. Near mint cond. $171.00

PHOTO ALBUM LUFTWAFFE: String bound leatherette covers with 85mm stamped Luftwaffe Eagle & silver leaf *Meine Dienstzeit* on front cover. 98 original photos which appear mostly Army troops on maneuvers. Various equipment & uniforms. Injured troops in hospital. Several interesting photos but none appear to pertain to the Luftwaffe. Above avg. cond. $175.00

PHOTO ALBUM NAVAL E-BOAT

PHOTO ALBUM NAVAL E-BOAT: 9x9" red leatherette *photo* album. Approx. 152 photos with most 2.5x3.5" & some 5x7" range. Almost all deal with ships or equipment shots. Looks to be Norway based with some snow & war damage shots. Torpedoes, supplies, winter deck uniforms, arty. shots & sinking of small ship. Remounted in this album with all photos removable. Above avg. cond. $181.00

PHOTO ALBUM NAVAL: *CRUISER SCHARNHORST.* 38 photos taken by sailor, many of Hitler's visit to ship with shots of Hitler reviewing officers, touring battle cruiser. Also some good shots of launching of battleship Tirpitz & shots showing her before main turrets put on. Album is very clean with excellent details. Also pictures of shakedown cruise, etc. Scharnhorst sank by British in mid-war when she was caught in a trap by battlecruisers. Cloth stock cover with gold KM eagle, Nazi battle flag, lettering *Meine Kriegserrinerungen auf Schlachtschiff Scharnhorst.* Exc. cond. $611.00

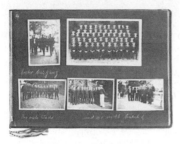

PHOTO ALBUM NAVAL
MEINE DIENSTZEIT

PHOTO ALBUM NAVAL *MEINE
DIENSTZEIT*: 9x12.5" brown leatherette
cover with metal eagle missing swastikas
& silver embossed title. Approx. 207
shots with most 2.5x3.5" size. Starts with
1936 RAD service pages., Naval EM
1936/37, ships, uniforms, 1937 Gibraltar,
Rome scenic cards, large group shot with
1 LW officer, 1942 service, Norway, E-
Boat, U-Boat, most pages captioned &
photos are removable. Well done. Above
avg. cond. $150.00
PHOTO ALBUM NAVAL: 1936-42. Book
loosely assembled by 40 year old sailor
who took clippings from local papers
about the Kriegsmarine, added pictures
of ships, personnel, etc. Also includes
maps, post-war discharge form in
compliance with allied occupation of
Germany, etc. All in soft cardboard
binder. A very nice period grouping of
about 100 items from ration cards
documents. A good personal view of the
Third Reich & the Kriegsmarine at war &
defeat. Avg. cond. $118.00
PHOTO ALBUM REICHSPARTEITAG 1934:
5x8" with 61 privately taken photos of the
1934 Reichsparteitag in Nurnberg. Nice
sharp photos of SA, SS, & HJ with
parades, marches & beer hall festivities.
Excellent studies of Nazi party uniforms
& insignia. String bound, Near mint
cond. $160.00
PHOTO ALBUM REICHSPARTEITAG IN
NURNBERG: 9x12" string bound. Beige
linen cover is imprinted with Der
Reichsparteitag, Erinnerungen on the
Tage in Nurnberg with photo of stone
bridge with tower in front. Has 24 press
released photos of Hitler, SS, SA, HJ in
parades, marches, & festivities. Some
photos missing. Exc. cond. $140.00
PHOTO ALBUM SS
OBERSTURMBANNFUHRER: 7.5x10.5"
green cover with silver printed SS runes
to center. Contains 36 interesting photos
ranging in size from 3x4.5" on down. Nice

typed captions to most pages. 2 good
uniform shots of Brandt at start with
caption listing him as Kommandeur
d.Aufklarungs Abt. der SS Standarte
Deutschland. Shows *Juni 1940
Culemborg-Holland* awards parade, 8 cm
mortar use, anti-tank rifle, 8 rad recon
car, MP-35, 3.7cm & various types of
uniform shots. Near mint
cond. $675.00

**THIRD REICH HISTORICAL BOOKS
(PUBLISHED BEFORE 1945)**

BOOK *ABC DES
NATIONALSOZIALISMUS*: Black title
print & large swastika to red cloth cover.
Written by Dr. Kurt Rosten, 1933 dated,
252 pages. German text & few photos.
Page edges have library stamps. Above
avg. cond. $45.00
BOOK *BAUSTEINE ZUM DRITTEN REICH*:
1941. Hb, German text, 600 pages.
Covers historical necessity for rebuilding
the Reich in an organized, disciplined
manner through the use of RAD units.
Cloth hb covers. Excellent wartime text
Above avg. cond. $34.00
BOOK *BAUWERK REICHS SPORT FELD*
1936: Hb, large format, 43 pages.
German text & 70 photos showing
architecture & construction for the 1936
Olympics in Berlin. Has fold-out map in
back. Also 7.75"x11" photo of sports
arena & smaller photo of track & stands.
2 additional brochures of the station are
enclosed. Linen cover with high quality
pages. Exc. cond. $164.00
BOOK *BAYERN IM ERSTEN
VIERJAHRESPLAN* 1937: Hb, large
format, red leather binding & gold
embossed party eagle in front. 575
pages. Filled with photos & illus. covering
Bayern economic & social development.
Many architectural shots. High quality
NSDAP book. Above avg.
cond. $125.00
BOOK *BLOCKADE BREAKER MARIE*:
1937. By Eckart. HC. German text. 230
pages with photos on the history of this
blockade runner ship. Covers WWI
period. Very nice unusual Imperial related
KM novel. Excellent reading. German
text. Mint cond. $20.00
BOOK *BLUTSCHUTZ UND
EHEGESUNDHEITSGESETZ*: Gesetze
und Erlaeutgerungen *Blood Protection &
Marriage/Health Law* Contains in overleaf
a green penciled signature of H. Himmler,
Reichsfuhrer SS. Book Is from Himmler's

personal library. Hb, med. format, 1936 dated, 354 pages. Incl. documentation of authenticity by 2 experts. Letter of person sending book back to the United States in 1946. Envelope is of brown paper with cancellation stamp dated 1946. Exc. cond. $588.00

BOOK *DAS NEUE REICH*: Medium format, SB, 1937, by Wehrmann, 18 pages, many color illustrations of maps. Above avg. cond. $20.00

BOOK *DAS WAR DER KRIEG IN POLEN*: Pictorial account of the Polish campaign. Hb, med. format, 111 pages, with text & 50 page photo section. 1939 dated personal note in front of book. Above avg. cond. $30.00

BOOK *DAS WELTJUDENTUM*

BOOK *DAS WELTJUDENTUM*: Sb, med. format, 1939, 62 pages. By Dieter Schwarz. Published by NSDAP. Eagle stamp by *Finanzamt Konigshutte* & is numbered. Near mint cond. $276.00

BOOK *DER DEUTSCHE SIEG IM WESTEN*: Sb, large format, 96 pages, by NSDAP, war issue. Historical & editorial account of the victory in the West. Many photos & maps. Large sword & oak leaves adorn cover. Shows some age. Above avg. cond. $50.00

BOOK *DER DEUTSCHE STAAT* (THE GERMAN STATE): Gottfried Feder, medium format, sb, 1932, 142 pages of German text. *Auf nationaler und sozialer Grundlage*. Some storage wear to the cover. Covers foundation & new laws of the Aryan Nazi state. Very early propaganda work of the Kampfzeit. Avg. cond. $26.00

BOOK *DER FUHRER*: By Konrad Heiden. Hb, med. format, 1944, 774 pages. Book on Hitler's rise to power. Exc. cond. $35.00

BOOK *DER GLAUBE AN DEUTSCHLAND* (A BELIEF IN GERMANY): Hans Zoberlein, medium format, hb, 1936, 890 pages with b/w graphics. Excellent propaganda book on how a belief in Hitler will make Germany strong; how he labors for the New Reich & how the people must put all their power behind him to create a new Germany that will reflect the highest ideals for Party & People. Gold embossed oak leave design on blue linen covers. Above avg. cond. $20.00

BOOK *DER NATIONAL-SOZIALISTISCHE STAAT* 1934: By Dr. Walther Gehl. sb, med., 239 pages, 2. heft. Above avg. cond. $20.00

BOOK *DER PARTEITAG DER EHRE*: Official report & speeches of Reichsparteitag 8.-14.Sept. 1936. Includes 16 page photo documentation. Clean red cloth cover with warriors, shields & party eagle. Exc. cond. $49.00

BOOK *DER PATROUILLENGANGER*: Medium format, hb, circa 1943. 237 pages & many color lithos. Above avg. cond. $20.00

BOOK *DER ROTE KAMPFFLIEGER* (THE RED BARON): Medium format, hb, dj, 1933. 261 pages with rare photos of Richthofen & other WWI fighter pilots. Beautiful cover showing him in dress tunic with plane in background. Near mint cond. $40.00

BOOK *DER STAAT IM AUFBAU* 1934: By Dr. Walther Gehl. Text & some photos. Sb, med. format, 1934, 239 pages. Above avg. cond. $20.00

BOOK *DER TECHNISCHE KRIEG* 1938: Hb, med. format, by Karl Justrow, 128 pages. with text & 62 photos/illus. of warfare. Avg. cond. $75.00

BOOK *DEUTSCHE KAMPFEN IN SPANIEN*: 1939. Published by Legion Condor, hb, med. format, 145 pages, cloth cover & text on Germans fighting in Spain. Above avg. cond. $20.00

BOOK *DEUTSCHLANDS AUSSENPOLITIK 1933-1940*: By Axel Freiherrn v. Freytagh. Sb, med. format, 1941, 266 pages. Publication for the Wehrmacht. Avg. cond. $20.00

BOOK *DIE DEUTSCHE KRIEGSFLOTTE*: Small format, SB, 1940, 72 pages & many photos & illustrations. Exc. cond. $40.00

BOOK *DIE DEUTSCHEN KRIEGSSCHIFFE 1815-1936* ON ID OF GERMAN SHIPS: Hb, 155 pages with profiles & specs on ships up to 1936, has warship & U-boats & others. Excellent reference & has a Luft ink stamp. Avg. cond. $20.00

BOOK *DIE GESPENSTER DIVISION*: 1942. By Alfred Tschimpke. Hb, red cover, 204 pages. With the panzer div. thru Belgian & France. Exc. cond. $20.00

BOOK *DIE KRIEGSMARINE EROBERT NORWEGENS FJORDE*: 1940. Hb. German text. 400 pages with some photos. Early book on the battle of the Kriegsmarine for the fjords of the Norwegian coast. KM lost many destroyers in the actions & this seriously eroded small ship operations later in the war. Superb text. Above avg. cond. $20.00

BOOK *DIE ROTEN TEUFEL FIND DIE HOLLE!* (RED DEVILS FROM HELL): Starch, medium format, hb, 1941, 111 pages of German text with b/w photos. Excellent photos of the Belgian French campaign with rare shots of field police, ordnance, knocked out French tanks, captured allied soldiers. Big emphasis on the use of black colonial troops against Germans. Nice early war propaganda book in very fine condition. Above avg. cond. $26.00

BOOK *DIE WEHRMACHT 1941*: Hb. 319 pages with photos & stories of the different arms, navy, army, SS. Breakage to glue binder, all pages intact. Early war photo history Avg. cond. $20.00

BOOK *DIE WEHRMACHT DAS BUCH DES KRIEGES 1939/40*: Published by the Wehrmacht. Hb, dj, med. format, 1940. 318 pages filled with photos & German text. Above avg. cond. $25.00

BOOK *DOKUMENTS ZUR VORGESCHICHTE DES KRIEGES*: Sb, large format, 1939, 344 pages. By Auswaertiges Amt 1939 Nr. 2. Party eagle & swastika printed on cover. Exc. cond. $20.00

BOOK *DURCH PULVER UND FIRN 1939/ 40*: Hb, dj, med. format, has 176 pages with photos & records of German ski team. Has photos of Nazi soldiers on skis. Avg. cond. $32.00

BOOK *ERNEUERUNG AUS BLUT UND BODEN*: Account of the Lappo movement to free the Finnish population from Bolschewismus. sb, med. format, 76 pages, 1932 dated. Exc. cond. ... $25.00

BOOK *FAHRTEN UND FLUGE GEGEN ENGLAND*: By Oberkommando der Wehrmacht, 1941, med. format, 208 pages, with 30+ page photo section on naval & air war activities. Blue cloth cover. Above avg. cond. $30.00

BOOK *FLIEGER STURZEN VOM HIMMEL*: Sb, dj, med. format, 1942, 31 pages. Text & 25 pages of photos of Stuka production & in action. By Kapprott. Above avg. cond. $20.00

BOOK *FLIEGERABENTEUR* (FLYERS ADVENTURES): Wartime German book. 160 pages with 31 illustrations, 6 maps. Stories of flyers & their unusual adventures in pre-WWII Arab lands, etc. 1941 book donation tag in front for a Luft. mine seeking squadron. Linen bound. Easy to read German text. Above avg. cond. $20.00

BOOK *FRAU IM FASCISTISCHEN ITALIEN*: 1934. By Louise Diel. Hb, med. format, 168 pages with photo study & history of women under Fascism in Italy by a German author. Has attached dedication on cover page with hand written note signed & dated by Mussolini in Rome & in German. Includes several newspaper clippings on the publication of this book in the back. In exceptional condition with only the expected yellowing of pages by age. Profusely illustrated with photos in b/w of Italian women in a variety of situations. Near mint cond. $800.00

BOOK *HITLER ABSEITS VOM ALLTAG*: By Hoffmann. Hb, large format, 1937 dated, 80+ pages. 100 pictures document Hitler in everyday activities. Exc. cond. $59.00

BOOK *HITLER IN BOHMEN-MAHREN-MEMEL*: By Hoffmann. sb, med. format, 30 pages. Pictorial & historical account of Hitler in titled countries. Dj shows fraying at edges. Exc. cond. $44.00

BOOK *HITLER IN POLEN*: By H. Hoffmann. Hb, med. format, 50+ unnumbered pages of Hoffmann photographs with good details of Hitler's visit to Poland. Each photo is captioned. In front of book is a personal note dated 1941. Nice clean gray & white cloth cover. Exc. cond. $44.00

BOOK *HITLER IN SEINEN BERGEN*: By Hoffmann. Hb, large format, 1938 dated, 96 pages. 86 pictures document Hitler & his daily surroundings. Exc. cond. $40.00

BOOK *HITLER OVER EUROPE*: 1934. By Henri. Hb, med. 306 pages on the Hitler & Rosenberg plan for Nazi Germanic Union & other ideals that were to come to pass during WWII. Very early book on Hitler expansion plans except for *Mein Kampf*. Avg. cond. $28.00

BOOK *HITLER REGIERT*: By Hans Wendt. Sb, med. format, 1933. 118 pages with German text & early portrait of Hitler on dj. Above avg. cond. $20.00

BOOK *HITLER WIE IHN KEINE KENNT*: By Hoffmann. Sb, dj, med. format, 96 pages. Filled with Hitler photos from birth thru WWI into 1930's as Fuehrer. Pre-war. Dj. Avg. cond. $80.00

BOOK *HITLER*

BOOK *HITLER*: A biography in 134 photos of early days of Hitler & his party by Hans Diebow & Kurt Goeltzer. sb, dj, med. format, 1931, 160 pages. Cover illustration of a saluting Hitler. Exc. cond. $229.00

BOOK *HOFJUDEN*: By Peter Deeg. 1938. Hb, med. format, 546 pages with illus. & has fold-out in back of the family tree of the Rothschilds, the Jewish bankers that Hitler blamed for Germanys decline in WWI & after. Has foreword by Hitler. All Gothic German text. Rare. Avg. cond. $129.00

BOOK *INFANTERIE GREIFT AN*: By Generalfeldmarschall Rommel. Hb, med. format, 1943, 400 pages. German text, illus. & maps. Has personal note in front of book. Avg. cond. $38.00

BOOK *JAHRBUCH 1941*: Published by NSDAP. Hb, med. format, dj, 1941. 448 pages filled with German text on Navy life with photos. Moisture damage to red cloth cover. Avg. cond. $35.00

BOOK *JAHRBUCH DER DEUTSCHEN LUFTWAFFE 1939*: Hb, large format, 1939, 186 pages. Many photos of Goering & Hitler/Facsimile signed by Goering. Cloth cover is embossed with gold like winged eagle & title. Shows some age. Above avg. cond. $40.00

BOOK *JESUITENSPIEGEL*: By Burghard Asmus. sb, med. format, 1938, 155 pages. Interesting facts about the Jesuits in text. Avg. cond. $45.00

BOOK *KAMERAD, LACH MIT!*: By W. Schlichting Humor for everyone. Sb, med. format, 1940, 123 pages. Cover depicts illus. of soldier telling joke. Shows usage. Exc. cond. $40.00

BOOK *KAMERADEN AUF SEE-ZWISCHEN MINEN UND TORPEDOS*: By Dr. Walter Lohmann, hb, med. format, 1943, 217 pages. German text, blue cover shows water stain. Avg. cond. $20.00

BOOK *KOHLER S FLOTTEN KALENDER 1939*: Sb, med. format with photo cover of a battleship. 295 pages with illustrations of the ships. With specs & all German text shows the pre-war Nazi Navy. Has a piece torn from the corner of the cover but in good condition. Avg. cond. $20.00

BOOK *KOLONIEN IM DRITTEN REICH* 1936: By Dr. H. W. Bauer. Hb, large format, red leather binder & color embossed colonial shield to cover. Ink stamped inside to *Stadt Fuerstenfeldbruck, Bayern*. 273 pages with some photos & illus. of colonial areas. Several pages have hand inked comments by a previous reader. Avg. cond. $125.00

BOOK *KOMMT KREIEG IN EUROPA?* (WILL WAR COME TO EUROPE?): Knickerbocker, medium format, 1934. 178 pages of German text. Also includes copied pages with a bio of the author. Book is hb with color dj. Dj has some tears. Nice early book about the plutocratic & corrupt democracies of England, France, Poland & Czechoslovakia. & how Hitler he will take by force what he should otherwise be given as rightful Leader of the Germans. A tinge of the horror of the coming war emanates from this small & seldom read book that predicted the coming of WWII. Avg. cond. $20.00

BOOK *LEISTEN UND DIENEN*: Published by weapon manufacturer Carl Eickhorn, Solingen in celebration of 75 years in business. Hb, large format, 1940 dated, 40 pages. Many photos. Exc. cond. $54.00

BOOK *MARSCH UND KAMPF DES D.A.K*: 1941. Hb, large format, 215 pages with war art & photos of the battle for North Africa. Very nice & well done while the battle was still in favor of Nazis. Avg. cond. $115.00

BOOK *MEIN KAMPF* 2 VOLUME SET

BOOK *MEIN KAMPF* 2 VOLUME SET: Hb, med. format, 1925 edition has glued Brandenburg Gate postcard inside. All pages in German text. 1927 edition with 354 pages. Light use only. Near mint cond. $1,400.00

BOOK *MEIN KAMPF* BOXED EDITION: 1937. Leather binder with gold embossed title, 780 pages all German text, med. size & very good condition. Box shows tearing & wear to ends Above avg. cond. $58.00

BOOK *MEIN KAMPF*: 1934. By Hitler. Hb, small format, 781 pages, with Hitler's portrait in front. Blue cloth cover with golden party eagle embossed. Exc. cond. $100.00

BOOK *MEIN KAMPF*: By Hitler. 1943. Hb, med. format, 781 pages, all German text, blue cover with gold embossed early Nazi eagle on cover & title on end panel. Some staining to cover. Avg. cond. $40.00

BOOK *MEIN KAMPF*: By Hitler. Hb, dj, med. format, 1939, 1001 pages. In English translation. Cover shows slight wear. Above avg. cond. $21.00

BOOK *MEIN KAMPF*: By Hitler. Hb, dj, med. format, 1939, 781 pages. With photo of Hitler in front. Above avg. cond. $69.00

BOOK *MEIN KAMPF*: By Hitler. Hb, med. format, 1934, 781 pages. Some water stains. Above avg. cond. $24.00

BOOK *MEIN KAMPF*: By Adolf Hitler. Hb, med. format, 1938 dated, 781 pages. with Hitler's portrait in front. This book was presented to a couple on their wedding day in 1939, With name, signature of mayor & official stamp. Leatherette binding with gold like embossing, & gold like finish on top of pages. Above avg. cond. $100.00

BOOK *MEIN KAMPF*: By Adolf Hitler. Hb, med. format, 1939 dated, 781 pages. With Hitler's portrait in front. This book was presented to a couple on their wedding day in 1940. With name, signature of mayor & official stamp.

Leatherette binding with gold like embossing & gold like finish on top of pages. Exc. cond. $84.00

BOOK *MIT HITLER IN THE MACHT*: By Otto Dietrich. Hb, dj, med. format, 1934, 209 pages. Personal account of author working with Hitler in the early years during the struggle for power. DJ shows the most wear. Above avg. cond. $93.00

BOOK *NARVIK IM BILD*: By Gerd Bottger, hb, large format, 1943, 150 pages. With 127 photos, some in color about the battle for Narvik in Norway. Cover Above avg. cond. $37.00

BOOK *NAUTICUS 1943*: Medium format, hb, 1943, 395 pages with b/w photos of naval vessels & related activity. Equivalent to *Jane's Fighting Ships*. Covers wartime activity of the KM with vital statistics on ships, shipping. Dust jack with men on sub conning tower. Very rare to get so late in the war. Avg. cond. $37.00

BOOK *OBERSALZBERG*: By Florentine Hamm, hb, med. format, 1938, 94 pages of text & special picture section of the Obersalzberg mountains where Hitler had his retreat. Red cloth cover. Exc. cond. $124.00

BOOK *PROTESTANTISCHE ROMPILGER* 1937: By Alfred Rosenberg. Sb, med. format, 86 pages. Deals with the betrayal of Luther & myth of the 20th century. Exc. cond. $20.00

BOOK *PROTESTANTISCHE ROMPILGER*: By Alfred Rosenberg. 1937. Sb, med. format, 86 pages, all German text, anti-Jewish propaganda. Avg. cond. . $20.00

BOOK *RASSE UND SEELE* 1934

BOOK *RASSE UND SEELE* 1934: Hb, med. format, by Dr. Ludwig Ferdinand Clauss.

188 pages of text with 176 photos covering racial differences. Near mint cond. $110.00

BOOK *REDEN DES FUHRERS AM PARTEITAG GROSSDEUTSCHLAND 1938*: Sb, med. format, 80 pages, German text on speeches of Hitler on title occasion. Exc. cond. $34.00

BOOK *REICHSTAGUNG IN NURNBERG 1935*: Hb, large format, 446 pages. German text with many photos of Nurnberg rally event. Map fold-out still in back. Blue cover shows age with clean inside. Avg. cond. $160.00

BOOK *REVOLUTION UBER DEUTSCHLAND*: 1930. By E.O. Volkmann, hb, med. format, dj, 390 pages. German text. Exc. cond. $37.00

BOOK *SCHACHT IN DER KARIKATUR*: 1937. Hb, large format, 105 pages. Filled with cartoons & jokes. German & French text. Above avg. cond. $21.00

BOOK *SOLDATEN FALLEN VOM HIMMEL*: 1940. By Belzig. Hb, med. format, 113 pages. German text with lots of photos on the history, the making of the chutes & the training of the troops. Excellent period book Avg. cond. $90.00

BOOK *SPENGLER IM DRITTEN REICH*: By Arthur Zweiniger, sb, med. format, 1933, 92 pages. Exc. cond. $20.00

BOOK *SS KAVALLERIE IM OSTEN* (SS CAVALRY IN EAST): Published only for the unit. This rare Vol. is serial #6. Hb, large format, 191 pages with photos & history of the SS in Russian. Has large photo section with great uniform references & a lot of candid photos of the Waffen SS in action. Above avg. cond. $675.00

BOOK *VIER JAHRE NATIONALSOZIALISTISCHE KOMMUNALPOLITIK IN SOLINGEN*: Hb, large format, covers 1933 thru 1937. 448 pages. Text with charts, photos & fold-out organization plan showing the improved standard for city of Solingen. High quality. Exc. cond. $149.00

BOOK *VOLK UND VERERBUNG* (THE PEOPLE & THEIR RACIAL PURITY): Medium format, 1938, sb, 86 pages with b/w photos & charts. C. Schaffer's German text propaganda book on determining the racial purity of individuals. Interesting background material for Hitler's theory that would justify the concentration camps & murder of millions. Seminal in the study of Judicaea. Above avg. cond. $37.00

BOOK *VOM 30. JANUAR ZUM 21. MARZ* WITH 2 LP RECORDS

BOOK *VOM 30. JANUAR ZUM 21. MARZ* WITH 2 LP RECORDS: 1933. 11x12" hb, large coffee table format with color embossed graphics on cover with 151 pages with b/w photos of the campaign & elections & all German text. But the rare part is having the 2 original 78 rpm records in back cover sleeve, undamaged & showing little play with speeches of Hitler on the *Czech-Jochberg*. Above avg. cond. $266.00

BOOK *WAS MAN UBER DIE KRIEGSSCHIFFS-TYPEN WISSEN MUSS*: 1940. By Korvettenkapitain Max Bartsch. Hb, med. format, 64 pages. About what must be known about the different types of Naval vessels. Near mint cond. $45.00

BOOK *WIR ARBEITSMAIDEN IN HESSEN*: Unit book for RAD district XI, Hessen. Hb, med. format, dj. 95 pages full with photos & text on female workers in RAD. Above avg. cond. $40.00

BOOK *WIR FLIEGEN GEGEN ENGLAND* (WE FLY AGAINST ENGLAND): Kohl, medium format, hb, 143 pages with numerous b/w photos of the attack on England. Excellent coverage of the air war against England in the early part of the war, the so-called Battle of Britain. Very fine stock covers with dust jacket. Exc. cond. $34.00

BOOK *WIR SOLDATEN*: 1939. Hb, large format, 288 pages. By Johannes von Kunowski. Filled with photos of inf., cav., pioneers, motorized, panzer, flyers, flak, navy, U-boats, etc. Excellent pre-war reference on Hitler's military might. Above avg. cond. $53.00

BOOK *WIR SUCHEN MINEN*: 1937. Hb, med. format, 77 pages, some illus. tells of a man's experience in mine sweeping training. Pre-WWII. Yellowing to pages. Avg. cond. $24.00

BOOKLET *ASSMANN & SOHNS* INSIGNIA, MEDALS & BUCKLES CATALOG: Hb. Large format. 89 pages filled with b/w photos & illus. of items produced. Lots of Nazi related insignia as well as Weimar & some imperial items. Excellent period ref. Avg. cond. $40.00

BOOKLET *DER DEUTSCHE SIEG IM WESTEN*: Sb, large format, 96 pages covering May & June 1940 battles. Many maps & photos of war leaders. Ends with map of England showing invasion ranges from captured France & Norway. Above avg. cond. $50.00

BOOKLET *DIE FREIMAUREREI*

BOOKLET *DIE FREIMAUREREI*: Sb, med. format, 1942, 68 pages, by Dieter Schwarz. Published by NSDAP, & editorial by SS Obergruppenfuhrer Heydrich. Has ink stamp by *Finanzamt Koenigshutte*. Near mint cond. . $315.00

BOOKLET *GROSSE ANTIBOLSCHEWISTISCHE AUSSTELLUNG*: 6x8" sb, with color illus. Russian soldier skeleton setting the globe on fire. 40 pages German text with several anti-Semitic & anti-Bolshevistic propaganda poster illus. Near mint cond. $100.00

BOOKLET PAUL SEIHEIMER SOLINGEN: Edged Weapons Catalog. Sb, large format, 8 pages b/w art of the swords & military & NSDAP daggers & bayonets, engraving for blades plates. Avg. cond. $40.00

BOOKLET *UNSERE KRIEGSFLOTTE*: Sb, med. format. 20 pages with glued in drawings of warships. German text. Avg. cond. $20.00

BOOKLET *WEHRHAFTES DEUTSCHLAND* VOL. 2: Sb, med.

format, 50 pages with photos on the rearming of Germany. All German text & swastika on cover. Avg. cond. $24.00

CIGARETTE ALBUM *OLYMPIA 1932*: By Reemtsma Cigarettenfabriken Album about the Olympic Games in Los Angeles 1932. Hb, large format, 142 pages. Blue cloth cover. Above avg. cond. $43.00

CIGARETTE ALBUM *OLYMPIA 1936*

CIGARETTE ALBUM *OLYMPIA 1936*: Hb, dj, large format, 1936, 126 pages. Facsimile Signed edition by the president of the Winter Olympics. Album complete in b/w & color photos. Has fold-out Olympic site map. Cover is of dark blue cloth with gold like imprint. Dj shows slight wear. Exc. cond. $108.00

CIGARETTE CARD ALBUM *ADOLF HITLER*: Hb, large format, 132 pages, 1936 dated. orange cover with gold print. complete, b/w photos, showing life of Fuehrer. Exc. cond. $90.00

CIGARETTE CARD ALBUM *ADOLF HITLER-BILDER AUS DEM LEBEN DES FUEHRERS*: Hb, large format, 132 pages, 1935 dated. Picture history of Adolf Hitler. Some loose pages. Avg. cond. $51.00

CIGARETTE CARD ALBUM *DEUTSCHE KULTURBILDER*: Sb, large format, 1934 dated, complete with all cards printed in color. Deals with German culture 1400-1900. Above avg. cond. $20.00

CIGARETTE CARD ALBUM *DEUTSCHLAND ERWACHE* 1933: Hb, gold embossed title & trooper to brown cover. 150 pages covering struggle, battle & victory of the NSDAP. Color & b/w photo cards, torn fold-out stadium photo at back. Avg. cond. $66.00

CIGARETTE CARD ALBUM *DEUTSCHLAND ERWACHE*: Hb, large format, 153 pages. 1933. Album contains many b/w & color printed photo cards from struggle of the NSDAP to power. Clean brown cloth cover with gold title print & embossed swastika. Exc. cond. $85.00

CIGARETTE CARD ALBUM *DIE DEUTSCHE WEHRMACHT*: Gold embossed title & 88 flak crew to cover. Sb, large format, 264 color printed photo cards with text. One missing print & several torn pages. Avg. cond. ... $75.00

CIGARETTE CARD ALBUM *DIE DEUTSCHE WEHRMACHT*: Sb, large format, with 270 color printed photos of German Army. Color embossed artillery design on cover. Shows slight age. Exc. cond. $85.00

CIGARETTE CARD ALBUM *FAHNEN UND STANDARTEN TRAEGER*: Sb, large format, 32 pages. Cover has damage. With color printed cards, complete. illus. of flag bearers 1100/1914. Nice. Avg. cond. $95.00

CIGARETTE CARD ALBUM *KAMPF UM S DRITTE REICH*: Album is 9.5x12.5" in size, sb, large format, 1933 dated, 91 pages. Color printed photos illustrate the Nazi party & Hitler's early history. A color photo of the victorious chariot flying the Nazi flag is affixed to the cover including gold like lettering. Exc. cond. $139.00

CIGARETTE CARD ALBUM *ZEPPELIN-WELTFAHRTEN II BUCH*

CIGARETTE CARD ALBUM *ZEPPELIN-WELTFAHRTEN II BUCH*: 1933. Sb, large format, with 155 photo cards of the world cruise of the Zeppelin airship during 1930's. 3 cards are missing. Cover shows airship in tow by ship. Including 2 press release photos of a camouflaged German battleship, one side view, the other from front view. Also 7x9.5" group photo of unidentified Kriegmarine crew. Avg. cond. $78.50

MANUAL *ARTILLERISTISCHES BILDERBUCH*: Sb, small format, 1931, with 45 photos & text on arty. weapons as Feldhaubitze 16 & Feldkanone 16. Near mint cond. $45.00

MANUAL *AUSBULDUNGSVORSCHRIFT FUR DIE INFANTERIE 1942*: Sb, med.

format, 255 pages. With photos, charts & German text. Avg. cond. $28.00

MANUAL *DAS KRAFTFAHRZEUG*: 1940. Hb, small format, 95 pages has NSKK eagle on cover, lots of color fold-out illus. on the working of a car & engine. 1 fold-out loose but in good shape Avg. cond. $37.00

MANUAL *DAS NEUE EXERZIEREN*: Das Schar, Trupp & Sturmerxerzieren nach den neuesten Vorschriften. Sb, med. format, 1936, 67 pages. By Heinz Denckler. Latest training material for infantry troops. 42 illus. Shows some age. Above avg. cond. $90.00

MANUAL *DAS REICHSFURSORGEWESEN 1936*: By Hermann Hess. Brown cloth 2 prong binder with text & tables on social issues. Binder has minor separation. Avg. cond. $20.00

MANUAL *DER DIESTUNTERRICHT IM HEERE*: By Reibert. Edition for Pioneers. Sb, med. format, 1939, 334 pages. Hitler's portrait in front of book & other high ranking officers. Many photos, illustrations, & charts. Exc. cond. $72.00

MANUAL *DER FEUERKAMPF DER SCHUETZENKOMPANIE*: Sb, med. format, 191 pages, 1940. With 132 photos & illus. Training Manual for infantry. Exc. cond. $72.00

MANUAL *DER REKRUT 1935*: Sb, small format, 162 pages. Has color plates showing uniforms & insignia & b/w photos & drawings. Has Army eagle on cover. Shows little age. Above avg. cond. $35.00

MANUAL *DIE LEICHTE FELDHAUBITZE 16 UND MUNITIONSWAGEN 98*: 1937, sb, med. format. 127 pages with illus., fold-out chart, & photos with official stamps. Exc. cond. $145.00

MANUAL *DIE SCHUTZENKOMPANIE*: By Ludwig Queckborner. Hb, med. format, 1939, 375 pages. Many photos & illus. of the German rifle company for the Military Intelligence Service Information Bulletin No. 15. For study & translation. Exc. cond. $40.00

MANUAL *DIE SOLDATENFIBEL*: Sb, med. format. 115 pages all German text with lots of illus. & photos on training. 1920-30's pre-Nazi with WWI style helmets & illus. Avg. cond. $40.00

MANUAL *DIE SOLDATENFIBEL*: Sb, med. format, 115 pages of text with photos & illus. covering inf. tactics in 1920s by Major A.D. Bodo Zimmermann. Slightly faded cover. Exc. cond. $75.00

MANUAL *FELDDIENST A B C FUER DEN SCHUETZEN*: Sb, med. format, by Kuehlwein, 106 pages. Photos & illus. of inf. tactics. Pages loose from cover at binding. Avg. cond. $50.00

MANUAL *GEFECHTSUNTERRICHTS A B C* 1935: Sb, med. format, 93 pages text with photos & illus. on early inf. tactics. By Hauptmann Queckborner. Near mint cond. $50.00

POCKET CALENDAR BOOKLET HITLER YOUTH 1934: Hb, gray cloth cover with mobile swastika & 1934. Has daily calendar for notes in front, rules, training info. & photos. Named & few entries. Exc. cond. $75.00

PRINT PORTFOLIO *GESCHICHTE IN BILDERN*: 125 8.5x12" b/w hand illus. WWI & pre-WWII subjects. Nice details of war leaders, heroes, combatants & early Nazi struggle. IV. Band by K.A. Mayer. Cardboard storage box & portfolio. Near mint cond. $150.00

PRINT PORTFOLIO *MEITERWERKE DEUTSCHER KRIEGS=BILDBERICHTER*: By Hoffmann. Complete 25 photo prints series. 15.5x20.5" matte bodies with nice printed details of original war photos. Show Hitler, war leaders, conquered Western countries & victorious combat troops, before the Russian campaign. Tattered coversheet & prints show age. Need to be framed. Above avg. cond. $250.00

SCRAP BOOK *ADOLF HITLER SCHULE*: 1942. Hb, med. format, with title *Arbeitsheft fur Naturkunde Biologie* & inked owner's name *Willrich Walter Servingen*. About 50 pages. filled with newspaper clippings & news photos of combatants, KC winners, LW planes, Hitler & several color Willrich illus. of war leaders. Unique youth scrap book. Avg. cond. $250.00

SONG BOOK *LIEDERBLATT DER HITLER-JUGEND*: 4 pages of notes & text of songs for summer camp. Above avg. cond. $23.00

STEREO VIEWER BOOK *DIE SOLDATEN DES FUHRERS IM FELDE*: Hb thick covers with area for storing 100 photo cards & viewer, appears to be complete. 61 pages of text on Polish campaign with some photos of war leaders. Near mint cond. $222.00

STEREO VIEWING BOOK *DER ERSTE GROSSDEUTSCHE REICHSKRIEGERTAG*: 1940. Hb, large format with approx. 86 of 100 photos & viewer placed in cover. 2.30x5.10" double take photos by Hoffmann depicting

festivities of the NS Reichskriegerbundes. All photos captioned. Center of book includes 67 pages of German text & 8 color photos of parades. Kyffhaeuser patch design on cover. Avg. cond. $160.00

STEREO VIEWING BOOK *DER KAMPF IM WESTEN*: Book includes about 100 2.25x5.25" approx. size double take photos & viewing fixture all placed in book cover. Text with color photos in center. Cover shows slight soiling. Avg. cond. $234.00

STEREO VIEWING BOOK *DIE SOLDATEN DES FUEHRERS IM FELDE*: Hb, large format, with approx. 100 photos. 2.25x5.25" size & viewer in cover. Each photo of Poland campaign captioned & taken by Heinrich Hoffmann. Center of book contains 60 pages of German text describing the invasion & includes photo of Hitler & other high ranking officers & 2 battle maps. Cover shows some wear. Avg. cond. $196.00

THIRD REICH POSTERS, MAPS & LEAFLETS

MAP LUFTWAFFE OILCLOTH OF WESTERN EUROPE: Color printed map is folded in 20 equal, separate squares 10x10.5" with party stamp *Fliegerhorstkommandatur Kolleda* & *Kartenstelle LZA Kolleda Blatt West etc.* Exc. cond. $35.00

MARKSMANSHIP TARGET HITLER YOUTH 22 CALIBER

MARKSMANSHIP TARGET HITLER YOUTH 22 CALIBER: Lot of 12. 13x13.5" b/w printed target & information. Unused

& yellowed from storage. Above avg. cond. $118.00

POSTER *MEIN KAMPF*: 12x19" size printed advertising poster showing Hitler, title & *Lerne Hitler durch sein buch kennen* print. Folded. Small tear at top. Above avg. cond. $30.00

POSTER ANTI-BRITISH

POSTER ANTI-BRITISH: *Heuchelei, Terror und Meuchelmord* 32x48" color printed poster as published by NSDAP in 1940. Poster illustrates large black print anti-British propaganda statements. With larger print in bottom section of poster. Photo of Chamberlain is illus. in left part of poster. Minor separation. Above avg. cond. $145.00

POSTER SS FROM OCCUPIED POLAND: 26x38". Light red poster with German, Polish text. Poster issued by order of the SS & Highest Police Fuhrer, Rosener at Chilli, Poland, 23 June 1942. Text announces the mass execution of Communist Jewish partisans who are claimed to have murdered German & pro-German persons. Long list of dead ranging from accountants to insurance salesmen to day laborers farmers. Also list of 6 women executed for murdering a German mother in front of her children. Old creases from storage but not detractive. A one of a kind item. In modern frame for display. Above avg. cond. $538.00

POSTER SS NACHRICTENTRUPPE: 20x28" orange body with 7 troops in action photos with captions for various communication styles. Title center with wording about communication use. Storage folded, brittle yellowed paper. Above avg. cond. $360.00

POSTER SS RECRUITING *DICH RUFT DIE WAFFEN SS*: 21.5x30" illustrated camo SS NCO trooper pointing finger over title. Done by *Anton* & lists *SS Hauptamt etc.Prag IV*. Shows folds & mounting age. Hard to find item. Exc. cond. $1,268.00

POSTER SS RECRUITING: 21.5x30.5" illustrated camo SS trooper & HJ trooper by *Anton* with title below. Report to SS Hauptamt etc. Prag IV. Folded from storage. Hard to find. Near mint cond. $1,268.00

POSTER SS RECRUITMENT 163E: 21.5x33" illustrated camo SS trooper & HJ trooper by *Anton* with title to upper corner & 12 combat photos of various trades of the Waffen SS in action with captions. Hard to find style by *SS-Hauptamt etc. Prag IV*. Folded from storage. Near mint cond. $1,125.00

POSTER STAHLHELM

POSTER STAHLHELM: 24x33" size color printed poster depicting powerful face under a German steel helmet. Lower lettering reads *UND DU?* & black background. Published by Der Stahlhelm. Rolled & ready for framing. Above avg. cond. $429.00

PROPAGANDA LEAFLET *HOW LONG HAS IT BEEN SINCE YOU HAD A GOOD NIGHT'S SLEEP*: 5x8" with red graphic of beautiful woman in a very sexy night-gown, asleep. Other side is 10 lines on how it would be not to sleep in the woods on pine needles & other good things you could do in bed. Has been folded in center & a small 1/8 hole on fold. Very convincing. Dropped on Allied troops fighting their way across France & Belgium in 1944. Avg. cond. $38.00

PROPAGANDA LEAFLET: Pamphlet gives short history of the murder of 12,000 Polish officers by the communists, finding of grave by Nazis. Complete with gruesome photos of decayed bodies in Polish uniforms. Anti-Communist propaganda leaflet in Flandish language for occupied Europe. 15x16". Has Polish cross on the front. Above avg. cond. $129.00

THIRD REICH NEWSPAPERS & PERIODICALS

BOUND NEWSPAPER *SIGNAL*: 1943. Issues 1 thru 12 & 13 thru 24 all hb in 2 vol. Near mint cond. $133.00

BOUND NEWSPAPER *WEHRFRONT*: Large format, 3" thick, gray cover with black print. Will hold a yearly supply of the newspaper. With instructions. Exc. cond. $20.00

PERIODICAL *AUSBAU*: 1940. Set includes copies 1 thru 12 dated 1940 with photos, text & teaching materials in the technical field. Sb, med. format, 60+ pages. Above avg. cond. $25.00

PERIODICAL *BERLIN, ROM, TOKIO*: Issued for cultural relations of the three powers. Dec. 1942 dated. Large format. Some color illus. In German & Italian language. Exc. cond. $23.00

PERIODICAL *BERLIN, ROM, TOKIO*: Issued for cultural relations of the three powers. Jul. 1943 dated. Large format. Some color illus. In German language. Exc. cond. $23.00

PERIODICAL *BERLIN, ROM, TOKIO*: Issued for cultural relations of the three powers. Oct. 1939 dated. Large format. Some color illus. In German & Italian language. Exc. cond. $23.00

PERIODICAL *BERLIN, ROM, TOKIO*: Issued for cultural relations of the three powers. Sept. 1943 dated. Large format. Some color illus. In German language. Exc. cond. $23.00

PERIODICAL *DAS DEUTSCHE ROTE KREUZ*: 1944. Captions on distribution of packages for enemy prisoners of war. Covers shows returning German soldier being greeting by nurse. Above avg. cond. $20.00

PERIODICAL *DAS SCHWARZE KORPS*: Berlin, 28 Aug. 1941. Lead article knocks allies belief that invasion of Russia will destroy Germany. Cartoon of FDR, Churchill trying to capture a German swastika bedecked eagle with the Atlantic Accord. Complete. Above avg. cond. $53.00

PERIODICAL *DER ADLER*: 15 Sept. 1942, Major Gordon Gollob received after 150 missions the Highest Award, the Oak Leaves with swords & diamonds to KC of

IC. 8 Dec. 1942. 3 at one stroke by KC Kloepper. Exc. cond. $31.00

PERIODICAL *DER ADLER*: 27. April 1943 issue reporting on the airplane construction of FW189, 190 & others developed by Kurt Tank. Exc. cond. $34.00

PERIODICAL *DER ADLER*: Lot includes 2 issues dated Dec. 1940 & Jul. 1943. Photo of Messerschmitt Me110 in air. Shows slight age. Avg. cond. $37.00

PERIODICAL *DER SCHULINGSBRIEF*: 1939. With photos & illus. popular during this era interesting reading now Exc. cond. $23.00

PERIODICAL *DER SCHULINGSBRIEF-VORWAERTS ZUM SIEG*: 3/4 issue, 1943 dated by NSDAP with pencil drawing of Hitler in foreground & fighting soldiers in back. Good condition. Exc. cond. $23.00

PERIODICAL *DER SCHULUNGSBRIEF*: 3 copies numbered 6, 7 & 11, 1938. Published by NSDAP with photos & articles of German life & culture. Cover depicts large party eagle with swastika. Exc. cond. $24.00

PERIODICAL *DER SCHULUNGSBRIEF-AUFBAU UND WERK DER PARTEI*: 9/10 issue 1941 dated by NSDAP, training published with photos & illus. Good Condition. Exc. cond. $23.00

PERIODICAL *DER SCHULUNGSBRIEF-DIE BESTEN DER WELD*: 3 issue 1940 dated by NSDAP. Good Condition. Exc. cond. $23.00

PERIODICAL *DER SCHULUNGSBRIEF-VOLK IN WAFFEN*: Nov. 1937 issue by the NSDAP. Training material with propaganda photos & illus. for the collector. Exc. cond. $23.00

PERIODICAL *DEUTSCHE KRAFTFAHRT*: Dec. 1943. with illus. on ignition & oil for winter. Avg. cond. $45.00

PERIODICAL *DEUTSCHE KRAFTFAHRT*: May 1941. With technical data on BMW R75 motorcycle. Avg. cond. $45.00

PERIODICAL *DEUTSCHE KUNST*: 1920s dated, large format, issue 10-2 with color or b/w art prints on sculptures, statues, goblets, cathedrals, etc. past & present. loose pages. Avg. cond. $23.00

PERIODICAL *DEUTSCHE KUNST*: 1930s dated, large format, issue 10-3 with color or b/w art prints on sculptures, statues, goblets, etc. past & present. Avg. cond. $23.00

PERIODICAL *DEUTSCHE STUDENTEN ZEITUNG*: 24 Jan. & 31 Jan. 1934 issues. Paper for students by NSDAP. Lead article on Hitler's victory in Saarland. Above avg. cond. $45.00

PERIODICAL *DIE AKTION*: Anti-US publication from May 1940. With illus. Exc. cond. $36.00

PERIODICAL *DIE AKTION*: Jan. 1942. Special Italian Edition. 181 pages. Exc. cond. $36.00

PERIODICAL *DIE AKTION*: July 1943 published for the New Europe, about freedom & justice. Exc. cond. $36.00

PERIODICAL *DIE DEUTSCHE POLIZEI*: 15 June 1942 dated, 10 pages. Published by Reichsfuhrer SS & Deutschen Polizei im Reichsministerium des Innern. Lead story on Heinhard Heydrich. Exc. cond. $29.00

PERIODICAL *DIE DEUTSCHE POST*: June 1938 dated with illus. & technical data on telephone & postal services. Above avg. cond. $20.00

PERIODICAL *DIE KUNST IM DEUTSCHEN REICH*: Dec. 1941 dated, large format, by NSDAP. With colored & b/w art prints, of sculptures & architectural structures. Past & present artists. Exc. cond. $68.00

PERIODICAL *DIE KUNST IM DEUTSCHEN REICH*: May 1940 dated by NSDAP, large format, With colored & b/w art prints, nude sculptures & military barracks. Exc. cond. $68.00

PERIODICAL *DIE KUNST IM DEUTSCHEN REICH*: Oct. 1941 dated, large format, by NSDAP. With colored & b/w art prints, of sculptures & architectural structures. past & present artists. Exc. cond. $68.00

PERIODICAL *DIE KUNSTKAMMER*: 4. Heft, April 1936, large format, 23 pages. with bronze bust of Hitler on cover. Exc. cond. $20.00

PERIODICAL *DIE POST DIE ZEITUNG FUR JEDEN SONDERHEFT 8*: Fold-out map of Black Sea area, article on Mercedes race cars, etc. Complete with special map of the Eastern Front. Issued to soldiers as a German version of *Stars & Stripes*. Above avg. cond. $20.00

PERIODICAL *DIE POST DIE ZEITUNG FUR JEDEN SONDERHEFT 7*: 64 pages. text with photos. Issued for field soldiers & covers propaganda, humor, news, home front advice. Similar to *Stars & Stripes* but a Nazi edition to keep up morale. Above avg. cond. $20.00

PERIODICAL *DIE WEHRMACHT*: 29 Jan. 1941 issued by Army. Pretty LW communication woman on cover. With reports on the U-boats. Above avg. cond. $23.00

PERIODICAL *DIE WEHRMACHT*: Issued by Army 2 July 1941. Front page illus. of bullet riddled car with its Soviet driver seated while awaiting arrest. Further reports on battles in the East. Above avg. cond. $22.00

PERIODICAL *DIE WOCHE*: With news reports & photos from battles, articles on military strategy, cultural events & medicine. Aug. 1944 dated. With picture report on Hitler's assassination. Exc. cond. $40.00

PERIODICAL *GEGEN ENGELAND*: Issue of 20. January 1943 with strong anti-Allied propaganda reports. In a Feldpost mailing wrapper. Exc. cond. $20.00

PERIODICAL *ILLUSTRIERTER BEOBACHTER*: Pictorial history on Aviation. 1939 dated. 160+ pages. Large format. Avg. cond $45.00

PERIODICAL *JULZEIT*: Dec. 1936. med. format, 16 pages. with stories, songs, & poems. Has party eagle on cover with early HJ type eagle inside. Above avg. cond. $34.00

PERIODICAL *LAIKMETS*: 3 issues 1942, & 1943 dated. Exc. cond. $20.00

PERIODICAL *LAIKMETS*: 3 issues dated 1942 & 1943 dated. One front page illus. Dr. Goebbels, other a pilot in HE111, & a Latvian legionnaire in German uniform. Exc. cond. $20.00

PERIODICAL *LUFTFLOTTE WEST*: Published by Luftflotte 3, 5, May 1944. Front page shows three pilots talking in front of plane. Reports on downing Allied planes. Exc. cond. $82.00

PERIODICAL *LUFTPOST*: Aug. 1941. Small format for airmail issue, 8x10, 4 pages on single sheet. Has articles on England, Russia, America. Has photos. Avg. cond. $26.00

PERIODICAL *LUSTICE BLATTER*: The cover has a cartoon of a Russian terrorist flying to America for protection by the Statue of Liberty. This is really interest-ing. Large format, 10 pages with lots of color & b/w cartoons on the allies, some very sexy. Aug.1943 issue & very interesting. Avg. cond. $41.00

PERIODICAL *LUSTIGE BLAETTER*: Feb. 1944. Cartoon periodical. The liberators, shows GI & British looking at freezing woman & her children. Exc. cond. $90.00

PERIODICAL *LUSTIGE BLATTER*: Dec. 1942. Cartoon illustrated periodical with anti-American jokes. Color printed cover shows a big red donkey on crutches eating dollars. With Roosevelt as an Indian on it's back. Exc. cond. $90.00

PERIODICAL *LUSTIGE BLATTER*: Feb. 1944. Cartoon periodical with anti-American motive. Shows the Statue of

Liberty on a blue background. Exc. cond. $90.00

PERIODICAL *LUSTIGE BLATTER*: Oct. 1942. Cartoon illustrated with anti-British motive. Color cover shows hay stack wrapped in royal red coat & crown attacked by small man with hammer & sickle. Exc. cond. $90.00

PERIODICAL *LUSTIGE BLATTER*: Oct. 1942. Cartoon periodical with anti-American & anti-capitalist propaganda. Color cover shows couple in tuxedo & gown dancing over grave side. Exc. cond. $90.00

PERIODICAL *NORDLICHTER*: Sb, med. format, 95 pages. 1941 dated. Magazine is published for the German soldier serving in the Northern occupied territories. Cover has powerful color drawing of the midnight sun. Above avg. cond. $55.00

PERIODICAL *NS FRAUEN-WARTE*: 1937. Sb, large format, Heft 27, pages 849 thru 879. Text with photos & W. Willrich profile illus. Large officer's belt buckle & SS runes on cover. Near mint cond. $108.00

PERIODICAL *OLYMPIA ZEITUNG*: 17 Aug. 1936 issue reporting on the Olympic Games & its winners. Exc. cond. $23.00

PERIODICAL *OLYMPIA ZEITUNGS*: 13 Aug. & 5 Aug. issues with news on events & winners. Exc. cond. $45.00

PERIODICAL *REICHSZEITUNG DER DEUTSCHEN ERZIEHER*: Feb. 1937 dated, issued by NS on Education & Family. Avg. cond. $23.00

PERIODICAL *SCHLESWIG-HOLSTEINISCHE TAGESZEITUNG*: 14 issues dated 1929-1931-1932. With political, cultural & sports news. Avg. cond. $20.00

PERIODICAL *SIEG DER WAFFEN-SIEG DES KINDES*: Sb. large format, 16 pages, 1940, with photos. Issued by the Reichsfuhrer SS, Exc. cond. $32.00

PERIODICAL *SIGNAAL*: 10 Aug. 1940 issue. Cover illus. parade under the Brandenburger Tor in Berlin. Above avg. cond. $22.00

PERIODICAL *SIGNAAL*: 25 Aug. 1940 Issue has bomber & pilot on cover. Above avg. cond. $23.00

PERIODICAL *SOLDATENBLATTER FUER FEIER UND FREIZEIT*: Reading material for solder. Sm. format. Sept. 1940 dated. Exc. cond. $20.00

PERIODICAL *SOLDATENBLATTER FUR FEIER UND FREIZEIT*: May 1941. Patriotic reading material for the soldier. Exc. cond. $20.00

PERIODICAL *SPORT DER JUGEND*: Aug. 1938 issue for youth in sports competition. Exc. cond. $40.00

PERIODICAL *SS LEITHEFT*: May 1943. Sb, med. format, 33 pages with photos & all German text. Cover has been taped Avg. cond. $50.00

PERIODICAL *SS LEITHEFT*: Sept./Oct. 1943. Sb, med. format, 48 pages with articles on the war & the homefront has photos & examples of German art. All German text. Avg. cond. $32.00

PERIODICAL *SS LEITHEFT*

PERIODICAL *SS LEITHEFT*: Year 7 1941. Sb, med. format, 25 pages with all German text & captioned b/w photos. Unusual one of Himmler not in uniform, but in mountain clothing & gray leather overcoat Avg. cond. $50.00

PERIODICAL *SS LEITHEFT*: Nov. 1943. Sb, med. format, 48 pages with articles on the war & the homefront has photos & examples of German art. All German text. Avg. cond. $32.00

PERIODICAL *SS LEITHEFT*: Sb, med. format, 30 pages. Heft 3, 1942. Published by Reichsfuhrer SS, with articles on duty, honor, loyalty. Near mint cond. ... $66.00

PERIODICAL *SS LEITHEFT* 1941: Sb, med. format, 25 pages with photos & articles on the SS & Nazi propaganda & news of the war. Has photos of SS troops in action & art of the pure Aryan race. Cover has crossed sword & battle ax. Some yellowing to cover. Above avg. cond. $45.00

PERIODICAL *WESTFRONT ILLUSTRIERTE*: April 1941 dated, Large format, 112 pages. Army propaganda journal. With pictures, some in color, about war in action. Caption on tomorrow we march on. Exc. cond. $60.00

IMPERIAL GERMAN FLAGS, ARTWORK, DECORATORS & REGIMENTAL STEINS

AERO SQUADRON INSIGNIA SHIELD: Hand painted. 9x12". Light metal body with black border. Dun yellow field with charging ruptured duck emblem in gray, black, yellow. Two holes on top for mount backing for plane of unit bierstube. Avg. cond. $370.00

AVIATION PHOTO DISPLAY FROM LT. VON CONTA ESTATE: 5x13" wood frame holds photo of Conta in uniform with Blue Max, biplanes on airfield & crashed plane against brick building that's reported to have killed Conta. Above avg. cond. $135.00

BUST OF FRANZ JOSEF IN
SILVER FINISHED METAL

BUST OF FRANZ JOSEF IN SILVER FINISHED METAL: Approx. 10" tall with black wooden cylindrical base bearing 1848-98 dates on Imperial crest with crown above, crossed scepter with orb & sword. Bust shows Emperor in open coat displaying hussar style tunic with many orders & decorations. Double shields below bust with arms of Austria & Hungary. Fine toned silver finish. Near mint cond. $450.00

COLOR ILLUSTRATED ARTY.36 OFFICER: 6x8" current black frame with ornate floral design. Glass, red, matte & hanger to back. 4x5" image is shown from waist up with nice details. Artist signed *B.Raimond de Bauer Berlin 1850*. Light age. Near mint cond. $100.00

COMMEMORATIVE PLATE 12TH JAGER BATL: Meissen. 10" diam. White field with blue worked oak & laurel wreath at sides. 1810 1910 commemorative centennial dates at top. Center has large royal crown with *JB 12* below. Mint cond. $375.00

COMMEMORATIVE PLATE 13TH UHLAND: Pewter. Very fine hand engraved 13th Uhlan cipher in the center of the plate. Raised beveled edge with center having circular disc showing royal unit crest. Engraved *9 Nov. 1893 - 1973. Decker Kolling Matthies. offermann Wurimann. 3 Esk./Konigs Ulanan Regiment 13*. Hmkd on verso. Near mint cond. $90.00

DESK WEIGHT AVIATION
RADIAL ENGINE ON MARBLE
MILITAR FLIEGERSCHULE

DESK WEIGHT AVIATION RADIAL ENGINE ON MARBLE *MILITAR FLIEGERSCHULE ETC.*: About 1x4x6.5" black marble with velvet backing. About 3" diam. silver engine center by *Oberursel Motorenfabrik* & 2 copper props. with EK to each. 30mm tall silver Prussian Pilot badge likeness affixed to corner. Engraved silver title plate below & *Herzog C.Eduard-Schule*. Above avg. cond. $375.00

DESK WEIGHT DEVICE FLAK: Cast brass. 5x5" device of winged, flaming bomb (AA unit). Posts for mounting to marble base. Above avg. cond. $60.00

MISC. MILITARIA

FLAG IMPERIAL BATTLE

FLAG IMPERIAL BATTLE: 2.5x4' printed cotton body with good details. Roped bunting with loop. Avg. cond. $278.00

FLAG IMPERIAL BATTLE: 4x6' printed wool body with good details, bunting & rope with looped ends. Above avg. cond. $500.00

FRAMED PHOTO REMEMBRANCE 1917 PILOT SCHOOL: 15x17.5" brown finished wood frame with ornate details in plaster. Glass front, 7x9" photo showing partial biplanes & 40 uniformed men in various dress. Most wear visor caps, 4 officers, some leather coats & 1 crash helmet. Gray matte nicely title marked in black & *(Herzog Carl Eduard-Schule) Gotha, August 1917.* Near mint cond. $234.00

FUNERAL SASH RIBBON: 32" long. Blue. 2" gilt bullion fringe on a beautiful water pattern ribbon & 4x4" black with silver border iron cross at base. Above avg. cond. $25.00

MARKSMANSHIP PRIZE LETTER & PEN HOLDER: 9x5x2". Gilt gold metal with hunting dogs on side: grouse on top with flip open lid having compartment for letters, paper. Front section has three holders for nips, pens, ink supplies with design of flying grouse. Inner lid inscribed to a winner of 80 meter free standing shooting prize of Dresden in black lettering. Near mint cond. $135.00

MEMORIAL CHAMPAGNE CAMPAIGNS: Plastic. Approx. 4" wide. Design is of memorial rock on broken pedestal of brick with impressed iron cross having 1914,15, 16, 17 dates & large inscription, *Gott Mit Uns* over *Champagne.* Tribute to the dead who fought in this area in France for 4 years. Above avg. cond. $36.00

MEMORIAL DOCUMENT ZEPPELIN DEATH: 14x11". Printed litho death memorial showing figure of Christ at sea holding out his hands above sinking cruiser. Bottom design shows furled

Imperial battle flag with inscription, *Zum Gedachtnis des Signal-Maaten Julius Petitjean. Marine-Luftschiff R34. Er starb fur das Vaterland* with facsimile Wilhelm signature. Top of document shows about 1" trimmed off to fit in old period frame that comes with it. The R-34 went down with all hands during a bombing run against England. Above avg. cond. $150.00

MEMORIAL TO A BAVARIAN INFANTRY OFFICER: Hand- made. Desk style wooden stand on base approx. 13x2" in black wood. Tall 9" fan in red & gold wood & paint. Large Bavarian reservist officer frontplate mounted on body with *Ludwig Konig von Bayern* lettering. Near mint cond. $217.00

MEMORIAL TO A BAVARIAN INFANTRY OFFICER

MEMORIAL TO SOLDIER DEATH: Hand embr. 12x15" gray cloth covers with hand embroidered black wreath having green oak leaves & Iron Cross at top. Center embr. in black, *Aus grosser Zeit.* Covers open to reveal folio carrier for picture (none included). Inside has two handwritten poems to honor the soldiers who fell for the Fatherland. Near mint cond. $72.00

MEMORIAL TO THE FIRST WORLD WAR: 16" tall. Cylindrical red wood column approx. 5" wide at base, tapering to 4" with removable lid. Body has officer frontplate with rare *Colberg 1807* battle honor. Rest decorated with chin scale base, flaming bomb buttons, black leather shield, etc. Ball topped on lid. Near mint cond. $643.00

OIL PAINTING OF A LANDSSTURM NCO IN DRESS TUNIC: 21x26" old frame with linen cloth field having superb painting of man in dress uniform with unit & NCO insignia on collar, 3 gold chevrons on left sleeve & 1914 Iron Cross ribbon in button hole. Artist signed & dated *Lille, 1916* showing it was done in occupied France. Nice perspective with fine details. Near mint cond. $349.00

OIL PAINTING OF IMPERIAL GERMAN GENERAL: Approx. 20x26" on original stretchers. Painting is full face with good details to tunic. Subject wears 1910 service tunic with general officer boards & collar tabs. On the neck are suspended the Red Eagle & Royal Crown Orders 2nd class with swords. Left breast has an Iron Cross 1914 & the Commander's Breast Badge of the Order of Malta, St. John of Jerusalem. Painting signed & dated 1936. Very good details: nice coverage of face & orders. Avg. cond. $492.00

OIL PAINTING OF SAXON GARDE REITER: Dated 1907 & artist signed. Approx. 18x24". 3/4 body painting of a young Garde Reiter in full Saxon helmet with lion top. Painting depicts subject in blue & white kurassier koller with white belt, brass buckle & brass epaulettes: nice details to helmet & lion with full Saxon crest. Painting is mounted on wooden stretchers. Mint cond. ... $292.00

behind a sword. Nice dark red background. Exc. cond. $175.00

OIL PAINTING OF UHLANS & KURASSIERS ON RECONNAISANCE: In modern frame measuring 19.5x14". Painting shows two Prussian uhlans in foreground with one man pointing at a small town with a tower while two mounted kurassiers in armor move off to examine it. Linen body. Near mint cond. $591.00

PATRIOTIC ASHTRAY BUST OF BIS-MARCK IN CENTER: 7X5" oval. White metal. Scrolled edges with Imperial crown & eagle design. Radiant sun above bust of Bismarck in center with *Unser Bismarck* lettering. Hmkd. Avg. cond. $72.00

PATRIOTIC ASHTRAY: Oval white porcelain. 7x3.75" in size. White field. Cigarette retainers on ends trimmed in national colors. Center field has oak & laurel wreath bound with ribbons of Germany & Austria. Center has litho b/w portraits of Kaiser & Franz Josef. Near mint cond. $27.00

OIL PAINTING OF THE KAISER, WILHELM II IN PERIOD FRAME

PATRIOTIC BEER STEIN

OIL PAINTING OF THE KAISER, WILHELM II IN PERIOD FRAME: 20x14" gold leaf frame. Beautiful portrait shows Kaiser standing in army fieldmarshal dress dark blue tunic with aigulettes neck order. Right hand clasps a GdC helmet by its spike. His left, withered arm is held

PATRIOTIC BEER STEIN: 6" tall overall with domed pewter lid having lyre design, wreath, edelweiss thumb lift & rim engraved *Ludwig Holzapfel*. White china body with handle, size *1/2L*, color front with *Gen.-Feldmarschall von Hindenburg*, Hindenburg profile, 1914 EK, wreath with crossed equipment & tri-color flags. Tri-color lower edge. Avg. cond. $176.00

PATRIOTIC BOX IRON CROSS: 1.25x3x4.5" black & gray cloth covered box with stamped metal full size EK affixed to lid with small ribbon above. Deluxe inside is lined with blue velvet. Above avg.cond. $114.00

PATRIOTIC BOX IRON CROSS: About 3x6x9" light shade of wood with color 1914 EK with ribbon in the center with wreath & tri-color corner stripe. Hook to front. Above avg. cond. $68.00

PATRIOTIC BRACELET WITH 6 MINIATURE MEDALS: Ladies. Includes Hindenburg cross with swords, Silver wound badge, Prussian long service, German WWI combat & more. Exc. cond. $85.00

PATRIOTIC BREAD BOWL WITH PORTRAIT OF U-BOAT ACE OTTO WEDDIGEN: China. Approx. 8x12" with integral gold trimmed handles, pierced side walls. Bottom has large green oak wreath with national colored rb. Center shows star with portrait of Capt. Lt. Weddigen of the navy in white summer dress uniform. Weddigen became an early ace after sinking 3 British cruisers in one day within the space of an hour. All sank with tremendous loss of life, causing a scandal in the admiralty offices. Mint cond. $215.00

PATRIOTIC BUTTER DISH IRON CROSS: White porcelain 3.25 diam. small personal butter pat dish. Ceramic dish with design of Iron Cross in bottom & motto black white & red border to rim. With wire stand. $70.00

PATRIOTIC CHINA VASE IRON CROSS: Meissen. White glazed china body with flared rim. Approx. 9" tall with 5.5" flared lip. Blue cobalt design of laurel on front encloses a radiant EK 1914 1st class. Reverse has oak leaf sprig with 1914-16 dates. Mint cond. $245.00

PATRIOTIC CHOCOLATE MUGS: Set of 6. 3.5" tall & 3.5" wide at top with gold rim. Colored panels around base Wreath with Iron Cross & black & white ribbon. Near mint cond. $152.00

PATRIOTIC CIGAR BOX IRON CROSS: 5x3.65" white metal. Two piece, hinged construction with cloth band inside to retain contents. Miniature black metal Iron Cross 1st class on upper left of lid. Avg. cond. $37.00

PATRIOTIC CIGARETTE CASE

PATRIOTIC CIGARETTE CASE: 1915 dated. Silver finished. Approx. 3x4". Flip open pattern. Scrolled silver field with blue enameled house order on lid with gilt crown, FR device. Miniature EK 1st class. Verso with silver oak leaf sprig with *Gorlice 2v 1915* lettering. Near mint cond. $280.00

PATRIOTIC COGNAC DECANTER NAVAL SAILOR: Porcelain. 10" tall. Decanter is in shape of Imperial signal man sailor in dress blues with rate on left sleeve, signal flags in hand, sailor carries M09 binoculars in left hand. White sailor cap removable with original cork stopper. Hand painted & fired. Above avg. cond. $75.00

PATRIOTIC CREAMER NAVAL MOTIF: 5.5". White china. National color rim with gold trim on pourer & handle. White field with oval green wreath enclosing fouled blue anchor with crossed national & battle flags above lettering, *Kriegsjahr 1914*. Near mint cond. $65.00

PATRIOTIC CUP FRANZ JOSEF 1898 JUBILEE

PATRIOTIC CUP FRANZ JOSEF 1898
JUBILEE: Enameled. Similar to pattern
associated with Czar Nicholas II
accession in 1896. Approx. 4" tall with
3.5" turned lid. Portrait of Franz Josef on
one side in sepia tone. Verso with
Imperial eagle. 1848-98 dates. Beautiful
colorful red, pink, green work of eagles,
floral motif. Above avg. cond. $91.00

PATRIOTIC CUP IRON CROSS: White
china. 2.5" wide, 2.45" tall with white
field. National color design on lip. Center
panel has green wreath with 1914 Iron
Cross in black work. Gold trimmed
handle. Near mint cond. $41.00

PATRIOTIC DEMI TASSE TEA SET: China
cup & saucer. 4" saucer, 2" tall cup.
Matching set. Cup lip trimmed in national
colors, design of two eagles on cup
German & Austrian with nice black gold
details. Saucer & cup trimmed also in
gold. Mint cond. $61.00

PATRIOTIC FACSIMILE COIN LUDWIG III
OF BAVARIA WITH PULL OUT: 2".
Obverse with bust of King, reverse with
Coat of arms. Flips open to reveal
complete circular pull out color litho
series of pictures of glorious victories of
Germans in early days of WWI. Bright
silver finish. Mint cond. $34.00

PATRIOTIC FELDPOST BOX: Pseudo black
pebbled leather body with *Feldpost
Grusse* (Field Post Greetings). Flip open
with white metal ornate hasp. Lettering is
done in raised work with miniature design
of EK 1914. 7x12". Above avg.
cond. $28.00

PATRIOTIC FELDPOST LETTER BOX:
11x8.5x2.5" hinged box with metal clasp
lock. Gray cloth body with black border.
EK 1914 2nd class on lid with ribbon.
Nice facsimile. National colored ribbon for
hinge opener. Inside has two lid compartments for letters & card. White & gray
paper work design liner. Exc.
cond. $100.00

PATRIOTIC FINGER RING: 1914 Austrian.
Nickel with bust of Franz Josef. Medium
size. Above avg. cond. $21.00

PATRIOTIC GLASSES: Both pressed glass
with raised details. 1: 4" tall with 1914 EK
in wreath & *Gott mit uns!*. 2: 3.5" tall gold
painted with 1914 EK in wreath &
v.Hindenburg profile in wreath. Above
avg. cond. $68.00

PATRIOTIC GOBLET *1914 KRIEGSJAHR*:
Etched bubble glass. 7.5" tall clear body
with nice wheel cut title to crowned
wreath with crossed swords. 9 small
bubble design to stem with 3" diam. base.
Mint cond. $225.00

PATRIOTIC GOBLET FROM OLDENBURG
1900: 6.5" tall body has relief views of
Imperial monuments featuring Bismarck
& Wilhelm I. Gray pewter color. Lip
inscribed in German, *Greetings from
Oldenburg from your brother Dietrich.*
Avg. cond. $84.00

PATRIOTIC GOBLET IRON CROSS: 5" tall
heavy clear glass body has 3.5" diam.
ground rim. Nice ruby red finish to body
with large base having ground clear
design & ruby outlines. Frosted/etched
1914 EK to side with excellent oak leave
wreath details having acorns & wrap-
around branches to body. Exc.
cond. $223.00

PATRIOTIC INK WELL IN FORM OF
SPIKED HELMET: 2.5" long nickel body
is 1.5" tall with removable 1" brass spiked
lid. Brass eagle frontplate & brass
bayonet placed thru helmet behind eagle.
Black leatherette chinstrap. Avg.
cond. $105.00

PATRIOTIC LETTER BOX IRON CROSS:
Pressed paper with black pebbled finish.
Silver impressed facsimile of 1914 Iron
Cross & national colors band on lid.
Brass worked key entry lug with silver
metal key. Functional lock. 6x4x2" in size.
Avg. cond. $69.00

PATRIOTIC LETTER BOX: 6x4x2". Black
simulated leather finish with metallic
crossed German, Austrian flags & motto
In treue fest 1914. Lower right has
lettering *Feld postkarten.* Box opens to
reveal photo of German sailor seated in
studio with 1915 Turkish Gallipoll badge
on his white blouse (picture dated 6 Aug.
1915 & 2 unused). Above avg.
cond. $40.00

PATRIOTIC MEMORIAL 1916
GREETINGS FROM STRASSFURT
UNITED WITH GERMANY

PATRIOTIC MEMORIAL 1916 GREETINGS FROM STRASSFURT UNITED WITH GERMANY: 4X5" polished granite block with silver Plaque, with draped battle flags, Kaiser crown, Iron Cross. Inset lettering *Gruss aus Stassfurt, 1916.* Maker hmkd *KO* & proofed on the lower edge. Near mint cond. $52.00

PATRIOTIC PITCHER & TUMBLER SET: 6 clear glass tumblers, each with ornate national color bowed ribbon & wreath in green on it, gold rimmed. 5.75" tall, 2.8" wide at mouth. Pitcher is fancy art deco clawed style with handle, gold work & Imperial tri-color flag, pole & oak leaves in bright green decor. Approx. 10" tall. Mint cond. $125.00

PATRIOTIC PLATE *1.GROSSHERZOGLICH MECKLENBURGISCHES DRAGONER-RGT.17*: Meissen. 10" diam. white porcelain with blue title to rim *Seybothenreuth Loigny Haelen Nery Dolginow*, crowned cipher center, oak leaf wreath, *1819-1919* & crossed blue maker swords. Back has wire loop & crossed blue swords trademark. Mint cond. $353.00

PATRIOTIC PLATE *DER KAISER RIEF UND ALLE ALLE KAMEN AUGUST-1914*: 8.5" diam. white porcelain with blue title to rim, 2 black EK's & color center with 3 gray Infantry soldiers charging into battle. Green maker *C.T.Altwasser Silesia etc.* with an eagle. Near mint cond. $150.00

PATRIOTIC PLATE *MIT GOTT FUR KONIG UND VATERLAND 1914*: 9.5" diam. white porcelain with blue title to rim & charging lancer to center. Green *von Professor Anton Hoffmann Munchen* & *Rosenthale Kunst-Abteilung Selb-Bavaria*. Mint cond. $176.00

PATRIOTIC PLATE BAVARIAN *LUDWIG III KONIG VON BAYERN GEKRONT 10.NOV.1913*: 8.5" diam. white porcelain with blue title to rim having 2 monument scenes. Blue crowned shield held by lions at center. Ludwig III takes the throne. Green maker *Rosenthal etc.* Mint cond. $203.00

PATRIOTIC PLATE CHRISTMAS 1914: 10" diam. china plate with blue Christmas scene showing 5 German soldiers in trench celebrating around small candlelit Christmas tree. Center soldier playing concertina while others enjoy gifts or letters. One soldier on watch. Dated 1914 on the rim. Marked on the back with blue crossed swords. Bottom rim is pierced for hanging. Near mint cond. $339.00

PATRIOTIC PLATE HEROES OF THE WORLD WAR: 10" white glazed porcelain plate with scalloped edges & alternating national color shields. Center has b/w litho of Wilhelm & Franz Josef in wreath with national eagles, national color ribbons. Top & bottom has b/w portraits of U-Boat Ace Weddigen & Hindenburg. *In grosser Zeiit. Weltkrieg 1914-15* lettering in gold. Above avg. cond. $135.00

PATRIOTIC PLATE IRON CROSS: Gold & silvered china. Maker is *C.T. Altwasser Silesia* with a green Eagle & serial numbered. 160 mm square with a perfect 1914 Iron cross in the center. Near mint cond. $220.00

PATRIOTIC PLATE SAXON 6TH INF REGT: 10" diam. White china body in glazed finish with cobalt blue toned view of a Cathedral, medieval town in center: blue cobalt style lettering on rim of plate *Kgl. Sachs. 6. Infanterie Rgt. No. 105. Konig Wilhelm II. v. Wurttemberg* with Imperial eagle, 1701 founding date. Each side of plate has crest of Wurttemberg & Saxony. Crossed sword maker mark on rev. Bright colors. Mint cond. $252.00

PATRIOTIC SERVING BOWL HINDENBURG: White china with national color bands on edges, center has green wreath with sepia toned portrait of Hindenburg in military attire. Portrait flanked by German national flags, cannons, rifles & fancy work Iron Cross. Ribbon with inscription *Generaloberst von Hindenburg.* Near mint cond. $72.00

PATRIOTIC SCHNAPPS SERVING TRAY IRON CROSS: White metal. 11.5x9" with ridged surface & rim having nicely struck raised Iron Cross in the center. Steel style finish. Near mint cond. $185.00

PATRIOTIC SMOKING PIPE BOWL: 3.5" ceramic pipe bowl. Nice hand painted details to 2 WWI medics with armbands, side packs & cloth service caps working on a wounded & bleeding soldier who has a severe chest wound. Background shows other medics with stretcher. Back of pipe is inscribed in German. *Badly Wounded.* Near mint cond. $50.00

PATRIOTIC SMOKING PIPE: Bavarian Peasant style. Long 13" cherry wood straight stem with horn pattern lip. 4.5" white china bowl with color design showing two young resting cherubim with wings on clouds. Silvered bowl lip & lid. Above avg. cond. $39.00

PATRIOTIC STEIN IRON CROSS: 4.5" fat body with 1/2 liter capacity. Blue & gray glazed work design of helmeted soldiers with field packs on charge flanked by two panels with 1914 Iron Crosses. Incised motto *Mit Gott fur Konig und Vaterland*. White metal domed lid with raised work Iron Cross & ball thumb lift. Minor 1mm separation at joint of lid & thumb lift. Above avg. cond. $284.00

PATRIOTIC STEIN METTLACH: 1/2 liter. 8" tall with raised work design of Imperial eagle on front bearing Hohenzollern eagle crest on shield in breast. Side flanking designs of gray oak leaves. Beaded style upper & lower rim with matching motif on handle. Lid is of gray metal with Mettlach raised Imperial crown. Thumb lift is floral pattern. Base bears Mettlach logo, castle & *2204* number. Bright colors. Near mint cond. .. $600.00

PATRIOTIC SUGAR BOWL: China. 3.2" tall. Bowl has national color design at top. Center has oval red & green laurel wreath with design of 1914 Iron Cross, Austrian & German national flags, marked *Krlegsjahr 1914* in black l ettering. Above avg. cond. $36.00

PATRIOTIC SUGAR BOWL: White china. 5" tall, 4.56" wide with double handles. Complete with lid. Lid & upper bowl trimmed in national colors. Oval green wreath on pot with blue fouled anchor & crossed national & Imperial battle flags above *Kriegsjahr 1914* lettering. Near mint cond. $65.00

PATRIOTIC TILE 1914 IRON CROSS: 6" diam. white body with black EK center & green oak leave wreath with acorns. Back is marked *1914* . Above avg. cond. $75.00

PATRIOTIC UTENSILS 6 PLACE DINNER KNIFE & FORK SET WITH CROWNED EAGLE ON HANDLES: 6 10" dinner knives & 6 8" forks with Wurttemberg maker marks on body, handles each have Imperlal crowned National eagle. Avg. cond. $93.00

PATRIOTIC WALL CALENDAR: 18x23". Stiff cardboard with gorgeous 4 color picture of all the crests of all the states of Imperial Germany in full color. Center shows Teutonia holding her crown aloft. Beside the date holder appear soldiers of the Napoleonic & 1913 period in full color uniforms. Holder on lower front center for dates. Company advertised for military provisions from old Hannover. Original hanging cord with Prussian crowned eagle in center. Avg. cond. $175.00

PATRIOTIC WOOD BOX
FOR CHESS PIECES

PATRIOTIC WOOD BOX FOR CHESS PIECES: About 2.5x5x7" body with slide out lid having 1914 EK affixed by 4 tabs, black stenciled owner *Schach* & hand inked details *Zur Erinnerung an den Feldzug 1914-1915 Lynwoldt 1916*. Divided inside holds 16 black & 16 natural wood turned & hand carved pieces. Above avg. cond. $139.00

PATRIOTIC WOODEN CIGAR BOX WITH STEEL PLATE LITHO DESIGNS: 5x7x2". HInged lid with brass stud pull. Yellow paper covering with scenes of 7 different historical homes & peasants. Inner liner has rubberized support for cigars. Lid has view of the Albrecht Hall in Landeck. Avg. cond. $25.00

PERSONALITY ITEM BAVARIAN KING LUDWIG PERSONAL CASED SILVER HUNTING CUP: The cup was used on hunting trips. It has a folding handle stamped *900* with proof & engraved side Crown L. Leather covered hinged storage case with traces of gold Crown L to top. Near mint cond. $565.00

PERSONALITY ITEM FROM THE COURT OF QUEEN LUISE (1776-1810) ANTIQUE GERMAN CLASSIC URN: 24" tall on 3 piece pedestal. 28" diam. White porcelain body with clear over glaze with white bisque eagle handles. Urn is classlc Greco-Roman style of the 2nd Empire as reflected in German art taste. Body is of Blanc de' Chine porcelain. Raised detailed eagle heads with classic flight wings drawn back. Fancy convoluted scroll work with flared double rim & tapered base. Work is separately fired in several pieces. Near mint cond. $1,300.00

PERSONALITY ITEM GENERAL LUTZOW'S LEAD CRYSTAL GOBLET: Finest of Quality. Goblet is approx. 11" tall with flared 4" gold trimmed lip. Matching gold trimmed 4" diam. base, stem is ground & faceted with 9 patterned bubbles. Front of goblet delicately etched with baronial helmet, with 3 Feather plume & von Lutzow's coat of arms, reverse has *v. Lutzow* inscription on glass. A fine item associated with a well known Prussian General. Mint cond. $275.00

PRESENTATION BASKET
TO A RESERVE OFFICER

PRESENTATION BASKET TO A RESERVE OFFICER: Nickel silver. Diamond shaped metal basket with plain style legs & matching metal handle with dbl. straps. 7.5x7.5 in size; 3" deep with raised 9" high handle. Handle hand engraved, *Zur Erinnerung a.d. 5 Res. Offz. Asp. Kursus. Harburg. September 1916* in two lines. Above avg. cond. $50.00

PRESENTATION GOBLET ROYAL PRUSSIAN: To Prince Oscar of Prussia. Enameled crystal on a pewter base. Delicate 6.5" flared lip crystal goblet with gold filled rim. Body has Prussian eagle shield showing *Kaiserhaus Goslar* above in wreath. Base has flared pewter base with banded arbor design above raised inscription. *21 July 1908. His Highness, the Crown Prince of the German Nation/ 18, 19, 20 July 1913 His Royal Highness, Oscar Prince of Prussia.* Mint cond. $538.00

PRESENTATION WINE DECANTER 49TH FIELD ARTILLERY: 1902 dated with presentation inscription on flat silver lid with spout cover & scrolled cipher with *49* below on center of lid. Edge dated 27 January 1902 having two men's names. Ball top lifter. Upper 2" of glass body sheathed in silver metal finish. Decanter

is 10.5" tall with clear crystal glass body in gentle flare configuration. Near mint cond. $225.00

PRINT GERMAN TROOPS CHEERING WILHELM I: 1870s. In old brown period frame with glass; print nicely matted & done by well known artist Franz Anling. Approx. 30x20". Sepia, b/w drawing shows 9th Laurenberg Jaeger troops cheering Wilhelm I as his carriage passes by destroyed French field artillery unit. Above avg. cond. $150.00

PROPELLER PHOTO DISPLAY

PROPELLER PHOTO DISPLAY: 6x13.5" propeller tip has hammered copper frame work to hold 2 photos. Affixed brass EK engraved 1918 & yellowed celluloid covers to photo postcard of *Rittmeister Manfred Frhr von Richthofen* & early uniformed photo of Lt. von Conta. Above avg. cond. $387.00

REMEMBRANCE PILLOW NAVAL PAINTED SCENE: 14x19.5" black velvet front with purple cloth backing & open seam to lower edge with no stuffing. Shows burning ship with sailor on floating wreckage holding small kriegs flag over head. Above avg. cond. $28.00

RESERVIST MAGIC STEIN 3 holes inside below the rim connect to a hole in the handle, result the drinker gets wet. 1 liter, cream colored crockery with green & tan highlight raised relief work of soldier, flags & shoulder board: bead work bottom rim with raised panels having various patriotic reservist slogans & devices. *Raise your glass on high to a Reserve man* motto at the top. Mint cond. $150.00

RESERVIST STEIN *4.GARDE FELD=ART.REGT.,POTSDAM 1919/ 1912*: 8.5" tall off-white crockery body with color details to raised designs around base, painted 3 arty. scenes to body with crowned display at center. Named to *Reservist Blohm* at rim, small roster at back near handle with crowned eagle thumb lift, metal garde star hanging from beak & view glass has named *Podsdam etc.* image. Domed pewter lid has fuse details, arty. crew & a mounted trooper finial. Near mint cond. .. $906.00

RESERVIST STEIN *INF.REGT.NO130 METZ 1906/1908*: 8" tall off-white crockery body with 6 picture panels around base each with saying, *Hoch Reserve!* etc. Raised colored details to body with *130* yellow shoulder board center, reservist in uniform, scroll *B.d.Comp.1.Lothring Inf.Regt. No130. Metz 1906/1908* & 2 painted soldier scenes to sides with wording. Soldier head to handle, wording to rim, domed pewter lid with military equipment, drinking soldier finial & eagle thumb lift. Exc. cond. $594.00

RESERVIST STEIN *RGT. DER FELD ART. SCHIESS SCHULE JUTERBOG 1911- 13:* 13" overall 8.5" crockery body with nice color arty. scenes, Kaiser profile & 50 shoulder strap. Named to *Reservist Olbert* & roster at back. Color soldier face to handle, mounted trooper thumb lift, domed pewter lid with arty. fuse, military motif & arty. gun/soldier finial. Near mint cond. $769.00

RESERVIST STEIN 8TH RHEINISH FOOT ARTILLERY REGT.: 12". 1/2 liter. Named to Reservist Heis of the 6th company, Metz, 1904-06. Double roster. Field howitzer finial with two ball topped helmeted soldiers: crowned spread winged eagle thumb lift. Bright colors. Man, woman departing in field litho. Front panel shows field gun being ready for firing with officer in background with telescope. Two side panels depict artillery in firing position. No damage. Cannon barrel moves on pewter lid. Near mint cond. $460.00

RESERVIST STEIN 9.WURTT.INFTR.REGT. NO.127 ULM.1907-09: 11.5" tall overall 7" white china body with color details, roster at back, named to *Musketier Rub.* Domed pewter lid with military motif & 2 soldier finial. Lithopane of soldier with woman. Avg. cond. $282.00

RESERVIST STEIN *RGT. DER FELD ART. SCHIESS SCHULE JUTERBOG 1911-13*

RESERVIST STEIN BAVARIAN
1901-1903 4TH INF REGT

RESERVIST STEIN BAVARIAN 1901-1903 4TH INF REGT: 10.5" tall overall 6.5" white china body with color details, roster at back, named to *Res. Zapf* & *8. Cp. Konigl. Bayr. 4. Inftr. Regt. (Koenig Wlh. v. Wurttemberg) Metz 1901-1903*. Domed pewter lid with military motif & soldier finial. Lion shield thumb lift. King lithopane. Avg. cond. $300.00

RESERVIST STEIN HOLSTEIN FIELD ARTY REGT 24 1906-08: 11" tall. Beautiful bright colors. Named to Gefreiter Wigger of the 5th Batt. Holstein Field Artillery Regt. 24, stationed at Gustrow, 1906-08. Gray domed lid with two artillery soldiers standing by field cannon. Crowned Prusssian eagle thumb lift. Lithopane of man & woman departing from one another. Center panel shows cannon & caisson pulled by horses. Lower device depicts shoulder strap, shells, crown, flags & swords. Two side panels show firing practice & the placement of weapons. Mint cond. $538.00

SIGN PRUSSIAN EAGLE *K.P. E.V.*: For Postal/Railway building use. 8x10" metal body with cut corner & 4 holes for mounting. Gray/white background with black eagle having colored details & yellow title below. Avg. cond. $76.00

SIGN PRUSSIAN EAGLE *KAIS.POSTAGENTUR*: Enameled. 21x29.5" size vaulted body has excellent 5 color details to the crowned eagle with eagle shield to chest with ornate chained order border. Has black title below on gray body with brown border trim. Metal backside. Above avg. cond. $675.00

SOUVENIR CUP: Pewter. 3.5". Turn of the Century. With equestrian statue of Wilhelm I & view of the Marine Academy. Avg. cond. $32.00

SOUVENIR FELDPOST BOX: 9x7x2". Black pseudo leather covering: raised title, *Feldpost Grusse* with EK 1914 design. White metal lock. Above avg. cond. $33.00

SOUVENIR GOBLET FROM GERMANY: Turn of the Century. Pewter. 3.75" tall with raised design of Imperial Reich's eagle plus bust of Kaiser Wilhelm I. Nice flanking floral, public building designs. Near mint cond. $65.00

STATUE OF GOTZ VON BERLICHLINGEN ON HORSE BACK: 17" tall. Dark bronze style statue detailed very nicely with man in half armor of the 16th century mounted on a war horse & carrying a mace in his right fist. Salade style helmet with good details to armor, horse fittings, stirrups. All mounted on large veined white & black marble base measuring approx. 6x13x2". Circa 1880s. Near mint cond. $950.00

STATUE OF VON MOLTKE

STATUE OF VON MOLTKE: 12" tall on black turned round wooden flared base. Base has 1870 1st class Iron Cross mounted on it. White metal bust of general with him in general spiked helmet with Garde star & field marshal shoulder boards. Near mint cond. $809.00

STATUES OF WILHELM & HINDENBURG: White plaster. Each studio marked to a Munich art company. Each offers full shoulder & bust with superb detail to neck orders, medal bars, general officer collar insignia & facial expressions. Plinth of Wilhelm statue has spread winged eagle, base of Hindenburg statue shows man battling with dragon. Nice tonal quality. Both date to circa 1915. Avg. cond. $675.00

STUDIO PORTRAIT OF SOLDIER WITH ORNATE MATTE

STUDIO PORTRAIT OF SOLDIER WITH ORNATE MATTE: 1918. 18.5x24.5" gray matte with gold embossed crowned eagle, 1914 EK & etc. 11x15" photo shows uniformed trooper outside with early bayonet, knot & pillbox cap. Script name & date to back. *Jos.Ott Singen etc.* photographer. Above avg. cond. $62.00

SWEETHEART ROUGE CASE GARDE: 3.25" diam., 1.2" tall. Silver metal. Brass Garde star on top. Flip-up silvered lid. Avg. cond. $65.00

TAPESTRY OF GENERAL HINDENBURG: 17.5x24.5" color shoulders-up portrait of Hindenburg in uniform with neck order. Current gold & black wood frame has good antique look, 23.5x30.5" size with wire. Exc. cond. $280.00

TAPESTRY OF GENERAL HINDENBURG: 19x28" size has been removed from frame & shows color, shoulders-up portrait of Hindenburg in uniform with neck order. Avg. cond. $59.00

TRENCH ART ASHTRAY: Made from wood aircraft propeller. 6x7.5" crosscut section is 3" tall with hammered brass inset tray. Above avg. cond. $100.00

TRENCH ART LAMP: Made from 1916 brass arty. shell. 19.5" tall brass body has about 4.5" diam. to brass lamp fitting that is 5.5" tall. The head is stamped *Karth 851 Dez.1916 etc.* Avg. cond. $24.00

TRENCH ART LETTER OPENER *VERDUN 1914-17* Made from arty shell driving band. 7.5" long copper band with 4" blade hand engraved *VERDUN 1914-17.* Avg. cond. $50.00

TRENCH ART LETTER OPENER: Copper. Made from pounded-out driving band of shell warhead. Approx. 10" long with handle & double edged dagger shaped blade. Above avg. cond. $22.00

TRENCH ART LETTER OPENER: Rough shrapnel style handle with polished diamond formed steel cutting blade. 5.7" long with nice soldier trench art work. Near mint cond. $25.00

TRENCH ART PHOTO FRAME WITH PHOTO: 4x8" 3 bullets on either side of a b/w photo of officer & wife with brass crown & small frame at top. Has wire stand on back. Avg. cond. $75.00

TRENCH ART SHELL: 75mm. 1923. 13.5" tall dark body with fluted lower end, female figure, leaves, date & *Jcnomeh*? Head stamp *A RS L481.* Above avg. cond. $50.00

WALL PLAQUE GENERAL OFFICER MEMORIAL: 11" with oak leaf border. Plaque has head of General with open collar type tunic, very heroic style. Back

of plaque has massive lugs for mounting. Above avg. cond. $265.00

WALL PLAQUE HINDENBURG PROFILE: 12" tall heavy & dark bronze casting. Profile of detailed head with collar, partial neck cross & partial shoulder board showing. 2 threaded mounting holes. Above avg. cond. $162.00

WALL PLAQUE KAISER WILHELM II: Silvered on copper. Approx. 5x7.5" in size. Raised profile relief of Kaiser from chest to head with all medals, decorations & laurel leaf trim with PAX (Peace) motto. Beautifully hand engraved. Artist signed & dated at Cassel, 1899. Avg. cond. $85.00

WALL PLAQUE MUSKETEER
DEATH MEMORIAL

WALL PLAQUE MUSKETEER DEATH MEMORIAL: 11x14" black painted plaster body with oak leaf wreath border. Copper paint to raised highlights, EK 1914/1918 *Aus unserer Mitte* & title *Verdun am 17.8.1917.* 2 hanger loops & has felt backing. Avg. cond. $116.00

WALL PLAQUE PATRIOTIC QUOTE: Polished steel. 7x8" with high raised letters, oak leaf borders. Patriotic quote by Karl Bosenius of the German Hero League, Sedan, 1912 to the effect that one should honor German heroes who shed their blood that our souls may be endowed with desire to follow them. Very heavy. Finely done with pebbled interior finish. Exc. cond. $125.00

WALL PLAQUE PILOT BADGE: All worked metal is hand cut out & hand detailed. 7x11.5" size. Dark Oak backing with hand made copper, white metal front having raised relief of 1913 style pilot badge with early Taube in flight above field, rising

sun. Green velvet backing. Near mint
cond. $300.00
WALL PLAQUE SERPENT & TORCH:
Bronze. 14" long with single serpent
intertwined on stylized torch with bulbous
head: Back of torch has two posts for
mounting. From Military Hospital. Near
mint cond. $79.00

IMPERIAL GERMAN PATRIOTIC
INSIGNIA & JEWELRY

CIGARETTE TIN GARDEKORPS BRAND:
3.75x3" size. Has Gardekorps star on lid.
Orange, white & black in color. Embossed. Has colorful paper label inside
for Egyptian Cigarette Co. Above avg.
cond. $80.00
FREI KORP BADGE: 28mm silvered bronze
oval with Prussian crown & IV at base,
Pb. Avg. cond. $50.00
PATRIOTIC BADGE AUSTRIAN 1915:
30MM. Silvered oak wreath with gilt brass
center having black lettered motto *Viribus
Unitis* (United Strength) & design of five
pointed enameled star with each ray
having the colors of a central power. PB.
Mint cond. $49.00
PATRIOTIC BADGE GERMAN ANTI-
ALLIES: Oval wreath with design of large
oak tree trunk in center bearing in black
all the names of the nations who fought
against the Central Powers. Wreath
bound with ribbons having names of
Austria, Germany, Bulgaria & Turkey.
Hmkd. PB. 40x50mm. Near mint
cond. $135.00
PATRIOTIC BADGE GERMAN AUSTRIAN
ALLIANCE: 45X15mm. Design of 5
silvered acorns on branch with Austrian &
German national ribbons in enamel work
wrapped about base of branch. Pb. Mint
cond. $30.00
PATRIOTIC BADGE IMPERIAL EAGLE:
27x29mm black enamel eagle with gold
details & blue enamel crown. Horizontal
Pb. Near mint cond. $20.00

PATRIOTIC BADGE IRON CROSS 1914:
Detailed 23mm EK affixed to frosted
silver 32mm oakleave wreath. With a
horizontal pin. Highest quality. Mint
cond. $168.00
PATRIOTIC BRACELET ARTY DRIVING
BADGE WITH IRON CROSS: Cut from
the brass shell with spiral body & hinged
with chained button catch. Has small
dedication silver plate attached inside &
wife to husband for war years 1914-15.
Attached black enameled 1914 IC & oak
leaf wreath on either side. 60mm &
heavy. Avg. cond. $160.00
PATRIOTIC BRACELET ARTY DRIVING
BAND WITH IRON CROSS: Gold finish
to fired band with hinge, chain, affixed
oak leaf branches & black enamel EK.
Avg. cond. $75.00
PATRIOTIC CIGAR CASE IRON CROSS:
Leather. 2 piece each 4x5" & slide
together & has silver color embossed IC
& other side is the Nurnberg castle with
oak leaf wreath. Avg. cond. $59.00
PATRIOTIC CIGAR TIN IRON CROSS: Full
color, outstanding EK on the lid. 7x5x3"
with hinged lid. Light checker board motif
with crossed green laurel branches
meeting at wreath under 1914 black Iron
Cross. Side panels have wreaths with
laurel berries having national shields of
Germany, Austria, Turkey & Bulgaria.
Avg. cond. $50.00
PATRIOTIC CIGARETTE CASE IRON
CROSS: 3x3.5". Domed pebble white
metal snap case with miniature EK 1914
on body. Avg. cond. $27.00
PATRIOTIC CIGARETTE CASE IRON
CROSS: Stamped pebbled dark gray
steel body with affixed 18mm EK device.
Hinged with 2 springs inside to hold
cigarettes. Exc. cond. $50.00
PATRIOTIC FINGER RING EAGLE SHIELD
1914-1918: Size 11.5 narrow silver band
stamped 800. 13mm tall black enamel
panel with siler eagle having tricolor
shield chest. Dates at each side. Avg.
cond. $139.00
PATRIOTIC FINGER RING GOLD FOR
IRON: Gray with inscription around body
with raised oak leaves on front with
cross. Small size. Avg. cond. $27.00
PATRIOTIC FINGER RING GOLD FOR
IRON: Size 11 gray metal body with cast
EK & oakleaves. Faint wording around
sides. Avg. cond. $35.00
PATRIOTIC FINGER RING GOLD FOR
IRON: Size 6.5 nickel/silver body with
stamped *Gold gab ich fur Eisen 1914*
Avg. cond. $22.00

PATRIOTIC BADGE IRON CROSS 1914

PATRIOTIC FINGER RING
GOLD FOR IRON

PATRIOTIC FINGER RING GOLD FOR
IRON: Size 10. Raised EK, oak leaves,
1914 to front with faint wording to sides.
Avg. cond. $76.00
PATRIOTIC FINGER RING IRON CROSS
1914/1917: About size 9.5 thin silver
finished band with 8mm black enamel
EK. Above avg. cond. $38.00

PATRIOTIC FINGER RING IRON CROSS

PATRIOTIC FINGER RING IRON CROSS:
Size 10 narrow dark silver band with faint
stamp proof. 10mm oval front with black
enamel EK & border design. Oak leaves
show wear at sides. Avg.
cond. $125.00
PATRIOTIC FINGER RING IRON CROSS:
Size 10.5. to narrow band with 10mm tall
shield. Black enamel EK & tri-color
corner with black *Wilna* to white stripe.
Stamped *800*. Avg. cond. $40.00
PATRIOTIC FINGER RING IRON CROSS:
Size 6.5 narrow silver band with stamped
800. 8mm tall panel with black EK & tri-
color corner. Avg. cond. $58.00

PATRIOTIC FINGER RING IRON CROSS

PATRIOTIC FINGER RING IRON CROSS:
Size 8.5 narrow silver band with brass
base coming thru. Nice EK to 11mm
black panel with tricolor swirl to each
side. Above avg. cond. $101.00
PATRIOTIC FINGER RING IRON CROSS:
Large size with IC on rectangle front.
brass Avg. cond. $40.00
PATRIOTIC FINGER RING IRON CROSS:
Small size with IC on square in front.
Steel. Avg. cond. $20.00
PATRIOTIC MATCH BOX SAFE HEL-
METED SOLDIER: Stamped gray zinc
with round center & stamped soldier. Avg.
cond. $27.00
PATRIOTIC MATCH BOX SAFE IRON
CROSS: Brass with stamped steel IC
with black painted center & soldered on
front. Avg. cond. $30.00
PATRIOTIC MATCHBOX SAFE GOTT MIT
UNS: 3 sided body with title roundel
having crown. Avg. cond. $20.00
PATRIOTIC MATCHBOX SAFE GOTT MIT
UNS: Brass 3 sided body with title
roundel having dented crown. Avg.
cond. $23.00
PATRIOTIC MEDALLION 1914/17 OCCU-
PIED ALSACE: 40mm gray metal round
with skyline & German soldiers in
combat. Avg. cond. $20.00
PATRIOTIC MEDALLION GOLD FOR IRON
1916 IN ROUND METAL FRAME WITH
HOOK: Designed to be worn in conjunction with a neck chain or fob. Avg.
cond. $20.00
PATRIOTIC MEDALLION GOLD FOR IRON:
In white metal frame. Pb. Above avg.
cond. $20.00
PATRIOTIC MEDALLION SINKING THE
LUSITANIA 1915 GERMAN COMMEMO-
RATIVE: 55mm round bronze high art
relief of ship sinking & other side is
skeleton selling tickets for ship. Above
avg. cond. $100.00
PATRIOTIC NECKLACE IRON CROSS
1914 TO 9 RUSSIAN COINS: 16mm
silver EK with black enamel center is
affixed to 1914-20 silver coin 4 smaller
coins linked to each side with early dates.
Neck chain & hooks. Near mint
cond. $95.00
PATRIOTIC PENDANT IRON CROSS 1914:
25mm diam. to dark silver wreath with
nice details to black enamel EK center.
Exc. cond. $27.00
PATRIOTIC PIN 1916: 18mm round with
relief of a person tied up & hanging
piece. Above avg. cond. $20.00
PATRIOTIC PIN GERMAN TAUBE AIR-
PLANE: 38mm brass struck with Pb &
marked, detail Avg. cond. $150.00

PATRIOTIC PIN IRON CROSS 1914: 16mm dark silver frame. Black enamel center. Stamped *830S*. Knurled pin. Above avg. cond. $177.00

PATRIOTIC PIN WELTKRIEG 1914-17: In form of 1" driving band of shell with *Weltkrieg 1914-17*. PB. Above avg. cond. $23.00

PATRIOTIC SPOON WILHELM II DEUTSCHLAND: Lot of 4. German silver. Has *Deutschland* Bust of the Kaiser & Imperial Eagle on the handle. On the back of the handle is design of 2 soldiers standing back to back with waving flag above. Marked to *Oneida Community A1 x*. Nearly 6" long. Mint cond. $95.00

PATRIOTIC VIVAT RIBBON *1914 KRONPRINZ WILHELM LONGWY 26.VIII ETC.*: Uncut silk gray with black printed title, Wilhelm profile, naked swordsman, etc. Mint cond. $32.00

PATRIOTIC VIVAT RIBBON *DER KRIEG VON 1914 ETC.*: Uncut rose silk with black printed title, Kaiser profile, mounted knight slaying dragon, etc. Mint cond. $32.00

PATRIOTIC VIVAT RIBBON *SCHLESISCHEN HERO ETC.*: Uncut yellow silk with black printed condor over scroll, profile, soldiers, etc. Mint cond. $32.00

PATRIOTIC VIVAT RIBBON *U21 GROSSADMIRAL VON TIRPITZ ETC.*: Uncut light blue with black printed title, U-Boat sinking ship, profile, etc. Mint cond. $32.00

PATRIOTIC WATCH CARRIER BAVARIAN OFFICER: Custom made. Silver metal finish: snap open with raised Iron Cross, In Treue Fest motto on front, reverse has clear celluloid viewer for watch face. Type carried in trench war to protect watch from shocks & impacts. Above avg. cond. $95.00

PATRIOTIC WATCH FOB SAXON WAR SERVICE RIBBON: 1933. 800 marked fitting on ends & a slide in center with colors of German flag with engraving on front & back. Avg. cond. $28.00

miniature pilot badge in center, Pb & with a catch hmkd 800 on pin & well made. Avg. cond. $157.00

TRENCH CRUCIFIX: 6" tall nickel plated body, dark wood inlay, affixed title scroll metal Jesus & skull/crossbones. Stamped *Germany* & hanger ring. Above avg. cond. $35.00

TRENCH CRUCIFIX: 55x110mm heavy cast nickel silver cross with 3-D Christ over skull & letters on each arm & hanging loop. Avg. cond. $213.00

THIRD REICH ORDNANCE

ARTILLERY ROUND 3.7CM WITH PROJECTILE: 13.5" long overall. Dark brass case head stamped *3.7cm Flak18 P 1939 WaA406 etc*. Black painted metal projectile with copper band stamped *WaA534 etc*. 1939 stamped lower rim with no threaded plug. Above avg. cond. $139.00

ARTILLERY ROUND NAVAL 3.7CM: 20.5" long with 2 part projectile having alum. tip to steel body. Brass colored magnetic case is pitted. Head stamped *aux 3.7cm 30 St 5 41* & Eagle M??. Avg. cond. $244.00

ARTILLERY SHELL CASE *2.5cm H* : 6.5" tall brass body. Title head stamped & *LUM.S 13g 42* with *WaA550*. 1940 dated primer. Above avg. cond. $30.00

ARTILLERY SHELL CASE NAVAL 4CM: 12" tall body lacks primer. Head stamped *enz 1941 4cm 28 38* & Eagle M V/2. Avg. cond. $95.00

BOMB LUFTWAFFE INCENDIARY: About 14" long body with silver paint & many stamped maker numbers. Red & green sheet metal tail. Paper label typed *Hyde Park, London Dec. 29th, 1940 etc*. Above avg. cond. $200.00

EXPLOSIVE DETONATOR PIONEER: Black leather. For M26 detonator. 5.5x7x11" body by *O.Reichel Lengefeld i/ Erzgeb. 1936 WaA142*. Roller buckle straps & handle pouch fittings. Wool padded lining. Above avg. cond. $129.00

SWEETHEART PIN MINIATURE PRUSSIAN PILOT BADGE

SWEETHEART PIN MINIATURE PRUS-SIAN PILOT BADGE: 50mm prop with

FLARE ROUND *FALLSCHIRMLEUCHTPATRONE*

FLARE ROUND
FALLSCHIRMLEUCHTPATRONE: 5" tall
alum. case with stenciled title etc. Avg.
cond. $133.00

FUZE *SP BU.37* TIMER STYLE WITH BOX:
Set of 4. 4x4x4" cardboard body with lid
& paper label *Zt.Z.f.Sp.Bu.37 etc.* 4
complete bakelite bodies with 1940 inked
dates. Near mint cond. $328.00

FUZE *SP BU.37* TIMER STYLE: Bakelite. 3"
tall body *RhS Zt.S.f. SpBu.37* & inked
date. Above avg. cond. $21.00

FUZE *SP BU.37* TIMER STYLE: Bakelite.
Title to body with endcap & key with
missing cover. Avg. cond. $30.00

FUZE CONTAINER *KART.VORL. L.F.H.16/
18*: Bakelite. Title to 1940 lid & 1942
base. 3.5" tall by 4.5" diam. Above avg.
cond. $22.00

FUZE CONTAINER *ZUNDERBUCHSE 1*:
Bakelite. 5 1/4" tall cone shaped body
with threading at the end. Near mint
cond. $20.00

GRENADE EGG STYLE

GRENADE EGG STYLE: Gray painted 2
part body. Gray wings to blue painted
fuze cover by *efy 43* & string intact. Avg.
cond. $220.00

GRENADE PULL CORD WITH DONUT
M1924 STICK-STYLE: White donut on
white string with wire from fuze intact.
Exc. cond. $38.00

GRENADE SMOKE *M2H* GLASS: 5" tall
clear glass light bulb shaped body with
glass tube inside & crack to fiber cap.
Avg. cond. $145.00

GRENADE STICK-STYLE WITH FRAG
SLEEVE: M1924 grenade with wood
turned handle has stamped *bab 43
WaA*??. Steel end cap with loose white
donut. Gray metal head by *RR 1940*
Force fit gray metal smooth frag sleeve.
Avg. cond $175.00

GRENADE STICK-STYLE WITH FRAG
SLEEVE: Wood handle stamped *HR791
1940 WaA136*. Gray painted metal head
has affixed gray smooth frag sleeve. Avg.
cond. $175.00

GRENADE STICK-STYLE

GRENADE STICK-STYLE: M1924.
WC1944 marked metal head & wood
turned handle with drilled center. Done
before fuze change to head mount. *WaA*
to end cap & lacks pull cord. Avg.
cond. $137.00

GRENADE STICK-STYLE: Wood turned
handle stamped *RR 1939 WaA*???.
Green metal head with white stenciled
wording, *WaA560* & top stamped *RR
1939*. End cap & donut with pull string.
Exc. cond. $345.00

GRENADE STORAGE BOX: Holds 15 stick
grenades. Stamped steel body by *kho43*
with original gray paint & white band
around center. Wood handle intact as is
metal rack inside. Avg. cond. $240.00

GRENADE STORAGE BOX

GRENADE TRAINING STICK-STYLE:
M1924. Wood turned handle
stamped *Ub 44 brb* inked WaA.
End cap. Red painted steel head
with 8 holes & stamped *44brb*. Exc.
cond. $282.00

IGNITOR *S.MI.Z.35* IGNITOR: Brown
finished alum. body by *blw41*, 3 wires,
safety pin & bakelite plug to end. Near
mint cond. $35.00

IGNITOR *Z.Z.35* PULL STYLE: 3" long
brass body with safety pin. Above avg.
cond. $20.00

MG ROUND LUFTWAFFE LW 20mm *MG-
151/20* with blunt steel projectile. Avg.
cond. $27.00

MINE ANTI-PERSONNEL *GLASMINE 43*

MINE ANTI-PERSONNEL *GLASMINE 43*: Complete example, heavy glass body, shear plate, glass top, metal inside disc & M-44 pressure ignitor. Above avg. cond. $177.00
MORTAR ROUND: 50mm mortar round, 9" tip to fin with well defined bakelite nose. Above avg. cond. $132.00
MORTAR ROUND: 50mm mortar round, 9" tip to fin with well defined bakelite nose. Above avg. cond. $145.00

PANZERFAUST *8.8CM RAKETENPANZERBUCHSE 54*

PANZERFAUST *8.8CM RAKETENPANZERBUCHSE 54*: Deactivated tube with large hole cut to side & welded rods inside. 64.5" long with recent camo paint & tan/green/reddish-brown. Comes with protective shield & only lacks sling. Exc. cond. $750.00

PANZERFAUST ANTI-TANK

PANZERFAUST ANTI-TANK: Steel tube has tan paint & red stenciled instructions. Sight & firing device intact. Tan painted head has paper firing instructions. Above avg. cond. $483.00

RIFLE GRENADE ANTI-PERSONNEL *WURFKORPER 361*

RIFLE GRENADE ANTI-PERSONNEL *WURFKORPER 361*: Style used with flare pistol that required smooth bore liner. 10" long with metal egg grenade, bakelite tube & head stamped *43 1a*. Avg. cond. $175.00
RIFLE GRENADE ANTI-PERSONNEL: 5.5" tall 4 part body, yellow painted steel body, gray metal tip, bakelite fuze & grooved tail. By *mne St 44 etc*. Above avg. cond. $93.00

RIFLE GRENADE ANTI-TANK

RIFLE GRENADE ANTI-TANK: 7" tall body, cone shaped, metal. Bakelite stem with grooved end. Avg. cond. $105.00
STORAGE CASE FLARE *6 STERNSIGNALPATRONEN*: Bakelite. 4.5" tall body with threaded lid & paper title label. Exc. cond. $55.00
TORPEDO GYRO UNIT *XSE M11600*: Non-magnetic unit is around 12x12" diam. with matching serial numbers to 2 part main cast alum. body. Removable domed cover to each end. Gyro cradle intact with many wired fittings dated *5.42 eyr etc*. Body is title stamped & by *brd* near wire hook up block. Above avg. cond. $433.00

THIRD REICH MILITARY VEHICLE & AIRCRAFT PARTS & EQUIPMENT

AIRCRAFT COMPASS *FUHRERKOMPASS FK 38*: 3" diam. bakelite body with 4 mounting tabs. Dark fluid filled inside, alum. ID plates *FL 23233 etc*. Exc. cond. $91.00
AIRCRAFT COMPASS FLUID FILLED *FK38 FL.23233*: 3" diam. bakelite body with 4 mounting hole tabs & 4" long. Metal front plate with title & inked *nfe*.

Chipped bakelite socket at bottom. Dark fluid filled body with luminous compass. Avg. cond. $160.00

AIRCRAFT ELECTRIC MOTOR FW190: 4.5" long body with about 3" diam. to body with no cover. Metal maker tag *eoa EM1-20K 24V 24 WL etc.* Base has 4 holes to mount & wire with 2 metal end loops. Above avg. cond. $35.00

AIRCRAFT ELECTRICAL TRANS- FORMER: Gray metal case with spec plate on top. Model FL22420. Attached to 4 bolt mounting frame. Exc. cond. $120.00

AIRCRAFT GAUGE *DOPPELDRUCKMESSER*: 2.5" diam. bakelite case with 4 mounting holes. Luminous needles & scale marks. Alum. maker plate with title, *Fl.20512-2*, etc. 2 threaded brass fittings at back. Above avg. cond. $142.00

AIRCRAFT GAUGE *FL20723 X100*: 2 1/4" diam. black finished metal case with 4 mounting hole tabs. Luminous needle & *X100* scale *1234* . Corrosion to stenciled wiring diagram with rest intact. 3 prongs to socket with wire loop. Avg. cond. $117.00

4 mounting tabs, dial below face with luminous needle & scale. Metal spec plate & 2 cut hose fittings. Exc. cond. $93.00

AIRCRAFT GAUGE *VARIOMETER FL.22384*: 3" diam. bakelite body with 4 mounting hole tabs & 2" long. Luminous needle & scales *0-5-10-15*. Title decal to back & by *oeq*. 2 hoses to fittings. Exc. cond. $92.00

AIRCRAFT GAUGE *VARIOMETER FL.22386*: 3" diam. bakelite body with 4 mounting hole tabs & 2" long. Luminous needle & scales *0-5-10-20-30*. Title decal to back & by *oeq*. 2 fittings at back for missing hoses. Exc. cond. $164.00

AIRCRAFT GAUGE *VORRATS-ANZEIGER FL20723*: 2" diam. black metal body with 4 mounting lugs & num'd scale with needle *x100*. 3 prongs to socket with wire loop. Above avg. cond. $370.00

AIRCRAFT GAUGE AIRSPEED *FAHRTMESSER FL 22230*: 3" diam. bakelite body with 4 mounting tabs, luminous needle & numbers to scale. 2 cut hose fittings at back with maker decal. Exc. cond. $53.00

AIRCRAFT GAUGE *FL20723 X100*

AIRCRAFT GAUGE AIRSPEED
FAHRTMESSER FL 22234

AIRCRAFT GAUGE *NAHE LN27002*: 2-1/4" diam. black alum. body with 4 mounting tabs. 2 luminous needles & *nahe* mark. Stenciled instructions near empty back socket with wire loop. Above avg. cond. $60.00

AIRCRAFT GAUGE *O2-WACHTER FL30489*: 2 1/4" diam. gray finished alum. case with 4 mounting hole tabs. Metal maker tag by *bwz etc.* Broken off tube at back nut. Luminous with 4 rectangles to face with title. Above avg. cond. $339.00

AIRCRAFT GAUGE *STAT. VARIOMETER FL22381-10*: 3" diam. bakelite body with

AIRCRAFT GAUGE AIRSPEED *FAHRTMESSER FL 22234*: 3" diam. bakelite body with 4 mounting tabs, luminous needle & numbers to scale. 2 cut hose fittings at back with maker decal. Exc. cond. $177.00

AIRCRAFT GAUGE ALTIMETER *FL 22320*: 3" diam. bakelite body with 4 mounting tabs. Dial adjustment knob moves scales & needle. *E* & *F* marked clips move red indicators at edge. Luminous numbers to scale. Maker decal at back with cut hose. Near mint cond. $139.00

AIRCRAFT GAUGE ARTIFICIAL HORIZON

AIRCRAFT GAUGE ARTIFICIAL HORI-
ZON: 7" tall 4" diam. with 4 mounting
lugs. Worn decal with *Fl.22411/1*. Plug to
cord with socket intact & cut cord.
Luminous painted detail & bubble level to
face with dial adjustment. Above avg.
cond. $145.00
AIRCRAFT GAUGE TURN & BANK
INDICATOR: FL22412. Black ball in
curved tube with vertical pointer. Black
metal case & spec label in back. Nice
piece. Above avg. cond. $120.00
AIRCRAFT NAVIGATION INSTRUMENT
FL.#23750 WITH CASE: 5.5x9x12"
brown repainted wood case with white
painted *P.A.Z.* to each side. Leatherette
handle to hinged lid with 2 latches &
metal capped corners. 12" long tan
finished metal body with many adjustment fittings & scales. Metal ID plate at
side *Libellen-Oktant etc.* All spare parts
appear to be intact with rubber eye cup,
brush, bulbs & etc. Exc. cond. .. $280.00
AIRCRAFT SWASTIKA: 16" square painted
black swastika with gray border & on gray
finished fabric. In current frame. Above
avg. cond. $555.00

AIRCRAFT WING CAMERA LUFTWAFFE
SIEMENS: 3.5x5.5x6.5" green painted
metal case, shade to lens, leather handle
at top & plug in cord with 2 hole socket
marked *FL32601* & *Siemens* marked film
cartridge inside. Above avg.
cond. $700.00
ID TAG *MECHANISCHE WERKE
COTTBUS*: 4x6" steel with 4 mounting
holes. Title, *D7.1943, WaA926* etc. Avg.
cond. $26.00
PANZER OPTIC SIGHTS WITH CASE
PZ.B.W.F.8 2,5X19: 10.5x12x22" gray
painted metal storage box, 2 handles, 2
latches with 1 hook broken & hinged lid.
Storage rack inside for 3 optics & small
wood box lacks contents. Both sights are
title marked, by *gwr* & *bvf*. Optics clear
with crosshair inside having scaled
numbers. 18" long L shaped bodies with
9" long end with eye cup. Above avg.
cond. $433.00
PANZER SCOPE *1.75X30 ZEISS* WITH
CASE: Finnish *SA* stamped green
painted wood box. White painted
T.Z.M.G.3a to lid with leather handle & 3
latch front. 4.5x4.5x48" box has metal
reinforced corners. 35" black crinkle
painted scope has clear optics with *7.62*
& *37mm* scales. Spanner wrench intact.
Exc. cond. $216.00
RAILWAY CAR EAGLE: Alum. 27" wing-
span. Avg. cond. $199.00
RAILWAY CAR ID PLATE: 6" long cast
alum. oval with 2 mounting holes. Black
painted. Raised letters *Waggonfabrik
Gebr.Luttgens G.m.b.H. 1943
Saarbrucken.* Above avg.
cond. $118.00

AIRCRAFT WING CAMERA
LUFTWAFFE *SIEMENS*

SEARCHLIGHT NAVAL STYLE
SCHEINWERFER ESW20 WITH CASE

SEARCHLIGHT NAVAL STYLE
SCHEINWERFER ESW20 WITH CASE:
10x13.5x16" gray painted wood box with
large metal handle to front, reinforced
metal corners, title ID tag to hinged lid &
added latch for padlock use. Paper
contents list inside lid with 6 items, still
has main light & 3 extra bulbs intact. 10"
diam. green painted metal body with
rough texture to handle having switch
lever. Rubber eye cup to tube sight, black
cord lacks plug & gray web neck strap.
Avg. cond. $248.00
SHIP BELL *EIDER BREMEN*: Comes with
hand written English note about it being
removed in 1944 by German salvage
diver, sunk in 1941 of Norway coast. 16
pound dark silver finished body with deep
engraved name to side. 8" tall & 8" diam.
Has bolt & striker. Original nautical item.
Exc. cond. $400.00
SIGNAL MIRROR DEVICE LUFTWAFFE
WITH CASE: 3x6x13" bakelite & riveted
alum. case with web shoulder strap.
Alum. ID/maker tag riveted to front
Fl.29730 etc., inside tag *Fl.29730-3* & to
alum. mirror frame *Fl.29730-1*. 1941 illus.
instruction booklet by *Zeiss Ikon* shows
tripod or hand use from ground. 12" long
frame to mirror with adjustments. 2 extra
mirrors in storage box. Contents illus. to
lid shows 2 small missing objects. Still
clean display. Exc. cond. $290.00
VEHICLE MEDICAL BOX: Gray lid with
white disc having Red Cross. Metal
handle to end, 2 latches to hinged lid,
metal splint inside & 5 other contents
remain. Avg. cond. $68.00
VEHICLE RECORD POUCH *MERCEDES
WH-637926*: 7x10" fold open heavy gray
cloth body with white stenciled title at
front. 2 inside pockets & cloth band for
map/papers. 2 original unused camera
film rolls *Voigtlander Film*. Above avg.
cond. $50.00

THIRD REICH FLAGS, BANNERS & PENNONS

DAF STANDARD *LUBECK TRAVEMUNDE
4*: 4x4.5' red wool body with alum. fringe
on 3 sides. Bunting lacks rings. Composite b/w cogged wheel swastika centers.
Tan wool with blue tape stripe borders &
white chain stitched title. Avg.
cond. $249.00
DAF STANDARD: 7x12' 2 part cotton body
with large composite cogged wheel
swastikas to sewn white centers. Rope to

bunting with swivel loop ends. Inked to
white center *Urting on the Rhine 45*. Exc.
cond. $115.00

DEUTSCHES JUNGVOLK STANDARD
11/541

DEUTSCHES JUNGVOLK STANDARD *11/
541*: 3.5x5' black cotton body with
composite white rune each side. 7 pole
rings to bunting stamped *RZM M3/40/38*.
White cotton corner panels with twisted
black piping & black chain stitched *11/
541*. Exc. cond. $382.00
FLAG POLE TOP KRIEGERBUND: Brass.
13" tall 2 part body. Black painted 1914
EK to swastika center & color painted EK
swastika shield above. Above avg.
cond. $130.00
FLAG POLE TOP NSKK: 5 1/4" wide
wingspan to nice nickel finished eagle
with scroll & swastika wreath. Black
painted letters & swastika. Large
threaded stud to base & 5" tall. Marked
RZM DRGM. Exc. cond. $200.00
FLAG POLE TOP REICHSNAHRSTAND:
14.25" tall. Brass with nickel finish. 2
piece construction. On sword & wheat
shaft. Deep pole socket. Hmkd
Priessmann Bauer & Co. Munchen Ges.
Gesch. Quality construction. Above avg.
cond. $275.00
FUHRER STANDARD: 10.5" wide pink
water pattern satin ribbon is 13' long with
gold bullion fringe to ends. Faded gold
printed *Adolf Hitler* towards 1 end with
resewn by hand gold bullion 7" wide
Party Eagle on red wool. Re-sewn Fuhrer
standard is 5.5x5.5" size with gold bullion
work. Avg. cond. $1,315.00
FUNERAL RIBBON *KAMERADSCHAFT
KREUZER BERLIN*: 7x38" blue water
pattern body with gold fringe & title. Avg.
cond. $125.00
FUNERAL RIBBON SS: 6.5" wide red satin
ribbon has black printed border stripes to
give armband look. 6.5' long with dark
silver fringe at ends. Printed black SS
runes in circle on sewn white disc to each
end. Avg. cond. $720.00

FUNERAL STREAMER
*NS.RECHTSWAHRERBUND
GAU BAYER. OSTMARK*

FUNERAL STREAMER
*NS.RECHTSWAHRERBUND GAU
BAYER. OSTMARK*: 7.5" wide red satin
ribbon is 8' long with fringe to ends. Silver
printed title shows fading & printed
swastika satin disc affixed near each end.
Above avg. cond. $75.00
FUNERAL WREATH RIBBON FUHRER:
Style used for High Party Officials with
combatant death in the family. Post-war
heavy wood frame with gold border,
20x34" size & glass front. 12" wide
bowtie red satin ribbon is 2' long with
gold bullion fringe to ends. 5.5" wide gold
bullion hand embr. Furher eagle on red
wool with black highlights. Area for death
notice paper with photo of Army soldier
Franz Deutsch killed in Russia 1942 etc.
Above avg. cond. $895.00
GORING STANDARD 2ND PATTERN:
30x30cm body is Reichsmarschall 2nd
pattern with blue printed body having
gold printed borders. Twisted gold piping
to 3 sides. No mounting devices so
appears to be style for weatherproof
case. Reichmarschall eagle with crossed
batons side & other with printed 1939 EK,
4 eagles at corners with crossed batons
below. Colorful printed style. Exc.
cond. $1,421.00
HITLER YOUTH FEMALE PENNANT *6
362* : 21x39.5" black cotton triangular
body. Early composite diamond centers &
white chain stitched numbers to corners.
Above avg. cond. $201.00

HITLER YOUTH FLAG

HITLER YOUTH FLAG: 3.5x6' 3 part red
& white body with 5 cloth pole loops
having 2 small clips. Printed swastikas

on sewn white centers. Above avg.
cond. $135.00
HITLER YOUTH PENNANT *10 767* :
20x36" black cotton triangular body.
Nice composite tri-color diamond to
each side. White chain stitched unit to
upper corners. Bunting with rope has 3
nickel clips on swivels. Shows honest
use. Above avg. cond. $231.00
HITLER YOUTH PENNANT *14 725* :
20x38" triangular black cotton body,
composite black/white/red HJ diamond
to each side & chain stltched white unit
to upper corner. Bunting has 3 gray
metal clips with 1 unsewn. Exc.
cond. $390.00
HITLER YOUTH PENNANT *LANDJAHR* :
21x37" triangular 3 piece sewn cotton
body. Composite swastika centers.
White chain stitched title on either
side. 3 nickel clips. Avg.
cond. $279.00
HITLER YOUTH PENNANT: 16x20.5"
triangular red cotton body with
composite centers. Large white pole
sleeve with tiestrings at 1 end. Avg.
cond. $50.00
KREIGS FLAG: 3x5' printed wool body.
Red cotton bunting has rope with loop
ends. Above avg. cond. $177.00
KREIGS FLAG: 6x8' printed wool body.
Variation cloth bunting with end loops.
Avg. cond. $125.00

KRIEGERBUND STANDARD

KRIEGERBUND STANDARD: 4x4' tri-color
body with swastika to center of EK. Black
pole sleeve. Avg. cond. $78.00
KRIEGERBUND STANDARD: 4x4.5' tri-
color printed body with swastika center to
large EK. Black bunting for pole wrapping. Above avg. cond. $111.00
KRIEGS FLAG NAVAL: 10x16' printed 2
part body. Rope to bunting with loop,
inked Eagle M *RKFl.Gr.10 300x500* &
bevo maker tag *Wurttembergische etc.*
Avg. cond. $110.00

KRIEGS FLAG NAVAL

KRIEGS FLAG NAVAL: 5x7.5' printed wool body with backside little faint. Rope to bunting with loop & inked *Reichskriegsflg. 1.5x2.5 Eagle-M* Above avg. cond. $160.00

KRIEGS FLAG NAVAL: 5x8' clean printed body with crisp details. White bunting with looped rope end & other cut off. Inked Eagle M *Reichskriegsflg. 150x250 Berliner etc.* Above avg. cond... $138.00

KRIEGS FLAG NAVAL: 5x8' clean printed body with crisp details. White bunting with rope & looped end. Inked Eagle M *Reichskriegsflg. 150x250 Berliner etc.* Mint cond. $200.00

KRIEGS FLAG NAVAL: 5x8' printed wool body with good details. Rope to bunting with loop & printed Eagle M *Kr.Fl.150x250 Johaun etc.* Minor mothing overall. Avg. cond. $135.00

KRIEGS FLAG NAVAL: 6x11' clean printed body with EK to corner. Very large inked script *Emil Benarcik May 7, 1945 Linbach Germany* to opposite corner from EK. Rope to bunting with loop & inked Eagle M *Kr.Fl.200x335 Berlin etc.* Above avg. cond. $113.00

KRIEGS FLAG NAVAL: 9x16' printed 2 part wool body. Rope to bunting with looped end. Inked Eagle M & *Loh.Kr.Fl.300x500.* Age soiling. Exc. cond. $162.00

LOTSEN FLAG NAVAL: 3x4' white wool body with printed party flag center. Rope bunting with hook ends. Black inked Eagle M Lotsenflg. 100x120'. Avg. cond. $120.00

LUFTWAFFE PENNANT FLAK KILL *LG.KDU.BELG.-NORDFR.*: 14.5x20" red cotton triangular body. Black stenciled title, LW eagle & white downed plane with smoke trail. 2 rings to white bunting. Avg. cond. $355.00

LUTSEN FLAG NAVAL: 5x6' white wool body with printed party flag center. Rope to bunting with clip ends. Black inked Eagle M *Sig.fl. Delta 150x18.* Bevo makers tag *Westdeutsche etc. Bonn.* Avg. cond. $120.00

NAVAL FLAG ADMIRAL: Approx. 38x39" white wool body with black printed EK. Bunting with rope & looped ends. Inked with an Eagle M & marked *Adm. 1.0x1.0.* Avg. cond. $223.00

NAVAL FLAG COMMANDER-IN-CHIEF: 5x5' printed wool body with black EK having gold crossed swords. Rope to bunting with loop, red inked Eagle M, black inked *Fl.d.Oberbefehlsh.d.m. 150x150.* Near mint cond. $1,200.00

NAVAL FLAG REAR ADMIRAL: 3x3' white wool body with black printed EK & dot to each bunting corner. Rope to bunting with loop end. Black ink stamped Eagle M *Kont.-Adm. 1.0x1.0.* Above avg. cond. $400.00

NAVAL PENNANT DESTRUCTION OF ENEMY SHIP: 10.5x21" triangular red printed body with white center disc having black EK on gold fouled anchor. Unmarked white bunting with rope having looped ends. Mint cond. $855.00

NSKK FLAG: 9x14' 2 part body. Gray printed eagle to white center with black details & title scroll. Bunting with rope having loop end & swivel brass loop. Exc. cond. $425.00

OLYMPIC PENNON *BERLIN 1936*

OLYMPIC PENNON *BERLIN 1936*: 10x15" white cotton triangle with nice color embr. title disc with rings & torch. Double sided & tie strings to bunting. Avg. cond. $300.00

PARTY BANNER *NSKK 13/M73*: 2' wide red cotton body is 6' long with angled sides that reduce lower edge to 4.5' long. Tiestrings to ends. Printed swastika on sewn white center with black inked title around edge. Single sided. Above avg. cond. $83.00

PARTY BANNER HONOR: 3.5x3' red cotton body with pole sleeve. Gold bullion fringe to bottom edge. 1.5" wide gold tape stripe border with same gold composite wreath to swastika center. Exc. cond. .. $486.00

PARTY BANNER: 17.5x22" red cotton body, white yarn fringe to lower edge, pole sleeve & printed swastika on white disc. Near mint cond. $79.00

PARTY BANNER

PARTY BANNER: 2.5x8' red cotton body with bunting having many wire rings & string with clip. Printed swastika to sewn white centers or disc. Above avg. cond. $150.00

PARTY FLAG NAVAL: 2.5x4' printed body. Rope to bunting with loop end & inked Eagle M, *Fahnen Kreisel, Zwickau Goschen 5 80-135.* Avg. cond. ... $76.00

PARTY FLAG NAVAL: 5x8' printed linen body. White bunting with rope & looped end. Inked Eagle M & *Gosch.150x250 etc.* Above avg. cond. $143.00

PARTY FLAG: 14x17" red cotton body with printed black swastikas on sewn white centers. Narrow pole sleeve. Above avg. cond. $28.00

PARTY FLAG: 14x19" red cotton body, printed swastikas to sewn white centers & sewn edges with no mounts. 17 inked names, towns & states to 1 side. Above avg. cond. $35.00

PARTY FLAG: 15x22" red cotton body, composite swastikas to sewn white centers & pole sleeve with bevo *Stetter etc.* Near mint cond. $150.00

PARTY FLAG

PARTY FLAG: 2.5x3.5' red cotton body with composite centers. Pole sleeve at bunting. Near mint cond. $61.00

PARTY FLAG: 2.5x4' red cotton body with pole sleeve. Printed centers. Avg. cond. $50.00

PARTY FLAG: 2.5x4' red cotton body with printed swastika sewn-on centers. Bunting with loop cord ends. Above avg. cond. $40.00

PARTY FLAG: 2.5x5' red cotton body with printed swastikas on sewn white centers. Pole sleeve inked *Deutsche Front Ortsgruppe Eiversberg.* Above avg. cond. $77.00

PARTY FLAG: 2.5x5' red cotton body with printed swastikas on sewn white centers. Small rope to bunting with looped ends. Avg. cond. $40.00

PARTY FLAG: 3.5x6' printed body. Rope to bunting with loop, inked *Gosch Gr.6 100x170* & bevo maker tag *Wuttembergische Cattunmanufactur Heidenheim a. Brz..* Avg. cond. .. $72.00

PARTY FLAG: 3.5x6' red cotton body with pole sleeve & printed swastikas to sewn white centers. Avg. cond. $30.00

PARTY FLAG: 3.5x6' red cotton body with printed swastikas on sewn white centers. Rope to bunting with looped ends. Black inked GI inscription over *France Belgium England Holland Germany* & 72 signatures of most men from Mass. Avg. cond. $160.00

PARTY FLAG: 4X12'. Double sided with sewn-on printed swastika centers. Avg. cond. $48.00

PARTY FLAG: 4x10' red wool body with pole sleeve, printed swastikas on sewn white centers. Avg. cond. $59.00

PARTY FLAG: 4x6' red cotton body printed black swastika on sewn white centers. Rope to bunting & loop to end. Above avg. cond. $50.00

PARTY FLAG: 4x6' red cotton body with printed swastika on sewn white centers. Avg. cond. $85.00

PARTY FLAG: 4x9' red cotton body with pole sleeve at both ends. Printed swastika centers. Avg. cond. $63.00

PARTY FLAG: 4x9' red cotton body with printed black swastika on sewn white centers. Pole sleeve. Avg. cond.. $50.00

PARTY FLAG: 5x12' 2 part red cotton body with pole sleeve & printed swastikas to sewn white centers. Avg. cond. .. $36.00

PARTY FLAG: 5x14' red cotton body with printed swastikas to sewn white centers. Rope to bunting with clip ends & small typed size tag *180x500.* Avg. cond. $80.00

PARTY FLAG: 5x8' red cotton body, large printed swastikas on sewn white centers & bunting has rope with clips to ends. Exc. cond. $100.00

PARTY PENNANT: 14x22" triangular red cotton body. Printed swastikas on sewn white centers. Avg. cond. $32.00

PARTY PENNANT: 3' wide white pole sleeve, faded red wool triangular body is 10' long with metal clip end, composite black cotton swastikas & sewn white centers. Avg. cond. $35.00

PARTY PENNANT

PARTY PENNANT: 4.5x9' red linen triangular 2 part body with blunt tip. Printed swastikas to sewn white centers. GI inked to white area *PFC.Leslie Wisuni Cannon Co. 30th Inf.3rd Division Schirmeck, France Gestapo Headquarters November 1944.* Pole sleeve has bevo maker tag *Westdeutsche etc.Bonn.* Above avg. cond. $196.00

PARTY PENNANT: 8x13" red cotton triangular body with string to bunting & printed swastikas on sewn white centers. Avg. cond. $20.00

PARTY PENNON: 8x12". 3 piece sewn construction single sided. With tie string. Above avg. cond. $34.00

PARTY PENNON: 8x14". 2 piece sewn construction single sided. Shield shaped with red tassel on end Above avg. cond. $36.00

PARTY STANDARD
*NSDAP KREISLEITUNG BECKUM,
AHLEN WESTF*

PARTY STANDARD *NSDAP KREISLEITUNG BECKUM, AHLEN WESTF*: 4x4.5' red twill wool body, silver fringe to 3 sides, 5 nickel pole rings & 1 clip to bunting. Composite swastikas on sewn white centers. Brown velvet corner panels with black tape stripe borders & white chain stitched title. Exc. cond. $661.00

PARTY STANDARD *OFFENBACH A.M. BUSING*: 4x4.5' red linen body, silver bullion fringe to 3 sides, 6 nickel pole rings with 1 missing to end. Composite swastikas on sewn white centers. Brown wool corner panels with blue tape stripe borders & white chain stitched title. Above avg. cond. $283.00

PARTY STREAMER *15.DEUTSCHES TURNFEST STUTTGART 1933*: 4.5x26.5" red side with embr. swastika on sewn white disc. Tricolor fringe to end & wire hanger loop at top. White side has red & black chain stitched title, *DT*, composite horse/shield & wool oak leaves with acorns. Avg. cond. ... $82.00

PARTY STREAMER: 2.5x5' red cotton body with composite swastikas on sewn white centers. 5 red cloth pole loops & other end has sewn in weights. Above avg. cond. $50.00

PARTY STREAMER: 2.5x5' red cotton body with composite swastikas on sewn white centers. 5 red cotton pole loops & other end has sewn in weights. Avg. cond. $50.00

PARTY STREAMER: 4.5x18' red cotton body with printed swastikas on white centers. Avg. cond. $90.00

PARTY STREAMER: 5x24' red cotton 2 part body with printed swastikas on white centers. Large pole sleeve. Above avg. cond. $75.00

PODIUM BANNER DAF: 4x4.5' red cotton body with white fringe to lower edge. Single sided with composite b/w cogged wheel swastika center. Small rope to bunting with nickel clip at each end. Near mint cond. $77.00

PODIUM BANNER PARTY *DEIN JA* : 22x32" red cotton body, white fringe to lower end, printed swastika on sewn white center, white painted title to corner & black outlined. Above avg. cond. $56.00

PODIUM BANNER PARTY EAGLE

PODIUM BANNER PARTY EAGLE: 3.5x4' red cotton body with off-white fringe to lower edge. 2 rings remain at top. White composite eagle has black swastika, border & stitched highlights. 2" wide white tape stripe border frame. Avg. cond. $300.00

PODIUM BANNER PARTY: 2.5x2.5' red cotton body with white fringe to end.

Printed swastika to sewn white center. Avg. cond. $39.00

PODIUM BANNER PARTY: 3x3.5' red cotton body with pole sleeve, gold bullion fringe to lower end, 1.5" gold tape border/frame, 3" wide gold brocade swastika arms with gold piping details. Near mint cond. $184.00

POLE TOP DAF: Nickel. 10" tall heavy nickel plated brass body. Pole cup with stamped *RZM M3/40* & 2 mounting holes. Age corrosion should polish off. Early example. Avg. cond. $100.00

POLE TOP DAF: Nickel. 10" tall with nice cogged/wheel swastika & cup stamped *RZM60*. 3 part construction that unscrews. Avg. cond. $126.00

POLE TOP LUFTWAFFE FLAK: 47mm round silver metal & edge for fitting on a pole. Has engraved down tail eagle with dates 15.7.34- 30. 9. 36 & named to Flak Regiment No.7. Above avg. cond. $100.00

POLE TOP NSKOV: 15" tall brass casting with silver finish worn at highlights. Black & red painted details to swastika/EK center. 2 mounting holes to pole cup & stamped *Ges.Gesch Ottogahr*. Avg. cond. $187.00

RAD FEMALE PENNANT

RAD FEMALE PENNANT: 3.5x6' red cotton triangular body, moisture blurred black printed swastika & wheat heads. Rope to bunting with looped ends. Avg. cond. $100.00

RAD FEMALE PENNANT: 3.5x6.5' triangular printed red cotton body. Black swastika & wheat heads to center. White bunting with looped ends to rope. Above avg. cond. $125.00

RAD FLAG: Approx. 7x13' with black printed spade/wheat heads to white center. Bunting with steel clips to rope loops, bevo maker tag *Bonner Fahnenfabrik Bonn* & *1 39 RADBA M/L* inked corner. Exc. cond. $444.00

RAD STANDARD: 4x4.5' red wool body with alum. fringe on 3 sides. Large bunting for wrapping pole. B/w composite swastika center with nice gray & black hand embr.

highlights. Spade & wheat head centers. Shows honest use. Above avg. cond. $664.00

RED CROSS PENNANT *ALTENKIRCHEN 3*: 26x36" triangular white wool body with printed black eagle holding Red Cross. Sewn gray upper corner panels with black inked title. 7 small nickel pole rings to bunting. Avg. cond. $268.00

REICHSPARTEITAG PENNANT 1939 NURNBERG: Rare example made for rally that wasn't held because the war started. 7x12" red linen triangular body with white cord piping. Nice color bevo disc has same look as tinnie with flat silver party eagle. Other side has composite swastika on white with couple frayed holes. Rope to bunting with clip. Above avg. cond. $248.00

RLB FLAG: 3x5' printed red body with black swastika to white starburst. Rope to bunting with looped ends. Near mint cond. $255.00

RLB FLAG

RLB FLAG: 4.5x8' printed body with excellent details to swastika/starburst. Bunting has rope with loop end. Near mint cond. $202.00

SPORTS BANNER *V.F.TURN U.JUGEND-SPIELE*: 5.5x7.5" double sided rectangle with gold brocade border, gold fringe to end & 8 loops. White satin side has red chain stitched *DT* in oval. Blue & red satin diagonal divided side has yellow chain stitched title with 2 gray gulls below. Avg. cond. $95.00

SPORTS FLAG *GEWIDMET VON GEORG LANG*: 3x5.5' printed wool body with black eagle to white centers. 4 nickel clips to bunting with inked Ges. Gesch. & makers shield. Heavy gold embr. title to each side. Avg. cond. $200.00

SPORTS PENNON *RUGBYSPIEL ITALIAN-NIEDERSACHSEN 20.MAI 1936*: 12x19" triangular satin cloth pennon. Red & white side has embr. yellow title & red side has printed swastika. Red/white twisted cord sewn around edges &

hanger. Brass rod to bunting. Avg.
cond. $175.00

SPORTS STANDARD: 4x4.5' red & white
satin body with black embr. eagle to
centers. 7 alum. pole rings to bunting.
Avg. cond. $150.00

SS FLAG: 5x8' black cotton body with white
composite runes to each side, 32" tall.
Rope to bunting with steel swivel clip.
Exc. cond. $551.00

SS STANDARD *I/103* : 4x4.5' red wool body
only has couple small moth holes.
Bunting shows 7 cut cloth loops. Black
fringe to 3 sides with faint alum. flecks.
Composite black swastikas on sewn
white centers. Black wool corner panels
with twisted alum. piping & alum. chain
stitched *I/103* . Exc. cond. $1,800.00

STANDARD POLE TOP
SS CAVALRY 1935

STANDARD POLE TOP SS CAVALRY
1935: 11.5" tall assembly is style with
pole cup having extra socket out back to
hold missing pole for Deutschland
Erwache standard. Gold finished hollow
metal eagle has 8" wide wingspan. Silver
oak leaf wreath with bright silver swasika.
Maker is marked *Gahr Munchen 1935*.
Mounting hole for each pole with gold
finished sockets. Near mint
cond. $6,156.00

STATE SERVICE FLAG

STATE SERVICE FLAG: 2.5x4.5' size
printed body. Bunting with loop end & cut
rope. Avg. cond. $140.00

STATE SERVICE FLAG: 6x10' printed 2
part linen body. White bunting has 2
metal clips. Avg. cond. $110.00

STATE SERVICE FLAG: 6x9' printed wool 2
part body. Rope to bunting with looped
ends. Bevo maker tag *Fahnenrichter etc.*
Avg. cond. $75.00

STATE SERVICE FLAG: 7x12' printed 2
part linen body. Rope to bunting with
metal swivel loop. 43" eagle to corner.
Avg. cond. $195.00

STATE SERVICE FLAG: 9x16' printed 2
part linen body. Rope to bunting with
metal swivel loop. 54" eagle to corner.
Above avg. cond. $180.00

TRI-COLOR FLAG: 2.5x1.5' 3 piece
construction. Pole sleeve bunting. Above
avg. cond. $37.00

TRI-COLOR FLAG: 3x5.5' printed red, white
& black body. Bunting lacks rope. Shows
age & small mothholes mostly to white.
Avg. cond. $80.00

TRI-COLOR FLAG: 4X10'. 3 piece
construction black/white/red, string tie
bunting Avg. cond. $30.00

TRUMPET BANNER ARMY *AR 27*

TRUMPET BANNER ARMY *AR 27*:
14.5x18.5" red wool side with b/w embr.
stylized eagle. Blue wool side with white
embr. title. White cloth fringe to 3 sides,
no fittings at bunting. Avg.
cond. $800.00

TRUMPET BANNER RAILWAY: 17x17"
black cotton body, alum. bullion fringe to
3 sides, nice composite centers with
alum. winged wheel having gray 2 tone of
chain stiched highlights, red swastika &
white center. Exc. cond. $1,100.00

VEHICLE ID FLAG: 3x6' 2 part red cotton
body with grommet at each corner.
Printed swastika on sewn white center.
Near mint cond. $48.00

VEHICLE ID FLAG: 3x6' red cotton body
with grommet at each corner. Printed

black cross on sewn white center. Above avg. cond. $60.00

VEHICLE ID FLAG: 3x6' red cotton body with printed swastika to sewn white center. Grommet at each corner. Mint cond. $114.00

VEHICLE ID FLAG: 3x6' 2 part red cotton body, printed swastika to sewn white center & 4 corner grommets. Near mint cond. $158.00

VEHICLE ID FLAG

VEHICLE ID FLAG: 3x6' red cotton body, black printed cross to sewn white center & 4 grommets. Avg. cond. $120.00

VEHICLE PENNANT ARMY: 8.5x12" triangular gray body with stiffener inside. 1/2" wide white cloth border around 3 sides. Cut rope to bunting with nickel clip end. Gray embr. eagle to each side with dark highlights. Above avg. cond. $125.00

VEHICLE PENNANT DAF HIGH RANKING LEADER: 29cm square body is high quality construction. Black & white satin ribbon border show 2 sides cut open with some fraying. Red wool or linen body has white center with composite swastika of 1914 EK style ribbon. B/w chain stitched cogged wheel & 4 b/w ribbons running to each corner. Avg. cond. $316.00

VEHICLE PENNANT DDAC
WITH FENDER POLE & TOP

VEHICLE PENNANT DDAC WITH FENDER POLE & TOP: 8x12" white triangular linen body with chain stitched black & red cross & bevo eagle centers. 14" alum. pole, threaded base, alum. bunting wire & nickel eagle/logo top. Avg. cond. $195.00

VEHICLE PENNANT NAVAL: 8.5x13" dark blue cotton body with bunting, cord & 2 clips. Yellow & black chain stitched eagle on either side. Yellow border. Above avg. cond. $170.00

VEHICLE PENNANT NAVAL

VEHICLE PENNANT NAVAL: 8x12" dark blue cotton body with bunting having cord & 2 nickel clips. Yellow & black chain stitched eagle. Yellow border. Above avg. cond. $120.00

VEHICLE PENNANT NSKK: 6.5x12" red cotton body with black leatherette borders. Bevo eagle centers with 3 color details. Rope to bunting with clip. Near mint cond. $250.00

VEHICLE PENNANT NSKK: 7x12" triangular red cotton body with black leather border & bevo eagle/scroll centers. Rope to bunting with clip. Above avg. cond. $120.00

VEHICLE PENNANT PARTY WITH WEATHERPROOF COVER: 7.5x12.5" triangular red cotton body with bevo swastikas on sewn white centers. Gold leatherette borders hold clear plastic covers. Rope to bunting with clip. Above avg. cond. $68.00

VEHICLE PENNANT PARTY: 7.5x12" red cotton triangular body, twisted white cord piping, bevo swastika centers & rope to bunting with clip. Above avg. cond. $55.00

VEHICLE PENNANT PARTY: 7x12" triangular red linen body with armband style composite centers. Rope to bunting with clip. Twisted white border piping. Avg. cond. $59.00

VEHICLE PENNANT PARTY: 9.5x15.5" red twill cloth body on wire frame with 2 mounting tabs. Bevo swastika on white to one side, other side missing. Avg. cond. $50.00

VEHICLE PENNANT POLE TOP NSKK: Aluminum. 2 1/4" wide wing span & 3" tall. *NSKK* to both sides of scroll. Cross threaded hole to base. Stamped *RZM M3/68*. Avg. cond. $127.00

VETERAN STANDARD *KAMERADSCHAFTSVEREIN*: Not the normal double sided standard but single sided 4.5x5.5' yellow satin body with blue & yellow triangle design border to 3 sides. Bunting edge has 12 small brass rings attached to sewn-in bars. Ornate design with color shaking hands center, oakleave branch wreath with acorns, gold bullion hand embr. title *gedienter Soldaten fur Endersdorf* & blue corner panels with excellent hand embr. gold 3 oak leaves with 2 acorns. Exc. cond. $256.00

THIRD REICH ARTWORK & DECORATORS

AIRCRAFT MODEL DORNIER 217: cast metal aircraft with O props. 7" wing span & limited details. Mounted on black metal rod from 3x2" white marble base. Above avg. cond. $164.00

ANTI-HITLER PLASTER SKUNK FIGU-RINE: 5" long & 5" tall painted b/w skunk body with likeness of Hitler's head. Solid plaster construction from 1940's. Exc. cond. $160.00

ANTI-HITLER WOOD CARVED CARICA-TURE: 8.5" carved body with defeated upset look. Avg. cond. $145.00

ASHTRAY *REICHSWERKE AG HERMAN GORING*: 6" diam. clear gray/green body with tltle impressed to bottom & 5 rests around rim for cigarettes/cigars. Near mint cond. $40.00

ATHLETIC STATUE: Bronze discus thrower. 24" Tall in a classic Greek pose. This is the type of art that was preferred during the Third Reich. Realism & the human figure. Mint cond. $945.00

BUILDING SIGHT *NATIONAL-ZEITUNG* NAZI NEWSPAPER: Red white & black with raised letters & NAZI EAGLE. 14.5x21" metal rectangular sign mounted on wooden backing. Old mounting holes visible on the front. Black raised wording *Neue National-Zeitung etc.Gau Schwaben etc.* Above avg. cond. $275.00

CAVALRY PARADE SADDLE WOOL TRADITION ORNAMENTS: Styled after

1800s dual pistol holsters. 8x10" white & yellow wool bodies with cloth backing having two leather belt loops & a single button hole strap to each. Exc. cond. $720.00

CHARCOAL & PIN DRAWING PRINT STUKAS IN BATTLE: 11X15" b/w Ju 87 Stukas & Ju 88 bombers attacking English ships. Printed litho on art paper & framed with paperboard. Shows Stuka Ju 87 & Ju 88 bombing the gun deck of a ship & an aircraft carrier. Excellent detail & well done. Captioned at base. Facsimile artist signature. Near mint cond. $40.00

COASTER/PLATE SET *UNSEREN VERWUNDETEN NSDAP KREISLEITUNG PASSAU*

COASTER/PLATE SET *UNSEREN VERWUNDETEN NSDAP KREISLEITUNG PASSAU*: 8.5" diam. wood serving plate having burned title to rim & *24.12.1942* to back. 4 coasters with handpainted flowers & ornate stand with flowers & painted title *20.4.1943*. Nice set. Near mint cond. $75.00

DESK WEIGHT 1937 NURNBERG PARTY EAGLE: On 2 piece Marble base. 7.5" tall stadium style silver eagle on pedestal mount. 2 part green 2 tone marble base & backing to eagle. 3/4x3.5x8". Inked script message to paper backing 35th birthday etc. Dated 1937. 1x4.5x6" base marble with both having chamfered edges. Above avg. cond. $880.00

DESK WEIGHT ARMY HELMET: 4" long gray metal hollow casting. Wear to gray paint, 75%. Eagle decal, 80%. National, 40%. Avg. cond. $75.00

DESK WEIGHT LUFTWAFFE TRANSITION HELMET: 2.5" long bronze finished WWI helmet with cast LW eagle & National decals. 3/4x3x3" white & red swirl marble base with chamfered corners & felt base. Exc. cond. $103.00

DESK WEIGHT SS: 6" tall overall. 4.5" tall brass hexagon base has threaded swastika to top & affixed brass SS runes to front. 1x2.5x2.5" gray & white marble. Above avg. cond. $450.00

DESK WEIGHT SWASTIKA: 11.5" tall overall. 5 part construction from solid brass, 3 tier base with threaded bolt to mount 7" tall octagon pillar & 2.5" square swastika that force fits top hole. Heavy duty display. Exc. cond. $200.00

DESK WEIGHT SWASTIKA

DESK WEIGHT SWASTIKA: Nickel. 3/8x 2 1/4x3" nickel base with green felt & affixed 2.5" tall swastika on ball mount. Exc. cond. $101.00

DESK WEIGHT WITH ENGRAVED PLATE *ZUR ERINNERUNG UFFZ.KORPS 1./ B.A.K.*: 5.5" tall metal casting of eagle perched on rocks, spread wings & holds 1.5" diam. swastika from beak. Silver finish has faded to dark gray. 3/4x3.5x5" gray marble base with affixed engraved alum. title plate. Above avg. cond. $675.00

DONATION CAN *GAU WIEN* : Red finish. bale handle. 1944 dated. Some wear to finish but no dings, dents, etc. Avg. cond $33.00

DONATION CAN *NSB HOLLAND*: 2.5" diam. & 3" tall metal body. Removable lid with slot lacks 3 screws. Red & black painted divided body with nice color NSB lion triangle to each side. Above avg. cond. $60.00

DRUM HITLER YOUTH: 14" diam. & 17" tall. Rope binders to black wood rims, leather skins with puncture to bottom & lacks snare fittings. Faint maker to nickel hanger loop. Black triangles instead of flames painted to white center. Avg. cond. $538.00

EAGLE STATUE WITH ENGRAVED PLATE *V.D. ARBEITSKAMERADEN 25.2.38*: 5.5" tall silver plated eagle mounted to 1x3x5" silver base. No swastika to design. Affixed engraved title plate to front. Above avg. cond. $200.00

FREDERICK THE GREAT STATUE: 10" tall overall. 7.5" gold/bronze finished metal casting in uniform with walking stick. Black wood block. Avg. cond. ... $177.00

FREDERICK THE GREAT STATUE: Color porcelain. 8.5" tall with dark blue tunic etc. & walking stick to right hand. Colored base. Blue trademark of crossed sword & trident with *Germany Dresden*. Near mint cond. $100.00

FREDERICK THE GREAT STATUE

FREDERICK THE GREAT STATUE: Porcelain. 11" tall white figure of standing Frederick in uniform with sword & walking stick. Green marked base *Hutschenreuther Germany Kunstabteilung* with 1814 lion trademark. Faint *Karl Tutter* above. Excellent details. Mint cond. $712.00

GRAVE MARKER CONVERTED TO WALL HANGER: 13x13" black painted iron cross with white border. 1939 date at bottom with white highlighted swastika in center. Old screw at rear top. Removed from grave & converted to a wall hanger. Macabre decorator. Above avg. cond. $328.00

HAND DRAWN SET OF PICTURES OF JEWISH GHETTO RESIDENTS: 24 different pencil hand drawn pictures, each approx. 7x11" with some variance in sizes. All drawn on a variety of papers that the Jewish artist had available to him. Drawings show old Jewish men & women, many with Stars of David insignia on them. Scenes of beggars, old rabbis, women in shawls, seated men, standing figures of men in old homburgs, great coats, etc. Artist apparently lived in a large ghetto & drew what he saw. An excellent group of 24 pictures that speak of the poverty & horror of the ghetto but show the undying spirit of the Jewish people under Nazi oppression. This one of a kind item is unique. Ideal for some Holocaust Museum display. Near mint cond. $2,400.00

HINDENBURG PORTRAIT: Hand painted on wood in oil. Very realistic fine Quality work by A. Pasche. Strong colors, excel. detail very life like. Brown wooden frame. 15x20". Hindenburg is painted in his fieldmarshal uniform with visor cap. long open coat showing Blue Max decoration. Above avg. cond. $250.00

HITLER BUST: Cast iron. Black finish. 23" tall. Not artist signed. Bust is very heavy (approx. 50 lbs.) & appears to be hollow cast with huge black iron base. Most probably displayed in some public building. Good likeness of Hitler. Avg. cond. $750.00

HITLER HEAD BUST ON MARBLE BASE: 10" tall overall. 3x3.5x3.5" gray marble base. Solid gray metal casting has good details. Black finish is showing some wear. Avg. cond. $282.00

HITLER HEAD BUST ON MARBLE BASE: 6.5" tall with imitation dark marble base & bronze/gold finished sculptured head by M. Heavy like metal but not bronze. Above avg. cond. $196.00

HITLER PORTRAIT TAPESTRY

HITLER PORTRAIT TAPESTRY: 21.5x28" color woven body showing Hitler from waist up with badges & party armband. Above avg. cond. $400.00

HITLER PROFILE BUILDING TILE: This unique type of tile was usually made in Italy. 8.5x9.5" body with raised profile having dark green finish. Very small chip to ear & nose. 2" thick with mounting rim for securing to wall. Above avg. cond. $400.00

HITLER PROFILE PLAQUE: 6.5x8.5", fine antique glazed bronze finished terra cotta. Nice profile of Hitler facing to his right. Hmkd on the back *MEISSEN*. Made in 1933 when Hitler came to power. Mint cond. $217.00

LETTER OPENER *WEIHN.1940 4./ H.U.V.S.DRESDEN*: 8.5" long with double edge & scroll design to flat handle. Hand engraved title. Above avg. cond. $55.00

MARKSMAN TARGET FRENCH TANK: Superb full color litho of tank crossing battle field. 8 small bullet holes, not detractive. Target is 15" diam. with lettering *Front Soldiers Leave Meeting, July 1942. To the Best Shot, Theodor Pauer.* (trans.). Very desirable type associated with traditional military groups. Men fired only once & winner was determined by exactness of his shot. Target is not framed. Original fiber board backing is intact. Above avg. cond. $137.00

MUSIC RECORD 78RPM *LILI MARIEN*: Printed paper sleeve to Electrola record that shows cracks. Recent black painted wood frame with glass & hanger. Record title is visible at center *Lied Eines Jungen Wachtpostens (Lili Marien) etc.* Above avg. cond. $135.00

NUDE FEMALE FIGURINE: Color porcelain. 10.5" long reclining nude with color face details & brown hair. White base has faint name to side *Steinel?* & green Crown W 1764 to bottom, also *1575/I*. Mint cond. $285.00

OFFICER SIGN *THURINGIA*: 4.5x7" stamped steel, black paint, 4 mounting holes, gold finish to raised title & eagle holding a spoked wheel. Near mint cond. $20.00

OFFICER SIGN *AMTSGERICHT*: Law officer. 12.5x14.5" cast heavy alum./alloy body with raised details. Silver painted border & eagle with black details. Black wording & orange background. 4 mounting holes. Exc. cond. $293.00

OFFICER SIGN *DEUTSCHE ARBEITSFRONT ORTSGRUPPE HOCHHEIDE*: 30.5x38.5" plywood is black painted front & back. Shows removal from frame as edges unpainted. One side has nicely painted white & red cogged wheel swastika & a white title with one arrow below. Above avg. cond. $150.00

OIL PAINTING OF ARMY HORSE DRAWN ARTILLERY CREW: 4x12'. Rolled canvas depicts 6 horse team pulling large wagon with 6 Army troopers. 3 Army troopers are riding horses as drivers. No arty. gun as the canvas appears cut from a larger section. Exc. cond. $1,450.00

OIL PAINTING WEHRMACHT NCO: 18x22" painting of oil on canvas. Chest & head of an NCO in the Army with a ribbon bar having War Service Cross 2nd class with swords & Russian Front ribbon. Nice details to face & good depth of field. Old original heavy wooden frame. Painting dated July 13, 1943 with artist initials at lower right. Near mint cond. $289.00

OIL PORTRAIT LW FLIGHT EM: Period done heavy wood frame 21.5x25.5" is painted silver, white & red. 15x19" nicely done flesh tones to blond hair/blue eyed soldier shown from chest up in gray uniform with yellow tabs having 2 gulls. Exc. cond. $325.00

OLYMPIC ATHLETE STATUE: 21.5" tall with rectangular 7.5x4" base with 1936 date & artist signed. Solid bronze. Beautiful statue of a naked running man with Olympic torch held in right hand, left hand clasps a Nazi eagle with wreath to breast while a portion of drapery conceals his lower groin. Figure's face very similar to Hitler's (sans mustache) with same hair cut. Mint cond. $1,647.00

OLYMPIC BELL FOR BICYCLE: Mounts to handle bar with thumb lever. Nice nickel bell with raised details of 5 ring pennant, Sport & laurel leaf wreath. Above avg. cond. $135.00

OLYMPIC SILK HANKIE: 16x17" white body with color border filled with flags & 4 sets of color Olympic rings at corners. 2 frayed corners from past hanging. Avg. cond. $113.00

OLYMPIC SILK HANKIE: 30x30" white silk body with color Olympic rings at 2 corners & 6 rows of flags, 48 total. Avg. cond. $102.00

OLYMPIC SILK HANKIE: 9.5x9.5" white body, colored flags to border with party flag & 4 sets of Olympic rings to center. Near mint cond. $75.00

PATRIOTIC BOX REICHSKANZLEI: BY JOH.WAGNER & SOHN 900: 3x8x10.5" wood body with burl walnut veneer covering overall. 4" wide affixed silver party eagle & 5.5" long silver title to lid.

Engraved silver swastika/EK rectangles affixed around sides with 9 total & center lock plate lacks key. Stamped title maker to latch assembly. Silver eagle foot at each corner with loose foot to back corner, is present for repair. Avg. cond. $2,400.00

PATRIOTIC BOX MUNICH TOWN SCENE: 6x10.5x14.5" body has cut out swastika/ scroll work around 4 sides & to lid border. Inlaid wood shield to front & back of Munich gate with maid & Party Eagle. No key to lock hinged lid. 6x8" inlaid wood town scene to lid with 1580 below. No contents remain to inside showing removed plate from lid with 4 holes. Highest quality woodwork. Near mint cond. $1,800.00

PATRIOTIC BOX RAD: 2.5x12x16" body shows 5 part lid construction having hand carved stylized party eagle with RAD spade/wreath to swastika & 1940 below. 9 part body has corner legs & 2 brass hinges to lid. Inside of the lid is hand carved OBERSTFELDMEISTER ARTHUR RUFFERT ALS DANK u.ERINNERUNG METTLACH-SAAR-JAN 1940 WOLDEMAR SCHMIDT. Mint cond. $279.00

PATRIOTIC BOX: Hand carved. 4.5x9x13.5" lightweight wood body with massive National style eagle perched on mountain peak without swastika. Checkered design to all sides & has one foot to each corner. Avg. cond. $135.00

PATRIOTIC CLASS: Crystal. Czech made for higher ups in the Nazis Party, design of pre-1939 Czech rampant lion with crown engraved & frosted on ochre colored oval to one side. Has rounded fluted base with walls of glass rising at an angle upward & outward. The base is also flashed in the ochre color with cut concave discs encircling it. The rim has another flashed ochre stripe & has an engraved patriotic slogan in sutterlin style script. Dated on this stripe 1938. Flat cut & polished bottom & rim. Has original maker sticker affixed. 4.5" high. Mint cond. $85.00

PATRIOTIC DESK SET GERMAN POW: 2 colors of pine wood used in const. of stand & 3 frames. 3x16" base with feet has slots for holding 3 frames for 2.5x3.5" & 3.5x5" pictures. Unique. Above avg. cond. $40.00

PATRIOTIC DESK WEIGHT ARMY HELMET ON MARBLE: 1x3.5x5" white/ gray marble base. 2" tall gray cast WWI helmet with double decals & traces of silver finish. Avg. cond. $73.00

PATRIOTIC PHOTO NAVAL E-BOOT

PATRIOTIC PHOTO NAVAL E-BOOT:
8.5x10.5" silver painted wood frame with glass front. 5x7" photo mounted at center showing E-Boot at speed in water. Typed label to back *Zur Erinnerung & Anerkennung an Ihre Frontfahrzeit bei der 2. Schnellbootsflottille vom 4.4.1940 bis 25.3.1944* with signature of the *Oberlt.zur See & Kommandant*. Hanger loop. Exc. cond. $165.00
PATRIOTIC PLAQUE *ATLANTIKKUSTE 1944*: 12" diam. very fine handcarved oak plaque with fouled-anchor in the center & deeply cut in old German style *ATLANTIKKUSTE 1944*. Dark brown finish Possible U-Boat sailor project. Mint cond. $100.00
PATRIOTIC PLAQUE ADMIRAL SCHEER: 18x14" black wooden frame with silver metal high relief view of the ship at speed with good detail to weapons, superstructure. Lower front has silver metal plaque inscribed *Gr. 4/1.9.41 - 30.9.41*. Reverse has large handwritten paper pasted to frame with 14 signatures of men who took the cruise in 1941. Above avg. cond. $195.00
PATRIOTIC PLAQUE LUFTWAFFE FLAK REGT. 804: A rare item probably came from regimental headquarters & is one of a kind. Bronze shield of Oak base. 5x7". Bronze plaque with 804 at upper left top, 88 guns in firing position above scrolled unit crest shield. Hook back. Above avg. cond. $124.00
PATRIOTIC PLATE PARTY EAGLE: 9.5x13" dark copper plate has a 12" wide party eagle at center. Above avg. cond. $185.00
PATRIOTIC PLATE WOOD: Plate is 8.75" diam. wood burned design around edges & color painted emblem of Munich in center with crest of 5 different cities/regions around edge. The Munich insignia is crested with the Nazi flag. Wall decoration. Exc. cond. $25.00
POW WAR ART SALT & PEPPER SHAKER WITH HOLDER: 4.5" square footed alum.

base with screw in 5" pine tree handle & 2 shakers all made out of alum. Etched on base *Made for S/Sgt. Mac Deretchin by Released Prisoner of War Erwin Holf Germany 1945*. Avg. cond. $28.00
PRESENTATION AWARD INFANTRY REGT 131: 18x14" mounted, shows fortress gate with unit history displayed on each side. Gate contains presentation from Infantry Regt. No. 131 in thanks to their comrade Lt. Colonel A.D. Von Ballujeck. dated May 8,1938 & signed. Fancy litho design work of Imperial & Nazi Party flags above gate. Near mint cond. $85.00
PRESENTATION PILOT PLAQUE: 10x8" green carian marble plaque with beautiful cast bronze high relief crowned wreath with airplane flying over medieval city. At lower section of wreath, an eagle rises to meet the plane, clasping a 1916 battle helmet in its talons. Integral plaque below with inscription in German, *The Stahlehlm Front Soldiers* Meeting, 11th National Front Soldier Day at Koblenz, October 4-5, 1930. For taking part in the welcoming fly by. Mint cond. $750.00

PRESENTATION PLAQUE
GENERAL VON BOCK

PRESENTATION PLAQUE GENERAL VON BOCK: Plaque hand carved of blond wood with large raised horse head in excellent detail. Rim of plaque is carved with inscription to commemorate the service of General von Bock of the Infantry. Beautiful finish with oak leaf inner ring. Near mint cond. $375.00
PRESENTATION PLAQUE SA SPORTS STANDARTE J.29: 3/4x8x54.5" Brown painted on wood with rounded top corners. Silver 5.5" diam. SA logo with black details. Gray gothic lettering & bronze painted sports badge, fine detail. Above avg. cond. $251.00

PRESENTATION VASE SA: 8" tall gray/
pewter colored narrow body. Ding to base
rim. Jeweler engraved in script at side
*Uns. lb. Sturmbann- Verwaltungsfuhrer
Zur Vermahlung 4.III.35 Sturm 2/L.* Faint
trademark to bottom. Avg. cond. $48.00

PRINTING PLATE NAVAL *THE SWORD
FROM THE SEA*: 3.5" wide & 4.5" tall.
SCHWERT UBER DEM MEER, large
sword at center with Party Eagle
crossguard & anchor pommel. Sword
runs through battleship with smaller
Viking ship beside. Mint cond. $90.00

REMEMBRANCE BOWL PARATROOPER:
Hand carved oak. 11" diameter bowl
carved raised lettering,
*FALSCHIRMJAGER- KRAFTFAHR
AUSB-ABTLG-HELMSTEDT* with
Oakleaves surrounding a *V* & 2 stars.
Mint cond. $250.00

REMEMBRANCE BOX
I.FRIESENBATAILLON I GR 489: Hard
carved oak. Excellent construction &
carving to dovetailed box. 5x6x10" size.
Removable lid is carved with helmeted
soldier holding broadsword, flowing flag
pole with *Eala Frya Frcsena* &
I.Friesenbataillon below boots. Carved
shield to front *I GR 489* & side shields
with bear *Esens* & eagle *Emden*. Near
mint cond. $153.00

REMEMBRANCE MUG NSDAP MEDICAL:
It is marked on the bottom *GMUNDNER*.
Lidless pattern in light pinkish shade with
turquoise green upper & lower stripes.
Front panel has ancient medieval crest of
the town of Gmunden ship, fish, three
leaves with black lettering *Erinnerung an
das Lazarett Gmunden. NSDAP
Lazarettbeireuung*. Mint cond. .. $165.00

REMEMBRANCE PLAQUE RAD: 9x6.5".
Oval bronze colored metal with raised
RAD spade, Wheat at lower center.
Raised lettering, *Nationalsozialistischer
Arbeitsdienst. Abtei- lung 7/234 Weimar.
Jahrgang 1934/35*. Cast metal hook at
top. Nice even age patina. Avg.
cond. $68.00

REMEMBRANCE PLATE LUFTWAFFE
GUNNER/ENGINEER WITH 14 SIGNA-
TURES: 8x9" silver plate has stamped
ring design to border. Stamped edge with
3 trademarks & *830S 7675*. Cast full-size
likeness of badge in silver. Nice engraved
facsimile signatures of 14 men. Very
unusual remembrance of service.
Scalloped bowl is high quality & would
make a fine Luftwaffe center piece. Mint
cond. $365.00

REMEMBRANCE PLATE PANZER
3.KOMPANIE 6.10.1936-31.5.1937:
Aluminum. 7" diam. with center having

gray affixed scene of large fist smashing
early tank. Engraved rim with title & *P20*.
Faint angel trademark to the back of the
plate. No loops for hanging. Near mint
cond. $133.00

REMEMBRANCE SIGN
D. TURNERBUND 1919

REMEMBRANCE SIGN *D. TURNERBUND
1919 ETC.*: 14" diam. heavy plate glass,
beveled edge & 2 mounting holes. Nice
b/w painted details with tricolor center
having 4 F logo with title & border
Manner Turn Verein Hernals. Near mint
cond. $90.00

REMEMBRANCE STEN LUFTWAFFE
FLAK: Hand made. 5.25" tall with barrel
style body. Gray glazed finish with raised
Flak unit crest in white, gray on front &
brown raised letters, *Leichte Bewegliche
Marine Flakbatteerie. Niederlande*. Above
avg. cond. $100.00

REMEMBRANCE TILE LUFTWAFFE
AIRFIELD: Hand painted. In old period
wooden & gilt frame with history of unit
handwritten on back by German owner.
Eagle shown in M-36 configuration (gray
on creme field). Below eagle is an oak
leaf branch with double heraldic unit &
district shields in red, yellow, white, blue
& black. Below is a hand painted gray &
black banner, *Flieger Horst Wurzburg*
(Military Air Field, Wurzburg). 6.75x6.75".
Near mint cond. $200.00

REMEMBRANCE WALL HANGER NSKOV:
Inlaid wood. This is a very artistic piece.
The border is made up of 3 different
kinds of wood set in a Greek key style
made up of little swastikas. The main
design is the NSKOV insignia made with
3 different shades of wood. This piece
was a named presentation award with the
hand written note on the back. 12x16"
size. Wording *National-Sozialistische
Kriegsopfer Versorgung*. Has 3 sided box
to front for date cards. Above avg.
cond. $175.00

RIFLEMAN STATUE: 11.5" tall overall with 9.5" tall cast metal rifleman shows standing & firing rifle. Some age darkening to frosted silver finish with full pack & equipment details. 1.5x4x4" black base with some gray flecks & silver mounted front plate engraved *4.Preis Unteroffisier Preisschiessen 27.9.1935.* Above avg. cond. $473.00

SHADOW BOX *EIN VOLK EIN REICH EIN FUHRER*: 6x9" with hand carved scene of 3 men in ethic German clothing playing cards in a cabin, has a picture of Hitler above cooking fire & lots of other small details. Very well done & has Nazi eagle label & makers name on back. Avg. cond. $45.00

SKETCHBOOKS REPRODUCED FOR ARTIST: Set of 2. Combat sketch artist's two sketchbooks reproduced during the war. Both pencil & watercolor washes capture the ebb & flow of German combat forces on the eastern front & thru the capture of Paris. Near mint cond. $240.00

SOLDIER BUST *14. KORPORALSCHAFT IM KRIEGSJAHR 1941*

SOLDIER BUST *14. KORPORALSCHAFT IM KRIEGSJAHR 1941*: 9" overall, 5" tall bronze finished casthead with WW1 helmet having Army double decals. 2 part gray marble base with affixed alum. plate engraved *Zur Erinnerung an die 14. etc.* Above avg. cond. $325.00

SOLDIER BUST ARMY: 5" tall gray/alum. metal casting with WWI transition helmet

having nice double decal details. Pole cup style with rim *DRGM* marked. Avg. cond. $86.00

SOLDIER BUST ARMY: 5" tall hollow casting, bronze finished shoulder/head & WWI double decal helmet. Recent 1x2.5x6" white marble base added. Above avg. cond. $76.00

SOLDIER BUST ARMY: 7" tall 2 part hollow casting, silver painted base & bronze finished 4.5" soldier from shoulders up with traces of the green finish to double decal helmet. Avg. cond. $90.00

SOLDIER BUST ARMY: 9" tall overall with 7" tall cast WWI helmeted bust with shoulders. Wear to frosted silver finish & has facsimile eagle & National decals to helmet. 2x3.5x3.5" painted stone base to resemble black marble. Avg. cond. $257.00

SOLDIER BUST HEROIC: This is a very important piece, not only historically & also artistically. First it was done by Fritz P. Zimmer one of Germany's greatest artist. & this is one of his Greatest works. Second this is the figure a Nation Rallied around, thousands of copies were made in all sizes. *1917 Fritz P.Zimmer* marked bronze bust & is the same bust Hitler is shown pictured with in early shots. 14.5" tall dark casting is life size & 100% bronze with casting marks to top of M16 combat helmet. Partial shoulders with title mark. Mint cond. $795.00

SOLDIER BUST LUFTWAFFE

SOLDIER BUST LUFTWAFFE: 8" tall overall, 4" frosted silver helmeted LW soldier bust, 4" gray/white marble tapered base with affixed engraved plate *Fldw.Stadler gewidmet von Deinen Kameraden L.Sch.Btl.18G.Kp. Juli 1940.* Avg. cond. $195.00

SOLDIER BUST PANZER CREWMAN: Wearing beret & wrap-around tunic, Heroic pose, on polished marble base, 7.25" tall, white metal, only example I have ever seen. Shows normal age. Above avg. cond. $271.00

SOLDIER STATUE ARMY: 5x2.5x2.5" white/gray marble base. 5" tall gray casting of helmeted soldier with rifle. Avg. cond. $56.00

SOLDIER STATUE LUFTWAFFE CONDOR LEGION STANDARD BEARER: 10.5" tall soldier on marble base with standard reaching 15.5" overall. Excellent details to 9" tall bronze finished standard bearer soldier in Legion uniform & o/seas cap. Removable bronze finished flowing standard has good details to each side. 1 1/4x2 3/4x4" black marble base with chamfered edges. Near mint cond. $625.00

SOLDIER STATUE STORM TROOPER THROWING A STICK GRENADE: Bronze. Very nice detail of the much feared Storm troops of WWI. Many interesting features the grenade bags, wire cutters. Engineer shovel. On a marbled cream & black marble base. With a Bronze plaque *EHRENGADE DES BUNDESMINISTERIUMS FUR HEERESWESEN 1928.* 13" tall. Artist signed A. Ka???. Mint cond. $1,450.00

SS ALLACH STANDING GOAT: White porcelain body is 6" tall & 5.5" wide, title marked & chip to right ear. Avg. cond. $500.00

SWAGGER STICK SS: 24.5" long black wood body with age fracture cracks to turned white tip & top. 4 white & silver bands that border inlaid silver swastika & SS runes. Above avg. cond. $702.00

TABLE COVER WITH SWASTIKA DESIGN: 40x40" tan cloth body shows light fading to top from use. Green zigzag sewn border rim. 21" square embr. design/border to center with green & brown thread, swastika & floral to center. Above avg. cond. $50.00

TABLE COVER WITH SWASTIKAS: 6x6' size with some age wear along center & edge. Ornate floral design with 12" swastika pattern at the center. Avg. cond. $66.00

TANK MODEL SD.KFZ.101: 4.5" long antique silvered metal tank with movable turret having 2 M.G. barrels. 2x3x5" black

painted wood base with chamfered top edge. Details to 1st of the Panzer line. Mint cond. $275.00

TORPEDO DRIVE MOTOR: Recovered from U-Boat sunk in North Sea. Big. 20x20x20" heavy brass/bronze assembly with corrosion & some steel fittings intact. Heavy, 200 lb. weight. Above avg. cond. $800.00

TRENCH ART AIRPLANE

TRENCH ART AIRPLANE: Aluminum & brass. 1.5" diam. brass cap base is filled with alum. & has brass 2.5" dish above. 3" tall alum. pole to center has mounted 3" long alum. plane to top that pivots & has 2 blade prop. that moves. Avg. cond. $85.00

TRENCH ART ASHTRAY: From bass arty case. 2" diam. body is 1.5" tall with unknown headstamps. Owner named *E Mayser* 3 cigarette rests to rim with anchor & 3 engraved scenes around sides. Small boat, 1941/1942 Krim shield & coastal flak badge. Above avg. cond. $107.00

TRENCH ART VASE: From brass arty case. 8.5" tall body with flared rim & 2" diam. unknown headstamps. Hammered details of 5 men flak crew with date. Above avg. cond. $139.00

WALKING CANE *WOLCHOWSTOCK*: 33" tall with entwined snake to body having wood burned details. Copper eyes & tongue to snake head near top with burned date & mammal head grip with burned details & brass eyes. Above avg. cond. $50.00

WALKING STICK DAF: 36" long wood body has carved twisted root design. Leather wrist strap to hole at handle with wood burned DAF cogged wheel swastika. 26 metal plaques of various towns & organizations. Nice copper DAF *Das Deutsche Handwerk Gesellenwandern*, stag heads, some color etc. Above avg. cond. $121.00

WATER COLOR PORTRAIT ARMY MT. TROOPER: 9x10.5" original wood frame with hangerloop. Artist signed & dated portrait with good facial details & M43 cap. Above avg. cond. $125.00

WATER COLOR PRINT *BOMBS FOR ENGLAND*: Full color very well done & artist facsimile signature. Printed litho on art paper & framed with paperboard. Shows ammo & bombs ready to load in a Stuka for England. Captioned at base. Near mint cond. $32.00

WATER COLOR PRINT *JU 87 IN THE FIELD*: 11X15" full color, nice likeness. printed litho on art paper & framed with paperboard. Shows 2 aircraft under cover of trees & brush. Captioned at base. Near mint cond $32.00

WORKER STATUE RAD: Porcelain. 440 mm muscular young man holding pick in hand. Wearing only work pants & boots. White glazed finish. Blue cipher on bottom with mold num. Signed on top of base *Otto Werner*. Mint cond. ... $680.00

THIRD REICH MILITARY & CIVIL PLAQUES

PLAQUE *12.U.13.AUG.1933 FERIENFAHRT DURCH DEUTSCHE BADER NACH BAD KREUZNACH ETC*: 3.5" diam. frosted silver metal with raised details of historic bridge houses, title border & *Veranstaltet v.SS Motorsturm IV/5 u. N.S.K.K. Schonheits Wettbewerb Flugzeugverfolgung*. 5 affixed enamel shields of various auto participants incl. SS runes. 2 mounting holes. Near mint cond. $405.00

PLAQUE *DDAC*: Wood. 3.5" diam. ornate disc with open center having *DDAC* eagle. 2 mounting screws to post-war black painted pine plaque with hanger. Above avg. cond. $135.00

PLAQUE *DEM BESTEN SCHUTZEN UFFZ.SCHIESSEN AM 19.4.1939*: 6x10" black wood body with hangerloop. 5" diam. frosted silver finish to raised details of pak gun crew. Engraved plate below. Disc needs 2 nails. Avg. cond. ... $75.00

PLAQUE *FELDHERRNHALLE MUNCHEN*: For walking stick. 1.75x1.5". Paper body with blue, silver & brown printed scene of the *Feldherrnhalle* with clear celluloid covering & thin silver finished metal frame. Near mint cond. $20.00

PLAQUE *GAULEITER* SPORTS AWARD: This is really an unusual piece it is made from a solid piece of pure limestone cut, polished, engraved, & colored. The central theme is a large black swastika on an antique white background & wide slanting red borders. This had to be for some very important event! The cost to make something like this had to be quite high. 1.5 thick by 9 3/4" square. Wording *Des Gauleiters Fuer Sportliche Leistung Der Eiserne Lorbeer*. Above avg. cond. ....,,, $625.00

PLAQUE *LANDESPOLIZEI 1933-35*: 8" diam. disc is brass/bronze casting with nice raised details. Title to border & *Der Mann Darf Fallen, Die Fahne Nicht*. Police swastika to WWI helmeted head with neck maker marked *Encke*. Hole to back rim lacks hanger ring. Exc. cond. $100.00

PLAQUE *LEGION CONDOR 2 F.88*

PLAQUE *LEGION CONDOR 2 F.88*: 7.5x9" black wood frame with loop & paper maker tag. Frosted silver metal body with 88 flak gun over map of Spain, LW eagle, title scroll & panel *Im Kampf gegen den*

PLAQUE *DDAC*

Bolschewismus 1936 Spanien 1938. Exc. cond. $275.00

PLAQUE *MITGLIED DER NS VOLKSWOHLFAHRT GAU KOLN AACHEN*: 77mm stamped steel with bronze finish, title border & logo center. With 2 mounting holes. Above avg. cond. $50.00

PLAQUE *NSKK 6.SAUERLANDISCHE GELANDEFAHRT 2.7.1939*: 4x5.5" dark varnished wood backing with hangerloop. 2x3.5" goldfinished metal shield with raised details of town, horse/shield, NSKK eagle & title. Above avg. cond. $177.00

PLAQUE *NSKK DDAC SAAR-TREUE FAHRT 1934*: 62x90mm frosted silver stylized party eagle, oath hand center & red enamel title. With three mounting holes & maker stamped. Near mint cond. $163.00

PLAQUE *NSKK MAGDEBURG 24.SEPT.1933*

PLAQUE *NSKK MAGDEBURG 24.SEPT.1933*: 62x84mm bronze finished 6 sided body with raised details, NSKK eagle over church towers, title border & *Sternfahrt Deutsche Woche Deutsche Arbeit Deutsche Ware*. 3 mounting holes. Inked maker to paper envelope. Mint cond. $150.00

PLAQUE *NSKK STERN-FAHRT BRESLAN 10.SEPTEMBER 1933*: 2 1/4x3 1/2" shield with raised NSKK eagle, title & oak leaf wreath border. 3 mounting holes. Rough finish. Avg. cond. $185.00

PLAQUE *NSKK TANGERMUNDE 10.SEPT.1933*: 60x86mm bronze finished rectangle with raised details, NSKK eagle, Goddess with eagle shield, town scene, title below & *Zielfahrt Nach Zur*

1000 Jahrfeier & Bruckenweihe. Four mounting holes. Inked maker to paper envelope. Mint cond. $282.00

PLAQUE *NSKK/DDAC VOGELSBERGGELANDEFAHRT SCHOTTEN 21.10.1934*: 67x95mm oval shape with 2 mounting holes. Bronze finish with perched hawk center, white border with title & 2 affixed eagle logo shields. By *E.F.Wiedmann etc*. Near mint cond. $328.00

PLAQUE *NSKK/DDAC VOGELSBERGGELANDEFAHRT SCHOTTEN 21.10.1934*

PLAQUE *NSKOV 1941*: Hand carved oak. 12x13x1" size. Hand carved design of crossed rifles, sword, Iron Cross swastika & oak leave wreath around. 1941 dated with NSKOV on cross guard of sword. Nicely detailed. Near mint cond. $143.00

PLAQUE *NUR IN DEN EIGENEN KRAFT 1937*: Cast iron. 4 1/4x6 1/4" body with raised factory scene, title & *ruht das Schicksal der Nation Oberhutten*. By *Moltke* with trademarks & wire hanger to back. Worn black paint with patina. Avg. cond. $60.00

PLAQUE *RAD ARBEIT ADELT*: 4x6" black wood body with chamfered edges & hanger loop to back metal frame for missing service booklet. 3x5" dark silver stamped panel with eagle holding swastika having shovel wheat heads center. Title below with oakleave bar. Faded paper unit name below. Avg. cond. $82.00

PLAQUE *RAD ARBEIT ADELT*: 4x6" black wood with affixed stamped brass title plate front having eagle & traces of silver frosted finish. Metal holder at back with clear celluloid & paper booklet with missing photo to cover *Zur Erinnerung an meine Arbeitsdienstzeit.* Lacks hanger loop. Avg. cond. $71.00

PLAQUE *RLB*: 72mm stamped steel disc, title starburst center & *Mitglied des Reichsluftschutzbundes Ldsgr. Rhld.Westf.* Mounted to 1x3.5x4" laminated wood backing. Near mint cond. $75.00

PLAQUE *RUDOLSTADT 1.GAU STAFFELFAHRT STAHLHELMGAU SAALE THURINGEN 3.JULI 1932*

PLAQUE *RUDOLSTADT 1.GAU STAFFELFAHRT STAHLHELMGAU SAALE THURINGEN 3.JULI 1932*: Stamped dark brass shield with raised title, WWI steel helmet & lion shield. Three mounting holes. Above avg. cond. $91.00

PLAQUE *TANNENBURG MEMORIAL*: 12.5x18" black wood backing with chamfered edges. 8x13" 3 D metal casting of monument with Hindenburg entrance at center. Frosted silver finish. Complete with 2 hanger loops for securing to wall. A very great Memorial to a Great leader of Germany in war & peace. Tannenburg is located outside Hamburg & must be seen. Above avg. cond. $72.00

PLAQUE *U-BOAT HONOR MEMORIAL*: 8.5x10.5" black wood backing. 5x7" cast plaque with good raised details to eagle monument with view of bay/harbor. Title along lower edge. Lacks 2 nails to front & has hanger loop. Minor age toning & good patina. 39,000 sailors died in WWII in the U-Boat service, including Doenitz's sons. Above avg. cond. $130.00

PLAQUE *ZUR ERINNERUNG AN DEINE KRIEGSZEIT MG08*: 7.5x11" black wood body with ornate border & hangerloop. 5"

diam. frosted silver disc with raised details of MG gunner. Engraved title plate below. Early one. Exc. cond. $119.00

PLAQUE ARMORED RADIO COMMAND CAR: 7x9.5" black wood backing with chamfered edges. 4x6.5" frosted metal car in high relief. *Pz.Fu.Wg.Sd.Kfz. 263.* Above avg. cond. $93.00

PLAQUE ARMY ARTY GUNNER: 9x12.5" black wood backing with chamfered edge & 2 hanger loops. 5.5x9.5" casting with silver frosted finish to raised details of WWI style 75mm gun being sighted by Army helmeted soldier. Maker *HB* to corner. 4 stud mounts lack nuts & 1 stud. Avg. cond. $110.00

PLAQUE ARMY MG08 GUNNER: 7" hexagon black wood backing with hanger loop. 4.5" diam. silver finished disc with raised details of prone Army trooper firing MG08. Clean & maker marked *HB*. Above avg. cond. $45.00

PLAQUE BIPLANE

PLAQUE BIPLANE: Wood. 16.5" diam. plywood lid has 10" diam. printed paper biplane *K6385* affixed to center. Colored details painted around border, oak leaves, crossed Party flags & scroll below *Ub Aug u.hand fur s Vaterland.* 5 repaired bullet holes from past target use. Hanger at top. Avg. cond. $175.00

PLAQUE GORING HEAD PROFILE: 11.5x15.5" non-magnetic casting with raised details to head with Blue Max between title name. Natural gray finish & is style with no hanger for frame use only. Above avg. cond. $180.00

PLAQUE HEROIC SOLIDER PROFILE: Silver painted profile of army soldier with helmet on. Mounted on black painted oak 10X13" rectangular base. Full profile of soldier in dress tunic with Nazi eagle on steel helmet. Antique toned silver finish. Heavy wood backing. Original hook. Avg. cond. $125.00

PLAQUE HINDENBURG HEAD PROFILE:
10x11.5" Black Japaned period wooden
frame. Head is in high relief. Rare to find
as most such plaques showed Hitler.
Complete with original folding stand at
rear. Near mint cond. $68.00

PLAQUE HINDENBURG HEAD PROFILE:
Artisted signed K.Kuhl. Very fine likeness.
Approx. 16.5" in diam. Circular raised
edge, center has raised head & shoulders of Hindenburg. Subject wears field
marshal uniform with Pour le Merite
medal on neck. Fine details. Bracket for
mounting on back. Very heavy construction. Near mint cond. $195.00

PLAQUE HITLER HEAD
PROFILE WITH CASE

PLAQUE HITLER HEAD PROFILE WITH
CASE: 1x5.5x7.5" black leatherette body,
off-white satin lid lining & fitted base.
4x5.5" cast body with bronze finish to
front, raised Hitler head & *Die
Voraussetzung etc.* More raised wording
in back, Hannover etc. & hangerloop.
Avg. cond. $282.00

PLAQUE HITLER HEAD PROFILE WITH
CASE: 1x5.5x7.5" black leatherette body,
off-white satin lid lining & fitted base.
4x5.5" cast body with bronze finish to
raised Hitler head & *Die Voraussetzung
etc.* More raised wording on back,
Hannover etc. & hangerloop. Avg.
cond. $150.00

PLAQUE HITLER HEAD PROFILE: Cast
iron. 8.5x12.5" heavy casting with raised
details repainted in gold, red & black.
Head profile looks to have faint *Wolff 33*
under paint at neck. Quote *Ich glaube an
Deutschland etc.* Back marked *ges.gesch*

A L.H. & hanger wire. Avg.
cond. $75.00

PLAQUE HITLER HEAD PROFILE: Cast
iron. 96x141mm dark body with bronze
finish to profile & *Die Voraussetzung etc.*
Raised wording to reverse, hangerloop &
stamped Hannover maker. Near mint
cond. $200.00

PLAQUE HITLER HEAD PROFILE: Looks
to be HJ school project. 6" tall silver
painted lead casting. Lacks 4 mounting
screws at back. Avg. cond. $23.00

PLAQUE LUFTWAFFE 1943 FINLAND AIR
DISTRICT STAFF ACHIEVEMENT WITH
CASE: 4.5x6.5" bronze casting with LW
eagle flying over globe with Finland
shown in a ray of sunlight. *Fur Besondere
Bewahrung etc.* below. Hanger loop &
stamped *#115X* to back. Original tan
cardboard storage box. Exc.
cond. $810.00

PLAQUE LUFTWAFFE ACHIEVEMENT
AIR DISTRICT *XI*: 4.5x5.75" bronze
finished non-magnetic casting with nice
details to raised down tailed eagle.
Engraved recipient *Masch.Ing.Genz* &
raised *Fur Hervorrangende Leistung Der
Kommandierende General Und
Befehlshaber Im Luftgau XI.* Hanger hole
to back. Avg. cond. $395.00

PLAQUE LUFTWAFFE ACHIEVEMENT
AIR DISTRICT *XI*: Looks to be silver/gray
finished class with 5x7" metal backing
with hanger loop. Affixed 4.5" wide silver
plated eagle over engraved recipient
Oberstleutnant karl Volbehr. Black
finished engraved *Fur Hervorrangende
Leistung Der Kommandierende General
Und Befehlshaber Im Luftgau XI* &
facsimile engraved signature of a *W????
General der Flieger.* Avg.
cond. $225.00

PLAQUE LUFTWAFFE ACHIEVEMENT
AIR DISTRICT *XI*: Variation cast metal
body with raised details is 4.5x5.5" size.
Style with early down tail eagle over
engraved *Hauptmann Gersdorf.* Raised
wording *Fur Hervorragende Leistung Der
Kommandierende General Und
Befehlshaber Im Luftgau XI.* Above avg.
cond. $522.00

PLAQUE LUFTWAFFE FLAK WAR
SERVICE: 6x8" black wooden plaque
having silvered round medallion showing
88 firing on aircraft. Plaque in white metal
below translates as *In Memory of the
Campaigns in Poland, France & the East.*
Avg. cond. $111.00

PLAQUE MOTORCYCLE: 10x8.5" oak wall
plaque painted black. Has superimposed
metal motorcycle with Army soldier & rifle
on his back. Side view. Nickel silvered

finish 3-D effect. Very nicely detailed. Exc. cond. $124.00

PLAQUE NAVAL: Hand carved oak shield. 13.5x18.5" dark oak shield has excellent carved raised details with party eagle to top of chain border, crossed anchors with sword & oak leaves center. Reads *Fur Verdienste um die Freizeitgestaltung in der Truppe 1941.* Wire hanger to back. Shows past glue repair to seam & 1 broken chain-link. Avg. cond. ... $400.00

PLAQUE PARTY EAGLE

PLAQUE PARTY EAGLE: 7x7.5" stamped non-magnetic body with raised eagle details & nickel finish. 4 mounting holes & shows age with some dings. Avg. cond. $58.00

PLAQUE RUNIC SHIELD: Hand carved oak. 1x7x10.5" dark wood body has divided design to shield with 7.5" long diagonal rune to center. Vertical halved shield has plain side & horizontal knurled side. Near mint cond. $125.00

PLAQUE SHOOTING: 7x7" dark stained wood with hanger loop. 4.5" diam. silver frosted disc with shooter & rifle. Avg. cond. $26.00

PLAQUE SS MOTOR SPORTS MEETING AWARD: 4.5" size shield shaped wood plaque with 3" metal plaque attached. Silvered finish. Reads *Motorsporttreffen Der SS Motorstaffel III/I In Bad Reichenhall Schlageter 1934.* Has design of cross, rayed swastika & mountains. Exc. cond. $167.00

PLAQUE SS SCHWARZE KORPS NEWSPAPER ACHIEVEMENT: In black fired glaze with large raised SS eagle above wreath & swastika with *1937. Das Schwarze Korps Furerfolgreiche Mitarbeit* lettering over SS runes. Back has circular maker mark with raised SS logo. Antique bronze finish. 6x9" in size. Given for

outstanding labor service to the paper. Above avg. cond. $950.00

PLAQUE TANNENBURG MEMORIAL: 10x13" black wood backing with alum. painted metal monument in 3-D. Hindenburg honor entrance. The Tannenburg memorial was evacuated by the Germans in 1945 & destroyed to prevent the Russians from taking it. Hindenburg's body was exhumed from the memorial & returned to the Reich on the cruiser *Leipzig* in secrecy. Near mint cond. $108.00

PLAQUE TWENTY-FIVE YEAR SERVICE 1939: 11x11.5" black wood frame. 7x8" silver body with gold raised design of Party eagle over train in cogged wheel with lightning bolts. Raised silver locomotive over engraved panel *Unserem Berufskameraden Max Mickan Zum 25 jahr etc. 1914-1939 14.11.39.* Loop to back. Exc. cond. $259.00

SIGN NSDAP DIRECTORY: 25x31" metal body is covered with black enamel with red & white details. White Party Eagle at top with red title & various party listings below. 4 mounting holes. 2 small chips. Above avg. cond. $342.00

THIRD REICH SILVER SERVICE & PERSONALITY RELATED ITEMS

BORMANN ITEM GOLDEN PARTY HONOR BADGE: 30.5mm size with flat style pin. Rounded oak leaves variant. Badge bears serial number 60508 which is listed also in the 1937 SS Diensteliste as being that of Bormann. Badge also marked *Ges. Gesch.* which is proper. No damage. This badge is the type only worn by high political officers & is undoubtedly Bormann's own party badge. Mint cond. $6,222.00

DOENITZ ITEM 1974 SIGNED PERSONAL LETTER: 6x8.25" on printed stationary, *Doenitz Grossadmiral A.D. etc.* Hand ink birthday greetings to Navy comrade. Large signature. Mint cond. $71.00

EVA BRAUN ITEM SILVER FORK MONOGRAMMED *E B*

EVA BRAUN ITEM SILVER FORK MONOGRAMMED *E B*: 7" long, floral design, EB resembles butterfly & *800* trademark. Near mint cond. $399.00

EVA BRAUN ITEM SILVER FORK
MONOGRAMMED *E B*: 8.5" long, floral
design, EB resembles butterfly & *800*
trademark. Near mint cond. $591.00
EVA BRAUN ITEM SILVER SPOON
MONOGRAMMED *E B*: 8.5" long, border
design, EB resembles butterfly & *800*
with 4 proofs. Near mint cond. .. $399.00
GORING ITEM GORING COAT OF ARMS
SILVER FORK: 8.5" long with ornate
border to silver handle with engraved
shield having arm holding ring. Stamped
Hulse 800. Near mint cond. $399.00

GORING ITEM GORING COAT
OF ARMS SILVER FORK

GORING ITEM GORING COAT OF ARMS
SILVER KNIFE: 8.5" long with ornate
border to silver handle with engraved
shield having arm holding ring. *800* with
proofs. Blade *Nicht Rostend J.A.
Henchels, etc.* with trademark twins. Near
mint cond. $426.00
GORING ITEM MINISTERPRASIDENT
GENERALFELDMARSCHALL GORING
INVITATION: 5.5x8" white card with
embossed Party Eagle, black title, *und
Frau Goring*, blank areas & *in Carinhall
etc.* Near mint cond. $48.00
GORING LOT 3 PIECE COFFEE/TEA SET:
All 3 pieces appear to be made from
brass with traces of silver wash to
insides. Includes 6" tall pot with spout &
handle. 3" tall creamer. 2.5" tall sugar
bowl. All 3 have hand engraved LW eagle
over *III/RGG* & pot has biplane to back
side. Not jeweler quality, no maker marks
& looks to have been done by Regiment
member at barracks *Berlin-Reinickendorf*.
Exc. cond. $280.00

GRAVY BOAT *REICH KANZELLEREI*

GRAVY BOAT *REICH KANZELLEREI*:
10" oval dish with attached pitcher
6x10", with engraved Nazi eagle & *RK*
at wreath. Heavy silver plated nickel
silver construction & hmkd *Wellner 40
cL.* & 30 in a circle. Well made & a
exceptional find for any collection.
Above avg. cond. $1,301.00
HIMMLER ITEM HEINRICH HIMMLER'S
PERSONAL LETTER OPENER WITH
CASE: Beautiful Damascus double
edged blade with dark bronze handle
having facsimile signature, *H. Himmler*
on it. Approx. 9.5" OA with verso of
handle having V checkered design.
Original black leatherette case with
double clasps. Pictured in *World War II
German War Booty,* Vol. 2 by Thomas
M. Johnson, p. 84. Case shows great
wear. Letter opener is in very fine
condition. Above avg.
cond. $9,715.00
HITLER ITEM PERSONAL BOOK PLATE:
3.5x4" in size with 95% of original glue
remaining on back. Dark brown &
sepia toned with pointed wing eagle on
wreath/swastika design imposed over
oak leaf with acorn. Banner above with
Ex Libris (From the Library of) & *Adolf
Hitler* below. Near mint
cond. $187.00
HITLER ITEM SILVER FORK WITH *A H*
MONOGRAM: 5.5" long, 3 tines,
variation engraved *A H* & stamped *BSF
800* 2 proofs. Near mint
cond. $399.00
HITLER ITEM SILVER FORK WITH *A H*
MONOGRAM": 5" long, variation
engraved *A H* & stamped *BSF 800* with
2 proofs. Near mint cond. $399.00

HITLER ITEM SILVER SPOON
A H FORMAL PATTERN

HITLER ITEM SILVER SPOON *A H*
FORMAL PATTERN: 7.5" long with Greek
border detailed party eagle & *A H*.
Stamped *800* with 3 proofs. Nick to the
back handle. Exc. cond. $496.00
MEAT PLATTER *REICH KANZELLEREI*:
18" round dish with engraved Nazi eagle
& RK at wreath. Heavy silver plated
nickel silver construction & hmkd *Wellner
40.* Well made & a exceptional find for
any collection. Above avg.
cond. $1,060.00

MEAT PLATTER *REICH KANZELLEREI*
WITH COVER

MEAT PLATTER *REICH KANZELLEREI*
WITH COVER: 25" oval dish with
engraved large Nazi eagle & RK at
wreath. Heavy silver plated nickel silver
construction & hmkd *Wellner 120 5x18*
top cover also engraved with large Nazi
eagle & *RK* at base. Hmkd *Wutt. Metallw
Fabrik Geislingen Steige* & heavy bar
handle also hmkd to a different maker.
Very beautiful & well made. Actual pieces
from Hitler's table. Above avg.
cond. $2,101.00
SERVING PLATE RAB: 9x14" oval body is
divided into 3 areas. Stamped rim with
RAB over split tail mermaid having trident
above head. By *Gebruder Hepp 90*. Avg.
cond. $110.00
SILVER CREAMER LUFTWAFFE
REICHSFLUGHAFEN AINRING 1938:
Only 2.25" tall body with handle & spout.
Bottom title stamped with eagle & *Wellner
7 1/2 cl*. Age darkening. Above avg.
cond. $40.00
SILVER GOBLET SS: 7.5" tall body with
short stem & base. Stamped *800 Gutruf*
with proofs. 3" diam. SS runes disc to
side, 3 alternating runic symbols to rim &
stem engraved *Deutsches Ahnenerbe
e.V.Berlin* with 3 oak leaves. Near mint
cond. $1,735.00

SILVER SALVER
OBERGRUPPENFUHRER FREIHERR VON
ERBERSTEIN

SILVER SALVER
OBERGRUPPENFUHRER FREIHERR
VON ERBERSTEIN: Salver of honor
marked. 835 silver with 3 hallmarks, two
of which are common to firm of CE
Juncker hallmark & crown. Other mark is
uncrowned Prussian eagle. Plate is
approx. 13" in diam. with flared winged
SS eagle in high relief in center with
raised dedication banners to von
Eberstein, top & bottom. Large flat rim
has raised SS motto - *Meine Ehre heisst
Treue* with large SS runes at bottom.
Near mint cond. $3,379.00
SILVER SALVER PRESENTED BY A
GENERAL OFFICER: 830 silver hmkd
with many jeweler marks. 12" diam. with
scalloped edge. Beautiful design of 3
heraldic shields in center & full lettering,
*Ehrenpreis des Kommandierenden
General des II Armeekorps 6.8.8.1937.
Schneidemuhl. Vielseitigkeit Lindenwirtin.*
Very finely made & given for merit. The
plate weighs approx. 446 grams. Near
mint cond. $275.00
SILVER SERVING TRAY WITH SWASTIKA:
1.5" tall & 8x10.5" overall. Stamped
Gebr.Hepp90 & swastika in wreath to
bottom. Above avg. cond. $100.00
SILVER TEA SERVER WITH PARTY
EAGLE: 6.5" tall pear shaped body with
large handle, spout & hinged lid. 1 1/4"
wide engraved eagle to side with couple
dents to body below. Bottom stamped
Krupp Berndorf 70cl. with bear trademark. Avg. cond. $68.00
SILVER TRAY ENGRAVED *PZ R 6
KOMMANDEUR* SILVER TRAY WITH
OFFICER SIGNATURES: 14x17.5" oval
silver tray with ridged design to border.
Maker stamped *F.J.Schroder 835 WTB*
with proofs. Engraved front with stylized
party eagle over *PzR6* cipher, crossed
swords below, Panzer-III tank to either
side & *Das Offizierkorps seinem
scheidenden Kommandeur in
Dankbarkeit* below. Reverse has approx.
62 facsimile signatures of loyal officers.
Mint cond. $2,800.00
TOASTING CUP LUFTWAFFE: WMF
Cromargan. 4" tall tapered silver body
with 1.5" wide silver LW eagle affixed to
side. Stamped title to bottom. Near mint
cond. $120.00

THIRD REICH GLASSWARE
(CHINA, GOBLETS, CRYSTAL)

BEER STEIN 1939/40 ARTY.
KRIEGSJAHAR CROCKERY: 5.5" tall off-
white body marked *10/20* near handle.

Nice color scene of horsedrawn large arty. gun, oak leaf wreath with crossed arty. shells, title & *Zur Erinnerung an das etc.* Slightly domed metal lid & pewter thumb lift. Named *Henny* to side. Bottom marked *Malerei Reinh. Gornemann Hohr-Grenzhausen.* Near mint cond. $216.00

BEER STEIN ARTILLERY: 5" tall gray crockery body with raised details of arty. crews & *Motorisierte Artillerie* crew. Dark blue background overall. Front has *Zur Erinnerung an Meine Dienstzeit & Feuerstellung* near blue handle. Gray thumb lift with age patina to domed silver lid. Trademark & *2963* to bottom. Exc. cond. $397.00

BEER STEIN NAVAL 1935-36 KREUZER KARLSRUHE: 5.5" tall crockery body with handle & size *0.5L* . Domed pewter lid. Black wording to front *Zur Erinnerung an die Weltriese 1935-1936 Unteroffizier-Kameradschaft Kreuzer Karlsruhe* with color Kriegs & tri-color EK flag center with large *Fidelitas* shield. Faint inked maker to bottom. Near mint cond. $507.00

BEER STEIN NAVAL KREUZER KOLN: 5" tall off white crockery body with handle & *10/20L* mark. Blue border stripes to rim & base. Black *Zur Erinnerung an meine Dienstzeit auf Kreuzer Koln.* with color divided crowns shield below. Near mint cond. $195.00

BEER STEIN PANZER REGT. 1 ERFURT ETC: Clear glass. 4.5" tall octagon body with ground base. Flat pewter lid engraved *Zur Erinnerung an meine Dienstzeit beim & title.* Size *0.4L* etched near handle. Cast Munich man figure to bottom. Near mint cond. $397.00

BEER STEIN RAD REMEMBRANCE 1935/36: 5" tall crockery body with handle & nickel lid with raised design of RAD man in uniform from chest up with robin hood cap. Pewter spade with wheat heads for thumb tab. Color oak leaf wreath to front with bright silver RAD spade & wheat heads with red & black *3/244* details. Dated 1935/36, *Arbeitsm. Wilh.Altmeier* to sides *Zur Erinnerung an Meine Arbeitsdienstzeit in Sohren.* Mint cond. $200.00

GRAVY BOAT DAF: White porcelain. round plate attached to round boat with pour spouts to sides. Maker marked on bottom DAF logo & hutschenreuther lelb. Near mint cond. $34.00

GRAVY BOAT DAF: White porcelain. round plate attached to round bowl with pour type spouts to either side. Has blue stripe around rim & rim to plate. Maker marked on the bottom, with DAF logo & *HUTSCHENREUTHER LELB.* Near mint cond. $25.00

MEISSEN PLATE 1941-42 LUFTWAFFE RUSSIAN FRONT (MOSCOW): 7" diam. White porcelain with *Winterfeldzug Luftgau Moskau 1941 1942* inscription in blue. Central design is of a Luft eagle with swastika in flight above St. Basil's church in the Kremlin. Very rare & with no damage. Meissen sword logo on bottom. Mint cond. $250.00

MEISSEN PLATE INFANTERIE REGIMENT 514 1940/41: 10" diam. white porcelain body with blue title, oak leaf wreath with numbers to scroll *185 101 10 173 187*, Party Eagle center with *514* oak leaves & red 4 leaf clover. Hanger wire to back with blue *Im Felde 1940/41.*, facsimile signature of *Oberst u.Rgts.-Kdew.* & crossed swords trademark. Mint cond. $350.00

MIXING BOWL WITH HANDLE: 2" tall white china body with 3.5" diam., 2.5" long handle, spout to rim & green marked side *1700 Haldenwanger Berlin.* Above avg. cond. $37.00

PATRIOTIC ASHTRAY HITLER PROFILE: white ceramic ashtray with picture of Hitler in brown with clear overglaze. Has gilt decorative stripe to upper edge, shows some wear from use. Maker marked on bottom, *CKW Buringia.* Three sided design, has rests for three cigerettes. Near mint cond. $145.00

PATRIOTIC GLASS OCCUPIED CZECHO-SLOVAKIAN LEAD CRYSTAL: Golden yellow tinted, engraved, ground & polished. Known by glass collectors as Czechoslovakian Art Glass. Made for higher-ups in the Nazi Party, design of pre-1939 Czech rampant lion with crown engraved & frosted in Golden yellow oval. Has rounded fluted base with walls of glass rising upward & outward. The base is also flashed in the same color with cut concave discs encircling it. The rim has another flashed stripe & has an engraved patriotic slogan in sutterlin style script. Dated on this stripe 1938. Flat cut & polished bottom & rim. 4.25" high. Still has original makers paper label. Mint cond. $160.00

PATRIOTIC PLATE HINDENBURG PORTRAIT: Beautiful gold worked porcelain plate with pierced edges having gold rim & side panel trim. Center of plate has fine color portrait of Hindenburg in his field marshal uniform with Grand Cross of the Iron Cross & Red Eagle, Orders bar from Franco-Prussian war & gold aiguelettes. Avg. cond. $75.00

ROSENTHAL DISH CONDOR LEGION:
7" diam. with 4 engine *Condor* flying
airplane with Swastika on the tail.
Bottom marked with crown & crossed
pikes, *Rosenthal Germany
Kunstabteilung selb*. Brown glaze is
crackled to give an antique look. Mint
cond. $145.00
SOUP BOW DAF: White porcelain. Maker
Hutschenreuther with Bavarian lion
trademark. Ceramic bowl with flared
lip. Has double red colored ring to lip.
8.75" diam. Above avg. cond. .. $20.00
SS ALLACH INK WELL & PEN HOLDER:
13x8" with scalloped edges. Alabaster
white. Concave rectangular surface for
old nib pens, small letters, desk
articles. Raised rear central 2x2.75"
rectangular pedestal with round hole
on top for accepting glass ink bottle
(none present). Front of ink holder has
large raised SS runes. Cap for hole
missing. SS marked to Allach on
bottom. Very rare. Personally used by
a high SS officer. No chips. Mint
cond. $750.00
SS ALLACH PLATE SS CHRISTMAS
FROM SS GENERAL OSWOLD POHL:
10" white china plate with blue edge &
flowered center wreath around a quote
from *Die weihe der nacht* by Hebbel.
Back dated 1944, with Christmas &
new year wishes. Signature POHE &
SS Obergruppenfuhrer U. General Der
Waffen SS. Plate is completely
described in *SS Porcelain Allach* by
Michael Passmore, pp. 92/93 with
photo of plate, translation of German &
even picture of SS General Pohl. Mint
cond. $387.00
SS ALLACH PORCELAIN FIGURE OF A
BROWN COLORED RESTING DOG:
Signed Prof. Th. Karner 13 with green
SS logo & Allach. See Passmore,
Figure. 54. No chips. Beautiful details
to muzzle with brown eyes, claws &
haunches. 7.5" long, 4.5" tall. No
damage. Colored Allach is rarer than
the white work. Mint cond. . $2,260.00
SS ALLACH PORCELAIN FIGURE OF A
JESTER OR CLOWN IN TWISTED
POISE: Figure stands approx. 8.75"
tall on a 5" base & is of white ceramic
with delicate fingers extended &
twisted. Each finger is an individual &
figure shows man in jester costume
with bells on lower legs, short boots &
tights, bell decorated vest & curled hair
with cloth band. Leer on face. No SS
logo but definitely Allach & quite
charming for size. Right thumb
missing. Near mint cond $450.00

SS ALLACH PORCELAIN FIGURE OF A
RESTING FAWN OR YOUNG DOE

SS ALLACH PORCELAIN FIGURE OF A
RESTING FAWN OR YOUNG DOE:
Signed *Prof. Th. Karner* with SS Allach
logo. 8" long, 5" high No chips or
damage. White ceramic with beautiful
details to hooves, eyes & body parts.
Logo & Allach in green work. Statue
numbered 41. Extremely rare to find in
large size. Mint cond. $750.00
SS ALLACH PORCELAIN FIGURE OF A
STANDING BAVARIAN PEASANT MAN:
See Passmore No. 39 for figure.
Passmore reports this is part of a
grouping of *Oberyabrisches Bauenpaar*
(Upper Bavarian Farmer Pair) made by
Prof. Richard Forster. This particular
flgure is artist signed *R. Forster* & is
numbered 48 which matches with
Passmore's evidence. 9.5" tall with
approx. 3" squared base having artist
name, number & impressed SS Allach
logo. White ceramic figure has slightly
yellow colored feather in Tyrol cap. Small
size. 005mm chip to lower leather tab on
left side of breeches. Near mint
cond. $375.00

**THIRD REICH MESS HALL CROCKERY
& UTENSILS**

1942 PARTY EAGLE PLATE: 9" diam. white
china. Black eagle, Crown W & *Bavaria
1942*. Above avg. cond. $27.00
ARMY BOWL: 9" diam. white china is 2"
tall. Black eagle & green maker
Hutschenreuther Hohenberg 1940 etc. to
bottom. Used. Avg. cond. $23.00
ARMY BOWL: 9" diam. white china. Black
Party Eagle to bottom & green *CM HR
1942 etc.* Avg. cond. $25.00

ARMY COFFEE CUP SAUCER: 5.5" diam. white china. Black eagle, *Seltmann Weiden 1942* to bottom with rust stains. Avg. cond. $20.00

ARMY COFFEE CUP: 2.5" tall white china body with handle. Black bottom *Rosenthal etc. 1940* & eagle. Exc. cond. $25.00

ARMY COFFEE CUP: White china with black eagle. Marked *TK Thun Germany 1939*. Stackable style. Above avg. cond. $27.00

ARMY FORK: 8.5" long with back stamped eagle *WSM 42* . Above avg. cond. $20.00

ARMY GRAVY SERVER

ARMY GRAVY SERVER: 10" long oval white china base with 9" long bowl & 4.5" tall. Black eagle to bottom with Crown W *Bavaria 1941*. Near mint cond. ... $72.00

ARMY PLATE: 9" diam. white china body with black eagle to back & green maker *Johann Haviland Bavaria 1938*. Above avg. cond. $30.00

ARMY PLATE: 9" diam. white china with black eagle, *Rosenthal 1938* to bottom. Avg. cond. $21.00

ARMY PLATE: 9" diam. white china with worn finish. Black eagle & green maker *CM HR 1814 1934 etc. 1937*. Avg. cond. $20.00

ARMY PLATE: 9" diam. white china. Black Party Eagle to bottom *LHS Bavaria 1938 etc.* Finish shows some use. Avg. cond. $34.00

ARMY PLATE: 9" diam. white china. Black eagle *1940 PMR Bavaria Jaeger & Co.* Above avg. cond. $25.00

ARMY SERVING BOWL: 8" square white china is 2.5" tall. Green eagle to bottom with lion trademark of *Elbogen Sudetengau 1939*. Shows use & fracture crack. Avg. cond. $66.00

ARMY SHALLOW BOWL: 9" diam. white china body. Black eagle, *Heinrich & Co. 1938 etc.* Exc. cond. $21.00

ARMY SHALLOW BOWL: 9" diam. white china. Black eagle *1939 Bauscher Weiden*. Avg. cond. $23.00

ARMY SHALLOW BOWL: 9" diam. white china. Black eagle *1939 Bauscher Weiden*. Avg. cond. $25.00

ARMY SHALLOW BOWL: 9" diam. white china. Black eagle *1941 Bauscher Weiden*. Avg. cond. $23.00

DAF 3 WAY DIVIDED PLATE: 11" diam. white china body. Green cogged wheel swastika, etc. By *Rosenthal* with trademark. Mint cond. $28.00

DAF COFFEE CUP: 3" diam. & 2.5" tall white body with brown bands around rim. Green cogged wheel swastika, etc. & *Rosenthal* /trademark to bottom. Avg. cond. $27.00

DAF SERVING BOWL: 7" diam. & 4" tall white china body with blue band to rim. Green cogged wheel swastika & is marked *Hutschenreuther etc.* Above avg. cond. $34.00

DAF SERVING PLATTER: 8x12.5" white china oval with worn brown border stripe to rim. Green maker *Rosenthal*, cogged wheel swastika, etc. to bottom. Avg. cond. $65.00

DAF SHALLOW BOWL: 9.5" diam. & 2" tall white china body. Green cogged wheel swastika, etc. & *Rosenthal* with trademark. Above avg. cond. $26.00

DAF TEA CUP: 3" diam. & 2.5" tall white body with green band around rim. Green cogged wheel swastika, etc. & *Bauscher Weiden* trademark to bottom. No handle style. Mint cond. $27.00

LUFTWAFFE BOWL: 9" diam. white china is 2" tall. Black eagle *Fl.U.V. 1938* & *Bauscher etc.* Used. Avg. cond. $23.00

LUFTWAFFE CELLAR: 4.5" long white china body with 2 rounded bowls. Nice black eagle to back *Fl.U.V. 1941 Epiag Elbogen* with Knight arm holding sword. Mint cond. $37.00

LUFTWAFFE COFFEE CUP: 2.5" tall white china body with handle. Black bottom *Fl.U.V.1942 Epiag Elbogen* with eagle & trademark. Exc. cond. $38.00

LUFTWAFFE COFFEE CUP: 2.5" tall white china body with handle. Black bottom with blurred 1941 maker & *FL.U.V.* with eagle. Above avg. cond. $25.00

LUFTWAFFE COFFEE CUP: 2.5" tall white china body with handle. Green bottom *Fl.U.V. Boheimia 1941* with eagle & lion trademark. Exc. cond. $26.00

LUFTWAFFE FORK: 7" with eagle to back *WMF etc.* Above avg. cond. $20.00

LUFTWAFFE GRAVY BOAT: 6.5x10.5" white china oval base with body having rest at each side for spoon. Green title maker to bottom with LW eagle *Fl.U.V.* Near mint cond. $40.00

LUFTWAFFE GRAVY BOAT: 9.5" long oval white china body, black LW eagle *FL.U.V.* & the maker's name is marked in green. *Hutschenreuther.* Near mint cond. $37.00

LUFTWAFFE GRAVY BOAT: 9.5" long white china body. Black eagle shows removal attempt as does maker mark with date. Avg. cond. $55.00

LUFTWAFFE KNIFE: 7" with eagle to side & *WMF etc.* Above avg. cond. $20.00

LUFTWAFFE RLM CREAMER: 2.5" tall white china pitcher with handle, spout & red title eagle at side. Faint green maker mark. Rare. Exc. cond. $30.00

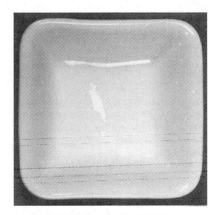

LUFTWAFFE SERVING BOWL

LUFTWAFFE SERVING BOWL (DETAIL)

LUFTWAFFE SERVING BOWL: 8" square white china is 2.5" tall. Black eagle to bottom *Fl.U.V.* & glider trademark of

Felda Rhon Stadtlengsfeld 1942. Near mint cond. $89.00

LUFTWAFFE SERVING BOWL: 8.5x8.5" white china body is 2.5" tall. Black early eagle *FL. U.V.* & green maker *H&Co. etc.* Avg. cond. $20.00

LUFTWAFFE SERVING PLATTER: White china 10.5x16.5" body stands 2" tall. Black marked *Fl.U.V.* eagle & green *H&Co 1938 etc.* Avg. cond. $30.00

LUFTWAFFE SHALLOW BOWL: 6.5" diam. white china is 1.5" tall. Black down tail eagle, *Fl.U.V. 1938 Bauscher Weiden* to bottom. Near mint cond. $29.00

LUFTWAFFE SHALLOW BOWL: 6.5" diam. white china is 1.5" tall. Green eagle, *Fl.U.V. 1941 Bohemia* to bottom with lion trademark. Avg. cond. $23.00

LUFTWAFFE SHALLOW BOWL: 9.5" diam. with blue stripe to rim, 2" tall & bottom marked *H&Co. Selb Bavaria Germany Heinrich Fl.U.V.* with 1941 eagle. Used. Avg. cond. $40.00

LUFTWAFFE SPOON: 8.5" long with eagle stamp top & back *H.M.Z41 Fl.U.V..* Avg. cond. $20.00

NAVAL BUTTER KNIFE: Eagle M stamped silver handle & *Rostfreier Stahl.* Patina to blade. Avg. cond. $20.00

NAVAL BUTTER KNIFE: Eagle M stamped silver handle & *Rostfreier Stahl.* Patina to blade. Avg. cond. $20.00

NAVAL BUTTER KNIFE: Eagle M stamped silver handle & *Rostfreier Stahl.* Patina to blade. Avg. cond. $26.00

NAVAL BUTTER KNIFE: Eagle M stamped silver handle & 8" long. Patina to blade. Avg. cond. $20.00

POLICE LADLE: 7" long silver body with back stamped *Sandrik Anticorro* & top eagle/wreath. Near mint cond. ... $30.00

POLICE SUGAR TONGS: 5" long silver body with side stamped *Sandrik Anticorro* & other eagle/wreath. Near mint cond. $30.00

POLICE SUGAR TONGS: 5" long silver body with side stamped *Sandrik Anticorro* & other eagle/wreath. Near mint cond. $34.00

SS DAS REICH BOWL: 9" diam. bowl for soup. Bottom has Bauscher-Weiden trademark with large green *SS Reich 1940* lettering. Bowl shows only normal chipping from use & no cracks. Lettering very clear. Avg. cond. $139.00

SS FS BRAUNSCHWEIG SPOON: 5.5" long by *WMF Cromargan* & title to back. Near mint cond. $158.00

SS REICH SERVING SPOON: 8.5" long. Stamped plain design. Underside has

unit stamp & *Roneusil*. No damage. Near mint cond. $40.00
SS REICH SPOON: 6" long silver body with darkening. Title stamped on back & marked *Roneusil Rostfrei*. Above avg. cond. $72.00
SS REICH SPOON: 8" long with stamped title to back & *Roneusil etc*. Above avg. cond. $65.00
SS REICH SPOON: 8.5" long, stamped title to underside & maker *Roneusil*. Near mint cond. $38.00
SS RF VERS FORK: Hmkd *WMF Patent 90 45*. Back stamped *RFSS Vers*. Above avg. cond. $221.00

THIRD REICH TABLE MEDALS & MEDALLIONS

MEDALLION *1933 MG SCHIESSEN PREISREICHTEN*: 50mm diam. with gold finish worn from bronze body, raised MG08 gunner & *Preisrichten 1933 6 Preis 8 Inf.Regt. 8 (M.G.) Komp*. to reverse. Avg. cond. $76.00
MEDALLION *1931/41 NSB 10 JAHRIG*: 65mm diam. to bronze casting with raised details. Title & *Der Nationaal Socialistische Beweging in Nederland* with various logos. Profile of *Ir Anton Adriaan Mussert*. Finish shows age. Above avg. cond. $301.00
MEDALLION *1933 ADOLF HITLER DEUTSCHLAND ERWACHE*: 59mm bronze disc with raised profile & *Reichskanzler Adolf Hitler 10. Januar 1933*. Reverse has party flag standard bearer & marked & dated *Deutschland Erwache 5.-12.Marz 1933*. Above avg. cond. $180.00

tan leatherette body with purple velvet fitted base. 36mm dark bronze disc with raised early party eagle *1933 Im Jahre Deutscher Schicksalswende*. Hitler head reverse *Unser die Zukunft Adolf Hitler* Stamped rim *Bayer. Hauptmunzamt*. Avg. cond. $54.00
MEDALLION *1933 HITLER HINDENBURG*: 38mm round bronze with profiles of both men on obverse & other side is Hitler quote *Fur ein Freies geeintes und stozeses Deutschland* -Hitler & shaking hands at top. Dated *30.1.1933/5.3 1933*. Avg. cond. $52.00
MEDALLION *1933 PREUSS. FEUERLOSCHWESEN FUER VERDIENSTE*: 29x42mm oval body with excellent raised details of fireman over burning house & *Fuer Verdienste um das Feuerloschwesen* reverse *Preuss. Staatsmunze Silber 900 Fein*. Mint cond. $250.00
MEDALLION *1934 20. DEUTSCHES BUNDESSCHIESSEN LEIPZIG*: 37mm diam. Brown finished porcelain. Single sided with obverse with shooter with swastika in background. Meissen marked. In a gilt metal frame with pin on back. Near mint cond. $40.00
MEDALLION *1934 SA GRUPPENAUFMARSCH DRESDEN*: Brown porcelain. 50mm diam. Obverse with raised SA logo & lettering. Reverse reads *Der SA Mann Ist Revolutionar! Er Ist Stark In Der Liebe Und Stark Im Hass*. Meissen. Mint cond. $79.00
MEDALLION *1936 OLYMPIADE BERLIN* WITH BOX: Red leatherette disc box with gold embossed eagle/bell to lid. 70mm dark bronze casting with raised title side having naked man. Bell to reverse with maker *Otto Placzek*. Near mint cond. $136.00

MEDALLION *1933 ADOLF HITLER SCHICKSALSWENDE* WITH BOX

MEDALLION *1933 ADOLF HITLER SCHICKSALSWENDE* WITH BOX: Soiled

MEDALLION *1936 OLYMPIADE BERLIN*

TABLE MEDAL *1939 DEUTSCHLAND-ITALIEN DRESDEN*: It is one of a collection of plaques made by Meissen for special events. 46mm off-white body. Raised title to side with Sports Eagle & *13.8.1939* date. Other has swastika & fasces over town scene. Maker trademark of crossed swords below town. Mint cond. $90.00

TABLE MEDAL *1927 NATIONALE VOORBEREID INC OLYMPISCHE SPELEN*: 50mm diam. Dark silver finish. Obverse with clock tower scene. Reverse engraved *IA. STERRIT 13-9-27 12e PRUS*. Near mint cond. $40.00

TABLE MEDAL *1932 MACHINE GUN UNIT SHOOTING*: has a highly detailed art of a solder w machine gun & other sided engraved with date, for a infantry regt. M.G. Komp. Mint cond. $26.00

TABLE MEDAL *1934 SA GRUPPE DRESDEN*: 50mm diam. reddish brown with raised SA logo & border. Other side *Der SA Mann ist Revolutionar! Er ist Stark in der Liebe und Stark im Hass.* with oak leaves & crossed swords Meisen maker. Mint cond. $124.00

TABLE MEDAL *1936 HJ HOCHLAND LAGER*: About 75x95mm size dark gold finished heavy shield, Mt. scene with tents, green enamel title & HJ diamond to edelweiss. Maker *Carl Poellath etc.* Exc. cond. $233.00

TABLE MEDAL *1937 NSKK NACHT-SUCHFAHRT MOTOR-GURPPE-HESSEN*

TABLE MEDAL *1937 NSKK NACHT-SUCHFAHRT MOTOR-GURPPE-HESSEN*: 88mm bronze finished disc with raised title, NSKK eagle/scroll, 4 shields, oak leaves & enamel tree disc center. Near mint cond. $200.00

TABLE MEDAL *1938 NSFK DEUTSCHLANDFLUG* WITH CASE: Black leatherette case, white satin lining with gold *Nationalsozialistisches Fliegerkorps Der Korpsfuhrer* & blue velvet fitted base is faded. No certificate behind lining that has been glued. 77x95mm copper finished oval with raised Icarus & *Nationalsozialistisches Fliegerkorps Deutschlandflug 1938.* Reverse has raised quotation of *Christiansen* & stamped # *8621*. Avg. cond. $225.00

TABLE MEDAL *1938 PI. BATL. 47 WASSERSPORTFEST 1 PREIS*: 35x60mm gray rectangle with raised details of man with kayak. Stamp reverse *Pi.Batl.47 Wassersportfest 1938 behelfsmassiges Uebersetzen 1.Preis.* Above avg. cond. $25.00

TABLE MEDAL *1939 NSKK MOTORGRUPPE HESSEN 1.HESS.HEIMATFAHRT*: 67x77mm bronze rectangle with 4 way divided front with title & 2 affixed devices. Silver NSKK eagle/scroll & black enamel double headed eagle with b/w shield chest. Stamped maker *E.F.Wiedmann etc.* Near mint cond. $200.00

TABLE MEDAL *1939 REICHSPARTEITAG*: 95mm heavy gray body with raised tinnie details. Reverse *N.S. Kampfspiele 1939 dem Sieger*. Some corrosion. Avg. cond. $75.00

TABLE MEDAL *1939 SA BERLIN REICHSWETTKAMPFE* WITH CASE: Blue leatherette body, white satin & gray velvet fitted base. 96mm frosted silver disc with raised title border, party eagle & SA sports badge to reverse *Zweiter Preis*. Near mint cond. $368.00

TABLE MEDAL *1940 LA VILLE DE GAND-DIE STADT GENT*

TABLE MEDAL *1940 LA VILLE DE GAND-DIE STADT GENT*: 70mm dark bronze disc with raised queen holding lion shield & *Gent Gand* scroll below. Title to reverse scroll with engraved *Die Stadt Kommandantur zum Frontbesuch 1.10.1940.* Avg. cond. $97.00

THIRD REICH JEWELRY

BRACELET WESTERN FRONT: Double link with nine round bronze panels, each being 16 mm in size. Catch present. Each panel depicts flying planes, tanks, motorcycles, pill boxes, etc. Central disc inscribed *Gruss von der West Front* (Greetings from the Western Front). Near mint cond. $112.00

CIGARETTE CASE DAK: Native made. Aluminum. About 3/4x3.5x4.5" body made from downed airplane. Ornate cut out design affixed to each side with red leatherette background, Africa continent side has engraved palm tree & set stones for major coastal cities. Nice Arabic domed building scene with set colored stones. Hinged with more engraved designs inside. Near mint cond. $114.00

CUFF LINKS NSDAP SWASTIKA (PAIR) WITH CASE

CUFF LINKS NSDAP SWASTIKA (PAIR) WITH CASE: Black leather case has gold border outline. Maker to white satin lid lining & black velvet base. 16mm diam. to red enamel border with black swastika on white center. Curved & pivoting fitting to backs. Above avg. cond. $174.00

FINGER RING ANTI-NAZI *EISERNE FRONT*: Small size. Silver finish fading to gray. Rectangular front panel with 3 arrows. Misshapen band. Avg. cond. $50.00

FINGER RING DAK CAMEL: 8.5 size. 19mm tall oval with raised camel, palm tree & pyramid. Silver finish is worn & shows brass base. Owner added

swastika engraved to backside of oval. Avg. cond. $61.00

FINGER RING LUFTWAFFE EAGLE WITH BOX

FINGER RING LUFTWAFFE EAGLE WITH BOX: Brown box with faint maker to lid *L.G.Nitz Hannover etc.* Size 9.5. 12mm tall panel with raised eagle details. Near mint cond. $342.00

FINGER RING LUFTWAFFE PARA-TROOPER: Size 12.5. 18mm tall rectangular front with raised badge details. Oak leaves & acorns to sides. Stamped *800*. Highlights show use. Avg. cond. $328.00

FINGER RING ORGT TODT *OT 357*: Size 8.5 to massive silver casting. 20mm tall oval front with title & nice floral sides. Inside stamped *800*. Nice custom ring. Near mint cond. $145.00

FINGER RING SS SKULL & RUNIC SYMBOL: Hmkd *800* silver. Black enameled rectangular front panel with silver SS style totenkopf skull over *SS* runes. Small size. Rare. Above avg. cond. $548.00

NECKLACE PENDANT SWASTIKA: 18mm diam. to cut out swastika with border ring. 2 loops to the hanger hole. Avg. cond. $27.00

WATCH FOB 1942 KEGELABTEILUNG: 3.5" long white ribbon with black strip, silver fittings & engraved title to back. Clip to chain & engraved *SVP* to front. Avg. cond. $26.00

WATCH FOB GEB. JAG. RGT. 100: 37mm brass body with raised title & Edelweiss. Reverse has raised 7 battle areas. *Cassino, Abruzzen etc.* Exc. cond. $79.00

GERMAN TERMS AND ORGANIZATIONS

BDM: *Bund Deutscher Madel*- League of German Girls.

Bevo: *Bandfabrik Ewald Vorsteher*- The major manufacturer of cloth badges.

DAF: *Deutsche Arbeitsfront*- German Labor Front.

DAK: *Deutsches Afrikakorps*- German Africa Corps.

DJ: *Deutsches Jungvolk*- German Young People.

DK: *Deutsches Kreuz*- German Cross.

DRGM: *Deutsches Reichsgebrauchsmuster*- Nationally used pattern.

DRK: *Deutsches Rotes Kreuz*- German Red Cross.

DRP: *Deutsches Reichspost*- German National Post Office.

EK: *Eisernes Kreuz*- Iron Cross.

EL: *Eichenlaub*- Oak Leaves.

Ges. Gesch: *Gesetzlich Geschutzt*- Legally Protected.

HJ: *Hitlerjugend*- Hitler Youth.

JG: *Jagdgeschwader*- Lufwaffe Fighter Wing.

JM: *Jungmadel*- Young Girls.

KVK: *Kriegsverdienstkreuz*- War Merit Cross.

KVM: *Kriegsverdienstmedaille*- War merit medal.

LDO: *Leistungsgemeinschaft der Deutschen Ordenhersteller*- Administration of German Manufacturers.

NPEA: *Nationalpolitische Erziehungsanstalten*- National Political Educational Institutes.

NSBO: *Nationalsozialistische Betriebsorganisation*- National Socialist Factory Organization.

NSDAP: *Nationalsozialistische Deutsche Arbeiterpartei*- National Socialist German Worker's Party.

NSFK: *Nationalsozialistisches Fliegerkorps*- National Socialist Flying Corps.

NSKK: *Nationalsozialistisches Kraftfahrkorps*- National Socialist Motor Corps.

NSRK: *Nationalsozialistisches Reiterkorps*- National Socialist Riding Corps.

NS: *Studentenbund*- National Socialist Student League.

OKH: *Oberkommando des Heeres*- High Command of the Army.

OKL: *Oberkommando der Luftwaffe*- High Command of the Air Force.

OKM: *Oberkommando der Kriegsmarine*- High Command of the Navy.

OKW: *Oberkommando der Wehrmacht*- High Command of the Armed Forces.

OT: *Organisation Todt*

RAD: *Reichsarbeitsdienst*- National Labor Service.

RB-NR: *Reichsbetriebsnummer*- National Factory Code Number.

RK: *Ritterkreuz*- Knight's Cross.

RL: *Reichsleiter*- NSDAP official.

RLB: *Reichsluftschutzbund*- National Air Raid Protection Force.

RZM: *Reichszeugmeisterie*- National Material Control Board.

SA: *Sturmabteilung*- Assault Detachment.

SS: *Schutzstaffel*- Protection Squad.

SS-BW: *SS Bekleidungswerk*- SS Clothing Factory.

SS-SD: *SS Sicherheitsdienst*- SS Security Service.

SS-TV: *SS Totenkopfverbande*- SS Death's Head Units.

SS-VT: *SS Verfugungstruppe*- SS Special Purpose Troops.

TENO: *Technische Nothilfe*- Technical Emergency Service.

WBA: *Wehrmachtbekleidungsamt*- Armed Forces Clothing Office.

ABBREVIATIONS

Alum: Aluminum
Arty: Artillery
B & W: Black and White
Bde: Brigade
Bds: Boards
Bn: Battalion
Cal: Caliber
Camo: Camouflage
Cav: Cavalry
Cb: Clasp Back
cm: Centimeter
col: Colonel
cond: Condition
dbl: Double
Diam: Diameter
Div: Division
Dj: Dust Jacket
EK: Iron Cross
EM: Enlisted Man

Embr: Embroidered
Engr: Engineer
GRP: Group
hb: Hard Bound
HBT: Herringbone twill
hmkd: Hallmarked
IC: Iron Cross
Inf: Infantry
KC: Knights Cross
KM: Kriegsmarine
Lt: Lieutenant
LW: Luftwaffe
M: Model
MG: Machine Gun
MK: Mark
mm: Millimeter
mtd: Mounted
NCO: Noncommisined Officer

OD: Olive Drab
OG: Olive Green
Pb: Pin Back
PO: Petty Officer
Qm: Quartermaster
QR: Quick Release
rb: Ribbon
rect: Rectangular
Regt: Regiment
Rt: Right
Sb: Screw Back
sb: Soft Bound
sgt: Sergeant
shd: Shoulder
Spec: Specification
Svc: Service
WWI: World War One
WWII: World War Two

INDEX

E very issue of *Military Trader* has thousands of items for sale and wanted, show listings and editorial features on the field of Militaria Collectibles.

Use the coupon below, or call toll free 1-800 334-7165 to subscribe today at a

special low rate of only $15 (a 40% savings off the regular price.)

SAVE 40%
